THEORY OF TECHNICAL CHANGE AND ECONOMIC INVARIANCE

Application of Lie Groups

This is a volume in
ECONOMIC THEORY, ECONOMETRICS, AND MATHEMATICAL ECONOMICS

A Series of Monographs and Textbooks

Consulting Editor: KARL SHELL

A complete list of titles in this series appears at the end of this volume.

THEORY OF TECHNICAL CHANGE AND ECONOMIC INVARIANCE

Application of Lie Groups

Ryuzo Sato

Department of Economics
Brown University
Providence, Rhode Island

1981

ACADEMIC PRESS
A Subsidiary of Harcourt Brace Jovanovich, Publishers
New York London Toronto Sydney San Francisco

ACADEMIC PRESS, INC.
111 Fifth Avenue, New York, New York 10003

United Kingdom Edition published by
ACADEMIC PRESS, INC. (LONDON) LTD.
24/28 Oval Road, London NW1 7DX

Library of Congress Cataloging in Publication Data

Satō, Ryūzō, Date.
Theory of technical change and economic invariance.

(Economic theory, econometrics, and mathematical economics)
Includes bibliographies and index.
1. Economics, Mathematical. 2. Technological innovations--Mathematical models. 3. Lie groups.
I. Title. II. Title: Economic invariance. III. Series.
HB135.S27 330'.0724 80-68563
ISBN 0-12-619460-2 AACR2

PRINTED IN THE UNITED STATES OF AMERICA

81 82 83 84 9 8 7 6 5 4 3 2 1

To
Richard A. Musgrave
Ichiro Nakayama

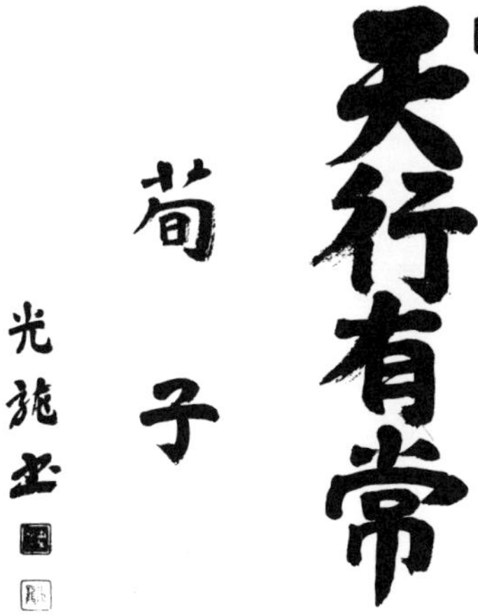

"Nature's ways are invariant"
Hsün Tzu
(ca. 305–235 B.C.)
CALLIGRAPHY BY REVEREND ROSHI KORYU

CONTENTS

Chapter 6 **Self-Dual Preferences and Technologies**

Chapter 7 **Dynamic Symmetries and Economic Conservation Laws**

Chapter 8 **A Lie Group Approach to the Index Number Problems**

FOREWORD

Mathematics is the handmaiden of the sciences. But mathematics also has a life of her own, gaining as much in her own development and fulfillment from the sciences as she gives to them. To help describe how apples and planets fall, and how ropes hang, Newton and Leibniz developed the calculus. By serendipity, that mode of analysis permitted economists to perfect the theory of general equilibrium two centuries later.

Sometimes the logical tools are forged long before their practical use becomes apparent. The calculus of variations was formulated in the eighteenth century and, in its classical form, perfected a century ago. Lying dormant for decades, it was brought back to life by the kiss of the dynamic programmer in pursuit of optimal control. Quaternions were something of an anticlimax until the spin matrices of quantum mechanics brought them back into vogue. Albert Einstein's quest for a general theory of relativity was helped by the fortuitous earlier development of the Ricci tensor calculus. Applied researchers even reinvent the wheel, as when Werner Heisenberg's rules for combining the elements in the array of quantum observables turned out to mimic the rules for matrix multiplication. Probability theory would remain a rather dry branch of measure theory were it not for its usefulness in describing how dice fall, multitudes die, and atoms collide.

Barely a century ago, the Norwegian Sophus Lie developed the theory of what have come to be called *Lie transformation groups*. Their original primary application was to the classical mechanics of Lagrange and Hamilton. Now Ryuzo Sato of Brown University is making a pioneering attempt to apply the Lie theory to modern economics. Here are only a few of his explorations.

1. It is popular to speak of "labor-saving inventions," which enable nine men to do the work of ten. This is the special case of a "factor-augmenting invention," in which land or labor or any input becomes equivalent in efficiency to a multiple of itself. Dr. Sato treats such technical processes, and more general ones, as examples of Lie groups.

2. I once posed the open question: What demand functions are *self-dual,* in the sense that their natural duals have *exactly the same mathematical form as themselves?* (The unit-elastic Cobb–Douglas case, in which any good's relative expenditure $p_i q_i / I = k_i$, is an obvious case; but what other cases are there in which

$$\mathbf{q} = \mathbf{f}(\mathbf{y}), \qquad \mathbf{y} = \mathbf{f}(\mathbf{q}),$$

$$\mathbf{q} = [q_1, \ldots, q_n], \qquad \mathbf{y} = [p_1 / \sum_1^n p_j q_j, \ldots, p_n / \sum_1^n p_j q_j],$$

and $\mathbf{f}(\mathbf{y}) = [f_1(\mathbf{y}), \ldots, f_n(\mathbf{y})]$?) Dr. Sato, using the methods of Lie groups, has extended the answers given by Professor Wahidul Haque and others.

3. Here is the final example from a long list of possible examples. Along an intertemporally efficient path of a *closed* von Neumann system, in which every good of a set of goods and its rate of growth are producible out of those *same goods as inputs* by a *constant-returns-to-scale* technology, the ratio of the total value of the capital goods to total income is a fundamental constant. Dr. Sato now shows that this 1970 finding of mine is essentially the only "energy integral" that such a dynamic system can in general possess.

I believe that Ryuzo Sato is the only scholar who has studied the application of Lie groups to economics. Not until economists have given his impressive treatise a thorough reading shall we be in a position to put useful bounds on the value added to economics by this powerful and elegant technique. The ball is now in our court.

Massachusetts Institute of Technology PAUL A. SAMUELSON

PREFACE

This book is based on lectures delivered at Brown University over a period of several years and at the University of Bonn, West Germany, during the academic year of 1974. It deals with a variety of topics in economic theory, ranging from the analysis of production functions to the general recoverability problem of optimal dynamic behavior. However, I treat the various selected topics, which interest me, from the unifying point of view of "transformation and invariance." In general, the book is concerned with the economic invariance problems of observable behavior under general transformations such as technical change and/or taste change. It is fundamentally a study of market behavior and economic invariance under "Lie types of technical change" (the exact definition being given in the text).

I became interested in the area of transformation and invariance through my continued involvement in the study of the theory of technical change. My initial contact with Lie group theory, however, goes back to my days at Johns Hopkins University in the early 1960s, when I was exploring different branches of mathematics, including differential geometry, for enjoyment. I was then unaware of any economic relevancy of the theory. The realization of the usefulness of this aspect of mathematics in economic theory came much later when I studied, as a Guggenheim Fellow, the physical applications of Lie groups. Samuelson's short note [1970] "Law of Conservation of the Capital–Output Ratio" (see Chapter 7 for the exact reference) was the catalyst that inspired my perception of the direct link between optimal economic behavior and Lie groups. Although Samuelson's article itself is not directly related to Lie groups, I realized that conservation laws can be deduced from the invariance properties of optimal dynamic behavior under (Lie group) transformations by application of Noether's theorem (see Chapter 7). This initial insight led me to the application of Lie group theory to other areas presented in the book.

This book is intended for economists, and hence emphasis is placed on economic interpretation rather than mathematical rigor. The book assumes a knowledge of the basic elements of modern economic theory as well as some amount of elementary mathematics used in economics. Beyond this it is self-contained: The reader who is not familiar with even the elementary aspects of Lie's theory of transformation groups can read this book by first studying the brief survey of Lie group theory presented in the Appendix. Although this book is not meant to be a textbook, it is hoped that the book may be used for advanced undergraduate courses and for graduate courses in economics. Specialists in applied mathematics and natural sciences may also find it useful, especially for learning the manner in which the same methodology is consistently applied in theoretical economics as in other branches of modern scientific endeavors.

The writing of this book was a long and arduous task, and I received help from many people. My greatest debt is to Paul A. Samuelson, who, in one way or another, is responsible for some of the topics discussed. His inspiration and encouragement are in evidence throughout the volume. I owe my deepest appreciation to Takayuki Nôno, who read the entire manuscript in various stages and offered numerous suggestions for its improvement. His careful criticism has saved me from many errors, and his advice and influence are reflected throughout the book.

I am grateful to the former and present members of the Mathematical Economics Workshop at Brown University, notably to Martin J. Beckmann, Yannis M. Ioannides, Allan M. Feldman, Gilbert Suzawa (in addition to his editing), Hajime Hori, Rama V. Ramachandran, Hiroshi Ono, Yasuo Kawashima, Philip S. Kott, Joel D. Scheraga, Behzad Diba, Thomas M. Mitchell, Mariko Fujii, Paul Calem, John Rizzo, Paul Segerstrom, Kazuo Mino, and Shun'ichi Tsutsui.

In addition, I have benefited greatly from useful comments and criticisms offered when I presented parts of this book at various universities. My special thanks go to Hendrik Houthakker, Dale Jorgenson, Wilhelm Krelle, Miyohei Shinohara, Karl Shell, Isamu Yamada, Thomas R. Saving, William R. Russell, Akira Takayama, Shujiro Sawada, Seichi Ota, Mineo Ikeda, Hukukane Nikaido, Eiji Ohsumi, Robert L. Basmann, Lawrence J. Lau, P. J. Hammond, Rolf Färe, Michael D. Intriligator, Bryan Ellickson, Yoshimasa Kurabayashi, Shuntaro Shishido, Taro Yamane, Noboru Sakashita, and I-Min Chiang.

The present book includes certain of my previous articles. Thanks are due to the editors of *Review of Economic Studies* and *Econometrica,* and to the Springer-Verlag and the J. C. B. Mohr publishing companies for permission to use my articles which were originally published by them. I gratefully acknowledge the support of the National Science Foundation and of the Guggenheim Foundation in enabling me to pursue and complete the present work.

I express my sincere gratitude to Marion Wathey for a superb typing job with her bionic fingers. Finally, I must express my great thanks to my wife, Kishie, and to my children, Luke (Ryuku) and Elly (Eri), for their patience and encouragement.

Brown University RYUZO SATO

CHAPTER 1

AN OVERVIEW

I. Introduction: Why Lie Groups?

1. The past 20 years have exhibited a remarkable progress in many branches of economic science. One notable area of research which has attracted the attention of a large number of competent economists is what may be called "the theory of observable market behavior." One of the oldest branches of this approach (started by Samuelson with finishing touches provided by Houthakker) is the theory of revealed preference. It is, in a way, the most direct challenge to the standard theory of consumer behavior, which begins with axiomatic assumptions in order to deduce theorems stating the properties of the consumer's optimal behavior. The theory of revealed preference takes a reverse process of, first, observing rational behavior in the market, and then deriving the theory of consumption and utility analysis consistent with the market behavior.

The theory of observable behavior has recently taken another important turn by the introduction of the "duality analysis" of consumer and firm's behavior. Rather than studying the market behavior generated from the direct (or primal) functions, one begins with the observation of the market behavior related to the indirect (or dual) functions. Here, contrasted with the direct approach, the analysis focuses on the recoverability problem of the expenditure (or indirect utility) function and of the cost function. The properties of the underlying functions such as the utility and production functions are then studied through the recovered indirect functions (see Fuss and McFadden [1978]). This indirect and dual approach not only contributes important insights of its own, but also offers more immediate empirical application. It enables one to formulate many problems in a way that is "natural" (Baumol [1977, p. 354]).

The primary purpose of this book is to develop still further the theory of observable behavior by analyzing the "invariant" relationships among economic variables, often represented by (partial) differential equation systems, by employing a relatively simple aspect of Lie's theory of continuous transformations. It is essential to recognize that the observable market behavior both in the direct and indirect approaches usually manifests itself in *the form of differential equation systems* (often partial). But thus far in the economic literature, very little effort has been given to the study of these differential equations from economic and formal (mathematical) points of view. This book deals with the *economic invariance problems of observable behavior under general "economic transformations" such as "technical change" and "taste change."* It is basically a study of economic invariance under "Lie types of technical change." The title of this volume may be somewhat misleading. This book does *not* deal with every aspect of technical change. Other than presenting a rather general theory of *endogenous* technical progress, the book does not directly deal with the standard problems of technical progress, such as the diffusion process and patent problems.

To demonstrate what is meant by a Lie group and to say why Lie groups are relevant here, let us consider a typical estimation problem of the underlying production function and technical change. Assume that technical progress in the production process is a priori known to have the simple "neutral" form

$$T_t\colon \quad \bar{K} = e^{\alpha t}K, \qquad \bar{L} = e^{\alpha t}L,$$

where K is the capital, L the labor, α the rate of technical progress ($\alpha \geqq 0$), $\bar{K}$ the "effective" capital, $\bar{L}$ the "effective" labor, and t the index of technical progress. The equations for $\bar{K}$ and $\bar{L}$, which may be called the technical progress functions for capital and labor, constitute a *one-parameter Lie group of continuous transformations* (Lie [1891]). Let the parameter of technical progress t change from t_0 to t_1. Then $\bar{K}$ and $\bar{L}$ change from

$$T_{t_0}\colon \quad \bar{K}_0 = e^{\alpha t_0}K, \quad \bar{L}_0 = e^{\alpha t_0}L, \qquad \text{to} \quad T_{t_1}\colon \quad \bar{K}_1 = e^{\alpha t_1}K, \quad \bar{L}_1 = e^{\alpha t_1}L.$$

The technical progress functions constitute a Lie group for the following reasons:

(i) (*Composition*) The result of the successive performance of T_0 and T_1 is the same as that of the single transformation

$$T_{t_2}\colon \quad \bar{K}_2 = \exp(\alpha(t_0 + t_1))K, \qquad \bar{L}_2 = \exp(\alpha(t_0 + t_1))L.$$

(ii) (*Identity*) When there is no technical change $t = 0$, then $\bar{K} = K$ and $\bar{L} = L$.

(iii) (*Inverse*) The inverse functions of T_t are also a member of T, when t is replaced by $-t$,

$$T_t^{-1} = T_{-t}: \quad K = e^{-\alpha t}\bar{K}, \qquad L = e^{-\alpha t}\bar{L}.$$

From the aggregate of the transformation included in the family T_t, where t varies continuously over a given range, any particular transformation of the family is obtained by assigning a particular value to t. Any successive transformations (including identity and inverse transformations) of the family are equivalent to a single transformation of the family. These are the basic properties of a Lie group. (See the Appendix and Chapter 2 for a more precise definition.)

Now assume that the estimation equation is derived from the market observation on the marginal rate of substitution between capital K and labor L by

$$p_K/p_L = Y_K/Y_L = f(K/L, t),$$

where p_K is the price of capital, p_L the price of labor, Y the output, $Y_K = \partial Y/\partial K$ the marginal product of K, and $Y_L = \partial Y/\partial L$ the marginal product of L. If K and L are related with $\bar{K}$ and $\bar{L}$ by the technical progress functions T_t given in the foregoing and if T_t is the only source of technical progress of the system, then it is seen immediately that the estimated marginal rate of substitution f should not contain t, because f coincides with the quantity known as the *invariant* of the group, i.e.,

$$f(K/L, t) = f(\bar{K}/\bar{L}) = f(e^{\alpha t}K/e^{\alpha t}L) = f(K/L).$$

This means that the efficiency increase of capital and labor α cannot be estimated from the observed behavior of the marginal rate of substitution. Furthermore, from the behavior of f, it is "impossible" to identify any "economies of scale" even if they exist. This is because the underlying production function is a member of the so-called *invariant family* of curves generated by this group.

In general, given a Lie type of technical progress T_t, one can always derive a family of production functions invariant under T_t (holothetic technology, see Chapter 2). Conversely, given the observable marginal rate of substitution in the form of a differential equation

$$M(K, L)\,dK + N(K, L)\,dL = 0, \quad \text{or} \quad -\frac{dL}{dK} = \frac{p_K}{p_L} = \frac{M(K, L)}{N(K, L)} = \frac{Y_K}{Y_L},$$

there exists a one-parameter Lie group of transformations (Lie type of technical change) which leaves the underlying production function invariant. If we know beforehand how this type of technical change acts on capital and labor, we can use this knowledge to find the underlying production function and to study its properties. This is an important reason why we may want to study the application of Lie groups.

Consider as another example the case of Shephard's lemma: One can observe the "optimal" production behavior from the factor demand functions

$$x_i = x_i(p, Y), \qquad 1 \leqq i \leqq n,$$

where x_i is the demand for the ith input, p the relative price vector of factor inputs, and Y the output. But in view of Shephard's lemma, the foregoing is equal to

$$\partial C/\partial p_i = x_i(p, Y) = x_i, \qquad 1 \leqq i \leqq n,$$

where C is the total cost function. There are two invariance properties in the preceding equation. First, in order to ascertain that this equation is derived from the *same* underlying cost function $C = C(p, Y)$ for all i, $1 \leqq i \leqq n$, the integrability condition of symmetry must be satisfied for all the x_i. But this is nothing but the *invariant* condition of the partial differential equations, known as the "involution condition" of a Lie group. By writing the factor demand functions in terms of their ratios

$$\frac{\partial C}{\partial p_i}\bigg/\frac{\partial C}{\partial p_j} = \frac{x_i(p, Y)}{x_j(p, Y)} = R^{ij}(p, Y), \qquad 1 \leqq i, j \leqq n,$$

or

$$\frac{\partial C}{\partial p_i} - \frac{\partial C}{\partial p_j} R^{ij}(p, Y) = 0,$$

the observable behavior of the demand system of the factor inputs may be expressed as the *invariant Lie group action of infinitesimal transformations* on the cost function, i.e., $L_{ij}C = 0$, where L_{ij} is an infinitesimal transformation equal to $(\partial/\partial p_i) - R^{ij}(p, Y)\, \partial/\partial p_j$ (the exact definition is given in Chapter 2 and the Appendix). Thus the study of observable market behavior of the demand functions of the factor inputs requires the study of the invariance property of partial differential equations. Second, to assume the *stable* relationships such as $R^{ij}(p, Y)$ implies that the forms of x_i and x_j are not affected or invariant under changes in some variables which are explicitly or implicitly observable. (One of the obvious variables is the index of technical change.) But from the mathematical point of view, the "stability" of the forms x_i and x_j is nothing but the "invariance" of differential equations under some transformations. Thus analysis of demand functions for factor inputs and of the cost and production functions requires again the study of invariant partial differential equations.

Another example may be taken from the area of dynamic optimization. Jürgen Moser in his address at the 1978 annual meeting of the National Academy of Sciences states

> I should like to present a glimpse into a new area of mathematics—one in which remarkable development has taken place over the last fifteen years. ... it is concerned with symmetries in dynamic systems that are not apparent at first and are only revealed through deep analysis. Such terms as, ..., integrable dynamic systems, and conservation laws fall into this area (Moser [1979]).

Paul A. Samuelson [1970] was the first to formally introduce "conservation laws" in theoretical economics.[1] Samuelson has in effect shown that the maximized value of the Hamiltonian in a simple optimal growth model of the von Neumann type is constant and *invariant* under a Lie translation group of the time variable—the "conservation law of the (aggregate) capital–output ratio." The translation group is the simplest type of Lie groups. Suppose one can find another more general Lie group (technical change) under which the dynamic system is *invariant*, then by Noether's [1918] theorem, one can derive another fundamental economic law of conservation. This is basically the study of the relationship between the (Lie) group invariances (often referred to as *dynamic symmetries*) of a system and its integrals, or "conservation laws." Economists have not yet been fully exposed to this aspect of dynamic analysis: they have been too busy devising economic interpretations of only the Euler–Lagrange equations.

2. It is becoming increasingly obvious that the study of observable market behavior can best be pursued via the application of Lie's theory of continuous groups. While this represents a new approach to the study of production (utility) functions and technical (taste) change, and to economic dynamics, in the natural sciences and in applied mathematics, it has been traditionally productive to use group theory for the study of *invariant* differential equations. Even outside of the traditional areas of physics and engineering, Lie groups have become increasingly useful. For instance, in the recent work on pattern recognition in visual perception (Hoffman [1968]), the visual integrative process is postulated to depend on a first-order differential equation. In order for recognition of a pattern as an entity to occur, this differential equation must be *invariant* under a Lie group. The results of this analysis are used to explain and interpret various visual phenomena.

[1] Ramsey's well-known rule for the optimal saving policy (Ramsey [1928]) was derived from the application of the conservation law of the Hamiltonian, although this aspect of the analysis has not been emphasized. (See Chapter 7.)

The theory of Lie groups was developed by the Norwegian mathematician Sophus Lie in the late 19th century in connection with his work on systems of differential equations. Lie groups arise in the study of solutions of differential equations just as finite groups arise in the study of algebraic equations. The possibility of solving many differential equations which arise in practical problems can often be traced to some geometrical or other symmetry property of the problem. Indeed, Lie groups play a fundamental role in many branches of geometry itself and have contributed significantly to the development of differential geometry of symmetric spaces and to abstract analysis (Chevalley [1946]).

The theory of Lie groups and Lie algebras is an area of mathematics in which we can see a harmony between the methods of classical analysis and modern algebra (e.g., Nôno [1968]). The application of Lie theory is one of the most powerful and most systematic approaches to the theory of invariant behavior. Belinfante and Kolman [1972, p. vii] observe: "Applications of the Theory of Lie Groups . . . are many and varied. This is a rapidly growing field through which one can bring to bear many powerful methods of modern mathematics." These fields include: "differential equations and their solvability; quantum mechanics and symmetries; harmonic oscillators; lattice; representation theory; analysis of integral variational problems; Hamiltonian approach conservation laws and equations of motion; etc."

Before proceeding with the formal analysis, we shall briefly give summaries of the basic results to be found in the following chapters so that the reader will have an overview of the contents of this book.

II. Holotheticity: Invariance of Production Function under Technical Change

3. We begin with the study of technical progress and production functions. Specifically, we address the question of what the impact of technical progress is upon different economic variables. At the forefront of this topic is the Solow–Stigler controversy; that is, can technical progress effects be independently isolated and identified from scale effects (i.e., growth in the capital–labor ratio)? Solow has argued that the portion of the increase in U.S. per capita output that is not explained by growth in the capital–labor ratio may be attributed to technical progress. In his econometric estimations, he assumes that technical progress is of the Hicks neutral type and that the underlying production function is linearly homogeneous (constant returns to scale). Stigler, on the other hand, has criticized the assumption of linear homogeneity of the production function and has emphasized the necessity of distinguishing between increasing returns to scale and technical progress.

We shall establish conditions under which the effects of technical progress and scale effects are independently identifiable. We begin with the definition of technical progress functions (ϕ and ψ). When technical progress is introduced into a production process, it changes the way in which factor inputs, capital (K) and labor (L), are combined. These technical progress functions combine the factor inputs through the technical progress parameter t:

$$\bar{K} = \phi(K, L, t), \qquad \bar{L} = \psi(K, L, t).$$

By using this definition, the new—and fundamental—concept of *holotheticity* is introduced (see Sato [1975]). Specifically, when the entire effect of technical progress can be represented by some monotonic transformation F, then the production function is said to be holothetic under that given type of technical progress. If we impose the condition that the technical progress functions possess the Lie group properties, then we can find a family of production functions under which the total effect of technical progress is completely transformed to apparent scale effects—*holothetic technology*.

In response to the Solow–Stigler controversy, we are now able to conclude that the effects of a given type of technical progress and scale effects are independently identifiable if and only if the production function is *not* holothetic under that particular type of technical progress. For example, since the well-known homothetic technology is holothetic under the uniform factor-augmenting type of technical progress, but not under the nonuniform type, scale effects and technical progress effects cannot be isolated in the first case; whereas in the latter situation under the nonuniform type, they are independently identifiable.

In practice, it is convenient to express technical progress functions as infinitesimal changes in the technical progress parameter. On using Lie's own notation, the *infinitesimal generator* is introduced ($U = \sum_{i=1}^{n} \xi_i(x)\, \partial/\partial x_i$). Given this infinitesimal transformation, the holothetic technology is simply derived as the family of curves that are invariant under the given group of technical progress transformations. As is well known, the optimal behavior of a cost-minimizing firm can be observed in the marketplace by studying the differential equation for the marginal rate of substitution (MRS). Given the Lie "representation" of the MRS, it is possible to test if a particular production technology is holothetic under a given Lie type of technical progress by the *compatibility condition* of the infinitesimal generators.

The basic analysis is extended to the case of a production function which is *simultaneously* subjected to more than one type of technical change. Here we are interested, for example, in an economy with more than one sector, each of which is subjected to a different type of technical progress. In such a framework our problem reduces to finding those conditions under which all of the different types of technical progress are transformed to an "aggregate scale effect" of the national economy. A unique family of nontrivial production functions, simultaneously holothetic under two independent types of technical progress, exists if and only if those types of technical progress are again compatible. If the two types are not compatible, then only a trivial production function is simultaneously holothetic under both types. It turns out that the compatibility condition on technical progress is nothing more than the well-known integrability condition. In particular, two independent types of technical progress are compatible if and only if the total differential equation consisting of their infinitesimal transformations satisfies the integrability condition.

III. Theory of Endogenous Technical Progress

4. In Chapter 3 we present a dynamic theory of endogenous technical progress. The purpose is to study the dynamic market forces of supply and demand which are responsible for invention and innovation activities. An important dimension of technical change is that it is the outcome of investment activities. Technical progress is regarded as the dynamic processes of efficient allocation of limited resources under technological and market constraints.

The process of accumulation of knowledge is *endogenous* and should be determined by the firm so as to maximize long-run profits. The firm may change its stock of *basic* and *applied* knowledge by producing a flow of the two. Basic knowledge is an intermediate product in the production of new technical knowledge. The idea behind this formulation is similar to the Böhm-Bawerk process applied to dynamic optimization with continuous lags. The firm is assumed to be a profit-maximizing monopolist, engaging in production (and sales) of the product and in research and development (R & D) activities. It buys capital and labor at given prices in competitive markets. The firm may increase the stock of basic knowledge or applied knowledge by employing specialized research workers and research capital. But there are time lags between inputs and outputs of the research activity. Formally writing the cumulative effects by the *integro-differential equation system*, we justify the existence of endogenous technical progress as the optimal solution of the long-run profit-maximization problem with a continuous time lag.

The model presented here is formally similar to the optimal control problem of a system with transport (or continuous) lag, first studied by Bate in 1969 and later applied to several economic problems (see Chapter 3,

Part III). However, one *basic and new feature* of the present analysis is that the model of optimal technical progress with *continuous lags* is reduced to a model with *no lags*, but with the appropriate *weights* to the corresponding differential equations. This enables one to study not only the steady state, but also the intertemporal paths even under more general conditions than the standard optimal model. This chapter is intended to justify the *existence of exogenous types of technical change* used throughout this book.

IV. *G* (Group)-Neutral Technical Change

5. Of the several well-known types of technical progress that have appeared in economic literature over the years, the most frequently encountered is the Hicks neutral type. It is demonstrated that the Lie type of technical progress under its own holothetic production function can always be expressed as a Hicks neutral type of product-augmenting technical progress. Since any production function has at least one type of technical change under which it is holothetic, this would appear to be a reasonable justification for using Hicks neutral technical change in empirical studies. Historically, though, the Hicks neutral type has been used because of its presumed "neutral" effect upon the distributive shares of the factors of production, given linearly homogeneous technology. Specifically, technical progress is Hicks neutral if the MRS is invariant under technical change, as long as the capital–labor ratio is invariant.

The concept of "neutrality" is basically the same as the group concept of invariance. Specifically we extend the concept of "neutrality" used in the earlier works to "neutrality in the sense of transformation groups"—"*G* (group)-neutral" type of technical change. If we now introduce two parameters of technical change (α and β), then technical change may be represented by a family of neoclassical production functions of the form $Y = F(K, L, \alpha, \beta)$. If y is used to represent the output–capital ratio and x the labor–capital ratio, then the production function may be written as $y = f(x, \alpha, \beta)$. Using this framework, we state that technical change expressed in this form is *G* neutral if this production function is invariant under a Lie transformation group (G) of r essential parameters. Specifically, for a given G, the second-order equations of neutrality can be obtained using the condition that for all $U \in L(G)$ (where $L(G)$ is the Lie algebra of infinitesimal transformations of G), $U''\phi = 0$ whenever $\phi(x, y, y_x, y_{xx}) = 0$. The family of production functions of *G*-neutral technical change can be obtained by simply solving this equation of neutrality. The approach taken here can not only justify the well-known types of neutral technical change, but also generate more meaningful and more general types of technical progress. This is the essence of the first topic discussed in Chapter 4.

V. Comparative Statics and Integrability Conditions

6. The second topic that is discussed in Chapter 4 is the application of infinitesimal transformations to comparative static analysis of economic systems. It is shown that under certain conditions comparative statics can be carried out in a most efficient and systematic way by the application of Lie groups and related concepts. By the *fundamental theorem* of comparative statics under r-parameter infinitesimal transformations, the comparative statics results of commodity and factor demand functions are systematically presented when the first-order conditions are parametrically affected by Lie group transformations.

As the last topic of Chapter 4, an alternative interpretation is given to the well-known integrability conditions of the theory of consumer's preference. The marginal rates of substitution may be regarded as the unconnected infinitesimal transformations of Lie groups. Then the integrability conditions are nothing but the *simultaneous holotheiticity conditions* of technical and taste change induced by these unconnected infinitesimal transformations. This way of looking at the integrability conditions should facilitate the understanding of the market behavior of a rational economic agent.

VI. Implicit Technology

7. At the forefront of economic analysis today is the study and development of implicit production functions. These implicit structures are appearing more frequently in the literature dealing with dual functions, cost of living indices, production and cost analyses, technical change and aggregation problems. In Chapter 5 the methodology applied to explicit technologies is extended to implicit technologies. We demonstrate, for example, that as with explicit technology, there is a systematic method for generating implicit technology from given Lie types of technical change. It is found that explicit holothetic technology is that class of production functions that is invariant under the so-called "once-extended" group for a particular Lie type of technical progress. Now it is shown that implicit holothetic technology is that type of production technology which is invariant under the "twice-extended" group.

Surprising, however, is the result that implicit technology need *not* possess any Lie type of technical progress under which it is holothetic; that is, *given an implicit technology in the form of the second-order differential equation, there generally does not exist any Lie type of technical progress under which the implicit technology is holothetic*! This nonexistence theorem, is in direct contrast to our existence theorem for explicit technology. In the implicit case there generally do not exist any, or at most a limited number of, Lie types of technical progress under which the implicit technology is holothetic.

This result leads us into the concept of r-degree holotheticity. If a production technology is holothetic under r linearly independent Lie types of technical progress, it is said to have the r-degree holotheticity. This result also provides us with a useful method for *classifying* implicit technologies according to the number of types of technical progress under which they are holothetic. The aggregate of all of the infinitesimal transformations of technical progress which will leave a given differential equation for an implicit technology invariant constitutes *an r-parameter group*. Hence an implicit technology of r-degree holotheticity has an r-parameter Lie type of technical change. It is also shown that if there are two inputs, then r must be less than or equal to 8. This result is used to classify implicit technologies according to their invariants. The two-parameter groups ($r = 2$) are applied to generate the basic four forms of implicit technology.

One of the most important cases of implicit technology holothetic under r-parameter Lie type of technical change is the "projective" technology. It is holothetic under the maximum number (eight) of different types of technical change: It is holothetic under the "projective group" of transformations. The projective type of technical change is applied to classify the general separable implicit technology. An important subset of this family is the general implicit constant elasticity of substitution (CES) function. It is possible to classify the different forms of CES production functions according to the basic (one-parameter) projective types of technical change. Thus the eight basic invariant forms of CES functions are additive types I and II, multiplicative types I and II, and ratio additive types I, II, III, and IV.

VII. Self-Duality

8. The versality of applications of the Lie theory does not end here. In Chapter 6 it is demonstrated that we can further apply this theory to the study of the duality and self-duality of preferences and technologies. After presenting the necessary and sufficient conditions for the self-duality of preferences as the set-symmetric conditions on the implicit functions of price and quantity vectors, we present a specific method of deriving such implicit functions. We consider the demand functions with r essential parameters as continuous transformations satisfying the budget constraint. If we place certain fundamental restrictions on these demand functions, we can assume that they satisfy the Lie group properties. It turns out that the self-dual demand functions that in fact satisfy these fundamental restrictions are simply the continuous transformations of the unitary elastic demand functions associated with a Cobb–Douglas preference ordering. In other words, we can make use of the fact that the system of demand functions arising from a Cobb–Douglas utility function with equal exponents can be used as the basis for the identical transformation.

We know from the theory of Lie groups that there are r linearly independent infinitesimal transformations associated with the demand functions. Given these infinitesimal transformations, the self-duality conditions, especially for a separable system, are stated as the invariance conditions of the group. Hence the *invariants* of the group together with the budget constraint constitute a separable system of set-symmetric functions of the self-dual demand system.

Although the basic duality principle of the utility and demand analysis will carry over to production and cost analysis, the self-duality of production and cost functions is usually different. The main reason for this is that here we are *not* comparing the direct and indirect production functions. Using the normalized cost function, we first state the necessary condition for the self-duality of the production and cost function: The production function must be *implicitly holothetic* under the uniform factor-augmenting type of technical progress. The observant reader will note that this implies that the production function must be implicitly homothetic. Hence we must deal with the problem of *implicit self-duality*. It is shown that such an implicitly homothetic production function has cost function of a particular form. If and only if the production function is implicitly homothetic can the cost function be written in the form $C = g(C_1(Y), \ldots, C_{n-1}(Y);\ p)C_n(Y)$. Using this, we formulate the necessary and sufficient conditions for the implicit self-duality of technologies.

The uniformity of factor demand functions is defined as the similarity of the functional forms of all demand functions. J. B. Clark's treatment of the marginal productivities of capital and labor clearly assumes this special property for the factor input demand functions (Clark uniformity). A theorem in Chapter 6 is designed to find the necessary and sufficient conditions for the Clark uniformity condition (Theorem 6).

Finally, we examine the correspondence of scale effects between production and cost functions. It is known that the cost function generated from any production function is holothetic under the uniform type of technical progress in the price vector. In other words, the dual rate of returns to scale of the cost function is a complete transformation of technical progress of the equiproportionate price-decreasing type. Alternatively, given a production function, usually implicit, the effect of technical progress is completely transformed to the dual rate of return to scale of the cost function if and only if the type of technical progress is of the uniform factor-augmenting type. Of special interest is the case of implicitly homothetic technology. Here the primal rate of returns to scale of the production function is in fact identical to the dual rate of returns to scale of the cost function.

VIII. Dynamic Symmetries and Economic Conservation Laws

9. Chapter 7 presents a self-contained and systematic analysis of conservation laws in economics. First, a fairly detailed mathematical treatment of Noether's theorem is given, so that the economist who is not familiar with this aspect of variational dynamics can understand its applications. Noether's theorem states that "if the fundamental integral of a problem in the calculus of variations and optimal control is *invariant* under the r-parameter (Lie) group of transformations, then there are r conservations laws." The Hamiltonian *canonical* transformation leaves a dynamic system invariant. By further extending this concept one can derive Noether's invariance identities, which are the system of partial differential equations involving the Lagrangian of the model, its derivatives, and the infinitesimal transformations. These identities can be used in two ways: Given the Lagrangian, an r-parameter group will be generated through the solutions of the partial differential equation system; given the r-parameter group, the corresponding Lagrangians will be integrated again through these solutions.

Second, the invariant variational principle is applied to general neoclassical optimal growth models of the Ramsey type. It is shown that there exist several (local) conservation laws in the neighborhood of the steady state. Noether's theorem applied to a typical problem of welfare maximization over time has an interesting economic interpretation. If a welfare function is dynamically invariant under an r-parameter family of transformations resulting from technical change and/or taste change, then the following expression is constant along any optimal path for the entire period:

$$\begin{pmatrix} \text{measure of welfare} \\ \text{per infinitesimal} \\ \text{change of time} \end{pmatrix} + \sum_{i=1}^{n} \begin{pmatrix} \text{value (effect)} \\ \text{of technical (taste) change} \\ \text{for the } i\text{th quantity} \end{pmatrix}$$

$$+ \text{ null term} = \text{const.}$$

One of the most interesting aspects of the conservation laws is that the Hamiltonian itself is *not* constant when the welfare function is discounted with a positive rate. However, in the neighborhood of the equilibrium position, the discounted welfare measured in terms of the "modified" Hamiltonian, which is the sum of the Hamiltonian and the value of technical change, remains unchanged.

Economic conservation laws and turnpikes are closely related. Thus the two additional local laws are the turnpike constants of the system. The weighted difference between investment and capital multiplied by the inverse of the negative turnpike exponent, and the weighted sum of investment and capital multiplied by the inverse of the positive turnpike exponent, are always constant.

Finally, the Samuelson conservation laws in a von Neumann growth model is derived through the application of the Noether theorem. It is shown that the Samuelson laws are the only laws *globally* operating for that system, although there are several *local* conservation laws. Again the turnpike constants are shown to be closely related with the local conservation laws.

IX. Invariance of Index Numbers

10. We next turn our attention to another area of application of Lie group theory: the index number problems. In Chapter 8 we present an alternative approach to the Fisher–Frisch test criteria of an index number. Furthermore, an analysis is extended to the invariant economic index number problem. It should be clear to the reader by now that Lie group theory presents us with a powerful tool for studying invariance properties of different types of economic behavior. Most of the well-known tests for index numbers can be looked upon as conditions on infinitesimal transformations of Lie groups. That is, in testing to determine if a particular index number can be used as an index of prices and quantities, we can check to see if it satisfies the invariance properties of group transformations.

We also spend a considerable amount of time examining the properties of index numbers that are derived from implicitly holothetic utility functions. In some cases, these index numbers satisfy the criterion of the factor-reversal test. Furthermore, the standard quantity index is *not* completely symmetric with the price index. However, using our theory, it is possible to derive a "dual" quantity index which is symmetric with the corresponding price index.

It should also be clear that technical progress and taste change effects can be brought into the analysis of index numbers most efficiently using the transformation groups. Once again, we may view these changes as transformations that leave the given index number invariant, taken under the holotheticity condition of equiproportionate changes.

Finally, we present the analysis of Divisia index numbers from the viewpoint of Lie groups. Most of the previous works are concerned with the path independence property of the index numbers. This condition is basically a problem of *static* behavior. Our concern here is to study the invariance property of *dynamic* behavior; that is, we are concerned with the *dynamic invariance* of the Divisia index numbers. This is a natural extension of the previous works, because the Divisia index numbers are the quantities equivalent to Lagrangians of dynamic systems. Again the Noether theorem proves to be indispensable for the derivation of the necessary and sufficient condition that a Divisia index is dynamically invariant under technical and/or taste change. We derive what may be called *the law of conservation of a Divisia index number.*

The concept of "general (or quasi)" Divisia index numbers is introduced to study a dynamic index number related to *nonhomothetic behavior*. The general Divisia index number is the *weighted* sum of percentage changes, the weights resulting from the relative shares and appropriate coefficients. Thus the almost homothetic Divisia index is a special case when the underlying utility (production) functions is of the almost homothetic type. The dynamic invariance condition is again applied to study the holotheticity property of the general index.

X. The Group Structure of Observable Market Behavior

11. In the final chapter we take up an introductory analysis of the theory of observable market behavior from the standpoint of the differential geometric approach. The emphasis is placed on the analysis and abstraction of the formal group structure exhibited in many observable market behaviors in economic theory. The purpose of Chapter 9 is to show that many of the well-known results in economic theory can be restated in the group theoretical framework in a more consistent manner and that some of the problems unresolved in economics thus far can be attacked in a more fruitful and unified manner. Thus the well-known theory of revealed preference in the consumer's demand analysis of Samuelson can be regarded as the "involution" condition of the "group action" of a Lie group on a differentiable manifold. In general, economic optimization such as cost minimization and utility maximization may be regarded as defining "contact transformations." If a rational economic behavior is market observable as a system of mixed variables of prices and quantities, then the underlying production technology or the preference ordering can be recoverable by the use of the fundamental properties of contact transformations.

Sometimes an optimal economic behavior may exhibit in the form of a system of differential equations. Here the recoverability problem becomes a *dynamic* one. From the knowledge of a system of observable differential equations, the underlying dynamic objective function of a rational economic agent may be reconstructed in the form of the Lagrangian and Hamiltonian functions. The well-known Hamilton–Jacobi transformation theory gives the necessary foundation for the study of the dynamic recoverability problem. After presenting a general formulation of the dynamic recovery problem, we analyze in detail the recoverability of simple neoclassical optimal growth models. As the methodology used here is quite general, it has a wide appeal for applicability in many different research areas of dynamic optimality. After stating a general theorem related to the recovery of an optimal growth model we derive a local recoverability theorem. It is shown that a *time-dependent* welfare function corresponding to the observable market behavior of the capital–labor ratio has its *surrogate* welfare function, independent of the time variable.

Most optimal economic systems possess some forms of symmetries. The group theoretic approach is the basic apparatus to uncover hidden and unhidden symmetries (static or dynamic) of optimal behavior. Here we study the relationship between the Hamilton–Jacobi transformation theory and the theory of technical and/or taste change. Instead of regarding the Hamilton–Jacobi theory as the practical computational method, we use it to study the *invariant* properties of a dynamic economic system, invariant under the transformations due to technical and taste change.

Chapter 9 is not intended to provide a complete analysis of observable behavior in terms of the application of the group theoretic and differential geometric framework. However, it can serve as a prelude to extensive future research in this area. The Frobenius existence theorem is quite fundamental to this approach. What the fixed point theorem is to general equilibrium theory, the Frobenius existence theorem is to the theory of observable behavior. Since some of the formal results may not be familiar to economists who are less inclined to the mathematical approach, we have presented briefly the necessary mathematics to follow the arguments.

Appendix: A Brief Survey of Lie's Theory of Continuous Transformation Groups

12. Those who are not familiar with the method of Lie's transformation groups may want to begin with the Appendix. We present a brief self-contained (but not complete) survey to introduce economists to the main feature of Lie's original work on transformation groups. With the use of examples and exercises, it is hoped that the reader can grasp the basic essentials of the theory. The references presented at the end of the Appendix (also some of the references at the end of each chapter) may be useful to those who are interested in further pursuing the study of Lie groups and their applications.

REFERENCES

Baumol, W. [1977]. *Economic Theory and Operations Analysis*, 4th ed. Prentice-Hall, Englewood Cliffs, New Jersey.

Belinfante, J. G. F. and Kolman, B. [1972]. *A Survey of Lie Groups and Lie Algebras with Applications and Computational Methods*. Society for Industrial and Applied Mathematics, Philadelphia, Pennsylvania.

Chevalley, C. [1946]. *Theory of Lie Groups*. Princeton Univ. Press, Princeton, New Jersey.

Fuss, M., and MacFadden, D. (eds.) [1978]. *Production Economics: A Dual Approach to Theory and Applications*, Vols. I and II, Contribution to Economic Analysis, No. 110. North-Holland Publ., Amsterdam.

Hoffman, W. C. [1968]. The neuron as a Lie group germ and a Lie product, *Quart. Appl. Math.*, **25**, 423–440.

Lie, S. [1891]. *Vorlesugen über Differentialgleichungen, mit Bekannten Infinitesimalen Transformationen*. Bearbeitet und herausgegeben von Dr. Georg Scheffers, Leipzig. Reprinted by Chelsea, New York, 1967.

Moser, J. [1979]. Hidden symmetries in dynamical systems, *American Scientists*, **67**, 689–695.

Noether, E. [1918]. Invariant variationsprobleme, *Nachr. Akad. Wiss. Göttingen, Math.-Phys. Kl. II*, 235–257. Translation by M. A. Tavel under the title of Invariant variation problems, *Transport Theory and Statistical Physics*, **1**, 186–207 [1971].

Nôno, T. [1968]. On the symmetry groups of simple materials: Application of the theory of Lie groups, *J. Math. Anal. Appl.*, **24**, 110–135.

Ramsey, F. [1928]. A mathematical theory of saving, *Economic Journal*, **38**, 543–559.

Samuelson, P. A. [1970]. Law of conservation of the capital-output ratio, *Proceedings of the National Academy of Sciences, Applied Mathematical Science*, **67**, 1477–1479.

Sato, R. [1975]. The impact of technical change on the holotheticity of production functions, presented at the World Congress of the Econometric Society in Toronto, Canada; *Review of Economic Studies*, **47** (1980), 767–776.

CHAPTER 2

HOLOTHETICITY OF A TECHNOLOGY[1]

I. Introduction and Motivation: Relative Significance of the Scale Economies and Technical Progress (the Solow–Stigler Controversy)

1. In recent years, many economists have attempted to study technical progress and production functions in order to ascertain the impact of technological changes under different assumptions on such economic variables as prices of factor inputs, their distributive shares, and factor requirements and the degree of scale effects. Several new concepts have been introduced, such as "homothetic" production functions (Shephard [1953]), "neutrality" of inventions (Hicks [1963], Sato and Beckmann [1968]), and "optimal returns to scale" (Sato and Ramachandran [1974]).

Motivation for this research topic is derived from the so-called Solow–Stigler controversy.[2] Solow [1957] shows that a substantial portion of the increase in per capita output in the United States cannot be explained by growth in the capital–labor ratio. The unexplained portion is attributed to technical progress. Solow [1957, p. 312] notes that he is "... using the phrase 'technical change' as a shorthand expression *for any kind of shift* in the production function. Thus slowdowns, speedups, improvements in education

[1] Parts of this chapter are based on my earlier paper (Sato [1975]), where the concept of holotheticity is first introduced.

[2] This is a revived controversy of the Pigou–Clapham exchange (see Solow [1961] and Ramachandran [1974]).

of the labor force, and all sorts of things appear as 'technical change.'" In this conglomerate of factors that enter into "technical change," there is one which is of special interest for the present discussion, and that is the effects of scale.

In his paper, Solow assumes that technical progress is Hicks neutral and that the production function is linear homogeneous. Stigler [1961] criticizes the latter assumption. This is followed by an exchange of comments between Stigler [1961] and Solow [1961]. After rejecting the possibility of estimating the extent of increasing returns by fitting cross-sectional production functions to numerous U.S. industries, Stigler attempts to fit an international cross-sectional production function, using U.S. and U.K. data. He also uses the Cobb–Douglas production function in his statistical analysis. His conclusion [1961, p. 63] deserves quotation:

> The conclusion to be drawn, aside from the inevitable one that more work should be done, is that economies of scale are potentially of the same order of magnitude as technical progress. I consider the problem of establishing the approximate magnitude of these economies a major one, not merely of productivity calculations, which are not especially important, but of the theory of economic growth.

In reply, Solow holds that he is in complete agreement with Stigler concerning the potential magnitude of scale effects. However, he considers the problem of measuring these effects and distinguishing these effects from those of technical progress to be extremely difficult, and that as an economic theorist he would prefer to stick to the assumption of constant returns.

Economies of scale can manifest themselves in many ways. They may generate a homogeneous but nonlinear production function with constant scale elasticity. They may underlie a homothetic production function with variable scale elasticity (Suzawa [1979]). Or they may even generate a nonhomothetic production function.

2. It is obvious that both Solow and Stigler are right in this controversy. Consider a cost-minimizing firm producing output under a homothetic production function:

$$Y = F[f(K, L)], \tag{1}$$

where Y is the output, K the capital, L the labor, and f a continuously differentiable function homogeneous of degree one with respect to K and L, with $f_i > 0$ and $f_{ii} < 0$ ($i = K, L$), and F any strictly monotone increasing (or homothetic) function of f. Suppose that the firm adopts the exogenous technical progress of "the uniform and equal multiplication type" (see

Sections 9 and 20), so that capital and labor measured in the efficiency units, $\bar{K}$ and $\bar{L}$, are expressed as

$$\bar{K} = T(t)K = e^{\alpha t}K, \qquad \bar{L} = T(t)L = e^{\alpha t}L, \qquad \alpha \geqq 0. \tag{2}$$

The production function after the introduction of technical progress of the uniform multiplication type is

$$\begin{aligned} \bar{Y} &= F[f(\bar{K}, \bar{L})] = F[f(e^{\alpha t}K, e^{\alpha t}L)] \\ &= F[e^{\alpha t}f(K, L)] = G_{(t)}[f(K, L)]. \end{aligned} \tag{3}$$

The impact of such a type of technical change is, of course, "neutral" in the sense of Hicks. This means that in terms of an isoquant map, the characteristics are unchanged or *invariant* (using the concept of the group theory which we plan to employ) before and after the technical progress, except for the relabeling of isoquants, and that there always exists some other homothetic function G which has the same labeling features as the production function with that type of technical progress. Thus *the impact of the type of technical progress* (2) *can always be represented by another member of the same family of homothetic production functions.* That is to say, *the impact of technical progress on the production function is transformed to a scale effect.*

The Solow–Stigler controversy occurs because the type of technical progress (2) is completely transformed to a Hicks neutral type and the Hicks neutral type is indistinguishable from the homotheticity (or returns to scale) property. In other words, technical progress and returns to scale are theoretically undifferentiable under the production function (1) combined with the technical progress type (2). Thus, in order to empirically identify both the scale and technical progress effects, one must know what type of technical progress is completely separable from the scale effect. When the impact of technical progress on the production function is transformed to a scale effect, then the production function is said to be *holothetic* under a given type of technical progress. (A more precise definition of holotheticity will be given in the next section.) Thus, to avoid the Solow–Stigler type of controversy, we must use a production function that is *nonholothetic* under a given type of technical progress (see Section 9, Theorem 3). This is the obvious reason we are interested in studying the conditions of holotheticity.

In addition, many later theoretical and empirical studies (Binswanger [1974], David and van de Klundert [1965], Samuelson [1965], Sato [1970]) suggest strongly that the nonuniform (or unequal) type of factor augmenting technical progress is more prevalent and that factor prices increase at uneven rates. Obviously, nonuniform types of factor-augmenting technical progress *cannot* be represented by any member of the "homothetic" family of production functions, except for the trivial case of the Cobb–Douglas type. Under what type of production functions, then, can the case of general factor-augmenting technical progress be completely transformed to a returns to scale feature? More specifically, what types of exogenous change will leave a given isoquant map (or factor price frontier) unaltered or invariant? We intend to explore these questions by applying the Lie theory of continuous groups of transformations.

Another reason we are interested in the holotheticity of a production function is that the concept itself is quite useful in analyzing the particular properties of a given production function. It will be shown that each family of production functions has a unique *invariance property* (again using the concept of the Lie groups) that is unaffected by the impact of technical change. Thus the homothetic family of production functions has the invariance property that the marginal rate of substitution between capital and labor for any given capital–labor ratio is unchanged under the impact and transformation of *unbiased* type of technical progress. This property is so unique to the homothetic family that it can be used to distinguish (or classify) the family from all other (nonhomothetic) families of production functions. On the other hand, the empirically useful type of Houthakker's addilog family (Houthakker [1960]) has another *invariance* property that differs from the homothetic family. The invariance property unique to the addilog family comes from the more general family of the "almost" homothetic class in which the relative shares of capital and labor are *invariant* under the transformation and impact of *biased* technical change. Hence the invariance property which is closely related to the holotheticity concept can be best used to delineate one family of production functions from another family. As a matter of fact, the Lie group theory provides one of the most efficient methods of studying invariance properties.

II. Holotheticity and the Group Properties of Technical Progress Functions

3. Although the exogenous changes that affect the factor combination in a production process may result from many different forces such as new inventions and new applications of known technology, we may simply identify them as "technical change" or "technical progress"[3] and represent it by a parameter t. Consider a general (strictly) quasi-concave and

[3] Thus, for the utility and demand analyses, the exogenous change may be identified as "taste change." Needless to say, everything we say about production technologies will carry over to preference orderings by substituting "technical change" with "taste change."

continuously differentiable neoclassical production function with the usual properties,

$$Y = f(K, L). \tag{4}$$

Assume that when exogenous technical progress is introduced, it will not change the form of the production function f, but will change the output level by affecting the way in which the factor inputs are combined, i.e.,

$$\overline{Y} = f(K, L, t). \tag{$4'_1$}$$

Definition 1 (*Technical Progress Functions*) When exogenous technical progress t is introduced, it will change the way in which K and L are combined. The functions which combine factor inputs through the technical progress parameter t may be called the technical progress functions of K and L, i.e.,

$$T_t\colon\quad \overline{K} = \phi(K, L, t), \qquad \overline{L} = \psi(K, L, t), \tag{5}$$

where $\overline{K}$ and $\overline{L}$ are "effective" factor inputs ("effective" capital and "effective" labor) and (ϕ, ψ) is a vector of *technical progress functions.*

Here T represents the set of transformations T_t, each one being determined by some value of the parameter t, technical progress. The technical progress (in general, technical change) functions ϕ and ψ are supposed to be generally analytic, real functions of the three variables K, L, and t. Besides, ϕ and ψ are independent functions with respect to K and L alone; i.e.,

$$\begin{vmatrix} \dfrac{\partial\phi}{\partial K} & \dfrac{\partial\phi}{\partial L} \\ \dfrac{\partial\psi}{\partial K} & \dfrac{\partial\psi}{\partial L} \end{vmatrix} \not\equiv 0,$$

so that Eq. (5) can be solved for K and L.

Following the example of homothetic production functions under the uniform factor-augmenting technical progress, we present

Definition 2 (*Holotheticity of a Production Function under a Given Type of Technical Progress*) When the whole or total effect of technical progress T, working through the technical progress functions ϕ and ψ in f, is represented by some strictly monotone transformation F, then the production function is said to be "holothetic" (complete-transformation type) under a given T,

$$\begin{aligned} \overline{Y} &= f(K, L, t) = f(\phi, \psi, 0) = f(\phi, \psi) = f(\overline{K}, \overline{L}) \\ &= f[\phi(K, L, t), \psi(K, L, t)] \\ &= g(h(K, L), t) = F_{(t)}[f(K, L)] = F_{(t)}[Y], \end{aligned} \tag{4''}$$

where $h(K, L) = f(K, L, 0) = f(K, L)$.

We present several interpretations of the holotheticity condition. First, we observe that if and when the *total effect of a given type of technical progress working through the technical progress functions is completely transformed into a scale effect of production without changing the shape of the isoquant map*, then the production function is said to be *holothetic* under a given type of technical progress T. The impact of technical progress is completely absorbed by the production function as a *scale effect*. Another way of stating this is that *if the isoquant map of a production function is not affected by a given type of technical progress transformation T, other than relabeling its isoquants, then the production function is said to be holothetic under the given T.* Let R be the marginal rate of substitution between capital and labor before technical progress takes place, $R = f_L/f_K$, where f_L and f_K are positive (or nonnegative). Let $\bar{R}$ be the marginal rate of substitution between K and L after a given type of technical progress takes place according to (5), i.e.,

$$\bar{R} = \bar{Y}_L/\bar{Y}_K = (f_\phi \phi_L + f_\psi \psi_L)/(f_\phi \phi_K + f_\psi \psi_K).$$

Then the holotheticity of a production function under a given ϕ and ψ implies that

$$R \equiv Y_L/Y_K \equiv (f_\phi \phi_L + f_\psi \psi_L)/(f_\phi \phi_K + f_\psi \psi_K) \equiv \bar{R}.$$

That is to say, the marginal rates of substitution between K and L, before and after technical progress, are exactly identical. Since R is independent of the technical progress parameter t by definition, $\bar{R}$ must also be independent under holotheticity after technical progress. Care must be taken not to confuse the preceding condition with the condition that R is equal to

$$R^* = \frac{\partial \bar{Y}/\partial \bar{L}}{\partial \bar{Y}/\partial \bar{K}} = \frac{f_{\bar{L}}}{f_{\bar{K}}} = \gamma(K, L, t).$$

In general, even under the holotheticity condition, R is not equal to R^*, the marginal rate of substitution (MRS) between effective capital $\bar{K}$ and effective labor $\bar{L}$, which depends not only on K and L but also on t, i.e., $R = f_L/f_K \not\equiv f_{\bar{L}}/f_{\bar{K}}$. Before technical progress, we have $Y_L/Y_K = f_L/f_K = R(K, L) = \text{MRS} = -dK/dL|_{Y=\text{const}}$. After technical progress under *holotheticity*, the marginal rate of substitution between K and L is

$$\bar{R} = \frac{\bar{Y}_L}{\bar{Y}_K} = \left(\frac{dF}{df}\right) f_L \Big/ \left(\frac{dF}{df}\right) f_K = \frac{f_L}{f_K} = R.$$

The marginal rate of substitution under *holotheticity* between *effective* capital and *effective* labor is $R^* = \bar{Y}_{\bar{L}}/\bar{Y}_{\bar{K}} = f_\psi/f_\phi = R(\bar{K}, \bar{L}) \neq R(K, L)$. An obvious exception to this statement is the case of the holothetic technology under the uniform factor-augmenting technical progress—the homothetic technology, where $R \equiv \bar{R} \equiv R^*$. This is coincidental because the *invariant*, which will be defined later, of ϕ and ψ happens to be equal to R. When T_t: $\phi = A(t)K$, $\psi = A(t)L$ (uniform factor-augmenting), the holotheticity condition must be equal to the homotheticity condition $\bar{Y} = F_{(t)}[KP(L/K)]$, and only in this case do we have $\bar{Y}_L/\bar{Y}_K = \bar{Y}_{\bar{L}}/\bar{Y}_{\bar{K}} = Y_L/Y_K$ (a straight line expansion path; see Section 20). In general, the slopes of the isoquant map measured in terms of K and L and in terms of $\bar{K}$ and $\bar{L}$ are different.

The second interpretation of the holotheticity condition is closely related to the concept of separability of technical progress. From condition (4″), it is seen that as t affects Y through the technical progress functions ϕ and ψ, t is separated from the basic technology $f(K, L)$. The function (4″) is said to be weakly separable with respect to K, L, and t if

$$\frac{\partial\left(\dfrac{\partial g}{\partial K}\Big/\dfrac{\partial g}{\partial L}\right)}{\partial t} \equiv 0.$$

Since $R = \bar{R}$, $\bar{R}$ is independent of t and $\partial\bar{R}/\partial t \equiv 0$. But this is exactly the conditions of weak separability. Hence, when the production function is holothetic under ϕ and ψ, the total effect of technical progress is *transformed* to a weakly separable form through the technical progress functions.[4] Again care must be taken to note that we are not assuming a weakly separable production function f, but that the continuous transformations of t through ϕ and ψ result in the weakly separable form $F_{(t)}$ if f is holothetic under ϕ and ψ.

Third, if the production function is *holothetic* under T, the production function is transformed into another function of the *same* family by the operation of technical progress. Consequently, the family of underlying curves is *invariant* as a whole under the transformations ϕ and ψ. Thus the concept of *holotheticity* is closely related to the concept of *invariance* under the technical progress transformation T. This last interpretation enables us to promulgate the analysis of holotheticity in terms of the analysis of invariance, which is central to the Lie theory of transformation groups.

In summary, the holotheticity of a production function means that:

(i) The total impact of technical progress is completely transformed to a scale effect. Hence the isoquant map, before and after technical progress, is unchanged other than the relabeling of its isoquants.

(ii) The marginal rate of substitution between capital and labor is unaffected by technical progress.[5] This is an alternative way of saying that the production function becomes weakly separable with respect to K, L, and t as a result of technical progress working through ϕ and ψ.

[4] I owe this interpretation to Paul A. Samuelson via private correspondence.

[5] Thus the so-called "neutrality" of technical progress in the Hicks sense is a special case of holotheticity when $F_{(t)}[f(K, L)] = A(t)f(K, L)$ (see Section 13).

(iii) The technical progress functions transform each production function into another function of the same family. Hence a family of production functions is invariant under the technical progress transformation.

Remark It is important to note that the concept of holothetic technology is defined in terms of "a given type of technical progress." Thus a class of production functions may be holothetic under a certain type of technical progress T_1, but may not be holothetic under a different type of technical progress T_2. This point will be discussed further in a later section.

4. We want to show that if we impose certain conditions on ϕ and ψ, we can find a general f (up to monotonicity) such that (4″) will always be satisfied. The interpretation of holotheticity as the invariance condition of the Lie group theory suggests that we must impose certain restrictions on the technical progress transformation T. We assume the following conditions:

Assumptions (*The Lie Group Properties*) The technical progress functions ϕ and ψ satisfy the following:

(A) The result of the successive performance of two transformations

$$T_t\colon \begin{cases} \bar{K} = \phi(K, L, t) \\ \bar{L} = \psi(K, L, t) \end{cases} \quad \text{and} \quad T_{\bar{t}}\colon \begin{cases} \bar{\bar{K}} = \phi(\bar{K}, \bar{L}, \bar{t}) \\ \bar{\bar{L}} = \psi(\bar{K}, \bar{L}, \bar{t}) \end{cases}$$

is the same as that of the single transformation,

$$T_{t+\bar{t}}\colon \quad \bar{\bar{K}} = \phi(K, L, t + \bar{t}), \qquad \bar{\bar{L}} = \psi(K, L, t + \bar{t}).$$

That is to say,

$$T_t T_{\bar{t}} = T_{t+\bar{t}}. \tag{6-i}$$

(B) The value $-t$ determines the transformation inverse to that obtained by using t:

$$T_t^{-1} = T_{-t} \tag{6-ii}$$

or

$$T_t^{-1}\colon \quad K = \phi(\bar{K}, \bar{L}, -t), \qquad L = \psi(\bar{K}, \bar{L}, -t),$$

and

(C) $t = t_0 = 0$ gives the identical transformation, $t_0 = 0$, i.e.,

$$T_0 = I, \tag{6-iii}$$

or

$$T_0\colon \begin{cases} \bar{K} = \phi(K, L, t_0) = K = \phi(K, L, 0), \\ \bar{L} = \psi(K, L, t_0) = L = \psi(K, L, 0). \end{cases}$$

When ϕ and ψ satisfy conditions (A)–(C), then the type of technical progress T is said to possess the *Lie group properties*[6] (see the Appendix, Part II). This type of technical progress may be referred to as the *Lie type of technical progress.* The Lie group properties (6-i)–(6-iii) amount to the assertion that the set of transformations (5), under the operation of composition, is a group isomorphic to the real line under the operation of addition.[7] More simply, it suffices to have

$$\text{(i)}\quad \phi[\phi(K, L; t), \psi(K, L; t); \bar{t}] = \phi(K, L; t + \bar{t}),$$
$$\psi[\phi(K, L; t), \psi(K, L; t); \bar{t}] = \psi(K, L; t + \bar{t});$$

$$\text{(ii)}\quad \phi[\phi(K, L; t), \psi(K, L; t); -t] = \phi^{-1}(\bar{K}, \bar{L}; t) = K,$$
$$\psi[\phi(K, L; t), \psi(K, L; t); -t] = \psi^{-1}(\bar{K}, \bar{L}; t) = L;$$

$$\text{(iii)}\quad \phi(K, L; 0) = K, \psi(K, L; 0) = L.$$

In summary, from the aggregate of the transformations included in the family (5), where t varies continuously over a given range and ϕ and ψ are differentiable with respect to t in the given range, any particular transformation of the family is obtained by assigning a particular value to t. Any two successive transformations (including identical and inverse transformations) of the family are equivalent to a single transformation of the family and thus these transformations form a *finite continuous group*, G_1 *of one parameter* (see the Appendix, Part III).

Economic Interpretation of the Lie Group Properties

5. The group properties of the technical progress functions can be given a simple and straightforward economic interpretation. We may assume that the technical progress parameter t also represents the year t in which technical progress takes place. Thus $\bar{K}$ and $\bar{L}$ may be considered as the "effective capital" and "effective labor" at year t. Property (A) implies that if the "effective capital" and "effective labor" at year t and the "effective capital" and "effective labor" at year $\bar{t}$ are expressed as the same functions ϕ and ψ of the previous year's values, then any year's "effective capital" and "effective labor" will be expressed only by the changes $(t + \bar{t})$ in the technical progress parameter. Property (B) implies that the initial capital and labor

[6] The associative law also holds trivially and thus is excluded. The aggregate here is represented by $T = \{T_t\}$. Hence $T_t T_{\bar{t}} \in T$, $T_{-t} \in T$, and $T_0 \in T$.

[7] Since any one-parameter group of transformations is equivalent to a one-parameter group of translations, it may be further transformed to a group isomorphic to the real line under the operation of addition (see the Appendix, Theorem 5).

can also be expressed by the same technical progress functions by assigning the appropriate parameter such as $(-t)$. Finally, property (C) implies that the initial capital and labor will always be equal to "effective" capital and "effective" labor if there is no technical progress ($t = 0$).

It may be argued that assumptions (A)–(C) are too restrictive, for there may be many types of technical progress operating in an economy which do not satisfy these restrictions. Certainly, it may be possible to construct a type of technical progress which is meaningful, yet does not satisfy the group properties. However, it should be noted that all of the known types discussed in the economic literature thus far do in fact satisfy the foregoing assumptions (see the later section on specific types, Part VI). Second, as it will be shown later, the Lie group properties are the characteristics that are useful for *distinguishing* one production function from another. In other words, the study of the essential nature of a production function can be best pursued by these assumptions regardless of their realistic values. Furthermore, it will be observed later that each known production function manifests the holothetic property compatible with at least one type of technical progress having these restrictions. Hence, starting with any given family of production functions, one can always derive at least one type of technical progress possessing these properties (Theorem 4). This line of approach, however, is, in many instances, more complicated and more involved from the mathematical point of view.

6. We require a few preliminary results. The effect of an "infinitesimal change" in the technical progress parameter t is first to change the technical progress function (5) by infinitesimal amounts, which in turn also changes the production function (4′) by an infinitesimal amount. Thus we first study the effect of changes in t on the technical progress functions. Since the technical progress functions ϕ and ψ are assumed to be generally analytic functions, the transformations changes K and L by infinitesimal amounts, i.e.,

$$\bar{K} = \phi(K, L; t_0 + \delta t) = \phi(K, L; \delta t), \qquad t_0 = 0,$$
$$\bar{L} = \psi(K, L; t_0 + \delta t) = \psi(K, L; \delta t), \qquad t_0 = 0,$$

where t_0 is the value of the parameter determining the identical transformation (6-iii), and δt is an infinitesimal. Then we have

$$\begin{aligned} \delta K &= \bar{K} - K = \xi(K, L)\,\delta t, \qquad \xi(K, L) = \left(\frac{\partial \phi}{\partial t}\right)_{t_0=0}, \\ \delta L &= \bar{L} - L = \eta(K, L)\,\delta t, \qquad \eta(K, L) = \left(\frac{\partial \psi}{\partial t}\right)_{t_0=0}. \end{aligned} \tag{7}$$

We shall call this an *infinitesimal transformation of technical progress*. Using the symbol introduced by Lie (Appendix), we shall write this as[8]

$$U = \xi(K, L)\frac{\partial}{\partial K} + \eta(K, L)\frac{\partial}{\partial L}. \tag{7'}$$

Lemma 1 (*Uniqueness of the Infinitesimal Transformation*) *Every Lie type of technical change* (5) *has one and only one independent infinitesimal transformation* (7′).

Proof This is the direct consequence of Theorem 2 of the Appendix.

Q.E.D.

We now give economic interpretation to the infinitesimal transformation applied to a production function.

Lemma 2 (*Measure of Technical Change*) *If a production function is subjected to a Lie type of technical change* (5), *then* the first-order measure *of the impact of technical change near the identical transformation* (*more simply, the* measure of technical change) $(\partial\bar{Y}/\partial t)_0$ *is equal to* Uf, i.e.,

$$\left(\frac{\partial\bar{Y}}{\partial t}\right)_{t=0} = Uf = \xi(K, L)\frac{\partial f}{\partial K} + \eta(K, L)\frac{\partial f}{\partial L} = \begin{pmatrix}\text{infinitesimal}\\ \text{transformation}\\ \text{of capital}\end{pmatrix}$$

$$\times\begin{pmatrix}\text{marginal}\\ \text{product}\\ \text{of capital}\end{pmatrix} + \begin{pmatrix}\text{infinitesimal}\\ \text{transformation}\\ \text{of labor}\end{pmatrix}\begin{pmatrix}\text{marginal}\\ \text{product}\\ \text{of labor}\end{pmatrix}. \tag{7''}$$

Proof Assuming f to be generally analytic, we expand $\bar{Y} = \bar{f}(\bar{K}, \bar{L}) = f(K, L, t)$ as

$$\bar{Y} = \bar{f} = f(K, L) + \left(\frac{\partial\bar{f}}{\partial t}\right)_0 t + \left(\frac{\partial^2\bar{f}}{\partial t^2}\right)_0 \frac{t^2}{2!} + \cdots. \tag{$4'_2$}$$

On writing $\bar{\xi} = \partial\bar{K}/\partial t$, $\bar{\eta} = \partial\bar{L}/\partial t$ of Eq. (5), and $\bar{U}\bar{f} = \bar{\xi}\,\partial\bar{f}/\partial\bar{K} + \bar{\eta}\,\partial\bar{f}/\partial\bar{L}$, so that $(\bar{\xi})_0 = \xi(K, L)$, $(\bar{\eta})_0 = \eta(K, L)$, and $(\bar{U}\bar{f})_0 = \xi(K, L)\,\partial f/\partial K +$

[8] If $f(K, L)$ is a generally analytic function of K and L, the effect of the infinitesimal transformation on it is to replace it by $f(K + \xi\,\delta t, L + \eta\,\delta t)$, which on expanding by Taylor's theorem becomes

$$f(K + \xi\,\delta t, L + \eta\,\delta t) = f(K, L) + \left(\xi\frac{\partial f}{\partial K} + \eta\frac{\partial f}{\partial L}\right)\delta t + \cdots.$$

But the expression within the parentheses of the second term is exactly equal to the effect of the infinitesimal transformation U on f, or $Uf = \xi\,\partial f/\partial K + \eta\,\partial f/\partial L$. That is the reason Lie introduced this symbol.

$\eta(K, L)\, \partial f/\partial L = Uf$, it follows that $\partial \bar{f}/\partial t = \bar{U}\bar{f}$ and hence $(\partial \bar{f}/\partial t)_0 = (\partial \bar{Y}/\partial t)_0 = Uf$ is the first-order measure of technical change. Q.E.D.

We may sometimes write (7″) as

$$Uf = UK\frac{\partial f}{\partial K} + UL\frac{\partial f}{\partial L} = \begin{pmatrix}\text{measure of}\\ \text{technical change}\\ \text{of capital}\end{pmatrix}\begin{pmatrix}\text{marginal}\\ \text{product}\\ \text{of capital}\end{pmatrix} + \begin{pmatrix}\text{measure of}\\ \text{technical change}\\ \text{of labor}\end{pmatrix}\begin{pmatrix}\text{marginal}\\ \text{product}\\ \text{of labor}\end{pmatrix}, \tag{7‴}$$

since $\xi(K, L)$ and $\eta(K, L)$ can also be expressed as

$$\xi(K, L) = UK \qquad \text{and} \qquad \eta(K, L) = UL,$$

where U is given by (7′). (See the Appendix, Part III.)

Definition 3 (*Invariant Family of Curves*) A family of curves is said to be *invariant* under a group G_1, if every transformation of the group transforms each curve into some curve of the same family, i.e.,

$$g = F(f), \tag{8}$$

where $g(K, L, t) = f[\phi(K, L, t), \psi(K, L, t)]$ (see the Appendix, Part III).

In this chapter we shall consider families containing a single infinity of curves only, i.e., those whose equations involve a single parameter of technical change t. As we suspected earlier, the concept of holotheticity is equivalent with the invariance property of the transformation group G_1, and hence we formulate

Lemma 3 (*Fundamental Lemma of Holotheticity*) *A family of production functions is* holothetic *under a given type of technical progress if and only if it is* invariant *under a group.*

Proof If a family of production functions is holothetic, we have (4″) from Definition 2. Hence the production function after technical progress $F_{(t)}$ is always a function of the production function before technical progress f. But this is exactly the condition of the invariance of a family of curves under a group. Conversely, writing the equation of the family in the form $f(K, L) = C$, it will be invariant, if $f(\bar{K}, \bar{L}) \equiv g(K, L, t) = C'$ is the equation of the same family of curves for every value of t, C, and C'. A single infinity of curves determined by an equation involving an arbitrary constant is equally determined by a unique differential equation of the first order, of which the equation involving the arbitrary constant is the general solution. If $f(K, L) = C$ and $g(K, L, t) = C'$ are to be the same family of curves, these equations must be solutions of the same differential equation of the first order. The differential equations arising from these equations are

$$\frac{\partial f}{\partial K}\,dK + \frac{\partial f}{\partial L}\,dL = 0 \qquad \text{and} \qquad \frac{\partial g}{\partial K}\,dK + \frac{\partial g}{\partial L}\,dL = 0.$$

In order that these be one and the same equation, it is necessary and sufficient that

$$\begin{vmatrix} \dfrac{\partial f}{\partial K} & \dfrac{\partial f}{\partial L} \\[2ex] \dfrac{\partial g}{\partial K} & \dfrac{\partial g}{\partial L} \end{vmatrix} \equiv 0 \qquad \text{or} \qquad \frac{\dfrac{\partial f}{\partial K}}{\dfrac{\partial f}{\partial L}} \equiv \frac{\dfrac{\partial g}{\partial K}}{\dfrac{\partial g}{\partial L}},$$

from which it follows that $g(K, L, t) = F_{(t)}(f(K, L))$. This condition is just the condition of holotheticity. Q.E.D.

III. Existence of General Holothetic Technology[9]

Necessary and Sufficient Condition for Holotheticity

7. Using the previous lemmas, we can now formulate the following important theorem:

Theorem 1 (*Necessary and Sufficient Condition for Holotheticity*) *The necessary and sufficient condition that a production function be holothetic under a given T is that the first-order measure of the impact of technical change is some function of the production function itself, i.e.,*

$$Uf = \xi(K, L)\frac{\partial f}{\partial K} + \eta(K, L)\frac{\partial f}{\partial L} = G(f), \tag{9}$$

where U is the infinitesimal transformation defined by (7′).

Proof In view of the fundamental lemma of holotheticity, Lemma 3, a production function is holothetic if and only if it is invariant under (7′). Assuming f to be generally analytic, by the fundamental theorem of Lie groups (Appendix, Theorem 4), f is invariant if and only if (9) holds.[10]

Q.E.D.

[9] Rather than stating "a technology holothetic under a given type of technical change," we may call it simply "a holothetic technology under a given type of technical change" or in short, "a holothetic technology."

[10] If $Uf \equiv 0$ for all values of K and L, we have $\bar{f} = f(\bar{K}, \bar{L}) \equiv f(K, L)$, the family of "path curves." In economics, we may exclude this case in order to include only nontrivial cases. $G(f)$ may take any convenient function of f such as $G(f) \equiv 1$.

Economic Interpretation of Theorem 1

The total effect of any technical change transformation (5) on f is given by

$$\begin{aligned}\bar{Y} &= \bar{f}(\bar{K}, \bar{L}) = f + Uf\frac{t}{1!} + U^2 f\frac{t^2}{2!} + \cdots + U^n f\frac{t^n}{n!} + \cdots \\ &= f(K, L) + g^1(K, L)\frac{t}{1!} + g^2(K, L)\frac{t^2}{2!} + \cdots + g^n\frac{t^n}{n!} + \cdots \\ &= e^{tU}f. \end{aligned} \tag{$4'_3$}$$

If the left-hand side of (9), which is the first-order measure of the impact of technical change, is equal to some function of f, then all of the higher-order measures of the impact of technical change $U^n f$ are also equal to some functions of f, because of $U^n f = UU^{n-1}f = UUU^{n-2}f = U\cdots Uf = U^{n-1}G(f)$. Hence, under holotheticity, (4′) reduces to

$$\bar{Y} = \bar{f} = f(\bar{K}, \bar{L}) = f + G(f)t + G'(f)G(f)\frac{t^2}{2!} + \cdots = g(f, t). \tag{$4'''$}$$

The result of the technical progress transformation (7′) applied on the production function does *not* change the form of f but changes only its scale effect. This is exactly the property of holotheticity required by the definition—*a complete transformation of technical change into the scale effect.*

Existence of the General Holothetic Technology

8. We are now in a position to demonstrate the existence of the general class of holothetic technology under technical change T.

Theorem 2 (*Existence*) *If the technical progress functions T_t of Eq.* (5) *satisfy the Lie group properties* (6-i)–(6-iii), *then there exists one and only one holothetic technology under T, such that Eq.* (4″) *holds. Hence there exists a general family of production functions under which the total effect of technical progress T is completely transformed to a returns to scale effect.*

Proof From Theorem 1, the problem is reduced to that of finding a general solution to the Lagrange linear partial differential equation (9). In view of the fundamental existence theorem (John [1971]), there exists a unique general solution (up to monotonicity) to (9). To solve (9), consider the corresponding system of ordinary differential equations

$$\frac{dK}{\xi(K, L)} = \frac{dL}{\eta(K, L)} = \frac{df}{G(f)}, \tag{$9'$}$$

and let its solutions be expressed as the so-called characteristics of the system,

$$u(K, L) = \alpha, \qquad v(K, L) = H(f) + \beta,$$

where $H(f) = \int df/G(f)$. Now since α and β are arbitrary constants, we can set $\alpha = -\beta$. Hence

$$H(f) = u(K, L) + v(K, L),$$

or

$$f = H^{-1}[u(K, L) + v(K, L)] = f(K, L) = Y.$$

Hence there exists a general type of families of holothetic production functions satisfying the partial differential equation (9), which establishes the existence of the holothetic technology. Q.E.D.

Estimation of Technical Progress and the Scale Effect

9. The preceding theorem will answer the basic question related to the Solow–Stigler controversy. Using this theorem, we can now find the condition under which both the scale economies and technical change may be theoretically identified. As the converse of the theorem, we formulate

Theorem 3 (*Possibility Theorem of the Estimation of Technical Progress*) *The effect of technical change T and the scale effect of f are independently identifiable if and only if the production function is* not *holothetic under the given type of technical change T.*

Proof This follows immediately from the definition of the holothetic technology under a given technical progress transformation. Q.E.D.

The preceding theorem makes it *possible* to estimate both the technical progress effect and scale effect of a production function, provided that the production function is not holothetic under the assumed type of technical progress. Thus, if technical progress is assumed to be the uniform (neutral) factor-augmenting type, i.e.,

$$T_t\colon\ \bar{K} = e^{\alpha t}K, \qquad \bar{L} = e^{\alpha t}L, \qquad \alpha \geqq 0,$$

then the holothetic technology is nothing but the *homothetic* technology

$$Y = g[f(K, L)], \qquad \lambda f = f(\lambda K, \lambda L), \qquad g' > 0.$$

Hence, after technical progress, we have

$$Y = g[f(\bar{K}, \bar{L})] = g(e^{\alpha t}f(K, L)) = F_{(t)}[f(K, L)].$$

In order to estimate both the uniform rate of technical progress and the scale effect, the preceding theorem requires that we should *never* use the homothetic technology under the neutral type of technical change.

On the other hand, if the underlying assumption of technical change is the nonuniform, biased type, the holothetic technology is the almost homothetic family of production functions (Lau [1978], Sato [1977]), and thus, any other families, including the homothetic family, should be used in order to isolate the effect of that type of technical progress from the effects of scale economies. This partly answers the question raised in the introduction.

To empirically identify the underlying type of technical change for a *non*-holothetic technology, we may utilize Lemma 2 [Eq. (7″)]. Thus, if the measure of technical change is independently estimated by, say the Kendrick method (Kendrick and Sato [1963]), we may be able to identify the infinitesimal transformation ξ and η using the price data of capital and labor from a simple regression of

$$\left(\frac{\partial \bar{f}}{\partial t}\right)_0 = \begin{pmatrix}\text{measure of}\\ \text{technical change}\end{pmatrix} = \xi(K, L)\begin{pmatrix}\text{marginal product}\\ \text{of capital}\end{pmatrix}$$

$$+ \eta(K, L)\begin{pmatrix}\text{marginal product}\\ \text{of labor}\end{pmatrix} + (\text{random term}).$$

We shall return to this approach later (see Part IX).

10. We now give examples to show how the theorems derived thus far can be utilized.

Examples[11] (a) *The nonuniform factor-augmenting type (biased type)* Here we have

$$T_t\colon \quad \bar{K} = e^{\alpha t}K, \quad \bar{L} = e^{\beta t}, \qquad \alpha \neq \beta, \quad \alpha > 0, \quad \beta > 0,$$

or

$$U = \alpha K\frac{\partial}{\partial K} + \beta L\frac{\partial}{\partial L}.$$

The holothetic technology under this type is obtained from

$$Uf = \alpha K\frac{\partial f}{\partial K} + \beta L\frac{\partial f}{\partial L} = G(f) \neq 0 \qquad \text{or} \qquad Y = f[K^{1/\alpha}Q(L^{\alpha}/K^{\beta})],$$

which is the almost homothetic class of production functions (Lau [1978], Sato [1977]). When $\alpha = \beta$, the above reduces to the homothetic family.

[11] These examples are provided to convey a feeling of reality and the operational aspect of these theorems. Part VI is devoted to special cases of holothetic technologies that are meaningful from an economic point of view.

(b) *The additive type* If we have

$$\bar{K} = K, \qquad \bar{L} = L + t \qquad \text{or} \qquad \bar{K} = K + t, \qquad \bar{L} = L,$$

then

$$U = \frac{\partial}{\partial L} \qquad \text{or} \qquad U = \frac{\partial}{\partial K}.$$

The holothetic technology under $U = \partial/\partial L$ is $Y = f[L + Q(K)]$, and under $U = \partial/\partial K$ is $Y = f[K + Q(L)]$, respectively.

IV. Existence of a Lie Type of Technical Progress

11. The next question is: Can we conversely show whether or not a given production function is holothetic under some type of technical progress functions? That is to say, is there always some T such that the given isoquant map is unaltered? The answer is affirmative. We wish to show that for any given production function there exists at least one type of technical progress which possesses the Lie group properties.

A given (continuous) isoquant map implies that there exists a differential equation for the marginal rate of substitution,

$$M(K, L)\,dK + N(K, L)\,dL = 0, \tag{10}$$

where N/M is the marginal rate of substitution f_L/f_K. A family of production functions is holothetic under a given Lie type of technical progress if and only if the differential equation for the isoquant map (10) is itself invariant under that type of technical progress.

Lemma 4 *(Integrating Factor and Lie Type of Technical Progress) If $I(K, L)$ is an integrating factor of* (10), *and $\xi(K, L)$ and $\eta(K, L)$ are any two functions such that*

$$I(K, L) = (\xi(K, L)M(K, L) + \eta(K, L)N(K, L))^{-1}, \tag{11}$$

then the family of integral curves of (10) *is holothetic under*

$$U = \xi(K, L)\frac{\partial}{\partial K} + \eta(K, L)\frac{\partial}{\partial L}.$$

Proof This is a direct consequence of Corollary 8-2 of the Appendix, Part IV. Q.E.D.

Theorem 4 *(Existence of a Lie Type of Technical Progress) Given an isoquant map, there exists at least one Lie type of technical change under which the production function is holothetic.*

Proof Since the isoquant map is given, the differential equation (10) and an integrating factor (11) are known. Lemma 4 immediately suggests that the differential equation (10) is invariant under $U = \xi\, \partial/\partial K + \eta\, \partial/\partial L$, where ξ and η are given by the integrating factor. However, since ξ and η are subject to the single condition (11), one of them may be chosen arbitrarily, and the other is determined uniquely. Hence there exists at least one U for any given M and N. Q.E.D.

Interpretation of Theorem 4

This theorem states that for any arbitrary production function (or its family), one can theoretically always identify at least one type of technical progress that satisfies all the Lie group properties. As a matter of fact, starting from a given production function, one can in principle identify an infinite number of Lie types of technical progress under which the production function is holothetic (see also Section 18).

However, there are several reasons why we did not begin with Theorem 4. First, since there are an infinite number of Lie types of technical progress for any given production function, the problem of finding U from a production function is *not* unique. Thus finding the Lie types of technical progress for a given production function cannot be effectively used as the method of studying the basic characteristics of the production function. On the other hand, in view of the existence theorem (Theorem 2) of a general type of holothetic technology, given a Lie type of technical progress, the inverse problem of the foregoing theorem is much more direct.

Second, in general the determination of U for a given isoquant is not an easy problem, especially when one is only given the differential equation (10). Consider the case of a market observation of the marginal rate of substitution between capital and labor under the assumption of cost minimization,

$$p_L/p_K = R(K, L) = f_L/f_K.$$

This gives the differential equation (10) from $f_L/f_K = -dK/dL$, or

$$dK + R\, dL = 0 \qquad \text{or} \qquad M\, dK + N\, dL = 0.$$

Unless one has a priori knowledge of the underlying production function, it is not in general easy to identify an integrating factor, and thus the Lie type of technical progress, although theoretically there always exists an integrating factor and a family of integral curves by the existence theorem of differential equations. Although such Lie types of technical progress always exist and one is sometimes suggested by the nature of the isoquant map giving rise to the differential equation of the marginal rate of substitution (such as homotheticity), the number of equations for which they are known is comparatively small.

Third, for practical purposes, the problem of finding the general class of production functions holothetic under a given Lie type of technical progress is much more direct. Under the condition of a one-parameter group of technical change, the infinitesimal transformation implies the system of differential equations for capital and labor. This is in many cases not a very unrealistic assumption. For this as well as other reasons, we first studied the problem of finding holothetic technology for a given type of technical progress.

Examples

12. The following will serve to illustrate the usefulness of Lemma 4 and Theorem 4.

(a) *Homothetic Cobb–Douglas functions*, $Y = F(K^\alpha L^\beta)$ The differential equation and an integrating factor are $\alpha L\, dK + \beta K\, dL = 0$ and $I = 1/KLQ(Y)$, respectively. Thus, from (11), $KLQ(Y) = \xi\alpha L + \eta\beta K$. By setting $\xi = a(Y)K$, we can immediately obtain $\eta = b(Y)L$, $b(Y) = (Q(Y) - \alpha a(Y))/\beta$. Hence it is holothetic under $U = a(Y)K\, \partial/\partial K + b(Y)L\, \partial/\partial L$. Obviously, if a and b are constants, we obtain the biased factor-augmenting type of technical progress under which the Cobb–Douglas family is known to be holothetic.

(b) *Homothetic CES functions* (Arrow *et al.* [1961]), $Y = F[\alpha K^{-\rho} + \beta L^{-\rho}]$ Here, we have $\alpha K^{-(1+\rho)}\, dK + \beta L^{-(1+\rho)}\, dL = 0$ and $I = 1/Q(Y)$. A Lie type of technical change is immediately obtained as

$$U = a(Y)K^{(1+\rho)} \frac{\partial}{\partial K} + b(Y)L^{(1+\rho)} \frac{\partial}{\partial L}.$$

If $Q(Y)$ in I is set equal to $\alpha K^{-\rho} + \beta L^{-\rho}$ and ξ equal to K, so that $\alpha K^{-\rho} + \beta L^{-\rho} = \xi\alpha K^{-(1+\rho)} + \eta\beta L^{-(1+\rho)}$ and $\eta = L$, we get $U = K\, \partial/\partial K + L\, \partial/\partial L$, which is the neutral type of technical progress.

"*Neutrality*" *of Technical Progress*

13. The concepts of "holothetic" production functions under a Lie type of technical change and the "neutrality" of technical progress in the sense of Hicks are closely related. As a corollary to the foregoing theorem, we can formulate

Corollary to Theorem 4 (*Product-Augmenting Type of Technical Progress*) *For any production function, there exists at least one type of technical progress function such that they can always be reduced to a "Hicksian neutral product-augmenting type" of technical progress, i.e.,*

$$f(K, L, t) = f(\bar{K}, \bar{L}) = A(t)f(K, L). \tag{12}$$

Proof Theorem 4 guarantees the existence of a Lie type of technical progress for a given production function f. Let that type be

$$U = \xi \frac{\partial}{\partial K} + \eta \frac{\partial}{\partial L}.$$

In view of Theorem 1 [Eq. (9)], holotheticity requires that we have $\xi\, \partial f/\partial K + \eta\, \partial f/\partial L = G(f)$. However, from (4‴), we can write $Y(K, L, t)$ as

$$\begin{aligned} Y(K, L, t) \equiv f(\bar{K}, \bar{L}) &= f(K, L) + Uft + U^2 f \frac{t^2}{2!} + \cdots \\ &= f + G(f)t + G'(f)G(f)\frac{t^2}{2!} + \cdots. \end{aligned}$$

In order that the impact of U on f be Hicks neutral, we must have (12) with $A(0) \equiv 1$. By setting

$$Uf = G(f) = \alpha f(K, L), \tag{13}$$

we obtain

$$f(\bar{K}, \bar{L}) = f(K, L) + t\alpha f(K, L) + \cdots = e^{\alpha t} f(K, L) = A(t)f(K, L),$$

$$\alpha = \partial A(0)/\partial t. \quad \text{Q.E.D.}$$

Remark Condition (13), which is a special case of $G(f)$, may be referred to as the *transformation of a Lie type to the Hicksian type of technical progress*.

V. Structures of Holothetic Technology

14. The problems arising from the Solow–Stigler controversy have now been completely resolved. The analysis thus far, however, strongly indicates that Lie groups are a powerful method to study general properties of a production function. More specifically, the existence theorem of a holothetic technology (Theorem 2) suggests that the analysis of a family of production functions by the holotheticity condition can provide a useful method for categorization of the basic characteristics of that family. In addition to the several interpretations already given in Parts II and III, we present here additional characterizations of a holothetic technology.

Existence of the General Type of Holothetic Differential Equation

Given a (Lie) type of technical progress, one can always obtain an alternative representation of the technical progress functions by introducing the so-called *extended* infinitesimal transformation (see the Appendix, Part IV). The (once) extended transformation includes not only capital and labor, but also the marginal rate of substitution between them. A given type of technical progress $\bar{K}$ and $\bar{L}$ can now be extended to include the marginal rate of substitution as

$$T': \begin{cases} \bar{K} = \phi(K, L, t), \\ \bar{L} = \psi(K, L, t), \\ \dfrac{d\bar{L}}{d\bar{K}} = \pi\left(K, L, \dfrac{dL}{dK}, t\right) = \left(\dfrac{\partial\psi}{\partial K} + \dfrac{\partial\psi}{\partial L}\dfrac{dL}{dK}\right)\Big/\left(\dfrac{\partial\phi}{\partial K} + \dfrac{\partial\phi}{\partial L}\dfrac{dL}{dK}\right). \end{cases} \tag{5'}$$

Starting with the one-parameter Lie type of technical progress (5), it is easily seen that the corresponding extended transformation (5′) also constitutes a one-parameter Lie type of technical progress in the three variables K, L, dL/dK (see the Appendix, Part IV). Hence there exists a unique infinitesimal transformation corresponding to (5′). Following Lie, we shall write the symbol of the *extended* transformation as

$$U' = \xi(K, L)\frac{\partial}{\partial K} + \eta(K, L)\frac{\partial}{\partial L} + \eta'\left(K, L, \frac{dL}{dK}\right)\frac{\partial}{\partial(dL/dK)}, \tag{14}$$

where ξ and η are defined by (5) and η' is the infinitesimal transformation corresponding to $\pi(K, L, dL/dK, t)$. The infinitesimal transformation for $d\bar{L}/d\bar{K} = \pi$ is reduced to [Appendix, Eq. (30′)]

$$\eta' = \frac{d\eta}{dK} - \frac{dL}{dK}\frac{d\xi}{dK} = \frac{\partial\eta}{\partial K} + \left(\frac{\partial\eta}{\partial L} - \frac{\partial\xi}{\partial K}\right)\frac{dL}{dK} - \frac{\partial\xi}{\partial L}\left(\frac{dL}{dK}\right)^2. \tag{15}$$

One basic property of (14) is that it provides an alternative (but equivalent) representation of the original technical progress functions. But this extension enables us to study the holotheticity condition from the perspective of the differential equation. We need

***Lemma* 5** (*Holothetic Differential Equation for the Marginal Rate of Substitution*) *Given U and therefore U', the general type of invariant differential equation $h(K, L, dL/dK) = 0$ is obtained by the condition that*

$$U'h = \xi(K, L)\frac{\partial h}{\partial K} + \eta(K, L)\frac{\partial h}{\partial L} + \eta'\frac{\partial h}{\partial(dL/dK)}$$
$$= 0, \qquad \textit{whenever} \quad h(K, L, dL/dK) = 0. \tag{16}$$

Proof This is a direct consequence of Theorem 6 of the Appendix, which defines the invariant condition for the differential equation. Q.E.D.

Here $h(K, L, dL/dK) = 0$ may be called the *holothetic* differential equation under a given Lie type of technical change.

This lemma enables us to speak of the holothetic differential equation for the marginal rate of substitution equation. Expressing

$$\frac{dL}{dK} = -\frac{M(K, L)}{N(K, L)}$$

from the solution $h(K, L, dL/dK) = 0$, we now have the differential equation invariant under U'. The family of production functions derived from $dL/dK = -M(K, L)/N(K, L)$ as the integral curves is then holothetic under the original technical progress U. As an illustration of the preceding result, consider the nonuniform factor-augmenting technical progress

$$U = \alpha K \frac{\partial}{\partial K} + \beta L \frac{\partial}{\partial L}.$$

The extended transformation is then

$$U' = \alpha K \frac{\partial}{\partial K} + \beta L \frac{\partial}{\partial L} + (\beta - \alpha) \frac{dL}{dK} \frac{\partial}{\partial(dL/dK)}.$$

Here $\xi = \alpha K$, $\eta = \beta L$, and $\eta' = (\beta - \alpha)\, dL/dK$ in (14). The holothetic differential equation under U' is a general solution of (16),

$$U'h = \alpha K \frac{\partial h}{\partial K} + \beta L \frac{\partial h}{\partial L} + (\beta - \alpha) \frac{dL}{dK} \frac{\partial h}{\partial(dL/dK)} = 0, \quad \text{whenever} \quad h = 0.$$

There are two independent solutions to the above, $L^\alpha/K^\beta = C_1$, $(dL/dK)^\alpha/K^{\beta-\alpha} = C_2$, so that the general type of holothetic differential equation is

$$h\left(\frac{L^\alpha}{K^\beta}, \frac{(dL/dK)^\alpha}{K^{\beta-\alpha}}\right) = 0 \qquad \text{or} \qquad \frac{(dL/dK)^\alpha}{K^{\beta-\alpha}} = H\left(\frac{L^\alpha}{K^\beta}\right).$$

The marginal rate of substitution $-dL/dK$ is then

$$-\frac{dL}{dK} = \frac{f_K}{f_L} = K^{(\beta-\alpha)/\alpha} G\left(\frac{L^\alpha}{K^\beta}\right) = \frac{M(K, L)}{N(K, L)},$$

which is the holothetic differential equation for the underlying technology. By further integrating the above, we can easily identify the family of production functions holothetic under the nonuniform factor-augmenting type of technical progress, as

$$Y = f[K^{1/\alpha} Q(L^\alpha/K^\beta)].$$

This is the class of almost homothetic production functions presented as Example (a) in Part III.

Invariants of Holothetic Technology

15. Equation (16) in Lemma 5, which is the condition for the holothetic differential equation under a given Lie type of technical change, has two solutions. A function of the variables K, L, dL/dK is said to be an *invariant* of a given Lie type of technical change if it is left unaltered by every transformation of the technical change (see the Appendix, Part III), i.e.,

$$u(\bar{K}, \bar{L}, d\bar{L}/d\bar{K}) = u(K, L, dL/dK). \tag{17}$$

Equation (16) involving three independent variables has two independent solutions. Let these solutions be u_1 and u_2. Then these two independent solutions are the two invariants of the system. The first invariant (the invariant of the technology) depends on K and L, while the second (differential invariant) depends on K, L, and dL/dK. Then the existence of the holothetic differential equation implies the existence of the general solution for (16) as a function of these two invariants:

$$h(K, L, dL/dK) = H(u_1(K, L), u_2(K, L, dL/dK)).$$

Hence the invariant differential equation is written as

$$u_2(K, L, dL/dK) = F[u_1(K, L)]. \tag{18}$$

It is clear then that *the holothetic differential equation is obtained by expressing the differential invariant as a function of the invariant of the production function.*

Reduction of a Holothetic Technology to the Normal Form

16. Consider the case of additive (to one factor) type of technical progress,[12]

$$\bar{K} = \phi(K, L, t) = K + t, \qquad \bar{L} = \psi(K, L, t) = L. \tag{19}$$

The additive type of technical progress is a Lie type of technical progress, for (19) satisfies the basic properties set by (6-i)–(6-iii). The infinitesimal transformations of this type of technical change are $\xi = 1$ and $\eta = 0$, i.e.,

$$U = \partial/\partial K. \tag{19'}$$

[12] Since the choice of one factor is arbitrary, we can have $\bar{K} = K$ and $\bar{L} = L + t$. The results will be exactly the same.

The holothetic technology associated with (19) or (19′) is obtained by

$$Uf = \partial f/\partial K = G(f) = 1. \tag{20}$$

Solving the above, we have

$$f = K + Q(L) \qquad \text{or} \qquad Y = F[K + Q(L)]. \tag{21}$$

Since $U' \equiv U$, and $\eta = 0$ and $\eta' = 0$, we can immediately obtain the holothetic differential equation for this technology from $U'h \equiv 0$, or from

$$\frac{dK}{1} = \frac{dL}{0} = \frac{d(dL/dK)}{0} \qquad \text{since} \quad h\left(\frac{dL}{dK}, L\right) = 0 \quad \text{or} \quad \frac{dL}{dK} = -R(L).$$

The invariant of (20) is simply L or $Q(L)$ and the differential invariant is dL/dK or $C(dL/dK)$. We observe that *the holothetic technology associated with* (19) *can always be written as the sum of the two components, one of which is the "invariant" of the technology*. We shall call (21) the *normal* (*or canonical*) *form of the holothetic technology*.

Consider now a general Lie type of technical progress defined by (5) with its associated infinitesimal transformation (7′).

Lemma 6 (*Reduction to an Additive Type*) *Any Lie type of technical progress can be reduced to an additive type of technical progress.*

Proof This is a direct consequence of Theorem 5 (Appendix, Part III), which enables one to reduce any one-parameter Lie type to a one-parameter translation (additive) type. Q.E.D.

The form of the transformations of technical change depends upon the choice of variables that are operated upon them. Let $\tilde{K}$ and $\tilde{L}$ be the new variables

$$S: \quad \begin{cases} \tilde{K} = P(K, L), & \text{(22-i)} \\ \tilde{L} = Q(K, L). & \text{(22-ii)} \end{cases}$$

Designating by J_t the transformation in the new variables corresponding to T_t in the old, we express

$$J_t = S^{-1}T_tS. \tag{23}$$

That the aggregate of J_t of all the transformations of the technical change (5) satisfy the Lie group properties follows, of course, from the fact that

$$J_tJ_{t'} = S^{-1}T_tSS^{-1}T_{t'}S = S^{-1}T_tT_{t'}S = S^{-1}T_{t+t'}S$$

and

$$J_tJ_{-t} = S^{-1}T_tSS^{-1}T_{-t}S = S^{-1}T_tT_{-t}S = S^{-1}IS = S^{-1}S = I,$$

while

$$J_tI = S^{-1}T_tSI = IS^{-1}T_tS = IJ_t = J_t.$$

It is always possible theoretically, and often practically, to find the change of variables that reduces the technical progress to a desired form. In particular, we can reduce the transformation to one of additive types in the direction of the axis of, say, $\tilde{K}$, i.e.,

$$\xi \frac{\partial \tilde{K}}{\partial K} + \eta \frac{\partial \tilde{K}}{\partial L} = 1, \tag{24-i}$$

$$\xi \frac{\partial \tilde{L}}{\partial K} + \eta \frac{\partial \tilde{L}}{\partial L} = 0. \tag{24-ii}$$

This is the so-called *canonical form*, in which the infinitesimal transformation in the new variables is exactly identical with (19′),

$$U = \partial/\partial \tilde{K}. \tag{24'}$$

The corresponding holothetic technology in the *normal form* is

$$Y = F[\tilde{K} + C(\tilde{L})] = F[P(K, L) + Q(K, L)]. \tag{25}$$

Since the particular forms of $\tilde{K}$ and $\tilde{L}$ chosen by (24) are arbitrary, sometimes it is more convenient to choose

$$\xi \frac{\partial \tilde{K}}{\partial K} + \eta \frac{\partial \tilde{K}}{\partial L} = \tilde{K}, \tag{26-i}$$

$$\xi \frac{\partial \tilde{L}}{\partial K} + \eta \frac{\partial \tilde{L}}{\partial L} = 0, \tag{26-ii}$$

where $\tilde{K}$ is *the Hicksian type* (see Remark in Section 13). Then the resulting new transformation has the form

$$U = \tilde{K}\, \partial/\partial \tilde{K}. \tag{26'}$$

This may be called the *multiplicative normal form*, in contrast to the additive form (24′). The family of holothetic production functions will now take the form

$$Y = F[P(K, L)Q(K, L)]. \tag{27}$$

As an illustration, consider the case of the uniform factor-augmenting technical progress and its associated homothetic technology. We wish to find $\tilde{K}$ and $\tilde{L}$ such that

$$K \frac{\partial \tilde{K}}{\partial K} + L \frac{\partial \tilde{K}}{\partial L} = 1, \qquad K \frac{\partial \tilde{L}}{\partial K} + L \frac{\partial \tilde{L}}{\partial L} = 0.$$

$\tilde{K}$ and $\tilde{L}$ are immediately obtained as

$$\tilde{K} = \log K, \qquad \tilde{L} = Q(L/K).$$

Here $Q(L/K)$ is the first *canonical* variable which is equal to the invariant and log K is the other *canonical* variable. Hence the homothetic technology in the (additive) normal form is[13]

$$Y = F[\log K + Q(L/K)].$$

By setting $K\,\partial\tilde{K}/\partial K + L\,\partial\tilde{K}/\partial L = \tilde{K}$, while maintaining the same form of $\tilde{L}$, we can get the new canonical form $\tilde{K} = K$, and the resulting holothetic technology will be reduced to the multiplicative normal form as

$$Y = F[KQ(L/K)],$$

which is the standard expression for the homothetic technology.

Compatibility of the Internal Structure with Exogenous Technical Change

17. There is yet another alternative necessary and sufficient condition for holotheticity of a technology. This alternative necessary and sufficient condition will play a very important role in subsequent chapters. In economic analysis, more often than not we observe a differential equation describing the optimal behavior of an economic agent. Thus, consider the case of a cost-minimizing (or profit-maximizing) firm. We observe that the marginal rate of substitution, which is a differential equation, is equal to the price ratio. It would be interesting to know something about its underlying production function from the observed properties of the differential equation. More specifically, we wish to study whether the family of production functions derived as the integral curves of the differential equation is holothetic under a certain Lie type of technical change. Although at times it is possible to tell from the nature of the problem whether or not it constitutes a holothetic technology, it is desirable to formulate a concrete condition under which the differential equation itself is holothetic.

We have seen that if $Y = f(K, L)$ is a family of production functions holothetic under a given Lie type of technical progress $U = \xi\,\partial/\partial K + \eta\,\partial/\partial L$, we must have $Uf = G(f)$. Suppose now that Eq. (10) is a differential equation for the marginal rate of substitution whose family of integral curves $Y = f(K, L)$ is holothetic under U.[14] Let f be chosen such that

$$Uf \equiv \xi\frac{\partial f}{\partial K} + \eta\frac{\partial f}{\partial L} = 1. \tag{28}$$

[13] Obviously we can use log L as one of the canonical variables so that $Y = F[\log L + P(K/L)]$.

[14] $Y = f(K, L)$ cannot be the so-called path curves of the group. The equation of path curves is derived from the invariant of the holothetic technology (Appendix, Part III).

Since $f(K, L) = Y$ is the solution of (10), $df \equiv (\partial f/\partial K)\,dK + (\partial f/\partial L)\,dL = 0$ must be the same equation as (10); hence $(\partial f/\partial K)/M = (\partial f/\partial L)/N$ or

$$N(K, L)\frac{\partial f}{\partial K} - M\frac{\partial f}{\partial L} = 0. \tag{29}$$

Equation (29) is an alternative representation of the marginal rate of substitution in the partial differential equation form.

Definition 4 (*Lie Group Representation of the Marginal Rate of Substitution*) Let A be defined as

$$A \equiv N(K, L)\frac{\partial}{\partial K} - M(K, L)\frac{\partial}{\partial L}.$$

Then A is said to be *the Lie group representation of the marginal rate of substitution.*

It is seen that A represents the *internal structure* of the production function, which itself may be regarded as the "internal technical progress" whose infinitesimal transformation is equal to N and $-M$ for K and L, respectively. Thus A may be alternatively called *the Lie group representation of the internal structure of the production function.* Using A as an operator, we can express the marginal rate of substitution equation as

$$Af \equiv N(K, L)\frac{\partial f}{\partial K} - M(K, L)\frac{\partial f}{\partial L} = 0, \tag{29'}$$

which is equal to (29).

Definition 5 (*Compatibility of Technical Progress*) A given exogenous Lie type of technical progress is said to be compatible with the internal structure of the technology if the following Lie bracket operation satisfies

$$\begin{aligned}(U, A)f &= UAf - AUf \\ &= (UN - A\xi)\frac{\partial f}{\partial K} - (UM + A\eta)\frac{\partial f}{\partial L} = \lambda(K, L)Af,\end{aligned} \tag{30}$$

where $U = \xi\,\partial/\partial K + \eta\,\partial/\partial L$ and $A = N\,\partial/\partial K - M\,\partial/\partial L$.

Alternatively, an exogenous technical progress is said to be compatible with the Lie group representation of the marginal rate of substitution if (30) is satisfied.

We observe *that the compatibility condition* (30) *is the alternative necessary and sufficient condition for holotheticity* (Appendix, Theorem 8).[15]

Interpretation of Compatibility Condition

On looking at U and A, as two distinct representatives of technical progress, one exogenous, the other internal, the first term of (30), UAf, measures the impact of the exogenous technical progress on the internal structure, but the second term, AUf, measures the impact of the internal (technical) change on the exogenous technical progress. By subtracting UAf from AUf, we express the *net impact* (*or effect*) *of two types of changes taking place simultaneously*. Since the second-order expressions will all cancel out, the resulting net impact will be expressed as the same type of transformation as the original two types. Equation (30) is an exact expression of this property. In general, there is no reason to believe that the coefficients $(UN - A\xi)$ and $(UM + A\eta)$ are related to the Lie group representation of the marginal rate of substitution. But if they are related as suggested by (30), this implies that the net effect of changes in both the internal and exogenous types of technical progress is completely absorbed by the internal structure. This is exactly the condition of holotheticity—a complete transformation of exogenous technical progress to the (internal) returns to scale effect.

Consider that we observe the Cobb–Douglas type of production function. Then the observed marginal rate of substitution satisfies

$$\alpha L\, dK + \beta K\, dL = 0.$$

The Lie group representation of the marginal rate of substitution is

$$A = \beta K \frac{\partial}{\partial K} - \alpha L \frac{\partial}{\partial L}.$$

The compatibility condition requires that

$$[U(\beta K) - A(\xi)] \frac{\partial f}{\partial K} - [U(\alpha L) + A(\eta)] \frac{\partial f}{\partial L} = \lambda A f = 0.$$

This is to say,

$$\frac{\beta\xi - (\beta K(\partial\xi/\partial K) - \alpha L(\partial\xi/\partial L))}{\beta K} = \frac{\alpha\eta + (\beta K(\partial\eta/\partial K) - \alpha L(\partial\eta/\partial L))}{\alpha L} = \lambda.$$

[15] The interested reader may want to prove that the compatibility condition (30) is also obtained by means of (16) by setting $h = M + N\, dL/dK = 0$ and by using (15). For non-economic reasons, λ may be nonnegative so that M and N are nonnegative. When $U = \rho(K, L)A$, U may be called trivial since the Lie bracket is identically zero.

By setting λ equal to any arbitrary nonnegative function, we can derive a general expression for ξ and η by solving the partial differential equations in terms of ξ and η. For instance, if we set $\lambda = 0$, we then have

$$\beta K \frac{\partial \xi}{\partial K} - \alpha L \frac{\partial \xi}{\partial L} = \beta \xi, \qquad \beta K \frac{\partial \eta}{\partial K} - \alpha L \frac{\partial \eta}{\partial L} = -\alpha \eta.$$

Solving the above, we get $\xi = Ka(K^{\alpha}L^{\beta})$ and $\eta = Lb(K^{\alpha}L^{\beta})$ or $U = Ka(K^{\alpha}L^{\beta})\, \partial/\partial K + Lb(K^{\alpha}L^{\beta})\, \partial/\partial L$, which is a general expression for the Lie type of technical progress compatible with the Cobb–Douglas structure. (Compare this result with that of Example (a), Section 12.)

General Expression of U by the Lie Representation A

18. The preceding example suggests that starting with a given production function (rather than a given technical progress function), there is a general expression for the Lie type of technical progress under which the differential equation for the marginal rate of substitution is holothetic. If $U_1 = \xi_1\, \partial/\partial K + \eta_1\, \partial/\partial L$ and $U_2 = \xi_2\, \partial/\partial K + \eta_2\, \partial/\partial L$ are any two Lie types of technical progress, we can obtain a general expression for U from the basic property of the holothetic differential equation (see the Appendix, Corollary 8-4). By using the Lie representation of the marginal rate of substitution A, every Lie type of technical progress compatible with a given technology can be expressed as

$$\begin{aligned} U_2 &= F(f)U_1 + \rho(K, L)A \\ &= (F(f)\xi_1 + \rho N)\frac{\partial}{\partial K} + (F(f)\eta_1 - \rho M)\frac{\partial}{\partial L}. \end{aligned} \tag{31}$$

That is to say, *every Lie type of technical progress under which a given production function is holothetic can be expressed as a linear combination of the Lie group representation of the marginal rate of substitution and some other Lie type of technical progress compatible with the given technology.*[16]

For instance, given the Cobb–Douglas technology $A = \beta K\, \partial/\partial K - \alpha L\, \partial/\partial L$, we can express a general type as

$$U_2 = F(K^{\alpha}L^{\beta})\left(\xi_1 \frac{\partial}{\partial K} + \eta_1 \frac{\partial}{\partial L}\right) + \rho(K, L)\left(\beta K \frac{\partial}{\partial K} - \alpha L \frac{\partial}{\partial L}\right).$$

[16] If $F(f) = \text{const}$, U_2 gives the same integrating factor as U_1. When $F(f) = 0$, we have $U_2 = \rho A$, which is the trivial case, discussed in footnote 15.

Since the uniform factor-augmenting case is compatible with A, we can use $U_1 = K\,\partial/\partial K + L\,\partial/\partial L$, and obtain

$$U_2 = (F + \rho\beta)K\frac{\partial}{\partial K} + (F - \rho\alpha)L\frac{\partial}{\partial L}.$$

When $\rho = 0$, the above corresponds to the case in the previous section.

Summary

19. We finally summarize the results in Part V in the following theorem:

Theorem 5 (*Structures of Holothetic Technology*) (i) *There exists the general type of differential equation for the marginal rate of substitution, holothetic under a given Lie type of technical progress.*

(ii) *The holothetic technology has an invariant.*

(iii) *Using the invariant, any holothetic technology may be expressed in the additive or multiplicative normal form.*

(iv) *A technology is holothetic under a given exogenous Lie type of technical progress if and only if the technical progress is compatible with the internal structure of the Lie representation of the marginal rate of substitution.*

(v) *Every Lie type of technical progress under which a given production function is holothetic may be expressed as a linear combination of the Lie group representation of the marginal rate of substitution and some other Lie type of technical progress compatible with the internal structure of the given technology.*

VI. Holothetic Technologies under Special Types of Technical Change

20. In this section we shall study in detail the special types of technical progress and the resulting holothetic technologies including those already given as illustrating examples in the previous sections.[17] It will be shown that all of the known types of technical progress which have appeared so far in the economic literature are special cases of the "projective" type.

[17] However, since some of these special cases have already been analyzed in the examples and exercises both in the text and in the Appendix, only a brief summary is given here for these cases. In many cases the second-order conditions are omitted, though they may be easily calculated following the standard method (see Carlson [1939], Frisch [1965]).

Homothetic Technology and the Uniform (Neutral) Factor-Augmenting Type of Technical Progress

Homothetic technology (Shephard [1953], Sato [1977], Clemhout [1968], Wolkowitz [1971]) is characterized by the fact that the production function is holothetic under the general type of uniform factor-augmenting technical progress. Suppose that the infinitesimal transformation of the technical progress functions for K and L is given by $U = \alpha K\,\partial/\partial K + \alpha L\,\partial/\partial L$, so that the technical progress transformation becomes

$$\bar{K} = T(t)K, \qquad \bar{L} = T(t)L, \qquad T(t) = e^t \quad (\alpha = 1 \text{ by normalization}).$$

Mathematically this is known as the *uniform magnification* (or perspective or similitudinous) group or as the group of *dilatations* or *homothetic* transformations.[18] The extended transformation is simply equal to

$$U' = K\frac{\partial}{\partial K} + L\frac{\partial}{\partial L} + \eta'\frac{\partial}{\partial(dL/dK)}, \qquad \eta' = 0,$$

from which the holothetic differential equation is obtained as $dL/dK = -Q(L/K) = -f_K/f_L$. Solving the above, we derive *the general class of holothetic production functions under the uniform factor-augmenting type* as

$$Y = F[KQ(L/K)] = F[f(K, L)]. \tag{32}$$

But this is nothing but the well-known class of Shephard's *homothetic production functions* in which f is a homogeneous function of degree k (or for simplicity $k = 1$). The *invariant* of this technology is $Q(L/K)$, the expansion path, while the *differential invariant* is $-dL/dK = f_K/f_L$, the marginal rate of substitution itself. The homothetic technology is characterized by the fact the marginal rate of substitution can be expressed simply in terms of the capital–labor ratio, because these are the two *invariants* of the technical progress functions. The holothetic differential equation for the homothetic family is the differential equation for the márginal rate of substitution itself.

Almost Homothetic Production Functions and the General Type of Factor-Augmenting Technical Progress

21. It is more reasonable and more realistic to assume that the infinitesimal transformation of technical progress is given by $U = \alpha K\,\partial/\partial K + \beta L\,\partial/\partial L$, which implies the technical progress functions for K and L as

$$\bar{K} = Ke^{\alpha t} = A(t)K, \qquad \bar{L} = Le^{\beta t} = B(t)L.$$

[18] Eisenhart [1933, p. 42], for example, has referred to this case as *homothetic* transformations.

This is nothing but the general type of factor-augmenting technical progress (general magnification group) and contains most of the known types of technical progress. (If $\alpha \equiv \beta$, then this reduces to the homothetic case.) The family of production function holothetic under this type of technical progress functions for K and L has already been derived in Section 14, as an illustrating example for Lemma 5. It has the form

$$Y = F[K^{\gamma/\alpha}Q(L^\alpha/K^\beta)] = F[L^{\gamma/\beta}P(K^\beta/L^\alpha)] = F[f(K, L)], \qquad (33)$$

where K and Q or L and P are the canonical variables of this technology. This is the *almost homothetic type* of production function, since (33) is a monotone transformation of the *almost homogeneous function* f (Lau [1978], Sato [1977]).

Examples of the almost homothetic class of production functions are the Cobb–Douglas type, $aK^\alpha L^\beta = f$, Houthakker's [1960] addilog function, $aK^{-\rho_1} + bL^{-\rho_2} = f$, and the nonhomothetic (almost homothetic) CES family $aY^{\alpha_1}K^{-\rho} + bY^{\alpha_2}L^{-\rho} = 1$ (Sato [1977]). Although the Shephard homothetic class is a special case of the general type of almost homothetic production functions when $\alpha \equiv \beta \neq 0$, there are two other special cases. When either α or β is equal to zero so that $U = \beta L\, \partial/\partial L$, $\alpha = 0$, or $U = \alpha K\, \partial/\partial K$, $\beta = 0$, we obtain the labor-augmenting and capital-augmenting types of technical progress, respectively.[19] The holothetic technology is given by

$$Y = F[f(K, L)] = F(LP(K)] \qquad \text{or} \qquad Y = F[f(K, L)] = F[KQ(L)]. \qquad (34)$$

We shall refer to these cases as "labor-homothetic" and "capital-homothetic" types of production functions, or simply as "L-homothetic" and "K-homothetic," respectively.

The isoquant map of an almost homothetic production function has an interesting property. In Fig. 1 the axes are measured in terms of log K and log L. The slope of an isoquant is nothing but the ratio of distributive shares of capital and labor. From

$$-\frac{dL}{dK}\frac{K}{L} = \frac{f_K K}{f_L L} = \frac{\text{share of } K}{\text{share of } L} = -H\left(\frac{L^\alpha}{K^\beta}\right),$$

or

$$-\frac{d \log L}{d \log K} = -H(\exp(\beta^{-1} \log L - \alpha^{-1} \log K)),$$

[19] When the production function is restricted to the constant returns to scale function, the uniform factor-augmenting type of technical progress reduces to the Hicks neutral case, while the labor-augmenting and capital-augmenting to the Harrod neutral and Solow neutral cases. The nonuniform case, then, reduces to the Sato–Beckmann–Rose neutrality. (See Chapter 4.)

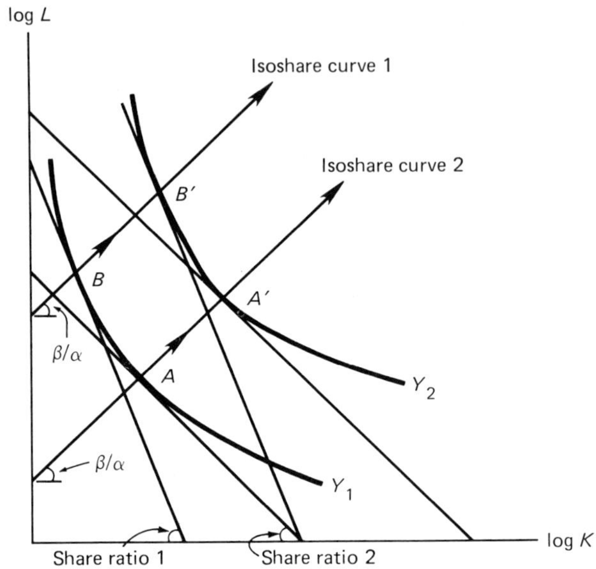

Figure 1 Isoquant map for almost-homothetic technology.

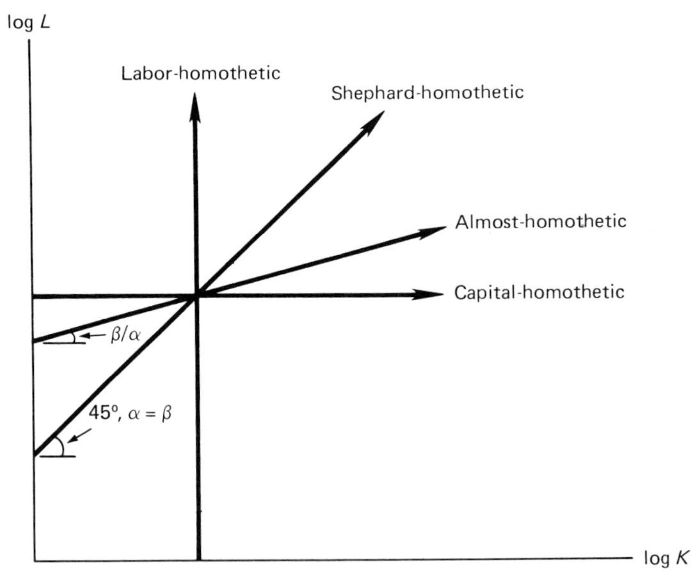

Figure 2 Isoquant map and isoshare curves for general homothetic technology.

the differential invariant is nothing but the share ratio of K and L and the *invariant* of the technology is L^{α}/K^{β}. Hence the share ratio remains constant under the factor-augmenting type of technical progress. As long as capital and labor change exponentially at the rate of α and β percent, respectively, then $\beta^{-1} \log L - \alpha^{-1} \log K$ remains constant. Hence the isoshare curves measured in terms of log K and log L (rather than K and L) are all straight lines, their slopes being all equal to β/α. The special case of the Shephard homothetic production function has the isoshare curves whose slopes are all equal to unity, 45° parallel lines, whereas the labor-homothetic and capital-homothetic production functions have the vertical and horizontal isoshare curves, respectively (see Fig. 2). In conclusion, we may say that *the general class of homothetic production functions has the straight line and parallel isoshare curves, whose slope depends on the degree of factor-augmenting technical progress*, β/α. In passing, we note that the only function which satisfies the conditions of Shephard's homotheticity, almost homotheticity, and labor and capital homotheticity at the same time is the Cobb–Douglas function. (This problem will be studied more extensively in Part VII.)

Separable Families

22. Let the infinitesimal transformation of technical change be either $U = u(K)\, \partial/\partial K$ or $U = v(L)\, \partial/\partial L$. This means that the efficiency of capital (or labor) is a function of capital (or labor), while the efficiency of labor (or capital) remains unchanged. The technical progress functions for these cases are either

$$\bar{K} = G^{-1}[G(K) + t], \qquad \bar{L} = L$$

or

$$\bar{K} = K, \qquad \bar{L} = H^{-1}[H(L) + t],$$

where $G(K) = \int dK/u(K)$ and $H(L) = \int dL/v(L)$. The holothetic differential equations for these cases are

$$-\frac{dL}{dK}u(K) = \frac{f_K}{f_L}u(K) = h(L), \qquad -\frac{dL}{dK}\frac{1}{v(L)} = \frac{f_K}{f_L}\frac{1}{v(L)} = h(K).$$

Thus the marginal rate of substitution multiplied (or divided) by the infinitesimal transformation of capital (labor) is invariant under that type of technical progress. Integrating the above, we immediately obtain the "separable" holothetic technology[20]:

$$Y = f(P(K)Q(L)). \tag{35}$$

The separable family contains the two special cases that we have already discussed earlier in Section 16; the *additive normal forms* and *multiplicative normal forms*. When $u(K) = 1$ and $v(L) = 0$ or $u(K) = 0$ and $v(L) = 1$, the holothetic technology associated with each of these cases of additive technical progress is

$$Y = f(K + Q(L)), \qquad \text{or} \qquad Y = f(L + P(K)), \tag{36}$$

respectively.[21] When $u(K) = K$ and $v(L) = 0$ or $u(K) = 0$ and $v(L) = L$, we obtain the multiplicative normal forms, which are exactly the same as the capital and labor homothetic technologies discussed in Section 21 [Eq. (34)].

"Projective" Holothetic Technology

23. One of the most general types of technical progress is the "projective" type.[22] In fact, this type contains all of the known types of technical progress which have thus far appeared in the economic literature, including the factor-augmenting (uniform and nonuniform), additive, etc. The general form of the one-parameter projective type of technical progress is

$$\begin{aligned} &\textit{for capital}: \quad \xi(K, L) = a_1 + a_3 K + a_5 L + a_7 K^2 + a_8 KL, \\ &\textit{for labor}: \quad \eta(K, L) = a_2 + a_4 K + a_6 L + a_7 KL + a_8 L^2, \end{aligned} \tag{37}$$

where $a_1, \ldots, a_8$ are constants.

An economic interpretation of the projective type of technical progress is obvious. The efficiency increase in capital and labor depends not only on a combination of capital and labor, but also on a combination of the products

[20] Since the holothetic technology which we have solved for is a production (or utility) function, it must satisfy $f_K = f'P'(K)Q(L) \geqq 0$, $f_L = f'P(K)Q'(L) \geqq 0$. Assuming $P(K) \geqq 0$, $Q(L) \geqq 0$ for $K \geqq 0$, $L \geqq 0$, the above implies that $P'(K) \geqq 0$ and $Q'(L) \geqq 0$. Furthermore, the quasi-concavity condition requires that $2P'^2Q'^2 - P''PQ'^2 - Q''QP'^2 \geqq 0$, which will be satisfied if $P'' \leqq 0$ and $Q'' \leqq 0$.

[21] Since the holothetic differential equation of the additive normal form is $-dL/dK = h(L)$ and $-dL/dK = h(K)$, respectively, the expansion path of the isoquant map is a straight line and parallel either to the K axis or the L axis.

[22] We shall call this the "projective" type, since it belongs to the so-called projective group (see the Appendix, Part VI). This is one of the most fundamental types of Lie groups developed by Lie himself. This includes all of the linear groups as special cases. Here we use (37) as a general expression for a one-parameter subgroup G_1 of the eight-parameter projective group G_8 studied in the Appendix, Part VI.

of capital and labor including own products and a constant term. Thus it represents a kind of a second-order approximation to the general expression disregarding the L^2 and K^2 terms in the ξ and η equations, respectively.

Given (37), we can derive the technical progress functions for K and L as

$$\bar{K} = \frac{e^{a_3 t}K + (a_5 L + a_1)t}{1 - (a_7 K + a_8 L)t}, \qquad \bar{L} = \frac{e^{a_6 t}L + (a_4 K + a_2)t}{1 - (a_7 K + a_8 L)t}. \tag{37'}$$

Virtually all of the different types of technical change that we have thus far discussed are special cases of (37′). When $a_i = 0$ for all i except $i = 1$, i.e., $\xi = a_1$, $\eta = 0$, we have the capital additive case, but if we have $\xi = 0$ and $\eta = a_2 \neq 0$, this reduces to the labor additive case. Now consider the case in which all of the parameters a_i, except a_3 and a_6, are equal to zero. Then we have the case of almost homothetic technology holothetic under the nonneutral type of factor augmentation. This, of course, contains the Shephard homothetic ($a_3 \equiv a_6 \not\equiv 0$), capital-homothetic ($a_3 \neq 0$, $a_6 = 0$), and labor-homothetic ($a_3 = 0$, $a_6 \neq 0$) families as special cases.

The family of production functions holothetic under (37)—"projective" holothetic family—may be derived from $Uf = H(f)$, or

$$\begin{aligned} Uf &= (a_1 + a_3 K + a_5 L + a_7 K^2 + a_8 KL)\frac{\partial f}{\partial K} \\ &\quad + (a_2 + a_4 K + a_6 L + a_7 KL + a_8 L^2)\frac{\partial f}{\partial L} \\ &= H(f) = A\frac{\partial f}{\partial K} + B\frac{\partial f}{\partial L} = H(f). \end{aligned}$$

The solution of the preceding partial differential equation requires the solution of $dK/A = dL/B$, which may be reduced to a *Jacobi equation*. Thus we have

$$W_1^{\lambda_2 - \lambda_3} W_2^{\lambda_3 - \lambda_1} W_3^{\lambda_1 - \lambda_2} = \text{const.}, \tag{38}$$

where $W_1 = \alpha_1 K + \beta_1 L + \gamma_1$, $W_2 = \alpha_2 K + \beta_2 L + \gamma_2$, and $W_3 = \alpha_3 K + \beta_3 L + \gamma_3$, ($\alpha_i$, β_i, γ_i are functions of a_i), and λ_1, λ_2, λ_3 are the characteristic roots of

$$\begin{vmatrix} 0 - \lambda & a_1 & a_2 \\ -a_7 & a_3 - \lambda & a_4 \\ -a_8 & a_5 & a_6 - \lambda \end{vmatrix} = 0.$$

Hence one of the canonical variables is equal to $\Phi(W_1^{\lambda_2 - \lambda_3} W_2^{\lambda_3 - \lambda_1} W_3^{\lambda_1 - \lambda_2})$, and the other canonical variable may be obtained from $dL/\eta(K, L) = df/H(f)$ using the first solution $K = K(L, c)$. Setting $B(L, c) = \eta(K, L)$, we have the canonical variable P and the holothetic technology as $P[L, c(K, L)] = P(K, L) = G(f) + c$, where $\int dL/B(L, c) = P$ and $\int df/H(f) = G(f)$. In summary, we have

Theorem 6 *(Projective Holothetic Family) The most general class of production functions holothetic under the general one-parameter "projective" type of technical change is*

$$Y = f[P(K, L) + Q[W_1^{\lambda_2 - \lambda_3} W_2^{\lambda_3 - \lambda_1} W_3^{\lambda_1 - \lambda_2}]], \tag{39}$$

where $P(K, L) = \int dL/B(L, c)$, $c = c(K, L)$, *and* W_i *satisfies* (38).

Obviously Eq. (39) contains all the types of production functions that we have thus far discussed. For instance, if $\alpha_1 = \beta_2$, $\beta_1 = \gamma_1 = \alpha_2 = \gamma_2 = \alpha_3 = \beta_3 = 0$, $\lambda_3 \neq 0$, and $\lambda_2 = \lambda_1 = 0$, and $P = \log L$, then we have $f = \log L + \Phi[(\alpha_1 K/\alpha_2 L)^{-\lambda_3}]$, the *homothetic class.* On the other hand, under the same conditions as the above, with the exception $\lambda_3 \equiv 0$, but $\lambda_1 \neq \lambda_2 \neq 0$, we have $f = \log L + \phi[K^{\lambda_2}/L^{\lambda_1}]$, the almost homothetic class $\lambda_1 \neq \lambda_2$. Another case which has not appeared so far in the previous sections is $a_3 \neq 0$, $a_5 = 0$, $a_1 = -1$, $a_4 = 0$, $a_6 = a_3$, $a_2 = 0$, $a_7 = -1$, and $a_8 = 0$. The Jacobi equation reduces to a simple form which yields[23]

$$Y = F(f),$$

$$f = -\tfrac{1}{2}\log(K^2 - a_3 K - a_1) + \frac{a_3}{\sqrt{B}} \tan^{-1}\left(\frac{2K - a_3}{\sqrt{B}}\right) + \log L,$$

$$B = 4 - a_3^2 > 0.$$

With appropriate restrictions on the coefficients, the above represents a holothetic technology.

Technical progress may occur for the *transformed* variables of capital and labor rather than capital and labor. Consider the projective type of technical change in the transformed variables $u(K)$ and $v(L)$. Technical progress now takes place for the transformed variables

$$\begin{aligned} \xi[u(K), v(L)] &= a_1 + a_3 u + a_5 v + a_7 u^2 + a_8 uv, \\ \eta[u(K), v(L)] &= a_2 + a_4 u + a_6 v + a_7 uv + a_8 v^2. \end{aligned} \tag{40}$$

The technology holothetic under (40) may be called the "transprojective-holothetic" technology whose general expression is to replace K and L with u and v in (39).[24] This represents a wide variety of technical change since u

[23] This equation is an example of the non-Cobb–Douglas self-dual functions (see Chapter 6).

[24] Chapter 5 develops the eight basic cases for the general infinitesimal generators using the transformed variables.

and v are in a sense arbitrary functions of K and L, respectively. The *trans-homothetic* case is one of them when $\xi = a_3 u$ and $\eta = a_6 v$ ($a_3 = a_6$). The holothetic technology is *homothetic* under the transformed variables.[25] The basic forms and special types of projective and other related technologies are summarized in Tables 1 and 2.

Cobb–Douglas, CES, *Addilog*, *Trans-Log*, etc.

24. We now want to characterize the well-known types of production functions by their Lie group representation and by their holothetic technical change. The (homothetic) Cobb–Douglas family belongs to (i) the homothetic, (ii) almost homothetic, (iii) labor-homothetic, and (iv) capital-homothetic families. It also belongs to the separable families. The Lie representation of the marginal rate of substitution for the *Cobb–Douglas* family is, as noted earlier, $A = \beta K\, \partial/\partial K - \alpha L\, \partial/\partial L$. Using Theorem 5(v), we can write a general expression of U as (see Section 18)

$$U_2 = (F(K^\alpha L^\beta) + \beta\rho(K, L))K \frac{\partial}{\partial K} + (F(K^\alpha L^\beta) - \alpha\rho(K, L))L \frac{\partial}{\partial L}.$$

For instance, if F and ρ are constant, the above reduces to the biased factor-augmenting case (the almost homothetic case), and if $F - \alpha\rho \equiv 0$ and $F + \beta\rho \equiv 0$, to the capital-homothetic case and to the labor-homothetic type, respectively. These are just a few examples.

The *homothetic* CES *and Houthakker's addilog* family has the differential equation

$$\alpha K^{-(1+\rho_1)}\, dK + \beta L^{-(1+\rho_2)}\, dL = 0.$$

Its Lie representation of the marginal rate of substitution is

$$A = \beta L^{-(1+\rho_2)} \frac{\partial}{\partial K} - \alpha K^{-(1+\rho_1)} \frac{\partial}{\partial L}.$$

The general expression of U for the CES case ($\rho_1 = \rho_2 = \rho$) is

$$U_2 = F(f)\left(K \frac{\partial}{\partial K} + L \frac{\partial}{\partial L}\right) + \rho(K, L)\left(\beta L^{-(1+\rho)} \frac{\partial}{\partial K} - \alpha K^{-(1+\rho)} \frac{\partial}{\partial L}\right)$$

$$= [F(f)K + \rho(K, L)\beta L^{-(1+\rho)}] \frac{\partial}{\partial K} + [F(f)L - \rho(K, L)\alpha K^{-(1+\rho)}] \frac{\partial}{\partial L}.$$

[25] An example of transhomothetic functions is the "power"-augmenting type $u = K^{-\rho_1}$, $v = L^{-\rho_2}$. This case is extensively analyzed by Kott [1979]. Kott started with a more general type, $U = K^{a_1}L^{b_1}\, \partial/\partial K + K^{a_2}L^{b_2}\, \partial/\partial L$.

TABLE 1

SPECIAL CASES OF THE PROJECTIVE AND OTHER TYPES OF TECHNICAL CHANGE

Type	Technical progress functions and infinitesimal transformation: $\bar{K}$	Technical progress functions and infinitesimal transformation: $\bar{L}$	Holothetic technology f	Regularity conditions: First order	Regularity conditions: Quasi-concavity	Holothetic differential equations	Remarks
(1) Additive to capital	$\bar{K} = K + a_1 t$ $\xi = a_1 \neq 0$	$\bar{L} = L$ $\eta = 0$	$K + g(L)$	$f_K = 1$ $f_L = g' > 0$	$g'' < 0$	$-\frac{dL}{dK} = \frac{1}{g'(L)}$	Additive normal form. Separable
(2) Additive to labor	$\bar{K} = K$ $\xi = 0$	$\bar{L} = L + a_2 t$ $\eta = a_2 \neq 0$	$L + g(K)$	$f_K = g' > 0$ $f_L = 1$	$g'' < 0$	$-\frac{dL}{dK} = g'(K)$	Additive normal form. Separable
(3) Capital-augmenting	$\bar{K} = e^{a_3 t}K$ $\xi = a_3 K$	$\bar{L} = L$ $\eta = 0$	$Kg(L)$	$f_K = g > 0$ $f_L = Kg' > 0$	$g'' < \frac{2g'^2}{g}$	$-\frac{dL}{dK}\frac{K}{L} = h(L)$	Multiplicative Normal form. Separable capital-homothetic
(4) Labor-augmenting	$\bar{K} = K$ $\xi = 0$	$\bar{L} = e^{a_6 t}L$ $\eta = a_6 L$	$Lg(K)$	$f_K = Lg' > 0$ $f_L = g > 0$	$g'' < \frac{2g'^2}{g}$	$-\frac{dL}{dK}\frac{K}{L} = h(K)$	Multiplicative normal form. Separable labor-homothetic
(5) Ratio additive to capital	$\bar{K} = K + a_5 Lt$ $\xi = a_5 L$	$\bar{L} = L$ $\eta = 0$	$\frac{K}{L} + g(L)$	$f_K = \frac{1}{L} > 0$ $f_L = \frac{-K}{L^2} + g' > 0$	$g'' < \frac{-2g'}{L}$	$\frac{K}{L} - \frac{dK}{dL} = h(L)$	

(6) Ratio additive to labor	$\bar{K} = K$ $\xi = 0$	$\bar{L} = L + a_4 Kt$ $\eta = a_4 K$	$\frac{L}{K} + g(K)$	$f_K = \frac{-L}{K^2} + g' > 0$ $f_L = \frac{1}{K}$	$g'' < \frac{2g'}{K}$	$\frac{L}{K} - \frac{dL}{dK} = h(K)$	
(7) Homothetic technology uniform factor-augmenting	$\bar{K} = Ke^t$ $\xi = K$	$\bar{L} = Le^t$ $\eta = L$	$KP(L/K)$	$f_K = P - \frac{L}{K} P' > 0$ $f_L = P' > 0$	$P'' < 0$ (concavity)	$-\frac{dL}{dK} = g\left(\frac{K}{L}\right)$	Straight line expansion path.
(8) Almost-homothetic nonuniform (biased) factor augmenting	$\bar{K} = Ke^{a_3 t}$ $\xi = a_3 K$	$\bar{L} = Le^{a_6 t}$ $\eta = a_6 L$	$K^{a_6} P\left(\frac{L^{a_3}}{K^{a_6}}\right)$	$f_K = a_6 K^{a_6 - 1} P' - a_6 \frac{L^{a_3}}{K} P' > 0$ $f_L = a_3 L^{a_3 - 1} p' > 0$		$-\frac{dL}{dK}\frac{K}{L} = g\left(\frac{K^{a_6}}{L^{a_3}}\right)$	Straight line expansion path for log K and log L
(9) Ratio additive III	$\bar{u}(\bar{K}) = \frac{u}{1 - a_7 ut}$ $\xi = a_7 u^2$	$\bar{v}(\bar{L}) = \frac{v}{1 - a_7 ut}$ $\eta = a_7 uv$	$u^{-1} + g(v/u)$	for $g' < 0$: $u' < 0$ $v' < 0$ $1 + vg' > 0$		$v - u\frac{dv}{du} = h\left(\frac{v}{u}\right)$	These two cases (9 and 10) with the original variables K and L have no economic meaning, as the first-order conditions do not satisfy the positivity requirement.

(continues)

TABLE 1 (*continued*)

Type	Technical progress functions and infinitesimal transformation: $\bar{K}$	$\bar{L}$	Holothetic technology f	Regularity conditions: First order	Quasi-concavity	Holothetic differential equations	Remarks
(10) Ratio additive IV	$\bar{u}(\bar{K})$ $= \dfrac{u}{1 - a_8 vt}$ $\xi = a_8 uv$	$\bar{v}(L)$ $= \dfrac{v}{1 - a_8 vt}$ $\eta = a_8 v^2$	$v^{-1} + g(u/v)$	for $g' < 0$: $u' < 0$ $v' < 0$ $1 + ug' > 0$		$u - v\dfrac{du}{dv} = h\left(\dfrac{u}{v}\right)$	
(11) Transhomothetic case	$\bar{u}(\bar{K}) = ue^t$ $\xi = u$	$\bar{v}(\bar{L}) = ve^t$ $\eta = v$	$uP(v/u)$	for $u' > 0$ $v' > 0$ Similar conditions can be found as the standard homothetic case		$-\dfrac{du}{dv} = g\left(\dfrac{v}{u}\right)$	Straight line expansion path for axes u and v
(12) Capital and labor additive	$\bar{K} = K + at$ $\xi = a$	$\bar{L} \doteq L + bt$ $\eta = b$	$L + g(bK - aL)$ or $K + g(bK - aL)$	$f_K = bg' > 0$ $f_L = 1 - ag' > 0$ or $f_K = 1 + bg' > 0$ $f_L = -ag' > 0$	$g'' < 0$	$\dfrac{dL}{dK} = h(bK - aL)$	Marginal rate of substitution is invariant under this technical progress

TABLE 2

OTHER SPECIAL CASES OF INTEREST

Type	$\bar{K}$	$\bar{L}$	f	Regularity conditions	Holothetic differential equations	Remarks
(13) General ratio additive type I	$\bar{K} = G^{-1}[G(K) + t]$ $\xi = \dfrac{K^2}{\phi(K)}$	$\bar{L} = G^{-1}[G(K) + t](L/K)$ $\eta = \dfrac{KL}{\phi(K)}$	$G(K) + h(L/K)$ where $G(K) = \int \dfrac{\phi(K)}{K^2}\,dK$	$0 < h' < \dfrac{\phi(K)}{L}$, $h'' < 0$, $\phi' < 0$ are sufficient	$L - K\dfrac{dL}{dK} = \dfrac{\phi(K)}{h'(L/K)}$	A special case of this will be reduced to Case 9
(14) General ratio additive type II	$\bar{K} = G^{-1}[G(L) + t](K/L)$ $\xi = \dfrac{KL}{\phi(L)}$	$\bar{L} = G^{-1}[G(L) + t]$ $\eta = \dfrac{L^2}{\phi(L)}$	$G(L) + h(K/L)$ where $G(L) = \int \dfrac{\phi(L)}{L^2}\,dL$	$0 < h' < \dfrac{\phi(L)}{K}$, $h'' < 0$, $\phi' < 0$ are sufficient	$K - L\dfrac{dK}{dL} = \dfrac{\phi(L)}{h'(K/L)}$	A special case of this will be reduced to Case 10
(15) Bernoulli type	$\bar{K} = K$ $\xi = 0$	$\bar{L} = \left[L^{1-s} + \dfrac{t}{1-s} \times \exp(\int(s-1) \times P(K)\,dK)\right]^{1/(1-s)}$ $\eta = L^s \exp \times (\int(s-1) \times P(K)\,dK)$	$g(K) + L^{1-s}\exp[\int(1-s) \times P(K)\,dK]$	First order: $s < 1$ $\Rightarrow f_L > 0$ and need $f_K = g'(K) + (1-s)P(K)L^{1-s} \times \exp[\cdot] > 0$	$-\dfrac{dL}{dK} = \dfrac{g'(K)L^s}{1-s} \times \exp[\int(1-s) \times P(K)\,dK] + LP(K)$	Holothetic differential equation is the Bernoulli differential equation
(16) Power-augmenting	$\bar{K} = [K^{-\rho_1} - \rho_1 t]^{-1/\rho_1}$ $\xi = K^{1+\rho_1}$	$\bar{L} = [L^{-\rho_2} - \rho_2 t]^{-1/\rho_2}$ $\eta = L^{1+\rho_2}$	$K^{-\rho_1} + g\left[\dfrac{K^{-\rho_1}}{\rho_1} - \dfrac{L^{-\rho_2}}{\rho_2}\right]$ or $L^{-\rho_1} + g[\cdot]$	First order: $g' > 0$, $\rho_1 < -g'$, $\rho_2 < -g'$	$\dfrac{L^{-(\rho_2+1)}\,dL}{K^{-(\rho_1+1)}\,dK} = \dfrac{-\rho_1 - g'}{g'}$	Addilog and CES are special cases of this type

For the addilog family, we have

$$U_2 = F(f)\left(aK\frac{\partial}{\partial K} + bL\frac{\partial}{\partial L}\right) + \rho(K, L)\left(\beta L^{-(1+\rho_2)}\frac{\partial}{\partial K} - \alpha K^{-(1+\rho_1)}\frac{\partial}{\partial L}\right)$$

$$= [F(f)aK + \rho(K, L)\beta L^{-(1+\rho_2)}]\frac{\partial}{\partial K}$$

$$+ [F(f)bL - \rho(K, L)\alpha K^{-(1+\rho_1)}]\frac{\partial}{\partial L}.$$

The above contains a number of interesting types, one of which is $U_2 = \beta L^{-(1+\rho_2)}\,\partial/\partial K - \alpha K^{-(1+\rho_1)}\,\partial/\partial L$, the power-augmenting type of technical progress.

The *trans-log family* (Christensen *et al.* [1973])

$$f = \log Y = \gamma_1 + \alpha_1 \log K + \beta_1 \log L + \frac{\alpha_2}{2}(\log K)^2 + \frac{\beta_2}{2}(\log L)^2$$

$$+ \gamma_2 \log K \log L$$

has the Lie group representation of the marginal rate of substitution,

$$A = [\beta_1 + \beta_2 v(L) + \gamma_2 u(K)]\frac{\partial}{\partial u} - [\alpha_1 + \alpha_2 u(K) + \gamma_2 v(L)]\frac{\partial}{\partial v}$$

$$= N\frac{\partial}{\partial u} - M\frac{\partial}{\partial v},$$

where $u(K) = \log K$ and $v(L) = \log L$. Notice that A belongs to the *trans-projective* type of (internal) technical progress, especially, a linear type. In view of Lemma 4 in Section 11 (also Corollary 8-3 in the Appendix), we can derive the Lie representation as

$$U_1 = \xi(u, v)\frac{\partial}{\partial u} + \frac{1}{(\beta_1 + \beta_2 v + \gamma_2 u)}\left(\frac{1}{G(f)} - (\alpha_1 + \alpha_2 u + \gamma_2 v)\xi(u, v)\right)\frac{\partial}{\partial v}.$$

Suppose we set a condition that $\eta(u, v) = a\xi(u, v)$, $a = \text{const}$, i.e., we look for the same type of technical progress for K and L. Then the above is simply equal to

$$U_1 = \frac{1}{G(f)}\frac{1}{(aN + M)}\frac{\partial}{\partial u} + \frac{1}{G(f)}\frac{a}{(aN + M)}\frac{\partial}{\partial v}.$$

From this expression, we finally get a general expression for U_2 as

$$U_2 = \frac{F(f)}{G(f)}\left(\frac{1}{aN + M}\frac{\partial}{\partial u} + \frac{a}{aN + M}\frac{\partial}{\partial v}\right) + \rho(u, v)\left(N\frac{\partial}{\partial u} - M\frac{\partial}{\partial v}\right)$$
$$= \left(\frac{H(f)}{aN + M} + \rho(u, v)N\right)\frac{\partial}{\partial u} + \left(\frac{aH(f)}{aN + M} - \rho M\right)\frac{\partial}{\partial v}, \qquad H = \frac{F(f)}{G(f)}.$$

VII. Simultaneous Holotheticity

Motivation

25. Suppose that one is interested in estimating the aggregate production function of an economy or of the "world" from that of each individual sector (or individual country's production function (Woodward [1979])). For simplicity let us assume that the production function in each sector (or country) is identical so that the aggregate production function has the same form as that of the individual sector. However, there is no reason to believe that technical change in each sector is also identical. (If technical changes were identical, there would be no reason for disaggregation.) The question to ask is: Under what conditions will all of the different types of technical progress be transformed to an aggregate scale effect of the production function of the economy? In order to give the answer to this question we must first know under what conditions the technical change of the individual sector is transformed to a scale effect of that sector. Since we are assuming that the individual sectors and the aggregate economy have an identical form of production function, this question is reduced to that of finding the conditions under which a production function is holothetic under *more than* one type of technical change *simultaneously*. We shall call this the *simultaneous holotheticity problem.*[26]

Another motivation may be derived from the analysis of demand functions under exogeneous *taste change*. The holotheticity of a utility function under a given Lie type of taste change implies that the demand functions for each commodity are *invariant* under that type of taste change.[27] Suppose that an

[26] If one is interested in isolating the effect of technical change from that of scale economies the *non*holotheticity condition becomes relevant.

[27] The impact of technical change on the production function is analogous with the impact of taste change on the utility function. Thus the marginal rates of substitution between commodities are not affected under the holotheticity condition (see footnote 3 and also the second interpretation of holotheticity in Section 3).

economy is composed of individuals identical in all respects except for taste changes. Under what types of taste change will the aggregate demand function remain invariant? This is again the simultaneous holotheticity problem given different types of technical change (or taste change), our problem now is to find a general class of production (or utility) functions holothetic under those simultaneous types of technical change (taste change).

26. If a production function is holothetic under given Lie types of technical progress U_a $(1 \leqq a \leqq r)$, then in view of the basic theorem of holotheticity (Theorem 1), we must have

$$U_a f = \xi^a(K, L)\frac{\partial f}{\partial K} + \eta^a(K, L)\frac{\partial f}{\partial L} = H^a(f) \not\equiv 0 \qquad (1 \leqq a \leqq r), \quad (41)$$

where ξ^a and η^a are infinitesimal transformations of the technical progress functions for K and L of the type a. We want to determine whether or not there exists any meaningful production function f such that it is holothetic under r given and different types of technical progress ξ^a and η^a, $1 \leqq a \leqq r$.

Trivial Production Function

If only $f = \text{const}$ for all K and L satisfies (41), then such a case is trivial, because the marginal products of K and L are identically equal to zero. We call such a production function with $\partial f/\partial K \equiv \partial f/\partial L \equiv 0$ a *trivial production function.* Otherwise, it is said to be nontrivial. Our purpose here is to find a (nontrivial) production function satisfying (41) and other neoclassical conditions. ($H^a \not\equiv 0$ excludes the possibility of a trivial function.)

It is actually more convenient to transform the holotheticity condition (41) into the following equivalent form (see Ince [1956]):

$$X_a\phi = \xi^a(K, L)\frac{\partial \phi}{\partial K} + \eta^a(K, L)\frac{\partial \phi}{\partial L} + H^a(f)\frac{\partial \phi}{\partial f} = 0 \qquad (1 \leqq a \leqq r), \quad (41')$$

where $\phi(K, L, f) = 0$, $\partial\phi/\partial f \not\equiv 0$. f is a solution of (41), where ϕ is a solution of (41′).

Unconnected Types of Technical Progress

If we have r types of technical progress $X_1, \ldots, X_r$ expressed by (41′), such that no identical relation of the form

$$\sum_{a=1}^{r} \psi_a X_a \equiv 0 \quad (42)$$

connects them, where the ψ_a are r functions of the variables K and L, not all zero, they are said to be *unconnected* types of technical progress.[28]

We now show that if the number of factor inputs is two, such as K and L, there *cannot* be more than two unconnected types of technical progress under which a nontrivial production function is holothetic. Suppose that there are, say, three unconnected and different types consistent with the nontrivial production function. That is to say, we must have

$$X_1\phi = \xi^1 \frac{\partial\phi}{\partial K} + \eta^1 \frac{\partial\phi}{\partial L} + H^1(f)\frac{\partial\phi}{\partial f} = 0, \tag{43-i}$$

$$X_2\phi = \xi^2 \frac{\partial\phi}{\partial K} + \eta^2 \frac{\partial\phi}{\partial L} + H^2(f)\frac{\partial\phi}{\partial f} = 0, \tag{43-ii}$$

$$X_3\phi = \xi^3 \frac{\partial\phi}{\partial K} + \eta^3 \frac{\partial\phi}{\partial L} + H^3(f)\frac{\partial\phi}{\partial f} = 0, \tag{43-iii}$$

where $\phi = \phi(K, L, f)$, $f = f(K, L)$ being defined by $\phi(K, L, f) = 0$. Since $\partial\phi/\partial f \neq 0$, we must have [Appendix, Eq. (46)]

$$M = \begin{vmatrix} \xi^1 & \eta^1 & H^1 \\ \xi^2 & \eta^2 & H^2 \\ \xi^3 & \eta^3 & H^3 \end{vmatrix} \equiv 0.$$

This means that three functions ψ_1, ψ_2, ψ_3 can be found such that

$$\sum_{a=1}^{3} \psi_a(K, L, f) X_a \phi \equiv 0,$$

which implies that Eqs. (43) are *not* unconnected. This is a contradiction and thus there cannot be three unconnected types. On the other hand, if the number of types is increased to more than three, with $\partial\phi/\partial f$ not being zero, the rank of M is still less than three, and hence the maximum number of unconnected types of technical progress is two. In summary, we have

***Lemma** 7* (*Number of Unconnected Lie Types of Technical Change*) *If the number of factor inputs is two, then there cannot exist more than two unconnected types of technical progress, under which a production function is holothetic.*

[28] Strictly speaking, unconnected types and independent types should be distinguished; independent types include unconnected types as a special case. Hence, unconnected types are necessarily independent, but independent types are not necessarily unconnected; thus, $\partial/\partial K$, $\partial/\partial L$, $\partial/\partial f$ are unconnected, but X_1, X_2, X_3 where $X_1 \equiv L\,\partial/\partial K - f\,\partial/\partial f$, $X_2 \equiv f\,\partial/\partial K - K\,\partial/\partial f$, $X_3 \equiv K\,\partial/\partial L - L\,\partial/\partial K$ are three connected types, since $KX_1 + LX_2 + fX_3 \equiv 0$, and yet they are independent.

Corollary 1 to Lemma 7 *If the number of factor inputs is two, there exists no production function simultaneously holothetic under three or more unconnected types of technical progress. Conversely*

Corollary 2 to Lemma 7 *If a production function is simultaneously holothetic under three or more types of technical progress, they are* not *unconnected.*

Next we present

Lemma 8 (*Holotheticity of the Lie Bracket Operation*) *If $f(K, L)$ is holothetic under two unconnected types of technical progress,*

$$X_1\phi \equiv \xi^1 \frac{\partial\phi}{\partial K} + \eta^1 \frac{\partial\phi}{\partial L} + H^1(f)\frac{\partial\phi}{\partial f} = 0, \tag{44-i}$$

$$X_2\phi \equiv \xi^2 \frac{\partial\phi}{\partial K} + \eta^2 \frac{\partial\phi}{\partial L} + H^2(f)\frac{\partial\phi}{\partial f} = 0, \tag{44-ii}$$

then it is also holothetic under the Lie bracket operation (alternant) of the two types of technical progress,

$$(X_1, X_2)\phi \equiv X_3\phi \equiv (X_1\xi^2 - X_2\xi^1)\frac{\partial\phi}{\partial K} + (X_1\eta^2 - X_2\eta^1)\frac{\partial\phi}{\partial L}$$
$$+ (X_1H^2 - X_2H^1)\frac{\partial\phi}{\partial f} = 0. \tag{45}$$

Proof $(X_1, X_2)\phi \equiv X_1(X_2\phi) - X_2(X_1\phi) = 0$, since $X_1\phi = 0$ and $X_2\phi = 0$. Q.E.D.

Lemma 9 (*Lie Bracket Condition*) *If Eqs.* (44), $X_1\phi = 0$ *and* $X_2\phi = 0$, *have a nontrivial solution, then Eq.* (45) *is expressed as*

$$(X_1, X_2)\phi = X_3\phi = \rho_1(K, L, f)X_1\phi + \rho_2(K, L, f)X_2\phi. \tag{46}$$

Proof It follows at once from Lemmas 7 and 8 (also see the Appendix, Theorem 9). Q.E.D.

Condition (46) may be called the *Lie bracket condition.*

Earlier we presented the compatibility of technical progress with the internal structure of a technology (Section 17, Definition 5). The Lie bracket condition (46) is a generalization of this concept applied to two exogenous types of technical change [compare Eq. (31) with Eq. (46)]. Generally we say that two unconnected types of technical change are *compatible* if the two types satisfy the Lie bracket condition (46). If they are compatible, then a pair of unconnected equations $X_1\phi = 0$ and $X_2\phi = 0$ is said to form a *complete system* (see the Appendix, Part V).

Theorem 7 (*Necessary and Sufficient Condition for Simultaneous Holotheticity*) *If and only if two unconnected types of technical progress are* *"compatible," then there exists a general family of nontrivial production functions f, simultaneously holothetic under those types of technical progress.*

Proof This is a direct consequence of Theorem 10 of the Appendix (for $\partial\phi/\partial f \neq 0$). Q.E.D.

Hence the Lie bracket condition is nothing but the simultaneous holotheticity condition. When ρ_1 and ρ_2 are *constant* in Eq. (46), the two different Lie types of technical change constitute a *two*-parameter group. Then (46) is the general simultaneous holotheticity conditions under a given two-parameter Lie type of technical change. It is often convenient to transform the two types of technical change and the simultaneous holotheticity condition in terms of a *Jacobian complete system* (see the Appendix, Part V) such as

$$Y_1\phi = \frac{\partial\phi}{\partial K} + R_1\frac{\partial\phi}{\partial f} = 0, \tag{44-i}$$

$$Y_2\phi = \frac{\partial\phi}{\partial L} + R_2\frac{\partial\phi}{\partial f} = 0, \tag{44-ii}$$

where $R_1 = (\eta^2 H^1 - \eta^1 H^2)/D$, $R_2 = (\xi^1 H^2 - \xi^2 H^1)/D$, and $D = \xi^1\eta^2 - \xi^2\eta^1 \not\equiv 0$. [Even when $D = 0$, X_1 and X_2 could be unconnected, but we exclude this possibility; see (47′).] The Jacobian complete system is the system which utilizes the normal (canonical) forms of the two Lie types of technical change. In terms of the Jacobian system, the simultaneous holotheticity condition becomes

$$(Y_1, Y_2)\phi = \rho_1 Y_1\phi + \rho_2 Y_2\phi = (Y_1R_2 - Y_2R_1)\frac{\partial\phi}{\partial f} \equiv 0, \qquad \rho_1 \equiv \rho_2 \equiv 0, \tag{46′}$$

because $(Y_1R_2 - Y_2R_1)\,\partial\phi/\partial f$ is free of both $\partial\phi/\partial K$ and $\partial\phi/\partial L$. The derivation of a family of production functions simultaneously holothetic under X_1 and X_2 is easily accomplished with this transformed Jacobian complete system using Y_1 and Y_2. The following is readily stated as a result of Theorem 7:

Corollary to Theorem 7 (*Trivial Production Function*) *If two unconnected types of technical progress are not "compatible," then the only production function simultaneously holothetic under both types is a trivial production function of $f \equiv$ const for all K and L.*

Further Results and Interpretation of the "Compatibility" Conditions

27. The last theorem presents the most fundamental results in studying the existence of holothetic technology under more than one type of technical progress. As far as is known, the foregoing theorem has never been derived in the past, although some authors have studied special cases of the Cobb–Douglas type and/or the factor-augmenting type (Eichhorn and Kolm [1974], Färe [1980]). This may be due to the fact that the present study adopts the powerful approach of Lie theory, whereas works in the past were limited to special cases.

We now present an alternative formulation of the compatibility condition and give a more obvious interpretation of it. If $\phi(K, L, f)$ is a solution of the complete system $X_1\phi = 0$ and $X_2\phi = 0$, then by multiplying H^2 and H^1 to $X_1\phi = 0$ and $X_2\phi = 0$, respectively, we obtain

$$H^2\xi^1 \frac{\partial\phi}{\partial K} + H^2\eta^1 \frac{\partial\phi}{\partial L} + H^2H^1 \frac{\partial\phi}{\partial f} = 0,$$

$$H^1\xi^2 \frac{\partial\phi}{\partial K} + H^1\eta^2 \frac{\partial\phi}{\partial L} + H^1H^2 \frac{\partial\phi}{\partial f} = 0.$$

Subtracting the second from the first equation, we get

$$(H^2\xi^1 - H^1\xi^2)\frac{\partial\phi}{\partial K} + (H^2\eta^1 - H^1\eta^2)\frac{\partial\phi}{\partial L} = 0,$$

or

$$\frac{\partial\phi}{\partial K}\bigg/\frac{\partial\phi}{\partial L} = \frac{H^2\eta^1 - H^1\eta^2}{H^1\xi^2 - H^2\xi^1}.$$

In the same way, we can show that

$$\frac{\partial\phi}{\partial K}\bigg/\frac{\partial\phi}{\partial f} = \frac{H^2\eta^1 - H^1\eta^2}{\xi^1\eta^2 - \xi^2\eta^1} \quad \text{and} \quad \frac{\partial\phi}{\partial L}\bigg/\frac{\partial\phi}{\partial f} = \frac{H^1\xi^2 - H^2\xi^1}{\xi^1\eta^2 - \xi^2\eta^1}.$$

For the solution $\phi(K, L, f)$ of $X_1\phi = 0$, $X_2\,\phi = 0$, we can express

$$d\phi = \frac{\partial\phi}{\partial K}\,dK + \frac{\partial\phi}{\partial L}\,dL + \frac{\partial\phi}{\partial f}\,df = 0$$

as

$$(H^2\eta^1 - H^1\eta^2)\,dK + (H^1\xi^2 - H^2\xi^1)\,dL + (\xi^1\eta^2 - \xi^2\eta^1)\,df = 0. \tag{47}$$

This is the total differential equation which has $\phi(K, L, f) = \text{const}$ for a solution. The problem of solving a complete system is thus reduced to that of solving a total differential equation (47).

Let the total differential equation (47) be written simply as

$$P(K, L, f)\,dK + Q(K, L, f)\,dL + R(K, L)\,df = 0, \tag{47'}$$

where $P = H^2\eta^1 - H^1\eta^2$, $Q = H^1\xi^2 - H^2\xi^1$, and $R = \xi^1\eta^2 - \xi^2\eta^1$ $(R \neq 0)$. If P, Q, and R are arbitrarily assigned functions of K, L, f, the total differential equation does *not* necessarily correspond to a primitive of the form

$$\phi(K, L, f) = 0, \qquad \frac{\partial \phi}{\partial f} \neq 0, \qquad \text{or} \qquad f = f(K, L).$$

The problem that arises is to find a necessary and sufficient condition that a given total differential equation should be integrable. The well-known condition of integrability is

$$P\left(\frac{\partial Q}{\partial f} - \frac{\partial R}{\partial L}\right) + Q\left(\frac{\partial R}{\partial K} - \frac{\partial P}{\partial f}\right) + R\left(\frac{\partial P}{\partial L} - \frac{\partial Q}{\partial K}\right) = 0. \tag{48}$$

We now show that the condition of the Jacobian complete system (46′) is identical to the integrability condition of the total differential equation. By using (44′) and (46′), the simultaneous holotheticity condition for the Jacobian complete system is

$$Y_1R_2 - Y_2R_1 = \frac{\partial(-Q/R)}{\partial K} + \frac{-P}{R}\frac{\partial(-Q/R)}{\partial f} - \frac{\partial(-P/R)}{\partial L} - \frac{-Q}{R}\frac{\partial(-P/R)}{\partial f} = 0, \tag{46″}$$

where $Y_1R_2 = \partial R_2/\partial K + R_1\,\partial R_2/\partial f$ and $Y_2R_1 = \partial R_1/\partial L + R_2\,\partial R_1/\partial f$. This will reduce to

$$\frac{1}{R_2}\left(-\frac{\partial Q}{\partial K}R + Q\frac{\partial R}{\partial K}\right) - \frac{P}{R}\frac{1}{R^2}\left(-\frac{\partial Q}{\partial f}R + Q\frac{\partial R}{\partial f}\right)$$
$$- \frac{1}{R^2}\left(-\frac{\partial P}{\partial L}R + P\frac{\partial R}{\partial L}\right) + \frac{Q}{R}\frac{1}{R^2}\left(-\frac{\partial P}{\partial f}R + P\frac{\partial R}{\partial f}\right) = 0.$$

For $R \neq 0$, the above implies (48), the integrability condition. Calculating the above for (47), we get

$$P\left(\frac{\partial H^1}{\partial f}\xi^2 + \frac{\partial \xi^2}{\partial L}\eta^1 + \frac{\partial \eta^1}{\partial L}\xi^2 - \frac{\partial H^2}{\partial f}\xi^1 - \frac{\partial \xi^1}{\partial L}\eta^2 - \frac{\partial \eta^2}{\partial L}\xi^1\right)$$
$$+ Q\left(\frac{\partial H^1}{\partial f}\eta^2 + \frac{\partial \eta^2}{\partial K}\xi^1 + \frac{\partial \xi^1}{\partial K}\eta^2 - \frac{\partial H^2}{\partial f}\eta^1 - \frac{\partial \eta^1}{\partial K}\xi^2 - \frac{\partial \xi^2}{\partial K}\eta^1\right)$$
$$+ R\left(\frac{\partial \eta^1}{\partial L}H^2 + \frac{\partial \xi^1}{\partial K}H^2 - \frac{\partial \eta^2}{\partial L}H^1 - \frac{\partial \xi^2}{\partial K}H^1\right) = 0. \tag{48′}$$

In summary, we have

Theorem 8 *(Equivalence of the Simultaneous Holotheticity Condition with the Integrability Condition) The two types of technical progress are "compatible" if and only if the total differential equation consisting of their infinitesimal transformations* (47) *satisfies the integrability condition* (48).

The well-known area where the condition of integrability appears in the traditional approach in economics is utility theory (Samuelson [1947]). And as Samuelson [1947, p. 3] correctly observed a long time ago, the same or similar mathematical conditions tend to reappear in many different branches of theoretical economics. The integrability condition is a case in point. Thus the condition of a (Jacobian) complete system, or the Lie bracket condition, may be given the interpretation more readily known to economists as the integrability condition of a total differential equation.

Compatibility under Well-Known Families of Production Functions

28. Here we study the compatibility question under various families of production function.

Homothetic Technology In Part VI, it was shown that the (Shephard) homothetic class is a holothetic function under the uniform factor-augmenting (or neutral) type of technical progress. Thus the compatibility of any technical change within the homothetic family must satisfy

$$X_1\phi = K\frac{\partial\phi}{\partial K} + L\frac{\partial\phi}{\partial L} + H^1(f)\frac{\partial\phi}{\partial f} = 0, \qquad \text{(49-i)}$$

$$X_2\phi = \xi^2\frac{\partial\phi}{\partial K} + \eta^2\frac{\partial\phi}{\partial L} + H^2(f)\frac{\partial\phi}{\partial f} = 0. \qquad \text{(49-ii)}$$

The above will be met if and only if

$$\begin{aligned} P&\left(\frac{\partial H^1}{\partial f}\xi^2 + \frac{\partial\xi^2}{\partial L}L + \xi^2 - \frac{\partial H^2}{\partial f}K - \frac{\partial\eta^2}{\partial L}K\right) \\ &+ Q\left(\frac{\partial H^1}{\partial f}\eta^2 + \frac{\partial\eta^2}{\partial K}K + \eta^2 - \frac{\partial H^2}{\partial f}L - \frac{\partial\xi^2}{\partial K}L\right) \\ &+ R\left(2H^2 - H^1\left[\frac{\partial\eta^2}{\partial L} + \frac{\partial\xi^2}{\partial K}\right]\right) = 0, \end{aligned} \qquad (50)$$

where $P = H^2L - H^1\eta^2$, $Q = H^1\xi^2 - H^2K$, and $R = K\eta^2 - L\xi^2$. Equation (50) is the fundamental equation which determines the other compatible type of technical progress with the homothetic technology.

As a special case of the above, let $H^1 = H^2 = f$, $\xi^2 = aK$, and $\eta^2 = bL$, or $X_2 = aK\,\partial/\partial K + bL\,\partial/\partial L + f\,\partial/\partial f$. Then we have $P = (1-b)fL$, $Q = (a-1)fK$, and $R = (b-a)KL$, $a \neq b$. The simultaneous holotheticity conditions under X_1 and X_2 are always satisfied, for $(X_1, X_2) = \rho_1 X_1 + \rho_2 X_2$, $\rho_1 \equiv \rho_2 \equiv 0$. Thus there exists a type of linearly homogeneous production functions compatible with the nonuniform (biased) factor-augmenting type, $X_2 = aK\,\partial/\partial K + bL\,\partial/\partial L + f\,\partial/\partial f$. Solving the equivalent total differential equation

$$(1-b)\frac{dK}{K} + (a-1)\frac{dL}{L} + (b-a)\frac{df}{f} = 0,$$

the family of production functions is found to be

$$(1-b)\log K + (a-1)\log L = (a-b)\log f - \log c$$

or simply

$$f = AK^{\alpha}L^{\beta}, \quad \alpha + \beta = 1, \quad (1-b)/(a-b) = \alpha, \quad (a-1)/(a-b) = \beta.$$

This is nothing but the well-known Cobb–Douglas type! Thus *the most general type of the constant returns to scale technology which is also holothetic under the general biased factor-augmenting type of technical progress is the Cobb–Douglas form.* (Compare this result with Eichhorn and Kolm [1974].)

A class of homothetic CES functions may be characterized as the most general type of production functions simultaneously holothetic under

$$X_1 = K\frac{\partial}{\partial K} + L\frac{\partial}{\partial L} + H^1(f)\frac{\partial}{\partial f}$$

and

$$X_2 = aK^{1+\rho}\frac{\partial}{\partial K} + bL^{1+\rho}\frac{\partial}{\partial L} + H^2(f)\frac{\partial}{\partial f}.$$

The reader may be interested in proving this result.

Almost Homothetic Technology Any production function within the almost-homothetic family, which is also holotehetic under some other type of technical change, must come from the general solution of

$$X_1\phi = \alpha K\frac{\partial\phi}{\partial K} + \beta L\frac{\partial\phi}{\partial L} + H^1(f)\frac{\partial\phi}{\partial f} = 0. \qquad \text{(51-i)}$$

$$X_2\phi = \xi^2\frac{\partial\phi}{\partial K} + \eta^2\frac{\partial\phi}{\partial L} + H^2(f)\frac{\partial\phi}{\partial f} = 0. \qquad \text{(51-ii)}$$

The Lie bracket condition of the above system is

$$P\left(\frac{\partial H^1}{\partial f}\xi^2 + \frac{\partial \xi^2}{\partial L}\beta L + \beta\xi^2 - \frac{\partial H^2}{\partial f}\alpha K - \frac{\partial \eta^2}{\partial L}\alpha K\right)$$
$$+ Q\left(\frac{\partial H^1}{\partial f}\eta^2 + \frac{\partial \eta^2}{\partial K}\alpha K + \alpha\eta^2 - \frac{\partial H^2}{\partial f}\beta L - \frac{\partial \xi^2}{\partial K}\beta L\right)$$
$$+ R\left(H^2[\alpha + \beta] - H^1\left[\frac{\partial \eta^2}{\partial L} + \frac{\partial \xi^2}{\partial K}\right]\right) = 0, \tag{52}$$

where $P = H^2\beta L - H^1\eta^2$, $Q = H^1\xi^2 - H^2\alpha K$, and $R = \alpha K\eta^2 - \beta L\xi^2$.

The Cobb–Douglas type is again a special case for $X_2\phi = aK\,\partial\phi/\partial K + bL\,\partial\phi/\partial L + H^2(f)\,\partial\phi/\partial f = 0$. By solving two partial differential equations, we have

$$(\beta - b)\log K + (a - \alpha)\log L + \log C = (a\beta - \alpha b)\log f$$

or

$$f = AK^{(\beta - b)/(a\beta - \alpha b)}L^{(a-\alpha)/(a\beta - \alpha b)}, \qquad a \neq \alpha, \qquad b \neq \beta, \qquad a\beta - \alpha b \neq 0.$$

Houthakker's addilog type is the most general class of production functions holothetic under (51) when Eq. (51-ii) takes the form

$$X_2\phi = aK^{1+\rho_1}\frac{\partial\phi}{\partial K} + bL^{1+\rho_2}\frac{\partial\phi}{\partial L} + H^2(f)\frac{\partial\phi}{\partial f} = 0.$$

Projective Holothetic Technology A family of production functions within the general projective technology, which is also compatible with any other types of technical change, must be a solution of

$$X_1\phi = (a_1 + a_3K + a_5L + a_7K^2 + a_8KL)\frac{\partial\phi}{\partial K}$$
$$+ (a_2 + a_4K + a_6L + a_7KL + a_8L^2)\frac{\partial\phi}{\partial L} + H^1(f)\frac{\partial\phi}{\partial f} = 0, \tag{53-i}$$

$$X_2\phi = \xi^2\frac{\partial\phi}{\partial K} + \eta^2\frac{\partial\phi}{\partial L} + H^2(f)\frac{\partial\phi}{\partial f} = 0. \tag{53-ii}$$

The interested reader is asked to work out several examples using (46) or (48′).

VIII. Multifactor Generalization[29]

Holotheticity of a Multifactor Technology

29. Although most of the basic results of the holotheticity property for a production function with capital and labor inputs hold for a multifactor technology, it may be of interest to investigate this case in some detail. Consider a general quasi-concave neoclassical production function with the usual regularity conditions

$$Y = f(x), \tag{54}$$

where Y is the output, $x = (x_1, \ldots, x_n)$ a vector of n factor inputs, and f a continuously differentiable function up to the second order. Technical progress first changes the way in which the inputs are combined through *the technical progress functions*

$$T_t\colon\quad \bar{x} = \phi(x:t) = \phi_t(x), \tag{55}$$

where t is the parameter of technical change, $\bar{x} = (\bar{x}_1, \ldots, \bar{x}_n)$ a vector of "effective" factor inputs, and $\phi_t = (\phi_t^1, \ldots, \phi_t^n)$ a vector of technical progress functions. The map $x \to \phi_t(x)$ is assumed to be a diffeomorphism. When the total effect of technical progress working through ϕ on f is represented by some monotone transformation F, such that

$$\begin{aligned} \bar{Y} &= f(x:t) = f[\phi(x:t):0] = h[\phi(x:t)] = g[h(x):t] \\ &= F_{(t)}[f(x)], \qquad h(x) = f(x:0) = f(x), \end{aligned} \tag{56}$$

then the production function is said to be "holothetic" under a given T. We assume as before that the technical progress functions ϕ satisfy the Lie group properties and thus technical change is of the Lie type. Then each Lie type of technical change has one and only one infinitesimal transformation represented by

$$\left(\frac{\delta \bar{x}_i}{\delta t}\right)_{t=0} = \xi_i(x) \qquad (1 \leqq i \leqq n) \tag{57}$$

or

$$U = \sum_{i=1}^{n} \xi_i(x) \frac{\partial}{\partial x_i}. \tag{57'}$$

Let y_i be a canonical variable of (55) and be equal to u^i,

$$y_i = u^i(x), \qquad 1 \leqq i \leqq n. \tag{58}$$

[29] This section may be skipped without a sacrifice of basic economic results.

Then (55) is equivalent to

$$\bar{y}_i = y_i + \delta_{in} t, \qquad 1 \leqq i \leqq n, \tag{55'}$$

or

$$V = \frac{\partial}{\partial y_n} \quad \Leftrightarrow \quad U = \sum_{i=1}^{n} \xi_i(x) \frac{\partial}{\partial x_i}. \tag{57''}$$

A family of production function f is holothetic under a given T *if and only if*

$$Uf = \sum_{i=1}^{n} \xi_i(x) \frac{\partial f}{\partial x_i} = G(f) \neq 0 \qquad (\text{say} \quad G(f) = 1) \tag{59}$$

or equivalently

$$Vf = 1. \tag{59'}$$

Solving the above equation, we immediately obtain

$$f = y_n + C(y_1, \ldots, y_{n-1}),$$

which is a family of the holothetic technology in *an additive normal form.* Rewriting the y_i in terms of x, we obtain a general family of holothetic production functions invariant under (55) as

$$Y = y_n(x) + C(y_1(x), \ldots, y_{n-1}(x)) = f(x), \tag{60}$$

which leads to

Theorem 9 (*Existence*) (i) *If the technical progress function* (55) *is of the Lie type, then there exists one and only one family of production functions holothetic under T, such that* $\bar{Y} = f(x:t) = f(\bar{x}) = g[f(x):t] = F_{(t)}[f(x)]$.

(ii) *Any holothetic technology can be reduced to an additive normal form*

$$Y = y_n + C(y_1, \ldots, y_{n-1}),$$

or to a multiplicative normal form

$$Y = z_n C(z_1, \ldots, z_n),$$

where $z_i = u^i$, $1 \leqq i \leqq n - 1$, *and* $z_n = \log u^n$.

The last part of the theorem is the direct result of the fact that *any Lie type of technical progress is equivalent to the Hicks neutral type*, i.e.,

$$U = \sum_{i=1}^{n} \xi_i(x) \frac{\partial}{\partial x_i} \quad \Leftrightarrow \quad V = z_n \frac{\partial}{\partial z_n}, \tag{61}$$

where $z_n = \log u^n$. It is seen that y_k and z_k $(1 \leqq k \leqq n-1)$ are solutions to

$$Uy_k = \sum_{i=1}^{n} \xi_i(x) \frac{\partial y_k}{\partial x_i} = 0 \qquad (1 \leqq k \leqq n-1), \tag{62}$$

and y_n and z_n are solutions to

$$Uy_n = \sum_{i=1}^{n} \xi_i(x) \frac{\partial y_n}{\partial x_i} = 1 \tag{63}$$

and

$$Uz_n = \sum_{i=1}^{n} \xi_i(x) \frac{\partial z_n}{\partial x_i} = z_n, \tag{64}$$

respectively.

Existence of a Lie Type of Technical Progress for Any Production Function

30. Conversely, starting with a given production function f, there exists at least one type of technical progress under which the given production function is holothetic. Since (59) is the only restriction for holotheticity, there would be $(n-1)$ degrees of freedom for choosing the ξ_i. Without loss of generality, let the infinitesimal transformation of the first factor be given together with f. Then (59) requires that

$$\sum_{i=2}^{n} \xi_i(x) \frac{\partial f}{\partial x_i} = 1 - \xi_1(x) \frac{\partial f}{\partial x_1}.$$

By choosing the ξ_i $(2 \leqq i \leqq n)$, a set of infinitesimal transformations for the remaining $(n-1)$ factors is determined for a given $\xi_1(x)$. One of the U may be the one in which $\xi_i \equiv 0$ $(2 \leqq i \leqq n)$. Hence we have

Theorem 10 (*Existence of a Lie Type of Technical Progress*) *Given an isoquant map with n factors $x_1, \ldots, x_n$, there exists at least one type of technical progress under which the given production function is holothetic.*

Capital and Labor Aggregates

We observe that the functions $y_k = u^k$, $1 \leqq k \leqq n-1$, in Eq. (62) are *invariants*. Any function of these invariants is also an invariant. Let K^* be such a function,

$$K^* = K^*(y_1, \ldots, y_{n-1}) = K^*(K_1^*, \ldots, K_{n-1}^*). \tag{65}$$

K^* may be called a "capital aggregate" with $y_k = K_k^*$ $(1 \leqq k \leqq n-1)$ being its "kth capital subaggregate." We call this an aggregate, because these quantities are *not* affected by the transformation (55) and thus may be treated as a single quantity. Let L^* be equal to y_n

$$L^* = y_n(x). \tag{66}$$

In contrast with (65), L^* then may be called a "labor aggregate." On using these aggregates, a multifactor production function is expressed in a normal form as

$$Y = L^* + C(K^*), \tag{67}$$

or, using $z_n = L^*$ in (64), as

$$Y = L^* C(K^*). \tag{68}$$

Simultaneous Holotheticity under r Types of Technical Change

31. Let

$$U_a = \sum_{j=1}^{n} \xi_j^a \frac{\partial}{\partial x_j} \qquad (1 \leqq a \leqq r)$$

be r unconnected types of technical change with each satisfying the Lie group properties. The simultaneous holotheticity condition requires that

$$U_a f = \sum_{j=1}^{n} \xi_j^a(x) \frac{\partial f}{\partial x_j} = H^a(f) \not\equiv 0, \qquad 1 \leqq a \leqq r. \tag{69}$$

We look for the neoclassical production function f which satisfies r equations of (69) simultaneously. Introducing a new function ϕ such that $Y = f(x)$ is defined by $\phi(x, f) = 0$ implicitly, with $\partial\phi/\partial f \neq 0$, we can rewrite (69) as

$$X_a \phi = \sum_{j=1}^{n} \xi_j^a(x) \frac{\partial \phi}{\partial x_j} + H^a(f) \frac{\partial \phi}{\partial f} = 0, \qquad 1 \leqq a \leqq r. \tag{69'}$$

Like the two-factor case, there *cannot* be a more than n independent types of technical progress under which a production function is holothetic. If the number of factor inputs is n, there exists no production function other than trivial one, simultaneously holothetic under $n + 1$ or more unconnected types of technical progress. Conversely, if a nontrivial production function is simultaneously holothetic under $n + 1$ or more types of technical progress, they are *not* unconnected.

Compatibility Conditions

The "compatibility conditions" stated in Part VII will carry over to this n-factor general case. If and only if r ($\leqq n$) different types of technical progress satisfy the Lie *bracket conditions* (or the *compatibility conditions*), then there exists a general family of production functions holothetic under the r types of technical progress. The compatibility conditions are

$$(X_a, X_b) = \sum_{c=1}^{r} \rho_{ab}^{c}(x) X_c, \qquad 1 \leqq a, b \leqq r. \tag{70}$$

Alternatively, there exists a general family of production functions satisfying all r holotheticity conditions, if and only if $X_a\phi = 0$ ($1 \leqq a \leqq r$) constitute a complete system. Summarizing these, we have

Theorem 11 (*Compatibility Conditions*) (i) *If and only if r ($\leqq n$) unconnected types of technical progress are "compatible," then there exists a general family of production functions simultaneously holothetic under those types.*

(ii) *If and only if r unconnected types of technical progress constitute a complete system, there exists a general family of holothetic production functions.*

Sometimes one might start with less than the maximum admissible number of unconnected types of technical change, but eventually one can obtain the maximum number. Consider the case in which r is initially less than or equal to, say, $s \leqq n$, i.e., $2 \leqq r \leqq s \leqq n$. Consider the case in which a system of r equations $X_a\phi = 0$, $1 \leqq a \leqq r$, is not complete.

By starting with r unconnected types of technical progress,

$$X_1\phi = 0, \quad X_2\phi = 0, \ldots, X_r\phi = 0, \qquad 2 \leqq r \leqq s \leqq n,$$

with a common solution ϕ, all the equations

$$(X_a, X_b)\phi = 0, \qquad 1 \leqq a, b \leqq r,$$

will also have this solution. Some or all of these equations may be unconnected to the original equations. By adjoining these to the latter, the process may be repeated as long as unconnected equations can be found. We have thus obtained a system of s equations $X_a\phi = 0$, $1 \leqq a \leqq s$ ($s \leqq n$), such that

$$(X_a, X_b) \equiv \sum_{c=1}^{s} \rho_{ab}^{c} X_c, \qquad 1 \leqq a, b \leqq s \ (s \leqq n).$$

Such a system constitutes a *complete system of order s*. We have shown that

Theorem 12 (*Complete systems of Order s*) *If a production function is holothetic under r ($\leqq s \leqq n$) different types of technical progress, then it is also*

holothetic under every member of technical progress (s of them) of the complete system determined by the first r types.

Lie Group Representation

Given a production function f, then we have a *Lie group representation* of the marginal rates of substitution of the production function as a system of $(n-1)$ partial differential equations,

$$R: \begin{cases} R_n^1 f = M_1(x)\dfrac{\partial f}{\partial x_1} - M_n(x)\dfrac{\partial f}{\partial x_n} = 0, \\ \quad\vdots \\ R_n^{n-1} f = M_{n-1}(x)\dfrac{\partial f}{\partial x_{n-1}} - M_n(x)\dfrac{\partial f}{\partial x_n} = 0, \end{cases} \tag{71}$$

where $M_j/M_n\ (1 \leqq j \leqq n-1)$ is the marginal rate of substitution between the jth and nth factor inputs. Let us assume that we have found a Lie type of technical change $U_1 = \sum_{i=1}^n \xi_i\, \partial/\partial x_i,\ \xi_1 \neq 0$, under which f is holothetic, i.e., $U_1 f = G(f) \neq 0$. This implies that

$$(U_1, R_n^j) = U^{*j} = \rho_{1j} U_1 + \sum_{i=1}^{n-1} \rho_{1j}^i R_n^i, \qquad 1 \leqq j \leqq n-1. \tag{72}$$

Equation (72) is a generalization of Eq. (31) for n-factor input case. It expresses the condition that any other Lie type of technical change U^{*j} under which a given production function is holothetic may be obtained from a combination of U_1 and R, the Lie group representation of the production function.

Special Types of Multifactor Technology

32. Let the infinitesimal transformation of the ith input be given by

$$\xi_i(x) = \alpha_i + \sum_{j=1}^n \alpha_{ij} x_j + \sum_{j=1}^n \alpha_j x_j x_i, \qquad 1 \leqq i \leqq n. \tag{73}$$

The technical progress functions for (73) are

$$\bar{x}_i = \phi(x:t) = \left(a_i(t) + \sum_{j=1}^n a_{ij}(t) x_j\right) \Big/ \left(1 + \sum_{j=1}^n b_j(t) x_j\right), \qquad 1 \leqq i \leqq n. \tag{74}$$

This is a general "projective" type of technical change. The invariant family of curves corresponding to the above is a *general projective technology*. The homothetic and almost homothetic families are again special cases of this technology. Thus, by solving $Uf = \sum_{i=1}^{n} \alpha_i x_i \, \partial f/\partial x_i = G(f)$, we derive a general expression for the almost homothetic technology,

$$Y = f[x_n C(y_1, \ldots, y_{n-1})], \tag{75}$$

where $y_k = x_k^{\alpha_n}/x_n^{\alpha_k}$ $(1 \leqq k \leqq n - 1)$ are the invariants of the technology. The *holothetic partial differential equations* for this family are given by

$$-\frac{\partial x_i}{\partial x_j}\frac{x_j}{x_i} = R_{ij}\frac{x_j}{x_i} = H_{ij}(y_1, \ldots, y_{n-1}). \tag{76}$$

Here, the H_{ij} are *the ratios of relative shares of the* jth *and* ith *factor inputs*.

When all the α_i are identical, we obtain the *homothetic family* with *the holothetic partial differential equations being identical with the marginal rates of substitutions*. When all of the α_i are zero except for one, say $\alpha_n \neq 0$, we obtain the x_n*-homothetic* technology which is the simplest type of a *separable* family, $Y = f[x_n C(x_1, \ldots, x_{n-1})]$. All other types of special families are left to the interested reader for analysis, including the *general separable* family, general *transprojective* family, etc.

IX. Estimation of Technical Change

33. Although it is not the purpose of this book to present empirical estimations of technical change, we shall briefly discuss the empirical implication of the application of the Lie group properties. In particular, we relate the present analysis to the existing works on the measurement of technical change (David and van de Klundert [1965], Sato [1970], Binswanger [1974], Diamond *et al.* [1978]).

kth *Measure of Technical Change*

Assuming a production function to be generally analytic, we expand $\bar{Y} = \bar{f} = f(x:t)$ as

$$\bar{f} = f(x) + \sum_{k=1}^{\infty}\left(\frac{\partial^k \bar{f}}{\partial t^k}\right)_0 \frac{t^k}{k!} = f(x) + \sum_{k=1}^{\infty} g^k(x)\frac{t^k}{k!}, \tag{77}$$

where $\bar{Y} = \bar{f}$ is the output after technical change, $f(x) = f(x:0)$ the output when there is no technical change, and $(\partial^k \bar{f}/\partial t^k)_0 = g^k(x)$ *the* kth *order measure of technical change near the identity* $t = 0$ $(k = 1, 2, \ldots)$. The total effect of technical change is the sum of $g^k(x)(t^k/k!)$ $(k = 1, 2, \ldots)$. Here we may regard the g^k as sort of a series of new "production" functions generated by the process of technical change.

If we now assume that technical change is of *the Lie type* with its infinitesimal transformation given by $U = \sum_{i=1}^{n} \xi_i(x)\, \partial/\partial x_i$, then (77) is expressed as

$$\bar{f} = f(\bar{x}) = f(x) + \sum_{k=1}^{\infty} U^k f \frac{t^k}{k!}, \tag{78}$$

where $U^k f = U^{k-1}(Uf) = U(U^{k-1}f)$, $Uf = \sum_{i=1}^{n} \xi_i(x)\, \partial f/\partial x = (\overline{U}\bar{f})_0 = (\sum_{i=1}^{n} \bar{\xi}_i\, \partial \bar{f}/\partial \bar{x}_i)_0$, and $(\bar{\xi}_i)_0 = (\partial \phi^i/\partial t)_0 = \xi_i(x)$. Hence, *under the assumption that technical change is of the Lie type, its* k*th-order measure near the identity is simply equal to the value of the infinitesimal transformation applied as many as k times to* f (extension of Lemma 2 in Section 6), i.e.,

$$\left(\frac{\partial^k \bar{f}}{\partial t^k}\right)_0 = U^k f \qquad (k = 1, 2, \ldots). \tag{79}$$

Using $g^k = (\partial^k \bar{f}/\partial t^k)_0$ and $Uf = g^1$, $U^2 f = Ug^1, \ldots, U^k f = Ug^{k-1}, \ldots,$ we write (78) as

$$\bar{f} = f(\bar{x}) = f(x) + Uf \frac{t}{1!} + Ug^1 \frac{t^2}{2!} + \cdots + Ug^{k-1} \frac{t^k}{k!} + \cdots. \tag{78'}$$

Hence, under the Lie group assumption, the kth (new) "production" function is equal to the infinitesimal transformation applied to the $(k-1)$th "production" function g^{k-1} $(g^0 = f)$, i.e.,

$$\begin{aligned} g^k = Ug^{k-1} &= \sum_{i=1}^{n} \xi_i(x) \frac{\partial g^{k-1}}{\partial x_i} \\ &= \sum_{i=1}^{n} \begin{pmatrix} \text{infinitesimal} \\ \text{transformation of } x_i \end{pmatrix} \begin{pmatrix} \text{marginal product} \\ \text{of } x_i \text{ in } g^{k-1} \end{pmatrix} \qquad (k = 1, 2, \ldots). \end{aligned} \tag{80}$$

When the original production function f is *holothetic* under a given U, then all the g^k functions are functions of f [Eq. (59)]. (Hence all the "new functions" are mere transformations of f.) On the other hand, when f is *not holothetic*, the g^k functions are not some transformations of f, but they are truly "new production functions."[30]

Consider a CES function $f = (aK^{-\rho} + (1-a)L^{-\rho})^{-1/\rho}$ and

$$\begin{aligned} U = {} & [aK^{-\rho} + (1-a)L^{-\rho}]^{1+1/\rho} K^{\delta_1} \frac{\partial}{\partial K} \\ & + [aK^{-\rho} + (1-a)L^{-\rho}]^{1+1/\rho} L^{\delta_2} \frac{\partial}{\partial L}. \end{aligned}$$

[30] Theoretically it is possible to have some of the g^k be mere transformations of f, while others are not. But there must exist at least one k such that $g^k \neq G(f)$ for the nonholothetic case.

Then the first-order measure of technical change is a new (addilog) function

$$Uf = g^1 = aK^{\delta_1 - \rho - 1} + (1 - a)L^{\delta_2 - \rho - 1} = aK^{-\rho_1} + (1 - a)L^{-\rho_2},$$

and the second-order measure is

$$U^2 f = Ug^1 = g^2 = [aK^{-\rho} + (1 - a)L^{-\rho}]^{1 + 1/\rho}[c_1 K^{2\delta_1 - \rho - 2} + c_2 L^{2\delta_2 - \rho - 2}],$$

$$c_1 = a(\delta_1 - \rho - 1), c_2 = (1 - a)(\delta_2 - \rho - 1), \text{ etc.}$$

Estimation of a Lie Type of Technical Change from the Kendrick–Solow Total Productivity Index

34. Now assume that f is a constant returns to scale production function. The Kendrick–Solow index of total productivity (Kendrick and Sato [1963]) is then nothing but the (relative) first-order measure of technical change, i.e.,

$$\frac{\dot{T}}{T} = \frac{\dot{\bar{f}}}{\bar{f}} - \sum_{i=1}^{n} \frac{x_i \bar{f}_{x_i}}{\bar{f}} \frac{\dot{x}_i}{x_i} = \frac{\dot{\bar{f}}}{\bar{f}} - \sum_{i=1}^{n} \tilde{\pi}_i \frac{\dot{x}_i}{x_i} = \frac{\partial \bar{f}/\partial t}{\bar{f}}, \tag{81}$$

where $\dot{T}/T$ is the index of "total productivity" and $\tilde{\pi}_i = x_i \bar{f}_{x_i}/\bar{f}$ the "actual" relative share of the ith input ($i = 1, \ldots, n$). If technical change is of the Lie type, we can express the total productivity index and the relative first-order measure (relative to $\bar{f}$) from Lemma 2 by

$$\frac{\dot{T}}{T} = \frac{\partial \bar{f}/\partial t}{\bar{f}} = \frac{\overline{Uf}}{\bar{f}} = \left(\sum_{i=1}^{n} \bar{\xi}_i \frac{\partial \bar{f}}{\partial \bar{x}_i}\right) \Big/ \bar{f} = \left(\sum_{i=1}^{n} \xi_i(\bar{x}) \frac{\partial f}{\partial \bar{x}_i}(\bar{x})\right) \Big/ f(\bar{x}) \tag{82}$$

Then *the total productivity index near the identity $t = 0$ is simply equal to the relative first-order measure of technical change near the identity $t = 0$*,

$$\left(\frac{\dot{T}}{T}\right)_0 = \left(\frac{\overline{Uf}}{\bar{f}}\right)_0 = \frac{Uf}{f} = \left(\sum_{i=1}^{n} \xi_i(x) \frac{\partial f}{\partial x_i}(x)\right) \Big/ f(x) \tag{83}$$

Equation (82) or (83) may be useful for the estimation of f and/or U. $\dot{T}/T$ and $(\dot{T}/T)_0$ are generally not identical for $t \neq 0$, but they may be almost identical for sufficiently small value of t. Hence

$$\frac{\dot{T}}{T} \doteqdot \frac{Uf}{f} = \left(\sum_{i=1}^{n} \xi_i(x) \frac{\partial f}{\partial x_i}(x)\right) \Big/ f(x) \qquad \text{for} \quad t \text{ sufficiently small.} \tag{84}$$

This equation may be used in a number of different ways. For instance, it may be used to test whether or not f is holothetic by fitting $\dot{T}/T$ to $G(f)$, say $G(f) = a \log f + b$, assuming f is known a priori. It may also be used to estimate the ξ_i from

$$\frac{\dot{T}}{T} = \sum_{i=1}^{n} \frac{\xi_i(x) f_i x_i}{x_i f} = \sum_{i=1}^{n} \frac{\xi_i(x)}{x_i} \pi_i,$$

where π_i is the relative share of the ith input, given $\dot{T}/T$, x_i, and π_i.[31]

There is another special case when $\dot{T}/T$ and $(\dot{T}/T)_0$ are almost identical. Let the Lie type of technical progress be the *nonneutral factor-augmenting* type, $U = \sum_{i=1}^{n} \alpha_i x_i\, \partial/\partial x_i$ ($\alpha_i = \text{const}, i = 1, \ldots, n$). Then the right-hand side of (82) becomes

$$\frac{\dot{T}}{T} = \left(\sum_{i=1}^{n} \alpha_i \bar{x}_i \frac{\partial f}{\partial \bar{x}_i}\right) \Big/ f(\bar{x}) = \sum_{i=1}^{n} \alpha_i \bar{\pi}_i = \sum_{i=1}^{n} \alpha_i \pi_i(\bar{x}), \tag{82'}$$

where $\bar{\pi}_i = \pi_i(\bar{x})$ is the relative share of the ith input measured in terms of the "effective" inputs $\bar{x}$. When the actual shares $\tilde{\pi}_i$ do not change drastically (the U.S. case in point), we may assume that

$$\tilde{\pi}_i \doteqdot \bar{\pi}_i \doteqdot \pi_i(x), \tag{85}$$

where $\pi_i(x)$ is the relative share of the ith input near the identity. Then by substituting $\tilde{\pi}_i$ into π_i, we may estimate the α_i, say by regression equations, from[32]

$$\frac{\dot{T}}{T} = \sum_{i=1}^{n} \alpha_i \tilde{\pi}_i = \sum_{i=1}^{n} \alpha_i \pi_i = \sum_{i=1}^{n} \frac{\dot{\bar{x}}_i}{\bar{x}_i} \pi_i, \tag{86}$$

for any given values of $\dot{T}/T$ and $\tilde{\pi}_i$.

Once the first-order measure of technical change is estimated, it may be possible to estimate higher-order measures by the use of higher-order changes of $\dot{T}/T$, i.e., $\partial^k(\dot{T}/T)/\partial t^k \doteqdot \Delta^k(\dot{T}/T)$ and the estimated U, thereby measuring the total impact of technical change. The total impact of technical change may sometimes be estimated directly from Eq. (78′) by sophisticated nonlinear econometric methods. But this aspect of empirical analysis is beyond the scope of the present work.

[31] If the $\xi_i(x)$ come from the projective type [Eq. (73)], then $\sum_{i=1}^{n} (\xi_i(x)/x_i)\pi_i$ may be estimated by some form of linear methods. This may be another way of avoiding the so-called impossibility theorem (see Sato [1970], Diamond *et al.* [1978]).

[32] Compare this equation with Eq. (3) in Sato [1970, p. 181].

REFERENCES

Arrow, K., Chenery, H., Minhas, B., and Solow, R. [1961]. Capital–Labor substitution and economic efficiency, *Review of Economics and Statistics*, **43**, 225–250.

Binswanger, H. P. [1974]. The measurement of technical change bias with many factors of production, *American Economic Review*, **64**, 964–976.

Carlson, S. [1939]. *A Study on the Pure Theory of Production*, Stockholm Economic Studies, No. 9. P. S. King & Sons, London.

Christensen, L. R., Jorgenson, D. W., and Lau, L. J. [1973]. Transcendental logarithmic production frontiers, *Review of Economics and Statistics*, **55**, 28–45.

Clemhout, S. [1968]. The class of homothetic isoquant production functions, *Review of Economic Studies*, **35**, 91–104.

David, P. A., and van de Klundert, T. [1965]. Biased efficiency growth and capital–labor substitution in the U.S., 1899–1960, *American Economic Review*, **55**, 357–394.

Diamond, P., McFadden, D., and Rodriguez, M. [1978]. Measurement of the elasticity of factor substitution and bias of technical change, in *Production Economics: A Dual Approach to Theory and Applications* (M. Fuss and D. McFadden, eds.), Vol. 2. North-Holland Publ., Amsterdam.

Eichhorn, W., and Kolm, S. C. [1974]. Technical progress, neutral inventions, and Cobb–Douglas, in *Production Theory: Proceedings of an International Seminar at the University of Karlsruhe*, (W. Eichhorn, R. Henn, O. Optitz, and R. W. Shephard, eds.), Lecture Notes in Economics and Mathematical Systems, Vol. 99. Springer-Verlag, Berlin and New York.

Eisenhart, L. P. [1933]. *Continuous Groups of Transformations*. Princeton Univ. Press, Princeton, New Jersey. Reprint, Dover, New York, 1961.

Färe, R. [1980]. *Laws of Diminishing Returns*, Lecture Notes in Economics and Mathematical Systems, Vol. 176. Springer-Verlag, Berlin and New York.

Frisch, R. [1965]. *Theory of Production*. Dordrecht.

Griliches, Z., and Ringstad, V. [1972]. *Economics of Scale and the Form of Production Function: An Econometric Study of Norwegian Manufacturing Establishment Data*, Contribution to Economic Analysis, Vol. 72. North-Holland, Publ., Amsterdam.

Hicks, J. R. [1963]. *The Theory of Wages*, 2nd ed. Macmillan, London.

Houthakker, H. S. [1960]. Additive preferences, *Econometrica*, **28**, 244–257.

Ince, E. L. [1956]. *Ordinary Differential Equations*. Dover, New York.

John, F. [1971]. *Partial Differential Equations*, Springer-Verlag, Berlin and New York.

Kendrick, W., and Sato, R. [1963]. Factor prices, productivity, and economic growth, *American Economic Review*, **53**, 974–1003.

Kott, P. S. [1979]. The Study and Estimation of Particular Technologies Consistent under Hypothesized Technical Progress Functions. Ph.D. Dissertation, Brown University, Providence, Rhode Island.

Lau, L. J. [1978]. Applications of profit functions, in *Production Economics: A Dual Approach to Theory and Applications*, (M. Fuss and D. McFadden, eds.), Vol. 1. North-Holland Publ., Amsterdam.

Ramachandran, R. V. [1974]. Long-Run Production Function and Endogenous Technical Progress—A Neoclassical Approach. Ph.D. Dissertation, Brown University, Providence, Rhode Island.

Samuelson, P. A. [1947]. *Foundations of Economic Analysis*. Harvard Univ. Press, Cambridge, Massachusetts.

Samuelson, P. A. [1965]. A theory of induced innovations along Kennedy–Weizsäcker lines, *Review of Economics and Statistics*, **47**, 343–356.

Sato, R. [1970]. The estimation of biased technical progress and the production function, *International Economic Review*, **11**, 179–208.

Sato, R. [1975]. The impact of technical change on the holotheticity of production function, presented at the World Congress of the Econometric Society, Toronto, Canada; *Review of Economic Studies*, **47** (1980), 767–776.

Sato, R. [1977]. Homothetic and non-homothetic functions, *American Economic Review*, **67**, 559–569.

Sato, R., and Beckmann, M. J. [1968]. Neutral inventions and production functions, *Review of Economic Studies*, **35**, 57–65.

Sato, R., and Ramachandran, R. [1974]. Models of Optimal Endogenous Technical Progress, Scale Effect and Duality of Production Functions, Discussion Paper, Department of Economics, Brown University, Providence, Rhode Island.

Shephard, R. W. [1953]. *Cost and Production Functions*. Princeton Univ. Press, Princeton, New Jersey.

Shephard, R. W. [1970]. *Theory of Cost and Production Functions*. Princeton Univ. Press, Princeton, New Jersey.

Solow, R. M. [1957]. Technical change and the aggregate production function, *Review of Economics and Statistics*, **39**, 312–320.

Solow, R. M. [1961]. Comment on Stigler, in *Output, Input and Productivity Measurement*, Income and Wealth Series, pp. 64–68. Princeton Univ. Press, Princeton, New Jersey.

Stigler, G. J. [1961]. Economic problems in measuring changes in productivity, in *Output, Input and Productivity*, Income and Wealth Series, pp. 47–63. Princeton Univ. Press, Princeton, New Jersey.

Suzawa, G. [1979]. A theory of long-run production function, in *Control Theory in Mathematical Economics: Proceedings of the Third Kingston Conference, Part B* (Pan-Tai Liu and J. G. Sutinen, eds.), Lecture Notes in Pure and Applied Mathematics, Vol. 47. Dekker, New York.

Wolkowitz, B. [1971]. A set of explicit homothetic production functions, *American Economic Review*, **61**, 980–983.

Woodward, G. T. [1979]. An Aggregate 'World' Production Function: Theory and Estimation. Ph.D. Dissertation, Brown University, Providence, Rhode Island.

Zellner, A., and Revankar, N. S. [1969]. Generalized production functions, *Review of Economic Studies*, **36**, 241–250.

CHAPTER 3

A THEORY OF ENDOGENOUS TECHNICAL PROGRESS

I. Introduction

1. This chapter does not deal directly with the application of Lie group theory, but deals with the analysis of exogenous technical change. The study of technical change, thus far, takes it for granted that there is a factor affecting the technology and that this factor is given exogenously to the economic system. The fact remains, however, that practically all types of technical change are determined within the economic system as the result of meaningful rational economic behavior of economic agents. That is to say, technical change is "endogenous." Our attention now is to study this process of endogenously determined technical progress—a process partly due to dynamic market forces of supply and demand and partly due to dynamic technological forces of inventions and innovations.[1] Technical progress is regarded as the result of dynamic processes of efficient allocation of limited resources under technological and market constraints.

[1] Historians, political scientists, sociologists, and economists will all agree that one of the major forces shaping human destiny has been technology and innovation. The discovery of cultivated grain is responsible for the agricultural surplus enabling the existence of urban society (Jacobs [1969]). The introduction of gunpowder in Europe was a major factor in terminating the feudal regime (Bloch [1961]). The printing machine helped Luther in the Reformation (McLuhan [1969]). The internal combustion machine is, of course, the basis for automobiles, airplanes, etc. The present book is not concerned with these types of technological advances which are considered "exogenous" in the short run, but "endogenous" in the very long run "subject to chance."

An important dimension of technical change is that it is the outcome of investment activities; society postpones a portion of present consumption for the benefit of increased consumption later. In the theory of the firm behavior, the firm postpones a fraction of present profits in the form of research and development (R & D) investment for the purpose of enjoying future cost-saving benefits. Viewing technological change in an intertemporal context affords us many possibilities to understand better the relationship between R & D and the efficiency increase in production of goods and services. Economists discovered long ago that a significant increase of productivity is largely due to R & D activities of the firm, industry, and economy as a whole. Quoting the conclusion drawn at the 1972 colloqium on R & D and economic growth/productivity sponsored by the National Science Foundation, Kamien and Schwartz [1975] write:

> despite methodological difficulties and debates, all the evidence—at the level of the firm, industry and economy—indicates that the contribution of R & D to economic growth/productivity is positive, significant, and high. Estimates of rates of return range between 10 percent and 50 percent with a bias toward the higher values.

Perhaps the most dramatic evidence for the direct effect of R & D is found in agriculture. Evenson and Kislev [1975] report: "We have found that very systematic relationships exist between levels of research activity and economic performance."

The studies done by industrial organization specialists have shown that the R & D cost relation to output follows the same (U-shaped) pattern as the cost relation of other commodities (Scherer [1970]; Schmookler [1966]; Mansfield [1968]). This indicates that R & D can be viewed as one of the factors of production and that we may apply the "production function" approach to the theory of endogenous technical progress. We abstract from problems of management and engineering, labor relations, and other factors. We recognize that much of the strength (and weakness) in the concept of the production function concept lies in its being a "black box," and that the black box can include the creative process, assimilation and processing of information, sociology of science and scientific society, and other factors.

Basic versus Applied Research

2. Review of the literature of technical progress and of production functions in general shows that the present approach is unique in the following two respects[2]:

(i) There are *two main categories of research*: *basic and applied*. Developments fall under the "applied" category. It is useful to think of basic knowledge obtained by basic research as an intermediate product in the production of technical knowledge by applied research. The combination of basic and applied research is responsible for productivity increase.

(ii) The production function depends not only on current research, but on a *stock* of technical knowledge accumulated by applied research done in several years. There exist *time lags* between research inputs and research outputs.[3]

Holotheticity and Endogenous Technical Progress

3. In Chapter 2 we have shown that for any given production function there exists an infinite number of different types of technical change that can be transformed to the scale effect—holotheticity. That is to say, there exists an infinite number of holothetic technical changes expressible in terms of "neutral type" of technical progress. This suggests that we are *not* required to justify the existence of *endogenous* technical change for every *different* type of *exogenous* technical change. It suffices to concentrate just on a "neutral type" of technical progress. It turns out, however, that it is much more convenient to use the neutral type of technical progress which generally applies to the cost function rather than to the production function itself. In short, our purpose is that, *rather than taking the neutral type (applied to the cost function) as exogenous, we formulate a model of technical change which is generated endogenously by efficient allocation of resources.*

II. Formulation of the Model

Dynamic Böhm-Bawerk Effects

4. The process of accumulation of knowledge is *endogenous*, and should be determined by the firm so as to maximize long-run profits. The firm may

[2] There is a number of excellent surveys of the area, and this is why we refrain from detailed bibliographical account. The surveys are: Kamien and Schwartz [1975], Nordhaus [1969], Scherer [1970, Chapter 15], and others. See also Griliches [1980].

[3] The present analysis is a direct extension of Sato and Ramachandran [1978]. Time lags considered here are the so-called "transport lags" (Bate [1969]). Thus, this is an application of optimal control with transport lags.

change its stock of *basic and applied* knowledge by producing a *flow* of the two. Basic knowledge is an intermediate product in the production of new technical knowledge. Consider the celebrated example of productivity increase by a roundabout production process of Böhm-Bawerk. A fisherman does not go to sea to catch fish with his barehands. He would rather use his labor first to make fishing nets and build boats, which are intermediate products for the final output—fish, to catch it more efficiently. The idea behind our formulation is similar to this type of the Böhm-Bawerk process, except that we assume here a dynamic process of continuous delays between research inputs and research outcomes. Next we assume that the firm is a profit-maximizing monopolist,[4] engaging in production (and sales) of the product and in R & D activities.[5] It buys capital (K) and labor (L) at given prices r and w, respectively. The firm may increase the stock of basic knowledge (B) or applied knowledge (A) by employing specialized research workers a and research capital b. But there are time lags between inputs and outputs of this research activity. If we allow for continuous time lags, the flow of outputs appears as cumulative. Formally we write the cumulative effects as

$$\dot{A}(t) = \int_{-\infty}^{t} G^1[A(\tau), B(\tau), a_A(\tau), b_A(\tau)]W_1(t-\tau)\,d\tau - vA(t), \tag{1}$$

$$\dot{B}(t) = \int_{-\infty}^{t} G^2[B(\tau), a_B(\tau), b_B(\tau)]W_2(t-\tau)\,d\tau - \mu B(t). \tag{2}$$

Looking at the second equation, we see that the potential flow of basic knowledge $\dot{B}$ without a time lag depends on the level of stock of basic knowledge itself B, the factor inputs a_B and b_B. Here, G^2 may be considered as a *production function* of the potential flow of basic knowledge, which represents the potential gross increase in B. Equation (1) without a time lag is, on the other hand, the production function of applied knowledge which has a direct influence on productivity increase. Thus G^1 represents the potential gross increase in the stock of applied knowledge resulting from A, a_A, and b_A, and more importantly from the value of basic knowledge B. The fact that G^1 contains B, but G^2 does *not* contain A shows the essential *asymmetric* property of technical change. *Basic knowledge B is "essential" for production of applied knowledge A*. Looking at the extreme case in which the stock of basic

[4] It is known that only big firms engage in research—the threshold is 5000 workers. It is conceivable that such firms view a negatively sloped demand curve.

[5] This is the general framework adopted by Sato and Ramachandran [1978]. They, however, do not separate basic and applied research. The present formulation follows closely with that of Sato and Nôno [1979].

knowledge is zero (a case which exists in principle, but not in practice), we find that the following conditions would hold:

$$G^1(A, 0, a_A, b_A) = 0 \tag{3-i}$$

$$\frac{\partial G^1(A, 0, a_A, b_A)}{\partial B} = +\infty. \tag{3-ii}$$

The first expression states that without basic knowledge, the production of applied knowledge is impossible. The assumption is quite realistic. Elementary language skills and fundamental numerical skills fall under the category of basic knowledge. It is clear, for example, that a student with no knowledge of Russian could not possibly formulate an intelligent interpretation of the original works of Tolstoy. Similarly, a researcher with no basic knowledge of a certain computer language could not possibly produce useful programs written in that language.

The second expression states that the marginal productivity of the first unit of basic knowledge in the production of technical knowledge is extremely high. As an approximation, one may envision the change in applied knowledge that is brought about by mastering simple arithmetic. Regarding the effects of other variables on G^1 and G^2, we shall simply assume the positivity (nonnegativity) of the marginal products and the *concavity* of G^1 and G^2 with respect to their arguments. In summary, we assume that

$$\frac{\partial G^1}{\partial A} \geqq 0, \qquad \frac{\partial G^1}{\partial B} > 0, \qquad \frac{\partial G^1}{\partial a_A} \geqq 0, \qquad \frac{\partial G^1}{\partial b_A} \geqq 0, \tag{4-i}$$

$$\frac{\partial G^2}{\partial A} = 0, \qquad \frac{\partial G^2}{\partial B} \geqq 0, \qquad \frac{\partial G^2}{\partial a_B} \geqq 0, \qquad \frac{\partial G^2}{\partial b_B} \geqq 0, \tag{4-ii}$$

G^1 and G^2 are concave functions. (4-iii)

Equations (1) and (2) allow for the existence of time lags between the inputs and increases in A and B. Because of time lags, the actual increase in A or B depends on the cumulative effect expressed by the integro-differential equation. We may call this as the *dynamic Böhm-Bawerk effect*, with W_i $(i = 1, 2)$ being a weighting function which has the property

$$\int_{-\infty}^{t} W_i(t - \tau)\, d\tau = 1, \qquad i = 1, 2. \tag{5}$$

Then Eq. (1) [or (2)] states that the realized gross increase in technical knowledge is a weighted average of past values of G^1 (or G^2 for $\dot{B}$). Both ν and μ $(\nu \geqq 0, \mu \geqq 0)$ are depreciation factors in applied and basic knowledge, respectively. It takes account of the fact that a part of the production effort of knowledge is aimed at renewing and transferring of knowledge. One may

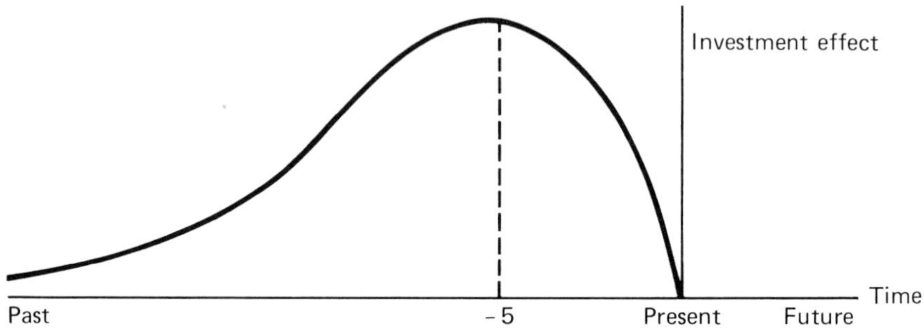

Figure 1 Continuous Böhm-Bawerk effect.

think on the beginning of the Middle Ages as a time where G^2 was near zero, and so the level of basic knowledge deteriorated.

The firm is faced with a discount rate ρ, time series of expected prices of a and b, $P_a(t)$ and $P_b(t)$, r_t and w_t the development of prices of capital and labor, and $P_t(Y)$ the demand function for the final output Y which is also subject to dynamic change. The firm may naturally expect the increasing scarcity of resource[6] to be reflected in knowledge, thus increasing its productivity and reducing its cost. We shall see that this indeed happens. Figure 1 depicts the cumulative effects of investment in research and development of new technology. The results of the past investments appear continuously, with the investment of, say, five years ago yielding the highest effect. The form and shape of this curve depend on a particular type of weighting functions we employ. It is found that a gamma distribution function is particularly appealing and useful for an empirical study (Sato and Suzawa [1980]).

Allocation of Resources

5. We assume that the firm produces the output (Y) from K and L using its neoclassical production function

$$Y(t) = F[A(t)K(t), A(t)L(t)]. \tag{6}$$

$A(t)$ is the level of factor augmentation at time t, and it is the measure of technical progress of the firm that we have already discussed.

[6] Scarcity of oil follows from its being an exhaustible resource. Scarcity of food follows from growth of population, and constancy of fertile land. So far the Malthusian famine was averted by a rate of technological innovation in production of food which was equal to the rate of population growth. This agrees with the predictions of our model.

From the production function we can derive the total cost function

$$TC(Y, w, r, A) = \frac{1}{A(t)} \overline{TC}(Y, w, r), \tag{6'}$$

where $\overline{TC}(Y, w, r)$ is the minimum cost of producing Y, given the production function with no factor augmentation. This property is valid for a general production function. We do not assume any homogeneity. Hence we want to justify the indirect holotheticity and indirect neutrality with respect to the cost function, as discussed in Section 3.[7]

The objective of the firm is to solve the maximization problem of the type

$$\max_{\substack{a_A(t),\, a_B(t) \\ b_A(t),\, b_B(t),\, Y(t)}} \int_0^\infty e^{-\rho t}\Bigg[Y(t)P(t, Y(t)) - \overline{TC}\left(Y(t), \frac{w(t)}{A(t)}, \frac{r(t)}{A(t)} \right) - P_a(t)(a_A(t) + a_B(t)) - P_b(b_A(t) + b_B(t)) \Bigg] dt \tag{7}$$

subject to the constraints (1) and (2) and the initial conditions.

The problem of the firm is to choose a time path of output and a program of research and development which maximizes the present value of future profits. In conducting its R & D program, the firm chooses the level of labor and capital inputs in the R & D process. In hiring inputs, there may be substantial interaction between firms. For example, the representative firm may hire researchers who have already been trained at another firm, or may purchase a device or process patented by another firm. It is assumed that these inputs are purchased in one competitive market. However, it may be that the firm recruits R & D inputs from two sources—(1) educational institutions and (2) other firms. As a first approximation, inputs into the production of basic knowledge a_B and b_B are probably hired more intensively in the educational sector, and applied inputs are most likely to be hired from

[7] If F is a homogeneous function of degree one, then the indirect neutrality $\overline{TC}/A(t)$ coincides with the direct neutrality $Y = A(t)F$. For a more general case, we must consider a nonuniform (biased) type of technical progress in (6) ($Y = F[A(t)K, B(t)L]$) in the context of endogenous technical change. This will enable one to analyze the implication of the *expanding* innovation frontier of Samuelson [1965]. A simple case of expanding innovation frontier where there is no distinction between basic and applied research is studied by Sato and Ramachandran [1978]. The relationship between the primal rate of return associated with the production function and the dual rate of return associated with the cost function is extensively studied in Chapter 6, Part IX.

other firms. Therefore, the wage and rental payments to basic and applied inputs are assumed to be the same. The validity of this assumption is an empirical question, and the assumption may easily be relaxed.

Additional Assumptions

6. In order to ensure the existence of a long-run steady-state equilibrium, we shall make the following additional assumptions:

$$P(t, Y(t)) = e^{\alpha t}\bar{P}(Y(t)), \tag{8-i}$$

$$r(t) = e^{\beta t}\bar{r}, \tag{8-ii}$$

$$w(t) = e^{\beta t}\bar{w}, \qquad \rho \geqq \beta \geqq \alpha \geqq 0, \tag{8-iii}$$

$$P_a(t) = e^{\alpha t}\bar{P}_a, \qquad \bar{P} > 0, \quad \bar{r} > 0, \tag{8-iv}$$

$$P_b(t) = e^{\alpha t}\bar{P}_b, \qquad \bar{w} > 0, \quad \bar{P}_a > 0, \quad \bar{P}_b > 0. \tag{8-v}$$

Here we assume that the commodity price $P(Y)$ is increasing at the same rate (α) as the prices of inputs in the R & D sector, while the wage rate and the return to capital both grow at the rate β.

Define a new state variable

$$g(t) = e^{-(\beta-\alpha)t}A(t). \tag{9}$$

Then we have by the homogeneity property

$$\begin{aligned} TC &= \overline{TC}(Y, w/A, r/A) = A^{-1}\overline{TC}(Y, w, r) \\ &= (e^{\beta t}/A)\overline{TC}(Y, \bar{w}, \bar{r}) \qquad \text{(by homogeneity);} \end{aligned}$$

therefore

$$TC = e^{\alpha t}g^{-1}C(Y), \qquad C(Y) = \overline{TC}(Y, \bar{w}, \bar{r}). \tag{10}$$

Also, the total revenue function can be expressed as

$$Y(t)P(t, Y(t)) = e^{\alpha t}Y(t)\bar{P}(Y(t));$$

therefore

$$Y(t)P(t, Y(t)) = e^{\alpha t}R(Y(t)), \qquad R(Y(t)) = Y(t)\bar{P}(Y(t)). \tag{11}$$

Equation (9) obviously implies

$$\dot{A}/A = (\dot{g}/g) + (\beta - \alpha). \tag{9'}$$

Using these new variables, our maximization problem of optimal endogenous technical change can be reformulated as

$$\max_{\substack{a_A(t),\, a_B(t)\\ b_A(t),\, b_B(t),\, Y(t)}} \int_0^{\infty} e^{-\gamma t}\Bigg[R(Y(t)) - \frac{1}{g(t)} C(Y(t)) - \bar{P}_a(a_A(t) + a_B(t))$$

$$- \bar{P}_b(b_A(t) + b_B(t))\Bigg]\, dt \tag{7'}$$

subject to[8]

$$\dot{g}(t) = -(\beta - \alpha + v)g(t) + \int_{-\infty}^{t} e^{-(\beta-\alpha)t} \tag{1'}$$

$$\times\, G^1[e^{(\beta-\alpha)\tau} g(\tau), B(\tau), a_A(\tau), b_A(\tau)]W_1(t-\tau)\, d\tau$$

and (2), where

$$\gamma = \rho - \alpha > 0. \tag{12}$$

III. Solution of the Model

7. The model we have just formulated is formally similar to the optimal control problem of a system with transport (or continuous) lag, first studied by Bate [1969], and later applied to economic analyses by Sethi [1973, 1974], Pauwels [1977], Sethi and McGuire [1977], Sato and Nôno [1979], and others. In order to guarantee the sufficiency conditions for the optimal control program, we assume that the production functions G^1, G^2, $F(K, L)$, and the profit function are all concave in such a way that the maximized Hamiltonian is concave in the state variables for each t. We may further assume that the maximized Hamiltonian is concave in the state variables for each given implicit price vector and for each t (Sethi [1974]).

[8] Equation (1′) was derived from (1) and (9) by

$$e^{(\beta-\alpha)t}\dot{g}(t) + (\beta - \alpha)e^{(\beta-\alpha)t}g(t) = -ve^{(\beta-\alpha)t}g(t)$$

$$+ \int_{-\infty}^{t} G^1[e^{(\beta-\alpha)\tau}g(\tau), B(\tau), a_A(\tau), b_A(\tau)]W_1(t-\tau)\, d\tau.$$

We shall basically follow the transformation suggested by Sethi [1973] to derive solutions to this type of problems. Thus the *current-value Hamiltonian* is equal to

$$\begin{aligned} &H[g(t), B(t), \lambda_1(\tau \geqq t), \lambda_2(\tau \geqq t), Y(t), a_A(t), b_A(t), a_B(t), b_B(t)] \\ &\quad = R(Y(t)) - \frac{1}{g(t)} C(Y(t)) - \bar{P}_a(a_A(t) + a_B(t)) - \bar{P}_b(b_A(t) + b_B(t)) \\ &\quad\quad - \lambda_1(t)(\beta - \alpha + v)g(t) - \lambda_2(t)\mu B(t) \\ &\quad\quad + \int_t^\infty e^{-\gamma(\tau - t)}\{\lambda_1(\tau)G^1[e^{(\beta-\alpha)t}g(t), B(t), a_A(t), b_A(t)]e^{-(\beta-\alpha)\tau} \\ &\quad\quad \times W_1(\tau - t) + \lambda_2(\tau)G^2[B(t), a_B(t), b_B(t)]W_2(\tau - t)\}\, d\tau, \end{aligned}$$

i.e.,

$$\begin{aligned} H &= R(Y(t)) - \frac{1}{g(t)} C(Y(t)) - \bar{P}_a(a_A(t) + a_B(t)) - \bar{P}_b(b_A(t) + b_B(t)) \\ &\quad - \lambda_1(t)(\beta - \alpha + v)g(t) - \lambda_2(t)\mu B(t) + G^1[e^{(\beta-\alpha)t}g(t), B(t), a_A(t), b_A(t)] \\ &\quad \times \int_t^\infty e^{-(\beta-\alpha)\tau}\lambda_1(\tau)e^{-\gamma(\tau-t)}W_1(\tau - t)\, d\tau + G^2[B(t), a_B(t), b_B(t)] \\ &\quad \times \int_t^\infty \lambda_2(\tau)e^{-\gamma(\tau-t)}W_2(\tau - t)\, d\tau. \end{aligned} \tag{13}$$

The current-value adjoint vector (λ_1, λ_2) of the implicit prices is given by

$$\begin{aligned} \dot{\lambda}_1(t) &= (\gamma + \beta - \alpha + v)\lambda_1(t) - \frac{1}{g^2(t)} C(Y(t)) \\ &\quad - e^{(\beta-\alpha)t}G_1^1 \int_t^\infty e^{-(\beta-\alpha)\tau}\lambda_1(\tau)e^{-\gamma(\tau-t)}W_1(\tau - t)\, d\tau, \end{aligned} \tag{14-i}$$

$$\begin{aligned} \dot{\lambda}_2(t) &= (\gamma + \mu)\lambda_2(t) - G_2^1 \int_t^\infty e^{-(\beta-\alpha)\tau}\lambda_1(\tau)e^{-\gamma(\tau-t)}W_1(\tau - t)\, d\tau \\ &\quad - G_2^2 \int_t^\infty \lambda_2(\tau)e^{-\gamma(\tau-t)}W_2(\tau - t)\, d\tau, \end{aligned} \tag{14-ii}$$

where

$$G^1 = G^1[e^{(\beta-\alpha)t}g(t), B(t), a_A(t), b_A(t)] = G^1(X_1, X_2, X_3, X_4),$$
$$G^2 = G^2[B(t), a_B(t), b_B(t)] = G^2(Y_2, Y_3, Y_4),$$

and

$$G_i^1 = \partial G^1/\partial X_i\ (i = 1, 2, 3, 4),\ G_j^2 = \partial G^2/\partial Y_j\ (j = 2, 3, 4).$$

By the maximum principle similar to the one developed by Pontryagin *et al.* [1962], we have

$$\frac{\partial H}{\partial Y} = R_Y(Y(t)) - g^{-1}C_Y(Y(t)) = 0, \tag{15-i}$$

$$\frac{\partial H}{\partial a_A} = -\bar{P}_a + G_3^1 \int_t^\infty e^{-(\beta-\alpha)\tau}\lambda_1(\tau)e^{-\gamma(\tau-t)}W_1(\tau - t)\,d\tau = 0, \tag{15-ii}$$

$$\frac{\partial H}{\partial b_A} = -\bar{P}_b + G_4^1 \int_t^\infty e^{-(\beta-\alpha)\tau}\lambda_1(\tau)e^{-\gamma(\tau-t)}W_1(\tau - t)\,d\tau = 0, \tag{15-iii}$$

$$\frac{\partial H}{\partial a_B} = -\bar{P}_a + G_3^2 \int_t^\infty \lambda_2(\tau)e^{-\gamma(\tau-t)}W_2(\tau - t)\,d\tau = 0, \tag{15-iv}$$

$$\frac{\partial H}{\partial b_B} = -\bar{P}_b + G_4^2 \int_t^\infty \lambda_2(\tau)e^{-\gamma(\tau-t)}W_2(\tau - t)\,d\tau = 0. \tag{15-v}$$

These equations give the optimality conditions for endogenous technical progress. The first is the familiar condition of the equality of the marginal revenue (R_Y) with the marginal cost (C_Y/g). The remaining conditions state that the ratios between the prices of the research factor inputs and their marginal products in creation of the basic and applied knowledge must be equal to their weighted averages of the implicit prices, i.e.,

$$\bar{P}_a/G_3^1 = \int_t^\infty e^{-(\beta-\alpha)\tau}\lambda_1(\tau)e^{-\gamma(\tau-t)}W_1(\tau - t)\,d\tau,$$

$$\vdots$$

$$\bar{P}_b/G_4^2 = \int_t^\infty \lambda_2(\tau)e^{-\gamma(\tau-t)}W_2(\tau - t)\,d\tau.$$

Further Simplifications

8. Rather than pursue the general line of analysis, we shall further simplify the model by assuming that *$A(t)$ in the production of $\dot{A}$ is multiplicative and $B(t)$ does not appear in the production of $\dot{B}$.* In addition, we shall consider the case in which a and b are highly substitutable so that a linear combination of these two inputs can be treated as one aggregate input θ. Let a linear combination be represented by

$$\theta(t) = \bar{P}_a a(t) + \bar{P}_b b(t)$$

with the weights $\bar{P}_a$ and $\bar{P}_b$ the (deflated) constant prices of a and b, respectively. Then we can express the dynamic Böhm-Bawerk effects of A and B as

$$\dot{A}(t) = -\nu A(t) + \int_{-\infty}^{t} A(\tau)G^1[B(\tau), \theta_1(\tau)]W_1(\tau - t)\, d\tau, \tag{16-i}$$

$$\dot{B}(t) = -\mu B(t) + \int_{-\infty}^{t} G^2[\theta_2(\tau)]W_2(\tau - t)\, d\tau, \tag{16-ii}$$

where

$$\theta_1(t) = \bar{P}_a a_A(t) + \bar{P}_b b_A(t), \tag{17-i}$$

$$\theta_2(t) = \bar{P}_a a_B(t) + \bar{P}_b b_B(t). \tag{17-ii}$$

We may *alternatively* look at G^1 and G^2 in (16) as the potential production functions of the flows of A and B depending on different research input factors θ_1 and θ_2 such as

$$\theta_1 = \bar{P}_a a_A, \tag{17-i$'$}$$

$$\theta_2 = \bar{P}_b b_B. \tag{17-ii$'$}$$

In this case, the production of the flow of A does not require the second factor b, whereas production of the flow of B does not require the first factor a.

By these simplifications we can reduce the number of control variables from five (Y, a_A, a_B, b_A, b_B) to three (Y, θ_1, θ_2). At the same time the model is changed to one more convenient for estimation purposes.[9] It is often not possible to estimate empirically the quantities of research factor inputs, while the deflated expenditures for these input costs θ_1 and θ_2 are readily available. These simplifications do not destroy the essential property of the Böhm-Bawerk effects in the model by allowing $B(t)$ to remain in the production of technical knowledge in G^1. Hence the production of basic knowledge is possible with research inputs only, while the production of applied knowledge requires not only research inputs but also the stock of basic knowledge.[10]

Our problem of optimal control is now reduced to

$$\max_{\{\theta_1(t), \theta_2(t), Y(t)\}} \int_0^{\infty} e^{-\gamma t}\left[R(Y(t)) - \frac{1}{g(t)}C(Y(t)) - \theta_1(t) - \theta_2(t)\right] dt \tag{18}$$

[9] This model has been tested against U.S. data in a paper by Sato and Suzawa [1980].

[10] One should not take the words basic and applied in a literary sense. Hence, in the Böhm-Bawerk example we used earlier, the skill of fishing is applied or technical knowledge, while the skill of making nets and building fishing boats is basic knowledge—basic for the purpose of fishing.

subject to

$$\dot{g}(t) = -(\beta - \alpha + v)g(t) + \int_{-\infty}^{t} g(\tau)G^1[B(\tau), \theta_1(\tau)]e^{-(\beta-\alpha)(t-\tau)}W_1(t-\tau)\,d\tau, \tag{19}$$

$$\dot{B}(t) = -\mu B(t) + \int_{-\infty}^{t} G^2[\theta_2(\tau)]W_2(t-\tau)\,d\tau, \qquad \gamma = \rho - \alpha > 0. \tag{20}$$

The current-value Hamiltonian for this is

$$\begin{aligned} H = {} & R(Y) - g^{-1}C(Y) - \theta_1 - \theta_2 - \lambda_1(\beta - \alpha + v)g - \lambda_2 \mu B \\ & + g(t)G^1[B(t), \theta_1(t)] \int_t^{\infty} \lambda_1(\tau)e^{-\gamma(\tau-t)}D_1(\tau-t)\,d\tau \\ & + G^2[\theta_2(t)] \int_t^{\infty} \lambda_2(\tau)e^{-\gamma(\tau-t)}D_2(\tau-t)\,d\tau, \end{aligned} \tag{21}$$

where $D_1(t) = e^{-(\beta-\alpha)t}W_1(t)$, $D_2(t) = W_2(t)$. By the maximum principle, we have

$$\frac{\partial H}{\partial Y} = R_Y(Y) - \frac{C_Y(Y)}{g} = 0, \tag{22-i}$$

$$\frac{\partial H}{\partial \theta_1} = -1 + g(t)G_2^1[B(t), \theta_1] \int_t^{\infty} \lambda_1(\tau)e^{-\gamma(\tau-t)}D_1(\tau-t)\,d\tau = 0, \tag{22-ii}$$

$$\frac{\partial H}{\partial \theta_2} = -1 + G^{2'}[\theta_2(t)] \int_t^{\infty} \lambda_2(\tau)e^{-\gamma(\tau-t)}D_2(\tau-t)\,d\tau = 0. \tag{22-iii}$$

The equations of motion are

$$\dot{g}(t) = -(\beta - \alpha + v)g(t) + \int_{-\infty}^{t} g(\tau)G^1[B(\tau), \theta_1(\tau)]D_1(t-\tau)\,d\tau, \tag{19$'$}$$

$$\dot{B}(t) = -\mu B(t) + \int_{-\infty}^{t} G^2[\theta_2(\tau)]D_2(t-\tau)\,d\tau, \tag{20$'$}$$

$$\begin{aligned} \dot{\lambda}_1(t) = {} & (\gamma + \beta - \alpha + v)\lambda_1(t) - g^{-2}C(Y(t)) \\ & - G^1[B(t), \theta_1(t)] \int_t^{\infty} \lambda_1(\tau)e^{-\gamma(\tau-t)}D_1(\tau-t)\,d\tau, \end{aligned} \tag{23}$$

$$\dot{\lambda}_2(t) = (\gamma + \mu)\lambda_2(t) - g(t)G_1^1[B(t), \theta_1(t)] \int_t^{\infty} \lambda_1(\tau)e^{-\gamma(\tau-t)}D_1(\tau-t)\,d\tau, \tag{24}$$

together with (22).

Using (22), we have

$$R'(Y) = g^{-1}C'(Y) = \text{marginal revenue} = \text{marginal cost}$$
$$\text{(to determine } Y\text{)}, \quad \text{(22-i}')$$

$$g(t)G_2^1 \int_t^\infty \lambda_1(\tau)e^{-\gamma(\tau-t)}D_1(\tau-t)\,d\tau = 1 = \text{price of } \theta_1$$
$$= \text{weighted average of its implicit price over time}, \quad \text{(22-ii}')$$

$$G^{2'} \int_t^\infty \lambda_2(\tau)e^{-\gamma(\tau-t)}D_2(\tau-t)\,d\tau = 1 = \text{price of } \theta_2$$
$$= \text{weighted average of its implicit price over time}, \quad \text{(22-iii}')$$

and substituting these into the equations of motion, we express (19′), (20′), and

$$\dot{\lambda}_1(t) = (\gamma + \beta - \alpha + v)\lambda_1(t) - g^{-2}C(Y(t)) - \frac{G^1[B(t), \theta_1(t)]}{g(t)G_2^1[B(t), \theta_1(t)]}, \quad (23')$$

$$\dot{\lambda}_2(t) = (\gamma + \mu)\lambda_2(t) - \frac{G_1^1[B(t), \theta_1(t)]}{G_2^1[B(t), \theta_1(t)]}. \quad (24')$$

Special Case: No Lags

9. The dynamic optimal behavior corresponding to these equations of motion is not easy to evaluate, as they involve integral-differential equations whose complete general solutions are still not known. We shall, therefore, first study a special case of the model for which

$$\int_t^\infty \lambda_1(\tau)e^{-\gamma(\tau-t)}D_1(\tau-t)\,d\tau = \lambda_1(t), \quad \text{(25-i)}$$

$$\int_t^\infty \lambda_2(\tau)e^{-\gamma(\tau-t)}D_2(\tau-t)\,d\tau = \lambda_2(t), \quad \text{(25-ii)}$$

with

$$D_1(t) = 1, \quad t = 0; \qquad D_2(t) = 1, \quad t = 0,$$
$$D_1(t) = 0, \quad t \neq 0; \qquad D_2(t) = 0, \quad t \neq 0.$$

Then the model is further reduced to a standard Pontryagin optimal control model with no lags. Hence, in this case, we have (18) subject to

$$\dot{g}(t) = -(\beta - \alpha + v)g(t) + G^1[B(t), \theta_1(t)]g(t), \quad (26)$$

$$\dot{B}(t) = -\mu B(t) + G^2[\theta_2(t)]. \quad (27)$$

We shall present a complete solution to this special case by first writing the current-valued Hamiltonian as

$$H = R(Y(t)) - (C(Y(t))/g(t)) - \theta_1 - \theta_2 - (\beta - \alpha + v)g(t)\lambda_1(t)$$
$$- \mu B(t)\lambda_2(t) + \lambda_1(t)G^1[B(t), \theta_1(t)]g(t) + \lambda_2 G^2[\theta_2(t)]. \quad (28)$$

The maximum principle gives immediately

$$R'(Y) - (C'(Y)/g) = 0 \quad \Rightarrow \quad Y = Y(g), \tag{29-i}$$

$$g(t)G_2^1[B(t), \theta_1(t)]\lambda_1 = 1 \quad \Rightarrow \quad \theta_1 = \theta_1(g, B, \lambda_1), \tag{29-ii}$$

$$G^{2'}[\theta_2(t)]\lambda_2 = 1 \quad \Rightarrow \quad \theta_2 = \theta_2(\lambda_2), \tag{29-iii}$$

with the equations of motion expressed by (26), (27), and

$$\dot{\lambda}_1(t) = (\gamma + \beta - \alpha + v)\lambda_1(t) - g^{-2}C(Y(t)) - G^1[B(t), \theta_1(t)]\lambda_1(t), \tag{30}$$

$$\dot{\lambda}_2(t) = (\gamma + \mu)\lambda_2(t) - g(t)G_1^1[B(t), \theta_1(t)]\lambda_1(t). \tag{31}$$

In order to avoid the complexity of partial derivatives, we shall change the notions by defining

$$G^1(B(t), \theta_1(t)) = h[B(t), \theta_1(t)], \tag{32-i}$$

$$G^2(\theta_2(t)) = f[\theta_2(t)]. \tag{32-ii}$$

If H is concave in the three control variables, then (29-i)–(29-iii) are sufficient for the maximization of H. This is equivalent to the assumptions that both the profit function and the production functions are concave. Arrow and Kurz [1970][11] have shown that the sufficient condition for optimality is that the maximized Hamiltonian H^* [obtained by substituting the values of the control variables from Eqs. (29)] be concave in B and g, and the transversality condition $\lim_{t\to\infty} e^{(\alpha-\rho)t} \to 0$ or $\alpha < \rho$. That means that the real rate of interest $\rho - \alpha$ should be positive. The economic rationale for that is simple; it prevents the situation in which the marginal revenue from increasing stock will be higher than the marginal costs, and the difference will increase with the increase of stock. This condition relates to both the revenue function and the production function.

IV. Analysis of the Solution

Steady State of the Special Case

10. Let g^*, B^*, λ_1^*, and λ_2^* be the *steady-state* or *equilibrium values* of the variables corresponding to $\dot{g} = \dot{B} = \dot{\lambda}_1 = \dot{\lambda}_2 = 0$. For convenience we may omit the asterisk (*) notation on the equilibrium values whenever obvious from the context. By equating Eqs. (26), (27), (30), and (31) to zero, we obtain $h(B, \theta_1) = \beta - \alpha + v$, $f(\theta_2) = \mu B$, $\gamma\lambda_1 = C(Y)/g^2$, and $(\gamma + \mu)\lambda_2 = g\lambda_1 h_1$, $h_1 = \partial h/\partial B$, $h_2 = \partial h/\partial \theta_1$, together with (29), $g = C'/R'$, $g\lambda_1 h_2 = 1$, $f'\lambda_2 = 1$ or alternatively, $Y = Y(g)$, $\theta_1 = \theta_1(g, B, \lambda_1)$, $\theta_2 = \theta_2(\lambda_2)$.

[11] Also see Mangasarian [1966], Kamien and Schwartz [1971], and Takayama [1974]. This case is, of course, covered by the result of Sethi [1974] and by the assumption stated in Section 7.

The analysis of the steady-state solution will proceed in two parts. From Eq. (26) we note that the current costs of maintaining a fixed positive amount of g is independent of g itself. The cost function is the solution of

$$\min \theta_1 + \theta_2$$

subject to

$$h(B, \theta_1) = \beta - \alpha + \nu,$$

$$f(\theta_2) = \mu B,$$

and nonnegativity of variables.

This problem always has a solution, because the functions are continuous, and the values permissible are bounded from below by 0. Denote this solution by m. We know that the profit function $\pi = R - (C/g)$ is ultimately a function of g, $\pi = \pi(g)$.

Given that there exists a value of g, say $\hat{g}$, such that the profits obtained from maintaining g are greater than the minimum cost $\underline{m}$, and given that there exists a $\bar{g}$ such that higher values of g cause profits to decline, then the optimum steady-state value of g is $\bar{g}$.[12] The value of B is determined independently in the solution to the minimization problem.

The argument so far confirms that under our assumptions the model possesses a steady-state solution. The second part of the analysis shows whether or not there is a stable solution, using the standard technique of the Taylor expansion of the differential equations in order to check the saddle-point stability properties.

Let the Jacobian matrix of Eqs. (26), (27), (30), and (31) at the steady-state position, which also satisfies Eq. (29), be equal to

$$J = \begin{bmatrix} \dfrac{\partial \dot{g}}{\partial g} & \dfrac{\partial \dot{g}}{\partial B} & \dfrac{\partial \dot{g}}{\partial \lambda_1} & \dfrac{\partial \dot{g}}{\partial \lambda_2} \\[2ex] \dfrac{\partial \dot{B}}{\partial g} & \dfrac{\partial \dot{B}}{\partial B} & \dfrac{\partial \dot{B}}{\partial \lambda_1} & \dfrac{\partial \dot{B}}{\partial \lambda_2} \\[2ex] \dfrac{\partial \dot{\lambda}_1}{\partial g} & \dfrac{\partial \dot{\lambda}_1}{\partial B} & \dfrac{\partial \dot{\lambda}_1}{\partial \lambda_1} & \dfrac{\partial \dot{\lambda}_1}{\partial \lambda_2} \\[2ex] \dfrac{\partial \dot{\lambda}_2}{\partial g} & \dfrac{\partial \dot{\lambda}_2}{\partial B} & \dfrac{\partial \dot{\lambda}_2}{\partial \lambda_1} & \dfrac{\partial \dot{\lambda}_2}{\partial \lambda_2} \end{bmatrix}, \quad \text{at} \quad \dot{g} = \dot{B} = \dot{\lambda}_1 = \dot{\lambda}_2 = 0.$$

[12] The nonexistence of $\hat{g}$ implies that the optimal value of g is zero. This solution is unlikely to occur in a monopoly setting, but certainly may occur in a purely competitive industry. The nonexistence of $\bar{g}$ given that $\hat{g}$ exists implies that the optimal steady-state stock of g is boundless. Even in the poorest of less developed countries, it is difficult to envision such a solution. Thus, it is almost certain that $\hat{g}$ and $\bar{g}$ exist for this model.

Using (29), $Y = Y(g), \theta_1 = \theta_1(g, B, \lambda_1), \theta_2 = \theta_2(\lambda_2)$, by the standard method of comparative statics, we first calculate

$$\begin{aligned}
&\frac{\partial Y}{\partial g} = \frac{C'(Y)}{g(C''(Y) - gR''(Y))}, \\
&\frac{\partial \theta_1}{\partial g} = \frac{-h_2(B, \theta_1)}{gh_{22}(B, \theta_1)}, \qquad \frac{\partial \theta_1}{\partial B} = \frac{-h_{21}(B, \theta_1)}{h_{22}(B, \theta_1)}, \\
&\frac{\partial \theta_1}{\partial \lambda_1} = \frac{-h_2(B, \theta_1)}{\lambda_1 h_{22}(B, \theta_1)}, \qquad \frac{\partial \theta_2}{\partial \lambda_2} = \frac{-f'(\theta_2)}{\lambda_2 f''(\theta_2)}.
\end{aligned} \tag{33}$$

Substituting (33) into

$$\frac{\partial \dot{g}}{\partial g} = -(\beta - \alpha + v) + h + gh_2 \frac{\partial \theta_1}{\partial g}, \qquad \frac{\partial \dot{g}}{\partial B} = gh_1 + gh_2 \frac{\partial \theta_1}{\partial B},$$

$$\frac{\partial \dot{g}}{\partial \lambda_1} = gh_2 \frac{\partial \theta_1}{\partial \lambda_1}, \quad \frac{\partial \dot{g}}{\partial \lambda_2} = 0, \quad \frac{\partial \dot{B}}{\partial g} = 0, \quad \frac{\partial \dot{B}}{\partial B} = -\mu, \quad \frac{\partial \dot{B}}{\partial \lambda_1} = 0, \quad \frac{\partial \dot{B}}{\partial \lambda_2} = f' \frac{\partial \theta_2}{\partial \lambda_2},$$

$$\frac{\partial \dot{\lambda}_1}{\partial g} = \frac{2C}{g^3} - \frac{C'}{g^2}\frac{\partial Y}{\partial g} - h_2 \lambda_1 \frac{\partial \theta_1}{\partial g}, \qquad \frac{\partial \dot{\lambda}_1}{\partial B} = -h_1\lambda_1 - h_2\lambda_1 \frac{\partial \theta_1}{\partial B},$$

$$\frac{\partial \dot{\lambda}_1}{\partial \lambda_1} = (\gamma + \beta - \alpha + v) - h - h_2\lambda_1 \frac{\partial \theta_1}{\partial \lambda_1}, \qquad \frac{\partial \dot{\lambda}_1}{\partial \lambda_2} = 0,$$

$$\frac{\partial \dot{\lambda}_2}{\partial g} = -h_1\lambda_1 - gh_{12}\lambda_1 \frac{\partial \theta_1}{\partial g}, \qquad \frac{\partial \dot{\lambda}_2}{\partial B} = -g\lambda_1\left(h_{11} + h_{12}\frac{\partial \theta_1}{\partial B}\right),$$

$$\frac{\partial \dot{\lambda}_2}{\partial \lambda_1} = -g\left(h_1 + h_{12}\lambda_1 \frac{\partial \theta_1}{\partial \lambda_1}\right), \qquad \frac{\partial \dot{\lambda}_2}{\partial \lambda_2} = \gamma + \mu,$$

and using (26′), (27′), (30′), and (31′), we obtain

$$J = \begin{bmatrix}
\dfrac{-h_2^2}{h_{22}} & g\left(h_1 - \dfrac{h_2 h_{21}}{h_{22}}\right) & -\dfrac{g}{\lambda_1}\dfrac{h_2^2}{h_{22}} & 0 \\
0 & -\mu & 0 & -\dfrac{1}{\lambda_2}\dfrac{f'^2}{f''} \\
\dfrac{S}{g^3} + \dfrac{\lambda_1}{g}\dfrac{h_2^2}{h_{22}} & -\lambda_1\left(h_1 - \dfrac{h_2 h_{21}}{h_{22}}\right) & \gamma + \dfrac{h_2^2}{h_{22}} & 0 \\
-\lambda_1\left(h_1 - \dfrac{h_2 h_{12}}{h_{22}}\right) & -g\lambda_1\left(\dfrac{h_{11}h_{22} - h_{12}^2}{h_{22}}\right) & -g\left(h_1 - \dfrac{h_2 h_{12}}{h_{22}}\right) & \gamma + \mu
\end{bmatrix}, \tag{34}$$

where $S = 2C(Y) - C'(Y)^2/(C''(Y) - gR''(Y))$.

After a considerable amount of complicated calculations as shown in the Mathematical Appendix to this chapter, we derive the characteristic equation

$$\det(J - XE) = X(X - \gamma)\left\{(X + \mu)(X - \gamma - \mu) - \frac{\lambda_1}{\lambda_2} g \frac{f'^2}{f''}\left(\frac{h_{11}h_{22} - h_{12}^2}{h_{22}}\right)\right\}$$
$$+ \left(\frac{S}{g^3} - \frac{\lambda_1}{g}\gamma\right)\left\{\frac{g}{\lambda_1}\frac{h_2^2}{h_{22}}(X + \mu)(X - \gamma - \mu)\right.$$
$$\left. - \frac{g^2}{\lambda_2}\frac{f'^2}{f''}\left(h_1^2 - 2\frac{h_1 h_2 h_{12}}{h_{22}} + \frac{h_2^2 h_{12}^2}{h_{22}^2}\right)\right\} = 0. \tag{35}$$

Saddle-Point Property of the Special Case of the Standard Optimal Control

11. In order to facilitate calculations, we further assume that the technical progress function of applied knowledge is a homogeneous function of degree one, i.e.,

$$h_1 B + h_2 \theta_1 = h, \tag{36}$$

which implies

$$h_{11}h_{22} - h_{12}^2 = 0 \quad \Leftrightarrow \quad \left\{\begin{matrix} h_{11}B + h_{12}\theta_1 = 0 \\ h_{21}B + h_{22}\theta_1 = 0 \end{matrix}\right\} \quad \Leftrightarrow \quad \frac{-B}{h_{22}} = \frac{\theta_1}{h_{21}} = \delta$$
$$\Leftrightarrow \quad \delta(-h_1 h_{22} + h_2 h_{12}) = h.$$

Then the characteristic equation becomes

$$X(X - \gamma)(X + \mu)(X - \gamma - \mu) + \left(\frac{S}{g^3} - \frac{\lambda_1}{g}\gamma\right)\frac{g}{\lambda_1}\frac{h_2^2}{h_{22}}(X + \mu)(X - \gamma - \mu)$$
$$- \left(\frac{S}{g^3} - \frac{\lambda_1}{g}\gamma\right)\frac{g^2}{\lambda_2}\frac{f'^2}{f''}\left(h_1 - \frac{h_2 h_{12}}{h_{22}}\right)^2 = 0, \tag{35'}$$

with $h_{11} < 0$, $h_{22} < 0$ and $f' > 0$, $f'' < 0$. By the concavity of the profit function and the Hamiltonian, we know that

$$S > 0, \tag{37}$$

because of

$$R'' - \frac{C''}{g} < 0, \qquad \frac{2C}{-g^3} < 0, \qquad \text{and} \qquad \begin{vmatrix} R'' - (C''/g) & C'/g^2 \\ C'/g^2 & 2C/-g^3 \end{vmatrix} > 0.$$

By rewriting (35′) as

$$X(X-\gamma)(X+\mu)(X-\gamma-\mu)+Z_1(X+\mu)(X-\gamma-\mu)+Z_2=0,$$
$$Z_1Z_2 \leqq 0, \quad (35'')$$

we study the characteristic roots. Observe that

$$\frac{S}{g^3}-\frac{\lambda_1}{g}\gamma=\frac{1}{g^3}(S-\lambda_1 g^2\gamma)=\frac{1}{g^3}(S-C)=\frac{1}{g^3}\left(C-\frac{C'}{C''-gR''}\right),$$

where $\lambda_1 g^2\gamma = C(Y)$ by (30′). Let $((S/g^3)-(\lambda_1/g)\gamma)$ be equal to

$$\frac{S}{g^3}-\frac{\lambda_1}{g}\gamma=\frac{1}{g^3}\left(C-\frac{C'}{C''-gR''}\right)=\zeta. \tag{38}$$

Then (35) becomes

$$F_\zeta(X)=X(X-\gamma)(X+\mu)(X-\gamma-\mu)+\zeta\frac{g}{\lambda_1}\frac{h_2^2}{h_{22}}(X+\mu)(X-\gamma-\mu)$$
$$-\zeta\frac{g^2}{\lambda_2}\frac{f'^2}{f''}\left(h_1-\frac{h_2h_{12}}{h_{22}}\right)^2=0.$$

It is easily seen that when $\zeta = 0$, we have four roots

$$F_0(X)=0, \quad X=-\mu, \quad 0, \quad \gamma, \quad \gamma+\mu. \tag{39}$$

When $\zeta > 0$, which implies from (35″), $Z_1 < 0$, $Z_2 > 0$, we have

$$F_\zeta(-\mu)=F_\zeta(\gamma+\mu)=Z_2>0, \quad F_\zeta(0)=F_\zeta(\gamma)=-Z_1\mu(\gamma+\mu)+Z_2>0,$$
$$F_\zeta(+\infty)>0, \qquad F_\zeta(-\infty)>0.$$

Hence *there are two positive and two negative roots for $\zeta > 0$, which gives the usual saddle-point property of the optimal path.* Figure 2 in the Mathematical Appendix to this chapter depicts the location of four roots for $\zeta > 0$ ($|\zeta| < 1$).

On the other hand, when $\zeta < 0$ so that the value of γ is relatively large, we have

$$F_\zeta(-\mu)=F_\zeta(\gamma+\mu)=Z_2<0, \quad F_\zeta(0)=F_\zeta(\gamma)=-Z_1\mu(\gamma+\mu)+Z_2<0,$$
$$F_\zeta(+\infty)>0, \qquad F_\zeta(-\infty)>0.$$

Hence *we have three positive roots and one negative root, which shows that the stead-state solution is not a saddle point.* This is shown in Fig. 3 in the Mathematical Appendix to this chapter. In summary, we could prove that unless the net discount rate γ is extremely large, we have the usual saddle-point stability of the optimal path.[13]

[13] The general result is due to Levhari and Liviatan [1972] and Samuelson [1972]. But here we are interested in specific conditions unique to this model.

Steady State of the General Case

12. Returning to the general case of optimal technical progress when lags are explicitly introduced, we note that the equations of motion are expressed by (19′), (20′), (23), and (24) with G^1 and G^2 replaced h and f, respectively. We present the following most important lemma:

Lemma *(Behavior near $t \to +\infty$) When $t \doteqdot +\infty$, we have*

$$\int_t^\infty \lambda_1(\tau)e^{-\gamma(\tau-t)}D_1(\tau - t)\,d\tau \doteqdot \omega_1\lambda_1(t),$$

$$\text{where} \quad \omega_1 = \int_0^\infty e^{-\gamma\sigma}D_1(\sigma)\,d\sigma,$$

$$\tau - t = \sigma, \tag{40-i}$$

$$\int_t^\infty \lambda_2(\tau)e^{-\gamma(\tau-t)}D_2(\tau - t)\,d\tau \doteqdot \omega_2\lambda_2(t),$$

$$\text{where} \quad \omega_2 = \int_0^\infty e^{-\gamma\sigma}D_2(\sigma)\,d\sigma, \tag{40-ii}$$

$$\int_{-\infty}^t g(\tau)h[B(\tau), \theta_1(\tau)]D_1(t - \tau)\,d\tau \doteqdot \omega_3 g(t)h[B(t), \theta_1(t)],$$

$$\text{where} \quad \omega_3 = \int_0^\infty D_1(\sigma)\,d\sigma, \tag{40-iii}$$

$$\int_{-\infty}^t f[\theta_2(\tau)]D_2(t - \tau)\,d\tau \doteqdot \omega_4 f(\theta_2(t)),$$

$$\text{where} \quad \omega_4 = \int_0^\infty D_2(\sigma)\,d\sigma, \tag{40-iv}$$

and $\omega_1, \omega_2, \omega_3, \omega_4$ are constants > 0.

Proof By setting

$$\int_t^\infty \lambda_1(\tau)e^{-\gamma(\tau-t)}D_1(\tau - t)\,d\tau = \int_0^\infty \lambda_1(t + \sigma)e^{-\gamma\sigma}D_1(\sigma)\,d\sigma, \qquad \sigma = \tau - t,$$

$t \doteqdot +\infty$, and

$$\lambda_1(t + \sigma) \doteqdot \lambda_1(t) \qquad (\sigma > 0),$$

we obtain

$$\int_0^\infty \lambda_1(t + \sigma)e^{-\gamma\sigma}D_1(\sigma)\,d\sigma \doteqdot \lambda_1(t)\int_0^\infty e^{-\gamma\sigma}D_1(\sigma)\,d\sigma = \omega_1\lambda_1(t),$$

$$\text{where} \quad \omega_1 = \int_0^\infty e^{-\gamma\sigma}D_1(\sigma)\,d\sigma. \tag{40-i}$$

In the same way we get (40-ii). To prove (40-iii) we can show that by setting $\sigma = t - \tau$,

$$\int_{-\infty}^{t} g(\tau)h[B(\tau), \theta_1(\tau)]D_1(t - \tau)\, d\tau$$

$$= -\int_{\infty}^{0} g(t - \sigma)h[B(t - \sigma), \theta_1(t - \sigma)]D_1(\sigma)\, d\sigma$$

$$= \int_{0}^{\infty} g(t - \sigma)h[B(t - \sigma), \theta_1(t - \sigma)]D_1(\sigma)\, d\sigma.$$

When $t \doteqdot +\infty$, we can assume

$$g(t - \sigma) \doteqdot g(t), h[B(t - \sigma), \theta_1(t - \sigma)] = h[B(t), \theta_1(t)]$$

for $t \doteqdot +\infty$ and for a rapidly decreasing $D_1(\sigma)$ $(\sigma > 0)$. Hence, we have

$$\int_{-\infty}^{t} g(\tau)h[B(\tau), \theta_1(\tau)]D_1(t - \tau)\, d\tau$$

$$\doteqdot g(t)h[B(t), \theta_1(t)] \int_{0}^{\infty} D_1(\sigma)\, d\sigma$$

$$= \omega_3 g(t)h[B(t), \theta_1(t)], \qquad \text{where} \quad \omega_3 = \int_{0}^{\infty} D_1(\sigma)\, d\sigma. \quad \text{(40-iii)}$$

In the same way we can show (40-iv). Q.E.D.

In view of this lemma we now write the equations of motion in (19), (20), (23), and (24) *near* $t \to +\infty$ as

$$\dot{g}(t) = -(\beta - \alpha + v)g(t) + \omega_3 g(t)h[B(t), \theta_1(t)], \quad \text{(41-i)}$$

$$\dot{B}(t) = -\mu B(t) + \omega_4 f[\theta_2(t)], \quad \text{(41-ii)}$$

$$\dot{\lambda}_1(t) = (\gamma + \beta - \alpha + v)\lambda_1(t) - g^{-2}C(Y(t)) - \omega_1\lambda_1(t)h[B(t), \theta_1(t)], \quad \text{(41-iii)}$$

$$\dot{\lambda}_2(t) = (\gamma + \mu)\lambda_2(t) - \omega_1\lambda_1(t)g(t)h_1[B(t), \theta_1(t)], \quad \text{(41-iv)}$$

together with the following equilibrium conditions resulting from the maximum principle:

$$R'(Y) - (C'(Y)/g) = 0, \quad \text{(42-i)}$$

$$\omega_1\lambda_1(t)g(t)h_2[B(t), \theta_1(t)] = 1, \quad \text{(42-ii)}$$

$$\omega_2\lambda_2(t)f'[\theta_2(t)] = 1, \quad \text{(42-iii)}$$

where

$$\omega_1 = \int_0^\infty e^{-\gamma\sigma} D_1(\sigma)\, d\sigma, \tag{43-i}$$

$$\omega_2 = \int_0^\infty e^{-\gamma\sigma} D_2(\sigma)\, d\sigma, \tag{43-ii}$$

$$\omega_3 = \int_0^\infty D_1(\sigma)\, d\sigma, \tag{43-iii}$$

$$\omega_4 = \int_0^\infty D_2(\sigma)\, d\sigma. \tag{43-iv}$$

In this formulation *when* $\omega_1 = \omega_2 = \omega_3 = \omega_4 = 1$, *the general model is reduced to the special case which we have already studied in the previous section.* Having established optimal behavior near the steady-state position, we now want to study the optimal path near the equilibrium position as $\dot{g} = \dot{B} = \dot{\lambda}_1 = \dot{\lambda}_2 = 0$ at $t = +\infty$. From (41), we obtain

$$\omega_3 h = \beta - \alpha + v, \tag{41-i$'$}$$

$$\omega_4 f = \mu B, \tag{41-ii$'$}$$

$$\lambda_1\{\gamma + (\omega_3 - \omega_1)h\} = C(Y)/g^2, \tag{41-iii$'$}$$

$$(\gamma + \mu)\lambda_2 = \omega_1 \lambda_1 g h_1. \tag{41-iv$'$}$$

As in the special case, we have (33). Using (33), we can calculate

$$\frac{\partial \dot{g}}{\partial g} = -\omega_3 \frac{h_2^2}{h_{22}}, \qquad \frac{\partial \dot{g}}{\partial B} = \omega_3 g\left(h_1 - \frac{h_2 h_{21}}{h_{22}}\right), \qquad \frac{\partial \dot{g}}{\partial \lambda_1} = -\omega_3 \frac{g}{\lambda_1} \frac{h_2^2}{h_{22}},$$

$$\frac{\partial \dot{g}}{\partial \lambda_2} = 0, \qquad \frac{\partial \dot{B}}{\partial g} = 0, \qquad \frac{\partial \dot{B}}{\partial B} = -\mu, \qquad \frac{\partial \dot{B}}{\partial \lambda_1} = 0, \qquad \frac{\partial \dot{B}}{\partial \lambda_2} = -\frac{\omega_4}{\lambda_2} \frac{f'^2}{f''},$$

$$\frac{\partial \dot{\lambda}_1}{\partial g} = \frac{S}{g^3} + \omega_1 \frac{\lambda_1}{g} \frac{h_2^2}{h_{22}}, \qquad \frac{\partial \dot{\lambda}_1}{\partial B} = -\omega_1 \lambda_1 \left(h_1 - \frac{h_2 h_{21}}{h_{22}}\right),$$

$$\frac{\partial \dot{\lambda}_1}{\partial \lambda_1} = \gamma + (\omega_3 - \omega_1)h + \omega_1 \frac{h_2^2}{h_{22}}, \qquad \frac{\partial \dot{\lambda}_1}{\partial \lambda_2} = 0,$$

$$\frac{\partial \dot{\lambda}_2}{\partial g} = -\omega_1 \lambda_1 \left(h_1 - \frac{h_2 h_{12}}{h_{22}}\right), \qquad \frac{\partial \dot{\lambda}_2}{\partial B} = -\omega_1 \lambda_1 g \frac{h_{11} h_{22} - h_{12}^2}{h_{22}},$$

$$\frac{\partial \dot{\lambda}_2}{\partial \lambda_1} = -\omega_1 g\left(h_1 - \frac{h_2 h_{12}}{h_{22}}\right), \qquad \frac{\partial \dot{\lambda}_2}{\partial \lambda_2} = \gamma + \mu,$$

where $S = 2C(Y) - C'(Y)^2/(C''(Y) - gR''(Y))$.

The Jacobian matrix near $t = +\infty$ is thus expressed as

$$J = \begin{bmatrix} -\omega_3 \dfrac{h_2^2}{h_{22}} & \omega_3 g\left(h_1 - \dfrac{h_2 h_{21}}{h_{22}}\right) & -\omega_3 \dfrac{g}{\lambda_1} \dfrac{h_2^2}{h_{22}} & 0 \\ 0 & -\mu & 0 & -\dfrac{\omega_4}{\lambda_2} \dfrac{f'^2}{f''} \\ \dfrac{S}{g^3} + \omega_1 \dfrac{\lambda_1}{g} \dfrac{h_2^2}{h_{22}} & -\omega_1 \lambda_1 \left(h_1 - \dfrac{h_2 h_{21}}{h_{22}}\right) & \gamma + (\omega_3 - \omega_1) + \omega_1 \dfrac{h^2}{h_{22}} & 0 \\ -\omega_1 \lambda_1 \left(h_1 - \dfrac{h_2 h_{12}}{h_{22}}\right) & -\omega_1 \lambda_1 g \dfrac{h_{11} h_{22} - h_{12}^2}{h_{22}} & -\omega_1 g \left(h_1 - \dfrac{h_2 h_{12}}{h_{22}}\right) & \gamma + \mu \end{bmatrix}. \tag{44}$$

After complicated calculations (see the Mathematical Appendix to this chapter), we can write down the characteristic equation for (44) as

$$\begin{aligned} \det(J - XE) &= (X + \mu)X(X - \gamma - (\omega_3 - \omega_1)h)(X - \gamma - \mu) \\ &+ \frac{h_2^2}{h_{22}}(X + \mu)(X - \gamma - \mu)\left\{(\omega_3 - \omega_1)X + \frac{\omega_3}{\lambda_1 g}\left(C - \frac{C'^2}{C'' - gR''}\right)\right\} \\ &- \omega_1 \frac{\lambda_1}{\lambda_2} g \frac{f'^2}{f''}\left(\frac{h_{11}h_{22} - h_{12}^2}{h_{22}}\right)X(X - \gamma - (\omega_3 - \omega_1)h) \\ &- \omega_1 \frac{\lambda_1}{\lambda_2} g \frac{f'^2}{f''}\left\{\left(h_1 - \frac{h_2 h_{21}}{h_{22}}\right)^2 + \frac{h_2^2(h_{11}h_{22} - h_{12}^2)}{h_{22}^2}\right\} \\ &\times \left\{(\omega_3 - \omega_1)X + \frac{\omega_3}{\lambda_1 g^2}\left(C - \frac{C'^2}{C'' - gR''}\right)\right\} = 0, \end{aligned} \tag{45}$$

where we normalize by $\omega_4 = 1$, $1 \geqq \omega_3 \geqq \omega_1 > 0$.

Optimal Behavior near the Steady-State Position

13. It is not very easy to determine how the optimal behavior should look for the case $\omega_3 > \omega_1$. As long as γ is sufficiently small, we may assume that $\omega_3 - \omega_1 \doteqdot 0$ so that (45) becomes

$$\begin{aligned} F(X) = (X + \mu)X(X - \gamma)(X - \gamma - \mu) &+ a(X + \mu)(X - \gamma - \mu) \\ &+ bX(X - \gamma) + c = 0, \end{aligned} \tag{46}$$

where

$$a = a_0 \sigma, \qquad \sigma = C - \frac{C'^2}{C'' - gR''} \qquad \left[\frac{\sigma}{g^3} = \zeta \text{ in Eq. (38)}\right],$$

$$a_0 = \frac{\omega_3}{\lambda_1 g} \frac{h_2^2}{h_{22}}, \qquad b = -\omega_1 \frac{\lambda_1}{\lambda_2} g \frac{f'^2}{f''} \frac{h_{11}h_{22} - h_{12}^2}{h_{22}},$$

$$c = c_0 \sigma, \quad c_0 = -\omega_1 \omega_3 \frac{1}{\lambda_2} \frac{f'^2}{f''} \left\{\left(h_1 - \frac{h_2 h_{21}}{h_{22}}\right)^2 + \frac{h_2^2(h_{11}h_{22} - h_{12}^2)}{h_{22}^2}\right\}.$$

Since $h_{22} < 0$, $h_{11}h_{22} - h_{12}^2 \geqq 0$, $f'' < 0$, we know that $a_0 < 0$, $b \leqq 0$, $c_0 \geqq 0$, and

$$a_0 b - c_0 = \omega_1 \omega_3 \frac{1}{\lambda_2 g} \frac{f'^2}{f''} \left(h_1 - \frac{h_2 h_{21}}{h_{22}}\right)^2 \leqq 0.$$

Letting $X^2 - \gamma X = Z$, we express (46) as

$$F(X) = G(Z) = (Z - \mu(\mu + \gamma))Z + a(Z - \mu(\mu + \gamma)) + bZ + c,$$

$$G(Z) = Z^2 + (a + b - \mu(\mu + \gamma))Z - a\mu(\mu + \gamma) + c = 0. \quad (46')$$

Let the discriminant of $G(Z)$ be represented by $\Delta(\sigma)$; then we have

$$\Delta(\sigma) = a_0^2\sigma^2 + 2\{a_0(\mu(\mu + \gamma) - b) + 2(a_0 b - c_0)\}\sigma + (\mu(\mu + \gamma) - b)^2. \quad (47)$$

Equation (47) itself is a quadratic equation whose discriminant D is equal to

$$\tfrac{1}{4}D = 4a_0(\mu(\mu + \gamma) - b)(a_0 b - c_0) + 4(a_0 b - c_0)^2 \geqq 0$$

(since $a_0 < 0, b \leqq 0, a_0 b - c_0 \leqq 0, \mu, \gamma \geqq 0$). Hence $\Delta(\sigma) = 0$ has real roots σ_1, σ_2 $(\sigma_1 \geqq \sigma_2)$, and since $\sigma_1 + \sigma_2 \geqq 0$ and $\sigma_1 \sigma_2 \geqq 0$, we conclude that

$$\sigma_1 \geqq \sigma_2 \geqq 0. \quad (48)$$

Theorem *(Stable and Unstable Optimal Paths) For sufficiently small value of γ, i.e., $\omega_3 - \omega_1 \doteqdot 0$, the optimal path is stable in the saddle-point sense if*

$$0 < \sigma < \sigma_2 \quad (49\text{-i})$$

or

$$\sigma_1 < \sigma, \quad (49\text{-ii})$$

and it is unstable if

$$\sigma_0 < \sigma < 0, \tag{50}$$

where

$$\sigma = C(Y) - \frac{C'(Y)^2}{C''(Y) - gR''(Y)},$$

$$\sigma_0 = \textit{the lower bound of} \quad \sigma = \frac{\frac{1}{4}\gamma^2(\frac{1}{4}\gamma^2 - b + \mu(\mu + \gamma))}{\frac{1}{4}a_0\gamma^2 + a_0\mu(\mu + \gamma) - c_0}$$

$$\sigma_1, \sigma_2 = \textit{real nonnegative roots of} \quad \Delta(\sigma) = 0\ (\sigma_1 \geqq \sigma_2).$$

Proof See the Mathematical Appendix to this chapter.

Economic Interpretation

14. Economic interpretation of this theorem is straightforward. Thus, when σ is positive which means that from $\sigma = C - C'^2/(C'' - gR'')$, $C'^2/(C'' - gR'') > 0$ is sufficiently small compared with C. σ is most likely positive whenever the profit function is *strongly concave* so that $C'' - gR''$ is very large. This condition is almost identical with the condition derived by Sato and Ramachandran [1974, 1978] for a less complicated model of technical progress. When σ is negative, and bounded by σ_0, which means that the profit function is not very concave, there is a chance of unstable optimal paths. There may be even a possibility of oscillating optimal behavior. (See a comment at the end of the proof of the theorem, Section 17.)

For the case in which $\omega_3 - \omega_1 > 0$, optimal behavior is similar to the one just described as long as ω_3 is not too different from ω_1. This will be true as long as the value of $\gamma = \rho - \alpha \geqq 0$ is sufficiently small. That is to say, as long as the discount rate ρ and the inflation rate α are not too afar apart.

One basic and new feature of the present analysis is that using the lemma we have reduced the model of optimal technical progress with *continuous lags* to a model with *no lags*, but with the appropriate weights ω_i. Hence, in the neighborhood of $t \to +\infty$, the model with continuous lags is equivalent to

$$\begin{pmatrix}\text{max (18) subject to (19)}\\ \text{and (20) with lags}\end{pmatrix} \Leftrightarrow \begin{pmatrix}\text{max (18) subject to (41-i)}\\ \text{and (41-ii) with no}\\ \text{lags, at } t \doteqdot +\infty\end{pmatrix}. \tag{51}$$

It is hoped that this type of new approach will also prove to be useful in other areas of economic analysis.

It may be of some interest to consider briefly a case in which the ω_i are determined by a special type of density function, say the gamma function. Let $D_i(\sigma)$ be given by

$$D_i = D_i(\sigma : n_i, s_i) = (a_i/n_i!\,s_i^{n_i+1})\sigma^{n_i}e^{-\sigma/s_i},$$

$$n_i = \text{integer}, \qquad a_i = \text{const}, \qquad s_i = \text{const}, \qquad i = 1, 2. \tag{52}$$

Then we have

$$\omega_1 = \int_0^\infty e^{-\gamma\sigma}D_1\,d\sigma = \int_0^\infty \frac{a_1}{n_1!\,s_1^{n_1+1}}\sigma^{n_1}e^{-(\gamma+s_1^{-1})\sigma}\,d\sigma = \frac{a_1}{(1+\gamma s_1)^{n_1+1}}, \tag{53-i}$$

$$\omega_2 = \int_0^\infty e^{-\gamma\sigma}D_2\,d\sigma = \int_0^\infty \frac{a_2}{n_2!\,s_2^{n_2+1}}\sigma^{n_2}e^{-(\gamma+s_2^{-1})\sigma}\,d\sigma = \frac{a_2}{(1+\gamma s_2)^{n_2+1}}, \tag{53-ii}$$

$$\omega_3 = \int_0^\infty D_1\,d\sigma = \int_0^\infty \frac{a_1}{n_1!\,s_1^{n_1+1}}\sigma^{n_1}e^{-\sigma/s_1}\,d\sigma = a_1, \tag{53-iii}$$

$$\omega_4 = \int_0^\infty D_2\,d\sigma = \int_0^\infty \frac{a_2}{n_2!\,s_2^{n_2+1}}\sigma^{n_2}e^{-\sigma/s_2}\,d\sigma = a_2. \tag{53-iv}$$

By normalization, we may set $\omega_4 = 1 = a_2$ and assume $0 < a_1 \leqq a_2$. In order to have $\omega_3 - \omega_1 \geqq 0$, we set $s_2 > 0$ for $\gamma \geqq 0$ and n_2 (integer) $\geqq -1$. The lag structure generated by (52) has the basic property exhibiting a continuous Böhm-Bawerk effect as depicted in Fig. 1. In the case of the exponential distribution ($n_i = 0$), ω_1 and ω_2 are simply equal to $\omega_1 = a_1/(1 + \gamma s_1)$ and $\omega_2 = a_2/(1 + \gamma s_2)$. On the other hand, as $s_i \to 0$ for $a_1 = a_2$, we have $\omega_1 = \omega_2 = \omega_3 = \omega_4$, the no-lag case.

Substituting the specific forms of the ω_i into the steady-state solution of the system (41′), we can calculate how the equilibrium values of the system change as one of the basic parameters of the distribution function changes. In particular, we may be interested in the comparative statics of the system with respect to the mean $[s_i(n_i + 1)]$ and variance $[s_i^2(n_i + 1)]$ of the gamma distribution. It is found that in general the sign pattern of the comparative statics is not definite, unless we impose additional restrictions on the production functions h and f and on the profit function. The reader may be interested in studying the case involving the Cobb–Douglas functions and the iso-elastic profit function (see Pauwels [1977]).

Mathematical Appendix

Proof of (45)

15. The characteristic equation of J is expressed as

$$|J - XE|$$

$$= \begin{vmatrix} -\omega_3 \dfrac{h_2^2}{h_{22}} - X & \omega_3 g\left(h_1 - \dfrac{h_2 h_{21}}{h_{22}}\right) & -\omega_3 \dfrac{g}{\lambda_1} \dfrac{h_2^2}{h_{22}} & 0 \\ 0 & -\mu - X & 0 & -\dfrac{\omega_4}{\lambda_2} \dfrac{f'^2}{f''} \\ \dfrac{S}{g^3} + \omega_1 \dfrac{\lambda_1}{g} \dfrac{g^2}{h_{22}} & -\omega_1 \lambda_1 \left(h_1 - \dfrac{h_2 h_{21}}{h_{22}}\right) & \begin{array}{l} \lambda + (\omega_3 - \omega_1)h \\ +\omega_1 \dfrac{h^2}{h_{22}} - X \end{array} & 0 \\ -\omega_1 \lambda_1 \left(h_1 - \dfrac{h_1 h_{21}}{h_{22}}\right) & -\omega_1 \lambda_1 g \dfrac{h_{11} h_{22} - h_{12}^2}{h_{22}} & -\omega_1 g \left(h_1 - \dfrac{h_2 h_{12}}{h_{22}}\right) & \gamma + \mu - X \end{vmatrix}$$

$$= \begin{vmatrix} -X & \omega_3 g\left(h_1 - \dfrac{h_2 h_{21}}{h_{22}}\right) & -\omega_3 \dfrac{g}{\lambda_1} \dfrac{h_2^2}{h_{22}} & 0 \\ 0 & -\mu - X & 0 & -\dfrac{\omega_4}{\lambda_2} \dfrac{f'^2}{f''} \\ \begin{array}{l} \dfrac{S}{g_3} - \dfrac{\lambda_1}{g} (\lambda + (\omega_3 - \omega_1)h) \\ + \dfrac{\lambda_1}{g} \left(1 - \dfrac{\omega_1}{\omega_3}\right) X \end{array} & 0 & \gamma + (\omega_3 - \omega_1)h - X & 0 \\ 0 & -\omega_1 \lambda_1 g \dfrac{h_{11} h_{22} - h_{12}^2}{h_{22}} & -\omega_1 g \left(h_1 - \dfrac{h_2 h_{21}}{h_{22}}\right) & \gamma + \mu - X \end{vmatrix}$$

Expanding in terms of the first and second columns, we get

$$\det(J - XE) = (-1)^{1+2}\Bigg[(-1)^{1+2}(-X)(-\mu - X)(\gamma + (\omega_3 - \omega_1)h - X)$$
$$\times (\gamma + \mu - X) + (-1)^{1+3}(-1)\omega_3 g\left(h_1 - \frac{h_2 h_{21}}{h_{22}}\right)$$
$$\times \left\{\frac{S}{g^3} - \frac{\lambda_1}{g}(\gamma + (\omega_3 - \omega_1)h) + \frac{\lambda_1}{g}\left(1 - \frac{\omega_1}{\omega_3}\right)X\right\}$$
$$\times (-1)\omega_1\omega_4 \frac{g}{\lambda_2}\frac{f'^2}{f''}\left(h_1 - \frac{h_2 h_{12}}{h_{22}}\right) + (-1)^{1+4}X\omega_1\lambda_1 g$$
$$\times \frac{h_{11}h_{22} - h_{12}^2}{h_{22}}\frac{\omega_4}{\lambda_2}\frac{f'^2}{f''}(\gamma + (\omega_3 - \omega_1)h - X)$$
$$+ (-1)^{2+3}(-1)(-\mu - X)\left\{\frac{S}{g^3} - \frac{\lambda_1}{g}(\gamma + (\omega_3 - \omega_1)h)\right.$$
$$\left. + \frac{\lambda_1}{g}\left(1 - \frac{\omega_1}{\omega_3}\right)X\right\}(-1)\omega_3 \frac{g}{\lambda_1}\frac{h_2^2}{h_{22}}(\gamma + \mu - X)$$
$$+ (-1)^{3+4}(-1)\left\{\frac{S}{g^3} - \frac{\lambda_1}{g}(\gamma + (\omega_3 - \omega_1)h)\right.$$
$$\left. + \frac{\lambda_1}{g}\left(1 - \frac{\omega_1}{\omega_3}\right)X\right\}\omega_1 g \frac{h_{11}h_{22} - h_{12}^2}{h_{22}}\frac{\omega_3\omega_4}{\lambda_2} g \frac{h_2^2}{h_{22}}\frac{f'^2}{f''}\Bigg] = 0.$$

Rearranging this, we get

$$(X + \mu)X(X - \gamma - (\omega_3 - \omega_1)h)(X - \gamma - \mu)$$
$$+ \omega_3 \frac{g}{\lambda_1}\frac{h_2^2}{h_{22}}(X + \mu)(X - \gamma - \mu)\left\{\frac{\lambda_1}{g}\left(1 - \frac{\omega_1}{\omega_3}\right)X + \frac{S}{g^3} - \frac{\lambda_1}{g}\right.$$
$$\left. \times (\gamma + (\omega_3 - \omega_1)h)\right\} - \omega_1\omega_4 \frac{\lambda_1}{\lambda_2}\frac{f'^2}{f''}\frac{h_{11}h_{22} - h_{12}^2}{h_{22}}$$
$$\times X(X - \gamma - (\omega_3 - \omega_1)h) - \omega_1\omega_3\omega_4 \frac{g^2}{\lambda_2}\frac{f'^2}{f''}\left\{\left(h_1 - \frac{h_2 h_{21}}{h_{22}}\right)^2\right.$$
$$\left. + \frac{h_2^2(h_{11}h_{22} - h_{12}^2)}{h_{22}^2}\right\} \times \left\{\frac{\lambda_1}{g}\left(1 - \frac{\omega_1}{\omega_3}\right)X + \frac{S}{g^3} - \frac{\lambda_1}{g}\right.$$
$$\left. \times (\gamma + (\omega_3 - \omega_1)h)\right\} = 0,$$

which is reduced to (45) by setting $\omega_4 = \int_0^\infty D_2(\sigma)\, d\sigma = 1$. Q.E.D.

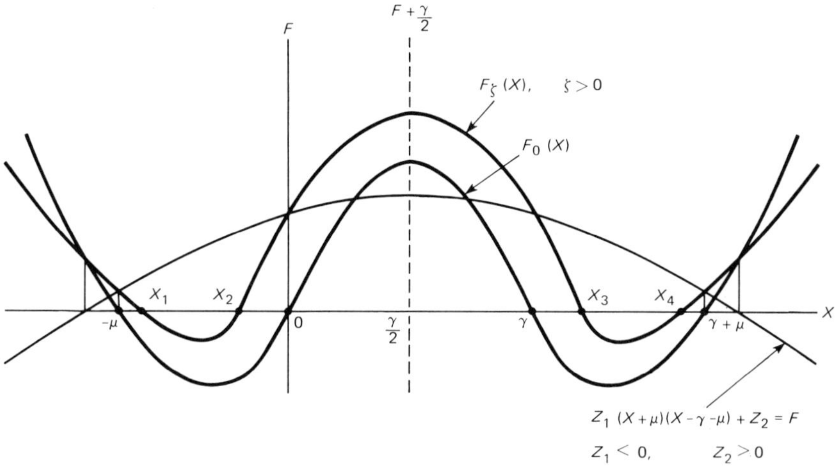

Figure 2 Location of roots $\zeta > 0$, $\zeta = 0$, $|\zeta| < 1$.

Proof of (35)

By setting $\omega_1 = \omega_2 = \omega_3 = \omega_4 = 1$, we immediately obtain Eq. (35). Q.E.D.

Location of Roots

16. The values of X are symmetric with respect to $\frac{1}{2}\gamma$, making the W-shaped curves for $F_\zeta(X)$ and $F_0(X)$ (see Fig. 2).

Location of Roots ($\zeta < 0$)

Again, the $F_\zeta(X)$ curve is symmetric with respect to $\frac{1}{2}\gamma$, but it is shifted downward from the $F_0(X)$ curve, making three positive roots and only one negative root (Fig. 3).

Proof of Theorem

17. By Eq. (48), $\Delta(\sigma) = 0$ has two positive (nonnegative) roots $\sigma_1 \geqq \sigma_2 \geqq 0$, since $\sigma_1 + \sigma_2 = -2\{a_0(\mu(\mu+\gamma) - b) + 2(a_0 b - c_0)\}/a_0^2 \geqq 0$, and $\sigma_1\sigma_2 = (\mu(\mu+\gamma) - b)^2/a_0^2 \geqq 0$. Hence, when $\sigma_1 \leqq \sigma$ or $\sigma \leqq \sigma_2$ [and $\Delta(\sigma) \geqq 0$], $G(Z) = 0$ has real roots. [On the other hand, when $\sigma_2 < \sigma < \sigma_1$,

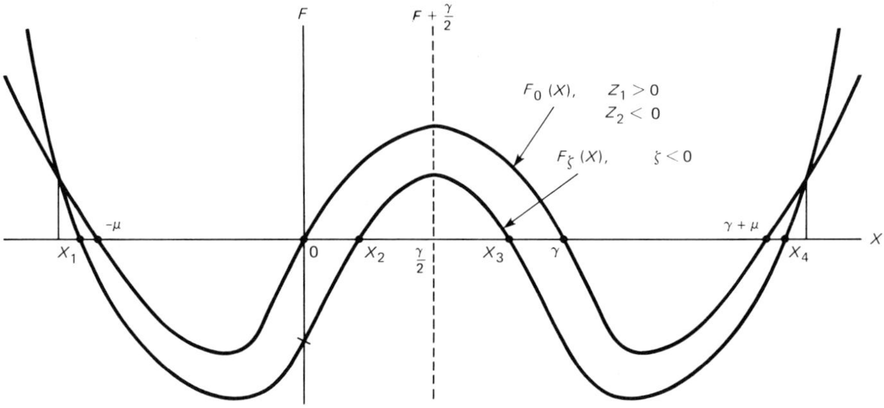

Figure 3 Location of roots when $\zeta < 0$.

$\Delta(\sigma) < 0$, $G(Z) = 0$ has all complex roots.] On looking at cases in which $\sigma_1 \leqq \sigma$ or $\sigma \leqq \sigma_2$ and $\Delta(\sigma) \geqq 0$, the two real roots Z_1 and Z_2 satisfy

$$Z_1 + Z_2 = -(a_0\sigma + b - \mu(\mu + \gamma)),$$
$$Z_1 Z_2 = (-a_0\mu(\mu + \gamma) + c_0)\sigma,$$

where $-a_0\mu(\mu + \gamma) + c_0 > 0$. First, when we have $\sigma > 0$ which implies $Z_1 Z_2 > 0$ and $Z_1 + Z_2 > 0$ and $Z_1 \geqq Z_2 > 0$, we conclude that $X = \frac{1}{2}(\gamma \pm \sqrt{\gamma^2 + 4Z_i})$, $i = 1, 2$. Hence there are two positive roots and two negative roots when (49) is satisfied. Second, when σ is negative which implies $Z_1 Z_2 < 0$, i.e., $Z_2 < 0$, $Z_1 > 0$, we have

$$X = \tfrac{1}{2}(\gamma \pm \sqrt{\gamma^2 + 4Z_1}): \quad \text{1 positive, 1 negative root,}$$
$$X = \tfrac{1}{2}(\gamma \pm \sqrt{\gamma^2 + 4Z_2}): \quad \text{2 positive roots if} \quad Z_2 > -\tfrac{1}{4}\gamma^2.$$

On the other hand, we note that

$$\begin{aligned} G(-\tfrac{1}{4}\gamma^2) &> 0 &\Leftrightarrow\quad & Z_2 > -\tfrac{1}{4}\gamma^2, \\ &= 0 &\Leftrightarrow\quad & Z_3 = -\tfrac{1}{4}\gamma^2, \\ &< 0 &\Leftrightarrow\quad & Z_2 < -\tfrac{1}{4}\gamma^2. \end{aligned}$$

Since we have $G(-\frac{1}{4}\gamma^2) = \sigma(-\frac{1}{4}a_0\gamma^2 - a_0\mu(\mu + \gamma) + c_0) + \frac{1}{4}\gamma^2(\frac{1}{4}\gamma^2 - b + \mu(\mu + \gamma))$, we conclude that

$$\begin{aligned} G(-\tfrac{1}{4}\gamma^2) &> 0 &\Leftrightarrow\quad & \sigma > \sigma_0, \\ &= 0 &\Leftrightarrow\quad & \sigma = \sigma_0, \\ &< 0 &\Leftrightarrow\quad & \sigma < \sigma_0, \end{aligned}$$

where

$$\sigma_0 = \frac{\frac{1}{4}\gamma^2(\frac{1}{4}\gamma^2 - b + \mu(\mu + \gamma))}{\frac{1}{4}a_0\gamma^2 + a_0\mu(\mu + \gamma) - c_0} \leqq 0$$

(since $\frac{1}{4}\gamma^2 - b + \mu(\mu + \gamma) \geqq 0, \frac{1}{4}a_0\gamma^2 + a_0\mu(\mu + \gamma) - c_0 \geqq 0$, and for $\gamma \neq 0$ $\sigma_0 < 0$). This proves the second part of the assertion as long as $0 > Z_2 > -\frac{1}{4}\gamma^2$, which means that σ is greater than the lower bound σ_0. In passing it is noted that there is a possibility of complex roots: When $\sigma < \sigma_0$, we have one positive, one negative, and two complex roots; when $\sigma_2 < \sigma < \sigma_1$, all of the roots are complex. This allows for a possibility of oscillatory optimal behavior. Q.E.D.

REFERENCES

Arrow, K. J. [1962]. Economic welfare and the allocation of resources for invention, in *The Rate and Direction of Inventive Activity* (R. R. Nelson, ed.), pp. 609–624. Princeton Univ. Press, Princeton, New Jersey.

Arrow, K. J., and Kurz, M. [1970]. *Public Investment, the Rate of Return and Optimal Fiscal Policy* (Resources for the Future). John Hopkins Press, Baltimore, Maryland.

Bate, R. R. [1969]. The optimal control of systems with transport lag, *Adv. Control Syst.*, **7**, 165–224.

Bloch, M. [1961]. *Feudal Society*. Univ. of Chicago Press, Chicago, Illinois.

Evenson, R. E., and Kislev, Y. [1975]. *Agricultural Research and Productivity*. Yale Univ. Press, New Haven, Connecticut.

Griliches, Z. [1975]. Returns to research and development in the private sector, in *New Developments in Productivity Measurement and Analysis*, (J. W. Kendrick and B. Vaccara, eds.), Vol. 41, Studies in Income and Wealth. Univ. of Chicago Press, Chicago, Illinois.

Jacobs, J. [1969]. *The Economy of Cities*. Random House, New York, 1969.

Kamien, M. I., and Schwartz, N. L. [1971]. Sufficient conditions in optimal control theory, *Journal of Economic Theory*, **3**, 207–214.

Kamien, M. I., and Schwartz, N. L. [1975]. Market structure and innovation: A survey, *Journal of Economic Literature*, **13**, 1–37.

Levhari, D., and Liviatan, N. [1972]. On stability in the saddle-point sense, *Journal of Economic Theory*, **4**, 88–93.

Mangasarian, O. L. [1966]. Sufficient conditions for the optimal control of nonlinear systems, *SIAM Journal on Control*, **4**, 139–152.

Mansfield, E. [1968]. *The Economics of Technological Change*. Norton, New York.

McLuhan, M. [1969]. *The Gutenberg Galaxy: The Making of Typographic Men*. New American Library, New York.

Nordhaus, W. D. [1969]. *Invention, Growth and Welfare*. MIT Press, Cambridge, Massachusetts.

Pauwels, W. [1977]. Optimal dynamic advertising policies in the presence of continuously distributed time lags, *Journal of Optimization Theory and Applications*, **22**, 79–89.

Pontryagin, L. S. *et al.* [1962]. *The Mathematical Theory of Optimal Processes*. Wiley (Interscience), New York.

Samuelson, P. A. [1965]. A theory of induced innovations along Kennedy–Weizsäcker lines, *Review of Economics and Statistics*, **47**, 343–356.

Samuelson, P. A. [1972]. The general saddlepoint property of optimal-control motions, *Journal of Economic Theory*, **5**, 102–120.

Sato, R., and Nôno, T. [1979]. A Theory of Endogenous Technical Change: Dynamic Böhm-Bawerk Effect and Optimal R & D Policy. Discussion Paper No. 79–20, Department of Economics, Brown University, Providence, Rhode Island.

Sato, R., and Ramachandran, R. [1974]. Models of Optimal Endogenous Technical Progress, Scale Effect and Duality of Production Functions. Discussion Paper, Department of Economics, Brown University, Providence, Rhode Island.

Sato, R., and Ramachandran, R. [1978]. A Contribution to the Microeconomic Analysis of Biased Technical Progress. Discussion Paper, Department of Economics, Brown University, Providence, Rhode Island.

Sato, R., and Suzawa, G. [1980]. An Analysis of the Effect of Basic and Applied Research on Productivity Gains. Research Project Sponsored by NSF Division of Policy Research and Analysis, Brown University, Providence, Rhode Island.

Scherer, F. M. [1970]. *Industrial Market Structure and Economic Performance*. Rand McNally, Chicago, Illinois.

Schmookler, J. [1966]. *Invention and Economic Growth*. Harvard Univ. Press, Cambridge, Massachusetts.

Sethi, S. P. [1973]. A useful transformation of Hamiltonians occurring in optimal control problems in economic analyses, *SCIMA Journal of Management Science and Applied Cybernetics*, **2**, (3), 1–17.

Sethi, S. P. [1974]. Sufficient conditions for the optimal control of a class of systems with continuous lags, *Journal of Optimization Theory and Applications*, **13**(5), 545–552.

Sethi, S. P., and McGruire, T. W. [1977]. Optimal skill mix: An application of the maximum principle for systems with retarded controls, *Journal of Optimization Theory and Applications*, **23**, 245–275.

Takayama, A. [1974]. *Mathematical Economics*. Dryden Press, Hinsdale, Illinois.

CHAPTER 4

"G-NEUTRAL" TECHNICAL CHANGE, COMPARATIVE STATICS, AND INTEGRABILITY CONDITIONS

1. In this chapter we consider three topics closely related to parametric changes under Lie groups and related transformations. Although these topics may appear to be entirely different, their fundamental formal structure shares the common property of (infinitesimal) transformations resulting from parametric changes in the economic system. We begin with "G (group)-neutral" types of technical change.

I. "*G*-Neutral" Types of Technical Change

Motivation

2. In Chapter 2, it was shown that the Lie type of technical progress under its own holothetic production function can always be expressed as a "Hicks" neutral type of product-augmenting technical progress (Corollary 1 to Theorem 4). On the other hand, it was also shown that any given production function has at least one type of technical change that leaves the isoquant map unchanged, the Hicks neutral type being, of course, one of them. This result may justify the frequent uses of the Hicksian product-augmenting technical progress in many theoretical and empirical analyses of cost and production functions (see, e.g., Arrow *et al.* [1961], Kendrick and Sato [1963], Solow [1957]).

Historically, the Hicks neutral type of technical progress came into existence in the economic literature from the assumption of a "neutral" effect of technical change on the *distributive shares* of factors of production under a constant returns to scale technology (Hicks [1963]). The closely related concept of "Harrod" neutral type of technical progress was first adopted by Harrod to accommodate the empirical fact of an increasing per capita income under a long-run balanced growth conjecture (Harrod [1948]). In order for a growth model to be consistent with a *constancy* of the capital–output ratio at a balanced growth path, Harrod found that only a special type of technical progress can generate increasing per capita income without disturbing the relative shares of capital and labor.

In order not to be repetitious of the earlier works (Sato and Beckmann [1968], Sato [1970], and Rose [1968]), we shall briefly present the theoretical foundations of various "neutral" types of technical progress that have frequently appeared in the economic literature. This is useful, because it will be shown that the earlier works of the above authors and others are the basis for the subsequent discussion of the concept of "G (group)-neutral" types of technical change.

The first comprehensive theoretical analysis of the relationships between the forms of production functions and the type of technical progress is given by Sato and Beckmann [1968]. They followed the leads provided by Robinson [1962] and Uzawa [1961]. Rose [1968], independently, presented the same framework as Sato and Beckmann's for *one* of the basic types of technical progress. In what follows we shall present a theoretical justification for the well-known types of neutral technical progress and then extend the concept of "neutrality" to "neutrality in the sense of transformation groups."

"Neutral Types" of Technical Progress

3. Assume that there are two inputs capital K and labor L, and one output Y which is subject to the following linear and (positively) homogeneous production function with technical progress t:

$$Y = F(K, L, t). \tag{1}$$

Assume further that F satisfies the usual regularity conditions. Define the output–capital ratio $Y/K = y$, the labor–capital ratio x, the output–labor ratio $Y/L = z = y/x$, and the capital–labor ratio $K/L = k = 1/x$. Then from (1) we have

$$y = f(x, t), \tag{1a}$$

$$z = g(k, t), \tag{1b}$$

where $f(x, t) = F(1, L/K, t)$ and $g(k, t) = F(K/L, t)$. The marginal productivities of capital and labor, which are equal to the return to capital r and the wage rate w under cost minimization, respectively, are written as

$$r = f - xf_x = g_k, \tag{2a}$$

$$w = g - kg_k = f_x. \tag{2b}$$

The regularity conditions require that

$$\begin{matrix} f_x > 0, & g_k > 0 \\ f_{xx} < 0, & g_{kk} < 0 \end{matrix} \quad \text{for} \quad f \geqq 0, \quad g \geqq 0, \quad x \geqq 0, \quad k \geqq 0. \tag{3}$$

Definition 1 (1) *Hicks Neutrality* Technical progress is Hicks neutral if the marginal rate of substitution is invariant under technical change as long as the capital–labor ratio is invariant.

(2) *Harrod Neutrality* Inventions are Harrod neutral if the output–capital ratio is invariant under technical change as long as the return to capital is unchanged.

(3) *Solow Neutrality* (Sato and Beckmann [1968, Case III, p. 59]) Technical progress is Solow neutral if the output–labor ratio is invariant under technical changes as long as the wage rate is constant (Solow [1962]).

(4) *Factor-Augmenting Type* (Sato and Beckmann [1968, Case XIV, p. 63], Rose [1968]) Inventions are neutral (Sato–Beckmann–Rose neutral[1]) in the sense that the elasticity of substitution is invariant under technical change as long as the income shares of factor inputs remain constant.

4. We can now write Eq. (1a) or (1b) and, therefore, Eq. (1) in a more specific manner that would satisfy the various definitions of neutrality. Following the earlier works we immediately obtain

Theorem 1 (i) *Hicks Neutrality Technical progress is product-augmenting if it is a Hicks neutral type*

$$Y = A(t)F(K, L). \tag{4a}$$

[1] See Gahlem [1972] and Sato and Beckmann [1975].

(ii) *Harrod Neutrality* *Technical progess is labor-homothetic if it is a Harrod neutral type*

$$Y = F[K, A(t)L]. \tag{4b}$$

(iii) *Solow Neutrality* *Technical progress is capital-homothetic if it is a Solow neutral type*

$$Y = F[A(t)K, L] \tag{4c}$$

(iv) *Factor-Augmenting* *Technical progress is factor-augmenting if it is neutral in the sense of Sato–Beckmann–Rose,*

$$Y = F[A(t)K, B(t)L]. \tag{4d}$$

Proof (i) Define the marginal rate of substitution between capital and labor as

$$R(x, t) = r(x, t)/w(x, t) = (f - xf_x)/f_x. \tag{5}$$

Then Hicks neutrality implies that $\partial R(x, t)/\partial t \equiv 0$, from which we have

$$R(x, t) = \bar{R}(x) = (f - xf_x)/f_x = (f/f_x) - x.$$

Integrating this with respect to f and x, we get

$$\log f(x, t) - \log A(t) = \int \frac{\partial x}{\bar{R}(x) + x} = \log f(x),$$

where $\log A(t)$ is the arbitrary constant, which measures the technical progress factor. From this we derive $f(x, t) = A(t)f(x)$ or (4a).

(ii) and (iii) Harrod neutrality implies

$$r = \psi(y) \tag{6}$$

or $r = y - xy_x = \psi(y)$, which will yield (4b). On the other hand, Solow neutrality is the "mirror image" of Harrod neutrality, i.e.,

$$w = \psi(z) = z - kz_k, \tag{7}$$

which yields (4c).

(iv) To prove this we first define the elasticity of substitution as

$$\sigma(x) = y_x(y - xy_x)/(-xyy_{xx}). \tag{8}$$

Neutrality in the sense of Sato–Beckmann–Rose implies that

$$\sigma(x) = \phi(xy_x/y), \tag{9}$$

where xy_x/y = share of labor = 1 − share of capital. From the definition of $\sigma(x)$, we can rewrite (9) as

$$\partial \log\left(\frac{y - xy_x}{y_x}\right) \Big/ \partial \log x = \phi\left(\frac{xy_x}{y}\right). \tag{9'}$$

Letting $xy_x/y = u$, we have $x(\partial/\partial x)\log[x(u^{-1} - 1)] = \phi(u)$, which yields $\partial x/x = \partial u/\phi(u)$. Integrating it, we get

$$\log x + \log C(t) = h(u) \qquad \text{or} \qquad u = H(C(t)x).$$

Since $u = xy_x/y$, this implies that

$$xy_x/y = H(C(t)x)$$

or

$$\int \frac{\partial y}{y} = \int \frac{\partial x}{xH(C(t)x)}, \qquad y = A(t)\exp \int^x \frac{C(t)\,\partial v}{C(t)vH(C(t)v)}.$$

Substituting $C(t)v = x$, we obtain

$$y = A(t)\exp \int^{B(t)x} \frac{\partial s}{sH(s)},$$

where integration is carried out at constant t. Then we finally obtain $y = A(t)f(C(t)x)$ so that $Y = F[A(t)K, A(t)C(t)L]$ or (4d). Q.E.D.

"*G-Neutral*" *Types of Technical Change*

5. In the previous section, the concept of "neutral" technical change is defined as that type of technical progress which leaves the differential equation unchanged by the introduction of a technical progress factor. This is essentially the same concept as the "invariance" of the group theory introduced in Chapter 2. Unlike the previous section, however, we shall introduce two parameters of technical change, α and β. Then technical change is expressed by a family of neoclassical production functions

$$Y = F[K, L, \alpha, \beta], \tag{1'}$$

where α and β are parameters of technical change.[2] On using y and x defined earlier, the production function is written as

$$y = f(x, \alpha, \beta). \tag{1a'}$$

We define "G-neutral" types of technical change as

Definition 2 (*Group-Neutrality*) Technical change expressed by (1a′) is said to be "G (Group)-neutral" if (1a′) is *invariant* under a Lie transformation group G of r *essential* parameters,[3]

$$\bar{x} = \phi(x, y, a_1, \ldots, a_r), \qquad \bar{y} = \psi(x, y, a_1, \ldots, a_r). \tag{10}$$

[2] Analyses and ideas of this section depend heavily on Nôno's work (Nôno [1971]).

[3] "G-neutrality" is obviously more general than "holotheticity" in that "G-neutrality" is in general not transformable to Hicks neutrality; "G-neutrality," however, is studied here only in the context of the constant returns to scale technology.

We may assume that the parameters of technical change in (1a′) are essential (see the Appendix, Part I), i.e.,

$$\frac{\partial f}{\partial \alpha} \not\equiv 0 \qquad \text{and} \qquad \frac{\partial f}{\partial \alpha}\frac{\partial^2 f}{\partial \beta\, \partial x} - \frac{\partial f}{\partial \beta}\frac{\partial^2 f}{\partial \alpha\, \partial x} \not\equiv 0. \tag{11}$$

Then by differentiating (1a′) with respect to x twice and by eliminating α and β from this result and from (1a′), we get a differential equation of the second order

$$\Phi(x, y, y_x, y_{xx}) = 0. \tag{12}$$

Equation (1a′) is a general solution of (12). We might say that (12) is *the equation for the definition of G-neutral technical change*, so that for a given G, the equation of "neutrality" can be obtained by the Lie theory of continuous groups.

Let $L(G)$ be the Lie algebra of infinitesimal transformations of G, and U be any element of $L(G)$ written as

$$U = \xi(x, y)\frac{\partial}{\partial x} + \eta(x, y)\frac{\partial}{\partial y}. \tag{13}$$

Then the twice extended group [Appendix, Eq. (34)] is given by

$$U'' = \xi(x, y)\frac{\partial}{\partial x} + \eta(x, y)\frac{\partial}{\partial y} + n'(x, y, y')\frac{\partial}{\partial y'} + \eta''(x, y, y', y'')\frac{\partial}{\partial y''}, \tag{14}$$

where

$$\eta' = \frac{\partial \eta}{\partial x} + \left(\frac{\partial \eta}{\partial y} - \frac{\partial \xi}{\partial x}\right)y' - \frac{\partial \xi}{\partial y}y'^2 \tag{14a}$$

and

$$\eta'' = \frac{\partial \eta'}{\partial x} + \frac{\partial \eta'}{\partial y}y' + \left(\frac{\partial \eta'}{\partial y'} - \frac{\partial \xi}{\partial x} - \frac{\partial \xi}{\partial y}y'\right)y''. \tag{14b}$$

Here we let $y' = y_x$ and $y'' = y_{xx}$. For a given G, the equations of neutrality of the second order can be determined by the following conditions:

$$\text{for all} \quad U \in L(G), \qquad U''\Phi = 0 \qquad \text{whenever} \quad \Phi(x, y, y_x, y_{xx}) = 0. \tag{15}$$

The family of production functions of G-neutral technical change can be obtained by solving the equation of neutrality satisfying (15).

Basic Results

6. The production function (1a′) must satisfy the regularity conditions $f_x > 0, f - xf_x > 0, f_{xx} < 0$. We shall now require that $f_{xx} < 0$ is invariant under any transformation of G.

Lemma 1 *(Invariance of the Law of Diminishing Marginal Product) The differential equation $f_{xx} = y'' < 0$ is invariant if and only if G is a Lie subgroup of the general projective group $GP(2, R)$ of the plane.*

Proof $y'' < 0$ is invariant if and only if $y'' = 0$ is invariant under G. From (15) we must have

$$y'' = 0 \qquad \text{implies} \quad U''(y'') = \eta''(x; y, y', y'') = 0. \tag{16}$$

Since η' and η'' are given by (14a) and (14b), (16) implies that $\partial\eta'/\partial x + (\partial\eta'/\partial y)y' = 0$, i.e.,

$$\frac{\partial^2\eta}{\partial x^2} + \left(2\frac{\partial^2\eta}{\partial x\,\partial y} - \frac{\partial^2\xi}{\partial x^2}\right)y' + \left(\frac{\partial^2\eta}{\partial y^2} - 2\frac{\partial^2\xi}{\partial x\,\partial y}\right)y'^2 - \frac{\partial^2\xi}{\partial y^2}\,y'^3 \equiv 0.$$

It follows that

$$\frac{\partial^2\eta}{\partial x^2} = 0, \qquad 2\frac{\partial^2\eta}{\partial x\,\partial y} - \frac{\partial^2\xi}{\partial x^2} = 0, \qquad \frac{\partial^2\eta}{\partial y^2} - 2\frac{\partial^2\xi}{\partial x\,\partial y} = 0, \qquad \frac{\partial^2\xi}{\partial y^2} = 0. \tag{17}$$

Solving the partial differential equations (17), we obtain

$$\begin{aligned}\xi &= a_1 + a_3 x + a_5 y + a_7 x^2 + a_8 xy,\\ \eta &= a_2 + a_4 x + a_6 y + a_7 xy + a_8 y^2,\end{aligned} \tag{18}$$

where the a_i are arbitrary constants. Equations (18) imply

$$\begin{aligned}U = {} & a_1\frac{\partial}{\partial x} + a_2\frac{\partial}{\partial y} + a_3 x\frac{\partial}{\partial x} + a_4 x\frac{\partial}{\partial y} + a_5 y\frac{\partial}{\partial x} + a_6 y\frac{\partial}{\partial y}\\ & + a_7 x\left(x\frac{\partial}{\partial x} + y\frac{\partial}{\partial y}\right) + a_8 y\left(x\frac{\partial}{\partial x} + y\frac{\partial}{\partial y}\right).\end{aligned} \tag{19}$$

Thus we have $U \in L(GP(2, R))$, the general projective group of the plane. Q.E.D.

7. The foregoing lemma enables us to concentrate on just the projective group [see Eq. (72) or (81) in the Appendix, Part IV]. We shall study the nature of technical change generated by the Lie subalgebras of the two-parameter subgroups G_2, which belong to $GP(2, R)$. We may express (19) by independent groups as

$$U = a_1 U_1 + a_2 U_2 + a_3 U_3 + \cdots + a_8 U_8. \tag{19′}$$

Among possible combinations of two groups from (19′), we shall study

Case (1) $L(G) = L(G_{(a)}) = \{aU_3 + (1-a)U_6\}$,[4]

Case (2) $L(G) = L(G_2) = \{U_3, U_6\}$,

where $U_3 = x\,\partial/\partial x$ and $U_6 = y\,\partial/\partial y$.

Case 1

Theorem 2 *(General $G_{(a)}$-Neutrality) The types of technical change invariant under $G_{(a)}$ can be expressed by the differential equation*

$$\Phi(y^a/x^{1-a}, s, \sigma) = 0, \tag{20}$$

where s is the relative share of labor and σ the elasticity of substitution.

Theorem 3 *(Special Cases) The equation of neutrality defined by (20) will include the well-known cases of Hicks neutral, Harrod neutral, and Solow neutral as special cases.*

Proof of Theorem Let $U = aU_3 + (1-a)U_6$; then we have

$$U'' = ax\frac{\partial}{\partial x} + (1-a)y\frac{\partial}{\partial y} + (1-2a)y'\frac{\partial}{\partial y'} + (1-3a)y''\frac{\partial}{\partial y''}.$$

By solving the ordinary differential equations associated with U'', we obtain the three independent differential invariants

$$I_1 = x, \qquad I_2 = \frac{y'}{y}, \qquad I_3 = \frac{y''}{y} \qquad \text{for} \quad a = 0,$$

$$I_1 = \frac{y}{x^c}, \qquad I_2 = \frac{y'}{x^{c-1}}, \qquad I_3 = \frac{y''}{x^{c-2}}, \qquad c = \frac{1-a}{a}, \qquad \text{for} \quad a \neq 0.$$

On letting $s = I_1 I_2$ and $\sigma = -I_2(1 - I_1 I_2)/I_1 I_3$ for $a = 0$, and $s = xy'/y = I_2/I_1$ and $\sigma = -I_2(I_1 - I_2)/I_1 I_3$ for $a \neq 0$, the equation of neutrality is obtained as (20). Q.E.D.

Proof of Theorem 3 By setting $a = 0$, $a = \frac{1}{2}$, and $a = 1$, we obtain $U = y\,\partial/\partial y$ (Hicks neutral), $U = \frac{1}{2}x(\partial/\partial x) + \frac{1}{2}y(\partial/\partial y)$ (Solow neutral), and $U = x\,\partial/\partial x$ (Harrod neutral). Q.E.D.

Theorem 4 *(Two-Parameter Family) The two-parameter family of production functions of $G_{(a)}$-neutral technical change is given by*

$$\begin{aligned} Y &= A(\alpha, \beta)F[K, L, B(\alpha, \beta)] && \text{for} \quad a = 0, \\ Y &= (L/K)^c F[K, A(\alpha, \beta, a)L, B(\alpha, \beta, a)] && \text{for} \quad a \neq 0. \end{aligned} \tag{21}$$

[4] In general, we assume that $-\infty < a < +\infty$, but for $a = \pm\infty$ we must replace y^a/x^{1-a} by xy and $c = -1$ in the subsequent discussion.

Proof The family of production function will be obtained by (20). Alternatively, we can obtain it from[5]

$$ax\frac{\partial f}{\partial x} + \delta(\alpha, \beta, a)\frac{\partial f}{\partial \alpha} + \gamma(\alpha, \beta, a)\frac{\partial f}{\partial \beta} = (1 - a)f.$$

Thus, we have

$$f = A(\alpha, \beta)\phi(x, B(\alpha, \beta)), \qquad a = 0,$$

$$f = x^c\psi[A(\alpha, \beta, a)x, B(\alpha, \beta, a)], \qquad a \neq 0,$$

which can be transformed to (21). Q.E.D.

As special cases we have the well-known types of neutrality:

Corollary to Theorem 4 (*Special Cases*)

$$f = A(\alpha, \beta)\phi(x), \qquad a = 0, \quad B = 0 \qquad \text{(Hicksian neutral)},$$

$$f = \psi[A(\alpha, \beta, 1)x], \qquad a = 1, \quad B = 0 \qquad \text{(Harrod neutral)},$$

$$f = \psi[x, B(\alpha, \beta, \tfrac{1}{2})], \qquad a = \tfrac{1}{2}, \quad A = 0 \qquad \text{(Solow neutral)}.$$

Case 2

We shall study the second case in which $L(G_2) = \{U_3, U_6\}$. Evidently, U_3 and U_6 form a two-parameter subgroup, i.e., $[U_3, U_6] = 0$. From (14a) and (14b), we have

$$U_3'' = x\frac{\partial}{\partial x} - y'\frac{\partial}{\partial y'} - 2y''\frac{\partial}{\partial y''} \tag{22a}$$

and

$$U_6'' = y\frac{\partial}{\partial y} + y'\frac{\partial}{\partial y'} + y''\frac{\partial}{\partial y''}. \tag{22b}$$

Theorem 5 (*Factor-Augmenting Type*) *The factor-augmenting type is nothing but the type of technical progress generated by the two-parameter Lie group $L(G_2)$, i.e., $f = A(\alpha, \beta)\psi[B(\alpha, \beta)x]$.*

[5] Here we follow the alternative method suggested by Lie [1888, pp. 458–497] (Kapitel 23, Invariance Schaaren von Mannigflaltigkeiten—Invariant Families of Manifolds). A family of production function (1a′) is invariant under G if and only if for each $U \in L(G)$ there corresponds an infinitesimal transformation $V = \delta(\alpha, \beta, a)\,\partial/\partial\alpha + \gamma(\alpha, \beta, a)\,\partial/\partial\beta$ such that $y - f(x, \alpha, \beta) = 0$ implies $(U + V)(y - f(x, \alpha, \beta)) = 0$. This condition is written as $\xi(x, f)\,\partial f/\partial x + \delta(\alpha, \beta, a)\,\partial f/\partial\alpha + \gamma(\alpha, \beta, a)\,\partial f/\partial\beta = \eta(x, f)$.

Proof By solving $U_3''f = 0$ and $U_6''f = 0$ simultaneously, we have two independent differential invariants up to the second order of G_2:

$$I_1 = xy'/y \qquad \text{and} \qquad I_2 = x^2y''/y.$$

Then from $s = I_1$ and $\sigma = I_1(I_1 - 1)/I_2$, the equation which satisfies both (22a) and (22b) is (9). However, this is nothing but the equation of neutrality, defined by Sato and Beckmann [1968] and Rose [1968] to obtain the factor-augmenting technical progress. Thus, the production function is (4d).

Q.E.D.

Corollary to Theorem 5 *(Cobb–Douglas Function) The one-parameter family of production functions of G_2-neutral technical change is given by*

$$Y = A(\alpha)K^cL^{1-c} \tag{23}$$

which is just the Cobb–Douglas production function.

Proof From $U_3' = x\,\partial/\partial x - y'\,\partial/\partial y'$ and $U_6' = y\,\partial/\partial y + y'\,\partial/\partial y'$, it is readily obtained that the only function which satisfies $U_3'f = 0$, $U_6'f = 0$ simultaneously is nothing but the Cobb–Douglas form. Q.E.D.

Remark Compare this result with the result in Chapter 2, Section 28.

G-Neutral Technical Change Generated by the One-Parameter Lie Subgroups of GP(2, R)

8. We shall next study the various types of G-neutral technical change derived from each of the one-parameter subgroups of the projective group. The general projective group with two variables x and y contains eight independent groups $U_1, \ldots, U_8$ [Eq. (19′)], and we study each case separately. Since the method has already been illustrated in the previous section, we simply summarize the results in Table 1.

G_3-Types of Neutral Technical Change

9. G-neutral types of technical change generated by $GP(2, R)$ contain many special cases including the ones which belongs to G_3, three-parameter groups. We now want to study the case of G_3 such that

$$L(G_3) = \{U_3, U_6, U_8\}, \tag{24}$$

where

$$U_3 = x\frac{\partial}{\partial x} = -\left(k\frac{\partial}{\partial k} + z\frac{\partial}{\partial z}\right), \qquad U_6 = y\frac{\partial}{\partial y} = z\frac{\partial}{\partial z},$$

$$U_8 = y\left(x\frac{\partial}{\partial x} + y\frac{\partial}{\partial y}\right) = -z\frac{\partial}{\partial k}.$$

TABLE 1

TECHNICAL CHANGE GENERATED BY ONE-PARAMETER SUBGROUP $G_1 \in GP(2,R)$ OF THE PLANE[a]

Type of technical change	Group form	Extended infinitesimal transformation	Three invariants	Equation of neutrality	Production function[b]
I. Labor combining					
$U_1 = \frac{\partial}{\partial x} = -k\left(k\frac{\partial}{\partial k} + z\frac{\partial}{\partial z}\right)$	$\bar{x} = x + a$ $\bar{y} = y$ or $c\bar{K} = K, \quad c > 0$ $c\bar{L} = L + aK$ $c\bar{Y} = Y$	$U_1'' = \frac{\partial}{\partial x}$	$I_1 = y$ $I_2 = y'$ $I_3 = y''$	$\phi\left(y, w, \frac{x}{r}\sigma\right) = 0$	$Y = F[K, L + A(\alpha,\beta)K, B(\alpha,\beta)]$
II. Capital additive					
$U_2 = \frac{\partial}{\partial y} = k\frac{\partial}{\partial z}$	$\bar{x} = x$ $\bar{y} = y + a$ or $c\bar{K} = K$ $c\bar{L} = L$ $c\bar{Y} = Y + aK$	$U_2'' = \frac{\partial}{\partial y}$	$I_1 = x$ $I_2 = y'$ $I_3 = y''$	$\phi\left(x, w, \frac{\sigma}{1-s}\right) = 0$	$Y = A(\alpha,\beta)K + F[K, L, B(\alpha,\beta)]$
III. Harrod (generalized)					
$U_3 = x\frac{\partial}{\partial x} = -\left(k\frac{\partial}{\partial k} + z\frac{\partial}{\partial z}\right)$	$\bar{x} = ax, \quad a > 0$ $\bar{y} = y$ or $c\bar{K} = K$ $c\bar{L} = aL$ $c\bar{Y} = Y$	$U_3'' = x\frac{\partial}{\partial x} - y'\frac{\partial}{\partial y'} - 2y''\frac{\partial}{\partial y''}$	$I_1 = y$ $I_2 = xy'$ $I_3 = x^2y''$	$\phi(y, r, \sigma) = 0$	$Y = F[K, A(\alpha,\beta)L, B(\alpha,\beta)]$

(continues)

TABLE 1 *(continued)*

Type of technical change	Group form	Extended infinitesimal transformation	Three invariants	Equation of neutrality	Production function[b]
IV. Labor additive					
$U_4 = x\frac{\partial}{\partial y} = \frac{\partial}{\partial z}$	$\bar{x} = x$ $\bar{y} = y + ax$ or $c\bar{K} = K$ $c\bar{L} = L$ $c\bar{Y} = Y + aL$	$U_4'' = \frac{\partial}{\partial z}$	$I_1 = k$ $I_2 = z'$ $I_3 = z''$	$\phi\left(k, r, \frac{\sigma}{s}\right) = 0$	$Y = A(\alpha, \beta)L + F[K, L, B(\alpha, \beta)]$
V. Quasi-Hicks I					
$U_5 = y\frac{\partial}{\partial x}$ $= -z\left(k\frac{\partial}{\partial k} + z\frac{\partial}{\partial z}\right)$	$\bar{x} = x + ay$ $\bar{y} = y$ or $c\bar{K} = K$ $c\bar{L} = L + aY$ $c\bar{Y} = Y$	$U_5'' = y\frac{\partial}{\partial x}$ $-y'^2\frac{\partial}{\partial y'}$ $-3y'y''\frac{\partial}{\partial y''}$	$I_1 = y$ $I_2 = \frac{y}{y'} - x$ $I_3 = \frac{y''}{y'^3}$	$\phi(y, R, xw\sigma) = 0$	$L = A(\alpha, \beta)Y + G[K, Y, B(\alpha, \beta)]$
VI. Hicks (generalized)					
$U_6 = y\frac{\partial}{\partial y} = z\frac{\partial}{\partial z}$	$\bar{x} = x$ $\bar{y} = ay, \quad a > 0$ or $c\bar{K} = K$ $c\bar{L} = L$ $c\bar{Y} = aY$	$U_6'' = y\frac{\partial}{\partial y}$ $+ y'\frac{\partial}{\partial y}$ $+ y''\frac{\partial}{\partial y''}$	$I_1 = x$ $I_2 = \frac{y'}{y}$ $I_3 = \frac{y''}{y}$	$\phi(x, s, \sigma) = 0$	$Y = A(\alpha, \beta)F[K, L, B(\alpha, \beta)]$

VII. Capital combining					
$U_7 = x\left(x\frac{\partial}{\partial x} + y\frac{\partial}{\partial y}\right)$ $= -\frac{\partial}{\partial k}$	$\bar{x} = \frac{x}{1-ax}, \quad ax < 1$ $\bar{y} = \frac{y}{1-ax}$ or $c\bar{K} = K - aL, \quad a < K/L$ $c\bar{L} = L$ $c\bar{Y} = Y$	$U_7'' = -\frac{\partial}{\partial k}$	$I_1 = z$ $I_2 = z'$ $I_3 = z''$	$\phi\left(z, r, \frac{k}{w}\sigma\right) = 0$	$Y = F[K + A(\alpha, \beta)L, L, B(\alpha, \beta)]$
VIII. Quasi-Hicks II					
$U_8 = y\left(x\frac{\partial}{\partial x} + y\frac{\partial}{\partial y}\right)$ $= -z\frac{\partial}{\partial k}$	$\bar{x} = \frac{x}{1-ay}, \quad ay < 1$ $\bar{y} = \frac{y}{1-ay}$ or $c\bar{K} = K - aY, \quad a < K/Y$ $c\bar{L} = L$ $c\bar{Y} = Y$	$U_8'' = -z\frac{\partial}{\partial k}$ $+ z'^2\frac{\partial}{\partial z'}$ $+ 3z'z''\frac{\partial}{\partial z''}$	$I_1 = z$ $I_2 = \frac{z}{z'} - k$ $I_3 = \frac{z''}{z'^3}$	$\phi(z, R, kr\sigma) = 0$	$K = A(\alpha, \beta)Y + H[Y, L, B(\alpha, \beta)]$

[a] r is the interest rate, w the wage rate, s the relative share of labor ($1 - s$ the relative share of capital), R the marginal rate of substitution, and σ the elasticity of substitution ($x = L/K$, $y = Y/K$, $k = K/L$, $z = Y/L$).

[b] As for a one-parameter family of production functions, replace $A(\alpha, \beta)$ by $A(\alpha)$ and omit B in the production function.

It is seen that all Lie subalgebras of $L(G_3)$ are given by

$$\{U_3, U_6, U_8\}: \qquad L_s(G_3) \in L(G_3), \tag{24-i'}$$

$$\{U_3, U_8\}, \{U_3, U_6 + aU_8\}, \{aU_3 + U_6, U_8\}: \quad L_s(G_2) \in L(G_3), \tag{24-ii'}$$

$$\{aU_3 + bU_6 + cU_8\}: \qquad L_s(G_1) \in L(G_3). \tag{24-iii'}$$

The extended infinitesimal transformations for U_3, U_6, and U_8 are

$$U_3'' = -k\frac{\partial}{\partial k} - z\frac{\partial}{\partial z} + z''\frac{\partial}{\partial z''},$$

$$U_6'' = z\frac{\partial}{\partial z} + z'\frac{\partial}{\partial z'} + z''\frac{\partial}{\partial z''},$$

$$U_8'' = -z\frac{\partial}{\partial k} + z'^2\frac{\partial}{\partial z'} + 3z'z''\frac{\partial}{\partial z''}.$$

By solving the invariance conditions simultaneously,

$$U_3''\phi = 0, \qquad U_6''\phi = 0, \qquad U_8''\phi = 0, \tag{25}$$

we obtain only one invariant

$$I = -z'^2(z - kz')/z^2 z'' \tag{26}$$

which can be written as

$$I = (1 - s)\sigma, \tag{26'}$$

where s is the share of labor and σ the elasticity of substitution. Hence the equation of neutrality of G_3 is simply

$$(1 - s)\sigma = c > 0. \tag{27}$$

By solving the above, we express the family of production functions

$$K = A(\alpha, \beta)Y + B(\alpha, \beta)L^{(1/c)+1}Y^{-1/c} \tag{27'}$$

with $A > 0$, $B > 0$.

The G-neutral technical change with $L_s(G_2) = \{U_3, U_8\}$ can be obtained from $U_3''\phi = 0$ and $U_8''\phi = 0$ as

$$\phi(r/s, s\sigma/y) = 0. \tag{28-i}$$

Also, the equation of neutrality for $L_s(G_2) = \{U_3, U_6 + aU_8\}$, $-\infty < a < +\infty$, can be written as

$$\phi\left(\frac{s}{1 - s}, \frac{k}{k + az}, \frac{\sigma}{1 - s}\right) = 0. \tag{28-ii}$$

Finally, for $L_s(G_2) = \{aU_3 + U_6, U_8\}$, $-\infty < a < +\infty$, the equation of neutrality becomes

$$\phi(z^a R^{a-1}, (1-s)\sigma) = 0. \tag{28-iii}$$

In summary, we obtain

Theorem 6 *(G_3-Neutrality)* (i) *A family of production functions invariant under the G_3-neutral type of technical progress, where G_3 is generated by $L(G_3) = \{U_3, U_6, U_8\}$, can be expressed as (27′).*

(ii) *The equations of neutrality corresponding to* (24-ii), *i.e.*, $L_s(G_2) \in L(G_3)$, are given by (28-i)–(28-iii).

It is interesting to see that there exists *no* G_4-neutral technical change of the second order based on $L(G_4) = \{U_3, U_5, U_6, U_8\}$. To show this we first derive

$$U_5'' = -kz\frac{\partial}{\partial k} - z^2\frac{\partial}{\partial z} - z'(z - kz')\frac{\partial}{\partial z'} + 3kz'z''\frac{\partial}{\partial z''},$$

and examine the determinant Δ of the coefficients of the operators U_3'', U_5'', U_6'', and U_8'',

$$\Delta = -kz^2z'(z + z')z'' > 0.$$

Since Δ is not zero, $L(G_4)$ has no invariant differential equation of the second order, which implies that there exists *no* G_4-neutral technical progress.

Invariance of the Regularity Conditions under Technical Change

10. Since the production function $y = f(x)$ is an economic function, it must satisfy certain regularity conditions such as

$$y = \text{output/capital} > 0 \tag{29-i}$$

$$x = \text{labor/capital} > 0 \tag{29-ii}$$

$$y' = \text{wage rate} > 0 \tag{29-iii}$$

$$y - xy' = \text{interest rate} > 0 \tag{29-iv}$$

$$y'' < 0 \quad \text{(diminishing marginal product).} \tag{29-v}$$

We shall study under what circumstances all or a subset of these regularity conditions are invariant under G-neutral technical change. We have

Theorem 7 *(Invariance of the Regularity Conditions) Each of the conditions stated in Table 2 in different cases is invariant by all transformations of G near the identity if and only if G is a Lie subgroup of the r-parameter*

TABLE 2

Case	Conditions	Lie algebra
(a)	$y' > 0$ $y - xy' > 0$ $y'' < 0$	$L(G_4) = \{U_3, U_5, U_6, U_8\}$
(b)	$y' > 0$ $y'' < 0$	$L(G_6) = \{U_1, U_2, U_3, U_5, U_6, U_8\}$
(c)	$y - xy' > 0$ $y'' < 0$	$L(G_6^*) = \{U_3, U_4, U_5, U_6, U_7, U_8\}$
(d)	$x > 0, \quad y' > 0$ $y - xy' > 0, \quad y'' < 0$	$L(G_3) = \{U_3, U_6, U_8\}$

Lie group G_r ($r = 3, 4, 6$), whose basis is given by the corresponding Lie algebra, where

$$L(G_r) \in L(GP(2, R)) = \left\{U_1 = \frac{\partial}{\partial x}, U_2 = \frac{\partial}{\partial y}, U_3 = x\frac{\partial}{\partial x}, \right.$$

$$U_4 = x\frac{\partial}{\partial y}, U_5 = y\frac{\partial}{\partial x}, U_6 = y\frac{\partial}{\partial y},$$

$$\left. U_7 = x\left(x\frac{\partial}{\partial x} + y\frac{\partial}{\partial y}\right), U_8 = y\left(x\frac{\partial}{\partial x} + y\frac{\partial}{\partial y}\right)\right\}.$$

Proof From Lemma 1 the invariance of $y'' < 0$ implies that the symmetry groups of technical change must be generated from the general projective group $GP(2, R)$ with the basis of infinitesimal transformation given by (18). To prove Case (a) we observe that each of the conditions $y' > 0$, $y - xy' > 0$, and $y'' < 0$ is invariant by all transformations of G if and only if each of the equations $y' = 0$, $y - xy' = 0$, and $y'' = 0$ is invariant by such transformations of G, i.e.,

$$y' = 0 \quad \text{implies} \quad U'y' = \eta'(x, y, y') = 0,$$

$$y - xy' = 0 \quad \text{implies} \quad U'(y - xy') =' \eta - \xi y' - x\eta' = 0,$$

$$y'' = 0 \quad \text{implies} \quad U''y'' = \eta''(x, y, y', y'') = 0.$$

Since η' is given by (14a) and $U'y' = 0$ is equivalent to $\partial\eta/\partial x = 0$, we must have that $a_4 = 0$ and $a_7 = 0$ in Eq. (18). In the same way, $U'(y - xy') = 0$ implies that

$$x\eta - y\xi - \left\{x^2\frac{\partial\eta}{\partial x} + xy\left(\frac{\partial\eta}{\partial y} - \frac{\partial\xi}{\partial x}\right) - y^2\frac{\partial\xi}{\partial y}\right\} = 0.$$

It follows that $a_1 = 0, a_2 = 0$, which proves $L(G_4)$. We shall leave the proofs of the remaining cases to the reader. Q.E.D.

One of the most interesting results is

Theorem 8 *(Invariance of the Elasticity of Substitution) The elasticity of factor substitution σ is invariant by a Lie transformation group G of the plane if and only if G is a Lie subgroup of G_2, where*

$$L(G_2) = \{U_3 = x\,\partial/\partial x,\ U_6 = y\,\partial/\partial y\}.$$

Proof The elasticity of substitution $\sigma = y'(y - xy')/(-xyy'')$ is invariant under G if and only if

$$U''(\sigma) = 0 \qquad \text{for all} \quad U \in L(G).$$

On using (14), after some complicated calculations, the foregoing implies

$$\left\{xyy'(xy' - y)\left(\frac{\partial\eta'}{\partial y'} - \frac{\partial\xi}{\partial x} - \frac{\partial\xi}{\partial y}y'\right) + xy(y - 2xy')\eta' + y'(-y^2\xi + x^2y'\eta)\right\}y'' + xyy'(xy' - y)\left(\frac{\partial\eta'}{\partial x} + \frac{\partial\eta'}{\partial y'}y'\right) = 0$$

from which we have

$$xyy'(xy' - y)\left(\frac{\partial\eta'}{\partial y'} - \frac{\partial\xi}{\partial x} - \frac{\partial\xi}{\partial y}y'\right) + xy(y - 2xy')\eta' + y'(-y^2\xi + x^2y'\eta) = 0 \tag{30}$$

and $\partial\eta'/\partial x + (\partial\eta'/\partial y)y' = 0$ $(xyy'(xy' - y) \neq 0)$. We have already proved (see the proof of Lemma 1) that $\partial\eta'/\partial x + (\partial\eta'/\partial y)y' = 0$ implies that G must be the general projective group (18). By substituting (18) into (30), we obtain $a_1 = a_2 = a_4 = a_5 = a_7 = a_8 = 0$, i.e.,

$$L(G_2) = \{U_3 = x\,\partial/\partial x,\ U_6 = y\,\partial/\partial y\}. \quad \text{Q.E.D.}$$

Remark In order to appreciate the power of the foregoing theorem, consider the expression for the elasticity of substitution. The invariance of σ under $\{U_3, U_6\}$ implies that the expression for the elasticity of substitution is unchanged before and after the simultaneous technical change due to U_3 and/or U_6. Since

$$U_3'' = x\frac{\partial}{\partial x} - y'\frac{\partial}{\partial y'} - 2y''\frac{\partial}{\partial y''},$$

$$U_6'' = y\frac{\partial}{\partial y} + y'\frac{\partial}{\partial y'} + y''\frac{\partial}{\partial y''}$$

are the twice extended groups, we have

$$T_3'':\quad \bar{x} = ax,\qquad \bar{y} = y,\qquad \bar{y}' = a^{-1}y',\qquad \bar{y}'' = a^{-2}y'',$$

$$T_6'':\quad \bar{x} = x,\qquad \bar{y} = by,\qquad \bar{y}' = by',\qquad \bar{y}'' = by''.$$

The expression for the elasticity of substitution

$$\sigma = y'(y - xy')/(-xyy'')$$

is unchanged by substituting $\bar{x}, \bar{y}, \bar{y}', \bar{y}''$ corresponding to U_3 and/or U_6. This is verified from

$$\bar{\sigma} = \frac{\bar{y}'(\bar{y} - \bar{x}\bar{y}')}{-\bar{x}\bar{y}\bar{y}''} = \frac{(b/a)y'(by - ax(b/a)y')}{-axby(b/a^2)y''} = \frac{y'(y - xy')}{-xyy''}.$$

Economic Interpretations of the Results

11. Before we leave this topic we shall briefly give economic interpretations to some of the results obtained in Part I. The concept of G-neutrality is closely related to the invariance condition of the differential equation for a production function under a given transformation group. Lemma 1 shows that, if we impose the condition that the law of diminishing marginal product is left unaffected under a G-neutral technical change, then we may restrict the analysis just to the general "projective" type of technical change. This again will justify the frequent uses of this type of technical change throughout this book (e.g., Chapters 2 and 5).

Among many different subgroups of the general projective type, we first choose a one-parameter group generated from a linear combination of $U_3 = x\,\partial/\partial x$ and $U_6 = y\,\partial/\partial y$; i.e., $G_{(a)} = aU_3 + (1 - a)U_6$. Theorem 2 derives the most general expression for the equation of neutrality under the one-parameter group $G_{(a)}$. The well-known cases of Hicks, Harrod, and Solow neutral types of technical change are just special cases of Theorem 2. In Theorem 4 we actually present the general (two-parameter) family of production functions generated from the one-parameter G-neutral type of technical change $G_{(a)}$.

Among possible two-parameter subgroups of the general projective group, we choose the one whose basis is again given by U_3 and U_6. Then the well-known factor-augmenting type, which is "neutral" in the sense of Sato–Beckmann–Rose, is just the G-neutral type of technical change generated by this (two-parameter) subgroup (Theorem 5).

The general projective group has the basic eight independent infinitesimal transformations. Section 8 presents a summary of production functions and types of technical change generated from these basic (one-parameter) subgroups (see Table 1). Of all the possible three-parameter subgroups, we have studied only the case corresponding to

$$\left\{U_3 = x\frac{\partial}{\partial x}, \qquad U_6 = y\frac{\partial}{\partial y}, \qquad U_8 = y\left(x\frac{\partial}{\partial x} + y\frac{\partial}{\partial y}\right)\right\}.$$

It may be interesting to observe how the regularity conditions are left unaffected under Lie group transformations. Theorem 7 summarizes the various cases: For instance, in Case (a), each of the conditions on the positivity of the marginal products of capital and labor and on the diminishing marginal product is invariant under the four-parameter Lie group whose basis is given by $\{U_3, U_5, U_6, U_8\}$.

Perhaps one of the most useful results from the practical estimation point of view is Theorem 8. The standard method of estimation of the elasticity of substitution is to use the formula

$$\sigma = \frac{\%\text{ change of } K - \%\text{ change of } L}{\%\text{ change of } w - \%\text{ change of } r}$$

(see Kendrick and Sato [1963]). This theorem shows that the method is still valid and unbiased if and only if technical change is a Lie (two-parameter) subgroup G_2, whose Lie algebra is given again by $L(G_2) = \{U_3, U_6\}$. (Compare this interpretation with the Remark at the end of the proof of Theorem 8.)

II. Comparative Statics under *r*-Parameter Infinitesimal Transformations

12. The second topic that we shall deal with in this chapter is the application of infinitesimal transformations to comparative static analysis of economic systems. Under certain conditions, comparative static analysis of an equilibrium system can be carried out in a most efficient and systematic way using Lie groups and related concepts. In many cases we may assume that the transformations form a group, more precisely a local Lie group of transformations. In the present work, however, we shall make less stringent assumptions on the transformations. Although many of the transformations which arise in actual applications may be groups of transformations, the group concept is *not* required for the investigation of comparative statics. We only require the related concept, the existence of the *r-parameter infinitesimal transformations* (*or generators*).[6]

[6] General mathematical properties of the r-parameter infinitesimal generators will be investigated in Chapter 7. Their applications to invariant optimal control problems and to economic conservation laws in particular, will be studied. See also Logan [1977].

Fundamental Equations of Comparative Statics

13. Consider a typical economic problem of maximization of a function

$$z = f(x), \qquad x = (x_1, \ldots, x_n), \qquad x_i \geqq 0, \tag{31}$$

subject to m constraints

$$g^j(x) \leqq b^j, \qquad b^j = \text{const}, \qquad j = 1, \ldots, m, \tag{32}$$

where $f(x)$ and $g^j(x)$ are smooth and single-valued functions of x with their continuous partial derivatives up to the desired order in a wide region. We choose f and g^j such that the second-order conditions are automatically satisfied. Thus, for instance, we may assume that f is strictly quasi-concave and that the g^j are all strictly convex. Now consider the situation that $f(x)$ and $g^j(x)$ are subject to the parametric change such that

$$f(x) \to f(x : \alpha), \tag{33-i}$$

$$g^j(x) \to g^j(x : \alpha), \tag{33-ii}$$

where $\alpha = (\alpha_1, \ldots, \alpha_r)$ is the vector of r essential parameters. We are interested in the comparative static analysis of displacement of equilibrium (Samuelson [1947, pp. 21–56]). The maximization problem after the parametric change is analyzed by formulating the Lagrangian with undetermined multipliers λ. Hence we have

$$h(x, \lambda : \alpha) = f(x : \alpha) + \sum_{j=1}^{m} \lambda^j [b^j - g^j(x : \alpha)]. \tag{34}$$

If we implicitly assume the positivity of the x_i and the existence of interior solutions, the Kuhn–Tucker first-order conditions become

$$\begin{aligned} h_i(x, \lambda : \alpha) &= \frac{\partial h}{\partial x_i} = f_i(x : \alpha) - \sum_{j=1}^{m} \lambda^j g_i^j(x : \alpha) = 0, \qquad i = 1, \ldots, n, \\ h_j(x : \alpha) &= \frac{\partial h}{\partial \lambda^j} = b^j - g^j(x : \alpha) = 0, \qquad j = 1, \ldots, m, \end{aligned} \tag{35}$$

where $f_i = \partial f / \partial x_i$ and $g_i^j = \partial g^j / \partial x_i$. Differentiating (35) with respect to the kth parameter,[7] we obtain

$$\begin{aligned} &\sum_{s=1}^{n} h_{ix_s} \frac{\partial x_s}{\partial \alpha_k} + \sum_{j=1}^{m} h_{i\lambda^j} \frac{\partial \lambda^j}{\partial \alpha_k} = -h_{i\alpha_k} \qquad (i = 1, \ldots, n), \\ &\sum_{s=1}^{n} h_{jx_s} \frac{\partial x_s}{\partial \alpha_k} = -h_{j\alpha_k} \qquad (j = 1, \ldots, m), \end{aligned} \tag{36}$$

[7] We may regard the b^j as a part of the α_k. Hence, in this case, the b^j are simply additive parametric change.

where $h_{ix_s} = \partial h_i/\partial x_s$, $h_i\lambda^j = \partial h_i/\partial\lambda^j$, $h_{jx_s} = \partial h_j/\partial x_s$, $h_{i\alpha_k} = \partial h_i/\partial\alpha_k$, $h_{j\alpha_k} = \partial h_j/\partial\alpha_k$, $i = 1,\ldots,n$, $j = 1,\ldots,m$. Expanding (36), we can rewrite the above as

$$\begin{bmatrix} f_{is} - \sum_{j=1}^{m} \lambda^j g^j_{is} & -g^j_i \\ -g^j_s & 0 \end{bmatrix} \begin{bmatrix} \partial x_s/\partial\alpha_k \\ \partial\lambda^j/\partial\alpha_k \end{bmatrix} = \begin{bmatrix} -h_{i\alpha_k} \\ -h_{j\alpha_k} \end{bmatrix}, \tag{36$'$}$$

where $f_{is} = \partial f_i/\partial x_s$, $g^j_{is} = \partial g^j_i/\partial x_s$ for i, $s = 1,\ldots,n$, $j = 1,\ldots,m$. Solving the above, we obtain the comparative static evaluations as

$$\begin{bmatrix} \partial x_s/\partial\alpha_k \\ \partial\lambda^j/\partial\alpha_k \end{bmatrix} = m_H \begin{bmatrix} -h_{i\alpha_k} \\ -h_{j\alpha_k} \end{bmatrix}, \tag{37}$$

where m_H is the inverse of the coefficient matrix of (36′). Hence, once $h_{i\alpha_k}$ and $h_{j\alpha_k}$ are known, $\partial x_s/\partial\alpha_k$ and $\partial\lambda^j/\partial\alpha_k$ are immediately derivable from (37).

The way in which the parameters α enter into (33) will certainly affect the values of $h_{i\alpha_k}$ and $h_{j\alpha_k}$, where[8]

$$h_{i\alpha_k} = \frac{\partial h_i}{\partial\alpha_k} = \frac{\partial f_i}{\partial\alpha_k} - \sum_{j=1}^{m} \lambda^j \frac{\partial g^j_i}{\partial\alpha_k}, \qquad h_{j\alpha_k} = \frac{\partial h_j}{\partial\alpha_k} = -\frac{\partial g^j}{\partial\alpha_k}. \tag{38}$$

Alternatively, we observe that the values of $h_{i\alpha_k}$ and $h_{j\alpha_k}$ depend on the way the first-order conditions (35) are affected by the parametric change of the essential parameters, i.e.,

$$h_i(x, \lambda) = 0 \to h_i(x, \lambda : \alpha) = 0, \qquad h_j(x) = 0 \to h_j(x : \alpha) = 0. \tag{39}$$

Let us assume that *the parametric change (in each of the h_i and h_j) specified by (39) is given by r-parameter transformations.* We then consider transformations, say due to technical change and taste change or due to any other exogenous impact such that

$$\begin{aligned} h_i(x_1,\ldots,x_n,\lambda:\alpha) &= h_i(\bar{x}^i_1,\ldots,\bar{x}^i_n,\lambda), \qquad & i &= 1,\ldots,n, \\ h_j(x_1,\ldots,x_n:\alpha) &= h_j(\bar{x}^j_1,\ldots,\bar{x}^j_n), & j &= 1,\ldots,m, \end{aligned} \tag{40}$$

where $\bar{x}^i_s$ and $\bar{x}^j_s$ are given by r-parameter transformations:

$$\begin{aligned} \bar{x}^i_s &= \phi^{is}(x_1,\ldots,x_n:\alpha), \\ \bar{x}^j_s &= \phi^{js}(x_1,\ldots,x_n:\alpha), \end{aligned} \qquad i, s = 1,\ldots,n, \quad j = 1,\ldots,m. \tag{41}$$

We may call the parametric change (40) under (41) the "*substitutional*" *parametric change under the r-parameter transformations* or simply the *r-parameter substitutional type*, since in (40) x_s in h_i and h_j are all substituted

[8] Here we are assuming that α_k is not equal to one of the b^j. Otherwise, the second equation of (38) will become $h_{j\alpha_k} = 1 - \partial g^j/\partial\alpha_k$ for one equation.

by $\bar{x}_s^i$ and $\bar{x}_s^j$ defined by (41). In many cases, $\bar{x}_s^i$ and $\bar{x}_s^j$ may actually satisfy the (r-parameter) Lie group properties so that the parametric change (40) is subjected to a Lie group transformation and is automatically the r-parameter substitutional type. This is certainly not necessary for our purpose. We simply assume *the existence of infinitesimal transformations* with α^0 being the set of parameters yielding the identical transformation[9] $\bar{x}_s^i = x_s^i$ and $\bar{x}_s^j = x_s^j$ ($x_s^i \equiv x_s^j = x_s$ for all i and j), i.e.,

$$X_i = \sum_{s=1}^{n} \xi_s^i \frac{\partial}{\partial x_s}, \qquad i = 1, \ldots, n,$$
$$X_j = \sum_{s=1}^{n} \xi_s^j \frac{\partial}{\partial x_s}, \qquad j = 1, \ldots, m, \tag{42}$$

where ξ_s^i and ξ_s^j are linear combinations of individual infinitesimal transformations with respect to each parameter $\alpha_1, \ldots, \alpha_r$,

$$\xi_s^i = \sum_{k=1}^{r} e_k^{is} \eta_k^{is} \qquad \text{and} \qquad \xi_s^j = \sum_{k=1}^{r} e_k^{js} \eta_k^{js}, \qquad e_k^{is}, e_k^{js} = \text{const}, \tag{43}$$

where $\eta_k^{is} = (\partial\phi^{is}(x:\alpha)/\partial\alpha_k)_{\alpha^0}$ and $\eta_k^{js} = (\partial\phi^{js}(x:\alpha)/\partial\alpha_k)_{\alpha^0}$, $k = 1, \ldots, r$. Hence X_i and X_j are infinitesimal transformations affecting the ith and the jth equations of the equilibrium conditions (35) ($i = 1, \ldots, n$, $j = 1, \ldots, m$). *Nothing has been said about the transformation affecting the original objective function* (33-i) *in general. Sometimes we may assume that without being contradictory to* (42) *the objective function is also subjected to an infinitesimal transformation*[10]

$$V = \sum_{s=1}^{n} \xi_s^v \frac{\partial}{\partial x_s}. \tag{44}$$

Let us now consider the comparative static evaluations due to changes in the kth parameter. The infinitesimal transformations due to changes only in the kth parameter in X_i and X_j are

$$X_i^k = \sum_{s=1}^{n} \eta_k^{is} \frac{\partial}{\partial x_s},$$
$$X_j^k = \sum_{s=1}^{n} \eta_k^{js} \frac{\partial}{\partial x_s}, \qquad i = 1, \ldots, n, \quad j = 1, \ldots, m, \quad k = 1, \ldots, r. \tag{45}$$

[9] We may look at (40) as $h_i(x, \lambda : \alpha) = h_i(\bar{x}^i, \bar{\lambda})$ and $h_j(x:\alpha) = h_j(\bar{x}^j)$ with $\lambda = \bar{\lambda}$. It is noted that in general the values of $\bar{x}_s$ entering into the ith equation and the lth equation $\bar{x}_s^i$ and $\bar{x}_s^l$ ($i, l = 1, \ldots, n$) are assumed to be different. They will be identical if α takes α^0 yielding the identical transformation $\bar{x}_s^i = x_s^i = \bar{x}_s^l = x_s^l = x_s$.

[10] Since the X_i are derived from the objective function and from the X_j, there may exist no V and X_i which are consistent with the given X_j. See the examples in Section 15, example (e).

Then we can immediately approximate (38) near the identity transformation as

$$
\begin{aligned}
h_{i\alpha_k}\Big|_{\alpha=\alpha^0} &= \frac{\partial h_i}{\partial \alpha_k}\Big|_{\alpha=\alpha^0} = X_i^k h_i = \sum_{s=1}^{n} \eta_k^{is}\frac{\partial h_i}{\partial x_s}, \qquad i = 1,\ldots,n, \\
h_{j\alpha_k}\Big|_{\alpha=\alpha^0} &= \frac{\partial h_j}{\partial \alpha_k}\Big|_{\alpha=\alpha^0} = X_j^k h_j = \sum_{s=1}^{n} \eta_k^{js}\frac{\partial h_j}{\partial x_s}, \qquad j = 1,\ldots,m.
\end{aligned}
\tag{46}
$$

Substituting (46) into (37), we get

$$
\begin{bmatrix} \dfrac{\partial x_s}{\partial \alpha_k} \\ \dfrac{\partial \lambda^j}{\partial \alpha_k} \end{bmatrix}_{\alpha=\alpha^0} = m_{H_{\alpha=\alpha^0}} \begin{bmatrix} -\sum\limits_{s=1}^{n} \eta_k^{is}\dfrac{\partial h_i}{\partial x_s} \\ -\sum\limits_{s=1}^{n} \eta_k^{js}\dfrac{\partial h_j}{\partial x_s} \end{bmatrix} = m_{H_{\alpha=\alpha^0}} \begin{bmatrix} -X_i^k h_i \\ -X_j^k h_j \end{bmatrix}. \tag{47}
$$

We shall call the above *the fundamental equations of comparative statics* when the equilibrium conditions are all subjected to the substitutional parametric change.

It is easy to evaluate the *total* effects of all parameters changing simultaneously by simply adding (47) and using (42). That is to say, we have

$$
\begin{bmatrix} \delta x_s = \sum\limits_{k=1}^{r} \dfrac{\partial x_s}{\partial \alpha_k} \\ \delta \lambda^j = \sum\limits_{k=1}^{r} \dfrac{\partial \lambda^j}{\partial \alpha_k} \end{bmatrix}_{\alpha=\alpha^0} = m_{H_{\alpha=\alpha^0}} \begin{bmatrix} -X_i h_i \\ -X_j h_j \end{bmatrix} = m_{H_{\alpha=\alpha^0}} \begin{bmatrix} -\sum\limits_{s=1}^{n} \xi_s^i \dfrac{\partial h_i}{\partial x_s} \\ -\sum\limits_{s=1}^{n} \xi_s^j \dfrac{\partial h_j}{\partial x_s} \end{bmatrix}, \tag{48}
$$

where e_k^{is} and e_k^{js} in ξ_s^i and ξ_s^j in (43) take unity.

In many cases it is possible to have

$$
V \equiv X_i \equiv X_j = X, \tag{49}
$$

in which the original parametric change in (33) and the parametric change in the first-order conditions are subjected to the same transformation. Then the comparative static evaluations in (47) is simply equal to

$$
\begin{bmatrix} \partial x_s/\partial \alpha_k \\ \partial \lambda^j/\partial \alpha_k \end{bmatrix}_{\alpha=\alpha^0} = m_{H_{\alpha=\alpha^0}} \begin{bmatrix} -Xh_i \\ -Xh_j \end{bmatrix}. \tag{50}
$$

We may also have cases in which $V = X_i = X \neq X_j$ or $V \neq X_i = X_j$, etc.

In summary, we present

Theorem 9 *(Fundamental Equations of Comparative Statics under r-Parameter Infinitesimal Transformations) If the first-order conditions are parametrically affected by the infinitesimal transformations* (42), *then the* *comparative static evaluations of the kth parameter change near the identity transformation are approximated by the fundamental equations of comparative statics* (47).

Comparative Statics of Demand Functions

14. Having established the general procedure in evaluating the partial derivatives, we shall now apply the method to demand analysis under taste change. Thus, let $U(x:\alpha)$ be the individual's utility function after taste change, where for simplicity we assume α is a scalar representing taste change caused by advertising and some other external forces. Demand functions of this individual for the x_i are optimal solutions to the problem

$$\max_x U(x:\alpha) \qquad \text{subject to} \quad \sum_{i=1}^{n} p_i x_i = I,$$

where p_i is the price of the ith commodity and I the income. The first-order conditions are

$$U_i - \lambda p_i = 0, \qquad i = 1, \ldots, n, \tag{51-i}$$

$$I - \sum_{i=1}^{n} p_i x_i = 0. \tag{51-ii}$$

Equations (51) are a special case of (35) when $j = 1$ (one constraint) and $r = 1$ (one parameter). Then (36) or (36′) becomes

$$\begin{bmatrix} U_{is} & -p_i \\ -p_s & 0 \end{bmatrix}\begin{bmatrix} \partial x_s/\partial\alpha \\ \partial\lambda/\partial\alpha \end{bmatrix} = \begin{bmatrix} -\partial U_i/\partial\alpha \\ \partial g/\partial\alpha \end{bmatrix} = \begin{bmatrix} -\partial U_i/\partial\alpha \\ 0 \end{bmatrix}, \qquad i, s = 1, \ldots, n,$$

where $g = \sum_{i=1}^{n} p_i x_i$ and $\partial g/\partial\alpha \equiv 0$ since the taste change does not affect the budget constraint (51-ii). Assuming that the utility function is strictly quasi-concave, we can solve for $\partial x_s/\partial\alpha$ and $\partial\lambda/\partial\alpha$ from

$$\begin{bmatrix} \partial x_s/\partial\alpha \\ \partial\lambda/\partial\alpha \end{bmatrix} = \begin{bmatrix} U_{is} & -p_i \\ -p_s & 0 \end{bmatrix}^{-1}\begin{bmatrix} -\partial U_i/\partial\alpha \\ 0 \end{bmatrix}.$$

Letting S_{is} be the Slutsky coefficients, we have

$$S_{is} = \frac{\lambda\Delta_{is}}{\Delta}, \qquad \Delta = \begin{vmatrix} U_{is} & U_i \\ U_s & 0 \end{vmatrix},$$

where the Δ_{is} are cofactors of Δ, $i, s = 1, \ldots, n$. Then the foregoing will be reduced to

$$\frac{\partial x_s}{\partial\alpha} = -\sum_{i=1}^{n} \Delta_{is}\frac{\partial U_i}{\partial\alpha}\bigg/\Delta = -\sum_{i=1}^{n} S_{is}\frac{\partial U_i}{\partial\alpha}\bigg/\lambda, \qquad s = 1, \ldots, n \tag{52-i}$$

$$\frac{\partial\lambda}{\partial\alpha} = \lambda\sum_{i=1}^{n} \Delta_{n+1,s}\frac{\partial U_i}{\partial\alpha}\bigg/\Delta. \tag{52-ii}$$

This is the basic equation of comparative statics for demand functions when they are subjected to an exogenous taste change.[11]

Let us assume that the marginal utility of the ith good is subjected to the ith infinitesimal transformation of taste change X_i $(i = 1, \ldots, n)$. Then, since we already have $X_j \equiv 0$ (no taste change in the budget constraint), (52) can be simply expressed as

$$\left.\frac{\partial x_s}{\partial \alpha}\right|_{\alpha=\alpha^0} = \left.\left(-\sum_{i=1}^{n} \Delta_{is} X_i U_i \Big/ \Delta\right)\right|_{\alpha=\alpha^0} = \left.\left(-\sum_{i=1}^{n} S_{is} X_i U_i \Big/ \lambda\right)\right|_{\alpha=\alpha^0}, \tag{53-i}$$

$$\left.\frac{\partial \lambda}{\partial \alpha}\right|_{\alpha=\alpha^0} = \left.\left(\lambda \sum_{i=1}^{n} \Delta_{n+1,s} X_i U_i \Big/ \Delta\right)\right|_{\alpha=\alpha^0}, \quad \text{where} \quad X_i U_i = \sum_{s=1}^{n} \eta^{is} \frac{\partial^2 U}{\partial x_s\, \partial x_i}. \tag{53-ii}$$

Concentrating our attention on $\partial x_s/\partial \alpha$, we can express (53-i) as

$$\left[\frac{\partial x_s}{\partial \alpha}\right]_{\alpha=\alpha^0} = -\frac{1}{\lambda}[S_{\alpha=\alpha^0}]\left(\begin{bmatrix} U_{11} & U_{12} & \cdots & U_{1n} \\ & 0 & & \\ & & & \end{bmatrix}\begin{bmatrix} \xi_1^1 \\ \xi_2^1 \\ \vdots \\ \xi_n^1 \end{bmatrix} + \begin{bmatrix} & 0 & & \\ U_{21} & U_{22} & \cdots & U_{2n} \\ & & & \\ & 0 & & \end{bmatrix}\begin{bmatrix} \xi_1^2 \\ \xi_2^2 \\ \vdots \\ \xi_n^2 \end{bmatrix} + \cdots + \begin{bmatrix} & 0 & & \\ & & & \\ & & & \\ U_{n1} & U_{n2} & \cdots & U_{nn} \end{bmatrix}\begin{bmatrix} \xi_1^n \\ \xi_2^n \\ \vdots \\ \xi_n^n \end{bmatrix}\right)\Bigg/_{\alpha=\alpha^0}. \tag{53-i$'$}$$

More compactly, we write

$$\frac{\partial x}{\partial \alpha} = -\frac{1}{\lambda} S\left(\sum_{i=1}^{n} M^i \xi^i\right), \qquad \text{where} \quad M_i = \begin{bmatrix} & 0 & & \\ U_{i1} & U_{i2} & \cdots & U_{in} \\ & 0 & & \end{bmatrix},$$

$$\xi^i = \begin{bmatrix} \xi_1^i \\ \vdots \\ \xi_n^i \end{bmatrix}, \quad \lambda = \text{scalar}, \quad \text{all quantities evaluated at } \alpha = \alpha^0.$$

[11] Equation (52) is in conformity with the results of Tintner [1951].

As a special case of the foregoing, when the marginal utilities U_i of all commodities are subjected to the same infinitesimal transformation of taste change

$$X_i = X_l = X = \sum_{s=1}^{n} \eta^s(x) \frac{\partial}{\partial x_s}, \qquad i, l = 1, \ldots, n, \tag{54}$$

then (53) is reduced to

$$\left.\frac{\partial x_s}{\partial \alpha}\right|_{\alpha=\alpha^0} = -\sum_{i=1}^{n} \left.\frac{\Delta_{is} X U_i}{\Delta}\right|_{\alpha=\alpha^0} = \left.\left(-\sum_{i=1}^{n} S_{is} X U_i \Big/ \lambda\right)\right|_{\alpha=\alpha^0}, \tag{55-i}$$

$$\left.\frac{\partial \lambda}{\partial \alpha}\right|_{\alpha=\alpha^0} = \left.\left(\lambda \sum_{i=1}^{n} \Delta_{n+1,s} X U_i \Big/ \Delta\right)\right|_{\alpha=\alpha^0}, \qquad \text{where} \quad X U_i = \sum_{s=1}^{n} \eta^s \frac{\partial^2 U}{\partial x_s\, \partial x_i}. \tag{55-ii}$$

Using (54), we can express the first part of the foregoing as

$$\begin{bmatrix} \partial x_1/\partial \alpha \\ \vdots \\ \partial x_n/\partial \alpha \end{bmatrix}_{\alpha=\alpha^0} = -\frac{1}{\lambda}[S_{\alpha=\alpha^0}][H^0_{\alpha=\alpha^0}] \begin{bmatrix} \eta^1 \\ \vdots \\ \eta^n \end{bmatrix}, \tag{56}$$

where S is the Slutsky matrix $\{S_{is}\}$ and H^0 the Hessian matrix $\{U_{is}\}$.

It is important to note that *nothing is said about the existence of an infinitesimal transformation V which applies to the utility function directly.*[12] In other words, although the existence of (53) automatically suggests the transformation of a taste change,

$$T: \quad U(x) \to U(x : \alpha), \tag{57}$$

T need not be, and usually is not, subjected to a parametric transformation like (40) and vice versa. Hence, although it is impossible to have taste change in the marginal utility functions U_i unless U itself is subjected to some kind of taste change, the taste change in U itself may not be the type suggested by (40). Conversely, even if U is subjected to an infinitesimal transformation of taste change V, the marginal utilities may not be subjected to any taste change of that type. Naturally, if taste change in U is of the r-parameter substitutional type with its infinitesimal transformation V and if the marginal

[12] After the work of this section had been completed, the author was informed of Ginsberg's work [1969] on this topic. However, the basic results of Ginsberg are unfortunately wrong since he always assumes $V \equiv X$. His example on p. 30 is incorrect because the direct differentiation $\partial x_1/\partial t$, $\partial x_2/\partial t$ does not yield the same result as that of a formula such as (56). Also, the Lie group assumption in his work is too strong for comparative statics analysis. See Example (d) in the next section.

utilities are subjected to the same type of taste change, then formula (56) can be applied with V substituted for X; i.e.,

$$\begin{bmatrix} \partial x_1/\partial\alpha \\ \vdots \\ \partial x_n/\partial\alpha \end{bmatrix}_{\alpha=\alpha^0} = -\frac{1}{\lambda}[S_{\alpha=\alpha^0}][H^0_{\alpha=\alpha^0}]\begin{bmatrix} \xi_1^v \\ \vdots \\ \xi_n^v \end{bmatrix}. \tag{58}$$

Examples

15. We now present a few examples:

(a) $(V = X_i = X)$ Let $V = \sum_{s=1}^n \partial/\partial x_s$ be the additive type; then the utility function after taste change is

$$U = U(x_1 + \alpha, x_2 + \alpha, \ldots, x_n + \alpha).$$

The first-order conditions after taste change are

$$U_i(x_1 + \alpha, x_2 + \alpha, \ldots, x_n + \alpha) - \lambda p_i = 0, \qquad U_i = \frac{\partial U}{\partial x_i}, \quad i = 1, \ldots, n.$$

Here the marginal utilities U_i for all i $(i = 1, \ldots, n)$ are subjected to the same type of taste change as the utility function; i.e.,

$$X_i = X = \sum_{s=1}^n \frac{\partial}{\partial x_s} = V.$$

Hence we have

$$\begin{bmatrix} \partial x_1/\partial\alpha \\ \vdots \\ \partial x_n/\partial\alpha \end{bmatrix}_{\alpha=0} = -\frac{1}{\lambda}[S_{\alpha=0}][H^0_{\alpha=0}]\begin{bmatrix} 1 \\ \vdots \\ 1 \end{bmatrix}.$$

This is a special case of (58) when $\xi_i^v = 1$ for all $i = 1, \ldots, n$.

(b) $(V \neq X_i = X)$ Let the utility function be given by a CES form, $U = x_1^{-\rho} + x_2^{-\rho}$. Assume that taste change takes place with

$$V = \frac{\partial}{\partial x_1} + \left(\frac{1+\rho}{\rho}\right) x_2 \frac{\partial}{\partial x_2},$$

which implies $\bar{x}_1 = x_1 + \alpha$, $\bar{x}_2 = e^{\alpha(1+\rho)/\rho}x_2$, yielding the utility function after taste change as $U = (x_1 + \alpha)^{-\rho} + e^{-\alpha(1+\rho)}x_2^{-\rho}$ $(\alpha = 0$, identity). The marginal utilities are

$$U_1 = -\rho(x_1 + \alpha)^{-\rho-1}, \qquad U_2 = -\rho e^{-\alpha(1+\rho)}x_2^{-\rho-1} = -\rho(e^{\alpha}x_2)^{-\rho-1}.$$

These may be considered as the result of continuous transformation of taste change with $X_i = X = \partial/\partial x_1 + x_2\,\partial/\partial x_2$ applied directly to the U_i. But X

is not the same as V as long as $\rho \neq +\infty$. The comparative static values of $\partial x_1/\partial\alpha$ and $\partial x_2/\partial\alpha$ are simply equal to

$$\begin{bmatrix} \partial x_1/\partial\alpha \\ \partial x_2/\partial\alpha \end{bmatrix}_{\alpha=0} = -\frac{1}{\lambda}[S_{\alpha=0}][H^0_{\alpha=0}]\begin{bmatrix} 1 \\ x_2 \end{bmatrix}.$$

(c) $(X_1 \neq X_2)$ Consider a utility function with taste changes, $U = U^1(x_1+\alpha) + (x_1+\alpha)x_2 + e^{-\alpha(1+\rho)}x_2^{-\rho}$. The marginal utilities are $U_1 = U^{1\prime}(x_1+\alpha) + x_2$ and $U_2 = (x_1+\alpha) - \rho(e^{\alpha}x_2)^{-\rho-1}$. U_1 may be considered as the result of application of $X_1 = \partial/\partial x_1$, while U_2 as the result of application of $X_2 = \partial/\partial x_1 + x_2\,\partial/\partial x_2$. $\partial x_1/\partial\alpha$ and $\partial x_2/\partial\alpha$ in this case are, from (53),

$$\begin{bmatrix} \partial x_1/\partial\alpha \\ \partial x_2/\partial\alpha \end{bmatrix}_{\alpha=0} = -\frac{1}{\lambda}[S_{\alpha=0}]\begin{bmatrix} X_1U_1 \\ X_2U_2 \end{bmatrix} = -\frac{1}{\lambda}[S_{\alpha=0}]\begin{bmatrix} U^{1\prime\prime} \\ 1+\rho(1+\rho)x_2^{-\rho-1} \end{bmatrix}.$$

(d) (V = *Lie Group*, $V \neq X_i$) Let the utility function be given by $U = x_1x_2$. Assume that there is a taste change of the rotation group in the utility function with the infinitesimal transformation $V = -x_2\,\partial/\partial x_1 + x_1\,\partial/\partial x_2$, yielding $\bar{x}_1 = x_1\cos\alpha - x_2\sin\alpha$, $\bar{x}_2 = x_1\sin\alpha + x_2\cos\alpha$. The utility function after taste change is

$$U = \bar{x}_1\bar{x}_2 = x_1^2\cos\alpha\sin\alpha + x_1x_2(\cos^2\alpha - \sin^2\alpha) - x_2^2\cos\alpha\sin\alpha.$$

The marginal utilities are

$$U_1 = 2x_1\cos\alpha\sin\alpha + x_2(\cos^2\alpha - \sin^2\alpha),$$
$$U_2 = x_1(\cos^2\alpha - \sin^2\alpha) - 2x_2\cos\alpha\sin\alpha.$$

The marginal utilities of x_1 and x_2 after taste change are not subjected to the same rotation type of infinitesimal transformation as V. The correct result obtained from the demand functions,[13]

$$x_1 = \frac{I[2p_1\cos\alpha\sin\alpha + p_2(\cos^2\alpha - \sin^2\alpha)]}{2p_1p_2(\cos^2\alpha - \sin^2\alpha) + 2(p_1^2 - p_2^2)\cos\alpha\sin\alpha},$$

$$x_2 = \frac{I[p_1(\cos^2\alpha - \sin^2\alpha) - 2p_2\cos\alpha\sin\alpha]}{2p_1p_2(\cos^2\alpha - \sin^2\alpha) + 2(p_1^2 - p_2^2)\cos\alpha\sin\alpha},$$

[13] This is the example used by Ginsberg [1969, p. 30], who erroneously applied a Lie group infinitesimal transformation to U_1 and U_2 when they do not form a Lie group. His result in our notation is

$$\frac{\partial x_1}{\partial\alpha} = \frac{I}{4p_2} + \frac{p_2I}{4p_1^2} \quad \text{and} \quad \frac{\partial x_2}{\partial\alpha} = -\frac{I}{4p_1} - \frac{p_1I}{4p_2^2},$$

which is obviously wrong. We may regard U_1 and U_2 after taste change as $U_1 = \bar{x}_2$ and $U_2 = \bar{x}_1$, where $\bar{x}_1 = -2x_2\cos\alpha\sin\alpha + x_1(\cos^2\alpha - \sin^2\alpha)$ and $\bar{x}_2 = 2x_1\cos\alpha\sin\alpha + x_2(\cos^2\alpha - \sin^2\alpha)$. Then the infinitesimal transformations are given by $X = -2x_2\,\partial/\partial x_1 + 2x_1\,\partial/\partial x_2$, which is different from the original transformation V applied to the utility function. The correct result can also be derived directly from $XU_1 = 2x_1$ and $XU_2 = -2x_2$, which confirms our basic theorem (Theorem 9).

is

$$\left.\frac{\partial x_1}{\partial \alpha}\right|_{\alpha=0} = \frac{I}{2p_2} + \frac{Ip_2}{2p_1^2} \qquad \text{and} \qquad \left.\frac{\partial x_2}{\partial \alpha}\right|_{\alpha=0} = -\frac{I}{2p_1} - \frac{Ip_1}{2p_2^2}.$$

(e) (*Nonexistence of V and No Utility Function, Although X Appears to Exist*) $U = x_1 x_2$, where $U_1 = x_2$, $U_2 = x_1$; we assume that we observe taste change in U_1 and U_2 such that $U_1 = e^{\alpha} x_2$, $U_2 = (x_1 + \alpha)$. Here $X = \partial/\partial x_1 + x_2\, \partial/\partial x_2$, but the above is not derived from any meaningful function, since there exists no utility function (*after* taste change) which generates $U_1 = e^{\alpha} x_2$, $U_2 = (x_1 + \alpha)$. To show this we check the integrability condition from $\partial U_1/\partial x_2 = U_{12} = e^{\alpha}$ and $\partial U_2/\partial x_1 = U_{21} = 1$ and find $U_{12} \neq U_{21}$ unless $\alpha = 0$.

(f) (*Holothetic Utility Functions*) If a utility function is *holothetic* under a certain (Lie type) taste change

$$V = \sum_{s=1}^{n} \xi_s^v \frac{\partial}{\partial x_s},$$

i.e.,

$$U = f(x) \rightarrow U = f(\bar{x}) = F(f(x), \alpha) = G_\alpha(f(x)), \qquad \bar{x} = \phi(x, \alpha),$$

then from the basic property of holotheticity, we have

$$\partial x_s/\partial \alpha \equiv 0 \qquad \text{for all} \quad s = 1, \ldots, n.$$

To study the case in which

$$\partial x_s/\partial \alpha \equiv 0 \qquad \text{for} \quad s = 1, \ldots, k, \qquad \partial x_t/\partial \alpha \neq 0 \qquad \text{for} \quad t = k+1, \ldots, n,$$

we may appeal to the *invariance theorem of Lie groups*. In particular, the case of a solitary increase in the want for x_k can be studied from the invariance conditions

$$X_s U_s = 0 \qquad \text{for} \quad s = 1, \ldots, n, \quad s \neq k \quad (X_k U_k \neq 0).$$

Once the X_s are given for which $X_s U_s = 0$, by solving a system of partial differential equations we may derive the underlying utility function which will generate $\partial x_i/\partial \alpha = -\lambda^{-1} S_{ik} X U_k$, where the S_{ik} are Slutsky terms (see Basmann [1954]).

Comparative Statics of Derived Demand

16. The comparative statics of derived demand correspond to the other extreme case of (33) in which, while the objective function (cost equation) is not subjected to a parametric transformation, the constraint function (production function) may be subjected to technical change. The first-order conditions for cost minimization require that

$$p_i - \lambda f_i(x:\alpha) = 0, \qquad i = 1,\ldots,n, \qquad Y - f(x:\alpha) = 0, \tag{59}$$

where Y is the output, x the vector of inputs, f the production function with the usual regularity conditions, and $f_i = \partial f/\partial x_i > 0$. Equations (59) are a special case of (35) when $j = 1$ (one constraint) and $r = 1$ (one parameter). Then (36) or (36′) becomes

$$\begin{bmatrix} f_{is} & f_i/\lambda \\ f_s & 0 \end{bmatrix} \begin{bmatrix} \partial x_s/\partial\alpha \\ \partial\lambda/\partial\alpha \end{bmatrix} = \begin{bmatrix} -f_{i\alpha} \\ -f_\alpha \end{bmatrix},$$

where $f_{i\alpha} = \partial f_i/\partial\alpha$ and $f_\alpha = \partial f/\partial\alpha$. Compared with the commodity demand functions, the last element of the right-hand side is not equal to zero. Solving the foregoing for $\partial x_s/\partial\alpha$ and $\partial\lambda/\partial\alpha$, we get

$$\begin{bmatrix} \partial x_s/\partial\alpha \\ \partial\lambda/\partial\alpha \end{bmatrix} = \begin{bmatrix} f_{is} & f_i/\lambda \\ f_s & 0 \end{bmatrix}^{-1} \begin{bmatrix} -f_{i\alpha} \\ -f_\alpha \end{bmatrix}.$$

Letting S_{is} be the Slutsky coefficients multiplied by λ, where $\lambda > 0$,

$$S_{is} = \frac{\lambda\,\Delta_{is}}{\Delta}, \qquad \Delta = \begin{vmatrix} f_{is} & f_i \\ f_s & 0 \end{vmatrix},$$

where the Δ_{is} are cofactors of Δ, $i, s = 1,\ldots,n$. The foregoing will be reduced to

$$\partial x_s/\partial\alpha = -\sum_{i=1}^{n} S_{is} f_{i\alpha} - S_{n+1,s} f_\alpha \tag{60-i}$$

($S_{n+1,s}$ = cofactors of Δ with respect to $n + 1$ and s divided by Δ),

$$\partial\lambda/\partial\alpha = -\lambda^{-1} \sum_{i=1}^{n} S_{i,n+1} f_{i\alpha} - \lambda^{-1} S_{n+1,n+1} f_\alpha. \tag{60-ii}$$

Let us now assume that technical progress in f is represented by the infinitesimal transformation

$$V = \sum_{s=1}^{n} \xi_s^f \frac{\partial}{\partial x_s}. \tag{61}$$

Then the operator X_j applied to the constraint function in (46) is equal to

$$X_j = V \qquad (j = 1, \text{ one constraint}).$$

Let us also assume that the marginal productivity functions f_i are also subjected to some kind of technical progress generated from V; i.e.,

$$X_i = \sum_{s=1}^{n} \xi_s^i \frac{\partial}{\partial x_s}, \qquad i = 1,\ldots,n. \tag{62}$$

From the examples in the last section we see that there is no reason to believe that the X_i always exist, and that even if the X_i exist they are not the same as V. When we have the special case

$$V = X_i = X,$$

our formula for (60) becomes

$$\left.\frac{\partial x_s}{\partial \alpha}\right|_{\alpha=\alpha^0} = -\sum_{i=1}^{n} S_{is} X f_i - S_{n+1,s} X f, \qquad 1 \leqq s \leqq n, \tag{63-i}$$

$$\left.\frac{\partial \lambda}{\partial \alpha}\right|_{\alpha=\alpha^0} = -\lambda\left(\sum_{i=1}^{n} S_{i,n+1} X f_i + S_{n+1,n+1} X f\right). \tag{63-ii}$$

In general, however, we must have

$$\left.\frac{\partial x_s}{\partial \alpha}\right|_{\alpha=\alpha^0} = -\sum_{i=1}^{n} S_{is} X_i f_i - S_{n+1,s} V f, \tag{64-i}$$

$$\left.\frac{\partial \lambda}{\partial \alpha}\right|_{\alpha=\alpha^0} = -\lambda\left(\sum_{i=1}^{n} S_{i,n+1} X_i f_i + S_{n+1,n+1} V f\right). \tag{64-ii}$$

By concentrating our attention on $\partial x_s/\partial \alpha$, we can rewrite (64) as

$$\left[\frac{\partial x_s}{\partial \alpha}\right]_{\alpha=\alpha^0} = -[S_{\alpha=\alpha^0}]\begin{bmatrix} X_1 f_1 \\ \vdots \\ X_n f_n \end{bmatrix} - Vf\begin{bmatrix} S_{n+1,1} \\ \vdots \\ S_{n+1,n} \end{bmatrix}. \tag{64-i'}$$

The reader can show that when $X_i = X_k = X$, the first part of the above will reduce to a similar expression as (56). The basic difference between the above and (53-i′) is that here the term involving Vf must be taken into consideration. Actually, it is easier to rewrite the first-order conditions by eliminating λ:

$$\begin{aligned} &R^i(x:\alpha) - \pi^i = 0, \qquad R^i = f_i/f_1, \qquad \pi^i = p_i/p_1, \qquad i = 2, \ldots, n, \\ &f(x:\alpha) - Y = 0. \end{aligned} \tag{65}$$

Differentiating (65) with respect to α, we obtain

$$\begin{bmatrix} R_1^i & R_2^i & \cdots & R_n^i \\ f_1 & f_2 & \cdots & f_n \end{bmatrix}\left[\frac{\partial x_s}{\partial \alpha}\right] = \begin{bmatrix} -\partial R^i/\partial \alpha \\ -\partial f/\partial \alpha \end{bmatrix}, \qquad R_s^i = \frac{\partial R^i}{\partial x_s}, \qquad \begin{matrix} i = 2, \ldots, n, \\ s = 1, \ldots, n, \end{matrix}$$

which can be solved to yield

$$\left[\frac{\partial x_s}{\partial \alpha}\right] = \begin{bmatrix} R_1^i & R_2^i & \cdots & R_n^i \\ f_1 & f_2 & \cdots & f_n \end{bmatrix}^{-1}\begin{bmatrix} -\partial R^i/\partial \alpha \\ -\partial f/\partial \alpha \end{bmatrix}.$$

If we assume infinitesimal transformations X_i $(i = 2, \ldots, n)$ and V operating on the marginal rates of substitution and on f in (65), the above can be expressed as

$$\left[\frac{\partial x_s}{\partial \alpha}\right]_{\alpha=\alpha^0} = [\tilde{R}_{\alpha=\alpha^0}]^{-1}\begin{bmatrix} -X_i R^i \\ -Vf \end{bmatrix}, \qquad i = 2, \ldots, n. \tag{64-i''}$$

This is an alternative formulation of (64-i′).

The case of *holothetic* technology under V corresponds to $X_i \equiv 0$ and $Vf = H(f)$. Hence, in this case we have

$$\frac{\partial x_s}{\partial \alpha} = -\tilde{R}_{sn} H(f), \qquad \tilde{R}_{sn} = \text{element of } (s, n) \text{ in } [\tilde{R}]^{-1}, \qquad s = 1, \ldots, n. \tag{66}$$

When the technology is homothetic and $V = \sum_{s=1}^{n} x_s\, \partial/\partial x_s$, we get

$$\frac{\partial}{\partial \alpha}\left(\frac{x_s}{x_r}\right) \equiv 0, \qquad \text{for} \quad s, r = 1, \ldots, n, \tag{67}$$

which is an alternative condition for "neutrality of technical change."

Derivation of Slutsky Equations

17. A word must be mentioned regarding the standard comparative static analysis of Slutsky equations. The first-order equilibrium conditions of utility maximization may be considered as r-parameter transformations with $p_1, \ldots, p_n$ and I being the $n + 1$ essential parameters. Thus, we have

$$\begin{aligned} h_i(x, \lambda : p, I) &= U_i(x) - \lambda p_i = 0, \qquad i = 1, \ldots, n, \\ h_{n+1}(x, \lambda : p, I) &= I - \sum_{i=1}^{n} p_i x_i = 0. \end{aligned} \tag{68}$$

Let p_i and I be represented by $e^{\alpha_i} = p_i$ and $e^{\beta} = I$. Then the h_i are expressed as $h_i = U_i(x) - e^{\alpha_i}\lambda = 0$, and h_{n+1} can be expressed as

$$h_{n+1}(x, \lambda : p, I) = e^{\beta} x_{n+1} - \sum_{i=1}^{n} e^{\alpha_i} x_i = 0,$$

where x_{n+1} is a dummy variable taking the value of unity $\equiv 1$. The infinitesimal transformations applied to h_{n+1} are, then,

$$V = \sum_{s=1}^{n+1} a_s x_s \frac{\partial}{\partial x_s}, \qquad a_s = \text{const}, \qquad s = 1, \ldots, n + 1, \tag{69}$$

while the h_i $(i = 1, \ldots, n)$ are subjected to

$$X_i = a_i \lambda \frac{\partial}{\partial \lambda}, \qquad i = 1, \ldots, n, \tag{70}$$

with the identical transformation $U_i - \lambda = 0$ and $\sum_{i=1}^{n} x_i = 1 = x_{n+1}$ when $\alpha_i = \beta = 0$. The total differentials of the h_i and h_{n+1} are

$$\begin{bmatrix} U_{ij} & -e^{\alpha_i} \\ -e^{\alpha_i} & 0 \end{bmatrix} \begin{bmatrix} dx_i \\ d\lambda \end{bmatrix} = \begin{bmatrix} -\dfrac{\partial h_i}{\partial \alpha_i} d\alpha_i \\ -\sum\limits_{i=1}^{n} \dfrac{\partial h_{n+1}}{\partial \alpha_i} d\alpha_i - \dfrac{\partial h_{n+1}}{\partial \beta} d\beta \end{bmatrix}.$$

Inverting the above, we get

$$\begin{bmatrix} dx_i \\ d\lambda \end{bmatrix} = \begin{bmatrix} U_{ij} & -e^{\alpha_i} \\ -e^{\alpha_i} & 0 \end{bmatrix}^{-1} \begin{bmatrix} -\dfrac{\partial h_i}{\partial \alpha_i} d\alpha_i \\ -\sum\limits_{i=1}^{n} \dfrac{\partial h_{n+1}}{\partial \alpha_i} d\alpha_i - \dfrac{\partial h_{n+1}}{\partial \beta} d\beta \end{bmatrix}.$$

The Slutsky equations are now readily obtained from the application of the infinitesimal transformations X_i and V to the h_i and h_{n+1}, respectively. Assume that only p_j changes, which means that $\alpha_j \neq 0$ and $\alpha_i = \beta = 0$, $i \neq j$ and $a_j \neq 0$, $a_s = 0$, $s \neq j$. Then the effects of changes in α_j alone are measured by

$$\frac{\partial h_j}{\partial \alpha_j} = X_j h_j = a_j \lambda \frac{\partial h_j}{\partial \lambda} = -a_j \lambda \tag{71}$$

and by

$$\frac{\partial h_{n+1}}{\partial \alpha_j} = V h_{n+1} = a_j x_j \frac{\partial h_{n+1}}{\partial x_j} = -a_j x_j. \tag{72}$$

Then we get the Slutsky equations as

$$\begin{bmatrix} \partial x_i/\partial \alpha_j \\ \partial \lambda/\partial \alpha_j \end{bmatrix} = \begin{bmatrix} U_{ij} & -1 \\ -1 & 0 \end{bmatrix}^{-1} \begin{bmatrix} 0 \\ \vdots \\ a_j \lambda \\ \vdots \\ 0 \\ \vdots \\ a_j x_j \end{bmatrix}, \qquad i, j = 1, \ldots, n. \tag{73}$$

By setting $a_j = 1$, we obviously get

$$\frac{\partial x_i}{\partial p_j} = \frac{\partial x_i}{\partial \alpha_j} = \frac{\lambda\, \Delta_{ji}}{\Delta} + \frac{x_j\, \Delta_{n+1,i}}{\Delta}, \qquad \text{where } \Delta = \begin{vmatrix} U_{ij} & -1 \\ -1 & 0 \end{vmatrix},$$

and the Δ_{ij} are cofactors of Δ. The last term can be replaced from income effect,

$$\begin{bmatrix} \partial x_i/\partial \beta \\ \partial \lambda/\partial \beta \end{bmatrix} = \begin{bmatrix} U_{ij} & -1 \\ -1 & 0 \end{bmatrix}^{-1} \begin{bmatrix} 0 \\ \vdots \\ -a_{n+1} \end{bmatrix}, \qquad \frac{\partial h_{n+1}}{\partial \beta} = a_{n+1} x_{n+1} \frac{\partial x_{n+1}}{\partial x_{n+1}} = a_{n+1},$$

$$\alpha_i = a_i = 0, \quad i = 1, \ldots, n, \tag{74}$$

by $\partial x_i/\partial \beta = -\Delta_{n+1,i}/\Delta$, $a_{n+1} = 1$ to yield

$$\frac{\partial x_i}{\partial p_j} = \lambda S_{ji} - x_j \left.\frac{\partial x_i}{\partial I}\right|_{\alpha_i = 0}. \tag{75}$$

The derivation of Slutsky equations using infinitesimal transformations seems much more difficult, but the purpose of this exercise is just to show that our general method works in a variety of comparative static analyses.[14]

Observable Market Behavior and Comparative Statics

18. Finally, comparative static analysis may be presented from the point of view of observable market behavior. Thus we may observe the marginal rates of substitution between factor inputs which include the effects of technical change. This gives a system of partial differential equations, yielding the underlying production function with technical progress if the integrability conditions are satisfied. Once $f(x, \alpha)$ is recovered, formula (64) may be used to study the comparative static evaluations of $\partial x/\partial \alpha$. The following example may illustrate the procedure: If we observe $f_1/f_2 = p_1/p_2 = e^\alpha x_2/(x_1 + \alpha)$, then the underlying production function is derived from $-dx_2/dx_1 = e^\alpha x_2/(x_1 + \alpha)$, yielding the production function

$$Y = \log(x_1 + \alpha) + e^{-\alpha} \log x_2,$$

which is a variant of the Cobb–Douglas function when $\alpha = 0$. The above may be considered as generated from $\log x_1 + \log x_2$ and from

$$V = \frac{\partial}{\partial x_1} - \log x_2 \frac{\partial}{\partial \log x_2}.$$

[14] The constancy (invariance) of the marginal utility of income may effectively be analyzed by Lie groups and the related concepts (see Samuelson [1947]).

Here the infinitesimal transformation applied to the marginal rate of substitution is given by

$$X = \frac{\partial}{\partial x_1} + x_2 \frac{\partial}{\partial x_2}, \qquad \text{yielding} \quad R = \frac{e^{\alpha} x_2}{x_1 + \alpha}.$$

III. Integrability Conditions

Marginal Rates of Substitution and Infinitesimal Generators

19. In Chapter 2, Part VII, it is shown that the simultaneous holotheticity and compatibility conditions can alternatively be interpreted as the well-known integrability conditions in economic analysis. In this section, we elaborate the assertion by studying the theory of utility and demand in the framework of Lie's theory of continuous transformations, in particular, infinitesimal transformations. This section serves as an introduction to a more rigorous approach to the problem studied in Chapter 9.

Consider the standard utility maximization problem under the budget constraint. The consumer's preferences are represented by a differentiable, strictly quasi-concave utility function $U : \mathbb{R}^n_+ \to \mathbb{R}$; i.e.,

$$U = U(x) \tag{76}$$

with $U_i > 0$ and with other regularity conditions. The budget constraint is given by

$$I = \sum_{i=1}^{n} p_i x_i. \tag{77}$$

Utility maximization under the budget constraint means that

$$\frac{p_j}{p_n} = \frac{U_j(x)}{U_n(x)} = r^j(x), \qquad j = 1, \ldots, n-1. \tag{78}$$

Solving for the x_i $(i = 1, \ldots, n)$ using (77) and (78), one can obtain the demand functions (or demand-quantity functions (Hurwicz [1971])),

$$x_i = f^i(p, I) \qquad (i = 1, \ldots, n). \tag{79}$$

The equation system (78) represents a relationship between the utility function U and the inverse demand (vector) functions $r = (r^1, \ldots, r^{n-1})$ generated by U from satisfaction maximization. This relationship can be exploited in two ways. When U is known, (78) enables one to obtain $r(x)$ and, thus, together with the budget constraint, to derive the demand functions

(79). On the other hand, one may consider (78) as the initial datum derived from observable market behavior of the consumer. The system (78) provides us with a test criterion as to whether r could have been generated from some utility function. In the affirmative case when the integrability conditions are satisfied, it is possible to "recover" an underlying utility function U from the knowledge of $r(x)$.[15]

With Antonelli [1886], Samuelson [1947, 1950], and Hurwicz [1971], we can look at the equilibrium conditions (78) as a system of linear partial differential equations

$$\frac{\partial U}{\partial x_j} - r^j(x)\frac{\partial U}{\partial x_n} = 0, \qquad j = 1, \ldots, n-1. \tag{78'}$$

Define $n-1$ unconnected infinitesimal transformations (or generators):

$$X_j = \sum_{s=1}^{n} \xi_j^s \frac{\partial}{\partial x_s} = \sum_{k=1}^{n-1} \delta_{jk}\frac{\partial}{\partial x_k} - r^j(x)\frac{\partial}{\partial x_n}, \qquad j = 1, \ldots, n-1, \tag{80}$$

where δ_{jk} is the Kronecker delta, the infinitesimal transformation of x_n is equal to $-r^j(x)$, and the infinitesimal transformation of x_k is equal to 1 $(j = k)$ or zero $(j \neq k)$. Then Eq. (80) can be considered as the transformations defining $n-1$ different types of exogenous "taste" change occurring simultaneously. Hence, the jth type of taste change X_j $(j = 1, \ldots, n-1)$ has the property that the jth commodity is subjected to additive type of taste change, and the nth commodity (considered as a kind of numéraire) is subjected to a type represented by its infinitesimal transformation $-r^j(x)$, while the kth commodity $(k \neq j, k = 1, \ldots, n-1)$ has no taste change.[16]

Suppose we are interested in deriving a utility function simultaneously holothetic under (80). First, the holotheticity condition (or invariance condition) under each type of taste change requires that

$$\begin{aligned} X_j U &= \sum_{k=1}^{n=1} \delta_{jk}\frac{\partial U}{\partial x_k} - r^j(x)\frac{\partial U}{\partial x_n} = 0 \\ &= \frac{\partial U}{\partial x_j} - r^j(x)\frac{\partial U}{\partial x_n} = 0, \qquad j = 1, \ldots, n-1. \end{aligned} \tag{81}$$

[15] In this chapter we intend to present a more general and rigorous analysis of integrability conditions and related concepts which may be useful to study the general theory of observable market behavior. Nothing, however, will be said about the methodology of actually recovering the underlying functions. This topic deserves an independent analysis, a part of which has already been accomplished by Scheraga [1979].

[16] Alternatively we may look at (80) as the infinitesimal transformations of the $n-1$ one-parameter Lie groups. This is certainly not necessary.

But this is exactly identical with (78′). Hence *the system of partial differential equations for the marginal rates of substitution represents nothing but the holotheticity condition of the utility function under* $n - 1$ *unconnected infinitesimal transformations of taste change.*

Compatibility and Integrability Conditions

20. We now look for the simultaneous holotheticity conditions of (81). Define the following Lie bracket (or "alternant" or "commutator").[17]

$$[X_a, X_b] \equiv X_a X_b - X_b X_a = \sum_{s=1}^{n} (X_a \xi_b^s - X_b \xi_a^s) \frac{\partial}{\partial x_s}, \quad a, b = 1, \ldots, n-1. \tag{82}$$

The necessary and sufficient condition for simultaneous holotheticity requires that (81) *constitute a complete system* (*Appendix, Part* V). The condition for a complete system is nothing but the condition that the above Lie bracket satisfies the conditions

$$[X_a, X_b] = \sum_{c=1}^{n-1} \gamma_{ab}^c X_c \qquad (a, b = 1, \ldots, n-1), \tag{83}$$

where the γ are functions of x. Since (81) is already written in the form of a standard system, the γ in (81) must be identically equal to zero, which constitutes a *complete Jacobian system* (see the Appendix and Eisenhart [1933, p. 8]). Hence the necessary and sufficient condition for simultaneous holotheticity of the utility function under $n - 1$ unconnected different types of taste change is

$$[X_a, X_b] \equiv 0. \tag{84}$$

Calculating (84) as

$$[X_a, X_b] = \left(\frac{\partial \cdot 1}{\partial x_a} - r^a \frac{\partial \cdot 1}{\partial x_n}\right) \frac{\partial}{\partial x_a} + \left(\frac{\partial \cdot 1}{\partial x_b} - r^b \frac{\partial \cdot 1}{\partial x_n}\right) \frac{\partial}{\partial x_b}$$
$$+ \left\{\left(\frac{\partial(-r^b)}{\partial x_a} - r^a \frac{\partial(-r^b)}{\partial x_n}\right) - \left(\frac{\partial(-r^a)}{\partial x_b} - r^b \frac{\partial(-r^a)}{\partial x_n}\right)\right\} \frac{\partial}{\partial x_n}$$

[17] Chipman's [1971] comment in the footnote to Antonelli's article [1886, p. 346, footnote 39] referring to Eisenhart's book [1933] and to the "Poisson operator" may be the first explicit reference to the so-called Lie bracket (operator) in the economic literature. However, Eisenhart's use of the term "Poisson operator" may not be appropriate in the present context, since the Poisson operator usually is defined in a more general framework such as in Hamiltonian dynamics (see Chapter 9).

and since the first two terms are equal to zero, we get

$$[X_a, X_b] = \left(-\frac{\partial r^b}{\partial x_a} + r^a \frac{\partial r^b}{\partial x_n} + \frac{\partial r^a}{\partial x_b} - r^b \frac{\partial r^a}{\partial x_n} \right) \frac{\partial}{\partial x_n}, \tag{84'}$$

which must be identically zero; i.e., from (84) and

$$\frac{\partial r^b}{\partial x_a} - r^a \frac{\partial r^b}{\partial x_n} = \frac{\partial r^a}{\partial x_b} - r^b \frac{\partial r^a}{\partial x_n}, \qquad a, b = 1, \ldots, n-1. \tag{85}$$

But this is nothing but the well-known integrability conditions of Antonelli [1886, Eq. (21b)] and Samuelson [1947, Chapter V, Eq. (14)]. Calculating

$$\frac{\partial r^b}{\partial x_a} = \frac{U_n U_{ba} - U_b U_{na}}{U_n^2}, \qquad \frac{\partial r^a}{\partial x_b} = \frac{U_n U_{ab} - U_a U_{nb}}{U_n^2},$$

$$\frac{\partial r^b}{\partial x_n} = \frac{U_n U_{bn} - U_b U_{nn}}{U_n^2}, \qquad \frac{\partial r^a}{\partial x_n} = \frac{U_n U_{an} - U_a U_{nn}}{U_n^2}, \qquad a, b = 1, \ldots, n-1,$$

we can show that (85) is always satisfied if and only if

$$U_{rs} = U_{sr}, \qquad r, s = 1, \ldots, n, \tag{85'}$$

i.e., the symmetry condition of the Hessian matrix of U.

The associated partial differential equation system (Eisenhart [1933]) of (78′) is represented by

$$\partial x_n / \partial x_j = -r^j(x), \qquad j = 1, \ldots, n-1, \tag{86}$$

which has the corresponding *total* differential equation

$$dx_n = -\sum_{j=1}^{n-1} r^j(x)\, dx_j. \tag{87}$$

We can study the properties of the original system (78′) by its associated partial differential equation system (86) or (87). This is exactly the procedure followed by Samuelson [1950].

21. Another connection between infinitesimal transformations and demand theory can be investigated in terms of an indirect utility function. Roy's identity states that

$$x_i = f^i(p, I) = -\frac{\partial V}{\partial p_i} \Big/ \frac{\partial V}{\partial I}, \qquad i = 1, \ldots, n, \tag{88}$$

where V, the indirect utility function, is defined as

$$V(p, I) = \max_x U(x) \qquad \text{subject to (77)} \tag{89}$$

Rewriting (88) as

$$\frac{\partial V}{\partial p_i} + f^i(p, I)\frac{\partial V}{\partial I} = 0, \qquad i = 1, \ldots, n, \tag{88$'$}$$

we can again look at (88) as the invariance conditions of *a system of n unconnected infinitesimal transformations of taste change defined by*

$$Y_i = \frac{\partial}{\partial p_i} + f^i(p, I)\frac{\partial}{\partial I} = \sum_{k=1}^{n} \delta_{ik}\frac{\partial}{\partial p_k} + f^i(p, I)\frac{\partial}{\partial I}, \qquad i = 1, \ldots, n. \tag{90}$$

Formally, (90) is exactly identical with (80). The necessary and sufficient condition for simultaneous holotheticity for this case is that the Lie bracket satisfy

$$[Y_a, Y_b] \equiv 0, \qquad a, b = 1, \ldots, n. \tag{91}$$

[Equation (90) is already in a standard form; see the Appendix.] Hence the integrability conditions are

$$[Y_a, Y_b] = \left(\frac{\partial f^b}{\partial p_a} + x^a\frac{\partial f^b}{\partial I} - \frac{\partial f^a}{\partial p_b} - x^b\frac{\partial f^a}{\partial I}\right)\frac{\partial}{\partial I} = 0, \qquad a, b = 1, \ldots, n,$$

which implies

$$\frac{\partial f^b}{\partial p_a} + x^a\frac{\partial f^b}{\partial I} = \frac{\partial f^a}{\partial p_b} + x^b\frac{\partial f^a}{\partial I} \tag{92}$$

or

$$S_{ab} = S_{ba}, \qquad a, b = 1, \ldots, n, \tag{92$'$}$$

where the S_{ab} are the Slutsky substitution effects. This is the well-known symmetry condition of the Slutsky matrix. The associated system of partial differential equations of (88′) is

$$\frac{\partial I}{\partial p_i} = f^i(p, I), \qquad i = 1, \ldots, n, \tag{93}$$

which is the counterpart of (88) (see McKenzie [1957]). This system is completely integrable if and only if (92) is met, yielding the indirect utility function $V(p, I)$.[18] A system (93) can also be solved by its related total differential equation

$$dI = \sum_{i=1}^{n} f^i(p, I)\, dp_i. \tag{94}$$

In summary, we obtain

Theorem 10 *(Integrability Conditions and the Lie Bracket)* (a) *Direct Utility Function*

(i) *The marginal rates of substitution may alternatively be looked at as $n - 1$ unconnected infinitesimal transformations representing "taste change."*
(ii) *The equilibrium conditions (78) may be considered as the simultaneous holotheticity (invariance) conditions of the $n - 1$ unconnected types of taste change.*
(iii) *The necessary and sufficient conditions for simultaneous holotheticity are identical with the integrability conditions.*

(b) *Indirect Utility Function*

(i) *The demand functions may alternatively be looked at as n unconnected infinitesimal transformations.*
(ii) *Roy's identity may be considered as the simultaneous holotheticity (invariance) and compatibility conditions of the n unconnected infinitesimal generators of taste change.*
(iii) *The necessary and sufficient conditions for compatibility of n unconnected infinitesimal transformations are exactly identical with the symmetry conditions of the Slutsky matrix.*

22. A brief mention must be made regarding the behavior of the firm. It is already shown that the marginal rates of substitution functions between the ith and the jth inputs constitute the invariance condition. Hence, the mathematical recoverability of the underlying production function from the marginal rates of substitution requires the same integrability conditions as

[18] By formulating the Lagrangian $L = U(x) + \lambda(I - px)$, one can write the equilibrium condition of the original problem as $X_i L = \partial L/\partial x_i + p_i\, \partial L/\partial \lambda = 0$, $i = 1, \ldots, n$, where $X_i = \partial/\partial x_i + p_i\, \partial/\partial \lambda$ $(i = 1, \ldots, n)$. This is exactly the counterpart of (90), where p_i is replaced by x_i, f^i by p_i, and I by λ. This formulation will enable us to compare the original and its dual in a completely symmetric form:

U (*Direct*)		V (*Indirect*)
$X_i = (\partial/\partial x_i) + p_i\, \partial/\partial \lambda$	$i = 1, \ldots, n$	$Y_i = (\partial/\partial p_i) + x_i\, \partial/\partial I$
$[X_a, X_b] = 0 \Leftrightarrow U_{ab} = U_{ba}$	$a, b = 1, \ldots, n$	$[Y_a, Y_b] = 0 \Leftrightarrow S_{ab} = S_{ba}$

Eq. (84) $[X_a, X_b] = 0$. On the other hand, *the counterpart of Roy's identity in the production and cost functions is Shephard's lemma*[19]

$$\frac{\partial C}{\partial p_i} = x^i(p, Y) \tag{95}$$

which is the simultaneous holotheticity condition of the infinitesimal transformations

$$X_i = \frac{\partial}{\partial p_i} - x^i \frac{\partial}{\partial C}, \qquad i = 1, \ldots, n. \tag{96}$$

The integrability conditions are stated as

$$[X_a, X_b] = 0 \quad \Leftrightarrow \quad \frac{\partial x^b}{\partial p_a} - x^a \frac{\partial x^b}{\partial C} = \frac{\partial x^a}{\partial p_b} - x^b \frac{\partial x^a}{\partial C}$$

which are equal to

$$\frac{\partial x^b}{\partial p_a} = \frac{\partial x^a}{\partial p_b} \quad \Leftrightarrow \quad S_{ab} = S_{ba}, \qquad a, b = 1, \ldots, n, \tag{97}$$

since $\partial x^b/\partial C = \partial x^a/\partial C \equiv 0$.

REFERENCES

Antonelli, G. B. [1886]. Sulla teoria matematica dell'economia politica, pisa, tipografia del folchetto, Reprinted English translation on the mathematical theory of political economy, in *Preferences, Utility, and Demand* (J. Chipman *et al.*, eds.). Harcourt, New York, 1971.

Arrow, K., Chenery, H., Minhas, B., and Solow, R. [1961]. Capital-labor substitution and economic efficiency, *Review of Economics and Statistics*, **43**, 225–250.

Basmann, R. L. [1954]. A note on an invariant property of shifts in demand, *Metroeconomica*, **6**, 69–71.

Chipman, J. [1971]. Introduction to part II, in *Preferences, Utility, and Demand* (J. Chipman *et al.*, eds.), Harcourt, New York.

Eisenhart, L. P. [1933]. *Continuous Groups of Transformations.* Princeton Univ. Press, Princeton, New Jersey. Reprint, Dover, New York, 1961.

Gahlem, B. [1972]. *Der Informationsgehalt der Neoklassischen Wachstumstheorie für Wirtschaftspolitik.* Mohr, Tübingen.

Ginsberg, P. M. [1969]. Consumption theory under variable preferences, Ph.D. Dissertation, Purdue University, Lafayette, Indiana.

Harrod, R. F. [1948]. *Towards a Dynamic Economics.* Macmillan, London.

Hicks, J. R. [1963]. *The Theory of Wages*, 2nd ed. Macmillan, London.

[19] Hotelling's lemma can also be considered as the equations generating infinitesimal transformations for the profit function.

Hurwicz, L. [1971]. On the problem of integrability of demand functions, in *Preferences, Utility, and Demand* (J. Chipman *et al.*, eds.), Harcourt, New York.

Kendrick, J. W., and Sato, R. [1963]. Factor prices, productivity and economic growth, *American Economic Review*, **53**, 974–1000.

Logan, J. D. [1977]. *Invariant Variational Principles*, Mathematics in Science and Engineering, Vol. 138. Academic Press, New York.

Lie, S. [1888]. *Theorie der Transformationgruppen*, u. Mitw. v. F. Engel, Vol. 1, Teubner, Leipzig. Reprinted by Chelsea, New York, 1970.

McKenzie, L. W. [1956–1957]. Demand theory without a utility index, *Review of Economic Studies*, **24**, 185–189.

Nôno, T. [1971]. A classification of neutral technical changes: An application of Lie theory, *Bulletin of Fukuoka University of Education*, **20**, 47–62.

Robinson, J. [1962]. *Essays in the Theory of Economic Growth*. Macmillan, London.

Rose, H. [1968]. The condition for factor augmenting technical change, *Economic Journal*, **78**, 966–971.

Samuelson, P. A. [1947]. *Foundations of Economic Analysis*. Harvard Univ. Press, Cambridge, Massachusetts.

Samuelson, P. A. [1950]. The problem of integrability in utility theory, *Economica*, **17**, 355–385.

Sato, R. [1970]. The estimation of biased technical progress and the production function. *International Economic Review*, **11**, 179–208.

Sato, R., and Beckmann, M. J. [1968]. Neutral inventions and production functions, *Review of Economic Studies*, **35**, 57–66; An Addendum, **35**, 366 [1968].

Sato, R., and Beckmann, M. J. [1975]. A note on economic growth, technical progress and the production function, *Jahrbüchern für Nationalökonomie und Statistik*, Band 189, Heft 1/2.

Scheraga, J. [1979]. A Systematic Methodology for the Solution of the Integrability Problems. Department of Economics, Brown University, Providence, Rhode Island.

Solow, R. M. [1957]. Technical change and the aggregate production function, *Review of Economics and Statistics*, **39**, 312–320.

Solow, R. M. [1962]. Technical progress, capital formation, and economic growth, *American Economic Review, Proceedings*, pp. 76–86.

Tintner, G. [1951]. Complementarity and shifts in demand, *Metroeconomica*, **4**, 1–4.

Uzawa, H. [1961]. Neutral inventions and the stability of growth equilibrium, *Review of Economic Studies*, **28**, 117–124.

CHAPTER 5

HOLOTHETICITY OF AN IMPLICIT TECHNOLOGY

I. Introduction and Motivation

1. Recent interest in implicit production and demand models has increased substantially as a result of the finding that implicit production (utility) structure play a central role in the rapidly expanding literature on dual functional structures, cost of living indices, production and cost analysis, implicit technical change, and aggregation problems.[1]

In this chapter we wish to show that there is a consistent and systematic way of generating implicit technology from a Lie type of technical change. Under certain conditions, the "implicit" formulation is shown to be the best approach to the study of the nonhomotheticity structure (Sato [1977b]). By defining an implicitly holothetic technology as that type of technology which is invariant under the twice-extend group of a Lie type of technical progress, one can formulate several useful theorems, one of which is the *nonexistence* theorem of technical change. In contrast to an "explicit" technology, it is in general impossible to find Lie types of technical change under which an implicit technology is holothetic. Even if an implicit technology is holothetic under several Lie types of technical change, this number

[1] Excellent presentations and extensions of much of this literature are available in Blackorby and Russell [1976], Blackorby *et al.* [1978]. Also see Gorman [1970], McFadden [1978], Diewert [1974], Hanoch [1975], Sato [1975a, 1977a], and Barnett *et al.* [1979]. Technical change in implicit technologies was first studied by Sato and Krelle [1975]. Parts of this chapter are based on my earlier papers (Sato [1975b, 1977b]).

is limited. Hence, by classifying implicit technologies according to the number of ways under which they are holothetic, one can analyze the structure of implicit technology in the most efficient manner.

2. Consider as an example a family of implicit CES production functions with two factor inputs, capital K and labor L (see Sato [1975a, 1977a]):

$$F[C_1(Y), C_2(Y), K, L] = C_1(Y)K^{-\rho} + C_2(Y)L^{-\rho} - 1 = 0, \quad \rho = \sigma^{-1} - 1.$$

In general, $C_1(Y)$ and $C_2(Y)$ are two independent functions of Y, and therefore Y *cannot* in general be written in an explicit form. This is not surprising, since the preceding form of the general CES family is a solution derived from the *second-order* differential equation which defines the constancy of the elasticity of substitution. Here $C_1(Y)$ and $C_2(Y)$ are derived as arbitrary constants of integration of the second-order differential equation in K and L. Unless we have a priori knowledge concerning $C_1(Y)$ and $C_2(Y)$, it is in general impossible to write the solution for Y in explicit form. For instance, C_1 may be proportionate to C_2 so that $C_2(Y) = aC_1(Y)$, which reduces the foregoing solution to a homothetic (explicit) CES case. Alternatively, either C_1 or C_2 may be constant, which reduces it to a separable (explicit) family, etc. (see Sato [1974]). But the very fact that there exist *two* (different) functions $C_1(Y)$ and $C_2(Y)$ makes it impossible to write the general class of CES functions in an explicit form.

Although an implicit formulation of a production function may *not* necessarily require the formulation with two different functions of Y, such as

$$F[C_1(Y), C_2(Y), K, L] = 0,$$

for our purpose we shall always write an implicit production function in this form. This is convenient because we always regard an implicit production function as a general solution of a second order differential equation in K and L with two arbitrary constants. As in the case of explicit formulation, it will be seen that the concept of (implicit) holotheticity is essential for the analysis of invariance properties of an implicit production function.

II. Implicit Formulation of a Technology Holothetic under a Given Lie Type of Technical Progress

3. We begin with definitions.

Definition 1 (*Implicit Technology*) A technology is said to be implicit if it can be regarded as a solution of a second-order differential equation in K and L.

Thus, given a second-order differential equation defining an economically meaningful relationship among K, L, dL/dK, and d^2L/dK^2 such that

$$h(K, L, dL/dK, d^2L/dK^2) = 0, \tag{1}$$

there exists a unique solution

$$F[C_1(Y), C_2(Y), K, L] = 0, \tag{2}$$

provided (1) satisfies certain continuity and Lipschitz conditions. Here $C_1(Y)$ and $C_2(Y)$ are constants of integration determined by initial conditions (Ince [1956, pp. 61–81]). Hence Eq. (2) is an implicit technology as already defined.

Another way of looking at this is to reverse the process of finding (2). Thus, suppose a family of production function of the type expressed by Eq. (2) is given, where C_1 and C_2 are the two essential parameters. The marginal rate of substitution between K and L at a given output $Y = \text{const}$ in (2) is

$$-\left.\frac{dL}{dK}\right|_{Y=\text{const}} = \frac{\partial Y/\partial K}{\partial Y/\partial L} = \frac{\partial F/\partial K}{\partial F/\partial L} = R(C_1(Y), C_2(Y), K, L) \geqq 0. \tag{3}$$

The law of diminishing (nonincreasing) marginal rate of substitution requires that

$$-(d^2L/dK^2)|_{Y=\text{const}} = dR/dK = M(C_1(Y), C_2(Y), K, L, dL/dK) \leqq 0. \tag{4}$$

Using (2)–(4), we can eliminate $C_1(Y)$ and $C_2(Y)$ to obtain the second-order differential equation (1). We may call (1) simply *the differential equation of the implicit technology*. It is seen that *if an implicit technology is given in the form of* (2), *then there exists a unique differential equation of the second order for that technology. Hence the properties of an implicit technology can be completely described by its differential equation.*

Recall that in Chapter 2 the holotheticity of an "explicit" technology was defined in a number of different ways. In particular, it was defined as the invariant condition of the (first-order) differential equation for the explicit technology (Lemma 3). Applying the same reasoning and assuming the Lie group properties for technical change, we can define the holotheticity condition of an "implicit" technology as

Definition 2 (*Holotheticity of Implicit Technology*) An implicit technology is holothetic under a given Lie type of technical progress $U = \xi(K, L)\,\partial/\partial K + \eta(K, L)\,\partial/\partial L$, if the (second-order) differential equation of the implicit technology is invariant under that type of technical progress.

Alternatively, a technology is said to be "implicitly holothetic" if the second-order differential equation of the implicit technology is invariant under a given Lie type of technical progress.

First, we need

Lemma 1 *(Necessary and Sufficient Condition for Implicit Holotheticity) A technology is implicitly holothetic under a given Lie type of technical progress* $U = \xi(K, L)\, \partial/\partial K + \eta(K, L)\, \partial/\partial L$ *if and only if*

$$
\begin{aligned}
U''h &= \xi(K, L)\frac{\partial h}{\partial K} + \eta(K, L)\frac{\partial h}{\partial L} + \eta'\left(K, L, \frac{\partial L}{dK}\right)\frac{\partial h}{\partial(dL/dK)} \\
&\quad + \eta''\left(K, L, \frac{dL}{dK}, \frac{d^2L}{dK^2}\right)\frac{\partial h}{\partial(d^2L/dK^2)} \\
&= 0, \qquad \text{whenever} \quad h\left(K, L, \frac{dL}{dK}, \frac{d^2L}{dK^2}\right) = 0,
\end{aligned}
\tag{5}
$$

where U'' *is the twice extended group of* U, *and* η' *and* η'' *are given by*

$$
\eta' = \frac{\partial\eta}{\partial K} + \left(\frac{\partial\eta}{\partial L} - \frac{\partial\xi}{\partial K}\right)\frac{dL}{dK} - \frac{\partial\xi}{\partial L}\left(\frac{dL}{dK}\right)^2, \tag{6-i}
$$

$$
\eta'' = \frac{\partial\eta'}{\partial K} + \frac{\partial\eta'}{\partial L}\frac{dL}{dK} + \left(\frac{\partial\eta'}{\partial(dL/dK)} - \frac{\partial\xi}{\partial K} - \frac{\partial\xi}{\partial L}\frac{dL}{dK}\right)\frac{d^2L}{dK^2}. \tag{6-ii}
$$

Proof This is a special case of Theorem 7 (Appendix, Part IV) when $s = 2$. Q.E.D.

4. We can now prove

Theorem 1 *(Existence of a General Implicit Technology Holothetic under a Lie Type of Technical Progress)* (i) *Given a Lie type of technical progress, there exists a general family of implicit production functions holothetic under that type of technical progress.*

(ii) *Given a Lie type of technical progress,* U *and therefore* U' *and* U'', *there exists a general form of differential equation of the second-order (a general holothetic differential equation of the implicit technology) invariant under* U''.

Proof We first prove the second part. From Lemma 1 we obtain a general solution h satisfying the partial differential equation of the twice-extended group U'' (5). Passing to the corresponding system of ordinary differential equations

$$\frac{dK}{\xi(K, L)} = \frac{dL}{\eta(K, L)} = \frac{d(dL/dK)}{\eta'(K, L, dL/dK)} = \frac{d(d^2L/dK^2)}{\eta''(K, L, dL/dK, d^2L/dK^2)}, \tag{7}$$

we obtain three invariants, $u(K, L) = \text{const}$, $u'(K, L, dL/dK) = \text{const}$ (first differential invariant), and $u''(K, L, dL/dK, d^2L/dK^2) = \text{const}$ (second differential invariant). On using these invariants, the general solution of (5) may be written in the form (1). This is the general form of the differential equation of the second-order invariant under U.

To prove the first part, we write

$$\tilde{K} = u(K, L), \qquad \tilde{L} = u'\left(K, L, \frac{dL}{dK}\right). \tag{8}$$

Then the second-order differential equation will be integrated as

$$\phi(\tilde{K}, \tilde{L}, C_1(Y)) = \phi(u, u', C_1(Y)) = 0, \tag{9}$$

which is a differential equation of the first order. Solving (9) again, we obtain a general family of implicit technology (2). Q.E.D.

Economic Interpretation of Implicit Holotheticity

5. There are similarities and differences between the economic interpretations of the explicit and implicit holotheticity conditions. As in the explicit case,

(a) the isoquant map before and after technical progress is unchanged other than the relabeling of its isoquants;

(b) the differential equation of the second order before and after technical progress is unchanged (symmetric property).

The first condition requires that the marginal rates of substitution, now not only a function of K and L, but also a function of output Y itself, have the exactly identical form before and after technical progress, i.e.,

$$R(K, L, Y) = \frac{Y_K}{Y_L} = \frac{Y_\phi \phi_K + Y_\psi \psi_K}{Y_\phi \phi_L + Y_\psi \psi_L} \equiv \bar{R}(\bar{K}, \bar{L}, \bar{Y}),$$

$$\bar{K} = \phi(K, L, t), \qquad \bar{L} = \psi(K, L, t), \qquad F[C_1(\bar{Y}), C_2(\bar{Y}), \bar{K}, \bar{L}] = 0. \tag{10}$$

The second condition implies that the differential equation of the second order, which has different economic interpretations depending upon specific assumptions on the technical progress functions (see Section 11), has the same form before and after technical progress, i.e.,

$$h(K, L, dL/dK, d^2L/dK^2) = h(\bar{K}, \bar{L}, d\bar{L}/d\bar{K}, d^2\bar{L}/d\bar{K}^2). \tag{11}$$

Unlike the explicit case, implicit holotheticity

(a) does not necessarily imply a complete transformation of technical progress into a scale effect, and

(b) does not necessarily imply weak separability of technical progress in the production function.

To understand these differences, consider the implicit CES example

$$F(K, L, C_1(Y), C_2(Y)) = C_1(Y)K^{-\rho} + C_2(Y)L^{-\rho} - C_1(Y) = 0.$$

By setting $C_1(Y) = Y$ and $C_2(Y) = Y^2$, we can obtain an explicit CES function as $Y = (1 - K^{-\rho})/L^{-\rho}$. Since the marginal rate of substitution of the foregoing is equal to $R = Y_K/Y_L = (K/L)^{-(1+\rho)}Y^{-1}$, it is invariant under the uniform factor-augmenting type of technical progress at any given Y, i.e., $\bar{K} = A(t)K$, $\bar{L} = A(t)L$, $\bar{Y} = (1 - \bar{K}^{-\rho})/\bar{L}^{-\rho}$, and

$$R = (K/L)^{-(1+\rho)}Y^{-1} = \bar{R} = (\bar{K}/\bar{L})^{-(1+\rho)}\bar{Y}^{-1} = (A(t)K/A(t)L)^{-(1+\rho)}\bar{Y}^{-1}.$$

But it is obviously not separable in terms of technical progress, since $\bar{Y} = (1 - (A(t)K)^{-\rho})/(A(t)L)^{-\rho}$ cannot be written in the form $\bar{Y} = F_{(t)}[f(K, L)]$. Hence the effect of technical progress cannot be transformed to increasing returns to scale.

Invariants of Implicit Technology

6. Despite these differences, the holotheticity concept can be used to analyze the basic properties—the invariance properties inherent in any production technology. The holothetic differential equation of the implicit technology is a differential equation satisfying condition (5). Since (5) is a partial differential equation in four variables K, L, dL/dK, and d^2L/dK^2, there are three independent solutions which constitute the three invariants of the technology. The first invariant is simply the solution of $dK/\xi(K, L) = dL/\eta(K, L)$, or

$$u(K, L) = u(\bar{K}, \bar{L}). \tag{12}$$

The second invariant, using the first invariant and

$$\frac{dK}{\xi(K, L(c, K))} = \frac{d(dL/dK)}{\eta'(K, L(c, K), dL/dK)},$$

is

$$u'(K, L, dL/dK) = u'(\bar{K}, \bar{L}, d\bar{L}/d\bar{K}). \tag{13}$$

Finally, the third invariant, using the first two invariants, is

$$u''(K, L, dL/dK, d^2L/dK^2) = u''(\bar{K}, \bar{L}, d\bar{L}/d\bar{K}, d^2\bar{L}/d\bar{K}^2). \tag{14}$$

The first two invariants are exactly the same as the explicit technology, but the third invariant applies only to the implicit technology. Using the first two invariants as the first and second canonical variables, we can write

$$\tilde{K} = u(K, L), \tag{15-i}$$

$$\tilde{L} = u'(K, L, dL/dK), \tag{15-ii}$$

$$d\tilde{L}/d\tilde{K} = F(\tilde{K}, \tilde{L}). \tag{15-iii}$$

The above has the same *invariant structure* as the original implicit technology. The reduction of the original technology to the invariant structure of the form (15) has an obvious advantage that the second-order system is now reduced to the first-order system. We have

Theorem 2 (*Invariant Structure of an Implicit Technology*) (i) *Any implicit technology holothetic under a given Lie type of technical progress has three unique* (*up to monotonicity*) *invariants, the first two of them being exactly identical with those of the corresponding explicit holothetic technology.*

(ii) *Using the first two invariants, the holothetic differential equation of the second order can be reduced to the first order with the same invariant structure.*

Proof See the Mathematical Appendix to this chapter.

III. General Nonexistence Theorem of a Lie Type of Technical Progress for a Given Implicit Technology

7. We shall next study the converse question of whether or not a given implicit technology is holothetic under some type of technical progress satisfying the basic Lie group properties. Here we have a completely different picture from the case of explicit technology. *Given an implicit technology in the form of a second-order differential equation, there exists in general no Lie type of technical progress under which the given implicit technology is holothetic.*

Assume that a differential equation for the implicit technology is given in the form

$$I: d^2L/dK^2 = N(K, L, dL/dK). \tag{1'}$$

The condition that it be left unaltered by a Lie type of technical progress

$$U = \xi(K, L)\frac{\partial}{\partial K} + \eta(K, L)\frac{\partial}{\partial L}$$

is (from Lemma 1)

$$-\xi\frac{\partial N}{\partial K} - \eta\frac{\partial N}{\partial L} - \eta'\frac{\partial N}{\partial(dL/dK)} + \eta'' = 0 \quad \text{whenever} \quad \frac{d^2L}{dK^2} = N\left(K, L\frac{dL}{dK}\right). \tag{16}$$

On using (6-i) and (6-ii), the preceding condition becomes

$$\begin{aligned}
&\left(\frac{\partial\eta}{\partial L} - 2\frac{\partial\xi}{\partial K}\right)N - \xi\frac{\partial N}{\partial K} - \eta\frac{\partial N}{\partial L} - \frac{\partial\eta}{\partial K}\frac{\partial N}{\partial(dL/dK)} + \frac{\partial^2\eta}{\partial K^2}\\
&\quad + \left[2\frac{\partial^2\eta}{\partial K\,\partial L} - \frac{\partial^2\xi}{\partial K^2} - 3\frac{\partial\xi}{\partial L}N - \left(\frac{\partial\eta}{\partial L} - \frac{\partial\xi}{\partial K}\right)\frac{\partial N}{\partial(dL/dK)}\right]\frac{dL}{dK}\\
&\quad + \left(\frac{\partial^2\eta}{\partial L^2} - 2\frac{\partial^2\xi}{\partial K\,\partial L} + \frac{\partial\xi}{\partial L}\frac{\partial N}{\partial(dL/dK)}\right)\left(\frac{dL}{dK}\right)^2 - \frac{\partial^2\xi}{\partial L^2}\left(\frac{dL}{dK}\right)^3 \equiv 0
\end{aligned} \tag{16'}$$

for all values of $K \geqq 0$, $L \geqq 0$, and $dL/dK \leqq 0$. Since (16′) is an identity with respect to K, L, and dL/dK, it is equivalent to a number of differential and finite equations in ξ and η, the exact number depending upon the form of N. Fixing our attention on dL/dK alone, we see that (16′) is equivalent to at least four equations. In general, it is impossible to find ξ and η other than $\xi \equiv \eta \equiv 0$, which satisfy all these conditions. Hence we have

Theorem 3 *(General Nonexistence Theorem of U) Given an implicit technology in the form of the second-order differential equation, there exists in general* no *Lie type of technical progress under which the implicit technology is holothetic, i.e., $\xi \equiv \eta \equiv 0$.*

Comparison with the Case of Explicit Technology

8. The case of a differential equation of the first order (the marginal rate of substitution) for an explicit technology is entirely different. The condition that

$$(dL/dK) - P(K, L) = 0 \tag{3'}$$

be holothetic under $U = \xi\, \partial/\partial K + \eta\, \partial/\partial L$ may be put into the form

$$\frac{\partial \eta}{\partial K} + \left(\frac{\partial \eta}{\partial L} - \frac{\partial \xi}{\partial K}\right)P - \frac{\partial \xi}{\partial L} P^2 - \xi \frac{\partial P}{\partial K} - \eta \frac{\partial P}{\partial L} = 0. \tag{17}$$

[This condition is derived from Lemma 5, Eq. (16) of Chapter 2 together with (3′) above.] Here one of the functions, say ξ, may be chosen at random, leaving a partial differential equation in η, which always has a solution. In fact, it has an infinite number of solutions. This is in complete accord with the results derived in Theorems 4 and 5 of Chapter 2.

Compatibility Condition and Alternative Interpretation of the Nonexistence Theorem

9. The differential equation of the second order for any given implicit technology (1) is equivalent to the system of equations of the first order (Ince [1956, p. 47]),

$$\frac{dK}{1} = \frac{dL}{(dL/dK)} = \frac{d(dL/dK)}{N(K, L, dL/dK)}. \tag{1″}$$

If the solutions of the latter are

$$u(K, L, dL/dK) = a, \qquad v(K, L, dL/dK) = b,$$

then the solution of (1′) may be obtained by eliminating dL/dK from the preceding two solutions. Alternatively, instead of (1″), one may find u and v as two independent solutions of the corresponding linear partial differential equation (see Ince [1956])

$$R'f = \frac{\partial f}{\partial K} + \frac{dL}{dK}\frac{\partial f}{\partial L} + N\left(K, L, \frac{dL}{dK}\right)\frac{\partial f}{\partial (dL/dK)} = 0. \tag{18}$$

Thus the problem of finding the implicit technology from (1′) is reduced to that of finding two independent solutions of (18).

***Definition* 3** (*Lie Group Representation of the Implicit Technology*) Let the infinitesimal generator R' be

$$R' = \frac{\partial}{\partial K} + \frac{dL}{dK}\frac{\partial}{\partial L} + N\left(K, L, \frac{dL}{dK}\right)\frac{\partial}{\partial (dL/dK)}. \tag{19}$$

Then R' said to be *the Lie group representation of the internal structure of the implicit technology corresponding to* (1′).

As in the case of explicit technology, the internal structure of an implicit technology can be treated as one type of internal technical progress (see

Definition 4 of Chapter 2). If (1′) is holothetic under some Lie type of technical progress Uf, then the equivalent system (1″) is holothetic under the extended group $U'f$, where

$$U' = \xi \frac{\partial}{\partial K} + \eta \frac{\partial}{\partial L} + \eta' \frac{\partial}{\partial(dL/dK)}.$$

This in turn implies that the internal structure must be compatible with a given exogenous transformation U'. If the internal structure $R'f = 0$ is compatible with $U'f$, the Lie operator must satisfy (see the Appendix, Theorem 11)

$$(U', R') \equiv \lambda R', \qquad \lambda = \lambda(K, L, dL/dK), \tag{20}$$

i.e., $U'f = 0$ and $R'f = 0$ form a *complete system.* It is desirable to have the condition expressed in terms of the differential equation itself,

$$\begin{aligned}(U', R')f &\equiv (U'1 - R'\xi) \frac{\partial f}{\partial K} + \left(U' \frac{dL}{dK} - R'\eta\right) \frac{\partial f}{\partial L} \\ &\quad + (U'N - R'\eta') \frac{\partial f}{\partial(dL/dK)} \\ &= \lambda\left(K, L, \frac{dL}{dK}\right)\left(\frac{\partial f}{\partial K} + \frac{dL}{dK}\frac{\partial f}{\partial L} + N \frac{\partial f}{\partial(dL/dK)}\right) = 0.\end{aligned}$$

The foregoing Lie bracket condition requires that

$$\begin{gathered} U'1 - R'\xi = \lambda, \qquad U'\, dL/dK - R'\eta = \lambda\, dL/dK, \\ U'N - R'\eta' = \lambda N. \end{gathered} \tag{21}$$

Alternatively, if u and v are common solutions of the system

$$\begin{aligned} R'f &= \frac{\partial f}{\partial K} + \frac{dL}{dK}\frac{\partial f}{\partial L} + N\left(K, L, \frac{dL}{dK}\right) \frac{\partial f}{\partial(dL/dK)} = 0, \\ U'f &= \xi \frac{\partial f}{\partial K} + \eta \frac{\partial f}{\partial L} + \eta' \frac{\partial f}{\partial(dL/dK)} = 0, \end{aligned}$$

they must satisfy the total differential equation (Appendix)

$$\left(\frac{dL}{dK}\eta' - \eta N\right) dK + (N\xi - \eta')\, dL + \left(\eta - \xi \frac{dL}{dK}\right) d\left(\frac{dL}{dK}\right) = 0. \tag{22}$$

Hence, in order that $R'f = 0$ and $U'f = 0$ form a complete system, (22) must have a solution. It is well known that (22) in general does not have any solution unless the "integrability condition" is satisfied. The integrability condition of (22) is (Ince [1956, p. 53])

$$\begin{aligned}&\left(\frac{dL}{dK}\eta' - \eta N\right)\left[\frac{\partial(N\xi - \eta')}{\partial(dL/dK)} - \frac{\partial(\eta - \xi\, dL/dK)}{\partial L}\right]\\&\quad + (N\xi - \eta')\left[\frac{\partial(\eta - \xi\, dL/dK)}{\partial K} - \frac{\partial(dL/dK\,\eta' - \eta N)}{\partial(dL/dK)}\right]\\&\quad + \left(\eta - \xi\frac{dL}{dK}\right)\left[\frac{\partial(dL/dK\,\eta' - \eta N)}{\partial L} - \frac{\partial(N\xi - \eta')}{\partial K}\right] = 0.\end{aligned} \tag{23}$$

Equations (16′), (21), and (23) are all identical conditions. (The interested reader is asked to prove this.) And hence we have

Theorem 4 (*Compatibility Condition and Nonexistence Theorem*) (i) *Given an implicit technology by its Lie group representation R′. Then the technology is holothetic under an exogenous type of technical progress if and only if the internal structure R′ is compatible with the exogenous technical change U′.*

(ii) *In general, R′ is not compatible with any U′ unless the integrability condition is satisfied. (There exists in general* no *exogenous technical progress under which the implicit technology is holothetic.)*

Remark 1 For the case of explicit technology, it is an entirely different picture, as can be observed from the corresponding total differential equation (22). Here the third term is absent and (22) is simply a total differential equation with two variables. The integrability condition is *always* satisfied.

Remark 2 The careful reader must have already realized the reason we started with a general Lie type of technical progress under which an implicit technology is holothetic rather than with a given implicit technology to find some Lie type of technical progress. Unlike the case of explicit technology, there may be no possibility of finding any Lie type of technical progress.

The reader will see in Section 15 that this property, together with the classification scheme of r-parameter groups, will enable us to distinguish one type of implicit technology from another.

Extensions

10. We shall briefly study two extensions: *simultaneous holotheticity* and a multifactor generalization. Given r independent (unconnected) types of technical change X_a ($1 \leqq a \leqq r$), we can derive a unique family of second-order differential equations, which is simultaneously invariant under all X_a, from

$$X''_a h = \xi^a(K, L)\frac{\partial h}{\partial K} + \eta^a(K, L)\frac{\partial h}{\partial L} + \eta^{a'}\frac{\partial h}{\partial(dL/dK)} + \eta^{a''}\frac{\partial h}{\partial(d^2L/dK^2)}$$

$$= 0, 1 \leqq a \leqq r. \tag{24}$$

Here the X''_a are the twice-extended group of the X_a, and $\eta^{a'}$ and $\eta^{a''}$ are defined by Eq. (6). If there are only two factor inputs, the maximum number of the unconnected types of technical change must be three.[2] If and only if the compatibility conditions [such as Eq. (70), Chapter 2] are satisfied among the X''_a does there exist a general form of the simultaneously holothetic differential equation for the implicit technology.

Let x be a vector of n factor inputs, $x = (x_1, \ldots, x_n)$. An implicit technology with multiple factor inputs is defined by

$$F[C(Y); x] = 0, \tag{25}$$

where $C(Y) = (C_1(Y), \ldots, C_n(Y))$ is a vector of n essential parameters. Assuming that there exists a vector of technical progress functions satisfying the basic Lie group properties, i.e.,

$$\bar{x} = \phi(x; t), \qquad \phi = (\phi^1, \ldots, \phi^n), \tag{26}$$

we can again obtain a general family of (25) from the holotheticity (invariance) condition of F under a Lie type of technical change (26). Also, as in the two-factor case, the converse problem of finding a Lie type of technical progress from a given implicit technology is in general not easy. There exists in general *no* Lie type of technical progress under which a given implicit technology is holothetic.

IV. Special Types of Implicit Technologies

Implicitly Homothetic Technology

11. The homothetic technology studied in Chapter 2 is an explicit technology holothetic under the uniform (neutral) factor-augmenting type of technical progress. The holothetic differential equation for the explicitly homothetic family is the differential equation invariant under the once-extended transformation. The implicitly homothetic technology is characterized by the fact that it is a general solution of the second-order differential

[2] Compare this with the case of explicit technology (Lemma 7, Chapter 2, Section 26), where the maximum number is only two.

equation invariant under the twice extended transformation of the uniform factor-augmenting type of technical progress.

Let the infinitesimal transformation of the technical progress functions be equal to

$$U = K\frac{\partial}{\partial K} + L\frac{\partial}{\partial L}. \tag{27}$$

The once-extended transformation is the same as (27) and, hence, the twice extended transformation is

$$U'' = K\frac{\partial}{\partial K} + L\frac{\partial}{\partial L} - \frac{d^2L}{dK^2}\frac{\partial}{\partial(d^2L/dK^2)}. \tag{28}$$

This implies that technical progress is given by

$$\bar{K} = e^tK, \qquad \bar{L} = e^tL, \qquad d\bar{L}/d\bar{K} = dL/dK, \qquad d^2\bar{L}/d\bar{K}^2 = e^{-t}\,d^2L/dK^2. \tag{29}$$

The *holothetic differential equation for the implicit homothetic family* is a solution to

$$U''h = K\frac{\partial h}{\partial K} + L\frac{\partial h}{\partial L} - \frac{d^2L}{dK^2}\frac{\partial h}{\partial(d^2L/dK^2)} = 0. \tag{30}$$

Using the three independent solutions of the above, we write

$$h(L/K, dL/dK, K\,d^2L/dK^2) = 0. \tag{31}$$

To find a general solution to the above, set $\tilde{K} = L/K$ and $\tilde{L} = dL/dK$ (see the proof of Theorem 1 of this chapter). Then from $h = h(\tilde{K}, \tilde{L}, d\tilde{L}/d\tilde{K}) = 0$, we get $\psi(\tilde{K}, \tilde{L}, C_1(Y)) = 0$ or $\tilde{L} = g(\tilde{K}, C_1(Y))$. Integrating once again, we obtain *a general family of implicitly homothetic production functions* as

$$K \exp \int \frac{d(L/K)}{(L/K) + g(L/K, C_1(Y))} = C_2(Y), \tag{32}$$

or

$$F(C_1(Y), C_2(Y), K, L) = KP[L/K, C_1(Y)] - C_2(Y) = 0. \tag{33}$$

Since $C_1(Y)$ and $C_2(Y)$ are arbitrary functions of Y, Eq. (33) represents an "implicitly homothetic" rather than "implicitly homogeneous" family. When $C_1(Y) = \text{const}$ ($dC_1/dY \equiv 0$) and $C_2(Y) = Y$, the foregoing reduces to the ordinary homogeneous production function of the first degree—the constant returns to scale technology. In Eq. (33) the marginal rate of substitution between K and L depends not only on the factor ratio but also on the output level.

An interesting example of implicitly homothetic technology is the case of $\sigma = \text{const}$—implicit CES technology. The implicit (or nonhomothetic) CES technology is derived as (Sato [1974, 1975a] and also Part VIII of this chapter)

$$C_1(Y)K^{-\rho} + C_2(Y)L^{-\rho} = 1, \qquad \sigma \neq 1, \tag{34-i}$$

$$C_1(Y)\log K + C_2(Y)\log L = 1, \qquad \sigma = 1. \tag{34-ii}$$

Looking at the general expression (33), we can easily infer that

$$\lambda KP[\lambda L/\lambda K, C_1(Y)] = \lambda C_2(Y). \tag{35}$$

This is obviously true for special cases (34) with appropriate choices of C_1 and C_2.

12. A multifactor form of an implicitly homothetic technology is easily shown as

$$F(C_1(Y), \ldots, C_{n-1}(Y); x_1, x_2, \ldots, x_n) = C_n(Y), \tag{36}$$

where F satisfies the condition

$$F[C_1, \ldots, C_{n-1}; \lambda x_1, \lambda x_2, \ldots, \lambda x_n] = \lambda C_n(Y), \tag{37}$$

or

$$F[C_1, \ldots, C_{n-1}; \lambda x] - \lambda C_n(Y) = 0. \tag{38}$$

It will be shown in the next chapter that this family is the only type of production function self-dual with its corresponding cost function.

Almost Homothetic Implicit Technology

13. It is not too difficult to extend the idea of implicit holothetic technology invariant under the general factor-augmenting type of technical change to a more general case. Let the infinitesimal transformation of technical progress be given by

$$U = \alpha K \frac{\partial}{\partial K} + \beta L \frac{\partial}{\partial L}, \tag{39}$$

with its twice-extended transformation

$$U'' = \alpha K \frac{\partial}{\partial K} + \beta L \frac{\partial}{\partial L} + (\beta - \alpha)\frac{dL}{dK}\frac{\partial}{\partial(dL/dK)} + (\beta - 2\alpha)\frac{d^2L}{dK^2}\frac{\partial}{\partial(d^2L/dK^2)}. \tag{40}$$

The holothetic differential equation is given by

$$h\left(\frac{L^\alpha}{K^\beta}, \frac{(dL/dK)^\alpha}{K^{\beta-\alpha}}, \frac{(d^2L/dK^2)^\alpha}{K^{\beta-2\alpha}}\right) = 0, \tag{41}$$

whose solution is a general family of almost homothetic implicit technology

$$F(K, L, C_1(Y)) = K\psi[L^\alpha/K^\beta, C_1(Y)] = C_2(Y). \tag{42}$$

It satisfies the condition

$$F[\lambda^\alpha K, \lambda^\beta L, C_1(Y)] = \lambda^\gamma C_2(Y). \tag{43}$$

The basic characteristic of (42) is that the share ratio is invariant under the nonneutral type of technical change at *each level* of Y, for we have

$$Y_K K/Y_L L = Q(L^\alpha/K^\beta, C_1(Y)). \tag{44}$$

Obviously, (42) contains a number of special cases:

(i) homothetic implicit technology when $\alpha \equiv \beta \neq 0$;
(ii) capital-homothetic implicit technology when $\alpha \neq 0, \beta = 0$;
(iii) labor-homothetic implicit technology when $\alpha = 0, \beta \neq 0$.

A multifactor representation of almost-homothetic implicit technology is simply given by

$$F[C_1(Y), \ldots, C_n(Y); x_1, \ldots, x_n] = 1, \tag{45}$$

satisfying the condition,

$$F[C_1(Y), \ldots, C_n(Y); \lambda^{\alpha_1}x_1, \ldots, \lambda^{\alpha_n}x_n] = \lambda^\gamma.$$

The reader can easily show that an implicit addilog family (Hanoch [1975], Sato [1977b], Barnett *et al.* [1979])

$$\sum_{j=1}^{n} C_j(Y)x_j^{-\rho_j} = 1 \tag{46}$$

is a special case of (45).

Projective and Transprojective Implicit Technologies

14. The implicit technology holothetic under a general (one-parameter) transprojective type of technical progress is a solution of the second-order differential equation obtained from the twice-extended transformation of

$$\begin{aligned} \xi[u(K), v(L)] &= a_1 + a_3 u + a_5 v + a_7 u^2 + a_8 uv, \\ \eta[u(K), v(L)] &= a_2 + a_4 u + a_6 v + a_7 uv + a_8 v^2. \end{aligned} \tag{47}$$

A special case of the foregoing when $u = K$ and $v = L$ is, of course, a general projective implicit technology. The general family of transprojective implicit technology is given by

$$P[u(K), v(L)] + Q[W_1^{\gamma_1} W_2^{\gamma_2} W_3^{\gamma_3}, C_1(Y)] = C_2(Y), \tag{48}$$

where P, Q, W_i, and γ_i are determined by Eq. (38) in Chapter 2 with K and L replaced by $u(K)$ and $v(L)$, respectively. The reader will find in Section 22 that the implicit technology generated by (47) is one of the most important families of technology that can be used to classify the separable implicit types of technologies, such as the implicit CES and implicit addilog types of production functions. The task of extending the two-factor implicit technology to a multifactor case is left to the interested reader.

V. Analysis of Implicit Technology by *r*-Parameter Lie Type of Technical Change

15. We have shown that there is a basic difference between explicit and implicit technologies in their relationship to the Lie group specification. For any given *explicit* technology in the form of the first-order differential equation in capital and labor, there exists at least one, and, in general, an infinite number of Lie types of technical progress under which the given differential equation is invariant. While for any *implicit* technology given in the form of the second-order differential equation, there exists in general none and, if any, only a limited number of Lie types of technical progress under which the given implicit technology is holothetic. We now utilize the nonholotheticity (or limited holotheticity) property of an implicit technology for the study of the basic structure of the technology. For simplicity, we restrict our analysis to the two input case.

r-Degree Holotheticity

Assume that an implicit technology is given by its second-order differential equation (1′). A set of infinitesimal transformations of technical progress $U_1, \ldots, U_r$ is said to be *linearly independent* if it is impossible to find a set of *constant coefficients* other than $c_i \equiv 0$ for all i such that

$$\sum_{i=1}^{r} c_i U_i \equiv 0. \tag{49}$$

Definition 4 (*r-Degree Holotheticity*) If I is holothetic under r linearly independent Lie types of technical progress, then I is said to have r-degree holotheticity.

We shall write the foregoing simply as

$$I \in H^r. \tag{50}$$

In Eq. (1′) when I contains no d^2L/dK^2 (explicit technology), we then have

$$I \in H^\infty. \tag{51}$$

Theorem 5 (*The Maximum Degree of Implicit Holotheticity* = 8) *A differential equation for an implicit technology cannot be holothetic under more than eight linearly independent Lie types of technical change, i.e.,*

$$I \in H^r, \qquad 0 \leqq r \leqq 8. \tag{52}$$

Proof See the Mathematical Appendix to this chapter.

Zero-Degree Holotheticity

16. A differential equation of the second (or higher) order is in general not invariant under any group. Here we present an example which is not invariant under any group. Consider the following differential equation without overemphasizing its validity as a meaningful function in economics:

$$I\colon\ d^2L/dK^2 = KL + \tan(dL/dK). \tag{53}$$

With a proper choice of K and L, this may be used as a differential equation representing an implicit technology. On using Eq. (16′), the necessary and sufficient condition in this case is calculated as

$$\left(\frac{\partial\eta}{\partial L} - 2\frac{\partial\xi}{\partial K}\right)\left[KL + \tan\left(\frac{dL}{dK}\right)\right] - \xi L - \eta K - \frac{\partial\eta}{\partial K}\sec^2\left(\frac{dL}{dK}\right) + \cdots$$

$$-3\frac{\partial\xi}{\partial L}\left[KL + \tan\left(\frac{dL}{dK}\right)\right]\frac{dL}{dK} - \left(\frac{\partial\eta}{\partial L} - \frac{\partial\xi}{\partial K}\right)\frac{dL}{dK}\sec^2\left(\frac{dL}{dK}\right)$$

$$+\frac{\partial\xi}{\partial L}\left(\frac{dL}{dK}\right)^2\sec^2\left(\frac{dL}{dK}\right) + \cdots \equiv 0,$$

where the dots represent terms free of $\tan(dL/dK)$ and $\sec(dL/dK)$, and also second derivatives of ξ and η. This identity implies

$$\text{(a)}\quad \frac{\partial \eta}{\partial L} - 2\frac{\partial \xi}{\partial K} = 0, \qquad \text{(b)}\quad \xi L + \eta K = 0, \qquad \text{(c)}\quad \frac{\partial \eta}{\partial K} = 0,$$

$$\text{(d)}\quad \frac{\partial \xi}{\partial L} = 0, \qquad \text{(e)}\quad \frac{\partial \eta}{\partial L} - \frac{\partial \xi}{\partial K} = 0.$$

From (a) and (e), we get $\partial\eta/\partial L = \partial\xi/\partial K = 0$. These together with (c) and (d) make it necessary that $\xi = \text{const}$ and $\eta = \text{const}$. But since (b) must hold for all K and $L \geqq 0$, we finally get $\xi = \eta = 0$. There exists no Lie type of technical progress under which the implicit technology representing a general solution of (53) is holothetic. The foregoing may be a good example of the general nonexistence theorem (Theorem 3) discussed in Section 7.

Holotheticity of Degree 1

Another case of interest is $I \in H^1$. That is to say, there exists only one Lie type of technical progress for I. We shall briefly discuss how we can derive the underlying implicit technology. Using (18) for Eq. (1′), if $R'h = 0$ is invariant under U'_1, we must have (20); i.e., $U'_1 h = 0$ and $R'h = 0$ form a complete system. Having found $\phi(K, L, dL/dK)$, a common solution of $U'_1 h = 0$ and $R'h = 0$, we can find a second solution of $R'h = 0$ in the following way. Since $\phi(K, L, dL/dK)$ is not a constant, it must involve at least one of the variables, say dL/dK. On replacing dL/dK by the new variable

$$Z = \phi(K, L, dL/dK),$$

$R'h = 0$ and $U'_1 h$ take the forms

$$Xh = P(K, L, Z)\frac{\partial h}{\partial K} + Q(K, L, Z)\frac{\partial h}{\partial L} = 0,$$

$$Yh = S(K, L, Z)\frac{\partial h}{\partial K} + T(K, L, Z)\frac{\partial h}{\partial L},$$

since $R'\phi = 0$ and $U'_1\phi = 0$. To solve $Xh = 0$, we proceed to the corresponding ordinary differential equation

$$Q\,dK - P\,dL = 0.$$

This is invariant under Yh. By Corollary 8-2 of the Appendix, we can always find an integrating factor to derive a first solution in a closed form. The second step is then again to solve the ordinary differential equation of the first order, yielding the deisred implicit technology.

r-Parameter Group and Holotheticity of Degree r

17. We now study the relationship between an r-parameter Lie type of technical change and the holotheticity of implicit technology. We present

Theorem 6 (*r-Parameter Lie Type of Technical Change*) *The aggregate of all the infinitesimal transformations of the Lie type of technical change that leave a given (second-order) differential equation of the implicit technology invariant constitute an r-parameter group, where* $0 \leqq r \leqq 8$.

Proof In Theorem 5, it was established that the degree of implicit holotheticity is limited, the maximum degree being eight. This means that the number of linearly independent infinitesimal transformations of technical change that leave (1′) invariant is limited. If this number is r, $0 \leqq r \leqq 8$, all the infinitesimal transformations are linear combinations, with constant coefficients, of any set of r linearly independent ones, $U_1, U_2, \ldots, U_r$. Theorem 16 of the Appendix states that if (1′) is invariant under U_i and U_j for $i, j = 1, 2, \ldots, r$, then it is also invariant under (U_i, U_j). Hence $(U_i, U_j) = U_{ij}$ must also be linear combinations with constant coefficients of the set $U_1, U_2, \ldots, U_r$, i.e.,

$$(U_i, U_j) = \sum_{k=1}^{r} a_{ij}^k U_k \qquad (0 \leqq i, j \leqq r), \tag{54}$$

where the a are constants. By *Lie's fundamental theorem* (Appendix, Theorem 15), the aggregates and all the transformations of $U = c_1 U_1 + \cdots + c_r U_r$ constitute an r-parameter Lie type of technical changes. Q.E.D.

Economic Interpretation of Theorem 6

Suppose that we are given a differential equation of the second order whose general solution represents an implicit technology. We assume that r linearly independent types of technical progress, under which the given differential equation is invariant, can be found. [To find these we may use the Lie operator (U_i, U_j).] Let us assume that we have found U_1 and U_2 under which the differential equation is invariant.[3] Next, the Lie operator (U_1, U_2), which is also an infinitesimal transformation, say $U_3 = (U_1, U_2)$, may or may not be linearly independent of U_1 and U_2. When U_3 is linearly independent, then we have found the third Lie type of technical progress under

[3] If there is only one U, we have found a one-parameter Lie type of technical change, and the process will end here.

which (1′) is holothetic. Again, the Lie brackets $(U_1, U_3) = U_4$ and $(U_2, U_3) = U_5$ can be tested with respect to their linear independency from U_1, U_2, and U_3. This process will continue until we finally get U_8 at most. In many cases, of course, the maximum number will be less than 8, say r.

Let the first parameter t_1 be a factor, say, the general educational level of workers, whose effect will induce a type of technical progress. Let the second parameter t_2 represent another factor, say, a specific skill of workers for a particular job, whose effect will induce a different type of technical progress. If these two parameters induce the same type of technical progress, we can treat them as the same parameter. Hence the existence of different parameters implies that their effects must be expressed by different forms U_1, $U_2, \ldots, U_r$. Let the aggregate of these different types of technical progress be represented by

$$\bar{K} = \phi(K, L; t_1, \ldots, t_r), \qquad \bar{L} = \psi(K, L; t_1, \ldots, t_r), \tag{55}$$

which satisfy the basic Lie group properties with r essential parameters $t_1, \ldots, t_r$. The holotheticity of the implicit technology under (55) means that $F[K, L; C_1(Y)] = C_2(Y)$ can be written in its original form after we substitute (55) into K and L in F, respectively. Hence the effects of all of these different types of technical progress are absorbed in the arbitrary constants $C_1(Y)$ and $C_2(Y)$, i.e., $F[\bar{K}, \bar{L}; C_1] = C_2$ can be expressed as $F[K, L; \bar{C}_1] = \bar{C}_2$. Hence *the r-degree holotheticity of the implicit technology means that the effects of each and every type of technical progress as well as of the aggregate of the r types will have no influence on an isoquant curve at a given output level, except relabeling the isoquant curve.*

s-Degree Subholotheticity

It is possible that a smaller number than $r > 2$, say s, of linearly independent infinitesimal transformations in an r-parameter group determine a group. This is an *s-parameter subgroup* of the larger group. If (1′) is invariant under an s-parameter Lie type of technical progress, then the implicit technology is said to have the *s-degree subholotheticity*, $1 \leqq s < r \leqq 8$.

Theorem 7 (*Subholotheticity of Degree* 2) *Every implicit technology of r-degree holotheticity* ($r > 2$) *has subholotheticity of degree* 2.

Proof This is a direct consequence of Theorem 18 in the Appendix which states that every r-parameter group ($r > 2$) contains two-parameter subgroups. Q.E.D.

This theorem may justify the use of two parameter groups for the analysis which follows.

VI. Two-Parameter Groups and Holotheticity of Degree 2

Classification of Two-Parameter Lie Types of Technical Change

18. We first prove

Lemma 2 (*Classification of Two-Parameter Group*) *Any two-parameter Lie type of technical progress can be classified by one of the following four types*:

Case A $(U_1, U_2) \equiv 0,\ U_2 \not\equiv \rho(K, L)U_1$;

Case B $(U_1, U_2) \equiv 0,\ U_2 \equiv \rho(K, L)U_1$;

Case C $(U_1, U_2) \equiv U_1,\ U_2 \not\equiv \rho(K, L)U_1$;

Case D $(U_1, U_2) \equiv U_1,\ U_2 \equiv \rho(K, L)U_1$.

Proof See the Mathematical Appendix to this chapter.

As an example, consider the case of the technical progress function of capital expressed by the two-parameter Lie type

$$U_1 = L\,\partial/\partial K \qquad \text{and} \qquad U_2 = (K + L)\,\partial/\partial K.$$

Here we assume that the technical progress of labor is zero. It is easy to show that

$$(U_1, U_2) = U_1 \qquad \text{and} \qquad U_2 = \rho(K, L)U_1,$$

where $\rho(K, L) = (K + L)/L$. Hence this type belongs to Case D.

Normal Forms of Two-Parameter Technical Progress

19. As for a one-parameter Lie type of technical progress, any two-parameter type can be reduced to normal forms. Recall that any one-parameter Lie type of technical progress is reduced to the additive (or multiplicative) form. We present

Theorem 8 *(Normal Forms of Two-Parameter Lie Types of Technical Change) By a proper choice of variables, a pair of transformations satisfying each one of the conditions A, B, C, D in Lemma 2 can be made to assume one of the following normal forms:*

Case A (Capital and Labor Additive)

$$U_1 = \partial/\partial K, \tag{56-i}$$

$$U_2 = \partial/\partial L \tag{56-ii}$$

or

$$\bar{K} = K + t_1, \tag{56-i'}$$

$$\bar{L} = L + t_2. \tag{56-ii'}$$

Case B (Labor Additive and Capital Multiplicative)

$$U_1 = \partial/\partial L, \tag{57-i}$$

$$U_2 = K\,\partial/\partial L \tag{57-ii}$$

or

$$\bar{K} = K, \tag{57-i'}$$

$$\bar{L} = L + Kt_2 + t_1. \tag{57-ii'}$$

Case C (Labor Additive and Uniform Factor Augmenting)

$$U_1 = \partial/\partial L, \tag{58-i}$$

$$U_2 = K\,\partial/\partial K + L\,\partial/\partial L \tag{58-ii}$$

or

$$\bar{K} = Kt_2, \tag{58-i'}$$

$$\bar{L} = Lt_2 + t_1. \tag{58-ii'}$$

Case D (Labor Additive and Labor Homothetic)

$$U_1 \equiv \partial/\partial L, \tag{59-i}$$

$$U_2 \equiv L\,\partial/\partial L \tag{59-ii}$$

or

$$\bar{K} = K, \tag{59-i'}$$

$$\bar{L} = Lt_2 + t_1. \tag{59-ii'}$$

Proof See the Mathematical Appendix to this chapter.

Normal Forms of Second-Degree Subholotheticity

20. We are now in a position to derive the basic normal forms of implicit technology holothetic under two-parameter Lie types of technical progress.

Theorem 9 (*Normal Forms of the Implicit Technology Invariant under Two-Parameter Groups*) *An implicit technology holothetic under two-parameter Lie types of technical change can always be expressed in one of the four basic forms given in Table* 1.

TABLE 1

Case	Differential equation	Technology	Characterization
A	$\dfrac{d^2L}{dK^2} = N\left(\dfrac{dL}{dK}\right)$	$L + \int \phi[K + C_1]\,dK = C_2$, $C_i = C_i(Y)$, $i = 1, 2$	Capital and labor additive
B	$\dfrac{d^2L}{dK^2} = N(K)$	$L + C_1K - \iint N(K)\,dK^2 = C_2$	Quasi-linear
C	$\dfrac{d^2L}{dK^2} = N\left(\dfrac{dL}{dK}\right)/K$	$L + \int \phi[C_1K]\,dK = C_2$	Labor additive and C_1K multiplicative
D	$\dfrac{d^2L}{dK^2} = \dfrac{dL}{dK}N(K)$	$L + C_1\int \exp[\int N(K)\ dK]\,dK = C_2$	Nonlinear in capital, labor additive, and labor homothetic

Proof *Case A* The general differential equation for implicit technology invariant under $U_1 = \partial/\partial K$ and $U_2 = \partial/\partial L$ is derived from their twice-extended groups (Lemma 1). For U_1 we have $\xi = 1$, $\eta = 0$, $\eta' = 0$, $\eta'' = 0$, and for U_2, $\xi = 0$, $\eta = 1$, $\eta' = 0$, $\eta'' = 0$. The general type of differential equation of the second-order invariant under U_1 is $d^2L/dK^2 = N(L, dL/dK)$, and under U_2 is $d^2L/dK^2 = N(K, dL/dK)$, respectively. Hence, it must have the form $d^2L/dK^2 = N(dL/dK)$ to be invariant under

U_1 and U_2 simultaneously. Integrating the above twice, we get the general expression for implicit technology invariant under U_1 and U_2 as

$$L + \int \phi(K + C_1)\, dK = C_2.$$

Case B The differential equation invariant under $U_1 = \partial/\partial L$ and $U_2 = K\, \partial/\partial L$ has the form $d^2L/dK^2 = N(K)$, which can be integrated to yield the general expression for implicit technology $L + C_1 K - \iint N(K)\, dK^2 = C_2$.

Cases C and D In the same manner we obtain $d^2L/dK^2 = K^{-1}N(dL/dK)$ for $U_1 = \partial/\partial L$, $U_2 = K\, \partial/\partial K + L\, \partial/\partial L$, and $d^2L/dK^2 = (dL/dK)N(K)$ for $U_1 = \partial/\partial L$, $U_2 = L\, \partial/\partial L$. Integration of these differential equations yields the desired forms of implicit technology. Q.E.D.

Remark If the normal forms of two-parameter Lie types of technical change in Theorem 8 are expressed in terms of their canonical variables $\tilde{K}$ and $\tilde{L}$, then the general forms of differential equations and implicit technologies in Theorem 9 must be likewise simply replaced by those in terms of $\tilde{K}$ and $\tilde{L}$. In particular, K and L are interchangeable in Theorems 8 and 9.

Recovery of the Implicit Technology from Its Differential Equation of the Second Order

21. Under certain conditions, Theorems 8 and 9 can be used to recover the underlying implicit technology most efficiently from a given differential equation. Assume that the differential equation of the second order is given, say, from market observation, by (1′). Let us assume that we have found an s-parameter Lie type which leaves (1′) unchanged, $s > 2$. Since the s-parameter Lie type of technical change always contains a two-parameter sub-Lie type, we shall assume that we have just found such a pair of infinitesimal transformations U_1 and U_2 such that they satisfy either $(U_1, U_2) \equiv 0$ or $(U_1, U_2) \equiv U_1$. Passing to the Lie group representation of the internal structure of the underlying implicit technology R' corresponding to (1′),

$$R'h = \frac{\partial h}{\partial K} + \frac{dL}{dK}\frac{\partial h}{\partial L} + N\left(K, L, \frac{dL}{dK}\right)\frac{\partial h}{\partial(dL/dK)} = 0, \tag{60}$$

we observe that $R'h = 0$ is invariant under the extended transformation U_1' and U_2' subject to either $(U_1', U_2') \equiv 0$ or $(U_1', U_2') \equiv U_1'$, where $(U_1', U_2') \equiv (U_1, U_2)'$.

Let us assume that U_1', U_2', and R' are found to be not independent (unconnected) operators, i.e.,

$$U_2' \equiv \alpha(K, L, dL/dK)U_1' + \rho(K, L, dL/dK)R'. \tag{61}$$

Equation (61) implies that we must have[4]

$$U_2 \neq \sigma(K, L)U_1. \tag{62}$$

This means, from Lemma 2, that we have only Cases A and C.

Let us assume that we have reduced the original variables to their canonical variables. Then from Theorem 9, Case A gives $d^2\tilde{L}/d\tilde{K}^2 = F(d\tilde{L}/d\tilde{K})$ invariant under $V_1 = \partial/\partial\tilde{K}$ and $V_2 = \partial/\partial\tilde{L}$. Hence, alternatively,

$$Xh = \frac{\partial h}{\partial \tilde{K}} + \frac{d\tilde{L}}{d\tilde{K}}\frac{\partial h}{\partial \tilde{L}} + F\left(\frac{d\tilde{L}}{d\tilde{K}}\right)\frac{\partial h}{\partial(d\tilde{L}/d\tilde{K})} = 0$$

is invariant under $V'_1 = \partial/\partial\tilde{K}$ and $V'_2 = \partial/\partial\tilde{L}$. But Eq. (61) means that V'_1, V'_2, and X are not independent (unconnected); i.e.,

$$\begin{vmatrix} 1 & d\tilde{L}/d\tilde{K} & F(d\tilde{L}/d\tilde{K}) \\ 1 & 0 & 0 \\ 0 & 1 & 0 \end{vmatrix} = F\left(\frac{d\tilde{L}}{d\tilde{K}}\right) \equiv 0.$$

Hence, when (61) holds, the introduction of canonical variables for the two-parameter Lie type of technical change reduces (1′) to the form

$$\frac{d^2\tilde{L}}{d\tilde{K}^2} = 0, \tag{63}$$

[4] Assume the contrary, $U_2 = \sigma(K, L)U_1$. If

$$U'_1 = \xi^1\frac{\partial}{\partial K} + \eta^1\frac{\partial}{\partial L} + \eta^{1'}\frac{\partial}{\partial(dL/dK)},$$

U'_2 would have the form

$$U'_2 \equiv \sigma\xi^1\frac{\partial}{\partial K} + \sigma\eta^1\frac{\partial}{\partial L} + \left(\sigma\eta^{1'} + \eta^1\frac{\partial\sigma}{\partial K} + \eta^1\frac{\partial\sigma}{\partial L}\frac{dL}{dK} - \xi^1\frac{\partial\sigma}{\partial K}\frac{dL}{dK}\right.$$

$$\left. - \xi^1\frac{\partial\sigma}{\partial L}\left(\frac{dL}{dK}\right)^2\right)\frac{\partial}{\partial(dL/dK)} = A\frac{\partial}{\partial K} + B\frac{\partial}{\partial L} + C\frac{\partial}{\partial(dL/dK)}.$$

A relation of the form (61) implies the vanishing of the determinant, i.e.,

$$\Delta \equiv \begin{vmatrix} 1 & dL/dK & N \\ \xi^1 & \eta^1 & \eta^{1'} \\ A & B & C \end{vmatrix} \equiv 0.$$

This reduces to

$$\left(\eta^1 - \xi^1\frac{dL}{dK}\right)\left[\eta^1\frac{\partial\sigma}{\partial K} + \left(\eta^1\frac{\partial\sigma}{\partial L} - \xi^1\frac{\partial\sigma}{\partial K}\right)\frac{dL}{dK} - \xi^1\frac{\partial\sigma}{\partial L}\left(\frac{dL}{dK}\right)^2\right] \equiv 0.$$

Since neither $\eta^1 - \xi^1\, dL/dK$ nor both ξ^1 and η^1 can be identically zero, Δ can vanish identically only in case $\partial\sigma/\partial K \equiv 0$ and $\partial\sigma/\partial L \equiv 0$ simultaneously; i.e., σ must be constant. This would make U_1 and U_2 one and the same transformation. Hence, no relation of the form $U_2 = \sigma(K, L)U_1$ holds under (61).

or integrating twice,

$$\tilde{L}(K, L) + C_1(Y)\tilde{K}(K, L) = C_2(Y). \tag{64}$$

In the same way, Case C gives $d^2\tilde{L}/d\tilde{K}^2 = F(d\tilde{L}/d\tilde{K})/\tilde{K}$ invariant under $V_1 = \partial/\partial\tilde{L}$ and $V_2 = \tilde{K}\,\partial/\partial\tilde{K} + \tilde{L}\,\partial/\partial\tilde{L}$. Alternatively,

$$Xh = \frac{\partial h}{\partial \tilde{K}} + \frac{\partial \tilde{L}}{\partial \tilde{K}}\frac{\partial h}{\partial \tilde{L}} + \frac{F(d\tilde{L}/d\tilde{K})}{\tilde{K}}\frac{\partial h}{\partial (d\tilde{L}/d\tilde{K})} = 0$$

is invariant under

$$V'_1 = \frac{\partial}{\partial \tilde{L}} \qquad \text{and} \qquad V'_2 = \tilde{K}\frac{\partial}{\partial \tilde{K}} + \tilde{L}\frac{\partial}{\partial \tilde{L}}.$$

Again V'_1, V'_2, and X are not independent; i.e.,

$$\begin{vmatrix} 1 & d\tilde{L}/d\tilde{K} & F(d\tilde{L}/d\tilde{K}) \\ 1 & 0 & 0 \\ \tilde{K} & \tilde{L} & 0 \end{vmatrix} = -F\left(\frac{d\tilde{L}}{d\tilde{K}}\right) \equiv 0. \tag{65}$$

This again implies (63) and (64). In summary, we have

Theorem 10 *(Recovery of the Implicit Technology by Canonical Variables) When a given differential equation of the second order* (1′) *is invariant under a two-parameter Lie type of technical change with the infinitesimal transformations U_1 and U_2, the underlying implicit technology can be simply recovered by the introduction of canonical variables and can be expressed in a linear form*

$$\tilde{L} + C_1(Y)\tilde{K} = C_2(Y),$$

if the following condition is met:

$$U'_2 \equiv \alpha U'_1 + \rho R'.$$

VII. Projective Holotheticity: Holotheticity of Degree 8

22. One of the most important cases of implicit technology holothetic under r-parameter Lie type of technical progress is the projective technology. It is holothetic under the maximum number of different Lie types of technical progress, i.e., eight different types. Consider the differential equation for an implicit technology given by

$$d^2v/du^2 = 0, \tag{66}$$

where $\tilde{K} = u$ and $\tilde{L} = v$. In view of Lemma 1 in Chapter 4, Section 6, $d^2v/du^2 = 0$ is invariant if and only if G is a Lie subgroup of the general projective group $GP(2, R)$ of the plane, whose Lie algebras are given by the eight linearly independent infinitesimal "projective" transformations

$$U = a_1 U_1 + a_2 U_2 + \cdots + a_8 U_8, \tag{67}$$

where

$$U_1 = \frac{\partial}{\partial u}, \qquad U_2 = \frac{\partial}{\partial v}, \qquad U_3 = u\frac{\partial}{\partial u}, \qquad U_4 = u\frac{\partial}{\partial v},$$

$$U_5 = v\frac{\partial}{\partial u}, \qquad U_6 = v\frac{\partial}{\partial v}, \qquad U_7 = u\left(u\frac{\partial}{\partial u} + v\frac{\partial}{\partial v}\right),$$

$$U_8 = v\left(u\frac{\partial}{\partial u} + v\frac{\partial}{\partial v}\right). \tag{68}$$

The differential equation (66) is a simple example of an equation that is left unaltered by the maximum number of infinitesimal transformations. The implicit technology (*translinear projective technology*)

$$v(K, L) + C_1(Y)u(K, L) = C_2(Y) \tag{69}$$

is left unaltered by every projective transformation

$$\bar{u} = \frac{a_1 + a_3 u + a_5 v}{1 - a_7 u - a_8 v}, \qquad \bar{v} = \frac{a_2 + a_4 u + a_6 v}{1 - a_7 u - a_8 v}. \tag{70}$$

General Linear Type of Technical Change

23. We shall briefly study subgroups of the general transprojective type of technical progress, viz.,

$$\bar{u} = a_1 + a_3 u + a_5 v, \qquad \bar{v} = a_2 + a_4 u + a_6 v,$$

whose infinitesimal operators are

$$\partial/\partial u, \quad \partial/\partial v, \quad u\,\partial/\partial u, \quad v\,\partial/\partial v, \quad u\,\partial/\partial v, \quad v\,\partial/\partial u.$$

They constitute the so-called *general linear* Lie type of technical change (see Campbell [1966, pp. 18, 349]).

The four types of technical change

$$U_1 = u\,\partial/\partial u, \qquad U_2 = v\,\partial/\partial u, \qquad U_3 = u\,\partial/\partial v, \qquad U_4 = v\,\partial/\partial v$$

determine a four-parameter group; for they are linearly independent, and besides

$$(U_1, U_2) \equiv -U_2, \qquad (U_1, U_3) \equiv U_3, \qquad (U_1, U_4) \equiv 0,$$

$$(U_2, U_3) \equiv U_4 - U_1, \qquad (U_2, U_4) \equiv -U_2, \qquad (U_3, U_4) \equiv U_3.$$

Of the subgroups of the four-parameter group, the following are immediately obvious:

The two-parameter subgroups: $\{U_1, U_2\}, \{U_1, U_3\}, \{U_1, U_4\},$
$\{U_2, U_4\}, \{U_3, U_4\}.$

The three parameter subgroups: $\{U_1, U_2, U_4\}, \{U_1, U_3, U_4\}.$

As examples of linear technical change we present

$$\bar{K}^\delta = e_1 + e_3 K^\delta + e_5 L^\gamma, \qquad \bar{L}^\gamma = e_2 + e_4 K^\delta + e_6 L^\gamma$$

or

$$\log \bar{K} = \log e_1 + e_3 \log K + e_5 \log L \quad \Leftrightarrow \quad \bar{K} = e_1 K^{e_3} L^{e_5},$$
$$\log \bar{L} = \log e_2 + e_4 \log K + e_6 \log L \quad \Leftrightarrow \quad \bar{L} = e_2 K^{e_4} L^{e_6}.$$

Multifactor Generalizations

24. We can immediately generalize the concept of implicit holotheticity for a multifactor technology. Rather than a single second-order differential equation for K and L, we now have a system of second-order partial differential equations for an implicit technology. They may be invariant under r different Lie types of technical change. Hence, they constitute an r-parameter group and the technology has r-degree holotheticity. Considering the general projective type of technical change of order 15 for three factor inputs, K, L, and N, we have

$$\bar{u} = \frac{a_{11}u + a_{21}v + a_{31}w + a_{41}}{a_{14}u + a_{24}v + a_{34}w + a_{44}},$$
$$\bar{v} = \frac{a_{12}u + a_{22}v + a_{32}w + a_{42}}{a_{14}u + a_{24}v + a_{34}w + a_{44}}, \tag{71}$$
$$\bar{w} = \frac{a_{13}u + a_{23}v + a_{33}w + a_{43}}{a_{14}u + a_{24}v + a_{34}w + a_{44}},$$

where $u = u(K, L, N)$, $v = v(K, L, N)$, and $w = w(K, L, N)$. A system of partial differential equations

$$\partial^2 v/\partial u^2 = 0, \qquad \partial^2 w/\partial u^2 = 0 \tag{72}$$

is invariant under 15 different types of technical progress, which are the linearly independent operators for (71). The implicit technology corresponding to (72) is simply

$$u + C_1(Y)v + C_2(Y)w = C_3(Y), \tag{73}$$

a transadditive technology. This can be further generalized to the case of n factor inputs as

$$\sum_{i=1}^{n} C_i(Y)X_i = 1, \tag{74}$$

where $X_i = X_i(x_1, \ldots, x_n)$, $x_i = i$th factor input, $1 \leqq i \leqq n$. This form of implicit technology has the advantage of direct application to study a class of implicitly *additive* functions including addilog and CES types. This will be discussed in the following sections.

VIII. Classification of Implicit CES and Related Technologies[5]

Introduction

25. We have shown that the twice-extended transformations of technical progress can be used to generate economically meaningful implicit types of production functions and that they all belong to the technologies classified according to r-parameter Lie types of technical change. Given two factor inputs, capital and labor, the maximum number of r (thus, the maximum degree of implicit holotheticity) is shown to be eight. Since the number of linearly independent Lie types of technical change under which an implicit technology is holothetic is limited at most to eight, any implicit technology can effectively be classified by these independent types. We have found in Part VII that the projective type of Lie technical change is one of the cases in which the number of parameters is the maximum. It is evident from Eq. (74) that any *implicitly additive technology* (or preference) may be considered as the technology generated by the differential equations invariant under the general (trans-) projective type of technical change.

A Justification for "Implicit" Formulation

26. If one can observe some "invariant" relationships among various economic variables in the form of second-order (partial) differential equations, then the underlying technology may be expressed as an "implicit" formulation and the "nonhomotheticity" property may be best reflected in this formulation. Among the many economic concepts, elasticities of substitution may be

[5] This section is heavily dependent on the author's published papers in the Krelle volume (Sato [1977b]) and in the Toba conference volume (Sato [1975b]). However, here more emphasis is given to the Lie group aspect of implicit holotheticity.

the prime candidate for this purpose since they are by definition the most well-known expressions of second-order differential equation. An equally useful concept may be the partial differential of $\log \omega_{ij}$, where ω_{ij} is the marginal rate of substitution between ith and jth factors, $1 \leqq i, j \leqq n$, $i \neq j$.

Let the "invariant" relationships under some transformation groups be

$$\partial \log \omega_{ij} = g^{ij}(\omega, \partial x, x), \qquad i \neq j, \quad 1 \leqq i, j \leqq n, \tag{75}$$

where ω, ∂x, and x are the vectors whose elements are ω_{ij}, ∂x_i, and x_i, respectively (x_i being the ith input). Since ω_{ij} is by definition equal to $-\partial x_i/\partial x_j$, Eq. (75) represents a system of partial differential equations of the second order. In order that Eq. (75) may yield a meaningful solution, the g^{ij} must satisfy a number of different conditions such as the integrability conditions. Assume that all of these requirements are met; then the "invariant" relationships represented by (75) will yield an underlying family of production functions as a solution of the differential equation system. Let the underlying function be equal to

$$F(x, C_1(Y), \ldots, C_n(Y)) = 0. \tag{76}$$

In general, the production function is expressed by an "implicit" formulation.

Our purpose here is not to study this general case, but to consider a special case which may warrant empirical investigation (see Barnett *et al.*, [1979]). The following special form of g^{ij} will yield a meaningful solution:

$$\frac{\partial \log \omega_{ij}}{\partial \log x_i} = \frac{\partial \log g^i(x_i)}{\partial \log x_i} + \frac{\partial \log g^j(x_j)}{\partial \log x_i}, \qquad 1 \leqq i, j \leqq n. \tag{77}$$

One can immediately derive

$$\omega_{ij} = C^{ij}(Y) g^i g^j = -\partial x_i/\partial x_j.$$

Integrating this again, one gets

$$\sum_{i=1}^{n} C_i(Y) F^i(x_i) = 1, \tag{78}$$

which is the "implicitly" additive type of production functions. This contains almost all of the known forms of additive functions. When all the C_i in expression (78) are the same, such that

$$C(Y) \sum_{i=1}^{n} F^i(x_i) = 1, \tag{78'}$$

we have an "explicitly" additive type.

Nonhomothetic CES *Functions: A Brief History*

27. Although the general implicit or nonhomothetic CES family can be derived as a special case of (78) by setting $F^i(x_i) = x_i^{-\rho}$, we shall study this family in some detail. Ever since Arrow *et al.* [1961] used the explicit constant returns to scale CES functions for empirical estimation of aggregate production functions in various countries, its variants have been widely used in both theoretical and empirical works on production analysis (e.g., McElroy [1967], Paroush [1964], Uzawa [1962], Yasui [1965]). Prior to its use in production analysis, this family was known in demand analysis as a Bergson family of utility functions (Samuelson [1965]). In mathematics, Courant [1959, Vol. 1, pp. 557, 601] has used this explicit form to show the applicability of the so-called Jensen inequalities. Earlier writers in economics, such as Dickinson [1955] and Solow [1956], have used special cases of CES such as $\sigma = 2$.

The nonhomothetic family of CES functions was supposed to have been introduced by McFadden[6] in his paper read at the Econometric Society Meetings in 1964. A published note by McElroy [1967] has the first reference to the form $\sum_{i=1}^{n} (x_i/A_i(Y))^{-\rho} = 1$. However, to the author's best knowledge, the "explicit" form of the separable nonhomothetic CES functions was never derived until 1974 (Sato [1974]).[7] This paper shows clearly that a rather simple form of CES functions can be used to incorporate nonhomotheticity property of production and utility analyses. Being encouraged by this development, the present author has attempted and derived the general (nonseparable) family of CES functions by solution of a nonlinear second-order partial differential equation which defines the constancy of the elasticity of substitution. The result was published in *Econometrica* (Sato [1975a]). An empirical work, also containing this derivation, was published in *American Economic Review* (Sato [1977a]).

It was not until 1975 that the author presented the first Lie group application to CES functions (Sato [1975b]). The purpose was to show that the nonlinear second-order differential equation is invariant under the projective type of technical change with eight essential parameters. This idea was further developed to study a general separable type of utility (or production) functions in the paper published in the Krelle volume (Sato [1977b]).[8]

[6] This information was provided by a referee of *Economic Studies Quarterly* when the present author first submitted a paper on the separable nonhomothetic CES functions (Sato [1974]). This was acknowledged in a footnote of that paper, p. 43.

[7] This result was derived by accident in the course of preparing homework assignments for an undergraduate class with the assistance of Hiroshi Ono, now of Hokkaido University. Due to inadequate proofreading, acknowledgment of Professor Ono's share of the credit was omitted from the final version of the paper (Sato [1974]).

[8] In the private communication commenting on this paper, Professor Samuelson shows alternative formulations of the invariance principle for the general CES functions.

Forms of Nonhomothetic CES

28. The elasticity of substitution between factor K and factor L is defined as

$$\begin{aligned}\sigma &= (Lf_L + Kf_K)\Big/ KL\left(\frac{-f_K f_{LL}}{f_L} + 2f_{KL} - \frac{f_L f_{KK}}{f_K}\right) \\ &= (L + KR)\Big/ KL\left(\frac{\partial R}{\partial L} - \frac{\partial R}{\partial K} R^{-1}\right),\end{aligned} \tag{79}$$

where $R = f_K/f_L$ is the marginal rate of substitution. Solution to the above is found to be (Sato [1975a])

Homothetic: (i) $aC(f)K^{-\rho} + C(f)L^{-\rho} = 1$,
ordinary CES ($\sigma \neq 1$)
(ii) $aC(f)\log K + C(f)\log L = 1$,
ordinary Cobb–Douglas ($\sigma = 1$),

and

Nonhomothetic: (i) $C_1(f)K^{-\rho} + C_2(f)L^{-\rho} = 1$, $C_1 \neq aC_2$,
nonhomothetic CES ($\sigma \neq 1$)
(ii) $C_1(f)\log K + C_2(f)\log L = 1$, $C_1 \neq aC_2$,
nonhomothetic Cobb–Douglas (C–D) ($\sigma = 1$).

The problem with this classification, however, is that the class of nonhomothetic CES (or C–D) contains an infinite number of different types again depending upon the relationship between C_1 and C_2 ($C_1 \neq aC_2$), while the homothetic class contains only one type of the ordinary CES and Cobb–Douglas functions. It is only natural to devise a more meaningful classification scheme which enables one to divide the nonhomothetic family into different subclasses corresponding to different economic situations. To accomplish this we now present an alternative expression for the differential equation for the general CES family.

The elasticity of substitution between K and L can be alternatively expressed as

$$\sigma = \frac{d\log(L/K)}{d\log R}, \qquad R = \frac{f_K}{f_L} = -\left.\frac{dL}{dK}\right|_{f=\text{const}}. \tag{79'}$$

(We may omit $|_{f=\text{const}}$ for simplicity.) Rewriting the above, we have

$$\sigma = \frac{dL/dK\;L - K\;dL/dK}{KL}\,\frac{}{-d^2L/dK^2}, \qquad -\frac{d^2L}{dK^2} = \frac{dR}{dK} = \frac{\partial R}{\partial K} - R\frac{\partial R}{\partial L}. \tag{80}$$

Assuming that σ is constant subject to $0 < \sigma < \infty$, the above is equal to

$$\sigma KL \frac{d^2L}{dK^2} + \frac{dL}{dK}\left(L - K\frac{dL}{dK}\right) = 0. \tag{81}$$

The second-order partial differential equation defined by (79′) is now converted into the ordinary differential equation of the same order.

We now make the following important transformations:

$$K^{-\rho} = u, \qquad L^{-\rho} = v \quad \text{for} \quad \rho = \sigma^{-1} - 1, \quad \text{i.e.,} \quad \sigma \neq 1, \tag{82-i}$$

$$\log K = u, \qquad \log L = v \quad \text{for} \quad \rho = 0, \qquad \text{i.e.,} \quad \sigma = 1. \tag{82-ii}$$

Then we have

$$\frac{dv}{du} = \left(\frac{L}{K}\right)^{-\rho-1}\frac{dL}{dK} \quad \text{for } \sigma \neq 1 \qquad \text{and} \qquad \frac{dv}{du} = \left(\frac{L}{K}\right)^{-1}\frac{dL}{dK} \quad \text{for } \sigma = 1.$$

The second derivative d^2v/du^2 may be expressed as

$$\frac{d^2v}{du^2} = \frac{\sigma L^{-\rho-2}}{-\rho K^{-2\rho-1}}\left[\sigma KL\frac{d^2L}{dK^2} + \frac{dL}{dK}\left(L - K\frac{dL}{dK}\right)\right]$$

$$\text{for} \quad \sigma \neq 1 \quad \text{or} \quad \rho \neq 0, \tag{83-i}$$

$$\frac{d^2v}{du^2} = \frac{K}{L^2}\left[KL\frac{d^2L}{dK^2} + \frac{dL}{dK}\left(L - K\frac{dL}{dK}\right)\right]$$

$$\text{for} \quad \sigma = 1 \quad \text{or} \quad \rho = 0. \tag{83-ii}$$

But the expression in brackets in (83) is nothing but the differential equation which defines the constancy of the elasticity of substitution in (81). Hence, for positive values of K and L, d^2v/du^2 will be zero if and only if (81) is satisfied, i.e.,

$$d^2v/du^2 \equiv 0. \tag{84}$$

In retrospect, the family of nonhomothetic CES functions which was first derived in *Econometrica* (Sato [1975a]) could have easily been obtained from (84) simply as

$$v = a(f)u + b(f), \qquad v - a(f)u = b(f)$$

or

$$\frac{1}{b(f)}v - \frac{a(f)}{b(f)}u = 1 = C_1(f)v + C_2(f)u,$$

where $u = K^{-\rho}$ for $\rho \neq 0$ or $u = \log K$, for $\rho = 0$ and $v = L^{-\rho}$ for $\rho \neq 0$ or $v = \log L$ for $\rho = 0$. From the standpoint of the Lie theory of transformation groups, Eq. (84) represents one of the most remarkable transformations which can be used to classify the resulting solutions.

We summarize the results in the following:

Theorem 11 *(Alternative Formulation of* CES) *For positive values of K and L, the second-order differential equation* (81), *which defines the general class of CES functions will be satisfied if and only if Eq.* (84) *is met, where* $u = K^{-\rho}$, $v = L^{-\rho}$ *for* $\rho \neq 0$, *i.e.,* $\sigma \neq 1$; *or* $u = \log K$, $v = \log L$ *for* $\sigma = 1$.

Classification by the Basic Projective Types of Technical Change

29. We have now reduced the problem of analysis of the implicit (CES) family into that of analysis of the second-order linear differential equation of the simplest type. All the discussions in Part VII may be applied to this case by simply setting $\tilde{K} = u = K^{-\rho}$ and $\tilde{L} = v = L^{-\rho}$, or $\tilde{K} = u = \log K$ and $\tilde{L} = v = \log L$. We have seen that Eq. (84) is invariant under the general transprojective type of technical change with eight essential parameters. The set of eight linear independent infinitesimal operators are given by Eq. (68). In view of the basic result in Chapter 2 (Theorem 2), we can determine the eight basic forms of CES functions invariant under each of the eight infinitesimal transformations. We list

Eight Basic Types

1. *Additive type I* $U_1 = \partial/\partial u$. $Y = F[f(u, v)] = F[u + g(v)]$.
2. *Additive type II* $U_2 = \partial/\partial v$. $Y = F[v + g(u)]$.
3. *Multiplicative I* $U_3 = u\,\partial/\partial u$. $Y = F[\log u + \log g(v)] = F[ug(v)]$.
4. *Multiplicative II* $U_6 = v\,\partial/\partial v$. $Y = F[\log v + \log g(u)] = F[vg(u)]$.
5. *Ratio additive I* $U_4 = v\,\partial/\partial u$. $Y = F[(u/v) + g(v)]$.
6. *Ratio additive II* $U_5 = u\,\partial/\partial v$. $Y = F[(v/u) + g(u)]$.
7. *Ratio additive III* $U_7 = u^2\,\partial/\partial u + uv\,\partial/\partial v$. $Y = F[u^{-1} + g(v/u)]$.
8. *Ratio additive IV* $U_8 = uv\,\partial/\partial u + v^2\,\partial/\partial v$. $Y = F[v^{-1} + g(u/v)]$.

Using these eight basic invariant families, we now present the basic classification of the CES functions. First, for additive type I, the CES must have the form

$$u + g(v) = f.$$

But, since d^2v/du^2 must identically vanish, $g(v)$ must be equal to $av + c$, where a and c are some constants. Thus the type of CES functions which is generated from the infinitesimal transformation of the group U_1 must be simply *homothetic*, i.e.,

$$Y = F[\beta_1 u + \beta_2 v]. \tag{85}$$

In the same way, the type of CES functions generated from the infinitesimal transformation U_2 must be also homothetic. On the other hand, the type of CES functions generated from U_3, or multiplicative I, must be of the form

$$Y = F[u/(av + c)], \tag{86}$$

while the type generated by U_6, multiplicative II, must be

$$Y = F[v/(au + c)]. \tag{87}$$

The CES function corresponding to ratio additive I or $U_4 = v\,\partial/\partial u$ may be obtained from

$$(u/v) + g(v) = f \qquad \text{satisfying} \quad d^2v/du^2 = 0.$$

This implies that $u = v[f - g(v)]$, $u' = f - g(v) - vg'(v)$, and $u'' = -g'(v) - g'(v) - vg'' = 0$; i.e., $2g' = -vg''$. Solving this differential equation, we immediately obtain

$$g(v) = c_1 v^{-1} + c_2.$$

Hence f must take the form $(u/v) + (c_1/v) + c_2 = f$ or

$$Y = F[(u + c)/v],$$

which is identical with the case of U_6. In the same way for ratio additive II, $U_5 = u\,\partial/\partial v$, we will have $Y = F[(v + c)/u]$, which is the same form as multiplicative I, or U_3. For the group U_7, we must have

$$f = u^{-1} + g(v/u), \qquad \text{which will yield} \quad Y = F[(v + a)/au].$$

This is again identical with the case of U_3. In the same way the CES production generated from U_8 must be of the form

$$y = F[(u + a)/av],$$

which is the same as the case of U_4.

In summary, we have

Theorem 12 *(Basic Forms of* CES*) The types of* CES *production functions generated from the basic eight groups of projective transformations must have the forms* (85)–(87), *where* $u = K^{-\rho}$, $v = L^{-\rho}$ *for* $\rho \neq 0$, *i.e.,* $\sigma \neq 1$, *or* $u = \log K$, $v = \log L$ *for* $\rho = 0$, *i.e.,* $\sigma = 1$.

Classification by the General One-Parameter Subgroups

30. In view of a fundamental theorem in the Lie group theory, the differential equation (84) will be invariant under the general one-parameter subgroups. These subgroups will be obtained from a linear combination of the eight basic types such as $a_1\,\partial f/\partial u + a_2\,\partial f/\partial v = a_1 U_1 f + a_2 U_2 f$, and $a_1\,\partial f/\partial u + a_3 u\,\partial f/\partial u = a_1 U_1 f + a_3 U_3 f$. They must, in general, come from

$$U = \sum_{i=1}^{8} e_i U_i, \tag{88}$$

where $e_i = \text{const}\ (1 \leqq i \leqq 8)$, and the U_i are given by (68). We begin with the case $e_3 u\,\partial/\partial u + e_6 v\,\partial/\partial v = U$ (almost-homothetic type). The family of CES functions then must have the form

$$\beta_1[C(Y)]^{e_3}K^{-\rho} + \beta_2[C(Y)]^{e_6}L^{-\rho} = 1. \tag{89}$$

Especially when $C(Y) = Y$, we have

$$\beta_1 Y^{e_3}K^{-\rho} + \beta_2 Y^{e_6}L^{-\rho} = 1. \tag{90}$$

This satisfies the condition of almost-homogeneity, for we have

$$\beta_1(\lambda^\rho Y)^{e_3}(\lambda^{e_3}K)^{-\rho} + \beta_2(\lambda^\rho Y)^{e_6}(\lambda^{e_6}L)^{-\rho} = \beta_1\lambda^{\rho e_3 - \rho e_3}Y^{e_3}K^{-\rho}$$
$$+ \beta_2\lambda^{\rho e_6 - \rho e_6}Y^{e_6}L^{-\rho} = \beta_1 Y^{e_3}K^{-\rho} + \beta_2 Y^{e_6}L^{-\rho} = 1.$$

It is noted that the three different types of CES functions derived from the basic groups (Theorem 12) are, in fact, special cases of Eq. (89): (a) $e_3 = e_6 \neq 0$, homothetic CES; (b) $e_3 \neq e_6 \neq 0$, almost homothetic; (c) $e_3 = 0 \neq e_6$, capital homothetic; (d) $e_3 \neq 0 = e_6$, labor homothetic.

Rather than presenting the remaining more general one-parameter groups, we shall present the general "projective holothetic" family of production functions, which includes all the general forms of one-parameter subgroups. Using the results in Chapter 2 (Theorem 6), we have

$$Y = F[\phi(u, v) + \phi[(\alpha_1 u + \beta_1 v + \gamma_1)^{\lambda_2 - \lambda_3}(\alpha_2 u + \beta_2 v + \gamma_2)^{\lambda_3 - \lambda_1}$$
$$\times (\alpha_3 u + \beta_3 v + \gamma_3)^{\lambda_1 - \lambda_2}]], \tag{91}$$

where $\alpha_1, \alpha_2, \ldots, \gamma_3$ are functions of $e_1, e_2, \ldots, e_8$, and u and v are defined by (82).

General Separable Nonhomothetic CES *Functions*

31. As a special case of (91), we shall briefly mention the explicit form of separable nonhomothetic CES functions derived from $f_{KL} \equiv 0$ in Eq. (79). It has the form

$$f = f((a_1 u + b_1)/(a_2 v + b_2)), \tag{92}$$

where $u = K^{-\rho}$, $v = L^{-\rho}$ for $\sigma \neq 1$ and $u = \log K$ and $v = \log L$ for $\sigma = 1$ (see Sato [1974]). It is, however, more convenient to write (92) as

$$f = A\left[\frac{\beta_1 K^{-\rho} + (\alpha - \beta_1)\rho - \beta_1}{\beta_2 L^{-\rho} + (\alpha - \beta_2)\rho - \beta_2}\right]^{-c\alpha/\rho}. \tag{93}$$

Because of the reasons which are obvious, we call β_1 and β_2 the distribution parameters, $\alpha^{-1} = \gamma$ the nonhomotheticity parameter, $\rho = (1 - \sigma)/\sigma$ the substitution parameter, and A the (neutral) efficiency parameter. Sometimes it is more convenient to define *the* distribution parameter as

$$\beta_1 = (1 + \beta_2) = \beta \quad \textit{the} \text{ distribution parameter.}$$

In Eq. (93) when $\rho \to 0$ or $\sigma \to 1$, it reduces to the nonhomothetic Cobb–Douglas family

$$f = \left[\frac{\beta_1 \log K - (\alpha - \beta_1)}{\beta_2 \log L - (\alpha - \beta_2)}\right]^{-\alpha}. \tag{94}$$

When in (93) the nonhomotheticity parameter $\alpha^{-1} = \gamma$ $(\gamma < 0)$ approaches zero, we get the ordinary homothetic CES function as (85). The homothetic Cobb–Douglas family may be obtained in either way as $\gamma = \alpha^{-1} \to 0$ in (94) or as $\sigma \to 1$, $\rho = \alpha^{-1}$, $c = \rho$. These cases have been fully discussed in the paper cited (Sato 1974]).

Generalizations

32. The method used in the CES case may be extended to other types of functions. Again limiting ourselves to the two-commodity (or factor) world, we can formulate the invariant differential equation as

$$\frac{d \log \omega}{d \log x} = \frac{d \log f(x)}{d \log x} + \frac{d \log g(y)}{d \log x} \tag{95}$$

or

$$\frac{d^2 y}{dx^2} = \frac{f'}{f}\frac{dy}{dx} + \frac{g'}{g}\left(\frac{dy}{dx}\right)^2.$$

The solution to the above is immediately obtained as

$$C_1(U)F(x) + C_2(U)G(y) = 1, \qquad U = \text{level of utility}. \tag{96}$$

Let $F(x) = u$ and $G(y) = v$. Then clearly from (78′), the invariant equation (95) implies (84). Here we have the differential equation of the second order in the transformed variables $F(x) = u$ and $G(y) = v$, of which $u = x^{-\rho}$ and $v = y^{-\rho}$ is a special case, invariant under the general projective group.

We can easily extend these results to the case of $n > 2$. The invariant differential equations (77) will be reduced to

$$\partial^2 u_i/\partial u_j^2 \equiv 0, \qquad i \neq j, \quad 1 \leqq i, j \leqq n. \tag{97}$$

We then must rely on the n-dimensional projective groups. The general projective group in n variables has the operators

$$p_i, \quad u_i p_k, \quad u_i u_j p_j, \qquad 1 \leqq i, j, k \leqq n, \tag{98}$$

where $p_i = \partial/\partial u_i$, $u_i p_k = u_i\, \partial/\partial u_k$, and $u_i u_j p_j = u_i u_j\, \partial/\partial u_j$. The group is of order $n(n+2)$ (see Eisenhart [1933, pp. 43, 184]). Since the properties of this group are completely known, the interested reader may want to derive the general family of "projective" holothetic production functions (see Campbell [1966, Chapter XXIV]).

Mathematical Appendix

Proof of Theorem 2[9]

33. This is the direct consequence of Lie's most ingenious method of finding a form for $u''(K, L, dL/dK, d^2L/dK^2)$. Lie has provided a method of finding a form for u'' in (14) without having to integrate whatsoever, when u in (12) and u' in (13) are known. Consider the differential equation

$$v - au = b, \qquad v = u',$$

where a and b are constants. Since u and v are invariants of the once-extended group $U'f$, $v - au = b$ is invariant under Uf. Keeping a fixed an invariant family of a single infinity of integral curves corresponds to each value of b. By allowing b to take successively all possible values but still keeping a fixed, an infinity of such families, constituting a double infinity of integral curves, is determined by $v - au = b$. This larger aggregate is invariant under Uf. It is the set of integral curves of the differential equation of the second order obtained by differentiating $v - au = b$; i.e.,

$$\frac{dv}{dK} - a\frac{du}{dK} = 0$$

or

$$\left(\frac{\partial v}{\partial K} + \frac{\partial v}{\partial L}\frac{dL}{dK} + \frac{\partial v}{\partial(dL/dK)}\frac{d^2L}{dK^2}\right)\Bigg/\left(\frac{\partial u}{\partial K} + \frac{\partial u}{\partial L}\frac{dL}{dK}\right) - a = 0$$

or

$$W(K, L, dL/dK, d^2L/dK^2) - a = 0, \qquad \text{where} \quad W = dv/du.$$

[9] Also see Lie [1891, Chapter 16, pp. 373–383].

Since the integral curves are interchanged among themselves by every transformation of the Lie type of technical change, we have

$$U''(W - a) = 0 \qquad \text{whenever} \quad W - a = 0.$$

But since $a = \text{const}$, $U''(W - a) \equiv U''W \equiv 0$, which is sufficient to make $W = dv/du$ an invariant of the twice-extended group. Also, since $\partial v/\partial(dL/dK) \not\equiv 0$, W must contain d^2L/dK^2. Hence $W = \text{const}$ may be used as the third solution of (7). The general solution of $U''f = 0$ may then be written in the form

$$f(u, v, W) = 0 \qquad \text{or} \qquad W = F(u, v).$$

By setting $u = \tilde{K}$, $v = \tilde{L}$, and $W = d\tilde{L}/d\tilde{K}$, we obtain (15). Q.E.D.

Proof of Theorem 5[10]

34. Suppose that we have $I \in H^9$. Then (1′) must be also holothetic under $U = \sum_{i=1}^{9} c_i U_i$ for all possible choices of the constants c_i. In general, a unique integral curve of (1′) passes two points, lying within a definite region determined by (1′). Suppose that P_1, P_2, P_3, P_4 are four points such that each of the six pairs determines a distinct integral curve associated with (1′). The nine constants $c_1, \ldots, c_9$ can be chosen such that $U = \sum_{i=1}^{9} c_i U_i$ leaves each of P_1, P_2, P_3, P_4 invariant. This is because, if their coordinates are, respectively, (K_1, L_1), (K_2, L_2), (K_3, L_3), (K_4, L_4), then the requirement for this is the simultaneous satisfaction of the eight equations

$$\xi(K_j, L_j) \equiv \sum_{i=1}^{9} c_i \xi^i(K_j, L_j) = 0,$$

$$\eta(K_j, L_j) \equiv \sum_{i=1}^{9} c_i \eta^i(K_j, L_j) = 0 \qquad (j = 1, 2, 3, 4).$$

These equations determine finite values of the ratios of eight of the cs to the ninth one because of the linear independence of the nine transformations. With the cs thus chosen, the transformation $U = \sum_{i=1}^{9} c_i U_i$ leaves the four points unaltered, and, therefore, also the integral curves determined by any two of the points. Thus, through each one of the points, e.g., through P_1, pass three of these invariant integral curves. The point P_1 on these being left invariant by $U = \sum_{i=1}^{9} c_i U_i$, and these slopes at this point ,L'_{12}, L'_{13}, L'_{14}, respectively, are also left unaltered by it. Hence, if η' is the coefficient of $\partial/\partial(dL/dK)$ in the extended transformation, it follows that

$$\eta' = \frac{\partial \eta}{\partial K} + \left(\frac{\partial \eta}{\partial L} - \frac{\partial \xi}{\partial K}\right)\frac{dL}{dK} - \frac{\partial \xi}{\partial K}\left(\frac{dL}{dK}\right)^2 = 0$$

[10] Also see Lie [1891, p. 405].

for $K = K_1, L = L_1, dL/dK = L' = L'_{12}, L'_{13}, L'_{14}$, where $U = \sum_{i=1}^{9} c_i U_i = \xi\, \partial/\partial K + \eta\, \partial/\partial L$. Letting a, b, c be the values of $\partial\eta/\partial K$, $\partial\eta/\partial L - \partial\xi/\partial K$, $-\partial\xi/\partial L$, respectively, when $K = K_1, L = L_1$, then $\eta' = 0$ gives $a + bL'_{12} + cL'^2_{12} = 0$, $a + bL'_{13} + cL'^2_{13} = 0$, $a + bL'_{14} + cL'^2_{14} = 0$. Since the determinant of the coefficients of the three equations is equal to

$$(L'_{13} - L'_{14})(L'_{14} - L'_{12})(L'_{12} - L'_{13}) \neq 0,$$

we must have $a = b = c$. Hence $\eta' \equiv 0$ for every integral curve through P_1, and every integral curve through P_1 is invariant under $U = \xi\, \partial/\partial K + \eta\, \partial/\partial L$. In exactly the same way, it can be shown that every integral curve through each of the other points P_2, P_3, P_4 is invariant under U. If P_5 is any fifth point in the region containing P_1, P_2, P_3, P_4, it will lie upon at least two integral curves, each of which passes through one of those points. These curves being invariant P_5 is left unaltered by $U = \xi\, \partial/\partial K + \eta\, \partial/\partial L$. In this way every point of the plane is found to be left unaltered under U. Hence we must have $U = \xi\, \partial/\partial K + \eta\, \partial/\partial L \equiv 0$. That is to say, any nine U_i which leave (1′) invariant cannot be linearly independent. Q.E.D.

Proof of Lemma 2

35. If a two-parameter Lie type of technical progress is determined by U_1 and U_2, which may be the case of $r = 2$ or the case of a two-parameter subgroup, $s = 2 < r$, we have from the condition of (54)

$$(U_1, U_2) = a_1 U_1 + a_2 U_2,$$

where a_1, a_2 are constant or zero. Assume that they are not zero. In this case it is always possible to find a pair of transformations to determine the two-parameter group for which one of these constants is unity and the other zero. If $a_1 \neq 0$, then $V_1 \equiv U_1 + (a_2/a_1)U_2$ and $V_2 \equiv (1/a_1)U_2$ are linearly independent and satisfy $(V_1, V_2) \equiv V_1$. On the other hand, if (U_1, U_2) is zero, or $a_1 \equiv a_2 \equiv 0$, then

$$(c_1 U_1 + c_2 U_2, b_1 U_1 + b_2 U_2) \equiv (c_1 b_2 - c_2 b_1)(U_1, U_2) \equiv 0$$

for all choices of c_i and b_i. Hence every two-parameter Lie type of technical progress can be represented by a pair of U_1 and U_2 such that either (i) $(U_1, U_2) \equiv 0$ or (ii) $(U_1, U_2) \equiv U_1$. These two possibilities are mutually exclusive. (See Eisenhart [1933, p. 60]. The case in which $(U_1, U_2) = 0$ is often referred to as an *Abelian* group.)

The second classification may be given as follows. If a two-parameter group is given by U_1 and U_2 which are connected by a relation of the form

$$U_2 \equiv \rho(K, L) U_1,$$

where $\rho(K, L)$ is *not* a constant, every pair of distinct transformations of the group are connected by a relation of this form. This is because if $V_1 = a_1 U_1 + a_2 U_2, V_2 = b_1 U_1 + b_2 U_2 (a_1 b_2 \neq a_2 b_1)$, then $V_2 = ((b_1 + b_2 \rho)/(a_1 + a_2 \rho))V_1$. Hence every two-parameter Lie type of technical progress can be divided into two classes according as their distinct transformations are connected either by (i) $U_2 \equiv \rho(K, L)U_1$ or (ii) $U_2 \not\equiv \rho(K, L)U_1$. Since the first and second classifications are independent of each other, we have four classifications. Q.E.D.

Proof of Theorem 8

36. We present only the basic steps.

Case A $((U_1, U_2) \equiv 0,\ U_2 \equiv \rho(K, L)U_1)$ Any one-parameter Lie type of technical progress can be reduced to $U_1 \equiv \partial/\partial K$. If the resulting form of U_2 is $U_2 \equiv \xi^2\, \partial/\partial K + \eta^2\, \partial/\partial L$, then we must have $\partial\xi^2/\partial K \equiv 0$ and $\partial\eta^2/\partial L \equiv 0$, since

$$(U_1, U_2) \equiv \frac{\partial \xi^2}{\partial K}\frac{\partial}{\partial K} + \frac{\partial \eta^2}{\partial K}\frac{\partial}{\partial L} \equiv 0$$

by assumption. Hence ξ^2 and η^2 are at most functions of L; i.e.,

$$U_2 \equiv \xi^2(L)\frac{\partial}{\partial K} + \eta^2(L)\frac{\partial}{\partial L},$$

where $\eta^2(L) \not\equiv 0$, since $U_2 \not\equiv \rho(K, L)U_1$. The transformation $U_1 = \partial/\partial K$ remains unaltered by a change of variables of the type $\tilde{K} = K - \phi(L)$, $\tilde{L} = \psi(L)$, where $\phi(L)$ and $\psi(L)$ are functions to be determined. This change of variable causes U_2 to take the form $[\xi^2(L) - \eta^2(L)\phi'(L)]\, \partial/\partial\tilde{K} + [\eta^2(L)\psi'(L)]\, \partial/\partial\tilde{L}$. If

$$\phi = \int \frac{\xi^2(L)}{\eta^2(L)}\, dL \qquad \text{and} \qquad \psi = \int \frac{dL}{\eta^2(L)},$$

then U_2 will assume the form $U_2 = \partial/\partial\tilde{L}$, which proves (56).

Case B $((U_1, U_2) \equiv 0,\ U_2 \equiv \rho(K, L)U_1)$ Assume that U_1 takes the form $U_1 = \partial/\partial L$. Then U_2 assumes the form $U_2 = \lambda(K, L)\, \partial/\partial L$, where $\lambda(K, L)$ is what ρ becomes when the old variables are replaced by the new. Since by assumption

$$(U_1, U_2) \equiv \partial\lambda/\partial L\ \partial/\partial L \equiv 0,$$

λ is a function of K only. Taking this as the new K, U_2 assumes the form $K\, \partial/\partial L$, which proves (57).

Case C $((U_1, U_2) \equiv U_1, U_2 \not\equiv \rho(K, L)U_1)$ As before, U_1 can be put in the form $U_1 = \partial/\partial L$. Since

$$(U_1, U_2) \equiv \frac{\partial \xi^2}{\partial L}\frac{\partial}{\partial K} + \frac{\partial \eta^2}{\partial L}\frac{\partial}{\partial L} \equiv U_1 \equiv \frac{\partial}{\partial L},$$

we must have $\partial \xi^2/\partial L = 0$ and $\partial \eta^2/\partial L = 1$, where ξ^2 and η^2 are the infinitesimal transformation of the second type. Hence U_2 must have the form

$$U_2 = \xi^2(K)\frac{\partial}{\partial K} + [C(K) + L]\frac{\partial}{\partial L},$$

where $\xi^2(K) \not\equiv 0$, because of $U_2 \not\equiv \rho(K, L)U_1$. The introduction of the new variables $\tilde{K} = \phi(K)$, $\tilde{L} = \psi(K) + L$ leaves U_1 unchanged in the form, but changes U_2 into

$$U_2 = \xi^2(K)\phi'(K)\frac{\partial}{\partial \tilde{K}} + [\xi^2(K)\psi'(K) + C(K) + L]\frac{\partial}{\partial \tilde{L}}.$$

This takes the form $U_2 = \tilde{K}\,\partial/\partial\tilde{K} + \tilde{L}\,\partial/\partial\tilde{L}$, where $\xi^2(K)\phi'(K) = \phi(K)$ and $\xi^2(K)\psi'(K) + C(K) = \psi(K)$. This proves (58).

Case D $((U_1, U_2) \equiv U_1, U_2 \equiv \rho(K, L)U_1)$ As before, we assume $U_1 \equiv \partial/\partial L$. This will cause U_2 to assume the form $U_2 = \eta^2(K, L)\,\partial/\partial L$. Since $(U_1, U_2) \equiv U_1$, $\partial \eta^2/\partial L \equiv 1$ and η^2 must be equal to $C(K) + L$, so that $U_2 \equiv [C(K) + L]\,\partial/\partial L$. The change of variables $\tilde{L} = C(K) + L$ leaves U_1 unaltered and changes U_2 to $U_2 \equiv \tilde{L}\,\partial/\partial\tilde{L}$, which proves (59). Q.E.D.

REFERENCES

Arrow, K., Chenery, H., Minhas, B., and Solow, R. [1961]. Capital-labor substitution and economic efficiency, *Review of Economics and Statistics*, **43**, 225–250.

Barnett, W. A., Kopecky, K. J., and Sato, R. [1979]. Estimation of implicit utility models. Special Study Paper—Division of Research and Statistics, # 127, Federal Reserve Board (forthcoming in *European Economic Review*, 1981).

Blackorby, C., and Russell, R. [1976]. Functional structure and the Allen partial elasticity of substitution: An application of duality theory, *Review of Economic Studies*, **43**, 285–291.

Blackorby, C., Primont, D., and Russell, R. [1978]. *Duality, Separability, and Functional Structure: Theory and Economic Applications*. Elsevier and North-Holland Publ., Amsterdam.

Campbell, J. E. [1966]. *Introductory Treatise on Lie's Theory of Continuous Transformation Groups*. Chelsea, New York.

Courant, R. [1959]. *Differential and Integral Calculus*, Vols. I, II. Wiley (Interscience), New York.

Dickinson, H. D. [1955]. A note on dynamic economics, *Review of Economic Studies*, **22**, 169–179.

Diewert, W. E. [1974]. Application of duality theory, in *Frontiers of Quantitative Economics* (M. Intriligator and K. Kendrick, eds.), Vol. II. North-Holland Publ., Amsterdam.

Eisenhart, L. P. [1933]. *Continuous Groups of Transformations*. Princeton Univ. Press, Princeton, New Jersey. Reprinted by Dover, New York, 1961.

Gorman, W. M. [1970]. Quasi-Separable Preferences, Costs and Technologies. Mimeo, London School of Economics and Political Science.

Hanoch, G. [1975]. Production and demand models with direct and indirect implicit additivity, *Econometrica*, **43**, 395–419.

Houthakker, H. S. [1960]. Additive preferences, *Econometrica*, **28**, 244–257.

Ince, E. L. [1956]. *Ordinary Differential Equations*. Dover, New York.

Lie, S. [1891]. *Vorlesungen über Differentialgleichungen, mit bekannten infinitesimalen Transformationen* (G. Scheffers, ed.). Teubner, Leipzig. Reprinted by Chelsea, New York, 1967.

McElroy, F. W. [1967]. Note on the CES production functions, *Econometrica*, **35**, 154–156.

McFadden, D. [1968]. Further results on CES production functions, *Review of Economic Studies*, **30(2)**, 73–83.

McFadden, D. [1978]. Costs, revenue, and profit functions, in *Production Economics: A Dual Approach to Theory and Applications*, M. Fuss and D. McFadden, (eds.), *Vol. 2*, Contributions to Economic Analysis, Vol. 111. North-Holland Publ., Amsterdam, 1978.

Paroush, J. [1964]. A note on the CES function, *Econometrica*, **32**, 213–214.

Samuelson, P. A. [1965]. Using full duality to show that simultaneously additive direct and indirect utilities implies unitary price elasticity of demand, *Econometrica*, **33**, 781–796.

Sato, K. [1967]. A two-level constant-elasticity-of-substitution production function. *Review of Economic Studies*, **34**, 201–218.

Sato, R. [1974]. On the class of separable non-homothetic CES production functions, *Economic Studies Quarterly*, 41–55.

Sato, R. [1975a]. The most general class of CES functions, *Econometrica*, **43**, 999–1003.

Sato, R. [1975b]. Analysis of production functions by Lie theory of transformation groups: Classification of general CES functions. Presented at the *International Symposium in Toba, Japan*, Proceedings published under the title of *Allocation of Resources and Division of Space* (R. Sato and T. Fujii, eds.), Lecture Notes in Mathematical Economics and Mathematical Systems, Vol. 147. Springer-Verlag, Berlin and New York, 1977.

Sato, R. [1977a]. Homothetic and non-homothetic CES production functions, *American Economic Review*, **67**, 559–569.

Sato, R. [1977b]. The implicit formulation and non-homothetic structure of utility functions, in *Quantitative Wirtschaftsforschung: W. Krelle zum 60. Geburtstag* (H. Albach, E. Helmstädter, and R. Henn, eds.). Mohr, Tübingen.

Sato, R., and Krelle, W. [1975]. Non-homothetic production functions subject to different types of technical progress: Theory and estimation. University of Bonn, Germany. Published in *Economic Review* (*Keizai Kenkyu, Hitotsubashi University, Tokyo*), **29**, 301–314.

Solow, R. M. [1956]. A contribution to the theory of economic growth, *Quarterly Journal of Economics*, **70**, 65–94.

Uzawa, H. [1962]. Production functions with constant elasticities of substitution, *Review of Economic Studies*, **29**, 291–299.

Yasui, T. [1965]. The CES production function: A note, *Econometrica*, **33**, 646–648.

CHAPTER 6

SELF-DUAL PREFERENCES AND TECHNOLOGIES

I. Introduction: Why Self-Duality?

1. In the preceding chapters we have shown that the *invariance property* of Lie group transformations serves as an extremely powerful tool for the study of production functions and thus of utility functions and preference orderings also. In this chapter we shall be concerned with a somewhat different, although basically the same, aspect of the invariance property exhibited in utility and production analysis—the self-duality property of preferences and technologies.

Recent papers by Houthakker [1960, 1965], Samuelson [1965, 1969], Sir John Hicks [1969], Pollak [1972], Lau [1969], Sato [1976], Samuelson and Swamy [1974], and Haque [1975] deal with the question of the existence of a nontrivial preference ordering which exhibits the same mathematical properties in terms of both the direct and indirect utility functions. Some of the mathematical properties investigated in these works are homogeneity, separability, additivity, and self-duality. It is shown that homogeneity and separability are compatible with both the direct and indirect utility functions, but that direct and indirect additivity is consistent with only limited classes of utility functions (Hicks [1969], Samuelson [1969]). Earlier, Samuelson [1965] raised the question of whether there exists a nontrivial "self-dual" preference ordering which may require more stringent conditions than homogeneity and separability. A "self-dual" preference is defined to be a preference ordering such that the direct utility function is exactly *identical* with the corresponding indirect utility function.[1] Although partial answers given by Houthakker [1965], Pollak [1972], and others are very illuminating, the solution is far from complete.

The purpose of this chapter is to present a more complete solution to the problem of self-duality by a group-theoretic approach.[2] We shall first discuss *why self-duality* in preference orderings (also in production and cost functions) may be important in demand analysis. Consider a typical estimation procedure of a system of demand functions and an underlying utility function of a representative individual. Here, even if we estimate the meaningful demand system (meaningful in the sense that all the symmetry and semidefiniteness conditions of the Slutsky matrix are fulfilled), we may not be able to identify the underlying (direct) utility function of the individual. This is because the system of demand functions can in general be used to recover (or integrate) only the underlying *indirect* utility function, but *not* the underlying *direct* utility function. Although theoretically all the properties of a direct utility function can be studied through its indirect form, there may be situations in which one may really want to recover the direct utility function, such as in the case of price and quantity indexes (see Samuelson and Swamy [1974]). The concept of self-duality is useful under the circumstances. Because by the assumption of the same form (weak or strong), one can determine not only the form of indirect utility functions from the demand functions, but also simultaneously the form of direct utility functions.

Since it is also known (Sato [1976], Samuelson and Swamy [1974]) that the self-dual type of preferences is not merely a limiting case, but that there exists an infinity of self-dual preferences, this concept is very useful from an empirical point of view. As a matter of fact, almost all of the known types of demand systems used in empirical analyses thus far fall into this category.

II. "Exact" (or Strong) Self-Duality

2. We begin by presenting formally the conditions of self-duality stated by Houthakker [1965]. Let x be a vector of commodities $x_1, \ldots, x_n$ and y a vector of prices (each divided by income, i.e., $y_i = p_i/I$, $i = 1, \ldots, n$). Then the demand and "inverse" demand functions are

$$x = f(y) \geqq 0 \tag{1}$$

and

$$y = g(x) \geqq 0, \tag{2}$$

[1] Compare footnote 7 of Samuelson's paper [1965, p. 793].

[2] A part of this chapter is taken from my earlier paper on the subject (Sato [1976]). It is seen, however, that this chapter has a heavier orientation toward Lie group applications than the earlier approach.

satisfying the budget constraint $x'y = 1$ (also the Slutsky equations satisfying the well-known conditions). Houthakker's question is whether or not there exists F such that $x = F(y, A)$ and $y = F(x, B)$ satisfying $F[F(x, B), A] = x$, where A and B are sets of r parameters. Those familiar with Lie's work on transformation groups would immediately notice that the foregoing condition is closely related to the conditions of an r-parameter transformation group. In his well-known paper, Lie [1880, p. 117] asks the following question:

> *Problem.* To determine the most general function f of x and r parameters $a_1, a_2, \ldots, a_r$ satisfying an equation of the form $f[f(x, a_1, \ldots, a_r), b_1, \ldots, b_r] = f(x, c_1, \ldots, c_r)$, in which it is assumed that the c_i depend only on the a's and the b's. This problem can perhaps be more clearly formulated by using the concept of a transformation group, ...

Although Houthakker's condition is not exactly identical to (but a special case of) Lie's condition (because in Houthakker's condition we look for the condition $F(F) = x$, while in Lie's formulation we look for $f(f) = f$ in general), one can look for a type of analysis necessary to answer the question of self-duality from the group theoretic approach. This is particularly true when one looks for empirically manageable types of self-dual conditions, i.e., separable self-duality conditions as shown in Section 16.

3. Let $\phi(x)$ and $\psi(y)$ denote a direct and indirect utility function, respectively. The demand functions $x = f(y)$ and their "inverse" demand functions $y = g(x)$ provide the unique solutions to the following dual problems, respectively:

$$\max_x N(x, y) \qquad \text{subject to} \quad y'x = 1$$

or

$$\max_y N(x, y) \qquad \text{subject to} \quad x'y = 1,$$

where $N(x, y) = \phi(x) - \psi(y)$. In view of the usual regularity assumptions on $\phi(x)$ (therefore, also on $\psi(y)$) the demand functions can be uniquely inverted to give the single-valued "inverse" demand functions and vice versa: $g = f^{-1}$ and $f = g^{-1}$.

"Exactly" (or Strongly) Self-Dual Preference Ordering

Following Samuelson [1965], a preference ordering is said to be *"exactly" (or strongly) self-dual* if it has a direct utility function $\phi(x)$ which is *identically* equal to its indirect utility function $-\psi(y)$. Alternatively, we say that a preference ordering is "exactly" or "strongly" self-dual if the demand and "inverse" demand functions (1) and (2) satisfy the relation

$$x \equiv f[f(x)], \qquad y \equiv g[g(y)]. \tag{3}$$

If it is obvious from the context, then we may omit the word "exactly" or "strongly" and simply say that a preference ordering is *self-dual* if the demand and their inverse demand functions are identical.[3]

The system of demand functions together with $x'y = 1$ may be viewed as a continuous transformation of y to x. When we define a series of transformations such that

$$\begin{aligned} T&: \quad x_i = f^i(y_1, \ldots, y_n) \qquad (i = 1, \ldots, n), \\ T^2&: \quad x_i' = f^i(x_1, \ldots, x_n), \\ T^3&: \quad x_i'' = f^i(x_1', \ldots, x_n'), \\ &\vdots \end{aligned}$$

then the system of demand functions is *"exactly" self-dual if and only if* $T^2: x_i' = f^i(x_1, \ldots, x_n) \equiv y_i = f^i[f^1(y), \ldots, f^n(y)]$, $1 \leqq i \leqq n$; i.e.,

$$T^2 \equiv Id \qquad \text{(identical transformation)}. \tag{4}$$

This implies that the demand function is an *involution*, i.e., a transformation which is its own inverse.[4] We will require the following concept.

Set-Symmetric Functions

Consider a function with m independent variables,

$$F(z_1, z_2, \ldots, z_m) = 0. \tag{5}$$

If $z = (z_1, z_2, \ldots, z_m)$ is partitioned into k subsets with each set containing the same number of s elements such that $z = (z^1, z^2, \ldots, z^k)$, $ks = m$, where $z^1 = (z_1, \ldots, z_s)$, $z^2 = (z_{s+1}, \ldots, z_{2s}), \ldots,$ then we have $F(z^1, z^2, \ldots, z^k) = 0$. The function F is said to be *set-symmetric* (or *invariant of the groups of permutations*) with respect to k vector if every permutation of sets z^i and z^j has no effect on F; i.e.,

$$F(z^{j1}, z^{j2}, \ldots, z^{jk}) \equiv F(z^1, z^2, \ldots, z^k), \qquad k = \text{integer} > 1. \tag{6}$$

[3] This is Samuelson's original definition. However, later the concept of "self-duality" is used to define a more general class of preference orderings in which the direct and indirect utility functions have the "same" mathematical form. Pollak's definition [1972, p. 435] is even more general. (In fact, it may be too general to be very useful.) Pollak refers to Samuelson's case as "strong self-duality."

[4] With appropriate redefinitions of x and y, demand functions can be rearranged to form a group. A *Legendre transformation* is an example of involution systems.

By a permutation of two sets z^i and z^j, we mean that each element of z^i is exchanged with the corresponding element of z^j without changing the order of these elements, i.e.,

$$\begin{array}{cccccc} z^i & = (z_1^i, & z_2^i, & \ldots, & z_s^i), \\ \uparrow\downarrow & \uparrow\downarrow & \uparrow\downarrow & & \uparrow\downarrow \\ z^j & = (z_1^j, & z_2^j, & \ldots, & z_s^j). \end{array}$$

Obviously, if $s = 1$, this definition reduces to the concept of ordinary "symmetric" function. Therefore, $F(z)$ is "set-symmetric" if it is *invariant* under the symmetric group of substitution of z^i with z^j.

If the demand functions are given, we can always find n independent implicit functions, including the budget constraint relating the $2n$ variables x and y, such that F^i is a monotone with respect to all elements in x and y and the Jacobian of the system of n implicit functions is nonvanishing; i.e.,

$$F^i(x, y) = 0, \qquad F^n(x, y) = x'y - 1 = 0, \qquad i = 1, \ldots, n - 1,$$

or more compactly

$$F(x, y) = 0. \tag{7}$$

The F^i may be the demand (or inverse demand) functions or the marginal rates of substitution, or any implicit relations yielding the system of given demand functions.

Theorem 1 *(Necessary and Sufficient Conditions for Self-Duality) The necessary and sufficient condition for a preference ordering to be "exactly" or "strongly" self-dual is that $F(x, y) = 0$ be set-symmetric in absolute value with respect to quantity and (real) price vectors, i.e.,*

$$F(x, y) = \pm F(y, x). \tag{8}$$

That is to say, $|F(x, y)|$ is an invariant of the group under substitution of x into y.

Proof We first observe that the budget constraint is in itself set-symmetric with respect to x and y, i.e., $x'y \equiv y'x = 1$. Since all other F's are also set-symmetric in absolute value, we can express any x_i and y_i in the identical form. (When $F(x, y) = -F(y, x) = 0$, we multiply -1 to get $F(y, x) = 0$.) Initiating with x_1 and y_1, and by solving F in terms of x_1 and y_1, we get

$$x_1 = H^1(x_2, \ldots, x_n, y_1, \ldots, y_n), \qquad y_1 = H^1(x_1, \ldots, x_n, y_2, \ldots, y_n).$$

Substitute these in F^2 and express x_2 and y_2 as

$$x_2 = H^2(x_3, \ldots, x_n, y_1, \ldots, y_n), \qquad y_2 = H^2(x_1, \ldots, x_n, y_3, \ldots, y_n);$$

we repeat this process until we finally obtain

$$x_n = H^n(y_1, \ldots, y_n) = f^n(y), \qquad y_n = H^n(x_1, \ldots, x_n) = f^n(x).$$

Substituting these results back into all other x_i and y_i, we have

$$x_i = f^i(y), \qquad y_i = f^i(x) \equiv g^i(x), \qquad i = 1, \ldots, n.$$

To demonstrate that this condition is also necessary, assume that $x = f(f(x))$, $g(g(y)) = y$. Define

$$F^i = x_i - f^i(y) + y_i - f^i(x) = 0, \qquad i = 1, \ldots, n-1,$$

$$F^n = \sum_{j=1}^{n} x_j y_j - 1 = 0.$$

Then we immediately obtain $F(x, y) \equiv F(y, x)$. Also define

$$F^i = x_i - f^i(y) - (y_i - f^i(x)) = 0, \qquad i = 1, \ldots, n-1,$$

$$F^n = \sum_{j=1}^{n} x_j y_j - 1 = 0.$$

Then we have $F^i(x, y) = -F^i(y, x) = 0, i = 1, \ldots, n-1$. Hence $|F(x, y)| = |F(y, x)|$. Q.E.D.

For homothetic utility functions, we have

Corollary to Theorem 1 *(Self-Duality of Homothetic Preferences) The necessary and sufficient condition for a homothetic utility function to be exactly self-dual is that the* $(n-1)$ *implicit functions relating* y_i/y_j *(the marginal rates of substitution between* x_i *and* x_j*) and* x_i/x_j *(demand ratios) be set-symmetric in absolute value with respect to*

$$x/x_i = (x_1/x_i, x_2/x_i, \ldots, x_n/x_i)$$

and

$$y/y_i = (y_1/y_i, y_2/y_i, \ldots, y_n/y_i)$$

for at least one i $(i = 1, \ldots, n)$*; i.e.,*

$$|F(x/x_i, y/y_i)| \equiv |F(y/y_i, x/x_i)| = 0 \tag{9}$$

subject to $x'y = 1$.

This follows directly from Theorem 1 and from the fact that for any homothetic utility function the marginal rates of substitution are only functions of demand ratios.[5]

[5] Professor Samuelson informs me that in 1973 he derived the necessary and sufficient conditions for the $n = 2$ and homothetic cases.

Examples

4. We now present a few examples.

(a) *Cobb–Douglas* When we have $F^i = \sum_{j=1}^n b_{ij}x_j y_j = c_i (1 \leqq i \leqq n-1)$ together with $x'y - 1 = 0$, we can solve for $x_j y_j = k_j$, $\sum_{j=1}^n k_j = 1$. This is the self-dual demand system associated with the Cobb–Douglas case.

(b) *Linear Demand Function* Consider $F^1 = x_1 + y_1 - b = 0$, $b > 0$, and the budget equation $F^2 = x_1 y_1 + x_2 y_2 - 1 = 0$. Then

Demand functions	*Inverse demand functions*
$x_1 = b - y_1 > 0,$	$y_1 = b - x_1 > 0,$
$x_2 = (y_1^2 - by_1 + 1)/y_2 > 0,$	$y_2 = (x_1^2 - bx_1 + 1)/x_2 > 0.$

Integrating the total differential equations for the direct and indirect utility functions, we obtain

$$\phi(x) = U = -\tfrac{1}{2}\log(x_1^2 - bx_1 + 1) + \frac{b}{\sqrt{B}}\tan^{-1}\left(\frac{2x_1 - b}{\sqrt{B}}\right) + \log x_2,$$

$$B = 4 - b^2 > 0, \qquad b - 1 < x_1 < b + 1,$$

and

$$-\psi(y) = -V = -\tfrac{1}{2}\log(y_1^2 - by_1 + 1) + \frac{b}{\sqrt{B}}\tan^{-1}\left(\frac{2y_1 - b}{\sqrt{B}}\right) + \log y_2,$$

which, of course, are exactly self-dual. (For $b = 1.9$, $0.9 < x_1 < 2.9$, and $0 < y_1 < 1$, we have $0.9 < x_1, y_1 < 1$ and $x_2 > 0$, $y_2 > 0$.)

(c) *Quadratic Self-Dual (Homothetic)* If we have $F^1 = x_1 y_1 + a(x_1 y_2 + x_2 y_1) + bx_2 y_2 = c$ and $F^2 = x_1 y_1 + x_2 y_2 = 1$, the demand functions are

$$x_1 = (\alpha y_2 - ay_1)/A > 0, \qquad \alpha = c - b = 1 - c > 0, \quad a > 0,$$

and

$$x_2 = (\alpha y_1 + ay_2)/A > 0, \qquad A = ay_2^2 + 2\alpha y_1 y_2 - ay_1^2,$$

which yield the self-dual quadratic (homothetic) utility function, $U = ax_2^2 + 2\alpha x_1 x_2 - ax_1^2$ ($U_1 > 0$, $U_2 > 0$, and $U_2 - U_1 > 0$).

(d) *Inverse Quadratic Self-Dual (Nonhomothetic)* Consider

$$F^1 = a_1(x_1 + y_1) + a_2(x_2 + y_2) = 1, \qquad a_1 > 0 \quad a_2 < 0,$$

$$F^2 = x_1 y_1 + x_2 y_2 = 1.$$

The demand functions are closely related to the inverse functions of the ordinary quadratic demand functions; i.e.,

$$x_1 = ((1 - a_1 y_1 - a_2 y_2)y_2 - a_2)/A > 0,$$

$$x_2 = ((1 - a_1 y_1 - a_2 y_2)y_1 - a_1)/-A > 0, \qquad A = a_1 y_2 - a_2 y_1.$$

The underlying self-dual indirect utility function is integrated to yield

$$\begin{aligned} -V &= B\log(a_1y_2 - a_2y_1) + \tfrac{1}{2}(1 - B)\log(a_1y_1 + a_2y_2 - \tfrac{1}{2}(1 + B)) \\ &\quad - \tfrac{1}{2}(1 + B)\log(a_1y_1 + a_2y_2 - \tfrac{1}{2}(1 - B)), \\ B &= 1 - 4(a_1^2 + a_2^2) > 0. \end{aligned}$$

For a sufficiently small value of $|z|$, $z = 1 - a_1y_1 - a_2y_2 < 0$, the above utility function will meet all the necessary properties of a utility function.

(e) *More General Case* Consider

$$F^i = \sum_j^n a_{ij}X_j = c_i, \qquad X_j = x_j + y_j + x_jy_j \qquad (1 \leqq i \leqq n - 1),$$

together with $x'y - 1 = 0$. The resulting demand system is self-dual, and the interested reader is asked to integrate the corresponding utility function.[6]

III. Uniform and Self-Dual Demand Functions

5. Examples (a) and (c)–(e) in the previous section show that some self-dual demand functions have a similar form. That is to say, x_i and x_j both have the same mathematical form. Following the suggestion of Professor Hendrik Houthakker, we shall call such demand functions *uniform* demand functions. Let the following be a precise definition. *The system of demand functions is said to be "uniform" if any demand function $x_i = f^i(y)$ is reduced to any other demand function $x_j = f^j(y)$ by simply interchanging y_i with y_j; i.e.,*

$$\begin{aligned} x_i &= f^i(y_1, \ldots, y_i, \ldots, y_j, \ldots, y_n) \qquad \text{for any} \quad i \neq j, \\ x_j &\equiv f^i(y_1, \ldots, y_j, \ldots, y_i, \ldots, y_n), \qquad 1 \leqq i, j \leqq n. \end{aligned} \tag{10}$$

Theorem 2 *(Necessary and Sufficient Condition for Uniform Demand Functions) The exactly self-dual demand functions are uniform if and only if the F^i are set-symmetric in absolute value with respect to $z = (z_1, z_2, \ldots, z_n)$, $z_i = (x_i, y_i)$, i.e.,*

$$\begin{aligned} |F^i(x, y)| &= |F^i((x_1, y_1), (x_2, y_2), \ldots, (x_n, y_n))| \\ &\equiv |F^i(z_1, z_2, \ldots, z_n)| \\ &\equiv |F^i(z_1^j, z_2^j, \ldots, z_n^j)| = 0, \qquad i = 1, \ldots, n - 1, \qquad (11) \\ F^n &= \sum_{j=1}^n x_jy_j - 1 = 0. \end{aligned}$$

[6] Examples (a) and (c) are homothetic, while examples (b), (d), and (e) are nonhomothetic self-dual functions. Examples (b) (linear) and (c) (non-Cobb–Douglas) were first found by Sato [1974, 1976]. Another interesting example may be derived from a linear and *idempotent* system of F^i functions.

That is to say, the value and the form of F^i are unchanged (*invariant* of the group) by all permutations of z_i and z_j or $x_i \rightleftarrows x_j$ and $y_i \rightleftarrows y_j$ (but not necessarily $x_i \rightleftarrows y_j$). The proof is left to the reader.

In actual demand analysis *some* x_i and *some* x_j may have the same mathematical form. In other words, we may have "partially" uniform and self-dual demand functions. This being the case, the "symmetric" conditions must hold for those demand functions which are partially uniform in all F^i functions. For instance, if x_1 and x_2 are uniform but not x_1 and x_3, then F^i must be set-symmetric with respect to (x_1, y_1) and (x_2, y_2), but not with respect to (x_1, y_1) and (x_3, y_3).

IV. Weakly Self-Dual Demand Functions

6. Although there is an infinite number of "exactly" self-dual preference orderings both in homothetic and nonhomothetic functions, for empirical estimation purposes, it may be more convenient to study the case of "weakly" self-dual demand functions (Houthakker [1965], Russell [1964]). As observed correctly by Houthakker [1965, p. 797], the "same" form of functions is an elusive concept and thus requires a more precise definition.

As in the theory of continuous groups, we employ the well-known concept of the *essential* or *effective* parameters (see Appendix). Consider a set of n functions f^i of n variables $y_1, \ldots, y_n$ and r parameters $a^1, \ldots, a^r$, say

$$f^i(y_1, y_2, \ldots, y_n; a^1, \ldots, a^r) \equiv f^i(y; a) \qquad (i = 1, \ldots, n),$$

which are continuous in y and a, as are their respective derivatives to as high an order as is desired.

Following the tradition of Lie group theory (Eisenhart [1933]), we shall call the system of demand functions "*weakly*" *self-dual* if the demand and inverse demand transformations can be arranged in pairs, the members of which are *mutually inverse*; that is to say, if, corresponding to a set of values of the essential parameters $a = (a^1, \ldots, a^r)$ of the demand functions, there is another set $b = (b^1, \ldots, b^r)$ such that b is some functions of a and the demand and inverse demand functions are mutually inverse. Thus, if there exists J: $a \to b$ such that

$$\begin{aligned} T_a\colon\ & x_i = f^i(y; a), \\ T_b\colon\ & y_i = g^i(x; b) = f^i(x; b) \qquad (1 \leqq i \leqq n), \end{aligned} \tag{12}$$

where $T_a^{-1} = T_b$ or $J^2 = Id$ (involution), then the system of demand functions is said to be "*weakly*" *self-dual* and can be written as[7]

$$\text{“} f \mathscr{S} g.\text{”} \tag{13}$$

In the above definition, the concept of effective parameters automatically rules out the case of $\partial f^i/\partial a^j \equiv 0$, so that a linear function, for instance, can never be the same function as a quadratic function. However, in some cases, the above definition still may be too general. We may consider the case of "*weakly*" *self-dual in the strict sense.* That is to say, if the demand and inverse demand functions satisfy $x_i = f^i(y; a)$, $y_i = f^i(x; b)$ $(1 \leqq i \leqq n)$, and furthermore, if there exists a set of essential parameters such that $J\colon a \to b$ and $J(\bar{a}) = \bar{a}$, i.e.,

$$x_i = f^i(y; \bar{a}), \qquad y_i = f^i(x; \bar{a}) \qquad \text{for} \quad a \equiv b = \bar{a} \quad (1 \leqq i \leqq n), \tag{14}$$

then the system of demand functions is said to be "*weakly*" *self-dual in the strict sense.*[8]

7. In the same manner in which we defined uniform self-dual, we can define the "*weakly*" *uniform* class of demand functions as: The system of demand functions is said to be "*weakly*" *uniform* if a demand function for the ith good $x_i = f^i(y_1, \ldots, y_i, \ldots, y_j, \ldots, y_n; a)$ is reduced to any other demand functions by interchanging x_i with x_j and y_i with y_j for some particular values of the essential parameters; i.e.,

$$\begin{aligned} x_i &= f^i(y_1, y_2, \ldots, y_i, \ldots, y_j, \ldots, y_n; \bar{a}) \\ &\equiv f^j(y_1, y_2, \ldots, y_j, \ldots, y_i, \ldots, y_n; \bar{a}) \\ &\qquad \text{for all} \quad i \neq j \quad (1 \leqq i, j \leqq n). \end{aligned} \tag{15}$$

8. In studying the properties of "weakly" self-dual and/or "weakly" uniform types of *demand functions,* caution must be taken not to immediately identify them as "weakly" self-dual and/or "weakly" uniform types of *utility functions.* Even though the demand functions are "weakly" self-dual and thus have the "same" mathematical form as their inverse demand

[7] This is the exactly the condition stated earlier as Houthakker's condition.

[8] Thus, if we can choose the values of a such that $a = b = \bar{a}$, then the system reduces to the case of an "exactly" or "strongly" self-dual preference ordering. In most cases these two definitions of "weakly" self-duality are the same. It is possible that by setting $a = b = \bar{a}$, the resulting functions may *not* meet the properties of demand functions. Nevertheless, we may still apply this criterion, since the resulting functions are simply used as reference functions.

functions, the direct and indirect functions may not have exactly the "same" form. Consider the example:

Demand functions	*Inverse demand functions*
$x_1 = a_1 - a_2 y_1,$	$y_1 = b_1 - b_2 x_1, \quad b_1 = a_1/a_2, \quad b_2 = 1/a_2,$
$x_2 = (a_2 y_1^2 - a_1 y_1 + 1)/y_2,$	$y_2 = (b_2 x_1^2 - b_1 x_1 + 1)/x_2,$
$a_1 > 0, \quad a_2 > 0,$	$b_1 > 0, \quad b_2 > 0.$

Integration yields the direct utility function

$$U = -\tfrac{1}{2}\log(b_1 x_1^2 - b_2 x_1 + 1) + \log x_2 \begin{cases} + \dfrac{b_2}{2\sqrt{B}} \log\left(\dfrac{2b_1 x_1 - b_2 - \sqrt{B}}{2b_1 x_1 - b_2 + \sqrt{B}}\right), \\ \qquad \text{if} \quad B > 0, \\ \text{or} \\ + \dfrac{b_2}{\sqrt{-B}} \tan^{-1}\left(\dfrac{2b_1 x_1 - b_2}{\sqrt{-B}}\right), \\ \qquad \text{if} \quad B < 0; \quad B = b_2^2 - 4b_1. \end{cases}$$

The corresponding indirect utility function will have the same type:

$$-V = -\tfrac{1}{2}\log(a_1 y_1^2 - a_2 y_1 + 1) + \log y_2 \begin{cases} + \dfrac{a_2}{2\sqrt{A}} \log\left(\dfrac{2a_1 y_1 - a_2 - \sqrt{A}}{2a_1 y_1 - a_2 + \sqrt{A}}\right), \\ \qquad \text{if} \quad A > 0, \\ \text{or} \\ + \dfrac{a}{\sqrt{-A}} \tan^{-1}\left(\dfrac{2a_1 y_1 - a_2}{\sqrt{-A}}\right), \\ \qquad \text{if} \quad A < 0; \quad A = a_2^2 - 4a_1. \end{cases}$$

But depending upon the values of a_1 and a_2, the positivity of $A = a_2^2 - 4a_1$ may imply the negative value of $B = b_2^2 - 4b_1 = (1/a_2^2) - 4a_1/a_2$; e.g., $a_1 = 1, a_2 > 2 \Rightarrow A > 0 \Rightarrow B < 0$. In this case, the direct utility function will take the form

$$\frac{b_2}{\sqrt{-B}} \tan^{-1}\left(\frac{2b_1 x_1 - b_2}{\sqrt{-B}}\right),$$

while the indirect utility function takes the form

$$\frac{a_2}{2\sqrt{A}} \log\left(\frac{2a_1 y_1 - a_2 - \sqrt{A}}{2a_1 y_1 - a_2 + \sqrt{A}}\right),$$

which is *not* exactly identical in form.[9] The same comment will apply to "weakly" *uniform* type of demand functions. Thus, in both cases of "weak" similarity, the (total) differential equations for direct and indirect utility functions will have the "same" form, but the solutions will not necessarily have the "same" form in the very strict sense.

Keeping these comments in mind, we can formulate

Theorem 3 *(Necessary and Sufficient Condition for Weak Self-Duality) The system of demand functions is "weakly" self-dual in the strict sense if and only if there exist* $F^i(x, y; a) = 0\ (1 \leqq i \leqq n-1)$ *and* $F^n = x'y - 1 = 0$, *such that*

$$F^i(x, y; \bar{a}) = \pm F^i(y, x; J(\bar{a})) \tag{16}$$

for some involution $J: a \to b$ *and* $J(\bar{a}) = \bar{a}$.

In view of Theorem 1 and in order to save space, the proof is omitted. The interested reader is asked to formulate a theorem for the "weakly" uniform types of demand functions. Like the "strongly" self-dual and uniform cases, there is an infinite number of "weakly" self-dual and "weakly" uniform types of demand systems (both homothetic and nonhomothetic).

V. Special Cases of Self-Dual Demand Functions

9. Depending upon the types of functions in F^i, there are a number of special cases of self-dual demand functions.

Separable between x and y

When F^i $(1 \leqq i \leqq n-1)$ takes the form

$$F^i[f^i(x; a), f^i(y; b)] = 0 \qquad (1 \leqq i \leqq n-1), \tag{17}$$

the demand system is "weakly" self-dual. When the F^i are additive, we have

$$F^i = f^i(x; a) \pm f^i(y; b) = 0 \qquad (1 \leqq i \leqq n-1). \tag{18}$$

Separable between $f^i(x_i, y_i)$ *and* $f^j(x_j, y_j)$

Another case of special interest is

$$F^i = F^i[f^{i1}(x_1, y_1; a, b), \ldots, f^{in}(x_n, y_n; a, b)] = 0 \qquad (1 \leqq i \leqq n-1) \tag{19}$$

[9] Although $\tan^{-1} f(x)$ and $\log g(x)$ can be reduced to the same type of functions by complex transformations, this procedure would require a more general concept of self-duality.

where $f^{ij}(x_j, y_j; a, b)$ are all symmetric functions with respect to x_j and y_j with some values of parameters $a \equiv b = \bar{a}$; i.e., $f^{ij}(x_j, y_j; \bar{a}) \equiv f^{ij}(y_j, x_j; \bar{a})$ for $1 \leqq i \leqq n-1$. On using the so-called *elementary symmetric polynomials*, $x_j + y_j$ and $x_j y_j$, f^{ij} may take the form $f^{ij} = f^{ij}(x_j + y_j, x_j y_j; a, b)$. Or as $g(x_j) + g(y_j)$ and $h(x_j)h(y_j)$ are also symmetric, f^{ij} may be $f^{ij}[g^i(x_j) + g^i(y_j), h^i(x_j)h^i(y_j); a, b]$.

Weakly self-dual and weakly uniform types of demand functions may be derived by further restricting the properties of F^i. If in (17) or in (19), f^i is symmetric [or f^{ij} is symmetric in (19)] with respect to all elements $x_1, \ldots, x_n$ at $a = b = \bar{a}$, then the resulting demand functions are weakly self-dual and weakly uniform (homothetic or nonhomothetic).

We shall next consider several special types of self-dual demand systems that are convenient for empirical applications, including those already known in the literature such as Houthakker's self-dual addilog type [1965].

Weakly Uniform and Weakly Self-Dual Preference Orderings

10. (a) *Houthakker's Self-Dual Addilog* Houthakker's "self-dual addilog" system may be reduced to the case of "weakly" self-dual demand functions if one can find $T(x) \equiv T(y)$ or more generally $T(x, a) \mathscr{S} T(y, b)$ such that

$$
\begin{aligned}
F^i &= \frac{a_i x_i^{1+b_i}}{a_j x_j^{1+b_j}} T(x)^{c(b_j - b_i)} - \frac{\alpha_i y_i^{1+\beta_i}}{\alpha_j y_j^{1+\beta_j}} T(y)^{\delta(\beta_i - \beta_j)} = 0, \\
F^n &= \sum_{j=1}^{n} x_j y_j - 1 = 0 \qquad (1 \leqq i \leqq n-1, \quad 1 \leqq j \leqq n),
\end{aligned}
\tag{20}
$$

$$a_i = \alpha_i^{-1/\beta_i}, \qquad b_i = \beta_i^{-1}, \qquad c = 1 - \delta,$$

where $T(x)$ and $T(y)$ are defined implicitly by

$$\sum_{j=1}^{n} a_j x_j^{1+b_j} T(x)^{-[\delta + (1-\delta)b_j]} = 1 \qquad \text{and} \qquad \sum_{j=1}^{n} \alpha_j y_j^{1+\beta_j} T(y)^{(1-\delta)+\delta\beta_j} = 1.$$

The demand and inverse demand functions are

$$x_i = \alpha_i y_i^{\beta_i} T(y)^{1-\delta+\delta\beta_i}, \qquad y_i = a_i x_i^{b_i} T(x)^{-[\delta+(1-\delta)b_i]}, \qquad 1 \leqq i \leqq n,$$

and they are weakly self-dual; i.e.,[10]

$$x_i \mathscr{S} y_i, \qquad 1 \leqq i \leqq n.$$

[10] See Pollak [1972] for derivation of x_i and y_i. One of the correct regularity conditions seems to be $-1 \leqq \beta_i \leqq 1$.

However, Houthakker's self-dual addilog system puts severe restrictions on $T(x)$, since $T(x)$ and also $T(y)$ must be extracted from the budget constraint and therefore cannot be any arbitrary function.[11]

11. (b) *Bergson Family* (*Homothetic* CES) For completeness and for the purpose of illustration of the theorems, we present the homothetic CES type. In (19), when F^i takes

$$F^i = \alpha_i x_j y_j^{-\beta} - \alpha_j x_i y_i^{-\beta} = 0 \qquad (i \neq j), \quad 1 \leqq i, j \leqq n-1), \tag{21}$$
$$F^n = \sum_{i=1}^{n} x_i y_i = 1,$$

then the resulting system of demand functions is that of the Bergson family and is "weakly" self-dual (also "weakly" uniform); i.e.,

$$x_i = \frac{\alpha_i y_i^\beta}{\sum_{j=1}^n \alpha_j y_j^{1+\beta}} \mathscr{S} \ y_i = \frac{\alpha_i^{-1/\beta} x_i^{1/\beta}}{\sum_{j=1}^n \alpha_j^{-1/\beta} x_j^{1+1/\beta}} \qquad (1 \leqq i \leqq n).$$

12. (c) *Quadratic Utility Functions* Another obvious case of weakly uniform and weakly self-dual demand functions is that of a (homothetic) quadratic utility function. Suppose that the direct utility function is of the quadratic form: $\phi(x) = x'Ax > 0$. Without loss of generality we can assume that A is symmetric with real coefficients, i.e., $A = A'$. Assume further that $\phi(x)$ is strictly quasi-concave with positive partial derivatives. The system

[11] Actually, it is not very easy to find $T(y) \equiv T(x)$ or $T(y; b) \mathscr{S} T(x; a)$ satisfying the budget constraint other than the already known types. Strictly speaking, the new demand system is not weakly self-dual for all combinations of the parameters. Consider the following example: $i = 1, 2$, $\delta = \frac{1}{2}$, $\beta_1 = -\frac{1}{2}$, $\beta_2 = -\frac{3}{4}$ (thus $\beta_i \neq \beta_j$). We have then $x_1 = \alpha_1 y_1^{-1/2} T(y)^{1/4}$ and $x_2 = \alpha_2 y_2^{-3/4} T(y)^{1/8}$. From the budget constraint $\alpha_1 y_1^{1/2} T(y)^{1/4} + \alpha_2 y_2^{1/4} T(y)^{1/8} - 1 = 0$, we can solve for $T(y)^{1/8}$ as

$$q = T(y)^{1/8} = (-\alpha_2 y_2^{1/4} + \sqrt{\alpha_2^2 y_2^{1/2} + 4\alpha_1 y_1^{1/2}})/2\alpha_1 y_1^{1/2} > 0.$$

Thus the demand functions for x_1 and x_2 are given by

$$x_1 = \alpha_1 y_1^{-1/2} q^2 = (\alpha_1 y_1^{-1/2}(\sqrt{\alpha_2^2 y_2^{1/2} + 4\alpha_1 y_1^{1/2}} - \alpha_2 y_2^{1/4})^2)/4\alpha_1^2 y_1,$$
$$x_2 = \alpha_2 y_2^{-3/4} q = (\alpha_2 y_2^{-3/4}(\sqrt{\alpha_2^2 y_2^{1/2} + 4\alpha_1 y_1^{1/2}} - \alpha_2 y_2^{1/4}))/2\alpha_1 y_1^{1/2}.$$

The inverse demand functions for y_1 and y_2 are $y_1 = 1/(x_1 + x_2 g)$, $y_2 = g/(x_1 + x_2 g)$, where

$$g = \frac{\alpha^4 z^2}{9\alpha^2}\Big[1 + 2\sqrt[3]{1 + t + \sqrt{t^2 + 2t}} + \sqrt[3]{2t^2 + 4t + 1 + 2(t+1)\sqrt{t^2 + 2t}}$$
$$+ 2(1 + \sqrt[3]{1 + t + \sqrt{t^2 + 2t}})(\sqrt[3]{1 + t - \sqrt{t^2 - 2t}})$$
$$+ \sqrt[3]{2t^2 + 4t + 1 - 2(t+1)\sqrt{t^2 + 2t}}\Big], \qquad t = (27/2)(\alpha_1^2/\alpha_2^4 z) \quad \text{and} \quad z = x_1/x_2.$$

Thus the demand functions and their own inverse do not seem to possess the same form.

of demand functions with the budget constraint $y'x = 1$ is "weakly" self-dual; i.e.,

$$x = (A^{-1}y/y'A^{-1}y) \mathscr{S} y = Ax/x'Ax.$$

One is tempted to say that the Taylor expansions of a nonlinear function up to the second order may yield a self-dual function. But this is not true unless the first-order terms identically vanish; i.e., $\phi(x) = \alpha x + x'Ax$ is not self-dual unless $\alpha \equiv 0$. One can also verify that nontrivial combinations of the Bergson and quadratic functions $F(x'Ax, \sum_{j=1}^{n} \alpha_j^{-1/\beta} x_j^{1+1/\beta})$ do *not* yield another type of self-dual functions.[12]

Weakly Self-Dual but Nonuniform Utility Functions

It was shown earlier that if and only if $(n-1)$ demand functions have the same mathematical forms as their respective inverse demand functions, then a preference ordering is self-dual. Among elementary functions, linear, fractional-linear, log-linear functions or their combinations in some special fashion are natural candidates, since their inverse functions are self-dual and they are statistically manageable.

13. (a) *Log-Linear Demand Functions* In (18), when F^i has a form

$$F^i = \prod_{j=1}^{n-1} x_j^{a_j} + \prod_{j=1}^{n-1} c y_j^{b_j} = 0 \qquad (1 \leqq i \leqq n-1),$$
$$F^n = \sum_{j=1}^{n} x_j y_j - 1 = 0, \tag{22}$$

the resulting demand functions are weakly self-dual and partially uniform (with respect to $n-1$ equations). Solving F^i $(i = 1, \ldots, n-1)$ to obtain x_i in terms of y, we have $(n-1)$ demand functions with *constant elasticities* with respect to $(n-1)$ prices such that

$$x_i = \alpha_i y_1^{\beta_{i1}} y_2^{\beta_{i2}} \cdots y_{n-1}^{\beta_{in-1}} \qquad (1 \leqq i \leqq n-1), \quad \alpha_i > 0, \tag{23}$$

and the demand function for the nth commodity is determined by the budget constraint

$$x_n = \frac{1}{y_n}\left[1 - \sum_{i=1}^{n-1} x_i y_i\right] > 0.$$

Because of the integrability conditions on the Slutsky matrix and the second-order conditions for a maximum of ϕ, the β_{ij} cannot take arbitrary constants. There are several interesting cases.

[12] Linear and/or log-linear nontrivial combinations of the Bergson and quadratic utility functions do not yield self-dual preferences.

Case 1 (*A Nonhomothetic* CES)

Demand functions		*Inverse demand functions*
$x_i = \alpha_i y_i^\beta$	$\mathscr{S}$	$y_i = \alpha_i^{-1/\beta} x_i^{1/\beta} \qquad (1 \leqq i \leqq n-1),$
$x_n = \left(1 - \sum_{i=1}^{n-1} \alpha_i y_i^{1+\beta}\right) \Big/ y_n > 0$	$\mathscr{S}$	$y_n = \left(1 - \sum_{i=1}^{n-1} \alpha_i^{-/\beta} x_i^{1+1/\beta}\right) \Big/ x_n > 0.$ (24)

In the preceding system, the Slutsky matrix is symmetric and thus the integrability conditions are satisfied. The own price elasticities of demand ($\partial \log x_i/\partial \log y_i$) are all *constant* and equal to $\beta < 0$ for $(n-1)$ commodities, while the own price elasticity of the nth commodity is equal to -1. [All cross elasticities are zero for $(n-1)$ commodities.] Solving the total differential equation for the direct utility function, we obtain

$$U(x) = \log x_n + \frac{\beta}{1+\beta} \log\left(1 - \sum_{i=1}^{n-1} \alpha_i^{-1/\beta} x_i^{1+1/\beta}\right). \tag{24'}$$

This type of utility function has a *constant elasticity of substitution* ($\sigma = -\beta$) (nonhomothetic CES) studied extensively by Sato [1974, 1975]. This function has the very interesting property that

$$\textit{own price elasticity of demand} = -\beta \equiv \sigma = \textit{elasticity of substitution} = \textit{const.}$$

When $\beta = -1$, this, of course, reduces to the Cobb–Douglas type. The demand equations (24) can be empirically tested by the usual linear method.[13]

Case 2 (*Other Log-Linear Demand Functions*) Other log-linear demand functions which satisfy the integrability conditions and necessary properties of the utility functions are (since x_n is always derived from the budget constraint, it will be omitted):

(i) If the demand system is

$$x_i = \alpha_i y_i^{-1} \quad (1 \leqq i \leqq n-2), \quad x_{n-1} = \alpha_{n-1} \prod_{j=1}^{n-2} y_j^{\alpha_j(1+\beta)/(1-\Sigma_j \alpha_j)} y_{n-1}^{\beta},$$

then the indirect utility function is

$$-V = c\left[1 - \sum_{j}^{n-2} \alpha_j - \alpha_{n-1} \prod_{j=1}^{n-2} y_j^{\alpha_j} y_{n-1}^{a_1}\right]^{a_2} \left(\prod_{j=1}^{n-2} y_j^{\alpha_j}\right)^{a_3} y_n,$$

$$a_j = \alpha_j(1+\beta) \Big/ \left(1 - \sum_{j=1}^{n-2} \alpha_j\right),$$

$$a_1 = 1 + \beta, \qquad a_2 = -1/(1+\beta), \qquad a_3 = (1+\beta) \Big/ \left(1 - \sum_{j=1}^{n-2} \alpha_j\right).$$

[13] A special case of (24) for $n = 2$ was derived by Wold [1952, pp. 106–107] long before the concept of self-duality was introduced in economics.

(ii) If

$$x_1 = \alpha_1 y_1^{-1}, \qquad x_i = \alpha_i y_1^{a_1} y_i^{\beta} \qquad (1 \leqq i \leqq n-1),$$

then

$$-V = c\left[1 - \alpha_1 - \sum_{j=2}^{n-1} \alpha_j y_1^{a_1} y_j^{1+\beta}\right]^{1/(1+\beta)} y_1^{a_2} y_n^{-1},$$

$$a_1 = \alpha_1(1+\beta)/(1-\alpha_1), \qquad a_2 = -\alpha_1/(1-\alpha_1).$$

(iii) If

$$x_i = \alpha_i \prod_{j=1}^{n-1} y_j^{a_j} y_i^{-1} \qquad (1 \leqq i \leqq n-1),$$

then

$$-V = c\left[1 - \prod_{j=1}^{n-1} \left(\sum_{i=1}^{n-1} \alpha_i\right) y_j^{a_j}\right] y_n^{a_n},$$

$$a_j = \alpha_j(1+\beta)/\alpha_1, \qquad a_n = -\left(\sum_{i=1}^{n-1} \alpha_i\right)(1+\beta).$$

(iv) For the demand functions

$$x_1 = \alpha_1 y_1^{\beta} y_2^{a_1}, \qquad x_2 = \alpha_2 y_1^{1+\beta} y_2^{a_1 - 1}, \qquad x_i = \alpha_i y_i^{\beta + a_1} \qquad (3 \leqq i \leqq n-1),$$

we have

$$-V = c\left[1 - (\alpha_1 + \alpha_2) y_1^{1+\beta} y_2^{a_1} - \sum_{j=3}^{n-1} \alpha_j y_j^{a_2}\right]^{1/a_2} y_n^{-1},$$

$$a_1 = \alpha_2(1+\beta)/\alpha_1, \qquad a_2 = (\alpha_1 + \alpha_2)(1+\beta)/\alpha_1.$$

(v) Given

$$x_1 = \alpha_1 y_1^{-1}, \qquad x_i = \alpha_i \prod_{j=2}^{n-1} y_1^{a_1} y_j^{a_j} y_i^{-1} \qquad (2 \leqq i \leqq n-1),$$

we have

$$-V = c\left[1 - \alpha_1 - \prod_{j=2}^{n-1} \left(\sum_{i=2}^{n-1} \alpha_i\right) y_1^{a_1} y_j^{a_j}\right]^{a_2} y_1^{a_3} y_n,$$

$$a_1 = (\alpha_1/(1-\alpha_1))\left(\sum_{i=2}^{n-1} \alpha_i/\alpha_2\right)(1+\beta), \qquad a_j = (\alpha_j/\alpha_2)(1+\beta),$$

$$a_2 = -\alpha_2 \Big/ \left(\sum_{i=2}^{n-1} \alpha_i\right)(1+\beta), \qquad a_3 = \alpha_1\left(\sum_{i=2}^{n-1} \alpha_i\right) \Big/ (1-\alpha_1)\alpha_2.$$

14. (b) *Composite Self-Dual Functions* Composite utility functions of quadratic, CES, and nonhomothetic CES will all yield "weakly" self-dual demand functions.

(i) *Composite quadratic* (3 goods):

$$-V = a(\alpha y_1^2 + \beta y_1 y_2 + \gamma y_2^2) + b(\alpha y_1^2 + \beta y_1 y_2 + \gamma y_2^2)^{1/2} y_3 + c y_3^2.$$

(ii) *Composite homothetic and Nonhomothetic CES*:

$$-V = c[1 - \alpha_2(a_1 y_1^{-\delta_1} + a_2 y_2^{-\delta_1})^{-\beta/\delta_1} + \alpha_3 y_3^{-\beta}]^{1/\beta} y_4.$$

(iii) *Composite nonhomothetic CES and quadratic functions*:

$$-V = c[1 - \alpha_2(a y_1^2 + b y_1 y_2 + c y_2^2)^{-\beta} + \alpha_3 y_3^{-\beta}]^{1/\beta} y_4.$$

15. (c) *Linear and Fractional Linear* The interested reader is asked to extend the case

$$x_1 = \frac{a_2 - a_4 y_1}{a_1 + a_3 y_1}, \qquad x_2 = \frac{a_4 y_1^2 + (a_3 - a_2) y_1 + a_1}{y_2(a_1 + a_3 y_1)}$$

$$-V = -\tfrac{1}{2}\log[a_4 y_1^2 - (a_2 - a_3) y_1 + a_1]$$

$$+ \frac{a_2 + a_3}{\sqrt{B}} \tan^{-1} \frac{2a_4 y_1 - (a_2 - a_3)}{\sqrt{B}} + \log y_2,$$

$$B = 4a_1 a_2 - (a_2 - a_3)^2 > 0$$

to the general case of

$$x_i = \left(\sum_{j=1}^{n-1} a_{ij} y_j + a_0\right) \Big/ \left(\sum_{j=1}^{n-1} b_{ij} y_j + b_0\right), \qquad i = 1, \ldots, n-1.$$

This type of demand function belongs to the projective group of transformation, and thus is known to have the similar (or self-dual) inverse functions.

VI. Method of Deriving Self-Dual Demand Functions by Infinitesimal Transformations

16. The basic theorems in the previous sections are sometimes too general for empirical applications. Rather we shall study in detail the special separable classes of the F^i in (8) or (16). Let z_i be equal to $1/ny_i$ or

$$z_i = 1/ny_i, \qquad 1 \leqq i \leqq n. \tag{25}$$

Then the demand functions with r essential parameters $a = (a_1, \ldots, a_r)$,

$$x = f(y; a) = f(z^{-1}; a) = \phi(z; a) \tag{26}$$

may be considered as continuous transformations $T: z \to x$ satisfying the budget constraint $x'/z = n$. By restricting $r = 1$ $(a_1 = t)$ and ϕ such that

$$x = z \qquad \text{at} \quad t = t_0, \tag{27-i}$$

$$z = \phi(x; t) \qquad \text{at} \quad t = \bar{t}, \tag{27-ii}$$

$$x = \phi[\phi(x; \bar{t}); t] = \phi[x; b(t, \bar{t})], \tag{27-iii}$$

$$x/z' = n, \tag{27-iv}$$

We can assume that (26) satisfies the Lie group properties with the self-duality conditions (27-iii). Here we are using the basic fact that the Cobb–Douglas demand functions with the *equal exponent* for each x_i can be used as the basis of identical transformation. That is to say, (27-i) implies $x = z = 1/ny'$, which is the system of demand functions associated with the Cobb–Douglas utility function with *identical exponents*. Thus the self-dual demand functions satisfying (27) are the continuous transformations of the unitary elastic demand functions associated with the Cobb–Douglas type of preference orderings.

Writing infinitesimal transformations associated with (26) when $r = 1$ in the usual form,

$$U = \sum_{i=1}^{n} \xi_i(z) \frac{\partial}{\partial z_i}, \tag{28}$$

we can express the self-dual conditions by their invariance conditions. Any function h will be invariant if and only if $Uh = 0$ whenever $h = 0$. This implies that

$$dz_1/\xi_1(z) = \cdots = dz_n/\xi_n(z) = dh/0. \tag{29}$$

There are $(n - 1)$ invariants corresponding to (29); i.e.,

$$\begin{array}{ll} (1) & F^1(z) = F^1(x), \\ (2) & F^2(z) = F^2(x), \\ \vdots & \\ (n-1) & F^{n-1}(z) = F^{n-1}(x). \end{array} \tag{30}$$

Together with the budget constraint, we shall be able to derive the system of self-dual demand functions. Thus we have

Theorem 4 (*Self-Duality of a Separable System under Lie Groups*) *The invariants of the transformation group associated with* (28), *together with the*

budget constraint, constitute a separable system of set symmetric functions of the self-dual demand system.

17. Consider as an example

$$U = \sum_{j=1}^{n} a_j z_j \frac{\partial}{\partial z_j}. \tag{31}$$

Then the invariants are derived from the first $(n - 1)$ terms of

$$dx_1/a_1x_1 = dx_2/a_2x_2 = \cdots = dx_n/a_nx_n = dt/1$$

as

$$x_i^{1/a_i}/x_j^{1/a_j} = z_i^{1/a_i}/z_j^{1/a_j}, \qquad i \neq j, \quad 1 \leqq i, j \leqq n. \tag{32}$$

Finally, using $(1/a_1)\log x_1 = (1/a_1)\log z_1 + t$ from $dx_1/a_1x_1 = dt/1$ and (32), we obtain the system of self-dual demand functions

$$x_i = e^{a_it}z_i = e^{a_it}/ny_i, \qquad 1 \leqq i \leqq n, \tag{32'}$$

together with the budget constraint $x'y = 1 = n^{-1}\sum_{i=1}^{n} e^{a_it}$. This is the system of demand functions associated with a general (unequal exponent) Cobb–Douglas utility function.

Another interesting aspect of the foregoing theorem is that by introducing the transformed variables of x and y and therefore x and z, such that

$$u_i(x_i; \alpha) = u_i(z_i; \beta), \qquad 1 \leqq i \leqq n, \tag{33}$$

we can generate a more general class of self-dual functions from the new infinitesimal transformations

$$U = \sum_{i=1}^{n} \xi_i(u) \frac{\partial}{\partial u_i}. \tag{34}$$

A special but important case would be the *transhomothetic case* of $\xi_i(u) = \xi_i(u_i)$, i.e., ξ_i depends only on the transformed variable of x_i. The interested reader is asked to work out a few examples.

18. Finally, we present a rather general method of constructing weakly self-dual demand functions using the transformed variables. In view of the special properties of the budget constraint which already satisfy the conditions of self-duality and uniformity, and in view of Samuelson's theorem [1969, p. 356], there is a rather general method of constructing weakly self-dual demand functions (but not necessarily uniform with respect to one commodity). Consider the following implicit systems of the demand and inverse demand functions, which satisfy the usual conditions of the Slutsky matrix:

Demand functions	*Inverse demand functions*
$h^i(x_i) - f^i[k^1(y_1), \ldots, k^n(y_n)] = 0$	$k^i(y_i) - g^i[h^1(x_1), \ldots, h^n(x_n)] = 0$
$(1 \leqq i \leqq n-1),$	$(1 \leqq i \leqq n-1),$
$x_n - \left(1 - \sum_{i=1}^{n-1} x_i y_i\right)\Big/ y_n = 0,$	$y_n - \left(1 - \sum_{i=1}^{n-1} x_i y_i\right)\Big/ x_n = 0.$

If $h^i \mathscr{S} k^i$ (also if $h^{i^{-1}} \mathscr{S} k^{i^{-1}}$) and $f^i \mathscr{S} g^i$ for all i $(1 \leqq i \leqq n-1)$, the above systems will be weakly self-dual. We then have

Demand functions		*Inverse demand functions*	
$x_i = h^{i^{-1}}[f^i(k(y))]$	$\mathscr{S}$	$y_i = k^{i^{-1}}[g^i(h(x))]$	$(1 \leqq i \leqq n-1),$
$x_n = \left(1 - \sum_{i=1}^{n-1} h^{i^{-1}} y_i\right)\Big/ y_n$	$\mathscr{S}$	$y_n = \left(1 - \sum_{i=1}^{n-1} k^{i^{-1}} x_i\right)\Big/ x_n,$	

where $k(y) = (k^1(y_1), \ldots, k^n(y_n))$ and $h(x) = (h^1(x_1), \ldots, h^n(x_n))$. The problem of finding specific mathematical forms of h^i, k^i, and f^i, which are all self-dual and warrant empirical considerations, can be more easily solved if we consider a special case of the foregoing system of the demand functions. *When the implicit demand system for $(n-1)$ commodities is independent of the price of the nth commodity*; i.e.,

$$h^i(x_i) - f^i(k^1(y_1), \ldots, k^{n-1}(y_{n-1})) = 0 \qquad (1 \leqq i \leqq n-1),$$

where $h^i \mathscr{S} k^i$ (also $h^{i^{-1}} \mathscr{S} k^{i^{-1}}$) and $f^i \mathscr{S} g^i$, then the implicit system of the inverse demand functions for $(n-1)$ prices can be obtained by the solution of k^i in terms of h^i irrespective of the demand function for the nth commodity (therefore, irrespective of the budget constraint) as

$$k^i(y_i) - g^i(h^1(x_1), \ldots, h^{n-1}(x_{n-1})) = 0, \qquad 1 \leqq i \leqq n-1.$$

By assumption, x_i is weakly self-dual with respect to y_i for all $1 \leqq i \leqq n-1$, and x_n and y_n are also self-dual because of the budget constraint. The resulting direct and indirect utility functions take the form

$$U = u(x_1, \ldots, x_{n-1}) + a_n \log x_n, \qquad -V = v(y_1, \ldots, y_{n-1}) + \alpha_n \log y_n,$$

where $u(x_1, \ldots, x_{n-1}) \mathscr{S} v(y_1, \ldots, y_{n-1})$.

To show how the method can be applied, consider the example[14]: $n = 3$, $h^1 = x_1^2$, $k^1 = y_1^2$, $h^2 = \log x_2$, $k^2 = \log y_2$, and both f^1 and f^2 are linear. Then we have

$$h^i = (a_{i1}k^1 + a_{i2}k^2) = 0 \qquad (1 \leqq i \leqq 2),$$

[14] This is a purely mathematical exercise to show how weakly self-dual demand functions can be obtained. This may not, therefore, satisfy the usual conditions on the Slutsky matrix.

or

$$x_1^2 - (a_{11}y_1^2 + a_{12}\log y_2) = 0, \qquad \log x_2 - (a_{21}y_1^2 + a_{22}\log y_2) = 0.$$

The inverse demand functions for the two commodities are simply

$$y_1^2 - (b_{11}x_1^2 + b_{12}\log x_2) = 0, \qquad \log y_2 - (b_{21}x_1^2 + b_{22}\log x_2) = 0,$$

which are self-dual. (The matrix $\{b\} = \{a\}^{-1}$.) By solving explicitly for x_1, x_2, y_1, and y_2, and using the budget constraint, we have the demand and inverse demand functions as

$$x_1 = \sqrt{a_{11}y_1^2 + a_{12}\log y_2} > 0 \quad \mathscr{S} \quad y_1 = \sqrt{b_{11}x_1^2 + b_{12}\log x_2} > 0,$$

$$x_2 = \exp(a_{21}y_1^2 + a_{22}\log y_2) > 0 \quad \mathscr{S} \quad y_2 = \exp(b_{21}x_1^2 + b_{22}\log x_2) > 0,$$

$$x_3 = (1 - y_1\sqrt{a_{11}y_1^2 + a_{12}\log y_2} - y_2\exp(a_{21}y_1^2 + a_{22}\log y_2))/y_3 > 0 \quad \mathscr{S}$$

$$y_3 = (1 - x_1\sqrt{b_{11}x_1^2 + b_{12}\log x_2} - x_2\exp(b_{21}x_1^2 + b_{22}\log x_2))/x_3 > 0.$$

Although the exact forms of f^i must be determined empirically by market observations, linear, fractional linear, log–linear, and fractional log–linear forms (or their appropriate combinations) will usually yield the self-dual inverse demand functions g^i. The log–linear demand functions in Section 13 are derived using this method.

VII. Implicit Self-Duality: Duality of Production and Cost Functions

19. Although the basic duality principle of the utility and demand analysis will carry over to the production and cost analysis, the self-duality condition in the two approaches is usually different. The main reason is that in utility analysis the constraint function is a linear equation of the budget equation, while in production theory, the constraint function is a nonlinear function of the production function itself. We must recognize the fact that unlike in utility and demand analysis, we are *not* comparing the direct and indirect production functions. (We are comparing the form of a direct utility function with that of its own expenditure function.)

The purpose of studying the self-duality of production and cost functions is the same as before. Thus, under the self-duality condition, by studying the properties of a cost function directly or indirectly through factor demand functions, one can determine the basic form of the corresponding production function, or vice versa. From the empirical point of view, it is often necessary or even imperative to know the underlying form of a production function when its dual (cost) function is estimated.

Normalized Cost Function

20. Let a cost function be given by

$$C = g(p_1, \ldots, p_n, Y), \tag{35}$$

where C is the minimized value of total expenditure to produce a given output Y, when the prices of factor inputs p_i $(1 \leqq i \leqq n)$ are given. The cost function C is a continuously differentiable function of $p = (p_1, \ldots, p_n)$ and Y, and is *of the homogeneous function of the first degree with respect to the* p_i. Hence (35) must satisfy

$$\lambda C = g(\lambda p_1, \ldots, \lambda p_n, Y). \tag{36}$$

We shall normalize (35) by setting $C = 1$, i.e.,

$$1 = g(p_1, \ldots, p_n, Y), \tag{35'}$$

which may be called the *normalized cost function*, satisfying the condition

$$\lambda = g(\lambda p_1, \ldots, \lambda p_n, Y). \tag{36'}$$

It is seen that in general the normalized cost function is an implicit function of output Y. In order to distinguish it from an explicit formulation, we shall write (35′) as

$$g(B_1(Y), \ldots, B_n(Y); p) - 1 = G[B(Y); p] = 0, \tag{35''}$$

where $B(Y) = (B_1(Y), \ldots, B_n(Y))$ and $p = (p_1, \ldots, p_n)$.

The foregoing formulation of the normalized cost function enables us to compare it with the implicit formulation of a production function. By the same reasoning as used in Chapter 5, we can regard (35″) as a general solution of the economically meaningful partial differential equation system with n essential parameters $B(Y)$. Let us assume that (35″) is a normalized dual (cost) function corresponding to the original production function of the implicit form

$$F[C(Y); x] = 0, \tag{37}$$

where $C(Y) = (C_1(Y), \ldots, C_n(Y))$ is a vector of n essential parameters, and $x = (x_1, \ldots, x_n)$ a vector of factor inputs. By self-duality in the strong sense of Samuelson, we mean the following: A production function is said to be *strongly* or *exactly self-dual* if (35″) and (37) satisfy the condition

$$G[B(Y); p] \equiv F[C(Y); p]. \tag{38-i}$$

$$F[C(Y); x] \equiv G[B(Y); x]. \tag{38-ii}$$

For simplicity, we shall call the above the condition of (implicit) self-duality. We omit the adjective, strongly or exactly, whenever it is obvious.

The normalized cost function (35″) is implicitly homothetic with respect to prices, satisfying condition (36′). We can regard the normalized cost function as a general solution to the meaningful partial differential equation system holothetic under *the equiproportionate type of price change*,

$$U = \sum_{j=1}^{n} p_j \frac{\partial}{\partial p_j}. \tag{39}$$

Then the self-dual production function must also satisfy the same condition of holotheticity as (39),

$$U = \sum_{j=1}^{n} x_j \frac{\partial}{\partial x_j}. \tag{40}$$

Equation (37) is also regarded as a general solution to the meaningful partial differential equation system holothetic under the type of technical progress (40). Hence, *in order that the production and cost functions may be self-dual, it is necessary that the production function be implicitly homothetic.*

Cost Function of an Implicitly Homothetic Production Function

21. We have assumed that (35″) is a normalized cost function corresponding to the original production function of implicit form (37). (And this assumption is always warranted because of the general duality theorem of production and cost functions regardless of whether a production function is explicit or implicit.[15]) If a production function is implicitly homothetic, its dual cost function, which is always implicitly homothetic, has a special form. In the previous chapter an implicitly homothetic function is always shown to be written as[16]

$$f[C_1(Y), \ldots, C_{n-1}(Y); x] = C_n(Y), \tag{41}$$

where f is a homogeneous function of degree one with respect to x.

Lemma 1 (*Cost Function of an Implicitly Homothetic Production Function*) *If and only if the production function is implicitly homothetic, then the cost function can be written as*

$$C = g[C_1(Y), \ldots, C_{n-1}(Y); p]C_n(Y). \tag{42}$$

[15] The interested reader may want to prove this assertion using a method similar to the one employed by Shephard [1970].

[16] Thus $f[C_1, \ldots, C_{n-1}; x] - C_n = 0$ is defined as $F[C_1, \ldots, C_n; x] = 0$ in Eq. (37).

Proof Minimization of total cost $p'x$ subject to $f[C_1(Y), \ldots, C_{n-1}(Y); x] = C_n(Y)$ requires the first-order conditions

$$\frac{p_i}{p_j} = \frac{\partial Y}{\partial x_i}\Big/\frac{\partial Y}{\partial x_j} = \frac{f_{x_i}}{f_{x_j}} \qquad \text{where} \quad f_{x_i} = \frac{\partial f}{\partial x_i} \quad \text{and} \quad f_{x_j} = \frac{\partial f}{\partial x_j},$$

$$i \neq j, \quad 1 \leqq i, j \leqq n.$$

Since f is homogeneous degree one, f_{x_i} must be homogeneous degree zero with respect to x. Let R_j^i be the marginal rate of substitution between x_i and x_j. Then it is a function of $C_1, \ldots, C_{n-1}$ and x; i.e.,

$$R_j^i = R_j^i[C_1(Y), \ldots, C_{n-1}(Y); x_2/x_1, x_3/x_1, \ldots, x_n/x_1],$$

$$i \neq j \quad (1 \leqq i, j \leqq n).$$

There are $(n-1)$ first-order conditions for $(n-1)$ unknowns, $x_2/x_1, \ldots, x_n/x_1$. Solving these conditions, we obtain $x_j/x_1 = S_j[p_2/p_1, \ldots, p_n/p_1; C_1(Y), \ldots, C_{n-1}(Y)]$, $j = 2, \ldots, n$. Because of the homogeneity condition of f, it can be written as $\sum_{k=1}^n f_{x_k} x_k = C_n(Y)$. Substituting $x_j = S_j x_1$ $(j = 2, \ldots, n)$ into x_k $(k = 2, \ldots, n)$ in the above, we can express

$$x_1 = C_n(Y)\Big/\left(\sum_{j=2}^{n} f_{x_j} S_j + f_{x_1}\right).$$

It is also seen that f_{x_k} $(k = 1, \ldots, n)$ must be a function of the S_j, using the conditions $x_j/x_1 = S_j$ $(j = 2, \ldots, n)$. Hence we can see that $x_1 = C_n(Y)/h^1[p; C_1(Y), \ldots, C_{n-1}(Y)]$. Substituting x_1 into $x_j = S_j x_1$ for all j, we can express the factor demand function of the kth input as

$$x_k = \frac{C_n(Y)}{h^k[p; C_1(Y), \ldots, C_{n-1}(Y)]}, \qquad 1 \leqq k \leqq n, \tag{43}$$

where the h^k are homogeneous of degree zero in p. This may be called *the factor demand function of the* k*th input for an implicitly homothetic production function.* Substituting (43) in the total cost equation $C = p'x$, we get

$$C = \sum_{k=1}^{n} \frac{p_k C_n(Y)}{h^k[p; C_1(Y), \ldots, C_{n-1}(Y)]} = g[C_1(Y), \ldots, C_{n-1}(Y); p]C_n(Y).$$

To prove necessity, we use Shephard's lemma. By differentiating total cost with respect to p, we have

$$\frac{\partial C}{\partial p_k} = x_k = C_n(Y)\frac{\partial g}{\partial p_k}, \qquad 1 \leqq k \leqq n.$$

Since g is a homogeneous degree one function with respect to p, $\partial C/\partial p_k$ must be of the homogeneous zero degree in p. The ratio x_i/x_j must also be of the homogeneous zero degree with respect to p. Solving x_i/x_j in terms of p_i/p_j, we obtain $p_i/p_j = R^i_j[C_1(Y), \ldots, C_{n-1}(Y);\ x_2/x_1, \ldots, x_n/x_1]$, which must also be equal to $(\partial Y/\partial x_i)/(\partial Y/\partial x_j)$, the marginal rate of substitution between x_i and x_j. At any given isoquant, the production function must satisfy $\sum_{k=1}^{n} f_{x_k}\, dx_k = 0$. Dividing by any f_{x_k}, say $k = 1$, we can write this as $dx_1 + \sum_{j=2}^{n} (f_{x_j}/f_{x_1})\, dx_j = 0$. Using the condition $(\partial Y/\partial x_j)/(\partial Y/\partial x_1) = R^j_1$ and substituting it into the total differential equation, we get

$$dx_1 + \sum_{j=2}^{n} R^j_1[C_1(Y), \ldots, C_{n-1}(Y); x_2/x_1, \ldots, x_n/x_1]\, dx_j = 0.$$

Finally, solving the above, we obtain the production function

$$f[C_1(Y), \ldots, C_{n-1}(Y); x] = C_n(Y),$$

which is the implicitly homothetic function. Q.E.D.

Corollary to Lemma 1 *(Cost Function of an Explicitly Homothetic Production Function) If and only if f is explicitly homothetic,*

$$f(x) = C_n(Y), \qquad f(\lambda x) = \lambda C_n(Y), \tag{44}$$

then the cost function can be written as

$$C = g(p)C_n(Y), \qquad g(\lambda p)C_n(Y) = \lambda C. \tag{45}$$

Proof This is a special case of Lemma 1 when $\partial f/\partial C_j \equiv 0, 1 \leqq j \leqq n - 1$. In this case, the factor demand function (43) is simply $x_k = C_n(Y)/h^k(p)$ $(k = 1, \ldots, n)$. Substituting it into $C = p'x$, we get (45). Starting with (45), we can also show that the original production function has the form (45). Q.E.D.

Implicit Self-Duality

22. We now require a more precise definition of self-duality between f and g. Let F and G be equal to, respectively,

$$F = f[C_1(Y), \ldots, C_{n-1}(Y); x]C_n(Y)^{-1} - 1 = 0,$$
$$G = g[C_1(Y), \ldots, C_{n-1}(Y); p]C_n(Y) - 1 = 0, \qquad C = 1.$$

By defining $C_n(Y) = B_n(Y)^{-1}$, we can apply the restrictions of self-duality given by (38) simply as

$$g[C_1(Y), \ldots, C_{n-1}(Y); p] = f[C_1(Y), \ldots, C_{n-1}(Y); p] \tag{38-i'}$$

or

$$f[C_1(Y), \ldots, C_{n-1}(Y); x] = g[C_1(Y), \ldots, C_{n-1}(Y); x]. \tag{38-ii'}$$

However, like the case of self-dual preferences, it is actually more convenient to define the self-duality conditions in terms of the factor demand or inverse demand functions. Moreover, since the factor demand functions are homogeneous of degree zero, it is natural to define them in terms of the ratio of factor demand functions or the marginal rate of substitution function. Let the marginal rate of substitution between x_i and x_j of (41) be

$$p_i/p_j = R_j^i[C_1(Y), \ldots, C_{n-1}(Y); x_1/x_j, \ldots, x_i/x_j, \ldots, x_n/x_j] \qquad (1 \leqq i, j \leqq n, \quad i \neq j). \tag{46}$$

Also, let the inverse function of (46), which is the demand ratio between x_i and x_j derived from (42), be

$$x_i/x_j = S_j^i[C_1(Y), \ldots, C_{n-1}(Y); p_1/p_j, \ldots, p_i/p_j, \ldots, p_n/p_j] \qquad (1 \leqq i, j \leqq n, \quad i \neq j), \tag{47}$$

or writing more compactly,

$$P = R[D(Y); X], \qquad D(Y) = (C_1(Y), \ldots, C_{n-1}(Y)), \tag{46'}$$

and

$$X = S[D(Y); P]. \tag{47'}$$

Then *the production and cost functions are self-dual if*

$$P = R[D(Y); R[D(Y); P]], \qquad X = S[D(Y); S[D(Y); X]], \tag{48}$$

that is to say, if P and X are exactly the same mathematical functions in terms of D(Y), X, and P. The reader can see that this manner of formulation will reduce the analysis exactly to Lie's problem discussed in Part II of this chapter.

Theorem 5 (*Necessary and Sufficient Conditions of Implicit Self-Duality*) *The necessary and sufficient conditions for the implicit self-duality of production and cost functions are that there exist* $(n - 1)$ *functions satisfying the conditions*

$$H(X, P; D(Y)) = |H(P, X; D(Y))| = 0. \tag{49}$$

where $H = (H^1, \ldots, H^{n-1})$.

Proof Following exactly the same steps as the proof of Theorem 1, we can prove the foregoing by replacing x and y with X and P. Q.E.D.

Corollary to Theorem 5 (*Explicit Self-Duality*) *If and only if there exists* $(n - 1)$ *functions satisfying*

$$H(X, P) = |H(P, X)| = 0,$$

then the production and cost functions are explicitly self-dual.

Proof This is a special case when the H^i contain no $D(Y)$, which corresponds to the case of the self-duality of an explicit homothetic production function.[17] Q.E.D.

Examples

23. We now present a few examples.

(a) *Implicit or Explicit Cobb–Douglas* When we have

$$H^i = \sum_{j=1}^{n-1} b_{ij}[D(Y)] \frac{x_j}{x_n} \frac{p_j}{p_n} = c_i \qquad (1 \leqq i \leqq n-1),$$

where all the H^i are independent, we can solve for $(x_j/x_n)(p_j/p_n) = k_j[D(Y)]$. This is the demand and price ratio associated with the self-dual implicit (nonhomothetic) Cobb–Douglas production function. When k_j is independent of Y, we get a special case of explicit (or ordinary) Cobb–Douglas family.

(b) *Linear Marginal Rate of Substitution* Consider

$$H^1 = \frac{x_1}{x_2} + \frac{p_1}{p_2} - b[D_1(Y)] = 0, \qquad b > 0 \qquad \text{for} \quad n = 2.$$

Then $x_1/x_2 = b(Y) - (p_1/p_2)$ and $p_1/p_2 = b(Y) - (x_1/x_2)$, which are implicitly self-dual. Integrating the total differential equations $(b - x_1/x_2)\, dx_1 + dx_2 = 0$ and $(b - p_1/p_2)\, dp_1 + dp_2 = 0$, we obtain

$$\log C_2(Y) = \log x_1 + \tfrac{1}{2}\log(v^2 + bv - 1) + \frac{b}{2\sqrt{b^2+4}} \log \frac{2v + b + \sqrt{b^2+4}}{2v + b - \sqrt{b^2+4}}, \qquad v = \frac{x_2}{x_1},$$

$$\log C_2(Y) = \log p_1 + \tfrac{1}{2}\log(u^2 + bu - 1) + \frac{b}{2\sqrt{b^2+4}} \log \frac{2u + b + \sqrt{b^2+4}}{2u + b - \sqrt{b^2+4}}, \qquad u = \frac{p_2}{p_1}.$$

VIII. Uniformity and Implicit Self-Duality

24. As we did for the uniformity conditions in the utility analysis, we can present the conditions under which the demand function for one-factor input has the same form as that for any other inputs. According to Samuelson,

[17] Theorem 1 can be reformulated for "implicit" self-dual preferences by simply introducing appropriate parameters $D(U)$ into the F^i in Eq. (8).

Clark [1899, p. 201] envisioned a type of production function which exhibits the uniform types of factor demand functions.[18] We shall call this the *Clark uniformity condition.*

We present the precise definition of *the Clark uniformity condition*: *The system of factor demand function is said to be "Clark uniform" if any demand function* $x_i = f^i[p; C(Y)]$ *is reduced to any other factor demand function* $x_j = f^j[p; C(Y)]$ *by simply interchanging* p_i *with* p_j, *i.e.,*

$$\begin{aligned} x_i &= f^i[p_1, \ldots, p_i, \ldots, p_j, \ldots, p_n; C(Y)] \qquad \text{for any} \quad i \neq j, \\ x_j &= f^i[p_1, \ldots, p_j, \ldots, p_i, \ldots, p_n; C(Y)], \qquad 1 \leqq i, j \leqq n. \end{aligned} \tag{50}$$

Theorem 6 (*Uniformity and Self-Duality*) *The exactly self-dual factor demand functions are Clark uniform if and only if the* F^i *are set-symmetric in absolute value with respect to*

$$\begin{aligned} z = (z_1, z_2, \ldots, z_n), &\qquad z_i = (x_i, p_i), \\ |F^i(x, p; C(Y))| &= |F^i[(x_1, p_1), \ldots, (x_n, p_n); C(Y)]| \\ &= |F^i[z_1, \ldots, z_n; C(Y)]| \\ &= |F[z_1^j, \ldots, z_n^j; C(Y)]| = 0, \qquad 1 \leqq i \leqq n. \end{aligned} \tag{51}$$

This is a direct extension of Theorem 2. The value of and the form of F^i are invariant by all permutations of z_i and z_j or $x_i \rightleftarrows x_j$ and $p_i \rightleftarrows p_j$. Since we have already assumed that the x_i are self-dual satisfying Theorem 5, condition (51) is an additional restriction. The implicit Cobb–Douglas function [Example (a)] is a good example of a uniform and self-dual production function with appropriate choice of b_{ij} and c_i.

Alternatively, we can present the Clark uniformity condition in a different framework. Let

$$\begin{aligned} \sigma(i, j)f &= f(p_1, \ldots, p_i, \ldots, p_j, \ldots, p_n; C(Y)) \\ &\quad - f(p_1, \ldots, p_j, \ldots, p_i, \ldots, p_n; C(Y)) \\ &= f(p_i p_j) - f(p_j p_i), \qquad i \neq j, \quad \text{for any } f. \end{aligned} \tag{52}$$

Also, let

$$\begin{aligned} \sigma(i, j, k)f &= f(p_i p_j p_k) - f(p_k p_i p_j) - f(p_j p_i p_k) + f(p_k p_j p_i), \\ &\quad i \neq j \neq k, \qquad \text{for any } f. \end{aligned} \tag{53}$$

[18] The author was informed of this property in a private conversation with Professor Samuelson. See Clark [1899] for the treatment of the marginal productivities of capital and labor (Figs. 1 and 2, p. 201). Our definition of the Clark uniformity condition is not exactly identical to the original picture envisioned by Clark, since we are dealing with factor demand functions, while Clark was dealing with their marginal productivity curves. Uniform marginal productivity functions seem to be a necessary condition for factor demand to be uniform.

Then we conjecture that *the necessary and sufficient condition for the system of factor demand functions to be Clark uniform is*

$$\sigma(i,j)f^i + \sigma(j,i)f^j = 0 \qquad \text{(as for skew commutative)}, \tag{54-i}$$

$$\sigma(i,j,k)f^i + \sigma(j,k,i)f^j + \sigma(k,i,j)f^k = 0$$
$$\text{for}\quad i \neq j \neq k, \quad 1 \leqq i,j,k \leqq n \quad \text{(as for Jacobi's identity)}. \tag{54-ii}$$

25. We can extend the analysis to the *weakly self-dual* case. By introducing the concept of *essential* parameters, we formulate the conditions that

$$x_i \mathscr{S} p_i \tag{55}$$

in the strict sense. The system of factor demand and inverse demand functions is "weakly" self-dual in the strict sense if and only if there exist $(n-1)$ functions $H^i = 0\ (1 \leqq i \leqq n-1)$ such that

$$H^i[X, P; D(Y, \bar{a})] = |H^i[P, X; D(Y, J(\bar{a}))]| = 0 \tag{56}$$

for some involution $J\colon a \to b$ and $J(\bar{a}) = \bar{a}$, where a and b are vectors of r essential parameters.

An obvious example of weakly self-dual implicit production functions is *an implicit CES production function*. Consider

$$H^i = \alpha_i(D(Y))\,\frac{x_j}{x_n}\,\frac{p_j^{-\beta}}{p_n} - \alpha_j(D(Y))\,\frac{x_i}{x_n}\,\frac{p_i^{-\beta}}{p_n}$$
$$= 0, \qquad i \neq j \quad (1 \leqq i, j \leqq n-1), \tag{57}$$

the resulting production and cost functions are weakly self-dual (and "weakly" uniform).

26. Again the separable case of the H^i may be useful for empirical applications. Let y_j and z_j be

$$y_j = x_j/x_i = x_j/x_n, \tag{58-i}$$

$$z_j = p_i/p_j = p_n/p_j, \qquad 1 \leqq j \leqq n-1, \quad i = n. \tag{58-ii}$$

Without loss of generality, we can choose $i = n$. Then the demand ratio and the marginal rate of substitution between the jth and nth factor inputs can be expressed as continuous transformations with r essential parameters $a = (a_1, \ldots, a_r)$ such that

$$y = f[z; D(Y, a)], \tag{59}$$

where $D(Y, a) = (C_1(Y, a), \ldots, C_{n-1}(Y, a))$. Equation (59) can be considered as a continuous transformation

$$T_a\colon \quad z \to y,$$

where $y = z$ at $a = a_0$. By assuming similar conditions as in Eq. (27), we can generate (implicit) self-dual technologies from the infinitesimal transformations. Again we use the basic fact *that the explicit Cobb–Douglas production function with equal exponent for x_i can be used as the basis of identical transformation.* The basic results stated in Theorem 4 apply to this case with appropriate modifications relevant to production and cost functions. Also, the transformed variables of y and z such as $u = u(y)$ and $v = v(z)$ may be used to generate more general implicit families of self-dual production functions. For instance, it is easier to derive the well-known functions of CES and addilog types by simply defining $u_j = y_j^{-\rho_j}$ and $v_j = z_j^{-\delta_j}$.

IX. Duality of Scale Effect between Production and Cost Functions

27. We derive

Theorem 7 *(Complete Transformation of Technical Progress in the Production Function to the Dual Rate of Returns to Scale of the Cost Function) Let the production (in general implicit) function be given together with technical progress t by*

$$F[x, t; D(Y)] = C_n(Y), \qquad D(Y) = (C_1(Y), \ldots, C_{n-1}(Y)). \tag{60}$$

Then the effect of technical progress is completely transformed to the dual rate of returns to scale of the cost function as

$$C = e^{-t}g[p; D(Y), C_n(Y)] \tag{61}$$

if and only if the type of technical progress in (60) *is of the uniform factor-augmenting type*

$$U = \sum_{j=1}^{n} x_j \frac{\partial}{\partial x_j}. \tag{62}$$

Proof By assumption, technology after technical progress of the type (62) is $F[\bar{x}; D(Y)] = C_n(Y)$, where $\bar{x} = (\bar{x}_1, \ldots, \bar{x}_n)$, $\bar{x}_i = e^t x_i$. The first-order conditions of cost minimization require that

$$p_i/p_j = R_j^i(\bar{x}; D(Y)).$$

Solving this together with F, we get the factor demand functions

$$x_i = f^i[p; D(Y), C_n(Y)]e^{-t}.$$

Substituting this into $x'p = C$, we get the cost function

$$C = \sum_{i=1}^{n} p_i f^i e^{-t} = e^{-t} g[p; D(Y), C_n(Y)].$$

Thus technical progress of production is completely transformed to the dual rate of returns to scale of the cost function.

On the other hand, since the cost function is homogeneous of degree one with respect to p, it is holothetic under the equiproportionate price (decreasing) type of technical progress, $U = -\sum_{i=1}^{n} p_i \, \partial/\partial p_i$. On using Shephard's lemma, the factor demand function for the ith input is

$$\frac{\partial C}{\partial p_i} = x_i = f^i[\bar{p}; D(Y), C_n(Y)]e^{-t} = f^i[p; D(Y), C_n(Y)]e^{-t},$$

where $\bar{p}_i = e^{-t} p_i$ from $U = -\sum_{i=1}^{n} p_i \, \partial/\partial p_i$. On using $\bar{x} = e^t x$, the foregoing implies

$$\frac{\bar{x}_i}{\bar{x}_j} = \frac{f^i[p; D(Y), C_n(Y)]}{f^j[p; D(Y), C_n(Y)]},$$

from which p_i/p_j can be written as $R_j^i[\bar{x}; D(Y)]$. Hence the production function is of the form $F[\bar{x}; D(Y)] = C_n(Y)$. Q.E.D.

Corollary to Theorem 7 *(Duality of Technical Progress under Implicitly Homothetic Technology) The primal rate of returns to scale of the production function is identical to the dual rate of returns to scale of the cost function if and only if production technology is implicitly homothetic.*

Proof If and only if production technology is implicitly homothetic, then the rate of uniform factor-augmenting technical progress is identical to the primal rate of returns to scale of the production function, because the implicitly homothetic technology is the only function holothetic under the uniform factor-augmenting type of technical progress. The rate of the uniform factor-augmenting type of technical progress is identical to the dual rate of technical progress of the cost function. Q.E.D.

Consider explicit technology as a special case of (60),

$$Y = F(x, t). \tag{63}$$

When technical progress is of the type specified by (62) so that we have

$$Y = F(e^t x), \tag{64}$$

then the cost function is of the form[19]

$$C = e^{-t} g(p, Y). \tag{65}$$

[19] The reader may recall that we have used (64) and (65) of Chapter 3 to justify the existence of technical change endogenously generated by R & D activities of a rational economic unit.

In particular, if (63) is a constant returns to scale function

$$Y = e^{t}f(x), \tag{66}$$

we have the cost function

$$C = e^{-t}g(p)Y. \tag{67}$$

There is a perfect symmetry between the primal and dual returns to scale in Y and C.

REFERENCES

Clark, J. [1899]. *The Distribution of Wealth: A Theory of Wages, Interest and Profits*. Macmillan, London, (Reprinted in 1924).

Eisenhart, L. P. [1933]. *Continuous Groups of Transformations*. Princeton Univ. Press, Princeton, New Jersey. (Reprinted by Dover, New York, 1961).

Haque, W. [1975]. Samuelson's self-dual preferences, *Econometrica*, **43**, 31–40.

Hicks, J. R. [1969]. Direct and indirect additivity, *Econometrica*, **37**, 353–354.

Houthakker, H. S. [1960]. Additive preferences, *Econometrica*, **28**, 244–257.

Houthakker, H. S. [1965]. A note on self-dual preferences, *Ecometrica*, **33**, 797–801.

Lau, L. J. [1969]. Duality and the structure of utility functions, *Journal of Economic Theory*, **1**, 374–396.

Lie, S. [1880]. Sophus Lie's 1880 transformation paper. Translated by M. Ackerman with comments by R. Hermann in *Lie Groups: History, Frontiers, and Applications*, Vol. 1. Math. Sci. Press, Brookline, Massachusetts. 1975.

Pollak, R. A. [1972]. Generalized separability, *Econometrica*, **40**, 431–454.

Russell, R. R. [1964]. The Empirical Evaluation of Theoretically Plausible Demand Functions. Ph.D. Dissertation, Harvard University, Cambridge, Massachusetts.

Samuelson, P. A. [1965]. Using full duality to show that simultaneously additive direct and indirect utilities implies unitary price elasticity of demand, *Econometrica*, **33**, 781–796.

Samuelson, P. A. [1969]. Corrected formulation of direct and indirect additivity, *Econometrica*, **37**, 355–359.

Samuelson, P. A., and Swamy, S. [1974]. Invariant economic index numbers and canonical duality: Survey and synthesis, *American Economic Review*, **64**, 566–593.

Sato, R. [1974]. On the separable class of non-homothetic CES functions, *Economic Studies Quarterly*, **25**, 42–55.

Sato, R. [1975]. The most general class of CES functions, *Econometrica*, **43**, 999–1004.

Sato, R. [1976]. Self-dual preferences, *Econometrica*, **44**, 1017–1032.

Shephard, R. W. [1970]. *The Theory of Cost and Production Functions*. Princeton Univ. Press, Princeton, New Jersey.

Wold, H. [1952]. *Demand Analysis: A Study in Econometrics*. Wiley, New York.

CHAPTER 7

DYNAMIC SYMMETRIES AND ECONOMIC CONSERVATION LAWS

I. Introduction

Motivation: Dynamic Symmetries in Natural Systems

1. One of the most fascinating aspects of the group-theoretic method in the different branches of physical sciences is the analysis of the connection between dynamic symmetries (invariances) and conservation laws of a mathematical system. When natural systems are idealized, unexpected symmetries tend to arise. These symmetries are not apparent at first and are only revealed through rigorous analysis. The past 50 years have exhibited remarkable development in this new area of mathematics, which has far-reaching significance in the fields of physics, engineering, and applied mathematics.[1]

The fundamental work on this problem was initiated in the early part of this century by Noether [1918] in a classic paper.[2] Influenced by the work of

[1] See Klein [1918], Lie [1891], Noether [1918], Bessel-Hagen [1921], Gelfand and Fomin [1963], Goldstein [1950], Rund [1966], Logan [1977], Nôno [1968], Nôno and Mimura [1975, 1976, 1977], Sagan [1969], Lovelock and Rund [1975], Lanczos [1970], Whittaker [1937], and Moser [1979].

[2] Her paper has recently been translated into English by Tavel, who also supplies a brief motivation and historical sketch (see Noether [1918]).

Klein [1918] and of Lie [1891] on the transformation properties of differential equations under continuous (Lie) groups, Noether proved the fundamental result, now known as the *Noether theorem*. Her work represents an ingeneous combination of the methods of the formal calculus of variations with those of Lie's group theory.

Noether's theorem has important consequences. For example, if L is the Lagrangian of some physical or economic system, then the invariance of the fundamental integral under an *r-parameter (Lie) group leads directly to conservation laws for the system.* This means that the invariance hypothesis leads to expressions which are *constant* along the extremals, or first integrals of the equations of motion. The Noether theorem was utilized by Bessel-Hagen [1921] to compute the conservation laws in particle mechanics, using the ten-parameter Galilean group, which consists of a time translation, spatial translations and rotations, and velocity translations. The resulting ten conservation laws are the classical ten integrals of the N-body problem: conservation of energy, linear momentum, angular momentum, and the uniform motion of the center of mass. A group invariance such as a rotation or translation invariance is often referred to as a *symmetry* of a dynamic system or simply a *dynamic symmetry.*[3]

Economic Conservation Laws

2. In his well-known article, Ramsey [1928, p. 547] states his famous rule of optimal saving as "rate of saving multiplied by marginal utility of consumption should always equal bliss minus actual rate of utility enjoyed." This rule was derived from

$$\dot{c} = \frac{dc}{dt} = f(a, c) - x = \frac{B - (U(x) - V(a))}{u(x)},$$

where f is the production function, a the labor, c the capital, x the consumption, $U(x)$ the utility of consumption, $V(a)$ the disutility of labor, and $u(x) = \partial U/\partial x$ the marginal utility of consumption. Although Ramsey did not mention it explicitly, his rule is closely related to and is derived from *the law of*

[3] It may happen, however, that these symmetries are not at all obvious but quite opaque. A famous example is the Kepler problem which asks for the motion of a single particle under the influence of a fixed mass point (say, the sun) according to Newton's inverse-square law of gravitation. The solutions are ellipses, hyperboles, or parabolas. This system is rotation symmetric, and therefore has a fixed angular momentum vector. But it turns out—and this is by no means obvious—that the Kepler problem admits not only the rotation group in three-dimensional space, but even in four-dimensional space. This additional symmetry was fully understood first for the quantum-theoretical Kepler problem (Moser [1979]).

conservation of energy. In a conservative dynamic system, the Hamiltonian defined by the Legendre transformation

$$H = \sum_{i=1}^{n} p_i \dot{x}_i - L \qquad (p_i = \partial L/\partial \dot{x}_i, \quad L = \text{Lagrangian})$$

is *constant*. By letting $L = -(U(x) - V(a))$ and Bliss $B = H$, the Ramsey rule is derived from the conservation law

$$H = B = u(x)\dot{c} + (U(x) - V(a)) = u(x)\dot{c} - L.$$

Samuelson [1970a, b] is the first economist *explicitly* to introduce conservation laws in theoretical economics. From the analogy of the law of conservation of (physical) energy, kinetic energy + potential energy = constant, Samuelson obtained the conservation law of the aggregate capital–output ratio in a neoclassical von Neumann economy, where all output is saved to provide capital formation for the growth of the system. Although he did not appeal explicitly to Noether's theorem, it is seen that Samuelson's conservation laws are the most fundamental laws for the closed, consumptionless system of the von Neumann type. (This will be proved in section 18 using the Noether theorem directly.)

As a basis of motivation and in order to show the apparent connection between the (static) holotheticity concept in earlier chapters and the dynamic invariance (or dynamic symmetry, or dynamic holotheticity) concept in this chapter, let us consider the problem posed by Samuelson [1970a, b]. The optimal-control problem is defined as

$$\max_{\{K^i(t)\}} \int_0^T \dot{K}^1(t)\, dt \qquad \text{subject to} \quad F(K(t), \quad \dot{K}(t)) = 0$$

and assigned boundary conditions, where F is a smooth, neoclassical, concave, first-degree homogeneous transformation function relating the vector of n capital goods $K(t) = \{K^i(t)\}$ and the vector of net capital formation $\dot{K} = \{dK^i/dt\}$. This variational problem is to maximize the functional

$$\begin{aligned} J(K(t)) &= \int_0^T L(K(t), \dot{K}(t), \lambda(t))\, dt \\ &= \int_0^T (\dot{K}^1(t) + \lambda(t)F[K(t), \dot{K}(t)])\, dt. \end{aligned}$$

Let us suppose that we are given the time translation $\bar{t} = t + \varepsilon$ with no technical progress for capital goods, $\bar{K}^i = K^i$ and $\bar{\lambda} = \lambda$. We are interested in finding the condition that the fundamental integral is invariant under the time translation, i.e.,

$$\int_c L(\bar{K}(\bar{t}), \dot{\bar{K}}(\bar{t}), \bar{\lambda}(\bar{t}))\, d\bar{t} = \int_c L(K(t), \dot{K}(t), \lambda(t))\, dt.$$

In order that this requirement be satisfied, it is necessary and sufficient that $L(\bar{K}(\bar{t}), \dot{\bar{K}}(\bar{t}), \bar{\lambda}(\bar{t}))\, d\bar{t}/dt = L(K(t), \dot{K}(t), \lambda(t))$. But, since $d\bar{t}/dt = 1$, this requirement is nothing but

$$L(\bar{K}(\bar{t}), \dot{\bar{K}}(\bar{t}), \bar{\lambda}(\bar{t})) = L(K(t), \dot{K}(t), \lambda(t)).$$

This condition is simply the (static) holotheticity condition, when the differential equation L does *not* contain the independent variable t explicitly. (This corresponds to the special case of the infinitesimal transformation $U = \partial/\partial t$, discussed as the additive case in Chapter 2.) Hence, in this case, the *(static) holotheticity condition is exactly identical with the dynamic invariance condition.*

In general, however, since L contains time t and also since there exists technical change for capital goods, the static condition is *not* equal to the dynamic invariance. We shall later present more precise definitions of dynamic invariance conditions.

3. The purpose of this chapter is to present a self-contained and systematic analysis of conservation laws in economic dynamics. First, a fairly detailed mathematical treatment of Noether's theorem will be given, so that the economist who is not familiar with this aspect of variational dynamics can learn its applications. Second, the invariant variational principle will be applied to *general* neoclassical optimal growth models of the Ramsey type. It is shown that there exist several (local) conservation laws operating in the neighborhood of steady positions. An attempt will be made to derive more general local conservation laws that operate in a variety of special dynamic systems. Finally, the Samuelson conservation laws in a von Neumann growth system will be derived through the application of the Noether theorem. It will be shown that the Samuelson conservation laws are the only laws operating globally for the system.

II. Preliminaries: Noether's Theorem and Invariance Identities[4]

r-Parameter Transformations: Technical Change with r Essential Parameters

4. To motivate interest and to introduce the idea of (dynamic) invariance of the *fundamental* or *action integral* of a given calculus of variations or optimal control problem, we consider a classical result concerning an integration

[4] The reader who is familiar with Noether's theorem and its applications can skip this part and proceed to Part III.

of the Euler–Lagrange equations. As in the case of Samuelson's problem cited in Section 2, if the Lagrangian L does not depend explicitly on t,

$$J(x) = \int_{t_0}^{t_1} L(x(t), \dot{x}(t))\, dt, \qquad x(t) = (x^1(t), \ldots, x^n(t)),$$
$$\dot{x}(t) = (\dot{x}^1(t), \ldots, \dot{x}^n(t)),$$

then the Euler–Lagrange equations have first integral

$$-L + \dot{x}^k \frac{\partial L}{\partial \dot{x}^k} = H = C \qquad \left(\dot{x}^k \frac{\partial L}{\partial \dot{x}^k} = \sum_{k=1}^{n} \dot{x}^k \frac{\partial L}{\partial \dot{x}^k}, \text{ summation convention}^5\right),$$

where H is the Hamiltonian and C is a constant (see Whittaker [1937]). To say that L does not depend explicitly on t could be interpreted as saying that the functional J is invariant under the transformation which takes t to $t + \varepsilon$. The Noether theorem can to a certain degree be considered as a generalization of this fact.

Let us consider a Lagrange function $L\colon I \times \mathbb{R}^n \times \mathbb{R}^n \to \mathbb{R}^1$, which is twice continuously differentiable in each of its $2n + 1$ arguments, $L \in C^2$, and $I \subseteq \mathbb{R}^1$ is an open interval of real numbers. We then have the variational integral

$$J(x) = \int_a^b L(t, x(t), \dot{x}(t))\, dt, \tag{1}$$

where $[a, b] \subseteq I$ and $x \in C_n^2[a, b]$ is the set of all vector functions $x(t) = (x^1(t), \ldots, x^n(t))$, $t \in [a, b]$. The type of invariance transformations that will be considered are (technical change) transformations of configuration space, i.e., $(t, x^1, \ldots, x^n)$ space, which depend on r real, independent (essential) parameters $\varepsilon^1, \ldots, \varepsilon^r$. In Noether's original paper [1918], as well as in more recent treatments of invariance problems, it is assumed that the transformations form a group; in fact, the groups considered are precisely local *Lie groups* of transformations. Although many of the transformations which arise in applications to mathematical physics and mathematical economics are group of transformations (e.g., the Galilean group, the Lorenz group, biased technical change), the group concept is not necessarily required. To be more precise, we require here that the transformations are given by

$$\begin{aligned} \bar{t} &= \phi(t, x, \varepsilon), \qquad & \varepsilon &= (\varepsilon^1, \ldots, \varepsilon^r), \\ \bar{x}^k &= \psi^k(t, x, \varepsilon) \qquad & (k &= 1, \ldots, n). \end{aligned} \tag{2}$$

[5] We adopt the so-called Einstein summation convention (Young [1978, pp. 333–334]. When a lowercase Latin index such as $j, h, k, \ldots$ appears twice in a term, summation over that index is implied, the range of summation being $1, \ldots, n$. For example, $a^i x^i$ means $\sum_{i=1}^n a^i x^i$.

In economic terms, ϕ can be considered as "subjective" time (Samuelson [1976]), while ψ^k represent "technical" or "taste" change. It is assumed that a domain U in $\mathbb{R}^r$ is given which contains the origin as an interior point and that the mappings

$$\phi\colon [a, b] \times \mathbb{R}^n \times U \to I, \qquad \psi^k\colon [a, b] \times \mathbb{R}^n \times U \to I \qquad (k = 1, \ldots, n)$$

are of class C^2 in each of their $1 + n + r$ arguments with

$$\phi(t, x, 0) = t, \qquad \psi^k(t, x, 0) = x^k \qquad (k = 1, \ldots, n). \tag{3}$$

Expanding the right-hand sides of (2) in a Taylor series about $\varepsilon = 0$, we obtain

$$\begin{aligned} \bar{t} &= t + \tau_s(t, x)\varepsilon^s + O(\varepsilon), \\ \bar{x}^k &= x^k + \xi_s^k(t, x)\varepsilon^s + O(\varepsilon) \qquad (k = 1, \ldots, n) \end{aligned} \tag{4}$$

($s = 1, \ldots, r$, summation convention in force). The principal linear parts τ_s and ξ_s^k are nothing but the *infinitesimal generators* (or *transformations*) of the transformation (2) given by

$$\tau_s(t, x) = \frac{\partial \phi}{\partial \varepsilon^s}(t, x, 0), \qquad \xi_s^k(t, x) = \frac{\partial \psi^k}{\partial \varepsilon^s}(t, x, 0). \tag{5}$$

Let $x\colon [a, b] \to \mathbb{R}^n$ be a curve of class C_n^2 given by $x = x(t)$; then, for sufficiently small ε, the transformation

$$\bar{t} = \phi(t, x(t), \varepsilon) \tag{6}$$

is invertible (see Logan [1977]).[6] Writing the unique inverse function of (6) as $t = T(\bar{t}, \varepsilon)$, and substituting into the equation $\bar{x}^k = \psi^k(t, x(t), \varepsilon)$, we get

$$\begin{aligned} \bar{x}^k &= \psi^k(T(\bar{t}, \varepsilon), x(T(\bar{t}, \varepsilon)), \varepsilon) \\ &\equiv \bar{x}^k(\bar{t}) = \bar{x}^k(\phi(t, x(t), \varepsilon)) = \psi^k(t, x(t), \varepsilon). \end{aligned} \tag{7}$$

Hence we may define the transformed curves $\bar{x} = \bar{x}(\bar{t})$ in $(\bar{t}, \bar{x})$ space. By setting

$$\bar{a} = \phi(a, x(a), \varepsilon), \qquad \bar{b} = \phi(b, x(b), \varepsilon), \tag{8}$$

$\bar{x}(\bar{t})$ is defined on $[\bar{a}, \bar{b}]$. As an example, consider a simple rotation group $(n = 1, r = 1)$ $\bar{t} = t - \varepsilon x$, $\bar{x} = x + \varepsilon t$. Here the infinitesimal transformation

[6] If we assume a local Lie group transformation, then by definition it is invertible and has the same inverse form as the original mapping.

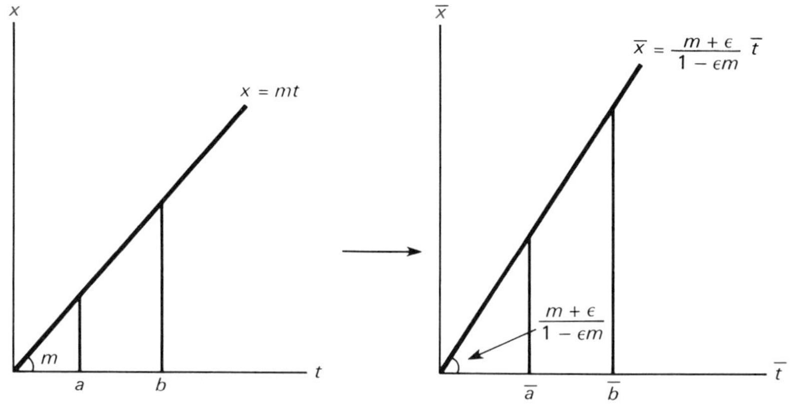

Figure 1

is given by $U = -x\,\partial/\partial t + t\,\partial/\partial x$. Consider the curve $x(t) = mt$, $m = \text{const}$. We then have $\bar{t} = t - \varepsilon mt$, $\bar{x} = mt + \varepsilon t$. Solving the first equation for t in terms of $\bar{t}$, we get $t = \bar{t}/(1 - \varepsilon m)$, $1 - \varepsilon m \neq 0$. Thus $\bar{x} = ((m + \varepsilon)/(1 - \varepsilon m))\bar{t} \equiv \bar{x}(\bar{t}, \varepsilon)$. If t is defined for $[a, b]$, then $\bar{a} = (1 - \varepsilon m)a$ and $\bar{b} = (1 - \varepsilon m)b$ and $\bar{t}$ is defined for $[\bar{a}, \bar{b}]$. Figure 1 depicts this transformation.

Invariance Definitions

5. We first present a geometrical interpretation of the transformation for a general case of $n = 1$ and $r = 1$. Given $x = x(t)$ in the tx plane, then the curve $x = x(t)$ is mapped to a one-parameter family of curves under the transformation $t \to \bar{t} = \phi(t, x(t), \varepsilon)$ and $x \to \bar{x} = \psi(t, x(t), \varepsilon)$. The resulting family of curves are the graphs of functions in the $\bar{t}\bar{x}$ plane, provided ε is sufficiently small. Figure 2 depicts this transformation with the curve drawn in the $\bar{t}\bar{x}$ plane showing one curve out of the one-parameter family for a particular value of ε. In the tx plane we can calculate the functional

$$J(x) = \int_a^b L(t, x(t), \dot{x}(t))\, dt, \qquad \dot{x}(t) = dx(t)/dt.$$

Also, for the $\bar{t}\bar{x}$ plane we can calculate

$$J(\bar{x}) = \int_{\bar{a}}^{\bar{b}} L(\bar{t}, \bar{x}(\bar{t}), \dot{\bar{x}}(\bar{t}))\, d\bar{t}, \qquad \dot{\bar{x}}(\bar{t}) = d\bar{x}(\bar{t})/d\bar{t}.$$

We say that J is invariant under the given transformation if $J(x) = J(\bar{x})$ or at least so up to the first-order terms in ε.

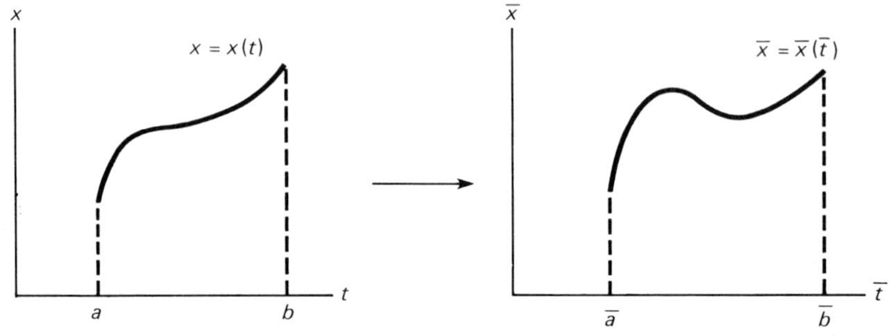

Figure 2

Definition 1 (*Dynamic Invariance or Dynamic Symmetry*)[7] (a) The fundamental integral (1) is absolutely invariant under the r-parameter family of transformations (2) if and only if given any curve $x\colon [a, b] \to \mathbb{R}^n$ of class C_n^2 and $a \leqq t_1 < t_2 \leqq b$, we have

$$\int_{\bar{t}_1}^{\bar{t}_2} L\left(\bar{t}, \bar{x}(\bar{t}), \frac{d\bar{x}(\bar{t})}{d\bar{t}}\right) d\bar{t} - \int_{t_1}^{t_2} L\left(t, x(t), \frac{dx(t)}{dt}\right) dt = O(\varepsilon) \tag{9}$$

for all $\varepsilon \in U$ with $|\varepsilon| < d$, where d depends on $x(t)$, where $\bar{x}(\bar{t})$ is defined by (7), and where $\bar{t}_i = \phi(t_i, x(t_i), \varepsilon)$, $i = 1, 2$.

(b) Alternatively, the fundamental integral is absolutely invariant if and only if

$$L\left(\bar{t}, \bar{x}(\bar{t}), \frac{d\bar{x}(\bar{t})}{d\bar{t}}\right) \frac{d\bar{t}}{dt} - L\left(t, x(t), \frac{dx(t)}{dt}\right) = O(\varepsilon). \tag{10}$$

By transforming the first integral in (9) back to the interval $[t_1, t_2]$, condition (9) is entirely equivalent to (10), which involves only the Lagrangian and not the action integral.

Remark 1 Definition 1 is somewhat more general than the one usually given (see Gelfand and Fomin [1963], Sagan [1969], Rund [1966], Lovelock and Rund [1975]), since $J(\bar{x}) - J(x)$ is not necessarily zero, but is equal to first-order terms in ε. If $J(\bar{x}) - J(x) = 0$, we can show that

$$J(\varepsilon) = \int_{\bar{t}_1(\varepsilon)}^{\bar{t}_2(\varepsilon)} L\left(\bar{t}, \bar{x}(\bar{t}, \varepsilon), \frac{d\bar{x}(\bar{t}, \varepsilon)}{d\bar{t}}\right) d\bar{t}$$

is independent of ε; i.e., $dJ(\varepsilon)/d\varepsilon = 0$ for all ε.

[7] In contrast to cases in which a function (rather than functional) is invariant, which was the main topic up to this chapter, we may call dynamic invariance as "dynamic holotheticity."

Remark 2 The invariance definition obviously holds true regardless of whether the Euler–Lagrange equations vanish or not.

Example 1 Consider $L = T - U$, where T is the kinetic energy given by $T = \frac{1}{2}m_k \dot{x}^k$, and U is the potential energy $U(t, x)$. Suppose that the potential energy is translation invariant, i.e., $U(t, \bar{x}) = U(t, x)$ where $\bar{x}^k = x^k + \varepsilon, \bar{t} = t$. From

$$\frac{d\bar{t}}{dt} = 1 \qquad \text{and} \qquad \frac{d\bar{x}^k}{d\bar{t}} = \frac{d\bar{x}^k}{dt}\Big/\frac{d\bar{t}}{dt} = \frac{dx^k}{dt},$$

condition (10) requires that

$$\begin{aligned}&\tfrac{1}{2}m_k \dot{\bar{x}}^k - U(t, \bar{x}) - (\tfrac{1}{2}m_k \dot{x}^k - U(t, x))\\ &\quad = \tfrac{1}{2}m_k \dot{\bar{x}}^k - \tfrac{1}{2}m_k \dot{x}^k - U(t, \bar{x}) + U(t, x) \equiv 0.\end{aligned}$$

In this case we have $L(\bar{t}, \bar{x}, \dot{\bar{x}}) - L(t, x, \dot{x}) \equiv 0$.

Example 2 Let $J(x)$ be given by

$$J(x) = \int_a^b \sqrt{1 + \dot{x}(t)^2}\, dt$$

and the one-parameter group of rotation by $\bar{t} = t - \varepsilon x$, $\bar{x} = x + \varepsilon t$. From $d\bar{t}/dt = 1 - \varepsilon\dot{x}$ and $d\bar{x}/dt = \dot{x} + \varepsilon$, we have

$$\frac{d\bar{x}}{d\bar{t}} = \frac{d\bar{x}}{dt}\Big/\frac{d\bar{t}}{dt} = \frac{\dot{x} + \varepsilon}{1 - \varepsilon\dot{x}}.$$

Therefore, condition (10) requires

$$\begin{aligned}\left(\sqrt{1 + \left(\frac{d\bar{x}}{d\bar{t}}\right)^2}\right)\frac{d\bar{t}}{dt} - \sqrt{1 + \dot{x}^2} &= \left(\sqrt{1 + \left(\frac{\dot{x} + \varepsilon}{1 - \varepsilon\dot{x}}\right)^2}\right)(1 - \varepsilon\dot{x}) - \sqrt{1 + \dot{x}^2}\\ &= \sqrt{(1 + \dot{x}^2)(1 + \varepsilon^2)} - \sqrt{1 + \dot{x}^2}\\ &= \sqrt{1 + \dot{x}^2}(\sqrt{1 + \varepsilon^2} - 1)\\ &= \sqrt{1 + \dot{x}^2}(1 + \tfrac{1}{2}\varepsilon^2 - \tfrac{1}{8}\varepsilon^4 + \cdots - 1)\\ &= \sqrt{1 + \dot{x}^2}(\tfrac{1}{2}\varepsilon^2 - \tfrac{1}{8}\varepsilon^4 + \cdots)\\ &= O(\varepsilon).\end{aligned}$$

Hence, according to Definition 1, the functional J in this case is also absolutely invariant under the rotation group.

Definition 2 (*Divergence-Invariant or Invariance with Nullity*) The fundamental integral is divergence-invariant, or invariant up to a divergence term, if there exist r functions $\Phi_s : I \times \mathbb{R}^n \to \mathbb{R}^1$, $s = 1, \ldots, r$, of class C^1 such that

$$L\left(\bar{t}, \bar{x}(\bar{t}), \frac{d\bar{x}(\bar{t})}{d\bar{t}}\right)\frac{d\bar{t}}{dt} - L(t, x(t), \dot{x}(t))$$

$$= \varepsilon^s (d\Phi_s/dt)(t, x(t)) + O(\varepsilon) \qquad \text{(summation convention on } s\text{)}, \quad (11)$$

with the remaining conditions of Definition 1 holding true.

This definition is more general than Definition 1 in that the left-hand side of (10) is equal to the sum of the exact differentials multiplied by the essential parameters and to first-order terms in ε. Since the addition of the total exact differentials does *not* change the original Euler–Lagrange equations associated with L (see Sagan [1969]), we may call this case the *dynamic symmetry condition with nullity*, or simply the *dynamic invariance with nullity*. Alternatively, Definition 2 is referred to as "invariance up to an exact differential" (see Rund [1966, p. 73]).

The Fundamental Invariance Identities, the Noether Theorem, and Conservation Laws

6. If the fundamental integral is invariant (either absolutely or up to an exact differential) under an r-parameter family (or group) of continuous transformations, the corresponding Lagrangian must satisfy certain conditions involving the Lagrangian, its derivatives, and the infinitesimal generators of the continuous transformations. On using the Euler–Lagrange expressions, the resulting formulation of these conditions is usually referred to as Noether's theorem. The importance of this theorem lies in the fact that it allows one to construct quantities which are constant along any extremal, i.e., a curve which satisfies the Euler–Lagrange equations. Hence it allows one to obtain relations which may be interpreted as "conservation laws."

We first derive the so-called *invariance* identities. By differentiating (11) with respect to ε^s and then setting $\varepsilon = 0$, we obtain

$$\left\{\frac{\partial L}{\partial t}\tau_s + \frac{\partial L}{\partial x^k}\xi_s^k + \frac{\partial L}{\partial \dot{x}^k}\left(\frac{\partial}{\partial \varepsilon^s}\left(\frac{d\bar{x}^k}{d\bar{t}}\right)\right)_0\right\}\left(\frac{d\bar{t}}{dt}\right)_0 + L\left(\frac{\partial}{\partial \varepsilon^s}\left(\frac{d\bar{t}}{dt}\right)\right)_0$$

$$= \frac{d\phi_s}{dt} \qquad \text{(summation on } k = 1, \ldots, n\text{)}, \qquad (12)$$

where $(\cdot)_0$ denotes $(\cdot)_{\varepsilon=0}$. In order to be able to exploit this condition, we must evaluate the various derivatives with respect to ε^s which appear on the left-hand side. We need the following expressions which are obvious from (2) and (3):

$$\begin{aligned}
&\left(\frac{\partial \bar{t}}{\partial t}\right)_0 = 1, \qquad \left(\frac{\partial \bar{x}^k}{\partial t}\right)_0 = \left(\frac{\partial \bar{t}}{\partial x^k}\right)_0 = 0, \\
&\left(\frac{\partial \bar{x}^k}{\partial x^h}\right)_0 = \delta_h^k \qquad \text{(the Kronecker delta)}, \\
&\left(\frac{\partial^2 \bar{x}^k}{\partial \varepsilon^s \, \partial t}\right)_0 = \frac{\partial \xi_s^k}{\partial t}, \qquad \left(\frac{\partial^2 \bar{x}^k}{\partial \varepsilon^s \, \partial x^h}\right)_0 = \frac{\partial \xi_s^k}{\partial x^h}, \\
&\left(\frac{\partial^2 \bar{t}}{\partial \varepsilon^s \, \partial t}\right)_0 = \frac{\partial \tau_s}{\partial t}, \qquad \left(\frac{\partial^2 \bar{t}}{\partial \varepsilon^s \, \partial x^h}\right)_0 = \frac{\partial \tau_s}{\partial x^h}.
\end{aligned} \tag{13}$$

We observe that, along any curve, we have by the chain rule

$$\frac{d\bar{t}}{dt} = \frac{\partial \bar{t}}{\partial t} + \frac{\partial \bar{t}}{\partial x^k} \dot{x}^k.$$

Differentiating this equation with respect to ε^s, and setting $\varepsilon = 0$ and using (13), we get

$$\left(\frac{\partial}{\partial \varepsilon^s}\left(\frac{d\bar{t}}{dt}\right)\right)_0 = \frac{\partial \tau_s}{\partial t} + \frac{\partial \tau_s}{\partial x^k} \dot{x}^k = \frac{d\tau_s}{dt}. \tag{14}$$

To calculate other expressions $((\partial/\partial\varepsilon^s)(\partial\bar{x}^k/\partial t))_0$, we differentiate (7) with respect to t to obtain

$$\frac{\partial \bar{x}^k}{\partial t} + \frac{\partial \bar{x}^k}{\partial x^h} \dot{x}^h = \frac{d\bar{x}^k}{d\bar{t}} \frac{d\bar{t}}{dt} = \frac{d\bar{x}^k}{d\bar{t}} \left(\frac{\partial \bar{t}}{\partial t} + \frac{\partial \bar{t}}{\partial x^h} \dot{x}^h\right). \tag{15}$$

Setting $\varepsilon = 0$ and using (13), we get

$$\delta_h^k \dot{x}^h = (d\bar{x}^k/d\bar{t})_0(1 + 0 \cdot \dot{x}^h);$$

i.e.,

$$\dot{x}^k = (d\bar{x}^k/d\bar{t})_0.$$

Again, differentiating (15) with respect to ε^s, we derive

$$\begin{aligned}
\frac{\partial^2 \bar{x}^k}{\partial \varepsilon^s \, \partial t} + \frac{\partial^2 \bar{x}^k}{\partial \varepsilon^s \, \partial x^h} \dot{x}^h &= \frac{d\bar{x}^k}{d\bar{t}} \left(\frac{\partial^2 \bar{t}}{\partial \varepsilon^s \, \partial t} + \frac{\partial^2 \bar{t}}{\partial \varepsilon^s \, \partial x^h} \dot{x}^h\right) \\
&\quad + \left(\frac{\partial}{\partial \varepsilon^s}\left(\frac{\partial \bar{x}^k}{\partial \bar{t}}\right)\right)\left(\frac{\partial \bar{t}}{\partial t} + \frac{\partial \bar{t}}{\partial x^h} \dot{x}^h\right),
\end{aligned}$$

after which we set $\varepsilon = 0$ while using (13). This yields

$$\frac{\partial \xi_s^k}{\partial t} + \frac{\partial \xi_s^k}{\partial x^h}\dot{x}^h = \dot{x}^k\left(\frac{\partial \tau_s}{\partial t} + \frac{\partial \tau_s}{\partial x^h}\dot{x}^h\right) + \left(\frac{\partial}{\partial \varepsilon^s}\left(\frac{\partial \bar{x}^k}{\partial \bar{t}}\right)\right)_0,$$

since

$$\left(\frac{\partial \bar{t}}{\partial t} + \frac{\partial \bar{t}}{\partial x^h}\dot{x}^h\right)_0 = \left(\frac{d\bar{t}}{dt}\right)_0 = 1.$$

Hence we obtain

$$\left(\frac{\partial}{\partial \varepsilon^s}\left(\frac{\partial \bar{x}^k}{\partial \bar{t}}\right)\right)_0 = \frac{d\xi_s^k}{dt} - \dot{x}^k\frac{d\tau_s}{dt}. \tag{16}$$

Substituting (14) and (16) into (12), we derive the invariance identities

$$\frac{\partial L}{\partial t}\tau_s + \frac{\partial L}{\partial x^k}\xi_s^k + \frac{\partial L}{\partial \dot{x}^k}\left(\frac{d\xi_s^k}{dt} - \dot{x}^k\frac{d\tau_s}{dt}\right) + L\frac{d\tau_s}{dt} = \frac{d\Phi_s}{dt} \tag{17}$$

($s = 1, \ldots, r$) (summation convention operative for $k = 1, \ldots, n$). The above are often referred to as the *fundamental invariance identities*, which involve the Lagrangian, its derivatives, and the infinitesimal generators τ_s and ξ_s^k of the transformations.

Noether's Theorem and Conservation Laws

7. The classical theorem of Noether on invariant variational problems can now be derived from the fundamental invariance identities when the Euler–Lagrange equations are introduced into this relation. Let the *Euler–Lagrange expressions* be given by

$$E_k = \frac{\partial L}{\partial x^k} - \frac{d}{dt}\frac{\partial L}{\partial \dot{x}^k} \qquad (k = 1, \ldots, n). \tag{18}$$

We note that

$$\frac{\partial L}{\partial t}\tau_s = \left(\frac{dL}{dt} - \frac{\partial L}{\partial x^k}\dot{x}^k - \frac{\partial L}{\partial \dot{x}^k}\ddot{x}^k\right)\tau_s$$

and

$$\frac{\partial L}{\partial \dot{x}^k}\frac{d\xi_s^k}{dt} = \frac{d}{dt}\left(\frac{\partial L}{\partial \dot{x}^k}\xi_s^k\right) - \frac{d}{dt}\left(\frac{\partial L}{\partial \dot{x}^k}\right)\xi_s^k,$$

together with

$$\frac{\partial L}{\partial \dot{x}^k}\dot{x}^k\frac{d\tau_s}{dt}+\frac{\partial L}{\partial \dot{x}^k}\ddot{x}^k\tau_s=\frac{d}{dt}\left(\frac{\partial L}{\partial \dot{x}^k}\dot{x}^k\tau_s\right)-\frac{d}{dt}\left(\frac{\partial L}{\partial \dot{x}^k}\right)\dot{x}^k\tau_s.$$

These three relations are substituted in turn into (17) to yield

$$\left[\frac{\partial L}{\partial x^k}-\frac{d}{dt}\left(\frac{\partial L}{\partial \dot{x}^k}\right)\right]\xi_s^k-\left[\frac{\partial L}{\partial x^k}-\frac{d}{dt}\left(\frac{\partial L}{\partial \dot{x}^k}\right)\right]\dot{x}^k\tau_s$$
$$+\frac{d}{dt}\left[L\tau_s+\frac{\partial L}{\partial \dot{x}^k}\xi_s^k-\frac{\partial L}{\partial \dot{x}^k}\dot{x}^k\tau_s\right]=\frac{d\Phi_s}{dt}\qquad (s=1,\ldots,r).$$

Using (18), this can be expressed as

$$E_k(\xi_s^k-\dot{x}^k\tau_s)+\frac{d}{dt}\left[L\tau_s+\frac{\partial L}{\partial \dot{x}^k}\xi_s^k-\frac{\partial L}{\partial \dot{x}^k}\dot{x}^k\tau_s-\Phi_s\right]=0,$$

which is now written in the form

$$-E_k(\xi_s^k-\dot{x}^k\tau_s)=\frac{d}{dt}\left[\left(L-\dot{x}^k\frac{\partial L}{\partial \dot{x}^k}\right)\tau_s+\frac{\partial L}{\partial \dot{x}^k}\xi_s^k-\Phi_s\right]\qquad (s=1,\ldots,r). \tag{19}$$

This relation represents r identities ($s = 1, \ldots, r$) known as the

Noether Identities *If the fundamental integral of a problem in the calculus of variations is invariant up to an exact differential under a given r-parameter family of transformations (or local Lie group of transformations), then there exist r distinct linear combinations of the Euler–Lagrange expressions which are exact differentials.*

If we set the Euler–Lagrange expressions to zero (necessary conditions for extremal),

$$E_k=\frac{\partial L}{\partial x^k}-\frac{d}{dt}\frac{\partial L}{\partial \dot{x}^k}=0\qquad (k=1,\ldots,n), \tag{18'}$$

then the following r expressions hold true:

$$\Omega_s\equiv\left(L-\dot{x}^k\frac{\partial L}{\partial \dot{x}^k}\right)\tau_s+\frac{\partial L}{\partial \dot{x}^k}\xi_s^k-\Phi_s=\text{const} \tag{20}$$

or

$$\Omega_s\equiv -H\tau_s+\frac{\partial L}{\partial \dot{x}^k}\xi_s^k-\Phi_s=\text{const}\qquad (s=1,\ldots,r), \tag{20'}$$

where H is the Hamiltonian function. This conclusion immediately gives rise to the usual formulation of

Noether's Theorem *If the fundamental integral of a problem in the calculus of variations is divergence-invariant under the r-parameter family of transformations* (2), *then r distinct quantities* Ω_s *defined by* (20) *or* (20′) *are constant along any extremal.*

Since the expressions Ω_s defined by (20) or (20′) are constant whenever $E_k = 0$ $(k = 1, \ldots, n)$, they are *first integrals* of the differential equations of motion, the Euler–Lagrange equations. *In physical and economic applications, Eqs.* (20) *or* (20′) *are thus interpreted as the "conservation laws" of the system.*

If we define the *canonical momenta* by $p_k \equiv \partial L/\partial \dot{x}^k$, and the *Hamiltonian*, which is in some mechanical systems is the total energy, then (20) or (20′) may be written simply in terms of these canonical variables as

$$-H\tau_s + p_k \xi_s^k - \Phi_s = \text{const} \qquad (s = 1, \ldots, r). \tag{21}$$

Examples

8. The following examples illustrate how the Noether theorem can be applied.

Example 1 (*Conservation of Energy*) Suppose that the potential energy does not explicitly depend on the time t: $U = U(x_1, \ldots, x_n)$. Then $L = T - U$, where T is the kinetic energy, is obviously invariant under the time translation $\bar{t} = t + \varepsilon$, $\bar{x}^k = x^k$, which has $\tau_s = 1$, $\xi_s^k = 0$, and $\Phi_s = 0$. Consequently, using (21), a first integral is given by

$$-H = L - p_k \dot{x}^k = -(T + U) = \text{const}.$$

Hence, *if the fundamental integral is invariant under a time translation, then the Hamiltonian, or total energy of the system, is constant—the conservation of energy theorem* (Whittaker [1937]).

Example 2 (*Conservation of Linear Momentum*) Suppose that (1) is absolutely invariant under translation of the form $\bar{t} = t$, $\bar{x}^k = x^k + \varepsilon^k$, which defines an n-parameter group of transformations with generators $\tau_s = 0$, and $\xi_s^k = \delta_s^k$, with $\Phi_s = 0$. This is the case in which the potential energy U is *translation invariant* in the directions of the coordinate axes. The first integrals are given, from (20), by

$$\frac{\partial L}{\partial \dot{x}^k} \delta_s^k = p_k \delta_s^k = \text{const} \qquad (s = 1, \ldots, r).$$

That is, the momentum remains unchanged—*conservation of linear momentum.*

Example 3 (*Uniform Motion of the Center of Mass* (Bessel-Hagen, 1921)) Invariance under the velocity transformations, which are sometimes called Galilean transformations, $\bar{t} = t$, $\bar{x}^k = x^k + \varepsilon^1 t$, $\bar{y}^k = y^k + \varepsilon^2 t$, $\bar{z}^k = z^k + \varepsilon^3 t$, with the group generators,

$$\tau_s = \left(\frac{\partial \bar{t}}{\partial \varepsilon^s}\right)_0 = 0, \qquad s = 1, 2, 3,$$

$$\xi_s^k = \left(\frac{\partial \bar{x}^k}{\partial \varepsilon^s}\right)_0 = \begin{cases} t, & s = 1, \\ 0, & s = 2, 3, \end{cases}$$

$$\eta_s^k = \left(\frac{\partial \bar{y}^k}{\partial \varepsilon^s}\right)_0 = \begin{cases} t, & s = 2, \\ 0, & s = 1, 3, \end{cases}$$

$$\zeta_s^k = \left(\frac{\partial \bar{z}^k}{\partial \varepsilon^s}\right)_0 = \begin{cases} t, & s = 3, \\ 0, & s = 1, 2, \end{cases}$$

leads to a result which describes how the center of mass of the n particle system moves. These velocity transformations provide us with an example of divergence-invariant, i.e., $\Phi_s \neq 0$. Assume now that the potential energy depends only on the mutual positions of the particles,

$$U = U(\ldots, x^i - x^j, y^i - y^j, z^i - z^j, \ldots).$$

Then it is invariant under the velocity transformations, for we have

$$\begin{aligned} U &= U(\ldots, \bar{x}^i - \bar{x}^j, \bar{y}^i - \bar{y}^j, \bar{z}^i - \bar{z}^j, \ldots) \\ &= U(\ldots, x^i - x^j, y^i - y^j, z^i - z^j, \ldots). \end{aligned}$$

Noether's theorem requires that

$$\Omega_s \equiv \sum_k \left(\frac{\partial L}{\partial \dot{x}^k} \xi_s^k + \frac{\partial L}{\partial \dot{y}^k} \eta_s^k + \frac{\partial L}{\partial \dot{z}^k} \zeta_s^k\right) - \Phi_s = \text{const} \qquad (s = 1, 2, 3).$$

If the kinetic energy has the form

$$T = \tfrac{1}{2} \sum_{k=1}^{n} m_k\{(\dot{x}^k)^2 + (\dot{y}^k)^2 + (\dot{z}^k)^2\},$$

then

$$\begin{aligned} \left(\frac{d\bar{x}^k}{d\bar{t}}\right)^2 &= \left(\frac{d\bar{x}^k}{dt}\right)^2 = \left(\frac{d}{dt}(x^k + \varepsilon^1 t)\right)^2 = (\dot{x}^k + \varepsilon^1)^2 \\ &= (\dot{x}^k)^2 + 2\varepsilon^1 \dot{x}^k + (\varepsilon^1)^2 = (\dot{x}^k)^2 + \varepsilon^1 \frac{d}{dt}(2x^k) + O(\varepsilon^1). \end{aligned}$$

Similar results apply for $(d\bar{y}^k/d\bar{t})^2$ and $(d\bar{z}^k/d\bar{t})^2$. Therefore, we have

$$\begin{aligned}\bar{T} - T &= \tfrac{1}{2}\sum_k m_k\left\{\left(\frac{d\bar{x}^k}{d\bar{t}}\right)^2 + \left(\frac{d\bar{y}^k}{d\bar{t}}\right)^2 + \left(\frac{d\bar{z}^k}{d\bar{t}}\right)^2\right\} \\ &\quad -\tfrac{1}{2}\sum_k m_k\left\{\left(\frac{dx^k}{dt}\right)^2 + \left(\frac{dy^k}{dt}\right)^2 + \left(\frac{dz^k}{dt}\right)^2\right\} \\ &= \varepsilon^1 \frac{d}{dt}\sum_k m_k x^k + \varepsilon^2 \frac{d}{dt}\sum_k m_k y^k + \varepsilon^3 \frac{d}{dt}\sum_k m_k z^k.\end{aligned}$$

The difference between the Lagrangians in the "barred" and "unbarred" coordinate systems is equal to

$$\bar{L} - L = \varepsilon^1 \frac{d}{dt}\Phi_1 + \varepsilon^2 \frac{d}{dt}\Phi_2 + \varepsilon^3 \frac{d}{dt}\Phi_3,$$

where $\Phi_1 = \sum_k m_k x^k$, $\Phi_2 = \sum_k m_k y^k$, and $\Phi_3 = \sum_k m_k z^k$. Substituting the preceding in the Noether identities, we get

$$\begin{aligned} t\sum_k m_k \dot{x}^k - \sum_k m_k x^k &= \text{const} = -B_1, \\ t\sum_k m_k \dot{y}^k - \sum_k m_k y^k &= \text{const} = -B_2, \\ t\sum_k m_k \dot{z}^k - \sum_k m_k z^k &= \text{const} = -B_3. \end{aligned}$$

Denoting $M = \sum_k m_k$ as the total mass of the n particles,

$$x_c = \frac{1}{M}\sum_k m_k x^k, \qquad y_c = \frac{1}{M}\sum_k m_k y^k, \qquad z_c = \frac{1}{M}\sum_k m_k z^k,$$

we observe that (x_c, y_c, z_c) are the coordinates of the center of mass of the system. From Example 2, the potential energy function also allows that the linear momentum is conserved, i.e.,

$$\sum_k m_k \dot{x}^k = \text{const} = A_1, \quad \sum_k m_k \dot{y}^k = \text{const} = A_2, \quad \sum_k m_k \dot{z}^k = \text{const} = A_3.$$

Hence, upon combining the above, we get

$$Mx_c = A_1 t + B_1, \qquad My_c = A_2 t + B_2, \qquad Mz_c = A_3 t + B_3.$$

These show that the center of mass moves uniformly in time or, with constant velocity given by $v_c = (A_1/M, A_2/M, A_3/M)$. This is *the law of the uniform motion of the center of mass—the center of mass theorem* (Hill [1951]).

Derivation of the Group of Transformation

9. If the Lagrangian and the group transformations are known, then Eq. (17) can be written down directly to obtain the fundamental identities for the system. Now we wish to consider the existence of the group of transformations as an a posteriori notion, and to show how a group can be determined under which a given variational problem is invariant. The fundamental invariance identities can be interpreted as a system of partial differential equations in unknowns τ_s and ξ_s^k for any given Lagrangian function.

Let us assume that a given integral functional (1) is twice continuously differentiable in each of its $2n + 1$ arguments, and $x^k(t) \in C^2[t_0, t_1]$ for $k = 1, \ldots, n$. According to the *fundamental invariance identities* (17), there exist the r relations (17), where τ_s and ξ_s^k are the generators of the group

$$\bar{t} = t + \tau_s(t, x)\varepsilon^s, \qquad \bar{x}^k = x^k + \xi_s^k(t, x)\varepsilon^s \qquad (s = 1, \ldots, r). \tag{5'}$$

Upon expanding the total derivatives in (17), we get

$$\frac{\partial L}{\partial t}\tau_s + \frac{\partial L}{\partial x^k}\xi_s^k + \frac{\partial L}{\partial \dot{x}^k}\left(\frac{\partial \xi_s^k}{\partial t} + \frac{\partial \xi_s^k}{\partial x^j}\dot{x}^j - \dot{x}^k\left(\frac{\partial \tau_s}{\partial t} + \dot{x}^j\frac{\partial \tau_s}{\partial x^j}\right)\right)$$
$$+ L\left(\frac{\partial \tau_s}{\partial t} + \frac{\partial \tau_s}{\partial x^j}\dot{x}^j\right) = \frac{d\Phi_s}{dt} \qquad (s = 1, \ldots, r). \tag{22}$$

Altering our viewpoint, Eq. (22) are identities in (t, x^k) for arbitrary directional arguments $\dot{x}^k$. That is to say, τ_s and ξ_s^k depend only on t and x^k but not on $\dot{x}^k$. Hence we can regard (22) as a set of partial differential equations in unknowns τ_s and ξ_s^k. *Due to the arbitrariness of the $\dot{x}^k$, (22) will be further reduced to a system of first-order partial differential equations in τ_s and ξ_s^k by equating to zero the coefficients of the powers of the $\dot{x}^k$*. The general method of the derivation of a group is then: *If this reduced system admits a solution, we have determined a group under which the fundamental integral is invariant, from which conservation laws will be derived by the Noether theorem.*

It may be best to illustrate this general method using the following Lagrangian which leads to the so-called Emden equation (see H. T. Davis [1962, p. 371 ff])

$$L = t^2(\tfrac{1}{2}\dot{x}^2 - \tfrac{1}{6}x^6).$$

The Emden equation is the Euler–Lagrange equation of L, i.e.,

$$\frac{\partial L}{\partial x} - \frac{d}{dt}\left(\frac{\partial L}{\partial \dot{x}}\right) = 0 \qquad \text{or} \qquad t\ddot{x} + 2\dot{x} + tx^5 = 0.$$

We look for a one-parameter group of transformations $\bar{t} = t + \tau(t, x)\varepsilon$, $\bar{x} = x + \xi(t, x)\varepsilon$ under which $J(x) = \int_{t_0}^{t_1} L\,dt$ is invariant. Calculating $\partial L/\partial t = t(\dot{x}^2 - \frac{1}{3}x^6)$, $\partial L/\partial x = -t^2x^5$, and $\partial L/\partial \dot{x} = t^2\dot{x}$ and substituting these quantities into the invariance identity (22) (with $s = 1, k = 1$, and $d\Phi/dt = 0$), we obtain

$$t\left(\dot{x}^2 - \frac{x^6}{3}\right)\tau + (-t^2x^5)\xi + t^2\dot{x}\left(\frac{\partial\xi}{\partial t} + \frac{\partial\xi}{\partial x}\dot{x} - \dot{x}\frac{\partial\tau}{\partial t} - \dot{x}^2\frac{\partial\tau}{\partial x}\right)$$
$$+ t^2\left(\frac{\dot{x}^2}{2} - \frac{x^6}{6}\right)\left(\frac{\partial\tau}{\partial t} + \dot{x}\frac{\partial\tau}{\partial x}\right) = 0.$$

Or by dividing with t and collecting the coefficients of the powers of $\dot{x}$, namely, $\dot{x}^0$, $\dot{x}^1$, $\dot{x}^2$, and $\dot{x}^3$, we get

$$\left(-\frac{x^6}{3}\tau - tx^5\xi - \frac{tx^6}{6}\frac{\partial\tau}{\partial t}\right)\dot{x}^0 + \left(t\frac{\partial\xi}{\partial t} - \frac{tx^6}{6}\frac{\partial\tau}{\partial x}\right)\dot{x}^1$$
$$+ \left(\tau + t\frac{\partial\xi}{\partial x} - \frac{t}{2}\frac{\partial\tau}{\partial t}\right)\dot{x}^2 + \left(-\frac{t}{2}\frac{\partial\tau}{\partial x}\right)\dot{x}^3 = 0.$$

The coefficients of the powers of $\dot{x}$ must be equal to zero due to the arbitrariness of directional argument $\dot{x}$ and due to the independence of τ and ξ from $\dot{x}$. Hence the following system of partial differential equations for τ and ξ must hold:

$$\text{(i)}\quad \frac{x}{3}\tau + t\xi + \frac{tx}{6}\frac{\partial\tau}{\partial t} = 0, \qquad \text{(ii)}\quad \frac{\partial\xi}{\partial t} - \frac{x^6}{6}\frac{\partial\tau}{\partial x} = 0,$$

$$\text{(iii)}\quad \tau + \frac{\partial\xi}{\partial x}t - \frac{t}{2}\frac{\partial\tau}{\partial t} = 0, \qquad \text{(iv)}\quad \frac{\partial\tau}{\partial x}\frac{t}{2} = 0.$$

Since t is not equal to zero, (iv) immediately gives that τ is a function of only t, $\tau = \tau(t)$, $\partial\tau/\partial x = 0$. As a result, from (ii) we have $\partial\xi/\partial t = 0$ or $\xi = \xi(x)$. Using these, the foregoing conditions reduce to

$$\frac{x}{3}\tau + t\xi + \frac{tx}{6}\frac{d\tau}{dt} = 0, \qquad \tau + t\frac{d\xi}{dx} - \frac{t}{2}\frac{d\tau}{dt} = 0,$$

which are simple ordinary differential equations. By differentiating the first equation with respect to x and noting that τ is independent of x, we get

$$\frac{\tau}{3} + t\frac{d\xi}{dx} + \frac{t}{6}\frac{d\tau}{dt} = 0, \qquad \tau + t\frac{d\xi}{dx} - \frac{t}{2}\frac{d\tau}{dt} = 0.$$

Elimination of $t\, d\xi/dx$ from these two equations gives

$$-\tfrac{2}{3}\tau + \tfrac{2}{3}t\frac{d\tau}{dt} = 0.$$

Then, τ is immediately derived as $\tau = ct$ or by setting $c = 1$, $\tau = t$. Substituting this in the first equation, we get $\xi = -\frac{1}{2}x$. From Noether's theorem, we obtain the first integral or constant of the motion,

$$\Omega \equiv \left(L - \dot{x}\frac{\partial L}{\partial \dot{x}}\right)\tau + \frac{\partial L}{\partial \dot{x}}\xi \equiv \frac{t^3x^6}{6} + \frac{t^3\dot{x}^2}{2} + \frac{t^2x\dot{x}}{3} = \text{const} = C.$$

This is the *conservation law* for the systems associated with the Emden equation.

III. Conservation Laws in Simple Models of the Ramsey Type[8]

Simple Models of the Ramsey Type

10. We are now in a position to derive conservation laws in dynamic economic systems. We begin with simple growth models of the Ramsey type. These models are characterized with the *linear* transformation function (linear production possibility frontier) between consumption and capital accumulation, i.e.,

$$c = c(\dot{k}, k) = f(k) - nk - \dot{k}, \qquad n \geqq 0, \tag{23}$$

where c is the consumption (per capita C/L), $f(k) = Y/L$ the neoclassical (aggregate) production function (per capita) with $f'(k) > 0$, $f''(k) < 0$, $k = K/L$ is the capital–labor ratio, n the sum of the constant population growth rate and the depreciation rate, and $\dot{k} = dk/dt$ the rate of capital (per capita) accumulation. Although Ramsey's original work [1928] considers the case of $n = 0$ and $k = K$, $c = C$, $\dot{k} = \dot{K}$, and $f = Y$, the qualitative properties of his model are basically the same as those developed later by Samuelson and Solow [1956], Cass [1965], Koopmans [1965], Burmeister and Dobell [1970], Samuelson [1965], Sato and Davis [1971], Shell [1967], and others. The basic feature of these models is that the production possibility frontier, as depicted by Fig. 3, is linear, i.e.,

$$\partial^2 c/\partial \dot{k}^2 \equiv 0. \tag{24}$$

The objective of society is to maximize the social welfare functional, i.e.,

$$J(k) = \int_0^T e^{-\rho t} U(c)\, dt \to \max \tag{25}$$

[8] The author gratefully acknowledges helpful assistance and suggestions rendered by Professor Takayuki Nôno.

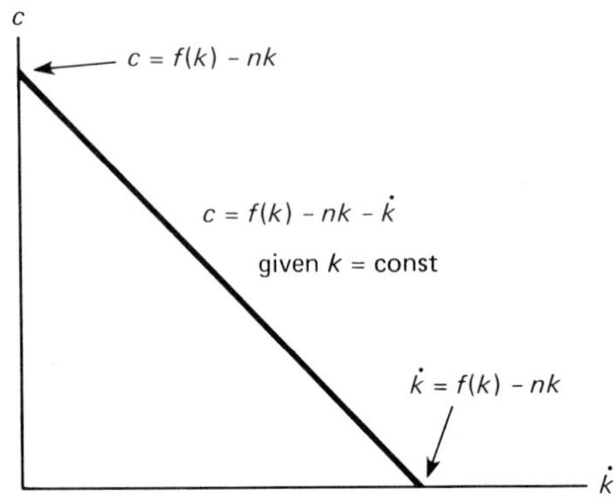

Figure 3

under condition (23), together with appropriate initial conditions. In (25), U is a utility (or welfare) function with the usual properties $U' > 0$, $U'' < 0$, and $\rho \geqq 0$ is the fixed discount rate. The terminal time T may or may not be finite. In many cases we may assume that it is infinite, $T = +\infty$. Substituting (23) into (25), we have the standard calculus of variation (or optimal control) problem (25), where c is defined by (23).

Here we have the Lagrangian

$$L(t, k(t), \dot{k}(t)) = e^{-\rho t}U[g(k(t)) - \dot{k}(t)], \tag{26}$$

where

$$g(k) = f(k) - nk. \tag{27}$$

We look for a family of transformations,[9]

$$\bar{t} = t + \varepsilon\tau(t, k), \tag{28-i}$$

$$\varepsilon = \text{parameter},$$

$$\bar{k} = k + \varepsilon\xi(t, k), \tag{28-ii}$$

under which (25) is *dynamically invariant*. In the invariance identity [Eq. (17) or (22)], we first assume $d\Phi/dt = 0$. Calculating $\partial L/\partial t = -\rho e^{-\rho t}U$, $\partial L/\partial k = e^{-\rho t}U'g'$, and $\partial L/\partial \dot{k} = -e^{-\rho t}U'$, and substituting these in the *invariance identity*, we get

$$U\left(\frac{d\tau}{dt} - \rho\tau\right) + U'\left(g'\xi - \frac{d\xi}{dt} + \dot{k}\frac{d\tau}{dt}\right) = 0. \tag{29}$$

[9] We may give economic interpretations to (28). The time transformation may be considered as the transformation of "objective time" to "subjective time" (Samuelson [1976]), where the subjective time depends not only on the objective time t, but also on the wealth k. The second equation of (28) is nothing but the technical change transformation depending also on the objective time and the wealth effect.

This is the *fundamental invariance equation for the simple Ramsey models.* In order that (25) may be invariant under *any arbitrary form* of U and that conservation laws may hold for *any* utility function, (29) must imply

$$\frac{d\tau}{dt} - \rho\tau = 0, \tag{29-i$'$}$$

$$g'\xi - \frac{d\xi}{dt} + \dot{k}\frac{d\tau}{dt} = 0. \tag{29-ii$'$}$$

On using $d\tau/dt = \partial\tau/\partial t + \dot{k}\,\partial\tau/\partial k$ and $d\xi/dt = \partial\xi/\partial t + \dot{k}\,\partial\xi/\partial k$, (29$'$) is equal to

$$\frac{\partial\tau}{\partial t} + \dot{k}\frac{\partial\tau}{\partial k} - \rho\tau = 0, \tag{29-i$''$}$$

$$g'\xi - \left(\frac{\partial\xi}{\partial t} + \dot{k}\frac{\partial\xi}{\partial k}\right) + \dot{k}\left(\frac{\partial\tau}{\partial t} + \dot{k}\frac{\partial\tau}{\partial k}\right) = 0. \tag{29-ii$''$}$$

Collecting the coefficients of the powers of $\dot{k}$, we have

$$\left(\frac{\partial\tau}{\partial t} - \rho\tau\right)\dot{k}^0 + \frac{\partial\tau}{\partial k}\dot{k}^1 = 0,$$

$$\left(g'\xi - \frac{\partial\xi}{\partial t}\right)\dot{k}^0 + \left(-\frac{\partial\xi}{\partial k} + \frac{\partial\tau}{\partial t}\right)\dot{k}^1 + \frac{\partial\tau}{\partial k}\dot{k}^2 = 0.$$

On setting these coefficients equal to zero, the invariance condition becomes

$$\frac{\partial\tau}{\partial t} - \rho\tau = 0, \tag{29-i$'''$}$$

$$\frac{\partial\tau}{\partial k} = 0, \tag{29-ii$'''$}$$

$$g'\xi - \frac{\partial\xi}{\partial t} = 0, \tag{29-iii$'''$}$$

$$-\frac{\partial\xi}{\partial k} + \frac{\partial\tau}{\partial t} = 0. \tag{29-iv$'''$}$$

From (29-ii$'''$), we immediately conclude that $\tau = \tau(t)$, and from (29-i$'''$)

$$\tau = ae^{\rho t} \qquad (a = \text{const}). \tag{30-i}$$

From (29-iv$'''$) and using (30-i), $\partial\xi/\partial k = \partial\tau/\partial t = a\rho e^{\rho t}$. Integrating (29-iii$'''$) partially with respect to t, we derive

$$\xi = A(k)e^{g'(k)t}. \tag{30-ii}$$

But from (29-iv‴), $\partial\xi/\partial k = \partial\tau/\partial t$, and from (30-i), $\tau = ae^{\rho t}$, we can show that $\partial^2\xi/\partial k^2 \equiv 0$. By differentiating ξ with respect to k once,

$$\frac{\partial\xi}{\partial k} = e^{g'(k)t}[A(k)g''(k)t + A'(k)],$$

and twice,

$$\frac{\partial^2\xi}{\partial k^2} = g''(k)te^{g'(k)t}[A(k)g''(k)t + A'(k)]$$
$$+ e^{g'(k)t}[(A(k)g''(k))'t + A''(k)],$$

and using the fact $\partial^2\xi/\partial k^2 \equiv 0$, we get

$$t^2 g''(k)^2 A(k) + t[g''(k)A'(k) + (g''(k)A(k))'] + A''(k) = 0.$$

The foregoing requires that

$$A''(k) = 0, \tag{31-i}$$

$$g''(k)^2 A(k) = 0, \tag{31-ii}$$

$$g''(k)A'(k) + (g''(k)A(k))' = 0. \tag{31-iii}$$

There are two cases depending upon $g''(k) \neq 0$ or $g''(k) = 0$.

Case 1 ($g''(k) \neq 0 \Leftrightarrow f''(k) \neq 0$ from (27), i.e., $f(k) \neq \alpha k + \beta$) Equation (31-ii) requires that $A(k) = 0$, which implies from (30-ii), $\xi = 0$ (no conservation law with respect to $\bar{k}$).

Also, from (29-iv‴) we must have $\partial\tau/\partial t = 0$. Substituting this into

$$\partial\tau/\partial t - \rho\tau = 0, \tag{29-i‴}$$

we have $\rho\tau = 0$, which means

$$\rho \neq 0, \qquad \tau = 0 \qquad \text{(no conservation law with respect to } \bar{t}\text{)}, \tag{32-i}$$

$$\rho = 0, \qquad \tau = \text{const} \qquad \text{(time translation)}. \tag{32-ii}$$

Case 2 ($g''(k) = 0 \Leftrightarrow f''(k) = 0$, i.e., $f(k) = \alpha k + \beta$, $\alpha > 0$ or $g(k) = (\alpha - n)k + \beta$) Here we have from (31-i), $A''(k) = 0$, or $A(k) = bk + d$. Substituting this into (30-ii), we get $\xi = (bk + d)e^{(\alpha - n)t}$, $g' = (\alpha - n)$. We must now determine the consistent values of α and b that satisfy (29‴). It is easily seen that (29-iii‴) is always met. Hence (29-iv‴) is the only restriction that must be satisfied, which relates ξ with τ. Thus

$$\partial\xi/\partial k = be^{(\alpha - n)t} = \rho ae^{\rho t} = \partial\tau/\partial t.$$

Therefore, we must have $b = \rho a$ and $\rho = \alpha - n$ or $\alpha = \rho + n$, which gives the final form of the generator of the group as

$$\tau = ae^{\rho t}, \tag{30-i'}$$

$$\xi = (a\rho k + d)e^{\rho t} \tag{30-ii'}$$

for $g(k) = \rho k + \beta = f(k) - nk = \alpha k + \beta - nk$, or $f(k) = g(k) + nk = \rho k + \beta + nk = (\rho + n)k + \beta$ (a, β, d are arbitrary constants).

In summary, we can write down the *conservation laws* as

Case 1 (General Production Function $f(k) \neq \alpha k + \beta$) (i) $\rho \neq 0$ (positive discount rate $\rho > 0$)

$$\xi = 0, \qquad \tau = 0, \qquad \text{no conservation laws.}$$

(ii) $\rho = 0$ (zero discount rate)

$$\xi = 0, \qquad \tau = \text{const} = 1, \qquad \text{time translation,}$$

$$\Omega = L\tau + \frac{\partial L}{\partial \dot{k}}(\xi - \dot{k}\tau) = L\tau - \frac{\partial L}{\partial \dot{k}}\dot{k}\tau,$$

or

$$\Omega = U + U'\dot{k} = \text{Hamiltonian} = \text{const} \qquad (\tau = 1). \tag{33}$$

Case 2 (Linear Technology $f(k) = (\rho + n)k + \beta$) (i) $\tau = ae^{\rho t}$, (ii) $\xi = (a\rho k + d)e^{\rho t}$ for

$$L = e^{-\rho t}U(\rho k + \beta - \dot{k});$$

$$\Omega = L\tau + \frac{\partial L}{\partial \dot{k}}(\xi - \dot{k}\tau) = \left(L - \frac{\partial L}{\partial \dot{k}}\dot{k}\right)\tau + \frac{\partial L}{\partial \dot{k}}\xi = -\text{Hamiltonian} \times \tau$$

$$+ \frac{\partial L}{\partial \dot{k}}\xi = \text{const} = e^{-\rho t}Uae^{\rho t} - e^{-\rho t}U'[(a\rho k + d)e^{\rho t} - \dot{k}ae^{\rho t}]$$

$$= aU - U'[a(g(k) - \dot{k}) + d - a\beta] \qquad (g(k) = \rho k + \beta),$$

or

$$\Omega = a[U(c) - U'(c)c] + (a\beta - d)U'(c) = \text{const} \qquad (g(k) - \dot{k} = c). \tag{34}$$

Up to this point we have sought conservation laws under the definition of absolute invariance (Definition 1). We now look for laws under the more general definition of divergence-invariant (Definition 2). The invariance equation (17) requires that

$$\frac{\partial L}{\partial t}\tau + \frac{\partial L}{\partial k}\xi + \frac{\partial L}{\partial \dot{k}}\left(\frac{d\xi}{dt} - \dot{k}\frac{d\tau}{dt}\right) + L\frac{d\tau}{dt} = \frac{d\Phi}{dt},$$

where $\Phi = \Phi(t, k)$ and $L = e^{-\rho t}U(g(k) - \dot{k})$. Substituting $\partial L/\partial t = -\rho e^{-\rho t}U$, $\partial L/\partial k = e^{-\rho t}U'g'$, $\partial L/\partial \dot{k} = -e^{-\rho t}U'$ into the foregoing and writing

$$\frac{d\xi}{dt} = \frac{\partial \xi}{\partial t} + \dot{k}\frac{\partial \xi}{\partial k}, \qquad \frac{d\tau}{dt} = \frac{\partial \tau}{\partial t} + \dot{k}\frac{\partial \tau}{\partial k}, \qquad \text{and} \qquad \frac{d\Phi}{dt} = \frac{\partial \Phi}{\partial t} + \dot{k}\frac{\partial \Phi}{\partial k},$$

we get

$$e^{-\rho t}\left[U\left(\frac{\partial \tau}{\partial t} - \rho\tau + \frac{\partial \tau}{\partial k}\dot{k}\right) + U'\left\{g'\xi - \frac{\partial \xi}{\partial t} - \left(\frac{\partial \xi}{\partial k} - \frac{\partial \tau}{\partial t}\right)\dot{k} + \frac{\partial \tau}{\partial k}\dot{k}^2\right\}\right]$$
$$= \frac{\partial \Phi}{\partial t} + \dot{k}\frac{\partial \Phi}{\partial k}.$$

Differentiating the above partially twice with respect to $\dot{k}$, we obtain

$$U'''\left\{\left(g'\xi - \frac{\partial \xi}{\partial t}\right) - \left(\frac{\partial \xi}{\partial k} - \frac{\partial \tau}{\partial t}\right)\dot{k} + \frac{\partial \tau}{\partial k}\dot{k}^2\right\}$$
$$+ U''\left\{\left(\frac{\partial \tau}{\partial t} - \rho\tau\right) + 2\left(\frac{\partial \xi}{\partial k} - \frac{\partial \tau}{\partial t}\right) - 3\frac{\partial \tau}{\partial k}\dot{k}\right\} = 0.$$

In order that the conservation laws may hold for any arbitrary utility function, we must have, after setting the coefficients of the powers of $\dot{k}$ to zero,

$$g'\xi - \frac{\partial \xi}{\partial t} = 0, \qquad \frac{\partial \tau}{\partial k} = 0$$

$$\frac{\partial \xi}{\partial k} - \frac{\partial \tau}{\partial t} = 0, \qquad \frac{\partial \tau}{\partial t} - \rho\tau + 2\left(\frac{\partial \xi}{\partial k} - \frac{\partial \tau}{\partial t}\right) = 0.$$

This implies that

$$\frac{\partial \tau}{\partial t} - \rho\tau = 0 \qquad \left(\text{from } \frac{\partial \xi}{\partial k} - \frac{\partial \tau}{\partial t} = 0\right), \tag{35-i}$$

$$\frac{\partial \tau}{\partial k} = 0, \tag{35-ii}$$

$$g'\xi - \frac{\partial \xi}{\partial t} = 0, \tag{35-iii}$$

$$\frac{\partial \xi}{\partial k} - \frac{\partial \tau}{\partial t} = 0. \tag{35-iv}$$

But *this is exactly identical with (29‴), the case of absolute invariance. Hence there exist no additional conservation laws, even if we allow for a more general definition of invariance.*

Economic Interpretation

11. We first give an economic interpretation to Noether's theorem [Eq. (20) or (21)] when it is applied to a typical welfare maximization problem with n state variables.

If a welfare function is dynamically invariant under an r-parameter family of transformations resulting from technical change and/or taste change, then the following quantities are constant along any optimal path for the entire planning period:

$$(\text{Hamiltonian})\begin{pmatrix}\text{infinitesimal}\\ \text{transformations}\\ \text{of time}\end{pmatrix} + \sum_{i=1}^{n}\begin{pmatrix}\text{implicit}\\ \text{price of}\\ \dot{x}_i\end{pmatrix}\begin{pmatrix}\text{infinitesimal}\\ \text{transformations}\\ \text{of } x_i \text{ due to}\\ \text{technical}\\ \text{(taste) change}\end{pmatrix} + (\text{null term})$$

$$= \text{const}$$

$$= \begin{pmatrix}\text{measure of}\\ \text{welfare per}\\ \text{infinitesimal}\\ \text{change of time}\end{pmatrix} + \sum_{i=1}^{n}\begin{pmatrix}\text{value (effect)}\\ \text{of technical}\\ \text{(taste) change}\end{pmatrix} + (\text{null term})$$

$$= \text{const.}$$

Turning our attention to the specific conservation laws derived in the previous section, we observe that conservation laws for the simple Ramsey models crucially depend on whether the discount rate is zero or not, and/or whether technology is linear or not. When production technology is of the general neoclassical type, $f(k) > 0, f'(k) > 0, f''(k) < 0, k > 0$, and when the discount rate is positive, then there exists *no* conservation law for an arbitrary form of utility function. On the other hand, when technology is linear with the marginal product equal to the exogenously determined rate of $\rho + n$, there exists an *invariance identity* $U(c) = \text{const}$, i.e., $c = \text{const}$ for every period.

When the discount rate is zero, that is to say, the Lagrangian does not contain t explicitly, the value of the Hamiltonian is, as is expected, constant. What is important here, however, is that *the constancy of the Hamiltonian is the only conservation law operating in the system when* $\rho = 0$. The economic interpretation of the constancy of the Hamiltonian [Eq. (33)] or the invariance under time translation (32-ii) is that the sum of the value of consumption

($U(c)$) and the value of investment ($q\dot{k}$, $q = U'$), which is the measure of welfare in terms of consumption, remains constant. That is to say, the value of income measured in terms of consumption ($U' = q$) does not change over the planning period.

The second case of singularity requires a further explanation. First, the conservation law (34) does *not* hold for *all* linear technology. It holds only for a special type of linear technology with the marginal product of capital identically equal to $\rho + n$, the sum of the discount rate and the population growth (and the Harrod neutral technical progress) rate. Since there are *two* parameters a and d in the infinitesimal transformation (30-i′) and (30-ii′), there are *two* quantities that are constant (Noether's theorem). Thus we have

$$\tau_1 = ae^{\rho t}, \quad d = 0, \qquad \tau_2 = 0, \quad a = 0,$$
$$\xi_1 = a\rho k e^{\rho t}, \quad d = 0, \quad \text{and} \quad \xi_2 = de^{\rho t}, \quad a = 0.$$

Corresponding to these cases using (34) we obtain

$$\Omega_1 = a[U(c) - U'(c)c + \beta U'(c)] = \text{const} \tag{34-i}$$

and

$$\Omega_2 = -dU'(c) = \text{const.} \tag{34-ii}$$

Looking at Ω_2, we immediately conclude that $U'(c) = \text{const}$ or $c = \text{const}$, that is to say, *the optimally controlled per capita consumption must remain unchanged during the planning horizon.* The conditions on Ω_1 do not say more than this, for if $c = \text{const}$, naturally, Ω_1, which is a function of only c, must also be constant. Hence, as the economic conservation law, we derive the constancy of *per capita consumption.*

This singular case of linear technology corresponds to the Arrow–Kurz example (Kurz [1968a]), when the marginal product in the Arrow–Kurz example $\alpha = \rho$ in our case. (Here our case applies to any utility function.) The optimal control program is to maximize

$$\int_0^\infty e^{-\rho t} U(c)\, dt$$

subject to $\dot{k} = (\rho + n)k - nk + \beta - c = \rho k + \beta - c,$

$$U' > 0, \quad U'' < 0, \quad k > 0.$$

The Euler–Lagrange equation (or the maximum principle) requires that

$$\dot{k} = \rho k + \beta - c(q) \qquad \text{and} \qquad \dot{q} = (\rho - \rho)q = 0, \qquad U'(c) = q,$$

where $q = U'(c)$ is the current value of the implicit price of investment. The phase diagram is shown in Fig. 4. Given the planning horizon, $U'(c) = q = \text{const} > 0$, because of the conservation law, $q = q^*$, while k must always be

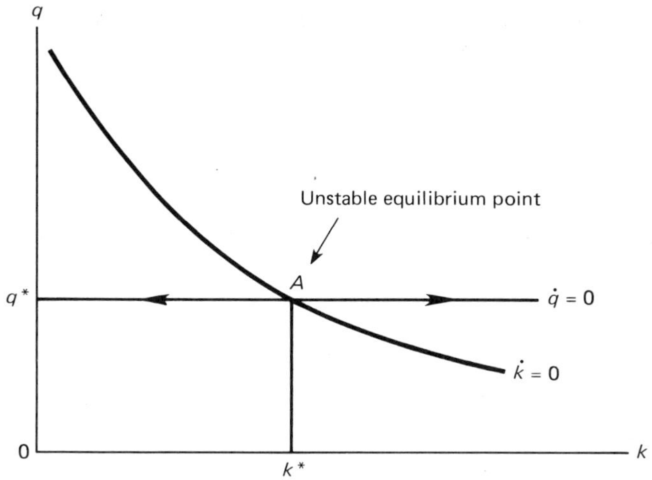

Figure 4

increasing determined by $\dot{k} = \rho k + \beta - c^*(q^*)$ or $k(t) = [k(0) - k^*]e^{\rho t} + k^*$, where $k^* = (c^* - \beta)/\rho$ and $k(0)$ is the initial condition. That is to say, k must be eventually increasing or decreasing at the rate of the discount rate ρ. Here, as Kurz demonstrates, the optimal program has the totally unstable feature.

The following theorem summarizes the results up to this point.

Theorem 1 *(Conservation Laws for Simple Models of the Ramsey Type)*

(i) *When the discount rate ρ is zero, there exists only one conservation law that the value of welfare measured in terms of consumption and investment remains constant, i.e.,*

$$H = U(c) + q \cdot \dot{k} = \text{const}, \qquad q = U'.$$

This is an alternative statement of the Ramsey rule in Section 2.

(ii) *When the discount rate ρ is positive, there exists* no *conservation law unless the production technology is a special linear type $f(k) = \alpha k + \beta = (\rho + n)k + \beta$, $\alpha = \rho + n$.*

(iii) *When the production function is of the form $f(k) = \alpha k + \beta = (\rho + n)k + \beta$, $\alpha = \rho + n$, $\rho > 0$, the value of per capita consumption c is always constant. Hence the (current value) implicit price of investment $q = U'$, and therefore, the utility level itself remains unchanged. The discounted welfare is decreasing at the constant rate ρ.*

(iv) *These results hold true even when the more general definition of invariance with nullity is adopted.*

IV. Conservation Laws in "General" Neoclassical Optimal Growth Models

The Liviatan–Samuelson Model—Concave Production Possibility Frontier

12. With Liviatan and Samuelson [1969], we now assume that the transformation function has a (strictly) concave frontier. Hence a production function of consumption is given by

$$c(t) = f(\dot{k}(t), k(t)), \tag{36}$$

where $c(t)$ and $k(t)$ represent, respectively, consumption and capital per capita, and $\dot{k}(t) = dk/dt$, the rate of capital accumulation. f specifies the *maximum* c for a given k and $\dot{k}$, and it already incorporates the parameter of exponential depreciation (or technical progress) and population growth.[10] The fundamental difference between this model and those of the Ramsey type is that $\partial^2 f/\partial \dot{k}^2$ is negative in this model, while in the Ramsey models $\partial^2 f/\partial \dot{k}^2$ is zero. Hence the production possibility frontier is concave to the origin as depicted in Fig. 5. More specifically, we assume that $\partial f/\partial \dot{k} < 0$, $\partial^2 f/\partial \dot{k}^2 < 0$ and the positivity of the Hessian determinant of c, i.e.,

$$\frac{\partial^2 f}{\partial \dot{k}^2} \cdot \frac{\partial^2 f}{\partial k^2} - \left(\frac{\partial^2 f}{\partial \dot{k}\, \partial k}\right)^2 > 0.$$

As usual, we also assume the existence of a golden rule, i.e., $\max_k f(0, k)$ at $k = \tilde{k}$, and hence we have $\partial f(0, k)/\partial k \gtreqless 0$ as $k \lesseqgtr \tilde{k}$.

Let the Lagrangian now be represented by

$$L(t, \dot{k}, k) = e^{-\rho t} U(c(t)) = e^{-\rho t} U[f(\dot{k}(t), k(t))]. \tag{37}$$

To derive conservation laws for this case, we apply the invariance identity (17) with $d\Phi/dt = 0$, where $\bar{t} = t + \varepsilon\tau(t, k)$ and $\bar{k} = k + \varepsilon\xi(t, k)$. Substituting $\partial L/\partial t = -\rho e^{-\rho t} U$, $\partial L/\partial k = e^{-\rho t} U'\, \partial f/\partial k$, $\partial L/\partial \dot{k} = e^{-\rho t} U'\, \partial f/\partial \dot{k}$, into (17), we get

$$U\left[-\rho\tau + \frac{d\tau}{dt}\right] + U'\left[\frac{\partial f}{\partial k}\xi + \frac{\partial f}{\partial \dot{k}}\left(\frac{d\xi}{dt} - \dot{k}\frac{d\tau}{dt}\right)\right] = 0. \tag{38}$$

In order to obtain (global) conservation laws for any *arbitrary* utility function and production function and for $\rho > 0$, i.e., independent of particular *forms*

[10] Kurz's model [1968b], which includes wealth in the utility function, has the same formal structure as the Liviatan–Samuelson model.

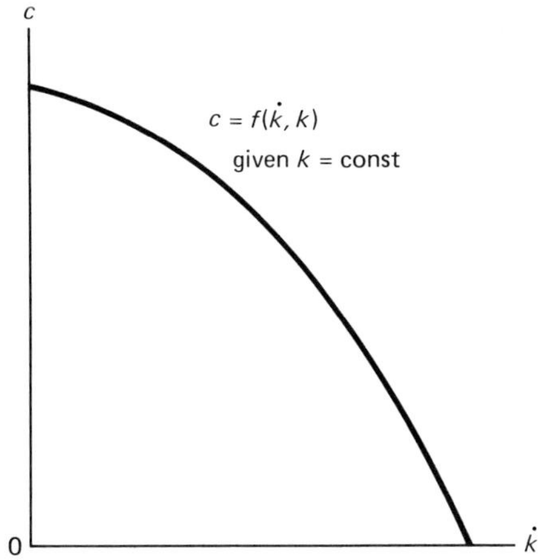

Figure 5

of utility and production functions, we must have

$$-\rho\tau + \frac{d\tau}{dt} = 0, \tag{38-i'}$$

$$\frac{\partial f}{\partial k}\xi + \frac{\partial f}{\partial \dot{k}}\left(\frac{d\xi}{dt} - \dot{k}\frac{d\tau}{dt}\right) = 0, \tag{38-ii'}$$

which in turn implies

$$\text{(i)}\quad \xi = 0, \qquad \text{(ii)}\quad d\xi/dt - \dot{k}\, d\tau/dt = 0,$$

or

$$\tau = 0, \tag{38-i''}$$

$$\xi = 0. \tag{38-ii''}$$

Hence there is *no* conservation law which is operating globally and is *independent of the forms of utility and production functions for* $\rho > 0$. This result again is not surprising, since conservation laws in physics and natural sciences usually refer to particular forms of the Lagrangian function.

Local Conservation Laws

13. Since most of the main results in economic dynamics are of *local nature*, such as turnpike theorems and catenary properties (see, e.g., Samuelson [1965], Levhari and Liviatan [1972]), we now look for what may be called the "*local*" *conservation laws* operating in the neighborhood of the stationary equilibrium point. We assume the existence of the stationary equilibrium point corresponding to $\dot{k} = 0$ of the optimal program, i.e., $k = k^*, \dot{k} = 0$. Let x and $\dot{x}$ be the deviation of $k(t)$ from k^* and its time derivative, respectively,

$$x = k(t) - k^*, \qquad \dot{x} = \dot{k}(t). \tag{39}$$

We begin with the local Lagrangian near $(0, k^*(0))$ in the form suggested by Samuelson [1972, p. 113, Eq. (46)],

$$L = e^{-\rho t}[-\tfrac{1}{2}\dot{x}^2 - ax\dot{x} - \tfrac{1}{2}x^2], \qquad -1 \leqq a \leqq 1. \tag{40}$$

For $-1 < a < 1$, L is strictly concave, and the characteristic exponents around the stationary point for the Euler–Lagrange equation,

$$\ddot{x} - \rho\dot{x} - (1 + \rho a)x = 0 \tag{41}$$

and

$$0 = \begin{vmatrix} a + \rho - \lambda & a^2 - 1 \\ -1 & -a - \lambda \end{vmatrix} = \lambda^2 - \rho\lambda - (1 + \rho a) = 0, \tag{42}$$

are (i) positive and negative or (ii) both positive, depending on the value of ρ relative to a (Samuelson [1972, p. 114]. This represents the "local" stable turnpike or unstable turnpike.

We seek conservation laws associated with (40). The Noether invariance identity under the infinitesimal transformation,

$$\bar{t} = t + \varepsilon\tau(t, x) \qquad \text{and} \qquad \bar{x} = x + \varepsilon\xi(t, x),$$

requires that

$$\frac{\partial L}{\partial t}\tau + \frac{\partial L}{\partial x}\xi + \frac{\partial L}{\partial \dot{x}}\left(\frac{d\xi}{dt} - \dot{x}\frac{d\tau}{dt}\right) + L\frac{d\tau}{dt} = \frac{d\Phi}{dt}.$$

Using $\partial L/\partial t = -\rho e^{-\rho t}f$, $\partial L/\partial x = e^{-\rho t}(-a\dot{x} - x)$, $\partial L/\partial \dot{x} = e^{-\rho t}(-\dot{x} - ax)$, where $f = -\frac{1}{2}\dot{x}^2 - ax\dot{x} - \frac{1}{2}x^2$, we derive

$$\begin{aligned} e^{-\rho t}\bigg[\frac{1}{2}\frac{\partial\tau}{\partial x}\dot{x}^3 &+ \left(\frac{\rho\tau}{2} - \frac{\partial\xi}{\partial x} + \frac{1}{2}\frac{\partial\tau}{\partial t}\right)\dot{x}^2 + \bigg(\rho a x\tau - a\xi - \frac{\partial\xi}{\partial t} - ax\frac{\partial\xi}{\partial x} \\ &- \frac{1}{2}x^2\frac{\partial\tau}{\partial x}\bigg)\dot{x} + \left(\frac{\rho x^2\tau}{2} - x\xi - ax\frac{\partial\xi}{\partial t} - \frac{1}{2}x^2\frac{\partial\tau}{\partial t}\right)\bigg] = \frac{\partial\Phi}{\partial t} + \dot{x}\frac{\partial\Phi}{\partial x}. \end{aligned} \tag{43}$$

Setting the coefficients of the powers of $\dot{x}$ equal to zero, we get

$$\frac{\partial \tau}{\partial x} = 0, \tag{43-i}$$

$$\frac{\rho\tau}{2} - \frac{\partial \xi}{\partial x} + \frac{1}{2}\frac{\partial \tau}{\partial t} = 0, \tag{43-ii}$$

$$e^{-\rho t}\left(\rho a x \tau - a\xi - \frac{\partial \xi}{\partial t} - ax\frac{\partial \xi}{\partial x} - \frac{1}{2}x^2\frac{\partial \tau}{\partial x}\right) = \frac{\partial \Phi}{\partial x}, \tag{43-iii}$$

$$e^{-\rho t}\left(\frac{\rho x^2 \tau}{2} - x\xi - ax\frac{\partial \xi}{\partial t} - \frac{1}{2}x^2\frac{\partial \tau}{\partial t}\right) = \frac{\partial \Phi}{\partial t}. \tag{43-iv}$$

Case A $(d\Phi/dt \equiv 0)$ We first study the case of *simple absolute invariance*, i.e.,

$$\frac{d\Phi}{dt} \equiv \frac{\partial \Phi}{\partial t} + \dot{x}\frac{\partial \Phi}{\partial x} = 0, \qquad \text{i.e.,} \quad \frac{\partial \Phi}{\partial t} = 0, \quad \frac{\partial \Phi}{\partial x} = 0 \quad \Leftrightarrow \quad \Phi = \text{const.} \tag{44}$$

Then the right-hand sides of (43-iii) and (43-iv) are identically equal to zero. First, we note that (43-i) implies that τ is a function of only t, i.e.,

$$\tau = \tau(t), \qquad \partial\tau/\partial x = 0. \tag{45}$$

Using this, we rewrite (43) as

$$\frac{\rho\tau}{2} - \frac{\partial \xi}{\partial x} + \frac{1}{2}\frac{d\tau}{dt} = 0, \tag{43-ii$'$}$$

$$\rho a x \tau - a\xi - \frac{\partial \xi}{\partial t} - ax\frac{\partial \xi}{\partial x} = 0, \tag{43-iii$'$}$$

$$\frac{\rho x \tau}{2} - \xi - a\frac{\partial \xi}{\partial t} - \frac{1}{2}x\frac{d\tau}{dt} = 0. \tag{43-iv$'$}$$

Substituting $d\tau/dt$ from (43-ii′) into (43-iv′), we obtain

$$\rho x \tau - \xi - a\,\partial\xi/\partial t - x\,\partial\xi/\partial x = 0.$$

Multiplying this by a and subtracting it from (43-iii′), we get

$$(a^2 - 1)\,\partial\xi/\partial t = 0. \tag{46}$$

Considering the case of strict concavity of L, i.e., $a^2 - 1 \neq 0$, we conclude that

$$\partial\xi/\partial t = 0 \qquad \text{or} \qquad \xi = \xi(x). \tag{47}$$

Partial differentiation of (43-iii′) with t after setting $\partial\xi/\partial t = 0$ gives $\rho a x\, \partial\tau/\partial t = 0$. For $\rho a \neq 0$, this implies, in view of (45),

$$\partial\tau/\partial t = d\tau/dt = 0 \qquad \text{or} \qquad \tau = \text{const} = \delta.$$

Then from (43-iv′) with $\partial\xi/\partial t = d\tau/dt = 0$, we immediately derive $\xi = (\rho\delta/2)x$. Hence the infinitesimal transformations become

$$\tau = \delta, \tag{48-i}$$

$$\xi = (\rho\delta/2)x. \tag{48-ii}$$

The conservation law corresponding to (48) is

$$\Omega = e^{-\rho t}\tfrac{1}{2}[\dot{x}^2 - \rho\dot{x}x - (1 + a\rho)x^2]\,\delta = \text{const}. \tag{49}$$

Economic Interpretation of the Conservation Law

We can give a meaningful economic interpretation to the foregoing conservation law: Equation (49) is obviously equal to

$$\Omega = \left(-H + \frac{\rho x}{2}\frac{\partial L}{\partial \dot{x}}\right)\delta = \frac{e^{-\rho t}}{2}\,[(\dot{x}^2 - x^2) - \rho x(\dot{x} + ax)]\,\delta = \text{const}, \tag{49′}$$

or by setting $\delta = -1$,

$$\Omega = H - \frac{\rho x}{2}\frac{\partial L}{\partial \dot{x}} = \frac{e^{-\rho t}}{2}(x^2 - \dot{x}^2) - \frac{\rho x}{2}\,e^{-\rho t}(-\dot{x} - ax) = \text{const},$$

where $H = (e^{-\rho t}/2)(x^2 - \dot{x}^2)$. The Hamiltonian H represents the (discounted) welfare measure of the sum of consumption and investment, while $-(\rho x/2)\,\partial L/\partial\dot{x} = (\rho/2)V$ represents *the value (or effect) of technical change measured* by the (cost) price of investment, $p = -\partial L/\partial \dot{x}$. Alternatively, $V = xp$ may be interpreted as the *value of capital* in terms of the investment price. Hence *the conservation law states that the value of the modified Hamiltonian, $H + (\rho/2)V$, which is equal to the Hamiltonian plus the value of capital V weighted by $\frac{1}{2}$ of the discount rate ρ, remains constant near the stationary equilibrium point k^**. We can also write

$$\Omega = e^{-\rho t}(\bar{H} + (\rho/2)\bar{V}) = e^{-\rho t}\,(\text{current modified welfare}) = \text{const}, \tag{50}$$

where $\bar{H}$ is the current value of Hamiltonian and $\bar{V}$ the current value of capital. In summary, we present

Theorem 2 *(Conservation Law of the Modified Hamiltonian) The discounted welfare measured in terms of the modified Hamiltonian, which is the*

sum of the Hamiltonian and the value of technical change, remains constant near the equilibrium point.

Case B ($d\Phi/dt \neq 0$, *Divergence-Invariant Case*) The second case of invariance requires the conditions that $\partial\Phi/\partial x \neq 0$ and $\partial\Phi/\partial t \neq 0$ in Eqs. (43-iii) and (43-iv). Hence we must have

$$\frac{\rho\tau}{2} - \frac{\partial\xi}{\partial x} + \frac{\tau'}{2} = 0, \qquad \tau' = \frac{d\tau}{dt} \quad \left(\frac{\partial\tau}{\partial x} = 0\right), \tag{43-ii''}$$

$$e^{-\rho t}\left(\rho a x\tau - a\xi - \frac{\partial\xi}{\partial t} - ax\frac{\partial\xi}{\partial x}\right) = \frac{\partial\Phi}{\partial x}, \tag{43-iii''}$$

$$e^{-\rho t}\left(\frac{\rho x^2\tau}{2} - x\xi - ax\frac{\partial\xi}{\partial t} - \frac{x^2\tau'}{2}\right) = \frac{\partial\Phi}{\partial t}. \tag{43-iv''}$$

Differentiating (43-ii″) partially with respect to x and using $\partial\tau/\partial x = 0$, we get $\partial^2\xi/\partial x^2 = 0$, and hence we obtain

$$\xi(x, t) = \xi_0(t) + \xi_1(t)x. \tag{51}$$

Then Eqs. (43″) can now be written as

$$2\xi_1 = \tau' + \rho\tau, \qquad \xi_1 = \frac{\partial\xi}{\partial x}, \tag{43-ii'''}$$

$$-e^{-\rho t}[ax(\xi_1 - \rho\tau) + a(\xi_0 + x\xi_1) + (\xi_0' + x\xi_1')] = \frac{\partial\Phi}{\partial x}, \tag{43-iii'''}$$

$$-e^{-\rho t}\left[\frac{x^2}{2}(\tau' - \rho\tau) + x(\xi_0 + x\xi_1) + ax(\xi_0' + x\xi_1')\right] = \frac{\partial\Phi}{\partial t}. \tag{43-iv'''}$$

Differentiating (43-iii‴) partially with t and (43-iv‴) partially with x, respectively, and then equating both expressions, we can derive the *integrability condition*:

$$\frac{\partial^2\Phi}{\partial t\,\partial x} = \frac{\partial^2\Phi}{\partial x\,\partial t}. \tag{52}$$

After using somewhat complicated calculations and the relation $2\xi_1 = \tau' + \rho\tau$, we can express (52) as

$$\{(1 + \rho a)2\tau' + \rho\xi_1' - \xi_1''\}x + \{(1 + \rho a)\xi_0 + \rho\xi_0' - \xi_0''\} = 0. \tag{52'}$$

Setting the coefficients of the powers of x to zero, we get

$$(1 + \rho a)2\tau' + \rho\xi_1' - \xi_1'' = 0, \tag{52-i'}$$

$$(1 + \rho a)\xi_0 + \rho\xi_0' - \xi_0'' = 0. \tag{52-ii'}$$

This is the set of conditions that must be satisfied by τ and ξ for the integrability of Φ. Using the relations $\xi_1' = \frac{1}{2}(\tau'' + \rho\tau')$ and $\xi_1'' = \frac{1}{2}(\tau''' + \rho\tau'')$, Eq. (52-i′) is reduced to

$$\tau''' - [\rho^2 + 4(1 + \rho a)]\tau' = 0,$$

whose solution is derived as

$$\tau(t) = \delta_1 e^{rt} + \delta_2 e^{-rt} + \delta_3, \tag{53}$$

where $r = \sqrt{\rho^2 + 4(1 + \rho a)}$ and the δ_i are arbitrary constants, $i = 1, 2, 3$. On the other hand, using (43-ii‴) and solving (52-ii′), we can express (51) as

$$\begin{aligned} \xi(t, x) &= \xi_0(t) + \xi_1(t)x \\ &= \delta_4 e^{(\rho + r)t/2} + \delta_5 e^{(\rho - r)t/2} \\ &\quad + \tfrac{1}{2}[\delta_1(\rho + r)e^{rt} + \delta_2(\rho - r)e^{-rt} + \rho\, \delta_3]x, \end{aligned} \tag{54}$$

where δ_4, δ_5 are other arbitrary constants.

Before presenting conservation laws and economic interpretations of (53) and (54), we shall determine Φ, the term of nullity. By integrating $\partial\Phi/\partial x$ [Eq. (43-iii‴)] with respect to x, we get

$$\begin{aligned} \Phi = \int \partial\Phi &= -\int e^{-\rho t}[ax(\xi_1 - \rho\tau) + a(\xi_0 + x\xi_1) + (\xi_0' + x\xi_1')]\,\partial x \\ &= -e^{-\rho t}\left[x^2\left(a\xi_1 + \frac{\xi_1'}{2} - \frac{a\rho\tau}{2}\right) + x(a\xi_0 + \xi_0')\right] + \psi(t). \end{aligned}$$

To determine $\psi(t)$, differentiate the foregoing Φ partially with respect to t and set it equal to Eq. (43-iv‴) in order to obtain

$$\begin{aligned} \frac{d\psi}{dt} = -e^{-\rho t}\Bigg[x^2\Bigg\{\rho\left(a\xi_1 + \frac{\xi_1'}{2} - \frac{a\rho\tau}{2}\right) - \left(a\xi_1' + \frac{\xi_1''}{2} - \frac{a\rho\tau'}{2}\right) \\ + (\tau' + a\xi_1')\Bigg\} + x\{\rho(a\xi_0 + \xi_0') - (a\xi_0' + \xi_0'') + (\xi_0 + a\xi_0')\}\Bigg]. \end{aligned}$$

The coefficients of the powers of x in the preceding equation will be reduced to zero by the integrability conditions (52-i′) and (52-ii′), i.e.,

$$\begin{aligned} x^2\!: \quad & \rho\left(a\xi_1 + \frac{\xi_1'}{2} - \frac{a\rho\tau}{2}\right) - \left(a\xi_1' + \frac{\xi_1''}{2} - \frac{a\rho\tau'}{2}\right) + (\tau' + a\xi_1') \\ & = (1 + \rho a)2\tau' + \rho\xi_1' - \xi_1'' = 0 \qquad \text{[Eq. (52-i′)]} \end{aligned}$$

and

$$\begin{aligned} x\!: \quad & \rho(a\xi_0 + \xi_0') - (a\xi_0' + \xi_0'') + (\xi_0 + a\xi_0') \\ & = (1 + \rho a)\xi_0 + \rho\xi_0' - \xi_0'' = 0 \qquad \text{[Eq. (52-ii′)]}. \end{aligned}$$

Hence we have

$$d\psi/dt = 0 \qquad \text{or} \qquad \psi = \text{const} = C.$$

The *final form* of Φ is then determined by

$$\Phi = -e^{-\rho t}\left[\frac{x^2}{2}(a\tau' + \xi_1') + x(a\xi_0 + \xi_0')\right] + C_0, \tag{55}$$

which is reduced to

$$\Phi = -e^{-\rho t}\left[\frac{rx^2}{4}\{(2a + \rho + r)\delta_1 e^{rt} + (2a + \rho - r)\delta_2 e^{-rt}\}\right.$$
$$\left. + \frac{x}{2}\{(2a + \rho + r)\delta_4 e^{(\rho + r)t/2} + (2a + \rho - r)\delta_5 e^{(\rho - r)t/2}\}\right],$$
$$r = \sqrt{\rho^2 + 4(1 + \rho a)}.$$

We are now in a position to delineate conservation laws in terms of Noether's theorem. Corresponding to Eq. (20), we have

$$\Omega = \left\{-e^{-\rho t}\left(\frac{x^2}{2} + ax\dot{x} + \frac{\dot{x}^2}{2}\right) + e^{-\rho t}(\dot{x} + ax)\dot{x}\right\}\{\delta_1 e^{rt} + \delta_2 e^{-rt} + \delta_3\}$$
$$- \{e^{-\rho t}(\dot{x} + ax)\}\{\delta_4 e^{(\rho + r)t/2} + \delta_5 e^{(\rho - r)t/2}$$
$$+ \frac{x}{2}[\delta_1(\rho + r)e^{rt} + \delta_2(\rho - r)e^{-rt} + \rho\,\delta_3]\}$$
$$+ e^{-\rho t}\left\{\frac{rx^2}{4}[(2a + \rho + r)\,\delta_1 e^{rt} + (2a + \rho - r)\,\delta_2 e^{-rt}]\right.$$
$$\left. + \frac{x}{2}[(2a + \rho + r)\,\delta_4 e^{(\rho + r)t/2} + (2a + \rho - r)\,\delta_5 e^{(\rho - r)t/2}]\right\}. \tag{56}$$

There are five conservation laws corresponding to five arbitrary constants δ_s, $s = 1, \ldots, 5$. We begin with δ_3 which gives

$$\delta_3\colon\ \Omega_3 = e^{-\rho t}\tfrac{1}{2}[\dot{x}^2 - \rho x\dot{x} - (1 + \rho a)x^2]\,\delta_3 = \text{const.} \tag{56-iii}$$

However, this is nothing but the *conservation law* which we have already derived as Theorem 2 when $d\Phi/dt = 0$.

It is not too difficult, though tedious, to show that the remaining four laws are not independent. By using $r = \sqrt{\rho^2 + 4(1 + \rho a)}$, it is shown that

$$\Omega_1 = (\Omega_4)^2, \qquad \Omega_2 = (\Omega_5)^2.$$

Hence *there are only three independent conservation laws including* Ω_1, Ω_2, and Ω_3, or alternatively Ω_3, Ω_4, and Ω_5; i.e.,

$$\delta_1\colon\ \Omega_1 = e^{(r-\rho)t}\left[\dot{x}^2 - (\rho + r)x\dot{x} + \left\{\frac{r(\rho + r) - 2(1 + \rho a)}{2}\right\}x^2\right]\delta_1 = \text{const}, \tag{56-i}$$

$$\Leftrightarrow\ \delta_4\colon\ e^{(r-\rho)t/2}\left[\dot{x} - \frac{(\rho + r)}{2}x\right]\delta_4 = \text{const}, \tag{56-iv}$$

$$\delta_2\colon\ \Omega_2 = e^{-(r+\rho)t}\left[\dot{x}^2 - (\rho - r)x\dot{x} - \left\{\frac{r(\rho - r) + 2(1 + \rho a)}{2}\right\}x^2\right]\delta_2 = \text{const}, \tag{56-ii}$$

$$\Leftrightarrow\ \delta_5\colon\ e^{-(r+\rho)t/2}\left[\dot{x} + \frac{(r - \rho)}{2}x\right]\delta_5 = \text{const}, \tag{56-v}$$

and (56-iii). It is interesting to observe that δ_1, δ_2, and δ_3 are arbitrary constants with their corresponding characteristic roots $r_1 = r$, $r_2 = -r$, and $r_3 = 0$, and that Ω_1 is the general expression for all of the conservation laws. Thus, Ω_2 and Ω_3 have the same expressions as Ω_1 when $r_1 = r$ is replaced by $r_2 = -r$ and $r_3 = 0$, respectively.

Economic Interpretation of the Additional Conservation Laws

14. The infinitesimal transformations for t and x are shown to be expressed as in (53) and (54). Notice that $\tau(t)$, $\xi_0(t)$, and $\xi_1(t)$ all have the *turnpike properties* that are so unique to an optimal programme of this type. Hence, the (infinitesimal) dynamic transformations that leave the Lagrangian invariant themselves satisfy the "turnpike theorem" with the two sets of roots r and $-r$ and $\frac{1}{2}(\rho + r)$ and $\frac{1}{2}(\rho - r)$. For sufficiently small value of $\rho > 0$, turnpikes are again shown to be *stable* with positive and negative roots. Even if ρ becomes large, the time transformation $\tau(t)$ always satisfies a stable turnpike property, while the x transformation now has the possibility of unstable turnpike. Because of the strict concavity condition of the Lagrangian, the infinitesimal transformations are not allowed to possess any imaginary roots like the solution of x itself. In summary, the infinitesimal transformations are expressible as

$$\begin{aligned}\text{time transformation} &= \text{turnpike expression I} + \text{const},\\ \text{state-variable transformation} &= \text{turnpike expression II}\\ &\qquad + x\,(\text{turnpike expression I} + \text{const}).\end{aligned}$$

The general expression for the conservation laws can now be expressible as

$$-\Omega = H\tau(t) - \frac{\partial L}{\partial \dot{x}}\,\xi(t, x) + \Phi = \text{const}$$

$$= \text{(Hamiltonian)(turnpike expression I + const)}$$

$$+ \text{(price of investment)\{turnpike expression II}$$

$$+ x\,\text{(turnpike expression I + const)\} + null term = const.}$$

Expressions (53) and (54) suggest that the two additional conservation laws may be related to the turnpike property of the optimal solutions. In fact, the additional laws are nothing but the *turnpike constants.* Let the general solution to the Euler–Lagrange equation (41) be equal to

$$x = C_1 e^{\lambda_1 t} + C_2 e^{\lambda_2 t}, \tag{57}$$

where λ_1 and λ_2 are the two characteristic (turnpike) roots $\lambda_1 = \frac{1}{2}(\rho + r)$, $\lambda_2 = \frac{1}{2}(\rho - r)$. Then differentiation of (57) with t gives

$$\dot{x} = C_1 \lambda_1 e^{\lambda_1 t} + C_2 \lambda_2 e^{\lambda_2 t}. \tag{57'}$$

Multiplication of λ_1 to (57) and subtraction of the resulting expression from (57′) yield $\dot{x} - \lambda_1 x = C_2 e^{\lambda_2 t}(\lambda_2 - \lambda_1)$, which is equal to

$$C_2(\lambda_2 - \lambda_1) = e^{-\lambda_2 t}(\dot{x} - \lambda_1 x) = \text{const.} \tag{56-iv'}$$

This is nothing but the first of the two additional laws (Ω_4). In the same manner, we can show

$$C_1(\lambda_1 - \lambda_2) = e^{-\lambda_1 t}(\dot{x} - \lambda_2 x) = \text{const}, \tag{56-v'}$$

which is the remaining conservation law (Ω_5). In retrospect, the reader may wonder why we had to apply the rather complicated Noether approach to obtain the simple turnpike constants. Recall that the Noether method is designed to uncover *all* conservation laws operating in the system, *hidden* or *unhidden.* The first conservation law (Theorem 2) of the constancy of the modified Hamiltonian was by no means easy to uncover because it was a hidden law. The additional two laws could have been derived without Noether's theorem, because they are not hidden. The point is, however, that the Noether theorem guarantees that *there are no other conservation laws.*

The turnpike constants and, therefore, the two additional conservation laws can be given the following economic interpretations. *Looking at* (56-iv) and (56-v) we can say that *the difference between investment* $\dot{x}$ *and capital* x *with the appropriate weight* $\frac{1}{2}(\rho + r)$ *attached to* x *must be "decreasing" at the rate* $\frac{1}{2}(r - \rho)\%$ *per year* $= \Omega_4$ ($\Leftrightarrow \Omega_1$), *while the sum of* $\dot{x}$ *and* x *with the weight* $\frac{1}{2}(r - \rho)$ *attached to* x *must be "increasing" at the constant rate* $\frac{1}{2}(r + \rho)\%$ *per year* $= \Omega_5$ ($\Leftrightarrow \Omega_2$).[11]

In summary, we have

Theorem 3 *(Additional Conservation Laws)* (i) *The two additional conservation laws are nothing but the turnpike constants of the system.*

(ii) *The weighted difference between investment* $\dot{x}$ *and capital* x *multiplied by the inverse of the negative turnpike exponent, and the weighted sum of investment and capital multiplied by the inverse of the positive turnpike exponent are always constant.*

More General Conservation Laws

15. Rather than linearizing near the stationary point, we shall briefly consider some specified forms of the production and utility functions as suggested by Liviatan and Samuelson [1969]. We begin with the form

$$L = e^{-\rho t} f(\dot{k}, k), \qquad \partial^2 f/\partial \dot{k}^2 = a = \text{const} < 0. \tag{58}$$

As f is a strictly concave function, we have assumed that $U' = \text{const} = 1$. We also have $\partial f(0, k)/\partial k \gtreqless 0$ as $k \lesseqgtr \tilde{k}$, $\partial f/\partial \dot{k} < 0$, $\partial^2 f/\partial k^2 < 0$, and $(\partial^2 f/\partial \dot{k}^2)(\partial^2 f/\partial k^2) - (\partial^2 f/\partial \dot{k}\, \partial k)^2 > 0$. ($\tilde{k}$ = the golden rule value of k.) More specifically, we may assume (58) to have a special quadratic form with respect to $\dot{k}$, i.e.,

$$L = e^{-\rho t}[(a/2)\dot{k}^2 + b(k)\dot{k} + c(k)]. \tag{58$'$}$$

The *Noether invariance condition* [Eq. (17)] for this case under $\bar{t} = t + \varepsilon\tau(t, k)$ and $\bar{k} = k + \varepsilon\xi(t, k)$ becomes

$$\begin{aligned} -\rho e^{-\rho t} f \tau + e^{-\rho t} \frac{\partial f}{\partial k} \xi + e^{-\rho t} \frac{\partial f}{\partial \dot{k}} \left[\frac{\partial \xi}{\partial t} + \dot{k}\left(\frac{\partial \xi}{\partial k} - \frac{\partial \tau}{\partial t} \right) - \dot{k}^2 \frac{\partial \tau}{\partial k} \right] \\ + e^{-\rho t} f \left(\frac{\partial \tau}{\partial t} + \dot{k} \frac{\partial \tau}{\partial k} \right) = \frac{\partial \Phi}{\partial t} + \dot{k} \frac{\partial \Phi}{\partial k}. \end{aligned} \tag{59}$$

[11] When $\rho = 0$, the two additional conservation laws take more apparent forms,

$$\Omega_4 = e^t(\dot{x} - x) = \text{const}, \qquad \Omega_5 = e^{-t}(\dot{x} + x) = \text{const}, \qquad \lambda_1 = 1, \quad \lambda_2 = -1.$$

Hence *the difference between investment* $\dot{x}$ *and capital* x *measured from the steady state is "decreasing" at the internally determined rate of* $\lambda\%$ (100%) *per year* $= \Omega_4$, *while the sum of investment* $\dot{x}$ *and capital* x *is "increasing" at that rate each year along the turn pike paths* $= \Omega_5$.

Differentiating the foregoing by $\dot{k}$ partially twice, we obtain

$$\frac{\partial^3 f}{\partial k\, \partial \dot{k}^2}\xi + \frac{\partial^3 f}{\partial \dot{k}^3}\left[\frac{\partial \xi}{\partial t} + \dot{k}\left(\frac{\partial \xi}{\partial k} - \frac{\partial \tau}{\partial t}\right) - \dot{k}^2\frac{\partial \tau}{\partial k}\right]$$
$$+ \frac{\partial^2 f}{\partial \dot{k}^2}\left[\left(\frac{\partial \tau}{\partial t} - \rho\tau\right) + 2\left(\frac{\partial \xi}{\partial k} - \frac{\partial \tau}{\partial t}\right) - 3\dot{k}\frac{\partial \tau}{\partial k}\right] = 0. \tag{60}$$

As $\partial^3 f/\partial k\, \partial \dot{k}^2 = 0$ and $\partial^3 f/\partial \dot{k}^3 = 0$, (60) implies that

$$\frac{\partial \tau}{\partial t} - \rho\tau + 2\left(\frac{\partial \xi}{\partial k} - \frac{\partial \tau}{\partial t}\right) - 3\dot{k}\frac{\partial \tau}{\partial k} = 0. \tag{60'}$$

Setting the coefficients of the powers of $\dot{k}$ equal to zero, (60′) gives

$$\frac{\partial \tau}{\partial t} - \rho\tau + 2\left(\frac{\partial \xi}{\partial k} - \frac{\partial \tau}{\partial t}\right) = 0, \tag{60-i''}$$

$$\frac{\partial \tau}{\partial k} = 0. \tag{60-ii''}$$

These two conditions with $2\,\partial\xi/\partial k = \partial\tau/\partial t + \rho\tau$ and $\partial^2\xi/\partial k^2 = 0$ imply

$$\xi(t, k) = \xi_0(t) + \xi_1(t)k \tag{60-i'''}$$

$$\tau = \tau(t). \tag{60-ii'''}$$

Substituting these into (59), we have

$$e^{-\rho t}[((a/2)\dot{k}^2 + b(k)\dot{k} + c(k))(\tau' - \rho\tau) + (b'(k)\dot{k} + c'(k))(\xi_0 + \xi_1 k)$$
$$+ (a\dot{k} + b(k))(\xi_0' + \xi_1' k + \dot{k}(\xi_1 - \tau')] = \frac{\partial \Phi}{\partial t} + \dot{k}\frac{\partial \Phi}{\partial k}. \tag{59'}$$

To determine τ, ξ, and Φ simultaneously, we write from (59′) the powers of $\dot{k}$ as

$$\dot{k}^2\colon\quad \frac{a}{2}e^{-\rho t}(2\xi_1 - \tau' - \rho\tau) = 0, \tag{59-i'}$$

$$\dot{k}^1\colon\quad \frac{\partial \Phi}{\partial k} = e^{-\rho t}[b(k)(\xi_1 - \rho\tau) + b'(k)(\xi_0 + \xi_1 k) + a(\xi_0' + \xi_1' k)], \tag{59-ii'}$$

$$\dot{k}^0\colon\quad \frac{\partial \Phi}{\partial t} = e^{-\rho t}[c(k)(\tau' - \rho\tau) + c'(k)(\xi_0 + \xi_1 k) + b(k)(\xi_0' + \xi_1' k)]. \tag{59-iii'}$$

The *integrability condition* $\partial^2\Phi/\partial t\, \partial k = \partial^2\Phi/\partial k\, \partial t$ is immediately derived as

$$a\{(\xi_0'' - \rho\xi_0') + k(\xi_1'' - \rho\xi_1')\} = (\rho b(k) + c'(k))(\xi_1 + \tau' - \rho\tau)$$
$$+ (\rho b'(k) + c''(k))(\xi_0 + \xi_1 k). \tag{61}$$

Liviatan–Samuelson Numerical Example A numerical example suggested by Liviatan and Samuelson [1969, p. 142] is a special case of our Lagrangian (58′), when $b(k)$ and $c(k)$ take the form

$$b(k) = b_0 + b_1 k + b_2 k^2 + b_3 k^3, \qquad b_i = \text{const}, \quad 0 \leqq i \leqq 3, \tag{62-i}$$

$$c(k) = c_0 + c_1 k + c_2 k^2, \qquad c_i = \text{const}, \quad 0 \leqq i \leqq 2, \tag{62-ii}$$

so that

$$L(t, \dot{k}, k) = e^{-\rho t}[(a/2)\dot{k}^2 + (b_0 + b_1 k + b_2 k^2 + b_3 k^3)\dot{k} + c_0 + c_1 k + c_2 k^2]. \tag{58″}$$

To look for "global" conservation laws for this case, we set

$$\begin{aligned} \rho b(k) + c'(k) &= (\rho b_0 + c_1) + (\rho b_1 + 2c_2)k + \rho b_2 k^2 + \rho b_3 k^3 \\ &= p_0 + p_1 k + p_2 k^2 + p_3 k^3, \qquad p_3 \neq 0, \end{aligned} \tag{63}$$

and substitute these into the integrability condition,

$$\begin{aligned} a\{(\xi_0'' - \rho\xi_0') + k(\xi_1'' - \rho\xi_1')\} &= (p_0 + p_1 k + p_2 k^2 + p_3 k^3)(\xi_1 + \tau' - \rho\tau) \\ &\quad + (p_1 + 2p_2 k + 3p_3 k^2)(\xi_0 + \xi_1 k). \end{aligned} \tag{61′}$$

Setting the coefficients of the powers of k to zero, we get

$$k^3: \quad 4\xi_1 + \tau' - \rho\tau = 0, \tag{61-i′}$$

$$k^2: \quad p_2(3\xi_1 + \tau' - \rho\tau) + 3p_3\xi_0 = 0, \tag{61-ii′}$$

$$k^1: \quad p_1(2\xi_1 + \tau' - \rho\tau) + 2p_2\xi_0 = a(\xi_1'' - \rho\xi_1'), \tag{61-iii′}$$

$$k^0: \quad p_0(\xi_1 + \tau' - \rho\tau) + p_1\xi_0 = a(\xi_0'' - \rho\xi_0'). \tag{61-iv′}$$

After complicated calculations,[12] *we can show that there exist no global conservation laws for this case*, i.e.,

$$\tau = 0, \qquad \xi = 0. \tag{64}$$

[12] From $\tau' - \rho\tau = -4\xi_1$, we have $-p_2\xi_1 + 3p_3\xi_0 = 0$, $-2p_1\xi_1 + 2p_2\xi_0 = a(\xi_1'' - \rho\xi_1')$, and $-3p_0\xi_1 + p_1\xi_0 = a(\xi_0'' - \rho\xi_0')$. Using (59-i′), (61-i′) becomes $3\tau' + \rho\tau = 0$ or $\tau = \alpha e^{-1/3\rho t}$, α = arbitrary constant. Substituting this into (59-i′), we get $2\xi_1 = \tau' + \rho\tau$ or $\xi_1 = \frac{1}{3}\rho\tau$. On the other hand, from $\xi_0 = \frac{1}{3}(p_2/p_3)\xi_1 = \frac{1}{9}(p_2/p_3)\rho\tau$, we have $(-2p_1 + \frac{2}{3}(p_2^2/p_3))\xi_1 = a(\xi_1'' - \rho\xi_1')$ and $(-9(p_0 p_3/p_2) + p_1)\xi_1 = a(\xi_1'' - \rho\xi_1')$. Subtracting the latter from the former, we derive $(3p_1 - \frac{2}{3}(p_2^2/p_3) - 9(p_0 p_3/p_2))\xi_1 = 0$. Since the value in the parentheses is never zero, we must have $\xi_1 = 0$, which implies that $\xi_0 = 0$. This in turn shows that $\tau = 0$ and $\xi = 0$. Hence there exist no groups under which (58′) is invariant.

General (Local) Conservation Laws

There exist conservation laws when $b(k)$ in Eq. (62-i) is linear, i.e., $b_2 = b_3 \equiv 0$. By setting

$$b(k) = b_0 + b_1 k, \tag{62-i'}$$

$$c(k) = c_0 + c_1 k + c_2 k^2, \tag{62-ii'}$$

in effect we have approximated the production function by a quadratic equation

$$f(\dot{k}, k) = (a/2)\dot{k}^2 + (b_0 + b_1 k)\dot{k} + c_0 + c_1 k + c_2 k^2,$$

so that the Lagrangian has the form

$$L(t, \dot{k}, k) = e^{-\rho t}[(a/2)\dot{k}^2 + (b_0 + b_1 k)\dot{k} + c_0 + c_1 k + c_2 k^2]. \tag{58'''}$$

The Euler–Lagrange equation is

$$a\ddot{k} - \rho a\dot{k} - (2c_2 + \rho b_1)k = c_1 + \rho b_0. \tag{65}$$

Let the equilibrium value of k be given by

$$k^* = -q_0/q_1 \geqq 0, \qquad q_1 = 2c_2 + \rho b_1 < 0 \quad \text{and} \quad q_0 = c_1 + \rho b_0 \geqq 0. \tag{66}$$

Then the deviation from the equilibrium

$$x = k - k^* \tag{67}$$

must satisfy the differential equation

$$\ddot{x} - \rho\dot{x} - (q_1/a)x = 0. \tag{68}$$

This is exactly identical to Eq. (41). Hence all the conclusions derived earlier must apply to this case. For completeness we write down the general conservation laws as

Theorem 4 *(General Local Conservation Laws) For the Lagrangian defined by* (58'''), *we have*

$$\text{modified Hamiltonian} = e^{-\rho t}[-(a/2)\dot{k}^2 + (a\rho/2)(q_0 + q_1 k)\dot{k} + (q_1/2)k^2 + q_0 k + (q_0^2/2q_1)] = \text{const}, \tag{69-i}$$

$$\text{turnpike const} = e^{-\lambda_2 t}[\dot{k} - \lambda_1(k - k^*)] = \text{const}, \tag{69-ii}$$

$$\text{turnpike const} = e^{-\lambda_1 t}[\dot{k} - \lambda_2(k - k^*)] = \text{const}, \tag{69-iii}$$

where $q_0 = c_1 + \rho b_0$, $q_1 = 2c_2 + \rho b_1$, $k^* = -q_0/q_1$, $\lambda_1 = \frac{1}{2}(\rho + r)$, $\lambda_2 = \frac{1}{2}(\rho - r)$, and $r = \sqrt{\rho^2 + (4q_1/a)}$. Also, for completeness the infinitesimal transformations used in the preceding theorem are shown to be

$$\tau(t) = \delta_1 e^{rt} + \delta_2 e^{-rt} + \delta_3, \qquad \delta_i = \text{arbitrary constants}, i = 1, 2, 3, \tag{70}$$

and

$$\xi(t) = \xi_0(t) + \xi_1(t)k, \tag{71}$$

where

$$\xi_0(t) = \delta_4 e^{\lambda_1 t} + \delta_5 e^{\lambda_2 t} + \delta_1 \frac{q_0(3r - \rho)}{2(ar^2 - a\rho r - q_1)} e^{rt}$$

$$+ \delta_2 \frac{-q_0(3r + \rho)}{2(ar^2 + a\rho r - q_1)} e^{-rt} + \delta_3 \frac{q_0}{2q_1} \rho, \tag{71-i'}$$

$$\xi_1(t) = \tfrac{1}{2}[\delta_1(\rho + r)e^{rt} + \delta_2(\rho - r)e^{-rt} + \rho\, \delta_3]. \tag{71-ii'}$$

V. Conservation Laws When There Exists "Technical Change"

16. We have seen that there usually exists no (global) conservation law independent of the forms of utility and/or production functions, when the discount rate ρ is *not* equal to zero. This conclusion applies to the cases in which the production possibility frontier is linear (Ramsey type) or nonlinear ("general" case) [see Eqs. (32) and (38″)]. The result is due to the fact that the time variable (the discount rate) appears only in the multiplicative form as

$$L(t, \dot{k}, k) = D(t)U[c(\dot{k}, k)] = e^{-\rho t}U[c(\dot{k}, k)].$$

One of the purposes of this section is to see how the conclusion is modified by introducing the time variable not only in the multiplicative form but also directly in the utility (or production) function itself. Thus we wish to study the case where L appears as

$$L(t, \dot{k}, k) = D(t)U[c(t, \dot{k}, k)]. \tag{72}$$

The appearance of t directly in c may be interpreted as the *representation of some form of "technical change"* in the production process of the consumption good. (We shall also give an alternative interpretation to the special case as "the repayment scheme" of the initial borrowing of the fund to set the growth process in motion.)

The invariance equation under $\bar{t} = t + \varepsilon\tau(t, k)$, $\bar{k} = k + \varepsilon\xi(t, k)$ corresponding to (72) is now

$$\left(D'U + DU'\frac{\partial f}{\partial t}\right)\tau + DU'\frac{\partial f}{\partial k}\xi + DU'\frac{\partial f}{\partial \dot{k}}\left(\frac{d\xi}{dt} - \dot{k}\frac{d\tau}{dt}\right) + DU\frac{d\tau}{dt} = 0, \quad (73)$$

where $c(t, \dot{k}, k) = f(t, \dot{k}, k)$. Rewriting (73), we have

$$U\left\{D'\tau + D\frac{d\tau}{dt}\right\} + U'\left\{D\frac{\partial f}{\partial t}\tau + D\frac{\partial f}{\partial k}\xi + D\frac{\partial f}{\partial \dot{k}}\left(\frac{d\xi}{dt} - \dot{k}\frac{d\tau}{dt}\right)\right\} = 0. \quad (73')$$

In order that the foregoing condition holds for any arbitrary utility functions, we must have

$$D'\tau + D\frac{d\tau}{dt} = 0, \quad (73\text{-i}'')$$

$$\frac{\partial f}{\partial t}\tau + \frac{\partial f}{\partial k}\xi + \frac{\partial f}{\partial \dot{k}}\left(\frac{d\xi}{dt} - \dot{k}\frac{d\tau}{dt}\right) = 0, \qquad D \neq 0. \quad (73\text{-ii}'')$$

Expressing $d\tau/dt$ as $\partial\tau/\partial t + \dot{k}\,\partial\tau/\partial k$ and $d\xi/dt$ as $\partial\xi/\partial t + \dot{k}\,\partial\xi/\partial k$, we rewrite (73″) as

$$D'\tau + D\left(\frac{\partial\tau}{\partial t} + \dot{k}\frac{\partial\tau}{\partial k}\right) = 0, \quad (73\text{-i}''')$$

$$\frac{\partial f}{\partial t}\tau + \frac{\partial f}{\partial k}\xi + \frac{\partial f}{\partial \dot{k}}\left[\left(\frac{\partial\xi}{\partial t} + \dot{k}\frac{\partial\xi}{\partial k}\right) - \dot{k}\left(\frac{\partial\tau}{\partial t} + \dot{k}\frac{\partial\tau}{\partial k}\right)\right] = 0. \quad (73\text{-ii}''')$$

Condition (73-i‴) implies that $dD(\tau)/dt + D\,\partial\tau/\partial t = 0$ and $D\,\partial\tau/\partial k = 0$ by setting the coefficients of the powers of $\dot{k}$ equal to zero, which in turn gives $\partial\tau/\partial k = 0$ for $D \neq 0$. Hence we must have

$$\tau = \tau(t). \quad (74)$$

Using $dD(\tau)/dt + D\,d\tau/dt = 0 = d(D\tau)/dt = 0$, we get $D\tau = a$ (const) or

$$\tau(t) = a/D(t). \quad (74')$$

If $D(t)$ is equal to the usual discounting expression

$$D(t) = e^{-\rho t}, \quad (75)$$

we must have

$$\tau(t) = ae^{\rho t}. \quad (76)$$

The forms of f and/or ξ will be determined from (73-ii‴), which is expression for the once-extended group of τ and ξ.[13] Hence to find the production function f is to find the differential invariants of the group under a given τ and ξ. Since $\partial\tau/\partial k$ is already known to be zero and τ is equal to $a/D(t)$, the extended group is now simply expressed as

$$\frac{\partial f}{\partial t}\frac{a}{D} + \frac{\partial f}{\partial k}\xi + \frac{\partial f}{\partial \dot{k}}\left\{\frac{\partial \xi}{\partial t} + \left(\frac{\partial \xi}{\partial k} - a\frac{d(D^{-1})}{dt}\right)\dot{k}\right\} = 0. \tag{77}$$

Case A ($\xi = 0$) We shall first derive the production function f and "technical change" consistent only with the time transformation. By setting $1/D(t) = \delta(t)$, Eq. (77) becomes

$$\frac{\partial f}{\partial t} a\delta(t) - a\frac{d\delta(t)}{dt}\dot{k}\frac{\partial f}{\partial \dot{k}} = 0.$$

The two independent solutions to the above are $f = k, f = \delta(t)\dot{k}$, which gives the general solution for f,

$$f(t, k, \dot{k}) = f(k, \delta(t)\dot{k}) \qquad \text{for} \quad a \neq 0. \tag{78}$$

Hence the "technical change" $\delta(t)$ must be multiplicative with $\dot{k}$ in the production function f.

Case B ($\xi \neq 0$) Using $\delta(t) = 1/D(t)$ and $\tau = a\,\delta(t)$, we rewrite (77) as

$$a\,\delta\frac{\partial f}{\partial t} + \xi\frac{\partial f}{\partial k} + \left\{\frac{\partial \xi}{\partial t} + \left(\frac{\partial \xi}{\partial k} - a\,\delta'\right)\dot{k}\right\}\frac{\partial f}{\partial \dot{k}} = 0. \tag{77'}$$

This is the fundamental equation which determines the form of ξ or of f. Obviously, we *cannot* determine both forms simultaneously since there is only one restriction (77′). We have worked out several cases, including

(a) $\partial f/\partial t = 0$,
(b) $f(t, \dot{k}, k) = f_0(t, k) + \dot{k}f_1(t, k) + (\dot{k}^2/2!)f_2(t, k) + \cdots + (\dot{k}^n/n!)f_n(t, k) + \cdots$,
(c) $\xi = k^\alpha$.

We shall, however, not present here the results of calculations to these cases, since economic interpretations for these cases are not as clear as that for Case A [$\xi = 0$, $\tau = \text{a}(t)$]. Instead, we shall turn our attention to economic interpretations of Eq. (77).

[13] Let X be equal to $\tau\,\partial/\partial t + \xi\,\partial/\partial k = X$; then the extended group X' is equal to $X' = \tau\,\partial/\partial t + \xi\,\partial/\partial k + (d\xi/dt - \dot{k}\,d\tau/dt)\,\partial/\partial\dot{k}$. But this is exactly identical with (73-ii″) or (73-ii‴).

Economic Interpretation and Conservation Laws When "Technical Change" Is Present

17. Returning to the production possibility frontier in Fig. 5, let us assume that the system experiences the exogenously determined "factor-augmenting" type of technical change as shown by

$$c(t) = f[A(t)k, B(t)\dot{k}] \tag{36'}$$

and by Fig. 6. Then Eq. (78) is a special case of (36′) when $A(t) = 1$ and $B(t) = \delta(t) = 1/D(t)$. Restricting ourselves to the case of $D(t) = e^{-\rho t}$, we have (36′) with $A(t) = 1$ and $B(t) = e^{\rho t}$. The rate of technical change of $\dot{k}$ is exactly equal to the discount rate ρ. The conservation law corresponding to this case is

$$\Omega = Hae^{\rho t} = -\{e^{-\rho t}U[f(k, e^{\rho t}\dot{k})] - U' \,\partial f/\partial(e^{\rho t}\dot{k})\dot{k}\}ae^{\rho t} = \text{const.}$$

That is to say, *the current Hamiltonian is constant along the optimal paths, or the discounted value of Hamiltonian is decreasing at the constant ρ over the planning period.*

When the production possibility frontier is linear—the Ramsey type, we can present an alternative interpretation to (36′), i.e.,

$$c = f(k) - nk - e^{\rho t}\dot{k}. \tag{36''}$$

By definition, $e^{\rho t}\dot{k}$ is the amount of saving that the society is required to deduct from income $f(k) - nk$, from which $\dot{k}$ amount is reinvested. The difference

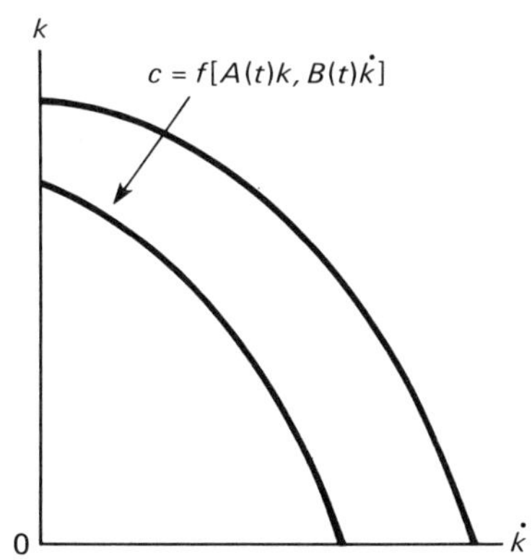

Figure 6

between $e^{\rho t}\dot{k}$ and $\dot{k}$, $(e^{\rho t} - 1)\dot{k}$, is the amount of repayment for the initial stock of fund borrowed (say from abroad), including the interest payment. The initial fund is necessary to start the business in operation.[14]

It is rather easy to show that the system with (36″) can generate a stable optimal path. Setting the Hamiltonian

$$H = e^{-\rho t}U(c) + pe^{-\rho t}[f(k) - nk - c],$$

where $\dot{k} = e^{-\rho t}[f(k) - nk - c]$, we obtain by the maximum principle,

$$\frac{\partial H}{\partial c} = e^{-\rho t}[U' - p] = 0 \qquad \text{or} \qquad U' = p$$

and

$$\dot{p} = -\frac{\partial H}{\partial k} = -e^{-\rho t}[f'(k) - n]p, \qquad \dot{k} = \frac{\partial H}{\partial p} = e^{-\rho t}[f(k) - nk - c(p)].$$

Let θ be equal to

$$\theta = \int_0^t e^{-\rho t}\, dt = [-\rho^{-1}e^{-\rho t}]_0^t = -\rho^{-1}(e^{-\rho t} - 1).$$

Then, in view of $d\theta/dt = e^{-\rho t}$, we have

$$\dot{p}e^{\rho t} = \frac{dp}{dt}\frac{dt}{d\theta} = \frac{dp}{d\theta} = -[f(k) - n]p, \quad \dot{k}e^{\rho t} = \frac{dk}{dt}\frac{dt}{d\theta} = \frac{dk}{d\theta} = f(k) - nk - c(p).$$

In the long run, as $t \to \infty$ or as $\theta \to \rho^{-1}$, we have a stable saddle-point path leading to the steady-state equilibrium, while by the conservation law

$$\Omega = e^{-\rho t}[U(c) + p(f(k) - nk - c(p))]e^{\rho t} = \text{const},$$

the current value of the Hamiltonian (the value in the bracket of the above expression) remains unchanged.

In summary, we present

Theorem 5 (*Conservation Law under Technical Change*) (i) *The only form of the infinitesimal transformation for the time variable, which leaves the Lagrangian* $L = D(t)U[f(t, \dot{k}, k)]$ *invariant, is* $\tau(t) = a/D(t)$, $a = \text{const}$.

[14] The total payment over the planning period is thus equal to $P = \int_0^\infty (e^{\rho t} - 1)\dot{k}\, dt$, while the actual amount of initial borrowing is $B = \int_0^\infty e^{-\rho t}(e^{\rho t} - 1)\dot{k}\, dt$, if the interest rate is equal to the discount rate ρ. It should be noted that Eq. (36″) can also be interpreted as the equation related to resource renewal. Thus $e^{\rho t}\dot{k}$ may be considered as the value of $\dot{k}$ at the increasing price $e^{\rho t}$.

(ii) *The current Hamiltonian is constant if and only if "technical change" in f takes the form* $c = f(\dot{k}/D(t), k)$.

(iii) *Alternatively, the Lagrangian is invariant under* $\tau(t) = a/D(t)$ *if and only if c takes the form* $c = f(\dot{k}/D, k)$.

VI. Conservation Laws in the von Neumann Model

Samuelson's Two Conservation Laws

18. The purpose of this section is to study conservation laws in a closed, consumptionless system of the von Neumann type. Samuelson [1970a, b] has already derived two conservation laws for such a system using the basic property that the Hamiltonian is constant when the Lagrangian contains no independent variable explicitly. In this section we apply a more general condition—the Noether invariance identity—to study completely the basic variational properties of the von Neumann system (Samuelson [1960]). It will be shown that *Samuelson's two conservation laws are the only conservation laws globally operating for such a system.*

Without loss of generality, we can assume that there are only *two* different types of capital goods K_1 and K_2 which are related to the net capital formations $\dot{K}_1$ and $\dot{K}_2$ by a smooth, neoclassical, concave, first-degree-homogeneous transformation function

$$F[K_1, K_2; \dot{K}_1, \dot{K}_2] = 0, \qquad \partial F/\partial K_i > 0, \qquad \partial F/\partial \dot{K}_i < 0, \qquad i = 1, 2. \tag{79}$$

The optimal-control problem is defined as

$$\max_{\{K_i\}} \int_0^T \dot{K}_1 \, dt \qquad \text{subject to} \quad F[K_1, K_2; \dot{K}_1, \dot{K}_2] = 0 \tag{80}$$

under (K_1^0, K_2^0) and (K_2^T) prescribed. Using the multiplier technique, the Lagrangian to this problem is reduced to

$$L(t, \lambda, K_1, K_2; \dot{\lambda}, \dot{K}_1, \dot{K}_2) = \dot{K}_1 + \lambda F[K_1, K_2; \dot{K}_1, \dot{K}_2]. \tag{81}$$

We look for conditions invariant under

$$\begin{aligned} \bar{t} &= t + \varepsilon\tau(t, \lambda, K_1, K_2), & \bar{\lambda} &= \lambda + \varepsilon\omega(t, \lambda, K_1, K_2), \\ \bar{K}_1 &= K_1 + \varepsilon\xi^1(t, \lambda, K_1, K_2), & \bar{K}_2 &= K_2 + \varepsilon\xi^2(t, \lambda, K_1, K_2), \end{aligned} \tag{82}$$

where τ, ω, ξ^1, ξ^2 are the infinitesimal transformation of the group. The invariance equation is

$$\frac{\partial L}{\partial t}\tau + \frac{\partial L}{\partial \lambda}\omega + \frac{\partial L}{\partial K_1}\xi^1 + \frac{\partial L}{\partial K_2}\xi^2$$
$$+ \frac{\partial L}{\partial \dot{\lambda}}\left(\frac{d\omega}{dt} - \dot{\lambda}\frac{d\tau}{dt}\right) + \frac{\partial L}{\partial \dot{K}_1}\left(\frac{d\xi^1}{dt} - \dot{K}_1\frac{d\tau}{dt}\right) + \frac{\partial L}{\partial \dot{K}_2}\left(\frac{d\xi^2}{dt} - \dot{K}_2\frac{d\tau}{dt}\right)$$
$$+ L\frac{d\tau}{dt} = \frac{d\Phi}{dt}(t, \lambda, K_1, K_2) = \frac{\partial \Phi}{\partial t} + \frac{\partial \Phi}{\partial \lambda}\dot{\lambda} + \frac{\partial \Phi}{\partial K_1}\dot{K}_1 + \frac{\partial \Phi}{\partial K_2}\dot{K}_2.$$

Substituting

$$\frac{\partial L}{\partial t} = 0, \qquad \frac{\partial L}{\partial \lambda} = F, \qquad \frac{\partial L}{\partial \dot{\lambda}} = 0, \qquad \frac{\partial L}{\partial K_1} = \lambda\frac{\partial F}{\partial K_1}, \qquad \frac{\partial L}{\partial K_2} = \lambda\frac{\partial F}{\partial K_2},$$
$$\frac{\partial L}{\partial \dot{K}_1} = 1 + \lambda\frac{\partial F}{\partial \dot{K}_1}, \qquad \frac{\partial L}{\partial \dot{K}_2} = \lambda\frac{\partial F}{\partial \dot{K}_2}, \qquad \text{and} \qquad L = \dot{K}_1 + \lambda F$$

into the above and using

$$F = K_1\frac{\partial F}{\partial K_1} + K_2\frac{\partial F}{\partial K_2} + \dot{K}_1\frac{\partial F}{\partial \dot{K}_1} + \dot{K}_2\frac{\partial F}{\partial \dot{K}_2},$$

we obtain

$$F\omega + \frac{d\xi^1}{dt} + \lambda\left[\frac{\partial F}{\partial K_1}\xi^1 + \frac{\partial F}{\partial K_2}\xi^2 + \frac{\partial F}{\partial \dot{K}_1}\frac{d\xi^1}{dt} + \frac{\partial F}{\partial \dot{K}_2}\frac{d\xi^2}{dt}\right.$$
$$\left. + \left(K_1\frac{\partial F}{\partial K_1} + K_2\frac{\partial F}{\partial K_2}\right)\frac{d\tau}{dt}\right] = \frac{\partial \Phi}{\partial t} + \frac{\partial \Phi}{\partial \lambda}\dot{\lambda} + \frac{\partial \Phi}{\partial K_1}\dot{K}_1 + \frac{\partial \Phi}{\partial K_2}\dot{K}_2.$$

On expressing total differentials by partial derivatives, the foregoing will be further reduced to

$$F\omega + \left(\frac{\partial \xi^1}{\partial t} + \frac{\partial \xi^1}{\partial \lambda}\dot{\lambda} + \frac{\partial \xi^1}{\partial K_1}\dot{K}_1 + \frac{\partial \xi^1}{\partial K_2}\dot{K}_2\right)$$
$$+ \lambda\left[\frac{\partial F}{\partial K_1}\xi^1 + \frac{\partial F}{\partial K_2}\xi^2 + \frac{\partial F}{\partial \dot{K}_1}\left(\frac{\partial \xi^1}{\partial t} + \frac{\partial \xi^1}{\partial \lambda}\dot{\lambda} + \frac{\partial \xi^1}{\partial K_1}\dot{K}_1 + \frac{\partial \xi^1}{\partial K_2}\dot{K}_2\right)\right.$$
$$+ \frac{\partial F}{\partial \dot{K}_2}\left(\frac{\partial \xi^2}{\partial t} + \frac{\partial \xi^2}{\partial \lambda}\dot{\lambda} + \frac{\partial \xi^2}{\partial K_1}\dot{K}_1 + \frac{\partial \xi^2}{\partial K_2}\dot{K}_2\right)$$
$$\left. + \left(K_1\frac{\partial F}{\partial K_1} + K_2\frac{\partial F}{\partial K_2}\right)\left(\frac{\partial \tau}{\partial t} + \frac{\partial \tau}{\partial \lambda}\dot{\lambda} + \frac{\partial \tau}{\partial K_1}\dot{K}_1 + \frac{\partial \tau}{\partial K_2}\dot{K}_2\right)\right]$$
$$= \frac{\partial \Phi}{\partial t} + \frac{\partial \Phi}{\partial \lambda}\dot{\lambda} + \frac{\partial \Phi}{\partial K_1}\dot{K}_1 + \frac{\partial \Phi}{\partial K_2}\dot{K}_2. \tag{83}$$

By separating the preceding expression according to the coefficients of the powers of λ, we can rewrite (83) as

$$\lambda^1: \quad \frac{\partial \xi^1}{\partial \lambda} + \frac{\partial F}{\partial \dot{K}_1}\left(\lambda \frac{\partial \xi^1}{\partial \lambda}\right) + \frac{\partial F}{\partial \dot{K}_2}\left(\lambda \frac{\partial \xi^2}{\partial \lambda}\right) + \left(K_1 \frac{\partial F}{\partial K_1} + K_2 \frac{\partial F}{\partial K_2}\right)\left(\lambda \frac{\partial \tau}{\partial \lambda}\right) = \frac{\partial \Phi}{\partial \lambda} \tag{83-i}$$

$$\begin{aligned}\lambda^0: \quad & F\omega + \left(\frac{\partial \xi^1}{\partial t} + \frac{\partial \xi^1}{\partial K_1}\dot{K}_1 + \frac{\partial \xi^1}{\partial K_2}\dot{K}_2\right) \\ & + \lambda\left[\frac{\partial F}{\partial K_1}\xi^1 + \frac{\partial F}{\partial K_2}\xi^2 + \frac{\partial F}{\partial \dot{K}_1}\left(\frac{\partial \xi^1}{\partial t} + \frac{\partial \xi^1}{\partial K_1}\dot{K}_1 + \frac{\partial \xi^1}{\partial K_2}\dot{K}_2\right)\right. \\ & + \frac{\partial F}{\partial \dot{K}_2}\left(\frac{\partial \xi^2}{\partial t} + \frac{\partial \xi^2}{\partial K_1}\dot{K}_1 + \frac{\partial \xi^2}{\partial K_2}\dot{K}_2\right) \\ & \left. + \left(K_1 \frac{\partial F}{\partial K_1} + K_2 \frac{\partial F}{\partial K_2}\right)\left(\frac{\partial \tau}{\partial t} + \frac{\partial \tau}{\partial K_1}\dot{K}_1 + \frac{\partial \tau}{\partial K_2}\dot{K}_2\right)\right] \\ & = \frac{\partial \Phi}{\partial t} + \frac{\partial \Phi}{\partial K_1}\dot{K}_1 + \frac{\partial \Phi}{\partial K_2}\dot{K}_2. \end{aligned} \tag{83-ii}$$

Differentiating (83-i) partially with respect to $\dot{K}_1$ and $\dot{K}_2$ and using

$$\begin{aligned}\frac{\partial}{\partial \dot{K}_i}\left(K_1 \frac{\partial F}{\partial K_1} + K_2 \frac{\partial F}{\partial K_2}\right) &= \frac{\partial}{\partial \dot{K}_i}\left(F - \dot{K}_1 \frac{\partial F}{\partial \dot{K}_1} - \dot{K}_2 \frac{\partial F}{\partial \dot{K}_2}\right) \\ &= -\sum_{i=1}^{2} \dot{K}_i \frac{\partial^2 F}{\partial \dot{K}_i\, \partial \dot{K}_j} \qquad (i, j = 1, 2),\end{aligned}$$

we obtain

$$\begin{aligned}\frac{\partial^2 F}{\partial \dot{K}_1^2}\left(\lambda \frac{\partial \xi^1}{\partial \lambda} - \dot{K}_1 \lambda \frac{\partial \tau}{\partial \lambda}\right) + \frac{\partial^2 F}{\partial \dot{K}_1\, \partial \dot{K}_2}\left(\lambda \frac{\partial \xi^2}{\partial \lambda} - \dot{K}_2 \lambda \frac{\partial \tau}{\partial \lambda}\right) &= 0, \\ \frac{\partial^2 F}{\partial \dot{K}_1\, \partial \dot{K}_2}\left(\lambda \frac{\partial \xi^1}{\partial \lambda} - \dot{K}_1 \lambda \frac{\partial \tau}{\partial \lambda}\right) + \frac{\partial^2 F}{\partial \dot{K}_2^2}\left(\lambda \frac{\partial \xi^2}{\partial \lambda} - \dot{K}_2 \lambda \frac{\partial \tau}{\partial \lambda}\right) &= 0. \end{aligned} \tag{84}$$

In order that conservation laws may hold for any arbitrary, strictly concave F, we must assume that[15]

$$\frac{\partial^2 F}{\partial \dot{K}_1^2}\frac{\partial^2 F}{\partial \dot{K}_2^2} - \left(\frac{\partial^2 F}{\partial \dot{K}_1\, \partial \dot{K}_2}\right)^2 > 0.$$

[15] When F is separable such as $F = Y(K_1, K_2) - I(\dot{K}_1, \dot{K}_2)$, we have $(\partial^2 F/\partial \dot{K}_1^2)(\partial^2 F/\partial \dot{K}_2^2) - (\partial^2 F/\partial \dot{K}_1\, \partial \dot{K}_2)^2 = 0$. We then can immediately determine $(\partial \xi^1/\partial \lambda)\dot{K}_2 = (\partial \xi^2/\partial \lambda)\dot{K}_1$, from which we can show $\partial \xi^1/\partial \lambda = \partial \xi^2/\partial \lambda = 0$. We shall discuss this singular case in detail in the next section.

Then (84) requires that

$$\lambda \frac{\partial \xi^1}{\partial \lambda} - \dot{K}_1 \lambda \frac{\partial \tau}{\partial \lambda} = 0, \qquad \lambda \frac{\partial \xi^2}{\partial \lambda} - \dot{K}_2 \lambda \frac{\partial \tau}{\partial \lambda} = 0.$$

Since ξ^1, ξ^2, and τ do not contain $\dot{K}_i$ and since λ cannot be zero, the above imply that $\partial \xi^1/\partial \lambda = \partial \xi^2/\partial \lambda = \partial \tau/\partial \lambda = 0$.

Hence ξ^1, ξ^2, *and* τ *do not involve* λ, *which in turn means that* Φ *also does not involve* λ *because of* (83-i), *i.e.*, $\partial \Phi/\partial \lambda = 0$.

Next, we want to show that the term of nullity Φ is related with ξ^1 by

$$\xi^1 = \Phi + C. \tag{85}$$

First by partially differentiating (83-ii) twice with respect to λ, we get $F\, \partial^2 \omega/\partial \lambda^2 = 0$, i.e., $\partial^2 \omega/\partial \lambda^2 = 0$, which implies that

$$\omega = \omega_0(t, K_1, K_2) + \lambda \omega_1(t, K_1, K_2). \tag{86}$$

Substituting this into (83-ii) and setting the coefficients of the powers of λ equal to zero, we obtain

$$\lambda^0: \quad F\omega_0 + \frac{\partial \xi^1}{\partial t} + \frac{\partial \xi^1}{\partial K_1}\dot{K}_1 + \frac{\partial \xi^1}{\partial K_2}\dot{K}_2 = \frac{\partial \Phi}{\partial t} + \frac{\partial \Phi}{\partial K_1}\dot{K}_1 + \frac{\partial \Phi}{\partial K_2}\dot{K}_2 \tag{87-i}$$

$$\begin{aligned}\lambda^1: \quad & F\omega_1 + \frac{\partial F}{\partial K_1}\xi^1 + \frac{\partial F}{\partial K_2}\xi^2 + \frac{\partial F}{\partial \dot{K}_1}\left(\frac{\partial \xi^1}{\partial t} + \frac{\partial \xi^1}{\partial K_1}\dot{K}_1 + \frac{\partial \xi^1}{\partial K_2}\dot{K}_2\right) \\ & + \frac{\partial F}{\partial \dot{K}_2}\left(\frac{\partial \xi^2}{\partial t} + \frac{\partial \xi^2}{\partial K_1}\dot{K}_1 + \frac{\partial \xi^2}{\partial K_2}\dot{K}_2\right) \\ & + \left(K_1 \frac{\partial F}{\partial K_1} + K_2 \frac{\partial F}{\partial K_2}\right)\left(\frac{\partial \tau}{\partial t} + \frac{\partial \tau}{\partial K_1}\dot{K}_1 + \frac{\partial \tau}{\partial K_2}\dot{K}_2\right) = 0. \end{aligned} \tag{87-ii}$$

Differentiating (87-i) partially with respect to $\dot{K}_1$ and $\dot{K}_2$, respectively, we can express

$$\frac{\partial}{\partial \dot{K}_1}: \ \frac{\partial \Phi}{\partial K_1} = \frac{\partial \xi^1}{\partial K_1} + \frac{\partial F}{\partial \dot{K}_1}\omega_0, \qquad \frac{\partial}{\partial \dot{K}_2}: \ \frac{\partial \Phi}{\partial K_2} = \frac{\partial \xi^1}{\partial K_2} + \frac{\partial F}{\partial \dot{K}_2}\omega_0,$$

and substituting these into (87-i), we get

$$\frac{\partial \Phi}{\partial t} = \frac{\partial \xi^1}{\partial t} + \left(F - \dot{K}_1 \frac{\partial F}{\partial \dot{K}_1} - \dot{K}_2 \frac{\partial F}{\partial \dot{K}_2}\right)\omega_0.$$

Next we show that ω_0 is zero. Rewriting these three expressions as

$$\frac{\partial}{\partial K_1}(\Phi - \xi^1) = \frac{\partial F}{\partial \dot{K}_1}\omega_0, \qquad \frac{\partial}{\partial K_2}(\Phi - \xi^1) = \frac{\partial F}{\partial \dot{K}_2}\omega_0,$$

$$\frac{\partial}{\partial t}(\Phi - \xi^1) = \left(F - \dot{K}_1 \frac{\partial F}{\partial \dot{K}_1} - \dot{K}_2 \frac{\partial F}{\partial \dot{K}_2}\right)\omega_0 = \left(K_1 \frac{\partial F}{\partial K_1} + K_2 \frac{\partial F}{\partial K_2}\right)\omega_0,$$

we differentiate the first expression partially with respect to $\dot{K}_1$, noting that Φ and ξ^1 do not contain $\dot{K}_1$, to obtain

$$\frac{\partial^2}{\partial \dot{K}_1\, \partial \dot{K}_1}(\Phi - \xi^1) = \frac{\partial}{\partial \dot{K}_1}\left(\frac{\partial F}{\partial \dot{K}_1}\omega_0\right) = \frac{\partial^2 F}{\partial \dot{K}_1^2}\omega_0 = 0.$$

Hence we conclude that $\omega_0 = 0$ for $\partial F/\partial \dot{K}_1^2 \neq 0$. Then we can write

$$\frac{\partial}{\partial K_1}(\Phi - \xi^1) = 0, \qquad \frac{\partial}{\partial K_2}(\Phi - \xi^1) = 0, \qquad \frac{\partial}{\partial t}(\Phi - \xi^1) = 0,$$

from which we derive $\Phi - \xi^1 = \text{const}$, with (85).

We are now in a position to determine the form of ξ^1, ξ^2, ω, and τ from the remaining condition (87-ii). Using the property of linear homogeneity

$$F = K_1 \frac{\partial F}{\partial K_1} + K_2 \frac{\partial F}{\partial K_2} + \dot{K}_1 \frac{\partial F}{\partial \dot{K}_1} + \dot{K}_2 \frac{\partial F}{\partial \dot{K}_2}$$

and substituting this into (87-ii), we write (87-ii) as

$$\begin{aligned}
&\frac{\partial F}{\partial K_1}\left[K_1\omega_1 + \xi^1 + K_1\frac{\partial \tau}{\partial t} + \frac{\partial \tau}{\partial K_1}K_1\dot{K}_1 + \frac{\partial \tau}{\partial K_2}K_1\dot{K}_2\right] \\
&\quad + \frac{\partial F}{\partial K_2}\left[K_2\omega_1 + \xi^2 + K_2\frac{\partial \tau}{\partial t} + \frac{\partial \tau}{\partial K_1}K_2\dot{K}_1 + \frac{\partial \tau}{\partial K_2}K_2\dot{K}_2\right] \\
&\quad + \frac{\partial F}{\partial \dot{K}_1}\left[\frac{\partial \xi^1}{\partial t} + \left(\omega_1 + \frac{\partial \xi^1}{\partial K_1}\right)\dot{K}_1 + \frac{\partial \xi^1}{\partial K_1}\dot{K}_2\right] \\
&\quad + \frac{\partial F}{\partial \dot{K}_2}\left[\frac{\partial \xi^2}{\partial t} + \frac{\partial \xi^2}{\partial K_1}\dot{K}_1 + \left(\omega_1 + \frac{\partial \xi^2}{\partial K_2}\right)\dot{K}_2\right] = 0.
\end{aligned} \tag{87-ii$'$}$$

Since the above condition must hold for any arbitrary function F, the coefficients of $\partial F/\partial K_1$, $\partial F/\partial K_2$, $\partial F/\partial \dot{K}_1$, and $\partial F/\partial \dot{K}_2$ must be identically equal to zero. Hence, by setting the coefficients of the powers of $\dot{K}_1$ and $\dot{K}_2$ equal to zero, we obtain

$$K_1\omega_1 + \xi^1 + K_1\frac{\partial \tau}{\partial t} = 0, \qquad \frac{\partial \tau}{\partial K_1} = \frac{\partial \tau}{\partial K_2} = 0,$$

$$K_2\omega_1 + \xi^2 + K_2\frac{\partial \tau}{\partial t} = 0, \qquad \frac{\partial \tau}{\partial K_1} = \frac{\partial \tau}{\partial K_2} = 0,$$

$$\frac{\partial \xi^1}{\partial t} = 0, \qquad \omega_1 + \frac{\partial \xi^1}{\partial K_1} = 0, \qquad \frac{\partial \xi^1}{\partial K_2} = 0,$$

$$\frac{\partial \xi^2}{\partial t} = 0, \qquad \omega_1 + \frac{\partial \xi^2}{\partial K_2} = 0, \qquad \frac{\partial \xi^2}{\partial K_1} = 0.$$

The above imply $\tau = \tau(t)$, $\xi^1 = \xi^1(K_1)$, and $\xi^2 = \xi^2(K_2)$. Using these and $\omega_1 + \partial\xi^1(K_1)/\partial K_1 = 0$, $\omega_1 + \partial\xi^2(K_2)/\partial K_2 = 0$, we conclude that

$$\partial\omega_1/\partial t = \partial\omega_1/\partial K_1 = \partial\omega_1/\partial K_2 = 0,$$

i.e.,

$$\omega_1 = \text{const} = -\alpha. \tag{88}$$

From $\partial\xi^1/\partial K_1 = \partial\xi^2/\partial K_2 = \alpha$, we immediately conclude that

$$\xi^i = \alpha K_i + \beta_i \qquad (i = 1, 2).$$

Substituting the above into $K_i\omega_1 + \xi^i + K_i\,\partial\tau/\partial t = 0$ $(i = 1, 2)$, we get

$$-\alpha K_i + (\alpha K_i + \beta_i) + K_i\,\partial\tau/\partial t = 0, \qquad \text{i.e.,} \quad \beta_i + K_i\,\partial\tau/\partial t = 0 \quad (i = 1, 2).$$

which implies that $\beta_2 = \beta_1 = 0$, $\partial\tau/\partial t = 0$, i.e.,

$$\tau = \text{const} = \gamma. \tag{89}$$

Hence we conclude that

$$\xi^i = \alpha K_i, \qquad i = 1, 2. \tag{90}$$

Using (85), we get

$$\Phi = \xi^1 + C = \alpha K_1 + C. \tag{91}$$

We have finally determined the infinitesimal transformations of the *two-parameter* group which leaves (81) invariant, i.e.,

$$\begin{aligned} &\tau = \gamma, \qquad \xi^1 = \alpha K_1, \qquad \xi^2 = \alpha K_2, \qquad \omega = -\alpha\lambda, \\ &\Phi = \alpha K_1 + C, \qquad \alpha, \gamma = \text{const}. \end{aligned} \tag{92}$$

Conservation laws are now derived from

$$\begin{aligned} \Omega &= \left(L - \frac{\partial L}{\partial \dot{K}_1}\dot{K}_1 - \frac{\partial L}{\partial \dot{K}_2}\dot{K}_2 - \frac{\partial L}{\partial \dot{\lambda}}\dot{\lambda}\right)\tau + \frac{\partial L}{\partial \dot{K}_1}\xi^1 + \frac{\partial L}{\partial \dot{K}_2}\xi^2 + \frac{\partial L}{\partial \dot{\lambda}}\omega - \Phi \\ &= \lambda\left(F - \frac{\partial F}{\partial \dot{K}_1}\dot{K}_1 - \frac{\partial F}{\partial \dot{K}_2}\dot{K}_2\right)\gamma + \lambda\left(\frac{\partial F}{\partial \dot{K}_1}K_1 + \frac{\partial F}{\partial \dot{K}_2}K_2\right)\alpha = \text{const}. \end{aligned} \tag{93}$$

Corresponding to the first parameter γ, we have

$$\begin{aligned} \gamma\colon \quad \Omega_1 &= \lambda\left(F - \frac{\partial F}{\partial \dot{K}_1}\dot{K}_1 - \frac{\partial F}{\partial \dot{K}_2}\dot{K}_2\right) = \lambda\left(K_1\frac{\partial F}{\partial K_1} + K_2\frac{\partial F}{\partial K_2}\right) \\ &= \lambda Y = \text{const}, \end{aligned} \tag{94}$$

and to the second parameter α,[16]

$$\alpha: \quad \Omega_2 = -\lambda\left(\frac{\partial F}{\partial \dot{K}_1} K_1 + \frac{\partial F}{\partial \dot{K}_2} K_2\right) = \lambda W = \text{const}, \tag{95}$$

where Y is the national income equal to $K_1\, \partial F/\partial K_1 + K_2\, \partial F/\partial K_2$, W the national wealth equal to $K_1 p_1 + K_2 p_2$ ($\partial F/\partial \dot{K}_1 = -p_1$, $\partial F/\partial \dot{K}_2 = -p_2$; p_1, p_2 are supply prices of K_1 and K_2). The two conservation laws Ω_1 and Ω_2 are exactly identical to the ones that have already been derived by Samuelson [1970a, b]. What is important and interesting here is, however, that they are the *only conservation laws* operating globally on the optimal paths of the von Neumann system. Dividing Ω_1 by Ω_2, we get the conservation law

$$\Omega_1/\Omega_2 = Y/W = \text{const}, \tag{96}$$

the *constancy of the aggregate output–capital (output–wealth) ratio* (Samuelson [1970a]). We summarize the result in the following

Theorem 6 (*Two Conservation Laws*) (i) *For the optimal control problem defined by* (80), $\Omega_1 = \lambda Y =$ const. *That is to say, the product of the implicit price* λ *and national income* Y *is always constant.*

(ii) $\Omega_2 = \lambda W =$ *const. That is to say, the product of the implicit price* λ *and national wealth* W *is always constant.*

(iii) $\Omega_1/\Omega_2 = Y/W =$ *const. That is to say, the aggregate output–capital (wealth) ratio is always constant.*

(iv) Ω_1 *and* Ω_2 *are the only conservation laws globally operating in the von Neumann model of optimal growth.*

Local Conservation Laws in the von Neumann Model

19. In order to determine if there exists any other conservation law operating for special types of technology, we consider a *separable type* of F, i.e.,

$$F = Y(K_1, K_2) - I(\dot{K}_1, \dot{K}_2) = 0, \tag{97}$$

where Y is the homogeneous-degree-one-concave-function and I the homogeneous-degree-one-convex function. We shall show, omitting intermediate

[16] The reader is reminded to appreciate the power of the second definition of dynamic invariance which includes the null term Φ. In this case without Φ, the second conservation law could not have been obtained, as α would be always zero.

calculations, that the following set of conditions must be met for this special case:

$$\frac{\partial \xi^1}{\partial \lambda} = \frac{\partial \xi^2}{\partial \lambda} = \frac{\partial \xi^1}{\partial t} = \frac{\partial \xi^2}{\partial t} = 0, \tag{98-i}$$

$$\frac{\partial \Phi}{\partial \lambda} = \lambda Y \frac{\partial \tau}{\partial \lambda}, \tag{98-ii}$$

$$\frac{\partial \Phi}{\partial t} = Y\omega + \lambda\left(\frac{\partial Y}{\partial K_1}\xi^1 + \frac{\partial Y}{\partial K_2}\xi^2 + Y\frac{\partial \tau}{\partial t}\right), \tag{98-iii}$$

$$\begin{aligned}\frac{\partial \Phi}{\partial K_1}\dot{K}_1 + \frac{\partial \Phi}{\partial K_2}\dot{K}_2 &= \frac{\partial \xi^1}{\partial K_1}\dot{K}_1 + \frac{\partial \xi^1}{\partial K_2}\dot{K}_2 + \lambda Y\left(\frac{\partial \tau}{\partial K_1}\dot{K}_1 + \frac{\partial \tau}{\partial K_2}\dot{K}_2\right),\\ &- I\omega + \lambda\left[-\frac{\partial I}{\partial \dot{K}_1}\left(\frac{\partial \xi^1}{\partial K_1}\dot{K}_1 + \frac{\partial \xi^1}{\partial K_2}\dot{K}_2\right) - \frac{\partial I}{\partial \dot{K}_2}\left(\frac{\partial \xi^2}{\partial K_1}\dot{K}_1 + \frac{\partial \xi^2}{\partial K_2}\dot{K}_2\right)\right].\end{aligned} \tag{98-iv}$$

To derive (98-i) and (98-ii), use (83-i) and (83-ii) with

$$F = Y(K_1, K_2) - I(\dot{K}_1, \dot{K}_2) = \frac{\partial Y}{\partial K_1}K_1 + \frac{\partial Y}{\partial K_2}K_2 - \frac{\partial I}{\partial \dot{K}_1}\dot{K}_1 - \frac{\partial I}{\partial \dot{K}_2}\dot{K}_2$$

and

$$\frac{\partial^2 Y}{\partial K_1^2}\frac{\partial^2 Y}{\partial K_2^2} - \left(\frac{\partial^2 Y}{\partial K_1\,\partial K_2}\right)^2 = \frac{\partial^2 I}{\partial \dot{K}_1^2}\frac{\partial^2 I}{\partial \dot{K}_2^2} - \left(\frac{\partial^2 I}{\partial \dot{K}_1\,\partial \dot{K}_2}\right)^2 = 0$$

or

$$\frac{\partial^2 Y}{\partial K_1^2} : \frac{\partial^2 Y}{\partial K_1\,\partial K_2} = -K_2 : K_1 \qquad \text{and} \qquad \frac{\partial^2 I}{\partial \dot{K}_1^2} : \frac{\partial^2 I}{\partial \dot{K}_1\,\partial \dot{K}_2} = -\dot{K}_2 : \dot{K}_1.$$

Differentiating (83-i), we immediately get

$$\frac{\partial^2 I}{\partial \dot{K}_1^2}\left(\lambda\frac{\partial \xi^1}{\partial \lambda}\right) + \frac{\partial^2 I}{\partial \dot{K}_1\,\partial \dot{K}_2}\left(\lambda\frac{\partial \xi^2}{\partial \lambda}\right) = 0,$$

from which we conclude that $\lambda\,\partial\xi^1/\partial\lambda = \lambda\,\partial\xi^2/\partial\lambda = 0$, i.e., $\partial\xi^1/\partial\lambda = \partial\xi^2/\partial\lambda = 0, \lambda \neq 0$. Substituting these into (83-i), we obtain $\partial\Phi/\partial\lambda = \lambda Y\,\partial\tau/\partial\lambda$. Using (83-ii) and differentiating it partially with $\dot{K}_1$ and $\dot{K}_2$, we shall also get

$$-\dot{K}_2\,\partial\xi^1/\partial t + \dot{K}_1\,\partial\xi^2/\partial t = 0,$$

which gives the remaining parts of (98-i), i.e., $\partial\xi^1/\partial t = \partial\xi^2/\partial t$. This will immediately yield (98-iii). Finally, substituting all of these into (83-ii), we get (98-iv).

Consequently, the integrability conditions of Φ from (98-ii) and (98-iii) are equal to

$$Y\left(\frac{\partial \omega}{\partial \lambda} + \frac{\partial \tau}{\partial t}\right) + \frac{\partial Y}{\partial K_1} \xi^1 + \frac{\partial Y}{\partial K_2} \xi^2 = 0, \tag{99-i}$$

$$\frac{\partial \Phi}{\partial t} = Y\left(\omega - \lambda \frac{\partial \omega}{\partial \lambda}\right) = Y\omega_0(K_1, K_2), \tag{99-ii}$$

$$\frac{\partial^2 \omega}{\partial \lambda^2} = \frac{\partial \omega}{\partial t} = 0, \qquad \text{i.e.,} \quad \omega = \omega_0(K_1, K_2) + \lambda\omega_1(K_1, K_2), \tag{99-iii}$$

$$\frac{\partial^2 \tau}{\partial t^2} = \frac{\partial^2 \Phi}{\partial \lambda\, \partial t} = 0, \qquad \text{i.e.,} \quad \tau = \tau_0(\lambda, K_1, K_2) + t\tau_1(K_1, K_2), \tag{99-iv}$$

$$\frac{\partial^2 \Phi}{\partial t^2} = \frac{\partial^2 \Phi}{\partial \lambda\, \partial t} = 0, \qquad \text{i.e.,} \quad \Phi = \Phi_0(\lambda. K_1, K_2) + t\Phi_1(K_1, K_2), \tag{99-v}$$

$$\lambda \frac{\partial \tau}{\partial \lambda} = \phi(\lambda Y), \qquad \phi\text{: arbitrary function} \qquad (\lambda Y = \text{const}). \tag{99-vi}$$

A special case of (97), which is often used in the literature (Samuelson [1970b], Caton and Shell [1971]), is the form

$$Y = AK_1^a K_2^{1-a}, \qquad A > 0, \quad 0 < a < 1, \qquad I = (\dot{K}_1^2 + \dot{K}_2^2)^{1/2}. \tag{100}$$

Substituting these into (98-iv) and setting

$$\dot{K}_1 = r\cos\theta, \qquad \dot{K}_2 = r\sin\theta, \qquad I = r, \tag{101}$$

we can express (98-iv) as

$$\begin{aligned}\left(-\frac{\partial \Phi}{\partial K_1} + \frac{\partial \xi^1}{\partial K_1} + \lambda Y \frac{\partial \tau}{\partial K_1}\right)\cos\theta + \left(-\frac{\partial \Phi}{\partial K_2} + \frac{\partial \xi^1}{\partial K_2} + \lambda Y \frac{\partial \tau}{\partial K_2}\right)\sin\theta - \omega \\ - \lambda \frac{\partial \xi^1}{\partial K_1}\cos^2\theta - \lambda\left(\frac{\partial \xi^1}{\partial K_2} + \frac{\partial \xi^2}{\partial K_1}\right)\cos\theta\sin\theta - \lambda \frac{\partial \xi^2}{\partial K_2}\sin^2\theta = 0,\end{aligned} \tag{102}$$

from which we conclude that

$$\begin{gathered}\frac{\partial \xi^1}{\partial K_2} + \frac{\partial \xi^2}{\partial K_1} = 0, \qquad \omega + \lambda \frac{\partial \xi^1}{\partial K_1} = 0, \qquad \omega + \lambda \frac{\partial \xi^2}{\partial K_2} = 0, \\ \frac{\partial \Phi}{\partial K_1} = \frac{\partial \xi^1}{\partial K_1} + \lambda Y \frac{\partial \tau}{\partial K_1}, \qquad \frac{\partial \Phi}{\partial K_2} = \frac{\partial \xi^1}{\partial K_2} + \lambda Y \frac{\partial \tau}{\partial K_2}.\end{gathered} \tag{102'}$$

From (99-iii), $\omega = \omega_0 + \lambda\omega_1$ and $\omega + \lambda\,\partial\xi^1/\partial K_1 = \omega + \lambda\,\partial\xi^2/\partial K_2 = 0$, we see that $\omega_0 = 0$ and $\partial\xi^1/\partial K_1 = \partial\xi^2/\partial K_2 = -\omega_1$. Summarizing these, we have

$$\frac{\partial\Phi}{\partial\lambda} = \lambda Y\frac{\partial\tau}{\partial\lambda}, \qquad \frac{\partial\Phi}{\partial t} = 0 \qquad (\omega_0 = 0),$$

$$\frac{\partial\Phi}{\partial K_1} = \frac{\partial\xi^1}{\partial K_1} + \lambda Y\frac{\partial\tau}{\partial K_1}, \qquad \frac{\partial\Phi}{\partial K_2} = \frac{\partial\xi^1}{\partial K_2} + \lambda Y\frac{\partial\tau}{\partial K_2}$$

which can now be written as

$$\frac{\partial}{\partial\lambda}(\Phi - \xi^1) = \lambda Y\frac{\partial\tau}{\partial\lambda}, \qquad \frac{\partial}{\partial t}(\Phi - \xi^1) = 0,$$

$$\frac{\partial}{\partial K_1}(\Phi - \xi^1) = \lambda Y\frac{\partial\tau}{\partial K_1}, \qquad \frac{\partial}{\partial K_2}(\Phi - \xi^1) = \lambda Y\frac{\partial\tau}{\partial K_2}.$$

From

$$\frac{\partial}{\partial\lambda}\left(\frac{\partial\tau}{\partial t}\right) = \frac{\partial}{\partial K_1}\left(\frac{\partial\tau}{\partial t}\right) = \frac{\partial}{\partial K_2}\left(\frac{\partial\tau}{\partial t}\right) = 0$$

and from (99-iv), $\tau = \tau_0 + t\tau_1$, we conclude that $\partial\tau/\partial t = \text{const} = \alpha$ or

$$\tau = \alpha t + \eta(\lambda, K_1, K_2). \tag{103}$$

Substituting this into (99-i) and using $\omega_1 = -\partial\xi^1/\partial K_1$, we obtain

$$Y\left(-\frac{\partial\xi^1}{\partial K_1} + \alpha\right) + \frac{\partial Y}{\partial K_1}\xi^1 + \frac{\partial Y}{\partial K_2}\xi^2 = 0. \tag{104}$$

Letting $Y = AK_1^aK_2^{1-a}$, Eq. (104) is now expressed as

$$K_1K_2\left(-\frac{\partial\xi^1}{\partial K_1} + \alpha\right) + aK_2\xi^1 + (1-a)K_1\xi^2 = 0. \tag{105}$$

The reader can show that

$$\eta = \phi(\lambda Y), \qquad \phi = \text{arbitrary function},$$
$$\lambda Y = \text{const (conservation law)}, \tag{106}$$

and

$$\begin{aligned}\Phi &= \xi^1 + \mu\phi(\mu) - \int\phi(\mu)\,d\mu, \qquad \mu = \lambda Y\\ &= \xi^1 + \text{const},\end{aligned} \tag{107}$$

and hence

$$\tau = \alpha t + \phi(\lambda Y) = \alpha t + \beta, \qquad \alpha, \beta = \text{const}. \tag{108}$$

To determine the remaining portion of the unknowns ξ^1 and ξ^2, we use

$$\frac{\partial \xi^1}{\partial K_1} = \frac{\partial \xi^2}{\partial K_2}, \qquad \frac{\partial \xi^1}{\partial K_2} + \frac{\partial \xi^2}{\partial K_1} = 0,$$
$$K_1 K_2\left(\alpha - \frac{\partial \xi^1}{\partial K_1}\right) + aK_2\xi^1 + (1-a)K_1\xi^2 = 0. \tag{109}$$

The reader can see immediately that $\alpha = 0$, $\xi^1 = \gamma K_1$, $\xi^2 = \gamma K_2$, $\omega = -\gamma\lambda$ represent a set of solutions which have already been derived in the previous theorem (Theorem 6). But (109) *may* include a more general solution for $\alpha \neq 0$ which gives a new conservation law. The interested reader is urged to pursue this line of approach further on his own.

Transformation to Unconstrained-Minimum Problem and Quadratic Approximation

20. It is well known (Samuelson and Solow [1956], Samuelson [1970b]) that the general optimal control problem (80) can be converted into an equivalent unconstrained-minimum problem

$$\min_{K_2(K_1)} \int_{K_1^0}^{K_1^T} \bar{L}(K_1, K_2; dK_2/dK_1)\, dK_1. \tag{80$'$}$$

When F takes a special separable form (97), the preceding problem is reduced to

$$\min_x \int \frac{I[(1+\dot{x})e^x]}{Y[e^x]}\, dy, \tag{110}$$

where $y = \log K_1$, $x = \log K_2 - \log K_1 = \log K_2 - y$, $\dot{x} = ((d \log K_2)/(d \log K_1)) - 1 = ((d \log K_1)/dy) - 1$, or $(1+\dot{x})e^x = dK_2/dK_1$. Hence the Lagrangian for this separable case is

$$L(t, x, \dot{x}) = I[(1+\dot{x})e^x]/Y(e^x). \tag{111}$$

Here the Lagrangian is a smooth convex function with respect to x and $\dot{x}$. To derive local conservation laws, in addition to the two conservation laws of Samuelson's, we consider a local quadratic approximation

$$\begin{aligned} L(x, \dot{x}) &= I[(1+\dot{x})e^x]/Y(e^x) \\ &= \tfrac{1}{2}a\dot{x}^2 + (b_0 + b_1 x)\dot{x} + c_0 + c_1 x + c_2 x^2 + \cdots, \end{aligned} \tag{112}$$

where

$$\begin{bmatrix} a & b_1 \\ b_1 & 2c_2 \end{bmatrix}$$

is positive definite. *This is a special case of the local Lagrangian for the general optimal control problem already considered in Part* IV *when the discount rate is zero,* $\rho = 0$ (*Theorem* 4). There are three conservation laws, one of which is already derived as *the constancy of the "energy" integral.* The remaining two laws are nothing but the *turnpike constants.* In summary, for the optimal control problem of (80), combining with the two global laws, we have uncovered altogether *four* conservation laws operating in the *neighborhood* of the equilibrium point:

Global laws

(i) $\Omega_1 = \lambda Y = \text{const},$ (ii) $\Omega_2 = \lambda W = \text{const},$ $Y/W = \text{const}.$

Local laws

(iii) $\Omega_3 =$ turnpike constant C_1, (iv) $\Omega_4 =$ turnpike constant C_2.

Economic interpretations of the turnpike constants are already given in Part IV.

REFERENCES

Bessel-Hagen, E. [1921]. Über die erhaltungssätze der elektrodynamik, *Math. Ann.*, **84**, 258–276.

Burmeister, E., and Dobell, R. [1970]. *Mathematical Theories of Economic Growth.* Macmillan, New York.

Cass, D. [1965]. Optimum growth in an aggregate model of capital accumulation. *Review of Economic Studies*, **32**, 233–240.

Caton, C., and Shell, K. [1971]. An exercise in the theory of heterogeneous capital accumulation, *Review of Economic Studies*, **38**, 13–22.

Davis, H. T. [1962]. *Introduction to Nonlinear Differential and Integral Equations.* Dover, New York.

Gelfand, I. M., and Fomin, S. V. [1963]. *Calculus of Variations*, (R. A. Siverman, transl.). Prentice-Hall, Englewood Cliffs, New Jersey.

Goldstein, H. S. P. [1950]. *Classical Mechanics.* Addison-Wesley, Reading, Massachusetts.

Hill, E. L. [1951]. Hamilton's principle and the conservation theorems of mathematical physics, *Reviews of Modern Physics*, **23**, 253–260.

Klein, F. [1918]. Über die differentialgesetze für die Erhaltung von Impuls und energie in der Einsteinschen gravitationstheorie, *Nachr. Akad. Wiss. Göttingen, Math.-Phys. Kl.*, II, 171–189.

Koopmans, T. C. [1965]. On the concept of optimal growth, in *The Econometric Approach to Development Planning.* Rand McNally, Chicago, Illinois.

Kurz, M. [1968a]. The general instability of a class of competitive growth processes, *Review of Economic Studies*, **35**, 155–174.

Kurz, M. [1968b]. Optimal economic growth and wealth effects, *International Economic Review*, **9**, 348–357.

Lanczos, C. [1970]. *The Variational Principles of Mechanics*, 4th ed., University of Toronto Press, Toronto.

Levhari, D., and Liviatan, N. [1972]. On stability in the saddle-point sense, *Journal of Economic Theory*, **4**, 88–93.

Lie, S. [1891]. *Vorlesungen über Differentialgleichungen, mit bekannten infinitesimalen Transformationen* (G. Scheffers, ed.). Teubner, Leipzig. Reprinted by Chelsea, New York, 1967.

Liviatan, N., and Samuelson, P. A. [1969]. Notes on turnpikes: Stable and unstable, *Journal of Economic Theory*, 1454–1475.

Logan, J. D. [1977]. *Invariant Variational Principles*, Mathematics in Science and Engineering, Vol. 138. Academic Press, New York.

Lovelock, D., and Rund, H. [1975]. *Tensors, Differential Forms, and Variational Principles*. Wiley, New York.

Moser, J. [1979]. Hidden symmetries in dynamical systems, *American Scientists*, **67**, 689–695.

Noether, E. [1918]. Invariante variationsprobleme, *Nachr. Akad. Wiss. Göttingen, Math.-Phys. Kl, II*, 235–257. Translation by M. A. Taval under the title of Invariant Variation Problems, *Transport Theory and Statistical Physics*, **1**(3), 186–207.

Nôno, T. [1968]. On the symmetry groups of simple materials: Application of the theory of Lie groups, *J. Math. Anal. Appl.*, **24**, 110–135.

Nôno, T., and Mimura, F. [1975]. Dynamic symmetries, I, *Bulletin of Fukuoka University of Education*, **25**.

Nôno, T., and Mimura, F. [1976]. Dynamic symmetries, III, *Bulletin of Fukuoka University of Education*, **26**.

Nôno, T. and Mimura, F. [1977]. Dynamic symmetries, IV, *Bulletin of Fukuoka University of Education*, **27**.

Ramsey, F. [1928]. A mathematical theory of saving, *Economic Journal*, **38**, 543–559.

Rund, H. [1966]. *The Hamilton–Jacobi Theory in the Calculus of Variations*. Van Nostrand-Reinhold, Princeton, New Jersey.

Sagan, H. [1969]. *Introduction to the Calculus of Variations*. McGraw-Hill, New York.

Samuelson, P. A. [1960]. Efficient paths of capital accumulation in terms of the calculus of variations, in *Mathematical Methods in the Social Sciences* (K. J. Arrow *et al.*, eds.), pp. 77–88, Stanford Univ. Press, Stanford, California.

Samuelson, P. A. [1965]. A catenary turnpike theorem involving consumption and the golden rule, *American Economic Review*, **55**, 486–496.

Samuelson, P. A. [1970a]. Law of conservation of the capital-output ratio, *Proceedings of the National Academy of Sciences, Applied Mathematical Science*, **67**, 1477–1479.

Samuelson, P. A. [1970b]. Two Conservation Laws in Theoretical Economics. Mimeo, Department of Economics, Massachusetts Institute of Technology, Cambridge, Massachusetts.

Samuelson, P. A. [1972]. The general saddlepoint property of optimal-control motions, *Journal of Economic Theory*, **5**, 102–120.

Samuelson, P. A. [1976]. Speeding up of time with age in recognition of life as fleeting, in *Evolution, Welfare, and Time in Economics, Essays in Honor of Nicholas Georgescu-Roegen* (A. M. Tang *et al.*, eds.). Lexington Books, Heath, Lexington, Massachusetts.

Samuelson, P. A., and Solow, R. M. [1956]. A complete capital model involving heterogeneous capital goods, *Quarterly Journal of Economics*, **70**, 537–567.

Sato, R., and Davis, E. [1971]. Optimal savings policy when labor grows endogenously, *Econometrica*, **39**, 877–898.

Shell, K. [1967]. Optimal programs of capital accumulation for an economy in which there is exogenous technical change, in *Essays on the Theory of Optimal Economic Growth* (K. Shell, ed.). MIT Press, Cambridge, Massachusetts.

Whittaker, E. T. [1937]. *A Treatise on the Analytical Dynamics of Particles and Rigid Bodies*, 4th ed. Cambridge Univ. Press, London and New York. Reprinted by Dover, New York, 1944.

Young, E. C. [1978]. *Vector and Tensor Analysis*, Monographs and Textbooks in Pure and Applied Mathematics, No. 48. Dekker, New York.

CHAPTER 8

A LIE GROUP APPROACH TO THE INDEX NUMBER PROBLEMS

I. Introduction

1. Recent contributions by Samuelson and Swamy [1974], Eichhorn and Voeller [1976], Afriat [1972], Diewert [1976], Fisher and Shell [1972], Richter [1966], Wold [1952], and others have almost perfected the theory of index numbers. Yet there are several unresolved problems which require a fresh and new approach. In this chapter we take a Lie group approach to study some of the basic problems of the index number theory. In particular, we present an alternative approach to the question of the Fisher–Frisch test criteria for an index number. We shall also deal with the "invariant" economic index number problem (both static and dynamic) so eloquently presented by such recent authors as Samuelson and Swamy, Fisher and Shell, and Richter.

As the reader of this book must have already realized, the Lie group approach has a decided advantage over the standard approach in dealing with "invariance" properties of economic behavior. It will be shown that the well-known tests of an index number can be looked at as the conditions on infinitesimal transformations of Lie groups. These tests are "actions" of Lie groups on the index number. Any index number must satisfy the invariance properties of group transformations in order that it may serve as a useful index of measurement of prices and quantities.

We shall also study the properties of index numbers derived from implicitly holothetic utility functions. Even under the nonhomothetic condition, some of these index numbers will satisfy the criterion of the factor-reversal test in a broad sense. It will be shown that the standard quantity index is not completely symmetric with the price index. To overcome this difficulty, a "dual" quantity index is derived, which is perfectly symmetric with the corresponding price index, satisfying all the requirements of the basic tests. Exogenous factors such as taste change and technical progress may be brought into the index number by this approach in the most natural way. Here again, under the holotheticity condition of equiproportionate change, they may be treated as transformations leaving the given index number invariant.

Finally, we shall present the analysis of the so-called Divisia index numbers (Divisia [1928]). Most of the previous works are concerned with the path independence property of the index numbers (Samuelson and Swamy [1974], Richter [1966], Hulten [1973], Hillinger [1970], Ville [1946]). The path independency condition is basically a problem of *static* behavior. Our concern here is to study the invariance property of *dynamic* behavior—*the dynamic invariance (or symmetry) of the Divisia index numbers.* Again, the Noether theorem proves to be indispensable for the derivation of the necessary and sufficient condition under which a Divisia index number is dynamically invariant under transformations of technical and taste change. There is the fundamental invariance condition which may be called the *law of conservation of a Divisia index number.*

II. Axioms and Basic Tests

Price Indices

2. For technical reasons, and unless stated otherwise, we assume that the domain of definition of all price and quantity indices is always restricted to the positive orthant, i.e., only positive components of the various vectors are admitted. Let

$$\mathbb{R}_{++} = \{x \mid x \in \mathbb{R}, \mathbb{R} \text{ the set of all real numbers}, x > 0\},$$

$$\mathbb{R}^n_{++} = \{X = (x_1, \ldots, x_n) \mid x_i \in \mathbb{R}_{++}, 1 \leqq i \leqq n\},$$

and let

$$P^0 = (p^0_1, \ldots, p^0_n) \in \mathbb{R}^n_{++}, \qquad X^0 = (x^0_1, \ldots, x^0_n) \in \mathbb{R}^n_{++},$$

$$P^1 = (p^1_1, \ldots, p^1_n) \in \mathbb{R}^n_{++}, \qquad X^1 = (x^1_1, \ldots, x^1_n) \in \mathbb{R}^n_{++}$$

be the price and quantity vectors of n commodities in a base year 0 and in a comparison year 1, respectively.[1] (Following Samuelson and Swamy [1974], we use capital letters for row vectors and lowercase or Greek letters for scalars. We may also use capital letters for Lie operators, but there will be no confusion from the context of analysis.)

Consider a one-parameter transformation group

$$\begin{aligned}&\phi_\lambda : \mathbb{R}^{2n}_{++} \to \mathbb{R}^{2n}_{++}, \qquad (P^0, P^1) \to \phi_\lambda(P^0, P^1),\\ &\phi_\lambda(P^0, P^1) = (\phi^0_1(P^0, P^1; \lambda), \ldots, \phi^0_n(P^0, P^1; \lambda), \phi^1_1(P^0, P^1; \lambda),\\ &\qquad\qquad \ldots, \phi^1_n(P^0, P^1; \lambda)),\end{aligned} \tag{1}$$

where $\lambda \in \mathbb{R}$ is a parameter and ϕ_λ a diffeomorphism, satisfying ϕ_{λ_0} equals identity for some λ_0. Let the infinitesimal generators of the group[2] be represented by

$$U = U^0 + U^1, \qquad U^0 = \sum_{i=1}^{n} \xi^0_i \, \partial/\partial p^0_i, \qquad U^1 = \sum_{i=1}^{n} \xi^1_i \, \partial/\partial p^1_i, \tag{1'}$$

where $\xi^0_i = \partial\phi^0_i/\partial\lambda|_{\lambda=\lambda_0}$ and $\xi^1_i = \partial\phi^1_i/\partial\lambda|_{\lambda=\lambda_0}$ are functions of P^0 and P^1 for $1 \leqq i \leqq n$.

A function

$$p : \mathbb{R}^{2n}_{++} \to \mathbb{R}_{++}, \qquad (P^0, P^1) \to p(P^0, P^1) \tag{2}$$

is called a price index, if p satisfies the following four axioms for all $(P^0, P^1) \in \mathbb{R}^{2n}_{++}$.

(A1) *Monotonicity Axiom* The function p is strictly increasing with respect to P^1 and strictly decreasing with respect to P^0:

$$\begin{aligned}p(P^0, P^1) &> p(P^0, P^2) \qquad \text{if} \quad P^1 \geq P^2,\\ p(P^0, P^1) &< p(P^2, P^1) \qquad \text{if} \quad P^0 \geq P^2,\end{aligned}$$

or alternatively,

$$\partial p/\partial p^1_i > 0, \qquad \partial p/\partial p^0_i < 0, \qquad 1 \leqq i \leqq n. \tag{3-i}$$

(A2) *Identity Axiom* If all prices remain constant, then the value of p equals unity: $p(P^0, P^0) = 1$, from which it follows that

$$\partial p/\partial p^1_i = -\partial p/\partial p^0_i \qquad \text{at} \quad P^1 = P^0 \quad \text{for all} \quad 1 \leqq i \leqq n. \tag{3-ii}$$

(A3) *Homogeneity Invariance Axiom* If all comparison prices change λ-fold ($\lambda \in \mathbb{R}_{++}$), then the value of p is changed by λ. That is to say, we assume

[1] This part is a restatement of some of the known results in terms of Lie groups, while most of the existing results depend on the functional equation analysis (see an excellent exposition by Eichhorn and Voeller [1976]).

[2] U^0 and U^1 are Lie's symbols for the infinitesimal transformations of the groups. They are not vectors, though they are written in capital letters.

that ϕ_i^1 in (1) or (1′) is a uniform magnification group with $\xi_i^1 = p_i^1$ and that p satisfies the "invariance" condition

$$U^1 p - p = 0. \tag{3-iii}$$

(A4) *Dimensional Invariance Axiom*[3] A dimensional change in the unit of the currency does not change the value of p. That is to say, we assume that ϕ_i^0 is also a uniform magnification group $\xi_i^0 = p_i^0$ and that p satisfies the invariance condition

$$Up = U^1 p + U^0 p = 0. \tag{3-iv}$$

Of course, the traditional way of writing (A3) and (A4) is

$$p(P^0, \lambda P^1) = \lambda p(P^0, P^1) \tag{3-iii′}$$

and

$$p(\lambda P^0, \lambda P^1) = p(P^0, P^1), \tag{3-iv′}$$

which are the solutions of our axioms (3-iii) and (3-iv) written in partial differential equation form. We take the Lie group approach since it proves to be more efficient to derive some results, such as the independency theorem of the four axioms (see Eichhorn and Voeller [1976]). If we use (3-i)–(3-iv), we can easily show that these four axioms are independent in the sense that any three can be satisfied by a function p which does not satisfy the remaining axiom. As a matter of fact, each axiom is seen to be independent of any other axioms. Thus, for instance, $\partial p/\partial p_i^1 > 0$ and $\partial p/\partial p_i^0 < 0$ do not imply $\partial p/\partial p_i^1 \equiv -\partial p/\partial p_i^0$ at $P^0 = P^1$. Condition (3-iii) $\sum_{i=1}^n p_i^1\, \partial p/\partial p_i^1 = p$ is, of course, an independent condition from $\partial p/\partial p_i^1 > 0$ and $\partial p/\partial p_i^0 < 0$. Condition (3-iv) is also independent in the sense that (3-i) does not imply $U^1 p + U^0 p$ to be zero. The reader can try all other combinations to show the independency conditions.

3. We now present various tests (Fisher [1922]):

(T1) *Proportionality Test: "General Mean of Price Relatives"* (A2) and (A3) imply that

$$p(P^0, \lambda P^0) = \lambda, \qquad \lambda \in \mathbb{R}_{++}, \tag{4-i}$$

which means that if all new prices change λ-fold compared with the base year prices, then p is equal to λ. Alternatively, since

$$p(P^0, \lambda P^1) = \lambda p(P^0, P^1) \qquad \text{from (A3)},$$

by setting $P^0 \equiv P^1$, we get $p(P^0, P^0) \equiv 1$ from (A2).

[3] Here we are not concerned with a more general definition of the dimensionality test suggested by Samuelson and Swamy.

(T2) *Homogeneity-of-Degree-Minus-One Test* Any function which satisfies (A3) and (A4) simultaneously must also satisfy

$$p(\lambda P^0, P^1) = p(P^0, \lambda^{-1} P^1) = \lambda^{-1} p(P^0, P^1). \tag{4-ii}$$

We shall first show that (A3) and (A4) are *compatible* in the sense that these two restrictions constitute the complete system (or the Jacobian complete system) of linear partial differential equations. (See Chapter 2 and the Appendix, Part V). Condition (3-iii) implies the existence of a new infinitesimal operator

$$V^1 = \sum_{i=1}^{n} p_i^1 \frac{\partial}{\partial p_i^1} + \sum_{i=1}^{n} 0 \frac{\partial}{\partial p_i^0} + p \frac{\partial}{\partial p}. \tag{5-i}$$

Also, condition (3-iv) implies the existence of a new infinitesimal generator

$$V^2 = \sum_{i=1}^{n} p_i^1 \frac{\partial}{\partial p_i^1} + \sum_{i=1}^{n} p_i^0 \frac{\partial}{\partial p_i^0} + 0 \frac{\partial}{\partial p}. \tag{5-ii}$$

The Lie bracket of V^1 and V^2 is

$$\begin{aligned}[V^1, V^2] = V^1 V^2 - V^2 V^1 = & \sum_{i=1}^{n} (V^1 p_i^1 - V^2 p_i^1) \frac{\partial}{\partial p_i^1} \\ & + \sum_{i=1}^{n} (V^1 p_i^0 - V^2 \cdot 0) \frac{\partial}{\partial p_i^0} + (V^1 \cdot 0 - V^2 p) \frac{\partial}{\partial p},\end{aligned} \tag{6}$$

which will be reduced to

$$[V^1, V^2] = \rho_1 V^1 + \rho_2 V^2, \qquad \rho_1 \equiv \rho_2 \equiv 0. \tag{6'}$$

Hence V^1 and V^2 are compatible types of infinitesimal generators satisfying the condition of the (Jacobian) complete system. Subtracting (3-iv) from (3-iii), we immediately obtain

$$U^1 p - p - (U^1 p + U^0 p) = -p - U^0 p = 0 \tag{7}$$

or

$$U^0 p = -p, \tag{7'}$$

the condition of homogeneity-of-degree minus one in terms of P^0.

(T3) *Mean Value Test* The value of p lies between the smallest and the largest of the price ratios of the corresponding prices, i.e.,

$$\min\{p_1^1/p_1^0, \ldots, p_n^1/p_n^0\} \leqq p(P^0, P^1) \leqq \max\{p_1^1/p_1^0, \ldots, p_n^1/p_n^0\}. \tag{4-iii}$$

To show this set $\min\{p_1^1/p_1^0, \ldots, p_n^1/p_n^0\} = \lambda$. Then

$$\begin{aligned}\min\{p_1^1/p_1^0, \ldots, p_n^1/p_n^0\} &= \lambda = \lambda p(P^0, P^0) = p(P^0, \lambda P^0) \\ &\leqq p(P^0, P^1), \qquad P^1 \geqq \lambda P^0.\end{aligned}$$

In the same way,

$$\max\{p_1^1/p_1^0, \ldots, p_n^1/p_n^0\} = \mu = \mu p(P^0, P^0) = p(P^0, \mu P^0)$$
$$\geqq p(P^0, P^1), \qquad P^1 \leqq \mu P^0.$$

It is seen, therefore, that any price index which satisfies the four axioms will also satisfy (T1)–(T3).

Theorem 1 *(Homogeneity of Degree One and Minus One) Every price index* $p: \mathbb{R}_{++}^{2n} \to \mathbb{R}_{++}$ *which satisfies the homogeneity invariance axiom* (A3) *and the dimensional invariance axiom* (A4) *simultaneously must be a homogeneous function of degree one with respect to* P^1 *and of degree minus one with respect to* P^0*, and must have the form*

$$p = (p_r^1/p_s^0)\phi(P^1/p_r^1, p_s^0/P^0) \qquad \textit{for any} \quad 1 \leqq r \neq s \leqq n, \tag{8}$$

where ϕ *is an arbitrary function of*

$$P^1/p_r^1 = (p_1^1/p_r^1, \ldots, p_n^1/p_r^1) \qquad \textit{and} \qquad p_s^0/P^0 = (p_s^0/p_1^0, \ldots, p_s^0/p_n^0).$$

Proof From the *compatibility condition* (6′), we have a complete Jacobian system

$$V^1 f = 0, \qquad V^2 f = 0,$$

where $f = f(p, P^0, P^1)$, and we choose a linear function of f with respect to p, i.e., $f = p - g(P^0, P^1)$. The corresponding systems of ordinary differential equations are

$$dp_1^1/p_1^1 = \cdots = dp_n^1/p_n^1 = dp_1^0/0 = \cdots = dp_n^0/0 = dp/p,$$
$$dp_1^1/p_1^1 = \cdots = dp_n^1/p_n^1 = dp_1^0/p_1^0 = \cdots = dp_n^0/p_n^0 = dp/0.$$

Or, alternatively, using (3-iii) and (7′),

$$U^1 p = p, \qquad U^0 p = -p$$

and their corresponding ordinary differential equation systems

$$dp_1^1/p_1^1 = \cdots = dp_n^1/p_n^1 = dp_1^0/0 = \cdots = dp_n^0/0 = dp/p,$$
$$dp_1^1/0 = \cdots = dp_n^1/0 = dp_1^0/p_1^0 = \cdots = dp_n^0/p_n^0 = dp/(-p),$$

we immediately obtain (8), which is a function of homogeneous degree one with respect to P^1 and degree minus one with respect to P^0. Q.E.D.

(T4) *Circular-Reversal Test* If in a first time period all prices change from P^0 to P^1, and in a subsequent time period from P^1 to P^2, and if the value of p for the entire time period is the product of the values of p for the two time intervals, then p is said to satisfy the circular-reversal test:

$$p(P^0, P^1)p(P^1, P^2) = p(P^0, P^2). \tag{4-iv}$$

(T5) *Time Reversal Test* By setting $P^2 = P^0$, $P^2 = P^1$ in (4-iv) and using (A2), the identity axiom, we get

$$p(P^0, P^2)p(P^2, P^0) = p(P^0, P^0) = 1. \tag{4-v}$$

The repeated application of (4-iv) together with (4-v) finally yields

$$p(P^0, P^1)p(P^1, P^2)\cdot\cdots\cdot p(P^s, P^0) = 1. \tag{4-v'}$$

Theorem 2 (*Ratio Form of a Price Index*) *Any price index function* $p\colon \mathbb{R}^{2n}_{++} \to \mathbb{R}_{++}$ *which satisfies the circular test must have the ratio form*

$$p(P^0, P^1) = e(P^1)/e(P^0), \tag{9}$$

where $e\colon \mathbb{R}^n_{++} \to \mathbb{R}_{++}$.

Proof By rewriting (4-iv) as $p(P^1, P^2) = p(P^0, P^2)/p(P^0, P^1)$, we immediately see that the left-hand side is independent of P^0. This is true if and only if $p(P^0, P^2)$ and $p(P^0, P^1)$ are multiplicative functions of P^0, P^2, and P^1, i.e., $p(P^0, P^2) = g(P^0)e_2(P^2)$ and $p(P^0, P^1) = g(P^0)e_1(P^1)$. But since $p(P^1, P^2) = e_2(P^2)/e_1(P^1)$ and must satisfy the same multiplicative condition as P^0, by setting $P^2 = P^1$ and $1 = p(P^1, P^1) = e_2(P^1)/e_1(P^1)$, we finally conclude that $g^{-1} \equiv e_1 \equiv e_2 \equiv e$. Q.E.D.

Theorem 3 (*Homogeneous Ratio Form*) *Any price index which satisfies the assumptions of both Theorems* 1 *and* 2 *must have the form*

$$p(P^0, P^1) = e(P^1)/e(P^0), \tag{10}$$

where $e(P)$ is a homogeneous function of degree one with respect to P such that $\partial e(P)/\partial p_i > 0$.

Proof Obvious from (8) and (9). Q.E.D.

Corollary to Theorem 3 (*Homogeneous Ratio Form and Basic Axioms*) *Any price index expressed in the form of* (10) *satisfies the basic four axioms of the index numbers* (A1)–(A4).

Proof Since (10) automatically satisfies the condition of (A3) and (A4) (Theorem 1), it suffices to show that (10) also satisfies (A1) and (A2). With positive partial derivatives of e with respect to its arguments, we get

$$\frac{\partial p}{\partial p_i^1} = \frac{1}{e(P^0)}\frac{\partial e(P^1)}{\partial p_i^1} > 0 \qquad \text{and} \qquad \frac{\partial p}{\partial p_i^0} = -e(P^1)e(P^0)^{-2}\frac{\partial e(P^0)}{\partial p_i^0} < 0,$$

and by setting $P^0 \equiv P^1$, we get $p = e(P^0)/e(P^0) = 1$. Q.E.D.

(T6) *Multiplicative Holotheticity Test.* A function $p\colon \mathbb{R}^{2n}_{++} \to \mathbb{R}_{++}$ is said to be *multiplicative holothetic* if the value of p at new prices

$$(\lambda_1^0 p_1^0, \ldots, \lambda_n^0 p_n^0, \lambda_1^1 p_1^1, \ldots, \lambda_n^1 p_n^1)\ (\lambda_i^0, \lambda_i^1 \in \mathbb{R}_{++}, 1 \leqq i \leqq n)$$

is equal to the value of p at the original prices (P^0, P^1) multiplied by a positive real number μ depending upon λ_i^0, λ_i^1 $(1 \leqq i \leqq n)$, i.e.,

$$p(\lambda_1^0 p_1^0, \ldots, \lambda_n^0 p_n^0, \lambda_1^1 p_1^1, \ldots, \lambda_n^1 p_n^1) = \mu(\lambda_1^0, \ldots, \lambda_n^0, \lambda_1^1, \ldots, \lambda_n^1) p(P^0, P^1). \tag{4-vi}$$

An alternative approach to (4-vi) is to consider a one-parameter transformation group of the nonuniform magnification type

$$\phi_\lambda: \mathbb{R}_{++}^{2n} \to \mathbb{R}_{++}^{2n}, \tag{11}$$

where the infinitesimal transformation is given by

$$U = U^0 + U^1, \qquad U^0 = \sum_{i=1}^n \alpha_i^0 p_i^0 \frac{\partial}{\partial p_i^0},$$

$$U^1 = \sum_{i=1}^n \alpha_i^1 p_i^1 \frac{\partial}{\partial p_i^1}, \qquad \alpha_i^0, \alpha_i^1 \geqq 0, \quad 1 \leqq i \leqq n. \tag{11$'$}$$

The multiplicative holotheticity condition in terms of (11′) (Hicks neutrality in technical change) requires that

$$Up = U^0 p + U^1 p = \gamma p. \tag{4-vi$'$}$$

Thus (4-vi) is nothing but the (multiplicative) invariance condition of p under the multiplicative change in the price vector (11). The reader can easily see the reason why this test may be called the multiplicative holotheticity test. (This is the condition of *almost homogeneity* discussed in the earlier chapters.)

Theorem 4 *(Cobb–Douglas Index Number) The most general index number which simultaneously satisfies the assumption of Theorem* 3 *and the multiplicative holotheticity test* (T6) *must be the Cobb–Douglas form, i.e.,*

$$p(P^0, P^1) = e(P^1)/e(P^0) = \prod_{i=1}^n p_i^{1^{a_i}} \Big/ \prod_{i=1}^n p_i^{0^{a_i}}, \qquad a_i > 0, \quad \sum_{i=1}^n a_i = 1 \tag{12}$$

Proof From Theorem 3 we have $p(P^0, P^1) = e(P^1)/e(P^0)$, where $e(P)$ is homogeneous degree one, i.e.,

$$\sum_{i=1}^n p_i \frac{\partial}{\partial p_i} e(P) = e(P).$$

From (11′) and (4-vi′), γ is a linear function of α_i^0 and α_i^1 $(i = 1, 2, \ldots, n)$, i.e., $\gamma = \sum_{i=1}^n (b_i \alpha_i^0 + a_i \alpha_i^1)$, so we must have

$$Up = U\left(\frac{e(P^1)}{e(P^0)}\right) = \sum_{i=1}^n (b_i \alpha_i^0 + a_i \alpha_i^1) \frac{e(P^1)}{e(P^0)}.$$

Hence

$$e(P^0)U^1(e(P^1)) - e(P^1)U^0(e(P^0)) = \sum_{i=1}^{n} (b_i\alpha_i^0 + a_i\alpha_i^1)e(P^0)e(P^1).$$

This condition must apply for all α_i^0 and α_i^1, and hence we have

$$-e(P^1) \sum_{i=1}^{n} \alpha_i^0 p_i^0 \frac{\partial e(P^0)}{\partial p_i^0} = \sum_{i=1}^{n} b_i \alpha_i^0 e(P^0)e(P^1)$$

for $\alpha_i^1 = 0$, i.e., for $U^1 = 0$, which in turn implies $p_i^0\ \partial e(P^0)/\partial p_i^0 = -b_i e(P^0)$ (no summation on i).

Also, for $\alpha_i^0 = 0$ and $U^0 = 0$, we must have

$$e(P^0)U^1(e(P^1)) = \sum_{i=1}^{n} a_i \alpha_i^1 e(P^0)e(P^1),$$

and hence $p_i^1\ \partial e(P^1)/\partial p_i^1 = a_i e(P^1)$ (no summation on i). But since $e(P)$ must satisfy Theorem 3,

$$p_i \frac{\partial}{\partial p_i} e(P) = a_i e(P) \qquad (a_i = -b_i),$$

the sum of the a_i must be equal to unity, i.e.,

$$\sum_{i=1}^{n} a_i = 1.$$

Let $\log p_i = q_i$. Then we have

$$\frac{\partial \log e}{\partial q_i} = a_i \qquad \text{(const)},$$

which implies $\log e = \sum_{i=1}^{n} a_i q_i + c$, $\sum_{i=1}^{n} a_i = 1$, or

$$e = C \exp\left(\sum_{i=1}^{n} a_i \log p_i\right) = C \prod_{i=1}^{n} p_i^{a_i}.$$

For $e > 0$ we must have $C > 0$, and for $\partial e/\partial p_i > 0$ we must have $a_i > 0$. Q.E.D.

(T7) *Additive Holotheticity Test* A function $e\colon \mathbb{R}_{++}^n \to \mathbb{R}_{++}$ is said to be *additive* holothetic if the value of e at new prices is equal to the value of e at the original prices added by some nonnegative real number μ such that

$$e(p_1 + t\lambda_1, \ldots, p_n + t\lambda_n) = e(p_1, \ldots, p_n) + \mu(t\lambda_1, \ldots, t\lambda_n),$$
$$t\lambda_i \in \mathbb{R}_+, \qquad 1 \leqq i \leqq n. \tag{4-vii}$$

This is a specification of the transformation group (1) by

$$A = \sum_{i=1}^{n} \lambda_i\ \partial/\partial p_i \tag{13}$$

and

$$Ae = \mu(\lambda_1, \ldots, \lambda_n). \tag{4-vii$'$}$$

Theorem 5 (*Additive Form*) *The most general index number which satisfies simultaneously Theorem 3 and the additive holotheticity test* (T7) *for e must have the form*

$$p = \sum_{i=1}^{n} a_i p_i^1 \Big/ \sum_{i=1}^{n} a_i p_i^0, \qquad a_i > 0, \quad 1 \leqq i \leqq n. \tag{14}$$

Proof The proof is left to the reader. (Follow the same steps as the proof of Theorem 4, showing that

$$\begin{aligned} \mu &= \lambda_1 \mu(1, 0, \ldots, 0) + \lambda_2 \mu(0, 1, 0, \ldots, 0) + \cdots + \lambda_n \mu(0, \ldots, 0, 1) \\ &= \sum_{i=1}^{n} a_i \lambda_i - \text{linear in } \lambda_i.) \quad \text{Q.E.D.} \end{aligned}$$

Price-Quantity Indices

4. Thus far, we have implicitly assumed that quantities do not change over the period and that they need not appear in the price index explicitly. Let

$$X^0 = (x_1^0, \ldots, x_n^0) \in \mathbb{R}_{++}^n, \qquad X^1 = (x_1^1, \ldots, x_n^1) \in \mathbb{R}_{++}^n$$

be the quantities of n goods in a base year and in a comparison year, respectively, corresponding to their respective prices P^0 and P^1. Then our price index is now defined as

$$p: \mathbb{R}_{++}^{4n} \to \mathbb{R}_{++}, \qquad (P^0, X^0, P^1, X^1) \to p(P^0, X^0, P^1, X^1). \tag{15a}$$

In addition to the preceding tests, we now consider:

(T8) *Commensurability Invariance Test* A change in the units of measurement of commodities does not change the value of p in (14), i.e.,

$$\begin{aligned} &p(\lambda_1^0 p_1^0, \ldots, \lambda_n^0 p_n^0, x_1^0/\lambda_1^0, \ldots, x_n^0/\lambda_n^0, \lambda_1^1 p_1^1, \ldots, \lambda_n^1 p_n^1, x_1^1/\lambda_1^1, \ldots, x_n^1/\lambda_n^1) \\ &\quad = p(P^0, X^0, P^1, X^1) \qquad (\lambda_i^0, \lambda_i^1 \in \mathbb{R}_{++}). \end{aligned} \tag{4-viii}$$

Alternatively, using the Lie group representation, we can write the preceding condition as

$$Up = 0,$$

$$U = \sum_{i=1}^{n} \alpha_i^0 \left(p_i^0 \frac{\partial}{\partial p_i^0} - x_i^0 \frac{\partial}{\partial x_i^0} \right) + \sum_{i=1}^{n} \alpha_i^1 \left(p_i^1 \frac{\partial}{\partial p_i^1} - x_i^1 \frac{\partial}{\partial x_i^1} \right), \tag{4-viii$'$}$$

$\forall \alpha_i^0, \alpha_i^1$. In many cases, $\alpha_i^0 \equiv \alpha_i^1$ for $1 \leqq i \leqq n$.

(T9) *Factor-Reversal* (*or* "*Self-Duality*") *Test* The result of an interchange of P^0 with X^0 as well as of P^1 with X^1 in p can be regarded as the value of a *quantity index q*,

$$q: \mathbb{R}^{4n}_{++} \to \mathbb{R}_{++}, \qquad (P^0, X^0, P^1, X^1) \to q(P^0, X^0, P^1, X^1). \tag{15b}$$

Then if the product of the two values p and q is the ratio of the values of the two baskets of goods in question, we have

$$\begin{aligned} p(P^0, X^0, P^1, X^1)p(X^0, P^0, X^1, P^1) &= e^1/e^0 = P^1X^1/P^0X^0, \\ = p(P^0, X^0, P^1, X^1)q(P^0, X^0, P^1, X^1) &= e^1/e^0 = P^1X^1/P^0X^0. \end{aligned} \tag{4-ix}$$

Since this condition implies that the same formula applies to p as to q, it may be called the "*strong*" *self-duality condition* discussed in Chapter 6. Instead of (4-ix), we may simply impose the second part of (4-ix), i.e.,

$$p(P^0, X^0, P^1, X^1)q(P^0, X^0, P^1, X^1) = e^1/e^0 = P^1X^1/P^0X^0, \tag{4-ix$'$}$$

which is known as the *product test*.

Theorem 6 (*Commensurability Invariance Theorem*) *The most general price index which satisfies the commensurability invariance test must have the form*

$$p(P^0, X^0, P^1, X^1) = f(p_1^0x_1^0, \ldots, p_n^0x_n^0, p_1^1x_1^1, \ldots, p_n^1x_n^1). \tag{16}$$

Proof Solving the invariance equation $Up = 0$ for $\forall\alpha_i^0$ and α_i^1, we must have

$$\left(p_i^0\frac{\partial}{\partial p_i^0} - x_i^0\frac{\partial}{\partial x_i^0}\right)p = 0, \qquad \left(p_i^1\frac{\partial}{\partial p_i^1} - x_i^1\frac{\partial}{\partial x_i^1}\right)p = 0 \qquad \text{for all } i.$$

Hence, we get $p = f(p_1^0x_1^0, \ldots, p_n^0x_n^0, p_1^1x_1^1, \ldots, p_n^1x_n^1)$. Q.E.D.

We also have

Theorem 7 (*Ratio Form of Price Index Containing Quantities*) *Any price index* $p: \mathbb{R}^{4n}_{++} \to \mathbb{R}_{++}$ *which simultaneously satisfies the circular test* (T4) *and the commensurability invariance test* (T8) *at* $\alpha_i^0 = \alpha_i$ *for all* i, $(1 \leqq i \leqq n)$ *must have the form*

$$p(P^0, X^0, P^1, X^1) = p(P^0, X^0, P^1, X^0) = \frac{e(x_1^0p_1^1, \ldots, x_n^0p_n^1)}{e(x_1^0p_1^0, \ldots, x_n^0p_n^0)}.$$

Proof This is the direct consequence of Theorems 2 and 6.[4] Q.E.D.

[4] Here we are concerned with the strong form of (T4). (T4) may be replaced by the so-called base test which only requires that $p(P^0, X^0, P^1, X^1)\rho(P^1, X^1, P^2, X^2) = p(P^0, X^0, P^2, X^2)$, where ρ is not necessary equal to the price index p. See Eichhorn and Voeller [1976].

Finally, we may add

(T10) *Determinateness Test* If any scalar argument in p tends to zero (or plus infinity), then p tends to a unique positive real number.

As Samuelson and Swamy [1974] eloquently argue, this test should not be applied to economic index numbers (to which we shall now turn our attention) since it violates the fundamental assumption of nonsatiation.

III. Economic Index Numbers

5. We begin with the case of an *explicit* utility function

$$u\colon \mathbb{R}^n_{++} \to \mathbb{R}, \qquad (X) \to u(f(X)), \quad u' > 0, \tag{17}$$

with the usual regularity conditions on u, such as the monotonicity and strict quasi-concavity conditions. From the analysis of the previous sections (Theorems 2, 3, and 7), it is seen that the index number must be expressed in the ratio form, if it is to simultaneously satisfy the circular test, the homogeneity test, etc. This will justify the following definitions of economic index numbers.

Definition (*Economic Price Index*—Samuelson and Swamy [1974]) The economic price index must equal the ratio of the (minimum) costs of a given level of living in two price situations, i.e.,

$$p\colon \mathbb{R}^{2n}_{++} \to \mathbb{R}_{++}|_{u=\text{const}}, \qquad (P^0, P^1 : u = \bar{u}) \to p(P^0, P^1 : u = \bar{u}), \tag{18}$$

$$p = \frac{e(P^1 : u = \bar{u})}{e(P^0 : u = \bar{u})} = \frac{e(P^1 : \bar{X})}{e(P^0 : \bar{X})}, \tag{18$'$}$$

where by definition

$$e(P : u = \bar{u}) = \min_X PX,$$

given $u(X) = \bar{u}$. (19)

Definition (*Economic Quantity Index*) The economic quantity index must equal the ratio of the minimum expenditure needed, in the face of a given price situation, to buy their respective levels of well-being; i.e.,

$$q\colon \mathbb{R}^{2n}_{++} \to \mathbb{R}_{++}|_{P=\text{const}}, \qquad (X^0, X^1 : P = \bar{P}) \to q(X^0, X^1 : P = \bar{P}), \tag{20}$$

q satisfying

$$q = \frac{e(u(X^1) : P = \bar{P})}{e(u(X^0) : P = \bar{P})} = \frac{e(X^1 : \bar{P})}{e(X^0 : \bar{P})}, \tag{20$'$}$$

where e is defined by (19).

For completeness we present

Theorem 8 (*Homogeneity Price and Quantity Theorem*—Samuelson and Swamy [1974]) *If and only if preferences are homothetic, p in* (18′) *and q in* (20′) *are invariant in the sense that*

$$\partial p/\partial \bar{x}_i \equiv 0 \tag{21-i}$$

and

$$\partial q/\partial \bar{p}_i \equiv 0, \; 1 \leqq i \leqq n, \tag{21-ii}$$

i.e.,

$$p = e(P^1)/e(P^0) \tag{22-i}$$

and

$$q = e(X^1)/e(X^0). \tag{22-ii}$$

Proof This result is the direct consequence of the *Corollary to Lemma* 1 in Chapter 6, i.e., $e = g(p)u(X)$. Furthermore, by reducing the utility function to its normal form $u(X) = \lambda^{-1}u(\lambda X)$, we can say that $e(X)$ is homogeneous of degree one with respect to X, as is $e(P)$ with respect to P. Q.E.D.

6. In view of the Corollary to Theorem 3 (homogeneous ratio form and basic axioms) in Part II, (22-i) and (22-ii) both satisfy the basic four axioms of the index number (A1)–(A4). Also, it is readily seen that p and q satisfy proportionality test (T1), homogeneity-of-degree-minus-one test (T2), mean value test (T3), circular reversal test (T4), time reversal test (T5), and factor-reversal test (T9) [in a weak form (4-ix′)]. We shall show that (4-ix′) is automatically satisfied with

$$pq = \frac{e(P^1)}{e(P^0)}\frac{e(X^1)}{e(X^1)}\frac{e(X^1)}{e(X^0)}\frac{e(P^0)}{e(P^0)} = \frac{e(P^1)e(X^1)}{e(P^0)e(X^0)} = \frac{e^1}{e^0} = \frac{P^1X^1}{P^0X^0}.$$

The question arises: Under what conditions will the strong-form of (T9) be met? Here the answer depends on the results of Chapter 6, self-duality of cost and production (in particular the Corollary to Theorem 5, Chapter 6). We then have

Theorem 9 (*Factor-Reversal Test or Strong Self-Duality Test*) *A homothetic preference ordering satisfies the factor-reversal or strong self-duality test, Eq.* (4-ix), *if and only if there exist* $(n - 1)$ *functions*

$$H^j(x_1/x_s, \ldots, x_n/x_s; p_1/p_s, \ldots, p_n/p_s) = 0, \qquad 1 \leqq j \leqq n - 1,$$

or

$$H^j(X_s, P_s) = 0 \qquad \textit{for any} \quad s, \quad 1 \leqq s \leqq n, \tag{23}$$

such that they satisfy the symmetry conditions

$$H^j(X_s, P_s) \equiv |H^j(P_s, X_s)|, \qquad 1 \leqq j \leqq n-1, \tag{24}$$

where $p_i/p_s = u_i/u_s$, $1 \leqq i, s \leqq n$, *are the marginal rates of substitution between* i *and* s *in* u.

Proof This is the direct consequence of the Corollary to Theorem 3 in Chapter 6, which guarantees the existence of the strongly self-dual utility and expenditure functions. We have implicitly assumed that u_i/u_s are the marginal rates of substitution, satisfying the integrability conditions. Q.E.D.

As an example other than the Cobb–Douglas type of utility function, consider a special case of example (b) in Chapter 6, Part VII ,when u is not an implicit function; i.e.,

$$H^1 = (x_1/x_2) + (p_1/p_2) - b = 0, \qquad b = \text{const} > 0, \qquad n = 2.$$

Then $x_1/x_2 = b - p_1/p_2$ and $p_1/p_2 = u_1/u_2 = b - x_1/x_2$, which are *explicitly* self-dual when $b =$ const. Integrating the total differential equation for x_1 and x_2, we get the underlying utility function from

$$\left(b - \frac{x_1}{x_2}\right) dx_1 + dx_2 = 0$$

since

$$\log u = \log x_1 + \tfrac{1}{2}\log\left(\frac{x_2^2}{x_1^2} + b\frac{x_2}{x_1} - 1\right) + \frac{b}{2\sqrt{b^2+4}}\log\frac{2(x_2/x_1) + b + \sqrt{b^2+4}}{2(x_2/x_1) + b - \sqrt{b^2+4}}.$$

The expenditure function associated with the preceding utility function is

$$e = p_1\left(\frac{p_2^2}{p_1^2} + b\frac{p_2}{p_1} - 1\right)^{1/2}\left(\frac{2(p_2/p_1) + b + \sqrt{b^2+4}}{2(p_2/p_1) + b - \sqrt{b^2+4}}\right)^{b/2(b^2+4)^{1/2}} u.$$

The price index number is then

$$p = \frac{e(P^1)}{e(P^0)} = \frac{p_1^1\left(\left(\dfrac{p_2^1}{p_1^1}\right)^2 + b\dfrac{p_2^1}{p_1^1} - 1\right)^{1/2}\left(\dfrac{2(p_2^1/p_1^1) + b + \sqrt{b^2+4}}{2(p_2^1/p_1^1) + b - \sqrt{b^2+4}}\right)^{b/2(b^2+4)^{1/2}}}{p_1^0\left(\left(\dfrac{p_2^0}{p_1^0}\right)^2 + b\dfrac{p_2^0}{p_1^0} - 1\right)^{1/2}\left(\dfrac{2(p_2^0/p_1^1) + b + \sqrt{b^2+4}}{2(p_2^0/p_1^0) + b - \sqrt{b^2+4}}\right)^{b/2(b^2+4)^{1/2}}}$$

which is exactly identical with the quantity index number q with P replaced by X in the foregoing formula.

The preceding theorem can be relaxed when we introduce the concept of *weak self-duality* (weak factor-reversal test) by defining some meaningful parameters $a = (a_1, \ldots, a_r)$ in (23). We simply state

Theorem 9' *(Weak Factor-Reversal Test) A homothetic preference ordering satisfies the weak factor-reversal test or weak self-duality test if and only if there exist* $(n-1)$ *functions with r parameters* $a = (a_1, \ldots, a_r)$,

$$H^j(X_s, P_s : a), \quad 1 \leqq j \leqq n-1 \quad \text{for any} \quad 1 \leqq s \leqq n, \tag{23'}$$

such that

$$H^j(X_s, P_s : \bar{a}) \equiv |H^j(P_s; X_s : \bar{a})|, \qquad 1 \leqq j \leqq n-1, \tag{24'}$$

where $\bar{a} = (\bar{a}_1, \ldots, \bar{a}_r)$, $\bar{a}_k$ *is the particular value of* a_k $(1 \leqq k \leqq r)$, *and the* H^j *satisfy the same conditions as those in Theorem* 9.

Proof The proof is omitted (see weak self-duality conditions in Chapter 6). Q.E.D.

Although the following seems obvious from Lemma 1 in Chapter 6, it may be of some interest to formulate it as a theorem.

Theorem 10 *(Impossibility of Strong Form of Factor-Reversal Test* (4-ix) *for Nonhomothetic Preferences) There exist "no" price and quantity index numbers which are self-dual if preference orderings are explicitly nonhomothetic.*

Proof This is the alternative way of stating the fact that p is always linear and homogeneous in P^1, but q is never homogeneous in X^1 by assumption. This violates the necessary condition for self-duality in Chapter 6. Q.E.D.

But nonhomothetic (explicit) utility functions will yield price indices (but not quantity indices always) which satisfy most of the foregoing tests. This, of course, corresponds with the statement by Samuelson and Swamy about the nonsymmetry properties of these two index numbers p and q.

Implicit Utility Functions

7. We now turn our attention to the case of *implicit* utility function,

$$F[C_1(u), \ldots, C_n(u); X] = 0. \tag{25}$$

We shall stress here that F involves n essential parameters $C_1, \ldots, C_n$ such that $F(\bar{C}; X) = 0$ defines ∞^n curves for all choices of $\bar{C}$ and $F(C; \bar{X}) = 0$ defines ∞^n curves for all choices of $\bar{X}$. Also, we assume that F is concave, increasing in X and decreasing in u. In view of the conditions of essential parameters (Appendix, Theorem 1), we must assume that

$$\Delta = \begin{vmatrix} 0 & F_{x_1} & \cdots & F_{x_n} \\ F_{C_1} & F_{x_1 C_1} & \cdots & F_{x_n C_1} \\ \vdots & \vdots & & \vdots \\ F_{C_n} & F_{x_1 C_n} & \cdots & F_{x_n C_n} \end{vmatrix} \neq 0 \qquad \text{when} \quad F = 0, \tag{26}$$

where $F_{x_i} = \partial F/\partial x_i$, $F_{C_i} = \partial F/\partial C_i$, $F_{x_i C_j} = \partial F/\partial x_i \, \partial C_j$, $1 \leqq i, j \leqq n$. The foregoing condition will guarantee that

$$\sum_{i=1}^{n} \psi_i(C) \, \partial F/\partial C_i \neq 0, \tag{26$'$}$$

which is the necessary and sufficient condition for $C_1, \ldots, C_n$ to be *essential* (Appendix, Theorem 1). Obviously, we are assuming that in general

$$\partial C_i/\partial u \neq 0, \qquad 1 \leqq i \leqq n. \tag{27}$$

Conditions (26) and (27) force us to say that *the implicit function* (25) *in general cannot be "expressed" in an explicit form.*

As far as the price index is concerned, the above formulation of a utility function does *not* change the basic properties of the index number, provided that Eq. (18′) is simply

$$p = \frac{e(P^1 : u = \bar{u})}{e(P^0 : u = \bar{u})} \tag{18$''$}$$

and *cannot* in general be expressed as a function of $\bar{X}$ explicitly. This does not, however, prevent us from applying all the necessary tests mentioned in the foregoing. Thus, p in (18″) satisfies (T1)–(T5) for any given $\bar{u}$. However, there is a serious problem regarding the factor-reversal test (T9), because of the very problem that *the quantity index number cannot be expressed in an explicit form.* That is to say, the quantity index

$$q = \frac{e(u^1(X^1) : P = \bar{P})}{e(u^0(X^0) : P = \bar{P})} \tag{20$''$}$$

is obtained from *implicitly* solving the functions

$$F[C(u^1); X^1] = 0 \tag{25-i}$$

and

$$F[C(u^0); X^0] = 0 \tag{25-ii}$$

We can still say that (20″) under (25-i) and (25-ii) satisfies circular-reversal test (T4) and time-reversal test (T5), since it is expressed in the ratio form, but not the other basic tests such as (T1) (proportionality test) and (T2) (homogeneity-of-degree-minus-one test). In particular, it fails to satisfy the (strong) factor-reversal test, since p in (18″) and q in (20″) are not expressible in the same mathematical form. This would require an alternative and new definition of the quantity index, to which we now turn.

IV. Alternative Definition of the Quantity Index Number—"Dual Quantity Index"

8. Looking at the procedure to derive the price index number from the (direct) utility function, we may utilize the duality principle involved in the (indirect) utility function. That is to say, we know that there always exists the indirect utility function $u^*\colon \mathbb{R}^n_{++} \to \mathbb{R}$ such that

$$u^*(P/e) = \max_X \{u(X) \text{ subject to } (P/e)X = 1\}. \tag{28}$$

It may be more convenient to utilize the complete symmetry suggested by defining

$$-u^* = v(P), \tag{28$'$}$$

where e is set to be equal to unity. For any given direct utility function (explicit or implicit), there exists a unique $v(P)$ such that v is (strictly) quasi-concave, (non)decreasing, and continuous like $u(X)$. Therefore, rather than starting with the implicit direct utility function, we may assume that its dual, the implicit *indirect* utility function, is given as

$$G[D_1(v), \ldots, D_n(v); P] = 0, \tag{29}$$

where G involves n essential parameters $D_1, \ldots, D_n$ satisfying the condition similar to (26). We can look at (29) as the "cost" condition at a given level of v. Then using the Legendre transformation (see Chapter 9, Section 29), we define

Definition ("*Dual Quantity Index*") The dual quantity index q^* for X^0 and X^1 is defined as the ratio of the minimum expenditure (with respect to P) needed to attain their respective highest standards of living at a given "cost" condition. Thus we define

$$q^* = \frac{e^*(X^1 : v = \bar{v})}{e^*(X^0 : v = \bar{v})}, \tag{30}$$

where

$$e^*(X : v = \bar{v}) = \min_P XP \qquad \text{such that} \quad v = \bar{v} \text{ in (29).} \tag{31}$$

Note that q^* *is completely dual to the price index defined by* (18′), *with P and X, and u and v interchanged.*

Alternatively, we can define the "dual" quantity index as *the ratio of the maximum income (standard of living) for given X^0 and X^1 under a given cost condition.* Thus,

$$q^* = \frac{I(X^1 : u^* = \bar{u}^*)}{I(X^0 : u^* = \bar{u}^*)}, \tag{30′}$$

where

$$I(X : u^* = \bar{u}) = \max_P XP \qquad \text{such that} \quad -v = u^* = \bar{u}^* \text{ in (29).} \tag{31′}$$

If we look at the implicit indirect utility function (29) as the unit "cost" function

$$1 - G[D(v) : P] = 0, \tag{29′}$$

then the "dual" quantity index can be obtained from

$$e^* = \min_P XP \qquad \text{given (29′)} \quad \text{at} \quad v = \bar{v}. \tag{31″}$$

Economic interpretation of q^* is obvious. Consider the two bundles X^0 and X^1. The problem of constructing the quantity index that measures the relative standards of living can be viewed as that of selecting (shadow) prices P at a given cost condition specified by the indirect utility function, which minimizes the total expenditure at a given X. We are now in a position to show that q^* like p satisfies most of the required tests.

Theorem 11 (*Properties of Dual Quantity Index*) *The dual quantity index defined by* (30) *satisfies* (T1)–(T5) *with P replaced by X in these tests.*

Proof From the definition of (31), we get $x_i/x_j = G_i/G_j$, $G_i = \partial G/\partial p_i$, and $G_j = \partial G/\partial p_j$. Together with $G[D(\bar{v}) : \mathrm{P}] = 0$, we solve for $p_i = g^i[X : D(\bar{v})]$, where g^i is the homogeneous degree zero with respect to X. Substituting the p_i into XP, we get $e^* = e^*(X : \bar{v})$, which is a homogeneous concave function of degree one with respect to X. This is the requirement for (T1). Since q^* is expressed in the ratio form it satisfies (T2)–(T5) (Theorem 3). Q.E.D.

Theorem 12 (*Homothetic Preference*) *If and only if preference orderings are (explicitly) homothetic, the dual quantity index is invariant under changes in the cost condition P.*

Proof This follows from the fact that q^* can be written as the product form if and only if preferences are homothetic, i.e.,

$$q^* = \frac{e^*(X^1 : v = \bar{v})}{e^*(X^0 : v = \bar{v})} = \frac{q(X^1)h(\bar{v})}{q(X^0)h(\bar{v})} = \frac{q(X^1)}{q(X^0)}. \qquad \text{Q.E.D.}$$

Corollary to Theorem 12 (*Quantity Index in the Homothetic Case*) *If and only if the preference ordering is homothetic* (*homogeneous*), *the dual quantity index* q^* *defined by* (30) *is equal to the original quantity index defined by* (20′).

Proof This follows from the fact that q^* is homogeneous of degree one with respect to X^1 for any preference ordering (homothetic or nonhomothetic, explicit or implicit), while q in (20′) can never be homogeneous degree one unless the underlying preference is homothetic (homogeneous degree one) (see Samuelson and Swamy [1974, Eq. (5.6)]). Q.E.D.

It is seen that the dual quantity index, therefore, has more satisfactory properties than q since it is completely *symmetric* with the price index (18′).

Turning our attention now to the factor-reversal test, we can show that q^* and p do satisfy the weak form of the factor-reversal test. This can be seen from

$$pq^* = \frac{e(P^1 : u = \bar{u})}{e(P^0 : u = \bar{u})} \frac{e^*(X^1 : v = \bar{v})}{e^*(X^0 : v = \bar{v})} = \frac{P^1X^1}{P^0X^1} \frac{P^0X^1}{P^0X^0} = \frac{P^1X^1}{P^0X^0} = \frac{e^1}{e^0}, \tag{32}$$

at $\bar{u} = u(X^1)$ and $\bar{v} = v(P^0)$.

p and q^* are symmetric in the sense that $F[C(u) : X] = 0$ and $G[D(v) : P] = 0$ are symmetric, with the latter reflecting all the properties of the former and vice versa. Although F and G are mirror images of one another, they may not be homogeneous functions. One advantage of p and q^* is that they are both (implicitly) homogeneous of degree one, with p being the mirror image of G and q^*, the mirror image of F. For any given P^0 and X^0, p and q^* are expressed as

$$p = p[P : C(u)], \qquad \lambda p = p[\lambda P : C(u)], \tag{33-i}$$

$$q^* = q^*[X : D(v)], \qquad \lambda q^* = q^*[\lambda X : D(v)], \tag{33-ii}$$

where p and q^* satisfy the homogeneity-of-degree-one condition for any given $C(u)$ and $D(v)$. Thus p and q^* are implicitly homogeneous degree one.

Lemma (*Necessary Condition for Implicit Self-Duality*) *p and q^* satisfy the necessary condition of* (*strong*) *self-duality of the cost and production functions.*

Proof This is nothing but the necessary condition for self-duality condition for the production and cost functions derived in Chapter 6. Q.E.D.

Theorem 13 (*Strong Self-Duality and Strong Factor-Reversal Test*) *p and q^* satisfy the condition of strong self-duality* (*strong factor-reversal test*) *if and only if there exist* $(n - 1)$ *functions satisfying the conditions*

$$H[X, P : E(\bar{u} = -\bar{v})] = 0 \tag{34}$$

such that

$$H[X, P : E(\bar{u} = -\bar{v})] = |H[P, X : E(\bar{u} = -\bar{v})]| = 0, \tag{35}$$

where X and P are the coefficients for the total differential equations for p and q^*, respectively, and they satisfy the integrability conditions.

Proof This is the direct consequence of Theorem 5, Chapter 6. Q.E.D.

Example As an example of the foregoing theorem, consider the implicit Cobb–Douglas direct utility function

$$F = \prod_{i=1}^{n} x_i^{C_i(u)} - 1 = 0, \qquad \sum_{i=1}^{n} C_i(u) = 1.$$

The indirect utility function is implicitly self-dual as shown by

$$F^* = \prod_{i=1}^{n} D_i(u) y_i^{-C_i(u)} - 1 = 0, \qquad D_i = C_i^{C_i}, \quad y_i = p_i/e.$$

Solving for e from the above, we get the price index p as

$$p = \prod_{i=1}^{n} p_i^{1 C_i(\bar{u})} \Big/ \prod_{i=1}^{n} p_i^{0 C_i(\bar{u})}.$$

The original quantity index defined by (20′) is

$$q = \prod_{i=1}^{n} p_i^{0 C_i(u(X^1))} \Big/ \prod_{i=1}^{n} p_i^{0 C_i(u(X^0))}.$$

Using $-F^* = 1 - \prod_{i=1}^{n} D_i(u(v)) y_i^{-C_i(u(v))} = 0$, we can derive the "dual" quantity index from $\min_P XP$ subject to $-F^* = 0$ at some given $v = \bar{v}$. From $x_j/x_i = C_j p_i / C_i p_j$ together with $-F^* = 0$, we get the p_i, and then substituting them into XP, we obtain the dual quantity index

$$q^* = \prod_{i=1}^{n} x_i^{1 C_i(\bar{v})} \Big/ \prod_{i=1}^{n} x_i^{0 C_i(\bar{v})}.$$

Note that since in this case the direct utility is already assumed to be implicitly homogeneous of degree one, q^* turns out to be nothing but the ratio of the F at a given $v = \bar{v}$. One can easily see that p and q^* are strongly self-dual and thus satisfies the strong factor-reversal test (4-ix). In many cases, the actual p and q^* do not, and need not, satisfy this *strong* condition, but they are the right match as good price and quantity indices, because of the very symmetric property of these indices regardless of whether preference orderings are expressed explicitly or implicitly. There is an obvious inherent difficulty in giving an economic interpretation to the dual quantity index from the point of view of the revealed preference approach.

V. Invariant Index Numbers under Taste Change

9. The recent work by Fisher and Shell [1972] on the study of taste change in index numbers has greatly contributed to our understanding of the effects of taste change on index numbers. Our purpose here is to use some of the basic results in earlier chapters and show that some index numbers are invariant under specific types of taste change.

Given the utility function

$$u = u(X, t), \tag{36}$$

where t represents an index of exogenous taste change, the price index number derived from (36) must in general be a function of t. Then we are interested in showing specifically under what conditions the price index (or quantity index) is invariant under the taste change in the sense

$$\partial p/\partial t \equiv 0 \qquad \text{at} \quad u = \bar{u}. \tag{37}$$

Here it is obvious that since p is expressed as the ratio of two minimum expenditures, the factor involving t must be expressed as the multiplicative form. But this is nothing but a specific case of "holotheticity" studied in earlier chapters.

Definition 1 (*Invariance of the Price Index under Taste Change at a Given Level of Utility*) The price index is said to be *invariant under taste change at a given level of utility* if

$$p = \frac{\alpha(t)e(P^1 : \bar{u})}{\alpha(t)e(P^0 : \bar{u})} = \frac{e(P^1 : \bar{u})}{e(P^0 : \bar{u})}. \tag{38}$$

Note here that the invariance condition assumes that $u = \text{const} = \bar{u}$.

We begin with the case of explicit representation of utility index function (36). In view of Theorem 7 in Chapter 6, we can formulate

Theorem 14 (*Equiproportionate Taste Change*) *If and only if taste change in any preference ordering* (36) *is of the equiproportionate and uniform magnification type,*

$$u = u[A(t)x_1, \ldots, A(t)x_n], \tag{36'}$$

then the price index is invariant in the sense of (38).

Proof If and only if taste change is equiproportionate, the expenditure function can be expressed as

$$e = (1/A(t))g(P : \bar{u}) = \alpha(t)g(P : \bar{u}), \qquad \alpha(t) = 1/A(t), \tag{39}$$

because of Theorem 7 in Chapter 6. This can be seen from the compensated demand function

$$x_i = f^i(P:\bar{u})(1/A(t)).$$

By forming the ratio function from (39), we get the index number

$$p = \frac{\alpha(t)g(P^1:\bar{u})}{\alpha(t)g(P^0:\bar{u})} = \frac{e(P^1:\bar{u})}{e(P^0:\bar{u})}. \qquad \text{Q.E.D..}$$

Definition 2 (*Absolute Invariance of the Price Index under Taste Change*) The price index is said to be *absolutely invariant under taste change for any levels of utility* if

$$\partial p/\partial t \equiv 0 \qquad \text{for any } X \text{ and any } t, \tag{40}$$

i.e., if p satisfies

$$p = \frac{\alpha(t)e(P^1:u(X,t))}{\alpha(t)e(P^0:u(X,t))} = \frac{e(P^1:X)}{e(P^0:X)}. \tag{40'}$$

Theorem 15 (*Homothetic Preference and Absolute Invariance*) *If and only if the preference ordering is homothetic, and taste change is equiproportionate, then the price index is absolutely invariant under the taste change. That is to say, if and only if*

$$u = F[f(A(t)X)], \qquad f = \lambda^{-1}f(\lambda X), \tag{41}$$

then

$$p = \frac{\alpha(t)g(P^1)h[u(A(t)X)]}{\alpha(t)g(P^0)h[u(A(t)X)]} = \frac{g(P^1)}{g(P^0)} = \frac{e(P^1)}{e(P^0)}. \tag{42}$$

Proof This is the direct consequence of the results of Theorems 8 and 14. Q.E.D.

Let us now turn our attention to the case of implicit representation of the preference ordering,

$$F[X, t: C(u)] = 0. \tag{43}$$

As written in Chapter 6, it is actually more convenient to express (43) in the form

$$F[X, t: C_1(u), \ldots, C_{n-1}(u)] = C_n(u). \tag{43'}$$

Theorem 16 (*Equiproportionate Taste Change*) *If and only if taste change in (43′) is equiproportionate, then the price index is invariant under that type of taste change at a given utility level*

$$p = \frac{\alpha(t)e[P^1: C_1(\bar{u}), \ldots, C_n(\bar{u})]}{\alpha(t)e[P^0: C_1(\bar{u}), \ldots, C_n(\bar{u})]} = \frac{e(P^1:\bar{u})}{e(P^0:\bar{u})}.$$

Proof Again this is a direct consequence of Theorem 7 in Chapter 6. Q.E.D.

Theorem 17 *(Implicit Homotheticity and Invariance of p under Taste Change) If and only if the preference ordering is implicitly homothetic and taste change is equiproportionate,*

$$\begin{aligned} F[A(t)X : C_1(u), \ldots, C_{n-1}(u)] &= F[X : C_1(u), \ldots, C_{n-1}(u)]A(t) \\ &= A(t)C_n(u), \end{aligned} \tag{44}$$

then price index can be written as

$$\begin{aligned} p &= \frac{e[P^1 : C_1(\bar{u}), \ldots, C_{n-1}(\bar{u})]A^{-1}C_n(\bar{u})}{e[P^0 : C_1(\bar{u}), \ldots, C_{n-1}(\bar{u})]A^{-1}C_n(\bar{u})} \\ &= \frac{e[P^1 : C_1(\bar{u}), \ldots, C_{n-1}(\bar{u})]}{e[P^0 : C_1(\bar{u}), \ldots, C_{n-1}(\bar{u})]}. \end{aligned} \tag{45}$$

Proof This is due to Corollary to Theorem 7 of Chapter 6. Q.E.D.

Remark Obviously, when (44) is explicitly homothetic, the results reduce to Theorem 15.

Everything that we have said regarding the price index can be applied to the "dual" quantity index by substituting the "equiproportionate taste change in prices $\sum_i^n p_i\, \partial/\partial p_i$" for the "equiproportionate taste changes in quantities $\sum_i^n x_i\, \partial/\partial x_i$" and by substituting the *indirect* utility function (explicit or implicit) for the *direct* utility function. This is left to the interested reader as an exercise.

VI. Dynamic Invariance (Symmetry) of Divisia Index Numbers

Static Invariance

10. Finally, we present analysis of the so-called Divisia index numbers. The Divisia index number is defined as[5]

$$\begin{aligned} D(x) &= \exp \int_{t_0}^{t_1} \left(\sum_{k=1}^{n} \frac{p_k(x(t))x_k(t)}{\sum_{j=1}^n p_j(x(t))x_j(t)} \frac{\dot{x}_k(t)}{x_k(t)} \right) dt \\ &= \exp \int_{t_0}^{t_1} \left(\sum_{k=1}^{n} \frac{p_k(x(t))\dot{x}_k(t)}{\sum_{j=1}^n p_j(x(t))x_j(t)} \right) dt, \end{aligned} \tag{46}$$

[5] The Divisia price index is defined exactly in the same form as (46) by simply interchanging the p with the x in (46).

or alternatively,

$$\log D(x) = \delta(x) = \int_{t_0}^{t_1} \left(\sum_{k=1}^{n} \frac{p_k(x(t))\dot{x}_k(t)}{\sum_{j=1}^{n} p_j(x(t))x_j(t)} \right) dt, \tag{46'}$$

where $x(t)$ is the quantity vector $(x_1(t), \ldots, x_n(t))$, and $p(t)$ the price vector $(p_1(t), \ldots, p_n(t))$.[6]

The problem that we are concerned with here is different from that studied in the existing literature. However, before we take up our problem, we shall present a summary of the existing results. Most of the past works are concerned with the *path independence property* of Divisia index numbers (Samuelson and Swamy [1974], Richter [1966], Hulten [1973], Hillinger [1970], Ville [1946], Wold [1952]). That is to say, they deal with the existence condition of a function $\phi(x)$ such that

$$\sum_{k=1}^{n} (p_k(x)\, dx_k) \Big/ \sum_{j=1}^{n} p_j(x)x_j$$

is the total (exact) differential $d\phi$ of ϕ; i.e.,

$$\sum_{k=1}^{n} (p_k(x)\, dx_k) \Big/ \sum_{j=1}^{n} p_j(x)x_j = d\phi, \tag{47}$$

where

$$p_k(x) \Big/ \sum_{j=1}^{n} p_j(x)x_j = \frac{\partial \phi}{\partial x_k}, \qquad k = 1, \ldots, n. \tag{48}$$

Hence, the line integral

$$\int_C \left(\sum_{k=1}^{n} (p_k(x)\, dx_k) \Big/ \sum_{j=1}^{n} p_j(x)x_j \right) \tag{46''}$$

taken along the curve C in $\mathbb{R}$ is *independent* of the particular choice of the path C and is determined solely by the initial and final point of the curve C if and only if (48) is met. Alternatively, the path independence condition is stated as the *closed cycle condition that the integral round a closed curve has the value zero.* This is the main reason the path independence condition is often referred to as the "path invariance" condition (Samuelson and Swamy [1974]) or as the "closed cycle condition" (Ville [1946]). The path invariance and closed cycle condition are closely related to the "condition of integrability." Thus, if $\mathbb{R}$ is a simply connected open region,[7] a necessary and

[6] Since there is no need to distinguish different base years, we use small letters $x(t)$ and $p(t)$ for vector notations.

[7] For example, a two-dimensional open region is said to be *simply connected* if every closed polygon within it can, by a continuous deformation within the region, be made to shrink up to a point. Hence there are no "holes" in $\mathbb{R}$.

sufficient condition that the line integral (46″) be independent of the path C joining two given points in $\mathbb{R}$ is that the coefficients of dx_k in (47) satisfy the *integrability conditions*

$$\operatorname{curl} A = 0, \tag{48'}$$

where $A = \operatorname{grad} \phi$ and $\phi = \log f$. Hence we see that the path independence condition, path invariance condition, closed cycle condition, and integrability condition all imply the same requirement that ϕ is the total differential of (47).

There is another concept of "invariance" of the Divisia index developed by Richter [1966]. Richter's recent study has shown that the Divisia index is the only index satisfying a reasonable set of axioms, at the center of which is the "axiom of invariance." This axiom is in general different from the "path invariance" property of the line integral. Richter's invariance axiom requires that the value of the Divisia index does not change as long as the path of the xs lies entirely along a given level set (e.g., indifference curve or isoquant) over the time interval t_0 and t_1. That is to say, along a given level set Eq. (47) is equal to zero

$$\sum_{k=1}^{n} \left(p_k(x)\, dx_k \Big/ \sum_{j=1}^{n} p_j(x) x_j \right) = 0. \tag{47'}$$

Hence the *invariance axiom* simply requires that there exists the total differential equation of the form (47′). Then it is obvious that the path independence condition automatically implies the invariance axiom since $d\phi$ is equal to zero along a given level set (Hulten [1973]). But the converse is not always true unless the integrability conditions are satisfied. It is known that the only function which satisfies the path independency condition of the Divisia index, therefore also the invariance axiom, is a class of linear homogeneous (or in general homothetic) functions ϕ. This is easily seen from the fact that the denominator of (47′) is the integrating factor of a total differential equation $\sum_{k=1}^{n} p_k(x)\, dx_k = 0$, where $p_k(x)$ are homogeneous functions of degree zero.

For completeness we write these results in the following

Theorem 18 (*Path Independence Condition*) (i) *If and only if*

$$\sum_{k=1}^{n} \left(p_k(x)\, dx_k \Big/ \sum_{j=1}^{n} p_j(x) x_j \right)$$

is the exact total differential $d\phi$ of ϕ, then the Divisia index (46) *or* (46′) *is path independent.*

(ii) *If and only if the line integral* (46″) *around a closed curve has the value zero—closed cycle condition, then the Divisia index is path independent.*

(iii) *If and only if the coefficients of dx_k in (47) satisfy the integrability conditions (48′), then the Divisia index is path independent.*

(iv) *If and only if $\sum_{k=1}^{n} (p_k(x)\, dx_k / \sum_{j=1}^{n} p_j(x)x_j)$ is equal to zero along a given level set, then the "invariance axiom" is satisfied.*

(v) *If the Divisia index is path independent, then the invariance axiom is automatically satisfied.*

(vi) *The only function which satisfies the path independency condition is a class of linearly homogeneous (or in general homothetic) functions ϕ.*

Dynamic Invariance

11. The path independency condition is basically a problem of static behavior. As stated earlier, our concern here is to study the invariance property of dynamic behavior. It may conveniently be called as the *dynamic invariance property* of the Divisia index number. This property is often referred to as the *dynamic symmetry condition* in natural sciences. We use them interchangeably. Consider a one-parameter family (or group) of transformations

$$\bar{t} = \phi(t, x, \varepsilon), \tag{49-i}$$

$$\bar{x}_i = \psi^i(t, x, \varepsilon), \qquad i = 1, \dots, n, \tag{49-ii}$$

where $\phi(t, x, \varepsilon)$ may be considered as the transformation of the "objective" time to a "subjective" time (Samuelson [1976]) and $\psi^1(t, x, \varepsilon)$ are technical progress (or taste change) functions for the x induced by the parameter ε. We assume that ϕ and $\psi \in C^2$ in an $(n + 2)$-dimensional domain that will contain the interval $[t_0, t_1]$ of values t, some interval $(\varepsilon_1, \varepsilon_2)$ of values ε, and the entire x space. More specifically, we may sometimes assume that (49) constitute a Lie group with the infinitesimal transformations[8] τ and ξ^i, i.e.,

$$\bar{t} = t + \varepsilon\tau(t, x), \tag{49-i′}$$

$$\bar{x}_i = x_i + \varepsilon\xi^i(t, x), \qquad i = 1, \dots, n, \tag{49-ii′}$$

where $\tau(t, x) = \partial\phi/\partial\varepsilon|_{\varepsilon_0}$ and $\xi^i = \partial\psi^i/\partial\varepsilon|_{\varepsilon_0}$, and ε_0 is the value of ε corresponding to the identity transformation. Consider any function $x = x(t) \in C^1[t_0, t_1]$ and subject it to the transformations (49) to get $\bar{t} = \phi(t, x(t), \varepsilon)$ and $\bar{x}_i = \psi^i(t, x(t), \varepsilon)$, $i = 1, \dots, n$. We solve the first of the above equations for t: $t = \chi(\bar{t}, \varepsilon)$ and substitute the result in the second equations

$$\bar{x}_i = \psi^i(\chi(\bar{t}, \varepsilon), x(\chi(\bar{t}, \varepsilon)), \varepsilon) = \bar{x}_i(\bar{t}, \varepsilon).$$

[8] As discussed in the previous chapter, the Lie group assumptions are not necessary to study the dynamic invariance condition.

Thus $\bar{x}_i = \bar{x}_i(\bar{t}, \varepsilon)$ is the image of $x_i = x_i(t)$ under (49). We note that the t coordinates of any two points $(t_0, x(t_0))$, $(t_1, x(t_1))$ on $x = x(t)$ are transformed into

$$\bar{t}_0 = \phi(t_0, x(t_0), \varepsilon) = \bar{t}_0(\varepsilon), \qquad \bar{t}_1 = \phi(t_1, x(t_1), \varepsilon) = \bar{t}_1(\varepsilon).$$

Then we define

The Divisia index $\delta(x)$ in Eq. (46′) is dynamically invariant on $[t_0, t_1]$ under the transformations (49) *if*

$$\int_{t_0}^{t_1}\left(\sum_{k=1}^{n}\frac{p_k(x(t))\dot{x}_k(t)}{\sum_{j=1}^{n} p_j(x(t))x_j(t)}\right)dt = \int_{\bar{t}_0(\varepsilon)}^{\bar{t}_1(\varepsilon)}\left(\sum_{k=1}^{n}\frac{p_k(\bar{x}(\bar{t}, \varepsilon))\, d\bar{x}_k/d\bar{t}}{\sum_{j=1}^{n} p_j(\bar{x}(\bar{t}, \varepsilon))\bar{x}_j(\bar{t}, \varepsilon)}\right)d\bar{t} \tag{50}$$

for any curve $x = x(t) \in C^1[t_0, t_1]$, and for all $\varepsilon \in (\varepsilon_1, \varepsilon_2)$.

Hence the dynamic invariance implies that the value of the Divisia index is constant under the transformations (49). Alternatively, we can define the dynamic invariance of $\delta(x)$ as[9]

$$d\delta(\varepsilon)/d\varepsilon = 0. \tag{50′}$$

Using the concept of holothetic differential equations which we studied in earlier chapters, we see that (50) implies

$$L(\bar{t}, \bar{x}(\bar{t}, \varepsilon), d\bar{x}(\bar{t}, \varepsilon)/d\bar{t})\, d\bar{t}/dt = L(t, x(t), \dot{x}(t)), \tag{50″}$$

where

$$L = \sum_{k=1}^{n}\frac{p_k(x(t))\dot{x}_k(t)}{\sum_{j=1}^{n} p_j(x(t))x_j(t)}. \tag{51}$$

In order to facilitate calculations, we use the summation convention to express L simply as

$$L = \frac{p_k(x(t))\dot{x}_k}{p_j(x(t))x_j(t)} \qquad \text{(summation on } j \text{ and } k,$$

$$j, k, \ldots = 1, 2, \ldots, n). \tag{51′}$$

In view of Noether's theorem (see Chapter 7, Part II), the fundamental invariance identity requires that

$$\frac{\partial L}{\partial t}\tau + \frac{\partial L}{\partial x_i}\xi^i + \frac{\partial L}{\partial \dot{x}_i}\left(\frac{d\xi^i}{dt} - \dot{x}_i\frac{d\tau}{dt}\right) + L\frac{d\tau}{dt} = 0 \qquad \text{(summation on } i\text{)}. \tag{52}$$

[9] Here we are concerned only with the case of "simple" dynamic invariance. In Chapter 7, we presented a more general definition of dynamic invariance. See Definition 2 (Part II), the case of "divergence-invariant."

But since $\partial L/\partial t = 0$ and $(\partial L/\partial \dot{x}_i)\dot{x}_i = L$, (52) is equal to

$$\frac{\partial L}{\partial x_i}\xi^i + \frac{\partial L}{\partial \dot{x}_i}\left(\frac{d\xi^i}{dt}\right) = \frac{\partial L}{\partial x_i}\xi^i + \frac{\partial L}{\partial \dot{x}_i}\left(\frac{\partial \xi^i}{\partial t} + \frac{\partial \xi^i}{\partial x_k}\dot{x}_k\right) = 0. \tag{52'}$$

Calculating the above from (51′), we get

$$\left[\frac{\partial}{\partial x_i}\left(\frac{p_k}{p_j x_j}\right)\xi^i + \left(\frac{p_i}{p_j x_j}\right)\frac{\partial \xi^i}{\partial x_k}\right]\dot{x}_k + \left(\frac{p_i}{p_j x_j}\right)\frac{\partial \xi^i}{\partial t} = 0, \tag{53}$$

which implies

$$\left(\frac{p_i}{p_j x_j}\right)\frac{\partial \xi^i}{\partial t} = 0, \qquad \frac{\partial}{\partial x_i}\left(\frac{p_k}{p_j x_j}\right)\xi^i + \left(\frac{p_i}{p_j x_j}\right)\frac{\partial \xi^i}{\partial x_k} = 0.$$

By setting

$$p_i/p_j x_j = P_i \geqq 0, \tag{54}$$

we write (53) as

$$P_i\, \partial \xi^i/\partial t = 0, \tag{53-i''}$$

$$(\partial P_k/\partial x_i)\xi^i + P_i\, \partial \xi^i/\partial x_k = 0. \tag{53-ii''}$$

We shall refer to (53″) as *the fundamental dynamic invariance conditions of the Divisia index number.*

The foregoing conditions imply that:

(i) Since they do not involve τ, the transformation on t, τ *can be any arbitrary function*

$$\tau = \tau(t, x); \tag{55}$$

(ii) if $P_i(x)$ are *arbitrary* functions, the only transformations which satisfy (53′) must be

$$\partial \xi^i/\partial t = 0, \qquad \partial \xi^i/\partial x_k = 0, \qquad \text{i.e.,} \quad \xi^i = 0. \tag{56}$$

That is to say, there exist no ξ^i. However, the second conclusion is, in general *not* valid, because $P_i(x)$ *cannot* be arbitrary functions if the Divisia index satisfies the *static* condition of path independence and the integrability conditions. Hence we may be able to find meaningful technical progress (taste change) functions for the x_i. Since P_i is nonnegative and by setting $p_i \neq 0$, $p_j = 0$, $i \neq j$, from (53-i′) we conclude that

$$\partial \xi^i/\partial t = 0, \qquad \text{i.e.,} \quad \xi^i = \xi^i(x). \tag{57}$$

Let us now assume that the path invariance condition is satisfied,

$$p_i \dot{x}_i/p_j x_j = d\phi/dt, \qquad \text{i.e.,} \quad P_i = \partial \phi/\partial x_i. \tag{58}$$

Then (53′) imply

$$\frac{\partial \phi}{\partial x_i}\frac{\partial \xi^i}{\partial t} = 0, \qquad \text{i.e.,} \quad \frac{\partial}{\partial t}\left(\frac{\partial \phi}{\partial x_i}\xi^i\right) = 0$$

and

$$\frac{\partial}{\partial x_i}\left(\frac{\partial \phi}{\partial x_k}\right)\xi^i + \frac{\partial \phi}{\partial x_i}\frac{\partial \xi^i}{\partial x_k} = 0, \qquad \text{i.e.,} \quad \frac{\partial}{\partial x_k}\left(\frac{\partial \phi}{\partial x_i}\xi^i\right) = 0,$$

from which we conclude that

$$(\partial \phi/\partial x_i)\xi^i = \text{const} = \text{a}, \qquad \text{summation on } i. \tag{59}$$

We may call this the conservation law of the Divisia index (see Chapter 7). Since $\partial\phi/\partial x_i = p_i/p_j x_j = p_i/$(total expenditure) is relative price of x_i, the conservation law states that *the sum of the products of the relative prices and the effects of taste change is always constant.* It is well known that the only family of functions which satisfy the integrability conditions and, thus, the path invariance condition is the homothetic family (Samuelson and Swamy [1974], Ville [1946], Hulten [1973]). With Ville we choose one special form as

$$\phi = \log f(x_1, \ldots, x_n), \tag{60}$$

where f is homogeneous degree one. Then from the optimality condition $\phi_i - \lambda p_i = 0$ of utility maximization, we have

$$P_i = \frac{p_i}{p_j x_j} = \frac{\phi_i/\lambda}{\phi_j x_j/\lambda} = \frac{\phi_i}{\phi_j x_j} = \frac{f_i/f}{f_j x_j/f} = \frac{f_i}{f_j x_j} = \frac{f_i}{f} = \frac{\partial \phi}{\partial x_i}, \tag{54′}$$

where $f_i = \partial f/\partial x_i$ is homogeneous degree zero. We can show that for Eq. (60), the uniform magnification type of taste change (multiplicative type)

$$\xi^i = a x_i, \qquad a = \text{const} \tag{61}$$

satisfies (59), because we have

$$(\partial\phi/\partial x_i)\xi^i = f_i\xi^i/f = f_i\xi^i/f_j x_j = a f_i x_i/f_j x_j = a. \tag{59′}$$

As a matter of fact, we can show that (61) is the only type which satisfies (59). To prove this assertion we rewrite one of the invariance conditions (53-ii) as

$$\left[\frac{1}{p_j x_j}\frac{\partial p_k}{\partial x_i} - p_k\frac{1}{(p_j x_j)^2}\left(\frac{\partial p_j}{\partial x_i}x_j + p_i\right)\right]\xi^i + \left(\frac{p_i}{p_j x_j}\right)\frac{\partial \xi^i}{\partial x_k} = 0,$$

i.e.,

$$\left[p_j x_j\frac{\partial p_k}{\partial x_i} - p_k\left(\frac{\partial p_j}{\partial x_i}p_j + p_i\right)\right]\xi^i + (p_i x_j)p_i\frac{\partial \xi^i}{\partial x_k} = 0. \tag{62}$$

In the preceding equations, we set $p_1(x) \neq 0$, $p_2(x) = \cdots = p_n(x) = 0$. Then we have

$$\left[p_1 x_1 \frac{\partial p_k}{\partial x_i} \xi^i - p_k\left(\frac{\partial p_1}{\partial x_i} x_1\right)\xi^i - p_k p_1 \xi^1\right] + (p_1 x_1) p_1 \frac{\partial \xi^1}{\partial x_k} = 0.$$

When $k = 1$, this becomes $x_1\, \partial\xi^1/\partial x_1 = \xi^1$, and when $k \neq 1$, it becomes $\partial\xi^1/\partial x_k = 0$ ($p_k \equiv 0$, $k \neq 1$). These two conditions imply that we must have

$$\xi^1 = a_{(1)} x_1, \qquad a_{(1)} = \text{const}.$$

Repeating this process, we obtain

$$\xi^i = a_{(i)} x_i, \qquad a_{(i)} = \text{const} \qquad (\text{no summation on } i).$$

Next in (62) we set $p_1, p_2 \neq 0$, $p_3 = \cdots = p_n = 0$. Then for $k = 1$, we have

$$(p_1 x_1 + p_2 x_2)\frac{\partial p_1}{\partial x_i}\xi^i - p_1\left[\left(\frac{\partial p_1}{\partial x_i} x_1 + \frac{\partial p_2}{\partial x_i} x_2\right)\xi^i + (p_1 \xi^1 + p_2 \xi^2)\right]$$
$$+ (p_1 x_1 + p_2 x_2)\left(p_1 \frac{\partial \xi^1}{\partial x_1} + p_2 \frac{\partial \xi^2}{\partial x_1}\right) = 0.$$

Since $p_1 > 0$ and $p_2 > 0$ and the above is satisfied for all values of p_1 and p_2, it must be satisfied for $p_1 = p_2 \neq 0$. Then for $\xi^1 = a_{(1)} x_1$, $\xi^2 = a_{(2)} x_2$, we must have

$$-(a_{(1)} x_1 + a_{(2)} x_2) + a_{(1)}(x_1 + x_2) = 0, \qquad x_i \neq 0, \quad i = 1, 2,$$

which implies that

$$a_{(1)} = a_{(2)}, \qquad \text{or in general} \qquad a_{(i)} = a_{(j)} = a.$$

Repeating this process, we conclude that (61) is the only transformation which leaves the Divisia index dynamically invariant. In summary, we have

Theorem 19 *(Dynamic Invariance of Divisia Index Numbers)* (i) *The Divisia index has the conservation law* (59). *That is to say, the sum of the values of taste change is constant.*

(ii) *The Divisia index number* (46) *is dynamically invariant under any arbitrary time transformation* (55).

(iii) *The Divisia index number* (46) *with the path invariance condition is dynamically invariant if and only if* (55) *and* (61) *hold. That is to say,* (46) *is dynamically invariant with respect to commodity transformations only under the uniform multiplicative type of taste change* $\bar{x} = e^{a\varepsilon} x$.

Remark (1) It is not surprising to see this result, since we know that the only function which satisfies the path invariance condition is the homothetic family and that the homothetic family is the only function holothetic under the uniform magnification group. Hence, here *the static holotheticity implies the dynamic holotheticity (invariance) at the same time.*

(2) The Divisia index satisfies the so-called "homogeneous problem" of calculus of variations since $L = p_i \dot{x}_i / p_j x_j$ is a homogeneous function with respect to $\dot{x}$. Hence the index (46) is also "parameter invariant" (see Lovelock and Rund [1975, p. 185]). Condition (55) states that the Divisia index is not only "parameter invariant," but also it is time-transformation invariant under *any* $\tau = \tau(t, x)$, $\partial\tau/\partial x \neq 0$.

Turning our attention briefly to the Divisia index of technical progress (Richter [1966], Solow [1957]),

$$D(T) = \exp \int_{t_0}^{t_1} \left(\frac{\dot{Y}}{Y} - \frac{w^i \dot{x}_i}{w^j x_j} \right) dt$$

$$(i, j = 1, \ldots, n, \quad \text{summation convention on } i \text{ and } j), \tag{63}$$

where $\dot{Y}/Y$ is the output index, $w^i \dot{x}_i / w^j x_j$ the input index, w^i the wage rate of x_i, and x_i the ith factor input. Let us assume that *technical progress is a Lie type whose infinitesimal transformation is given by*

$$U = \xi^i(x)\, \partial/\partial x_i \qquad (\text{summation convention on } i). \tag{64}$$

Then from the basic result of Lie group theory (see Chapter 2, Section 34) we can express

$$(\partial Y/\partial t)|_{t=0} = \xi^i(x)\, \partial Y/\partial x_i.$$

Hence, near the identity transformation, we have

$$\frac{\dot{Y}}{Y} - \frac{w^i \dot{x}_i}{w^j x_j} = \left. \frac{\partial Y/\partial t}{Y} \right|_{t=0} = \frac{\xi^i(x)\, \partial Y/\partial x_i}{Y}.$$

Assuming constant returns to scale on Y, this may be expressed as

$$\frac{\dot{Y}}{Y} - \frac{w^i \dot{x}_i}{w^j x_j} = \frac{\xi^i(x)\, \partial Y/\partial x_i}{\partial Y(x_j)/\partial x_j} = \frac{w^i \xi^i}{w^j x_j}.$$

The Divisia index of technical progress when technical progress is a Lie type can now be expressed as

$$D(T) = \exp \int_{t_0}^{t_1} (w^i \xi^i / w^j x_j)\, dt. \tag{65}$$

Obviously, when $\xi^i = a x_i$ (Hicks neutral), then we obtain the exponential index $D(T) = e^{a(t_1 - t_0)}$. Equation (65) may prove useful for empirical analysis once the $\xi^i(x)$ are known, since it does *not* involve $\dot{x}$ and integration is easily performed.

General (or Quasi-) Divisia Index Numbers

12. We now consider a generalization of the Divisia index related to *nonhomothetic* behavior. Let $\mathscr{D}(x)$ be given by

$$\mathscr{D}(x) = \exp \int_{t_0}^{t_1} \left(\sum_{k=1}^{n} \frac{p_k(x)x_k}{(\sum_{j=1}^{n} \alpha_j(x)p_j(x)x_j)} \frac{\dot{x}_k}{x_k} \right) dt. \tag{66}$$

This expression may be called the "general" or "quasi" Divisia index, for when the $\alpha_j(x)$ are identically equal to unity, we obtain the standard Divisia index. The Lagrangian corresponding to (66) is

$$L(t, x, \dot{x}) = \frac{p_k(x)\dot{x}_k}{\alpha_j(x)p_j(x)x_j}$$

$$(j, k, \ldots = 1, \ldots, n, \quad \text{summation convention}) \tag{66$'$}$$

We assume that the α_j and therefore the coefficients

$$Q_k(x) = p_k/\alpha_j p_j x_j \geqq 0 \tag{67}$$

are well-behaved and possess all the desired properties of smoothness, simple-connectedness, etc. In order that $\mathscr{D}(x)$ may be a meaningful index, we also assume that it satisfies the *path independence condition*; i.e.,

$$Q_k(x)\, dx_k = d\phi, \qquad \text{summation on } k. \tag{68}$$

That is to say, we assume that

$$Q_k(x) = \partial\phi/\partial x_k. \tag{68$'$}$$

Hence we assume that the integrability conditions are automatically satisfied, which also implies the axiom of invariance; i.e.,

$$Q_k\, dx_k = 0 \qquad \text{for} \quad \phi = \text{const.} \tag{69}$$

The *dynamic invariance condition* of the quasi-Divisia index must be derived from (52) or (52′), i.e.,

$$\left[\frac{\partial}{\partial x_i}(Q_k)\xi^i + Q_i \frac{\partial \xi^i}{\partial x_k}\right]\dot{x}_k + Q_i \frac{\partial \xi^i}{\partial t} = 0. \tag{70}$$

This implies

$$Q_i \frac{\partial \xi^i}{\partial t} = 0, \tag{70-i$'$}$$

$$\frac{\partial}{\partial x_i}(Q_k)\xi^i + Q_i \frac{\partial \xi^i}{\partial x_k} = 0. \tag{70-ii$'$}$$

Since $Q_i \neq 0$ for $p_i \neq 0$, $\alpha_i \neq 0$ and by setting $Q_j = 0$, $i \neq j$, we immediately conclude

$$\partial \xi^i / \partial t = 0, \qquad \text{i.e.,} \quad \xi^i = \xi^i(x). \tag{71}$$

Calculating further under the assumption of path independence (68′) and under (71), we get

$$\frac{\partial \phi}{\partial x_i} \frac{\partial \xi^i}{\partial t} = 0, \qquad \text{i.e.,} \quad \frac{\partial}{\partial t}\left(\frac{\partial \phi}{\partial x_i} \xi^i\right) = 0, \tag{70-i″}$$

$$\frac{\partial}{\partial x_i}\left(\frac{\partial \phi}{\partial x_k}\right)\xi^i + \frac{\partial \phi}{\partial x_i}\frac{\partial \xi^i}{\partial x_k} = 0, \qquad \text{i.e.,} \quad \frac{\partial}{\partial x_k}\left(\frac{\partial \phi}{\partial x_i} \xi^i\right) = 0, \tag{70-ii″}$$

which in turn implies

$$\Omega = (\partial \phi / \partial x_i)\xi^i = Q_i \xi^i = \text{const} = a. \tag{72}$$

This is the *fundamental invariance condition*[10] of the "general" Divisia index number. This is not affected by $\partial \alpha_j / \partial x_i \neq 0$ since we have already obtained the same expression for the simple Divisia index [Eq. (59)]. Actual derivation of the group of transformations now depends on how $\alpha_j(x)$ is specified.

A special case will be studied by assuming that $\alpha_j = \text{const}$ for all $j = 1, \ldots, n$. We then have a weighted sum of relative costs, weights given by the α_j. The resulting "quasi"-Divisia index is the *almost homothetic Divisia index number*. When all $\alpha_j = 1$, we get the original (homothetic) Divisia index defined by (46). Let the Lagrangian for the almost homothetic Divisia index be given by

$$L = \frac{p_k \dot{x}_k}{\alpha_j p_j(x) x_i} = \frac{p_k \dot{x}_k}{\tilde{p}_j x_j}, \qquad \text{summation on } j \text{ and } k,$$

$$\tilde{p}_s = \alpha_s p_s \qquad (\text{no summation on } s = 1, \ldots, n), \tag{73}$$

$$\alpha_j > 0, \qquad \text{and} \qquad \alpha_j = \text{const} \qquad \text{for all} \qquad j = 1, \ldots, n.$$

Then *the almost homothetic Divisia index is dynamically invariant under the nonuniform magnification group*

$$\xi^i = a_{(i)} x_i = \text{const} \qquad (\text{no summation on } i). \tag{74}$$

To prove the preceding assertion, we expand (70-ii′) as

$$\left[(\tilde{p}_j x_j)\frac{\partial p_k}{\partial x_i} - p_k\left(\frac{\partial \tilde{p}_j}{\partial x_i} x_j + \tilde{p}_i\right)\right]\xi^i + (\tilde{p}_j x_j) p_i \frac{\partial \xi^i}{\partial x_k} = 0.$$

[10] Since $\partial \phi / \partial x_i = \partial L / \partial x_i$, the fundamental invariance condition may be stated as $(\partial L / \partial \dot{x}_i)\xi^i = \text{const}$, which may be interpreted as a conservation law.

Setting $p_1(x) \neq 0$, $p_2(x) = p_3(x) = \cdots = p_n(x) = 0$, we get

$$\left[\tilde{p}_1 x_1 \frac{\partial p_k}{\partial x_i}\xi^i - p_k\left(\frac{\partial \tilde{p}_1}{\partial x_i} x_1\right)\xi^i - p_k \tilde{p}_1 \xi^1\right] + (\tilde{p}_1 x_1) p_1 \frac{\partial \xi^1}{\partial x_k} = 0.$$

When $k = 1$, this reduces to $x_1\, \partial\xi^1/\partial x_1 = \xi^1$, and when $k \neq 1$, it implies $\partial\xi^1/\partial x_k = 0$. Hence we must have $\xi^1 = a_{(1)} x_1$. In general, we must have (74). Finally, to determine the relationship between α_i and $a_{(i)}$, we use the fundamental invariance equation (72). Substituting (74) into (72), we obtain

$$\Omega = \frac{\partial \phi}{\partial x_i}\xi^i = Q_i \xi^i = \sum_{i=1}^{n}\left(p_i a_{(i)} x_i \Big/ \sum_{j=1}^{n} (\alpha_j p_j x_j)\right) = \text{const} = b. \tag{75}$$

This expression is constant if and only if

$$\xi^i = b\alpha_i x_i \qquad \text{(no summation on } i\text{)}.$$

Hence, by setting $b = 1$, we obtain the group under which the almost homothetic Divisia index is dynamically invariant as

$$\xi^i = \alpha_i x_i \qquad (i = 1, \ldots, n) \qquad \text{(no summation on } i\text{)}. \tag{76}$$

We call the index as the almost homothetic index because ϕ is a monotonic transformation of the almost homogeneous functions of the degrees α_i. Consider an example:

$$L = \frac{p_1 \dot{x}_1 + p_2 \dot{x}_2}{\alpha_1 p_1 x_1 + \alpha_2 p_2 x_2} = \frac{\delta_1 x_1^{\delta_1 - 1}\dot{x}_1 + \delta_2 x_2^{\delta_2 - 1}\dot{x}_2}{\alpha_1 \delta_1 x_1^{\delta_1 - 1} x_1 + \alpha_2 \delta_2 x_2^{\delta_2 - 1} x_2}.$$

The path independence condition of $\mathscr{D}(x)$ requires $\partial Q_1/\partial x_2 \equiv \partial Q_2/\partial x_1$, which in this case is reduced to $\alpha_1\delta_1 = \alpha_2\delta_2$. We set $\alpha_1 = \delta_1^{-1}$ and $\alpha_2 = \delta_2^{-1}$. Then we obtain

$$L = \frac{\delta_1 x_1^{\delta_1 - 1}\dot{x}_1 + \delta_2 x_2^{\delta_2 - 1}\dot{x}_2}{x_1^{\delta_1} + x_2^{\delta_2}}.$$

This will be invariant under $\xi^1 = \alpha_1 x_1 = \delta_1^{-1} x_1$ and $\xi^2 = \alpha_2 x_2 = \delta_2^{-1} x_2$, since

$$\Omega = \frac{\delta_1 x_1^{\delta_1 - 1}\, \delta_1^{-1} x_1 + \delta_2 x_2^{\delta_2 - 1}\, \delta_2^{-1} x_2}{x_1^{\delta_1} + x_2^{\delta_2}} = \frac{x_1^{\delta_1} + x_2^{\delta_2}}{x_1^{\delta_1} + x_2^{\delta_2}} = 1.$$

Alternatively, we can check

$$L = \frac{\delta_1 x_1^{\delta_1 - 1}\dot{x}_1 + \delta_2 x_2^{\delta_2 - 1}\dot{x}_2}{x_1^{\delta_1} + x_2^{\delta_2}} \equiv \frac{\delta_1 \bar{x}_1^{\delta_1 - 1}\dot{\bar{x}}_1 + \delta_2 \bar{x}_2^{\delta_2 - 1}\dot{\bar{x}}_2}{\bar{x}_1^{\delta_1} + \bar{x}_2^{\delta_2}} = \bar{L},$$

where $\bar{x}_1 = e^{1/\delta_1}x_1$ and $\bar{x}_2 = e^{1/\delta_2}x_2$. The almost homothetic Divisia index in this case is obviously a class of *addilog* functions since we have

$$\mathscr{D}(x) = \exp \int_{t_0}^{t_1} \left(\frac{\delta_1 x_1^{\delta_1 - 1}\dot{x}_1 + \delta_2 x_2^{\delta_2 - 1}\dot{x}_2}{x_1^{\delta_1} + x_2^{\delta_2}} \right) dt = \exp \int_c d\phi$$

$$= \exp(\log(x_1^{\delta_1} + x_2^{\delta_2}) = (x_1^{\delta_1} + x_2^{\delta_2}).$$

We summarize the results in the following

Theorem 20 (*Dynamic Invariance of the General Divisia Index*) (i) *The general Divisia index related to nonhomothetic behavior is invariant under any arbitrary time transformation* $\tau = \tau(t, x)$. (*Therefore, it is automatically "parameter invariant."*)

(ii) *The quantity transformations do not depend on t,* $\partial \xi^i / \partial t = 0$.

(iii) *The general Divisia index will always satisfy the fundamental invariance condition*

$$\Omega = \frac{\partial \phi}{\partial x_i} \xi^i = \frac{\partial L}{\partial \dot{x}_i} \xi^i = Q_i \xi^i = \text{const.}$$

This may be called the "fundamental conservation law" of the general Divisia index.

(iv) *The standard (or homothetic) Divisia index is a special case of the almost homothetic Divisia index when the relative weights are the same.*

Remark The general Divisia index satisfies the Noether theorem on conservation laws, because of the path independence condition which in turn automatically guarantees the vanishing of the Euler–Lagrange expressions. Hence we have

$$\frac{\partial L}{\partial \dot{x}_i} \xi^i + (L - \dot{x}_i \, \partial L / \partial \dot{x}_i) \tau(t, x) = \text{const.}$$

But since $L - \dot{x}_i \, \partial L / \partial \dot{x}_i = L - L \equiv$ zero value of the Hamiltonian, we have $\Omega = (\partial L / \partial \dot{x}_i) \xi^i = \text{const.}$ The fact that the value of the Hamiltonian is identically zero implies the arbitrariness of the time transformation (1); i.e., $\tau = \tau(t, x)$. (See Chapter 7.)

REFERENCES

Afriat, S. N. [1972]. The theory of international comparisons of real income and prices, in *International Comparisons of Prices and Output* (D. J. Daley, ed.). Columbia Univ. Press, New York.

Diewert, W. E. [1976]. Exact and superlative index numbers, *Journal of Econometrics*, **4**, 115–145.

Divisia, F. [1928]. *Economic Rationelle*. Paris.

Eichhorn, W., and Voeller, J. [1976]. *Theory of the Price Index*, Lecture Notes in Economics and Mathematical Systems, Vol. 140. Springer-Verlag, Berlin and New York.

Fisher, F. M., and Shell, K. [1972]. *The Economic Theory of Price Indices*. Academic Press, New York.

Fisher, I. [1922]. *The Making of Index Numbers*, 3rd ed. revised, 1927. Houghton-Mifflin, Boston, Massachusetts. Reprinted by Augustus M. Kelley, New York, 1967.

Hillinger, C. [1970]. Comment on invariance axioms and economic indexes, *Econometrica*, **38**, 773–774.

Hulten, C. R. [1973]. Divisia index numbers, *Econometrica*, **41**, 1017–1025.

Lovelock, D., and Rund, H. [1975]. *Tensors, Differential Forms, and Variational Principles*. Wiley, New York.

Richter, M. K. [1966]. Invariance axioms and economic indexes, *Econometrica*, **34**, 739–755.

Samuelson, P. A. [1976]. Speeding up of time with age in recognition of life as fleeting, in *Evolution, Welfare, and Time in Economics, Essays in Honor of N. Georgescu-Roegen* (A. M. Tang *et al.*, eds.). Lexington Books, Heath, Lexington, Massachusetts.

Samuelson, P. A., and Swamy, S. [1974]. Invariant economic index numbers and canonical duality: Survey and synthesis, *American Economic Review*, **64**, 566–593.

Solow, R. M. [1957]. Technical change and the aggregate production function, *Review of Economics and Statistics*, **39**, 312–320.

Ville, J. [1946]. The existence condition of a total utility function and of an index of price, *Review of Economic Studies*, **19**, 128–132, a translation of a 1946 paper from *Annales de l'Université de Lyon*.

Wold, H. [1952]. *Demand Analysis*. Wiley, New York.

CHAPTER 9

THE GROUP STRUCTURE AND THE THEORY OF OBSERVABLE MARKET BEHAVIOR

I. Introduction

· **1.** The main purpose of this chapter is to present an *introductory analysis* of the mathematical foundation of the theory of observable market behavior. Emphasis will be placed on the analysis and abstraction of the formal group structure exhibited in many observable market behaviors dealt with in economic theory. It will be shown that many of the well-known results in economic theory can be restated in the group theoretical and differential geometric framework in a more consistent manner. This will enable one to study some of the basic problems still unresolved in economics in a more fruitful and unified manner. Thus, for instance, the well-known theory of revealed preference in the consumer's demand analysis of Samuelson can be regarded as the "involution" conditions of the "group action" of a Lie group on a differentiable manifold. Economic optimization such as cost minimization and utility maximization may be regarded as defining "contact transformations." If rational economic behavior is market observable as a system of mixed variables of prices and quantities, the underlying production technology or the preference ordering can be recoverable by the use of the fundamental properties of contact transformations.

Sometimes optimal economic behavior may be exhibited in the form of a system of differential equations. Here the recoverability problem becomes a *dynamic* one. From the knowledge of a system of observable differential equations, the underlying dynamic objective function of a rational economic agent may be reconstructed in the form of the Lagrangian and Hamiltonian functions. The well-known Hamilton–Jacobi transformation theory gives the necessary foundation for the study of the dynamic recoverability problem. Most optimal economic systems contain some forms of symmetries. The group theoretic approach is the basic apparatus that one can use to uncover hidden and unhidden symmetries (static or dynamic) of optimal behavior.

This chapter is *not* intended to provide a complete analysis of observable behavior in terms of the application of the group theoretic and differential geometric framework of analysis. However, it can serve as a prelude to extensive future research in this area. The Frobenius existence theorem is quite fundamental to the group theoretic/differential geometric approach to the theory of observable behavior. What the fixed-point theorem is to general equilibrium theory, the Frobenius existence theorem is to the theory of observable behavior. Since some formal results may not be familiar to economists who are less inclined to the mathematical approach, we shall briefly discuss the mathematics necessary to follow the arguments.[1]

II. Preliminaries: Manifolds and Existence Theory

Differentiable Manifolds

2. Throughout Part II, A and J will denote arbitrary sets of indices. Let M be a set, $\mathscr{U}$ a family of subsets of M satisfying:

(i) $\varnothing \in \mathscr{U}$, $M \in \mathscr{U}$ (M itself and the empty set $\varnothing$ both belong to $\mathscr{U}$);
(ii) if $U, V \in \mathscr{U}$, then $U \cap V \in \mathscr{U}$;
(iii) if $U_\alpha \in \mathscr{U}$ ($\alpha \in A$), then $\bigcup_{\alpha \in A} U_\alpha \in \mathscr{U}$.

A *topological structure* (or, briefly, a *topology*) on a set M is $\mathscr{U}$, a collection of subsets of M, which satisfies the foregoing three axioms. We call the subsets of M belonging to $\mathscr{U}$ *open sets* of this topology. When such a structure is given on

[1] Thanks are due to John D. Logan (Department of Mathematics, Kansas State University), who suggested several relevant articles in this area, and to Robert Kotzen (Department of Mathematics, Brown University), who made many helpful comments on this chapter. There are a number of excellent works in this area, among them we refer to Matsushima [1972], Chevalley [1946], Boothby [1975], Varadarajan [1974], Hermann [1968, 1973], Lang [1972], Abraham and Marsden [1978], Nôno [1972], and Nôno and Mimura [1972, 1975].

a set M, we call it a *topological space* denoted by $(M, \mathscr{U})$. (Whenever it is obvious, we may omit $\mathscr{U}$ and call M a topological space.) In addition to the three axioms:

(iv) if there exist $U, V \in \mathscr{U}$ for $p, q \in M$, $p \neq q$, such that $p \in U$, $q \in V$, $U \cap V = \varnothing$, is satisfied, then we call M a *Hausdorff space.*

Let $(M, \mathscr{U})$ be a topological space. For $p \in M$ we set

$$\mathscr{U}(p) = \{U \in \mathscr{U} \mid p \in U\}.$$

We call any element $U \in \mathscr{U}(p)$ an *open neighborhood* of p. For $(M, \mathscr{U})$ and $p \in M$, we consider $\mathscr{U}_p \subset \mathscr{U}(p)$. If for every $U \in \mathscr{U}(p)$, there exists V such that $V \subset U$ and $V \in \mathscr{U}_p$, then we call $\mathscr{U}_p$ a *fundamental neighborhood system* of p in the topological space M. Let $(M_1, \mathscr{U}_1)$ and $(M_2, \mathscr{U}_2)$ be topological spaces with fundamental neighborhood systems. Then $(M_1 \times M_2, \mathscr{U})$, where $\mathscr{U} = \{\mathscr{U}_p\}$, $\mathscr{U}_p = \{U_1 \times U_2 \mid U_1 \in \mathscr{U}_1(p_1), U_2 \in \mathscr{U}_2(p_2)\}$, is called the *product space* of the topological spaces $(M_1, \mathscr{U}_1)$ and $(M_2, \mathscr{U}_2)$. If a family $\{U_i\}_{i \in J}$ of open sets of $(M, \mathscr{U})$ has the property $M = \bigcup_{i \in J} U_i$, $U_i \in \mathscr{U}$, then $\{U_i\}_{i \in J}$ is called an *open covering* of M. For an arbitrary covering $\{U_i\}_{i \in J}$ of M, if one can choose a finite number of indices $i_1, \ldots, i_N \in J$ such that

$$M = U_{i_1} \cup \cdots \cup U_{i_N},$$

then the topological space M is said to be *compact*. If K is a subset of $(M, \mathscr{U})$ and is compact, then K is called a *compact subset* of M. A topological space $(M, \mathscr{U})$ is said to be *locally compact* if there exists a compact neighborhood.

Let $(M_1, \mathscr{U}_1)$, $(M_2, \mathscr{U}_2)$ be topological spaces. A correspondence f which associates to each element p of M_1 an element $f(p)$ of M_2 is called a *mapping* from M_1 to M_2, i.e., $f: M_1 \to M_2$. If, for any two distinct elements p and q of M_1, the corresponding elements $f(p)$, $f(q)$ are distinct, i.e., if $f(p) \neq f(q)$ for $p \neq q$, then f is said to be a *one-to-one map* or an *injection* from M_1 into M_2. If, for an arbitrary element q of M_2, there is always an element p of M_1 such that $f(p) = q$, then f is called an *onto map* or a *surjection.* When f is an injection and a surjection, we call f a *bijection.* A correspondence f is said to be a *continuous* map from M_1 to M_2, if, for an arbitrary open set $V \in \mathscr{U}_2$, the *inverse image* of V, $f^{-1}(V) = \{p \in M_1 \mid f(p) \in V\}$, is always an open set of M_1, i.e., $f^{-1}(V) \in \mathscr{U}_1$. If f is a bijection from M_1 to M_2, and if f and its inverse f^{-1} are both continuous maps, then f is said to be a *homeomorphic map* or simply a *homeomorphism* from M_1 onto M_2.

Let W_i be two open subsets W_i $(i = 1, 2)$ of a topological space $(M, \mathscr{U})$ satisfying $W_i \neq \varnothing$ $(i = 1, 2)$. If $W_1 \cap W_2 = \varnothing$ and $M = W_1 \cup W_2$, then M is said to be disconnected. If M is not disconnected, then M is said to be *connected.* If N is a topological subspace of M and connected, then N is a *connected subset* of M. $(M, \mathscr{U})$ is said to be *locally connected* if each point has a fundamental neighborhood system consisting of connected neighborhoods, i.e., if there exists a connected $V \in \mathscr{U}(p)$, $V \subset U$ for any $p \in M$ and $U \in \mathscr{U}(p)$.

Let d be a map $d: M \times M \to \mathbb{R}$, where $\mathbb{R}$ is a set of real numbers. If d satisfies the following conditions, then d is called a *metric* on M;

(i) when $x \neq y$, then $d(x, y) > 0$ $(x, y \in M)$, $d(x, x) = 0$,
(ii) $d(x, y) = d(y, x)$,
(iii) $d(x, y) \leqq d(x, z) + d(z, y)$ $(x, y, z \in M)$.

A set M with a metric d is called a *metric space* and is denoted by (M, d). If an arbitrary Cauchy sequence in M always converges to a point in M, then the metric space M is said to be *complete*.

3. Let $(M, \mathscr{U})$ be a Hausdorff space. If each point of M has open neighborhood homeorphic to an *open* set in $\mathbb{R}^n$, then M is called an n-dimensional *topological manifold*. In particular, if $\phi: U \to V$ is a homeomorphism from $U \in \mathscr{U}$ onto some open set V of $\mathbb{R}^n$, then each pair (U, ϕ) is called a *coordinate neighborhood* or a *chart*. Let $(U_i, \phi_i) \in \text{Chart}(M, \mathbb{R}^n)$. To $q \in U_1$ we assign the n coordinates $x^1(q), \ldots, x^n(q)$ of its image $\phi_1(q)$ in $\mathbb{R}^n$, where each $x^i(q)$, with the ith *coordinate function*, is a real-valued function on U_1. If q lies also in a second coordinate neighborhood (U_2, ϕ_2), then it has (in general different) coordinates $y^1(q), \ldots, y^n(q)$ in this neighborhood. It is generally not possible to construct one suitable chart for an entire set M. That is, there is in general no ϕ whose domain is all of M. Let $U_{12} = U_1 \cap U_2$. (U_1, ϕ_1) and (U_2, ϕ_2) are said to be C^k-*compatible* ($0 \leqq k$ is an integer or $k = \infty$) if either (i) $U_{12} = \varnothing$ or (ii) $U_{12} \neq \varnothing$ and

$$\phi_1 \circ \phi_2^{-1} \in C^k(\phi_2(U_{12}), \phi_1(U_{12})) \quad \text{and} \quad \phi_2 \circ \phi_1^{-1} \in C^k(\phi_1(U_{12}), \phi_2(U_{12})).$$

For simplicity we may henceforth assume that $k = \infty$. A *differentiable or* C^∞ (*or smooth*) *structure* on M is a family $\mathscr{A} = \{U_\alpha, \phi_\alpha | \alpha \in A\}$ of coordinate neighborhoods such that (i) $M = \bigcup_{\alpha \in A} U_\alpha$, i.e., the U_α cover M, (ii) for any $\alpha, \beta \in A$, (U_α, ϕ_α) and (U_β, ϕ_β) are C^∞-compatible, (iii) any coordinate neighborhood (U, ϕ) compatible with every $(U_\alpha, \phi_\alpha) \in \mathscr{A}$ is itself in $\mathscr{A}$. A topological manifold M which has a C^∞-differentiable structure is called *an n-dimensional differentiable manifold of class* C^∞ *or a* C^∞ *manifold.*

4. Let f be a real-valued function defined on open set of a C^∞ manifold M, possibly all of M, as $f: M \to \mathbb{R}$. f is a C^∞ *function* if for $(U_\alpha, \phi_\alpha) \in \mathscr{A}$, $f \circ \phi_\alpha^{-1} \in C^\infty(\phi_\alpha(U_\alpha))$. Let $(M, \mathscr{A})$ and $(M', \mathscr{A}')$ be C^∞ manifolds of dimensions m and m', respectively. Φ is a *differentiable map* or a C^∞ *map* from M to M' if $g \in C^\infty(M')$ and $g \circ \Phi \in C^\infty(M)$. If a differentiable map Φ from a manifold M to a manifold M' has the property that it is a bijection and its inverse Φ^{-1} is also differentiable, then Φ is called *a diffeomorphic map* or *a diffeomorphism from M onto M'*, or simply a C^∞ *diffeomorphism.*

5. Let Φ be a differentiable map from a manifold M into a manifold M', and let the dimensions of M and M' be n and m, respectively. Suppose that $n \leqq m$; then Φ is an *immersion* of M in M' if rank $\Phi = n$ at every point.[2] If an immersion $\Phi: M \to M'$ is univalent (injective), then the image $\tilde{M} = \Phi(M)$ (endowed with the topology and C^∞ structure which makes $\Phi: M \to \tilde{M}$ a diffeomorphism) is a *submanifold*. If Φ is an immersion, and if moreover Φ is an injective map, i.e., if $\Phi(p) \neq \Phi(q)$ for $p \neq q$, then Φ is called *imbedding* of M into M'. Alternatively, if the manifolds M and M' satisfy the following two conditions, then M is a submanifold of M':

(i) The set M is a subset of M'.
(ii) The identity map from M into M' is an imbedding of M into M'.

If the topology of M coincides with the topology of M as a subspace of M', then M is called a *regular submanifold* of M'.

Lie Groups and Lie Algebras

6. A Lie group G is a group which is a C^∞ manifold whose group operation is a C^∞ mapping. Formally, let G be a C^∞ manifold with a countable base. If G is a group, and if the map $(x, y) \to xy$ from the product manifold $G \times G$ to G and the map $x \to x^{-1}$ from G to G are both C^∞ mappings, then G is called a *Lie group*. If G_1 and G_2 are Lie groups, then the direct product $G_1 \times G_2$ of these groups with the C^∞ structure of the Cartesian product of manifolds is a Lie group. Let H be a subgroup of a Lie group G, which is also a regular submanifold. Then H with its differentiable structure as a submanifold is also a Lie group. Hence a (Lie) subgroup H is any subgroup which is a submanifold and is a Lie group with its C^∞ structure as an (immersed) submanifold. If H is a regular submanifold and a subgroup of a Lie group G, then H is closed as a subset of G.

Let G be a group and X a set. Then G is said to *act on* X (on the left) if there is a mapping $\theta: G \times G \to X$ satisfying two conditions:

(i) If e is the identity element of G, then $\theta(e, x) = x$ for all $x \in X$.
(ii) If $g_1, g_2 \in G$, then $\theta(g_1, \theta(g_2, x)) = \theta(g_1 g_2, x)$, for all $x \in X$.

[When we define *right* action, (i) and (ii) become (i) $\theta(x, e) = x$ and (ii) $\theta(\theta(x, g_1), g_2) = \theta(x, g_1 g_2)$.]

7. Given any point $p \in M$, we define $C^\infty(p)$ as the algebra of real-valued C^∞ functions whose domain of definition includes some open neighborhood

[2] Let $\Phi: M \to M'$ be a differentiable mapping of C^∞ manifolds and let $p \in M$. If (U, ϕ) and (V, ψ) are coordinate neighborhoods of p and $\Phi(p)$, respectively, and $\Phi(U) \subset V$, then $\hat{\Phi} = \psi \circ \Phi \circ \phi^{-1}: \phi(U) \to \psi(V)$. The *rank of* Φ *at* p is defined as the rank of $\hat{\Phi}$ at $\phi(p)$.

of p. (The objects so obtained are called "germs" of C^∞ functions.) The *tangent space* $T_p(M)$ to M at p is the set of all mappings $X_p: C^\infty(p) \to \mathbb{R}$ satisfying, for all $\alpha, \beta \in \mathbb{R}$ and $f, g \in C^\infty(p)$, the following two conditions:

(i) $X_p(\alpha f + \beta g) = \alpha(X_p f) + \beta(X_p g)$ (linearity),
(ii) $X_p(fg) = (X_p f)g(p) + f(p)(X, g)$ (Leibniz rule).

$T_p(M)$ can be made into a vector space by defining

$$(X_p + Y_p)f = X_p f + Y_p f, \qquad (\alpha X_p)f = \alpha(X_p f).$$

A *tangent vector* to M at p is any $X_p \in T_p(M)$. A *vector field* X on M is a "function" assigning to each point p of M an element X_p of $T_p(M)$. It is a function whose range is the set $T(M)$ consisting of all tangent vectors at all points of M, i.e., $T(M) = \bigcup_{p \in M} T_p(M)$ and whose domain is M itself. Formally, a *vector field X of class C^∞ on M* is a function assigning to each point p of M a vector $X_p \in T_p(M)$ whose components in the frames of any local coordinates (U, ϕ) are functions of class C^∞ on the domain U of the coordinates. We usually use the words vector field to mean C^∞ vector field. If $(x^1, \ldots, x^n)$ is a local coordinate system on an open set U of M, then at each point p of U, X_p can be expressed uniquely as

$$X_p = \sum_{i=1}^{n} \xi^i(p)\phi^{*-1}\left(\frac{\partial}{\partial x^i}\bigg|_p\right),$$

where $\phi^*: T_p(U) \to T_{\phi(p)}(\mathbb{R}^n)$ is the map induced by $\phi: U \to \mathbb{R}^n$. Then ξ^i $(i = 1, \ldots, n)$ on U are called the *components* of X with respect to the local coordinates.

8. Let θ_t be diffeomorphisms of M, defined for each real value t, and satisfying the conditions

(i) $\theta_s \circ \theta_t = \theta_{s+t}$ $(s, t \in \mathbb{R})$,
(ii) $(t, p) \to \theta_t(p)$ gives a differentiable map from $\mathbb{R} \times M$ to M.

Then the family $\{\theta_t | t \in \mathbb{R}\}$ of diffeomorphisms θ_t is called a *one-parameter group of transformations of the manifold M*. For a one-parameter group of transformations $\{\theta_t\}$, for each $p \in M$ we can define a vector field $X_p: C^\infty(p) \to \mathbb{R}$ by

$$X_p f = \left[\frac{df(\theta_t(p))}{dt}\right]_{t=0}.$$

This vector field X is called the *infinitesimal transformation* (or *infinitesimal generator of θ*) of the one-parameter group of transformations $\{\theta_t\}$. If $\theta: G \times M \to M$ is the action of a group G on a manifold M, then a vector field X on M is said to be *invariant under the action of G or G-invariant* if X is invariant under each of the diffeomorphisms θ_g of M to itself. Let

$$\{\theta_t(p) \mid t \in \mathbb{R}\}$$

be the *orbit* of the one-parameter group of transformations through the point p of M. Define a curve F_p by $F_p(t) = \theta_t(p)$. The image of F_p is the orbit of p. Then F_p is an integral curve of X such that $F_p(0) = p$. A vector field X on M is said to be *complete* if it generates a (global) action of $\mathbb{R}$ on M. It is known that if M is a compact manifold, then every vector field X on M is complete. An infinitesimal transformation of a one-parameter group of transformations of M is a complete vector field. The correspondence between the set of all one-parameter groups of transformations on M and the set of all complete vector fields on M is 1:1, and we denote the one-parameter group of transformations, whose infinitesimal transformation is the complete vector field X, by

$$\theta_t = \exp tX.$$

Hence $\exp sX \circ \exp tX = \exp(s + t)X$ and $\theta_s \circ \theta_t = \theta_{s+t}$.

9. Let $\mathscr{X}(M)$ be the set of all C^∞ vector fields defined on the C^∞ manifold M. It is itself a vector space over $\mathbb{R}$, since if X and Y are C^∞ vector fields on M, so is any linear combination of them with constant coefficients. In fact, $\mathscr{X}(M)$ is a *vector space* over $\mathbb{R}$ and a *module* over $C^\infty(M)$. A vector space $\mathscr{L}$ over $\mathbb{R}$ is said to be a (real) *Lie algebra* if in addition to its vector space structure it possesses a product, i.e., a map $\mathscr{L} \times \mathscr{L} \to \mathscr{L}$, taking the pair (X, Y) to the element $[X, Y]$ of $\mathscr{L}$, which has the properties:

(i) $[\alpha_1 X_1 + \alpha_2 X_2, Y] = \alpha_1[X_1, Y] + \alpha_2[X_2, Y]$ (it is bilinear over $\mathbb{R}$);
(ii) $[X, Y] = -[Y, X]$ (it is skew commutative);
(iii) $[X, [Y, Z]] + [Y, [Z, X]] + [Z, [X, Y]] = 0$ (it satisfies the *Jacobi identity*).

Let $X, Y, Z \in \mathscr{X}(M)$ and $Z = [X, Y] = XY - YX =$ *the (Lie) bracket of X and Y*. Then $\mathscr{X}(M)$ with the Lie bracket $[X, Y]$ is a Lie algebra. In general, if G is a Lie group, the left-invariant vector fields on G form a Lie algebra with the bracket (or product) $[X, Y]$. This is the *Lie algebra of the Lie group G*. If a Lie group G has dimension n, then the Lie algebra of G also has dimension n.

Existence Theory

10. We shall formally present the integrability theorem, originally due to Frobenius, in a group-theoretic framework.

Definition 1 Let M be a C^∞ manifold with a point $p \in M$. Let $D(p)$ be a k-dimensional vector space of tangent vectors $T_p(M)$ or simply T_pM at $p \in M$. Then a set of $D(p)$ such that $\mathscr{D} = \{D(p) \mid p \in M\}$ is called a *k-dimensional C^∞ differential system* if it satisfies[3]

(A1) There exists a neighborhood U at $p \in M$ with $X_1, \ldots X_k \in \mathscr{X}(U)$ such that

$$D(q) = \{X_1(q), \ldots, X_k(q)\}_{\mathbb{R}}, \qquad q \in U.$$

Definition 2 Let (W, τ) be a submanifold of M (see Section 5). Then (W, τ) is an *integral manifold* of a k-C^∞ differential system if for each $w \in W$,

(A2) $(T\tau)(T_w W) \subset D(\tau(w))$, where $T\tau$ is the differential (or tangential map) of τ. When $k = 1$, (W, τ) is called an *integral curve*.

Definition 3 A k-dimensional C^∞ differential system (or vector-field system) is said to be *completely integrable* at $p \in M$, if there exists a neighborhood system (U, ϕ), $\phi(p) = 0$, $\phi(U) = \{x \in \mathbb{R}^n \mid |x| < a\}$ $(a > 0)$, and if for $c = (c_{k+1}, \ldots, c_n) \in \mathbb{R}^{n-k}$ $(|c| < a)$, the following condition is satisfied.

(A3) $U_c = \{q \in U \mid x^j(q) = c_j \ (k < j \leqq n)\}$ is an integral manifold of $\mathscr{D}$, where U_c is a *slice* and $\phi = (x^1, \ldots, x^n)$.

Lemma 1 *If (W, τ) is an integral manifold of D and $\tau(W) \subset U$ and W is connected, then there exists $c \in \mathbb{R}^{n-k}$ such that $\tau(W) \subset U_c$.*

Proof For a point $p \in U$, let $\phi(p) = (t_1, \ldots, t_k, c(p))$, $c(p) \in \mathbb{R}^{n-k}$, then we have $\dim T_p(U_{c(p)}) = k$ and $T_p(U_{c(p)}) \subset D(p)$, and therefore $T_p(U_{c(p)}) = D(p)$. For any $X \in T_w W$, we have

$$(T\tau)X \in (T\tau)(T_w W) \subset D(\tau(w)) = T_{\tau(w)}(U_{c(\tau(w))})$$

and

$$(T\tau)X = \sum_{i=1}^{k} a^i \left(\frac{\partial}{\partial x^i}\right)_{\tau(w)}, \qquad a^i \in \mathbb{R}.$$

Hence, for any j, $k < j \leqq n$, we have

$$X(x^j \circ \tau) = (T\tau X)x^j = \left(\sum_{i=1}^{k} a^i \left(\frac{\partial}{\partial x^i}\right)_{\tau(w)}\right) x^j = 0.$$

Since $x^j \circ \tau = c_j = \text{const}$, we have $\tau(W) \subset U_c$, where $c = c_{k+1}, \ldots, c_n$. Q.E.D.

[3] Thus a k-dimensional C^∞ differential system forms a so-called C^∞ *distribution* of dimension k on M. Here we intend to present a differential geometric formulation of the classical Frobenius theorem. This theorem has been extended in various directions (see, e.g., Hartman [1964]). Hartman's recent paper [1970] derives the "generalized" Frobenius theorem under Carathéodory-type conditions. His paper deals with the condition of Lipschitz continuity and the integrability conditions that apply "almost everywhere."

Definition 4 A k-dimensional differential system $\mathscr{D}$ is said to be *involutive* if there exists a neighborhood V of p, for $p \in M$ and $X_1, \ldots, X_k \in \mathscr{X}(V)$ such that

(A4) $\{X_1(q), \ldots, X_k(q)\}_{\mathbb{R}} = D(q)$.
(A5) $[X_i, X_j](q) \in D(q)$, $q \in V$.

Lemma 2 *The necessary and sufficient condition that $\mathscr{D}$ be involutive is that if X_p, $Y_p \in D(p)$ $(p \in U)$, then*

$$[X, Y](p) \in D(p) \qquad (p \in U) \qquad \text{for} \quad U \subset M \quad \text{and} \quad X, Y \in \mathscr{X}(U).$$

Proof Assume that $\mathscr{D}$ is involutive. Then, for $p_0 \in U$, there exists a neighborhood $V \subset U$ and $X_1, \ldots, X_k \in \mathscr{X}(V)$ satisfying (A4) and (A5). Then X and Y on V can be written as

$$X = \sum_{i=1}^{k} \xi_i X_i, \qquad Y = \sum_{i=1}^{k} \eta_i X_i, \qquad \xi_i, \eta_i \in C^\infty(V).$$

Hence $[X, Y] = \sum \xi_i \eta_j [X_i, X_j] + \sum \xi_i X_i \eta_j X_j - \sum \eta_j X_j \xi_i X_i$. Using (A4) and (A5), we see that $[X, Y](p) \in D(p)$ for any $p \in V$. Conversely, any $\mathscr{D}$ which satisfies the lemma clearly is involutive. Q.E.D.

We can next show that any involutive differential system can be transformed in such a way that $[X_i, X_j] \equiv 0$ (Eisenhart [1933, p. 49]). Then we have

Theorem (*Frobenius Integrability Theorem*) *Let $\mathscr{D}$ be a k-dimensional differential system (vector-field system). Then $\mathscr{D}$ is completely integrable if and only if $\mathscr{D}$ is involutive.*

Proof If $\mathscr{D}$ is involutive, there exist $X_1, \ldots, X_k \in \mathscr{X}(U)$ for any point p_0 and its neighborhood U. We also have $\{X_1(p), \ldots, X_k(p)\}_{\mathbb{R}} = D(p)$, $p \in U$ and $[X_i, X_j] = 0$, $1 \leqq i, j \leqq k$. By using $U = M$, there exists a neighborhood coordinate system (U_0, ϕ) such that $\phi = (x^1, \ldots, x^n)$ and

$$X_i(p) = \left.\frac{\partial}{\partial x^i}\right|_p, \qquad p \in U_0.$$

This system (U_0, ϕ) satisfies (A3), and thus $\mathscr{D}$ is completely integrable.

Conversely, if $\mathscr{D}$ is completely integrable and if we take (U, ϕ) such that it satisfies (A3), then $X_i = \partial/\partial x^i$ $(1 \leqq i \leqq k)$ satisfies $[X_i, X_j] \equiv 0$, or (A4) and (A5). Q.E.D.

III. Revealed Preference, Integrability, and Lie Groups

11. We are now in a position to study the theory of observable behavior applied to a consumer's utility maximization, from the standpoint of Lie groups. Recent contributions (Chipman *et al.* [1971], Hurwicz and Richter

[1979]) to the recoverability question of a utility function has brought a revived interest in the classical problem of integrability of preference fields. In particular, the paper by Hurwicz[4] [1971] focuses attention on a more general approach to the revealed preference and integrability question with the use of exterior derivatives. This line of approach formally belongs to a *differential geometric* analysis, especially, of *Lie groups*. Our purpose here is, therefore, to reformulate the classical revealed preference and integrability problem of Samuelson in a (Lie) group theoretical framework. It will be shown that the utility maximization behavior expressed in the observable equations may be regarded as the action of a Lie group. This fact presents the most fundamental justification for the use of such a relatively new approach as the theory of Lie groups and differential geometry.

Consider an individual consumer whose rational behavior is exhibited in maximizing satisfaction over the nonnegative orthant $\mathbb{R}_+^{n+1}$ of the $(n + 1)$-dimensional (Euclidean real) commodity space. The local coordinates for $\mathbb{R}_+^{n+1}$ are denoted by $(x_1, \ldots, x_{n+1})$. The corresponding prices $P \in \mathbb{R}_+^{n+1}$ are denoted by $(P_1, \ldots, P_{n+1}) \in \mathbb{R}_+^{n+1}$. The consumer's income is expressed by $I \in \mathbb{R}_+$. The consumer's preferences are given by a preference relation $\succcurlyeq$ which is reflexive, transitive, and total on $\mathbb{R}_+^{n+1}$, such as $x'' \succcurlyeq x'$. Focusing our attention on the local aspect of the problem, we shall now assume that preferences are represented by a differentiable concave utility function $U: \mathbb{R}_+^{n+1} \to \mathbb{R}$. In many *economic manifolds*, which are the manifolds related to *economic optimization* (usually $M \subset \mathbb{R}_+^{n+1}$), we may assume a C^r-differentiable structure ($1 \leqq r$ is an integer or $r = \infty$) with $x \in \mathbb{R}_+^{n+1}$.

Infinitesimal Generators

12. Utility maximization under the budget constraint $Px \leqq I$ implies that

$$r^j(x) = P_j/P_{n+1} = U_j/U_{n+1}, \qquad 1 \leqq j \leqq n, \quad U_{n+1} > 0, \quad r^j(x) > 0, \tag{1-i}$$

$$Px = I. \tag{1-ii}$$

We have implicitly assumed that preferences are strictly monotone and thus $P > 0$ for $I \geqq 0$. Condition (1-i) can be written alternatively as

$$U_j - r^j(x)U_{n+1} = 0, \qquad 1 \leqq j \leqq n, \tag{1-i$'$}$$

[4] This article is an excellent survey on this field, containing many useful original ideas about how to proceed and many new results of great importance. By applying Hartman's recent result (Hartman [1970]), it studies the "qualitative" aspects of the integrability conditions under the less restrictive conditions of Lipschitz continuity and symmetry conditions that apply "almost everywhere."

i.e.,

$$\frac{\partial U}{\partial x_j} - r^j(x)\frac{\partial U}{\partial x_{n+1}} = 0, \qquad 1 \leqq i \leqq n. \tag{1-i''}$$

Then, as already shown in Chapter 4 (Theorem 10), the utility maximization behavior expressed in the equilibrium conditions may be regarded as the action of the *unconnected n infinitesimal generators*, where the *n infinitesimal generators* are given by

$$X_j = \frac{\partial}{\partial x_j} - r^j(x)\frac{\partial}{\partial x_{n+1}}, \qquad 1 \leqq j \leqq n, \tag{2}$$

and the underlying one-parameter groups of transformations by

$$G^j\colon \mathbb{R}_+^{n+1} \to \mathbb{R}_+^{n+1}, \qquad 1 \leqq j \leqq n. \tag{3}$$

In many cases G^j may be regarded as a Lie group.

Recoverability

13. We now want to study the process of "recovering" the underlying preference from "observable" market behaviors exhibited in the marginal rates of substitution. We have implicitly assumed that the utility function is quasi-concave, i.e., *the level set is convex*. One can set conditions on the Slutzky matrix in such a way that the quadratic form generated from the elements of the matrix be negative semidefinite. These conditions can be expressed in a more general formulation and can thus be extended to a more general situation. (Here the reader is asked to study Hartman [1970], Theorems 9.1 and 9.2, and also Yorke's extension mentioned by Hartman [1970, p. 332].) In what follows we assume that the convexity condition is implicitly met, thus avoiding further complications of the analysis.

We begin with the assumption that one can observe the behavior of the marginal rates of substitution $r^j(x)$ of a rational individual in the neighborhood V of each point $x \in \mathbb{R}_+^{n+1}$. Suppose that there are n unconnected independent C^∞ vector fields generated from the marginal rate of substitution such that

$$X_j = \frac{\partial}{\partial x_j} - r^j(x)\frac{\partial}{\partial x_{n+1}}, \qquad 1 \leqq i \leqq n,$$

which form a local basis of a differential system Δ. A C^∞ vector-field system is *involutive* or *closed* when it is closed under the bracket operation. More specifically, the C^∞ vector-field system is *involutive* if there exists a local basis $X_1, \ldots, X_n$ in a neighborhood of each point such that

$$[X_i, X_k] = \sum_{j=1}^{n} \rho_{ik}^{j}(x) X_j, \qquad 1 \leqq i, k \leqq n. \tag{4}$$

We then present

Theorem 1 (*Local Integrability Conditions*) *Let Δ be a C^∞ vector-field system of the observable marginal rates of substitution on $\mathbb{R}_+^{n+1}$. Then there exists an (integral) utility function of Δ passing through $x \in \mathbb{R}_+^{n+1}$ if and only if Δ is involutive.*

Proof This is a special case of the Frobenius integrability theorem presented in Section 10. Q.E.D.

Corollary to Theorem 1 (*Jacobian Complete System and Integrability*) *If and only if $X_j U = 0$ $(1 \leqq j \leqq n)$ satisfy the conditions of the Jacobian complete system, then the underlying utility preference is recoverable.*

Proof This is the direct consequence of the preceding theorem, which gives the integrability conditions

$$\frac{\partial r^j}{\partial x_k} - \frac{\partial r^j}{\partial x_{n+1}} r^k = \frac{\partial r^k}{\partial x_j} - \frac{\partial r^k}{\partial x_{n+1}} r^j, \qquad 1 \leqq j, k \leqq n \tag{5}$$

(see Samuelson [1950]). Q.E.D.

Alternative Formulation of the Integrability Conditions (Exterior Differentiation)

14. We shall next give yet another version of the integrability conditions in terms of differential forms using tensor and exterior algebras. It is well known that there is a dual description of vector-field systems; that is to say, there is corresponding differential systems and one-differential forms for any vector-field (distribution) systems. In terms of our analysis of optimal market behavior of the rational individual, this means that there exists a total differential equation representation (Pfaffian equation) of the optimal behavior (see also Hurwicz [1971, p. 191]). Hence the differential form of the utility maximization behavior can now be expressed as

$$\omega = \sum_{j=1}^{n} r^j(x)\, dx_j + dx_{n+1}, \tag{6}$$

where $r^j(x)$ is the marginal rate of substitution between the jth and $(n+1)$th commodities $(j = 1, \ldots, n)$.

Let $F(V, W)$ be the free vector space over $\mathbb{R}$ whose generators are the points of $V \times W$. Thus $F(V, W)$ consists of all finite linear combinations of pairs (v, w), $v \in V$, $w \in W$. Let $R(V, W)$ be the subspace of $F(V, W)$ generated by the set of all elements of $F(V, W)$ of the forms

$$(v_1 + v_2, w) - (v_1, w) - (v_2, w), \qquad (v, w_1 + w_2) - (v, w_1) - (v, w_2),$$

$$(av, w) - a(v, w), (v, aw) - a(v, w) \qquad (a \in \mathbb{R}, v, v_1, v_2 \in V, w, w_1, w_2 \in W).$$

The quotient space $F(V, W)/R(V, W)$ is the *tensor product* of V and W and is denoted by

$$V \otimes W.$$

The tensor space $V_{r,s}$ of type (r, s) associated with V is the vector space

$$\underbrace{V \otimes \cdots \otimes V}_{r \text{ copies}} \otimes \underbrace{V^* \otimes \cdots \otimes V^*}_{s \text{ copies}},$$

where V^* is the dual space of V consisting of all real-valued linear functions on V. The direct sum

$$T(V) = \sum V_{r,s} \qquad (r, s \geqq 0),$$

where $V_{0,0} = \mathbb{R}$ is the *tensor algebra* of V, and elements of $T(V)$ are *tensors*. Let $C(V)$ denote the subalgebra $\sum_{k=0}^{\infty} V_{k,0}$ of $T(V)$. Let $I(V)$ be the two-sided ideal in $C(V)$ and set $I_k(V) = I(V) \cap V_{k,0}$. Then $I(V) = \sum_{k=0}^{\infty} I_k(V)$. $I(V)$ is the graded ideal in $C(V)$. The *exterior algebra* $\Lambda(V)$ of V is the graded algebra $C(V)/I(V)$. We denote multiplication in the algebra $\Lambda(V)$ by the *wedge* or *exterior product* $\wedge$.

A C^∞ mapping of M into $T_{r,s}(M)$, $\Lambda_k^*(M)$, or $\Lambda^*(M)$ whose composition with the canonical projection is the identity map, is called a (*smooth*) *tensor field of type* (r, s) *on* M, a (*differential*) *k-form* on M, or a (*differential*) *form* on M, respectively, where $T_{r,s}$ is a tensor bundle of type (r, s) over M, i.e.,

$$T_{r,s}(M) = \bigcup_{m \in M} (M_m)_{r,s},$$

$\Lambda_k^*(M)$ is an exterior k bundle over M, i.e.,

$$\Lambda_k^*(M) = \bigcup_{m \in M} \Lambda_k(M_m^*),$$

and $\Lambda^*(M)$ is an exterior algebra bundle over M, i.e.,

$$\Lambda^*(M) = \bigcup_{m \in M} \Lambda(M_m^*)$$

(M_m^* is the dual tangent space of M). If $f \in C^\infty(M)$, then the differential df is a smooth mapping of $T(M)$ into $\mathbb{R}$ which is linear on each tangent space. Thus df is a 1-form $df : M \to \Lambda_1^*(M)$. The 1-form df is called the *exterior derivative* of the 0-form f.

Theorem 2 *(Integrability Conditions of a Differential Form) Let Δ be a C^∞ vector-field system of the observable marginal rates of substitution on $\mathbb{R}_+^{n+1}$. Then the underlying preference is recoverable in the neighborhood of each $x \in \mathbb{R}_+^{n+1}$ if and only if the* 1*-form* (6) *vanishes on Δ and it satisfies*

$$d\omega = \tilde{\omega} \wedge \omega, \tag{7}$$

where $\omega = \sum_{j=1}^{\infty} r^j(x)\, dx_j + dx_{n+1}$, and $\tilde{\omega}$ is some suitable differential 1*-form.*

Proof This is a dual statement of our earlier condition on Δ in terms of the existence of a local bases $X_1, \ldots, X_n$ at each point. We shall merely present the steps of the proof. Suppose that Δ is given. Then in a neighborhood V of each point, an appropriate local canonical basis $X_1, \ldots, X_n$ of Δ can be completed to a field of frames. Δ is involutive if and only if in the expressions $[X_i, X_k] = \sum_{j=1}^{n} \rho_{ik}^j X_j$, giving $[X_i, X_k]$ as linear combinations of the basis, we have $\rho_{ik}^j = 0$ (Jacobi system) for $1 \leqq i, j, k \leqq n$. We can compute $d\omega$ as

$$d\omega(X_i, X_k) = -\omega([X_i, X_k]) = -\sum_{j=1}^{n} \rho_{ik}^j \omega(X_j) = -c_{ik}.$$

On the other hand,

$$d\omega = \tfrac{1}{2} B\omega \wedge \omega,$$

where B is uniquely determined by $\{b_{ik}\} = \{-b_{ki}\}$. From this we have $b_{ik} = -c_{ik}$, and so the system is involutive if and only if the terms involving b_{ik} vanish. Q.E.D.

We can state Theorem 2 in a more elegant way if we use the concept of an *ideal* of exterior differential forms. Let $E^*(M)$ be the set of all differential forms. An *ideal* of $E^*(M)$ is a subspace $\mathscr{I}$, which has the property that whenever $\omega \in \mathscr{I}$ and $\tilde{\omega} \in E^*(M)$, then $\omega \wedge \tilde{\omega} \in \mathscr{I}$. Obviously, let $\mathscr{I}$ be a subspace of $E^*(M)$, i.e., a collection of 1-forms closed under addition and multiplication by real numbers. Then the set $E^*(M) \wedge \mathscr{I} = \{\tilde{\omega} \wedge \omega \mid \omega \in \mathscr{I}\}$ is an ideal generated by $\mathscr{I}$. Now suppose that Δ is a vector-field system on M and suppose that $\mathscr{I}$ is the collection of 1-forms ω on M which vanishes on Δ, i.e., for each $p \in M$, $\omega_p(X_p) = 0$ for all $X_p \in \Delta_p$. $\mathscr{I}$ is a subspace. In fact, if $f \in C^\infty(M)$ and $\omega \in \mathscr{I}$, then $f\omega \in \mathscr{I}$.

Theorem 3 *(Integrability Conditions in Terms of a Differential Ideal) A vector-field system of the marginal rates of substitution Δ is completely integrable if and only if the ideal $\mathscr{I}(\Delta)$ is a differential ideal, i.e.,*

$$d\mathscr{I} \subset \mathscr{I}, \tag{8}$$

where $d\mathscr{I} = \{d\omega \mid \omega \in \mathscr{I}\}$.

Proof We merely present the steps of the proof. Let ω be a 1-form in $\mathscr{I}(\Delta)$, and let $X_1, \ldots, X_n$ be smooth vector fields lying in Δ. Then the involutiveness of Δ implies that $d\omega \equiv 0$. Hence $d\omega \in \mathscr{I}(\Delta)$, and $\mathscr{I}(\Delta)$ is a differential ideal. Conversely, suppose that $\mathscr{J}(\Delta)$ is a differential ideal. Let Y_0 and Y_1 be vector fields lying in Δ. On writing the extended form as

$$\omega[Y_0, Y_1] = -d\omega(Y_0, Y_1) + Y_0\omega(Y) - Y_1\omega(Y_0),$$

the right-hand side of the above is shown to be identically zero since $\mathscr{J}(\Delta)$ is a differential ideal and since $\omega \in \mathscr{J}(\Delta)$. Thus $\omega([Y_0, Y_1])(x) \equiv 0$. The final step is to show that $[Y_0, Y_1](x) \in \Delta(x)$ and Δ is involutive. Q.E.D.

Recovery of a Preference from a Demand System

15. We have thus far studied the integrability conditions in terms of the marginal rates of substitution functions. We can apply the same reasoning to a given system of observable demand functions. Suppose that the demand system

$$x = f(P, I), \qquad P = (P_1, \ldots, P_{n+1}), \tag{9}$$

is given from observation satisfying $Px = I$. Then from Roy's identity, we can write

$$x_j = -\frac{\partial V}{\partial P_j}\bigg/\frac{\partial V}{\partial I} = f^j(P, I), \qquad 1 \leqq j \leqq n + 1, \tag{9'}$$

where V is the indirect utility function associated with the direct utility function U. Writing

$$X_j = \frac{\partial}{\partial P_j} + f^j(P, I)\frac{\partial}{\partial I}, \tag{10}$$

we can formulate theorems formally identically with the previous theorems.

An alternative way of recovering a preference from observable demand functions is to consider the compensated (Hicks) demand functions

$$x^* = f^*(p, U), \tag{11}$$

where the $p = \{P_j/I\}$ are real prices, $1 \leqq j \leqq n$. Here x^* is a solution of $\min_x px$ subject to $U = U(x)$. The compensated demand function system $f^*(p, U)$ together with $U = U(x^*)$ constitutes a 1-differential form. Formally, this is again identical to the case (6), and all the results in the previous theorems can be applied with appropriate changes in the notations. Here we have

$$\omega = \sum_{j=1}^{n+1} f^{*j}(p, U)\, dp_j. \tag{12}$$

We shall leave the formal statement for (12) to the interested reader.

IV. Economic Equilibrium as a Contact Transformation: Recoverability of a Mixed System

Optimality and Contact Transformation

16. In many cases market behavior may be observable as a system of *mixed* variables, such as quantity and price vectors (Houthakker's addilog case in point). Part IV deals with the recoverability problem of such a system—a *mixed* system. Turning our attention now to the behavior of the rational firm, we first show that cost minimization may be regarded as a contact transformation of Lie's theory. By applying the theory of contact transformation, the underlying production function may be recoverable as the "generating function" of the given contact transformation (Campbell [1966], Eisenhart [1933], Hermann [1973], Lovelock, and Rund [1975]). This type of approach is particularly useful when the underlying technology is expressed in the form of a second-order differential equation system of, say, the partial elasticities of substitution.

Let $(x_1, \ldots, x_{n+1}) \in \mathbb{R}^{n+1}_{++}$ be the vector of factor inputs. Let $R = (R_1, \ldots, R_n)$ be the vector of the marginal rates of substitution between the x_ith and the x_{n+1}th factor inputs multiplied by (-1); i.e., $-R_i = F_i/F_{n+1}$, $F_i = \partial F/\partial x_i$, $F_{n+1} = \partial F/\partial x_{n+1}$, where F is a technology with the usual regularity conditions such as $-R \in \mathbb{R}^n_{++}$ and concavity. For the sake of the notational convenience, we set

$$z = x_{n+1}. \tag{13}$$

Optimal behavior of cost minimization under the technological constraint is expressed by the *Pfaffian equation*

$$dz - \sum_{i=1}^{n} R_i\, dx_i = 0. \tag{14}$$

Assume that the optimal market behavior is observable by the following $(n + 1)$ unconnected transformations in the $2n + 1$ variables of z, x, and R:

$$\bar{z} = Z(z, x_1, \ldots, x_n, R_1, \ldots, R_n), \tag{15-i}$$

$$\bar{x}_i = X_i(z, x_1, \ldots, x_n, R_1, \ldots, R_n), \qquad 1 \leqq i \leqq n. \tag{15-ii}$$

The transformation scheme (15-i), (15-ii) and

$$\bar{R}_i = P_i(z, x_1, \ldots, x_n, R_1, \ldots, R_n), \qquad 1 \leqq i \leqq n, \tag{15-iii}$$

defines a *contact transformation*[5] if the Pfaffian equation (14) is *unaltered* (*invariant*) under the transformation (15); i.e.,

$$d\bar{z} - \sum_{i=1}^{n} \bar{R}_i \, d\bar{x}_i = \rho\left(dz - \sum_{i=1}^{n} R_i \, dx_i\right), \tag{16}$$

where $\rho = \rho(z, x_1, \ldots, x_n; R_1, \ldots, R_n) \neq 0$.

When the $n + 1$ quantities $Z, X_1, \ldots, X_n$ are obtained as $n + 1$ functionally independent integrals of the equations

$$[Z, X_i] = 0, \qquad [X_i, X_j] = 0, \qquad 1 \leqq i, j \leqq n, \tag{17}$$

where $[f^r, f^s]$ are the *Poisson brackets* defined by

$$[f^r, f^s] = \sum_{i=1}^{n} \frac{\partial f^r}{\partial R_i}\left(\frac{\partial f^s}{\partial x_i} + R_i \frac{\partial f^s}{\partial x_{n+1}}\right) - \sum_{i=1}^{n} \frac{\partial f^s}{\partial R_i}\left(\frac{\partial f^r}{\partial x_i} + R_i \frac{\partial f^r}{\partial x_{n+1}}\right), \tag{18}$$

$$1 \leqq r, s \leqq n + 1, \qquad f^k = X_k \quad (1 \leqq k \leqq n), \qquad f^{n+1} = Z;$$

and when the quantities $P_1, \ldots, P_n$ are determined, either from the n equations

$$\frac{\partial Z}{\partial x_i} + R_i \frac{\partial Z}{\partial z} = \sum_{r=1}^{n} P_r\left(\frac{\partial X_r}{\partial x_i} + R_i \frac{\partial X_r}{\partial z}\right), \qquad 1 \leqq i \leqq n, \tag{19}$$

or from the equations

$$\frac{\partial Z}{\partial R_i} = \sum_{r=1}^{n} P_r \frac{\partial X_r}{\partial R_i}, \qquad 1 \leqq i \leqq n, \tag{20}$$

the two sets of n equations being equivalent to one another; and finally, when ρ denotes the nonvanishing quantity

$$\rho = \frac{\partial Z}{\partial z} - \sum_{r=1}^{n} P_r \frac{\partial X_r}{\partial z}, \tag{21}$$

then the relation

$$dZ - \sum_{i=1}^{n} P_i \, dX_i = \rho\left(dz - \sum_{i=1}^{n} R_i \, dx_i\right) \tag{22}$$

is satisfied identically. These conditions are *both necessary and sufficient for* (15) *to form a contact transformation.* When (15) is a contact transformation, we also have the *Poisson brackets* satisfying

$$\begin{aligned} &[Z, P_i] = \rho P_i, \qquad [P_i, X_i] = -\rho \qquad (1 \leqq i, j \leqq n), \\ &[P_i, X_j] = 0, \qquad [P_i, P_j] = 0 \qquad (i \neq j). \end{aligned} \tag{23}$$

[5] The distinctive idea of contact transformations is derived from geometrical considerations applied to hyperspace. A contact transformation obviously transforms two elements of surface, that *touch* one another, into two other elements of surface that also *touch* one another.

When $Z, X_1, \ldots, X_n$ satisfy (17), they are said to be in *involution*. The conditions for the existence of the contact transformation do not require any equation to be satisfied by any one of the quantities $Z, X_1, \ldots, X_n$ alone, and the preceding relation for coexistence holds for all functions which satisfy the equations. Hence there is an arbitrary element in the equations that define the contact transformation. Thus we could choose any *one* of the observable relations $Z, X_1, \ldots, X_n$ arbitrarily, or any other arbitrary relation could be chosen that is not inconsistent with the aggregate of conditions and equations.

Theorem 4 *(Recoverability of a Technology from a Mixed System) When the optimal behavior of the firm is observable in the $(n + 1)$ unconnected "mixed" equations $Z, X_1, \ldots, X_n$, then the underlying technology is completely recoverable if and only if the Poisson brackets satisfy the conditions of involution.*

Proof If and only if (17) is met, then $Z, X_1, \ldots, X_n$ from the Pfaffian system, yielding the underlying technology as the generating function (Campbell [1966]). Q.E.D.

17. The economic implication of the foregoing theorem can be observed directly from the following: Consider a firm which produces output Y using a given technology with $(n + 1)$ inputs,

$$F[C(Y); z, x] = 0, \tag{24}$$

where $C(Y) = (C_1(Y), \ldots, C_{n+1}(Y))$, $z = x_{n+1}$, $x = (x_1, \ldots, x_n)$. Assume that (24) satisfies the usual conditions of a neoclassical technology with $\partial F/\partial C_i \neq 0$, $\partial F/\partial z \neq 0$, $\partial F/\partial x_i \neq 0$. The objective of the firm is to choose z and x such that the total cost $w_z z + \sum_{i=1}^{n} w_i x_i$ be minimum subject to $F = 0$, where the w are given prices of the factor inputs. Assume further that the bordered determinant

$$\Delta = \begin{vmatrix} 0 & F_{x_i} \\ F_{C_j} & F_{x_i C_j} \end{vmatrix}, \qquad 1 \leqq i, j \leqq n + 1,$$

is nonvanishing. Then

(a) The first-order conditions for cost minimization together with the constraint

$$\frac{w_i}{w_z} = -R_i = \frac{\partial F}{\partial x_i}\bigg/\frac{\partial F}{\partial z} = \frac{\partial Y}{\partial x_i}\bigg/\frac{\partial Y}{\partial z} > 0, \qquad i = 1, \ldots, n, \quad F = 0, \tag{25}$$

satisfy the conditions of "involution."

(b) The optimal solutions for (25) and functions generated by (19) or (20) constitute a *contact transformation.*

Obviously, the factor demand functions for z and x are in "involution," with $Z = z - f^{n-1}$ and $X_i = x_i - f^i$, and $x_i = f^i(R; C(Y))$, $1 \leqq i \leqq n$, and $z = x_{n+1} = f^{n+1}(R; C(Y))$ together with $\bar{R}_i = R_i$ constitute a (primal) contact transformation. Since the cost minimization process under a given technology constitutes a contact transformation, the underlying technology is a *generating function of the transformation.* Since the parameters

$$C = (C_1, \ldots, C_{n+1})$$

are essential, the existence of the generating function (24) is guaranteed. By eliminating $R_1, \ldots, R_n$ among $(n + 1)$ demand equations, we get (24).

There is a *dual* to (25). Consider any cost function

$$G = g(w_1, \ldots, w_{n+1}; C(Y)) - \gamma = 0. \tag{26}$$

Then the partial differentiation process of deriving the factor demand functions (Shephard's lemma) together with the cost function itself can be used to obtain a *dual* contact transformation. By defining

$$\frac{x_i}{z} = -Q_i = \frac{\partial g}{\partial w_i} \bigg/ \frac{\partial g}{\partial w_{n+1}}, \qquad 1 \leqq i \leqq n, \tag{27}$$

and using (26), we can solve for $w_i = h^i(Q; C(Y))$, $1 \leqq i \leqq n$, and $w_{n+1} = h^{n+1}(Q; C(Y))$. Then they satisfy the involution conditions

$$[h^{n+1}, h^i] = 0, \qquad [h^i, h^j] = 0, \qquad 1 \leqq i, j \leqq n, \quad i \neq j.$$

The contact transformation obtained from h^i, h^{n+1}, and $\bar{Q}_i = Q_i$ $(1 \leqq i \leqq n)$ is the *dual contact transformation* to (25). Here the generating function of the dual contact transformation is the cost function (26) itself. The primal and dual contact transformations are special cases of Theorem 4 when the observable equations are *not* mixed. (Here the involution conditions become the symmetry condition of the Slutsky matrix.)

Illustrations

18. Let $x_1 = K$ (capital) and $x_2 = L$ (labor), and let $-R_1 = -R$ be the marginal rate of substitution between capital and labor Y_K/Y_L, which is also equal to their price ratio w_K/w_L. Consider the transformation scheme of the coordinates of a lineal element (K, L, R),

$$\bar{K} = \bar{K}(K, L, R), \qquad \bar{L} = \bar{L}(K, L, R), \qquad \bar{R} = \bar{R}(K, L, R).$$

Among the possible transformations on the coordinates of a lineal element, those which transform every union of elements consisting of K, L, R into a union consisting of $\bar{K}$, $\bar{L}$, $\bar{R}$ are *contact transformations*. The necessary and sufficient conditions that $\bar{K}$, $\bar{L}$, and $\bar{R}$ form a contact transformation are: The Poisson bracket satisfies the condition $[\bar{K}, \bar{L}] = 0$ and $\bar{R} = \bar{L}_R/\bar{K}_R$, i.e.,

$$[\bar{K}, \bar{L}] = 0 = \frac{\partial \bar{K}}{\partial R}\left(\frac{\partial \bar{L}}{\partial K} + R\frac{\partial \bar{L}}{\partial L}\right) - \frac{\partial \bar{L}}{\partial R}\left(\frac{\partial \bar{K}}{\partial K} + R\frac{\partial \bar{K}}{\partial L}\right)$$

$$= \begin{vmatrix} \bar{K}_R & \bar{K}_K + R\bar{K}_L \\ \bar{L}_R & \bar{L}_K + R\bar{K}_L \end{vmatrix} = 0, \qquad \text{and} \qquad \bar{R} = \frac{\bar{L}_R}{\bar{K}_R} = \frac{\bar{L}_K + R\bar{L}_L}{\bar{K}_K + R\bar{K}_L}.$$

The common ratio ρ can be shown as

$$\rho = (\bar{L}_L - \bar{R}\bar{K}_L)/1 = (\bar{L}_K - \bar{R}\bar{K}_K)/-R.$$

Here in the contact transformation scheme, we assume explicitly that

$$\partial\bar{K}/\partial R \not\equiv 0 \qquad \text{or} \qquad \partial\bar{L}/\partial R \not\equiv 0.$$

When $\partial\bar{K}/\partial R \equiv \partial\bar{L}/\partial R \equiv 0$, the contact transformation will be reduced to the (once) extended point transformation studied in Chapter 2. We have excluded this special case unless specific mention is made to the contrary.

The foregoing can be used to recover the underlying technology from the observable market behavior of the three variables K, L, and R by two relations if and only if the condition of involution is satisfied. Consider the following (general CES) example: If we observe a mixed system

$$\bar{K} = C_1(Y) = L^{-\rho} - KRL^{-(1+\rho)}, \qquad \bar{L} = C_2(Y) = -R(L/K)^{-(1+\rho)},$$

the underlying technology is recoverable since the involution condition is always met; i.e.,

$$\begin{aligned}[C_1, C_2] = {} & -RL^{-(1+\rho)}[(1+\rho)L^{-(1+\rho)}K^{(1+\rho)} \\ & - (1+\rho)RL^{-(1+\rho)-1}K^{(1+\rho)+1} - (1+\rho)L^{-(1+\rho)}K^{(1+\rho)} \\ & + (1+\rho)RL^{-(1+\rho)-1}K^{(1+\rho)+1}] \equiv 0.\end{aligned}$$

By eliminating R between C_1 and C_2, we obtain a family of general CES functions $C_1(Y) = L^{-\rho} + C_2(Y)K^{-\rho}$. It should be noted that of the three functions $\bar{K}$, $\bar{L}$, $\bar{R}$ in the contact transformation, either *one* of $\bar{K}$ and $\bar{L}$ may be selected arbitrarily and the other one is then determined as a solution of the linear partial differential equation of *involution*. With $\bar{K}$ and $\bar{L}$ thus selected, $\bar{R}$ is uniquely determined. Hence, among three equations of the contact transformation, only $\bar{K}$ and $\bar{L}$ should be initially determined.

Next consider the cost-minimizing firm with a given technology,

$$F[C_1(Y), C_2(Y); K, L] = 0,$$

where the functions $C_1(Y)$ and $C_2(Y)$ are the two essential parameters.[6] Then the first-order equilibrium condition for cost minimization together with the constraint function

$$w_K/w_L = -R = F_K/F_L, \qquad F = 0,$$

satisfies the condition of "involution"; and the optimum solutions expressed in terms of C_1 and C_2 and the third variable C_3,

$$C_1(Y) = \bar{K}(K, L, R), \qquad C_2(Y) = \bar{L}(K, L, R),$$

$$C_3(Y) = -\frac{\partial F}{\partial C_1}\bigg/\frac{\partial F}{\partial C_2} = \bar{R}(K, L, R),$$

constitute a *contact transformation*

$$(K, L, R) \to (C_1, C_2, C_3),$$

i.e.,

$$dC_2 - C_3\, dC_1 = \rho(K, L, R)(dL - R\, dK), \qquad \rho \neq 0.$$

Here a production function

$$F[C_1(Y), C_2(Y); K, L] = 0,$$

operating under the cost-minimizing firm, is the *generating function* of the contact transformation.

The cost function is the minimized value of the total cost as a function of the factor prices and the output level, $G = g[w_K, w_L; C_1(Y), C_2(Y)] - \gamma = 0$. The partial differentiation process of deriving the factor demand functions for K and L by Shephard's lemma from a cost function constitutes a "*dual*" *contact transformation* together with the definition of

$$\bar{Q} = -\frac{\partial g}{\partial C_1}\bigg/\frac{\partial g}{\partial C_2} \qquad \text{and} \qquad Q = -\frac{\partial g}{\partial w_K}\bigg/\frac{\partial g}{\partial w_L}.$$

The original (or primal) and dual contact transformations are *equivalent* since they generate the identical factor demand and inverse factor demand functions. The *duality* of contact transformations for (K, L, R) and for (w_K, w_L, Q) can be used to derive the equivalent form of a production function, the "dual" (or "shadow") production function. Any original (primal) production function

$$F[K, L; C_1(Y), C_2(Y)] = 0$$

has its equivalent representation as the "dual" ("shadow") production function

$$F^*(K, L; C_1(Y), C_2(Y)] = 0$$

[6] Hence F may be considered as a general solution of the holothetic differential equation of the second order with C_1 and C_2 being two arbitrary constants.

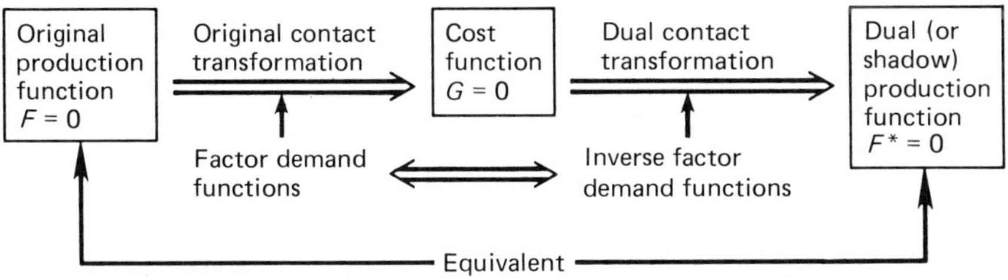

Figure 1

which is implicitly homogeneous degree one, in K and L. The cost function and the "shadow" production functions are *truly dual* in the sense that both functions are concave and homogeneous degree one with respect to w_K and w_L, and with respect to K and L. The partial differentiation of the cost and "shadow" production functions with their respective arguments gives the system of the factor demand and its inverse factor demand functions, respectively.[7] Figure 1 illustrates the link and equivalency of the three functions related to the contact transformations.

Contact Holotheticity

19. We now study the case of technical progress in which the technical progress functions for the x_i depend not only on their quantities but also the marginal rates of substitution. We assume

$$\begin{aligned} &\bar{x}_i = \bar{x}_i(x_1, \ldots, x_n, z = x_{n+1}, R_1, \ldots, R_n : t), && \text{(28-i)} \\ T^c: \quad &\bar{z} = \bar{x}_{n+1}(x_1, \ldots, x_n, z = x_{n+1}, R_1, \ldots, R_n : t), && \text{(28-ii)} \\ &\bar{R}_i = \bar{R}_i(x_1, \ldots, x_n, z = x_{n+1}, R_1, \ldots, R_n : t), \quad 1 \leqq i \leqq n. && \text{(28-iii)} \end{aligned}$$

(28) will be a Lie type of technical progress provided that T^c defines *a one-parameter group of contact transformation—a Lie "contact type" of technical progress*. Like any other group, it has the infinitesimal transformations ; i.e.,

$$\begin{aligned} &\bar{x}_i = x_i + \xi_i(x, z, R)t, && \text{(29-i)} \\ T^c: \quad &\bar{z} = z + \zeta(x, z, R)t, && \text{(29-ii)} \\ &\bar{R}_i = R_i + \pi_i(x, z, R)t, \qquad 1 \leqq i \leqq n, && \text{(29-iii)} \end{aligned}$$

[7] Let the generating function of a contact transformation be $F = \sum_i^n u_i \bar{u}_i + z + \bar{z} = 0$, where $u_i = u_i(x_i)$, $\bar{u}_i = \bar{u}_i(Y)$, $z = z(x_{n+1})$, and $z = \bar{z}(Y)$, $1 \leq i \leq n$. Then the resulting transformation defines the *Legendre contact transformation*. The technology here is implicitly separable.

where $z = x_{n+1}, x = (x_1, \ldots, x_n), R = (R_1, \ldots, R_n)$. The transformation is an infinitesimal contact transformation if the Pfaffian equation

$$dz - \sum_{i=1}^{n} R_i\, dx_i = 0$$

is *unaltered*; that is to say, if we have

$$d\bar{z} - \sum_{i=1}^{n} \bar{R}_i\, d\bar{x}_i = (1 + \rho t)\left(dz - \sum_{i=1}^{n} R_i\, dx_i\right), \qquad 1 + \rho t \neq 0, \tag{30}$$

where ρ is some function of the coordinates of the elements. Now since $d\bar{z} = dz + t\, d\zeta$, $d\bar{x}_i = dx_i + t\, d\xi_i$, $d\bar{R}_i = dR_i + t\, d\pi_i$, by defining the *characteristic* function associated with (29) as

$$W = \sum_{i=1}^{n} R_i \xi_i - \zeta, \tag{31}$$

we have

$$\begin{aligned} d\bar{z} - \sum_{i=1}^{n} \bar{R}_i\, d\bar{x}_i &= dz - \sum_{i=1}^{n} R_i\, dx_i + t\left(d\zeta - \sum_{i=1}^{n} R_i\, d\xi_i - \sum_{i=1}^{n} \pi_i\, dx_i\right) \\ &= dz - \sum_{i=1}^{n} R_i\, dx_i - t\, dW + t\left(\sum_{i=1}^{n} (\xi_i\, dR_i - \pi_i\, dx_i)\right) \end{aligned}$$

(neglecting small quantities of the order t^2); and therefore,

$$\sum_{i=1}^{n} (\xi_i\, dR_i - \pi_i\, dx_i) - dW = \rho\left(dz - \sum_{i=1}^{n} R_i\, dx_i\right),$$

so that

$$\xi_i = \frac{\partial W}{\partial R_i}, \qquad \rho = -\frac{\partial W}{\partial z}, \qquad \pi_i = -R_i \frac{\partial W}{\partial z} - \frac{\partial W}{\partial x_i},$$

$$\zeta = \sum_{i=1}^{n} R_i \xi_i - W = \sum_{i=1}^{n} R_i \frac{\partial W}{\partial R_i} - W.$$

We then have the infinitesimal contact operator

$$U^{c} = \sum_{i=1}^{n} \frac{\partial W}{\partial R_i} \frac{\partial}{\partial x_i} + \left(\sum_{i=1}^{n} R_i \frac{\partial W}{\partial R_i} - W\right) \frac{\partial}{\partial z} - \sum_{i=1}^{n} \left(R_i \frac{\partial W}{\partial z} + \frac{\partial W}{\partial x_i}\right) \frac{\partial}{\partial R_i}. \tag{32}$$

The effect of any infinitesimal transformation on ϕ can be expressed as

$$U^{c}\phi = [W, \phi] - W\, \partial\phi/\partial z, \tag{33}$$

where $[W, \phi]$ is the Poisson bracket

$$[W, \phi] = \sum_{i=1}^{n} \left[\frac{\partial W}{\partial R_i}\left(\frac{\partial \phi}{\partial x_i} + R_i \frac{\partial \phi}{\partial z}\right) - \frac{\partial \phi}{\partial R_i}\left(\frac{\partial W}{\partial x_i} + R_i \frac{\partial W}{\partial z}\right)\right].$$

The *contact holotheticity* is the *invariance* of ϕ under (33). Hence, the *necessary and sufficient condition* that the function ϕ should admit the infinitesimal contact transformation with the characteristic function W is

$$[W, \phi] = W\, \partial\phi/\partial z. \tag{34}$$

Given a Lie contact type of technical progress with its characteristic function (32), there exists a general family of technology holothetic under this type of technical progress (see the Appendix, Theorem 19).

In summary, we have

Theorem 5 *(Lie Contact Type of Technical Change) Given a Lie contact type of technical progress by its characteristic function W, then the infinitesimal technical progress functions can be written as*

$$\zeta = \sum_{i=1}^{n} R_i \frac{\partial W}{\partial R_i} - W, \qquad \xi_i = \frac{\partial W}{\partial R_i},$$

$$\pi_i = -R_i \frac{\partial W}{\partial z} - \frac{\partial W}{\partial x_i}, \qquad 1 \leqq i \leqq n.$$

V. Simultaneous Recovery Problems: Externality of Production and Preference

Motivation—Conglomerate's Operations

20. Consider a conglomerate which has two operating units, one in the domestic country and the other in a foreign country, each producing and selling Y^1 and Y^2 types of products. The production technologies of the conglomerate are given by usual neoclassical production functions $Y^1 = f^1(x_1, x_2)$ and $Y^2 = f^2(x_1, x_3)$, where x_1 may be considered as a common factor input such as "management" which applies to the main operation f^1 and to the subsidiary operation f^2, while x_2 and x_3 are aggregates of all other factor inputs "locally" used by each operation. The advantage of the conglomerate is to utilize the "externality" of x_1 in two distinct operations. The objective of the conglomerate is first to choose the optimal combinations of x_1, x_2, and x_3 such that the total cost of the conglomerate is minimized subject to the two technological constraints under the fixed input prices, and then to choose the optimal output combinations of Y^1 and Y^2 such that total profit is maximized. The problems that concern us here are not only to study the basic properties of the cost and profit functions, thus of the factor demand and product supply functions, but also to investigate the possibilities of "recovering" the underlying two technologies simultaneously from market observations and from some other available data. The latter presents us with the "simultaneous recovery problem" of two total differential equations.

A similar situation arises when there exists "consumption externality." Thus the ith individual's preference may be affected by the jth individual's preference when both individuals share common consumption goods in their utility functions, such as common public goods (Musgrave [1959]). The situation is basically the same as the conglomerate example, except that in this case it may be more difficult to observe market behavior and to collect other information necessary to recover the two individuals' preference orderings simultaneously. In what follows we shall study these simultaneous recovery problems from a formal point of view.[8]

Theory of the Firm under Multiple Production Processes

21. The firm (conglomerate) has m different (independent) production processes for m different outputs given by

$$Y^j = f^j(x), \qquad j = 1, \dots, m, \quad x = (x_1, \dots, x_n), \quad n > m, \tag{35}$$

where the x are factor inputs. Some x_i in the jth production may be zero, indicating that the factor may only be used for "local" production of the jth output. In general, we assume $\partial f^j/\partial x_i \geqq 0$, and when $\partial f^j/\partial x_i \equiv 0$, the factor may be called a "local" or "subsidiary" factor, while when $\partial f^j/\partial x_i > 0$, it is a common factor used for different processes. Assume further than the f^j have at least one factor input whose marginal product is always positive (the f^j have the usual regularity conditions of concavity, smoothness, etc.). If we eliminate the possibility of corner solutions, the Kuhn–Tucker optimal solutions for cost minimization at a given set of factor prices $p = (p_1, \dots, p_n)$ will yield

$$p_i - \lambda^j f^j_i(x) = 0 \qquad \text{for } x \geqq 0, \quad 1 \leqq i \leqq n, \tag{36-i}$$

$$Y^j - f^j(x) = 0 \qquad \text{for } x \geqq 0, \quad 1 \leqq j \leqq m, \tag{36-ii}$$

(summation convention operative)

[8] One might argue that if we begin with an "aggregate" production (or transformation) function $F(Y^1, Y^2, x_1, x_2, x_3) = 0$, rather than with two production functions f^1 and f^2, the "simultaneous" recovery problem will disappear. But in many cases, it is more realistic to consider two distinct operations such as domestic versus foreign. It is hardly justifiable to assume one aggregate operation in such a case. The conglomerate uses two distinct production technologies of domestic and foreign types. However, it will be shown later that there always exists a sort of "surrogate" aggregate production function combining two distinct technologies.

Solving this system of equations, we get the factor demand functions g^i and the marginal cost functions λ^j as

$$\begin{aligned} x_i &= g^i(p, Y), & 1 \leqq i \leqq n, && p = (p_1, \ldots, p_n), \\ \lambda^j &= = h^j(p, Y), & 1 \leqq j \leqq m, && Y = (Y^1, \ldots, Y^m). \end{aligned} \tag{37}$$

It is seen that the x_i *are homogeneous functions of degree zero with respect to p, while the* λ^j *are homogeneous functions of degree one with respect to p.* The factor demand functions also satisfy the usual Slutsky equations

$$\begin{aligned} \partial x_i/\partial p_s &= \Delta_{is}/\Delta, & 1 \leqq i, s \leqq n, \\ \partial x_i/\partial Y^j &= \Delta_{i, n+j}/\Delta, & 1 \leqq j \leqq m, \end{aligned} \tag{38}$$

where Δ is the bordered determinant of $(n + m) \times (n + m)$ defined by

$$\Delta = \begin{vmatrix} \lambda^j f^j_{is} & f^j_s \\ f^j_i & 0 \end{vmatrix}, \qquad 1 \leqq i, s \leqq n, \quad 1 \leqq j \leqq m$$

and Δ_{is} and $\Delta_{i,n+j}$ are cofactors of Δ with appropriate positions. We observe that $\partial x_i/\partial p_s = S_{is}$ are the Slutsky (aggregate) substitution terms and $\partial x_i/\partial Y^j = Q_{ij}$ are the output effects on the x_i. From the assumption of the stability (the second-order conditions) of the relative cost minimum, the own substitution effects $\partial x_i/\partial p_i$ are negative, while the output effects may or may not be positive. Also the Slutsky equations are symmetric and negative semidefinite due to the symmetric property and the second-order conditions of Δ and due to the homogeneity of x with respect to p.

The aggregate (minimized) cost function is obtained by substituting x into $C = p_i x_i$ as

$$C = C(p, Y) = p_i g^i(p, Y), \qquad \text{summation on } i, \tag{39}$$

which satisfies the usual property of degree-one-homogeneity and concavity in p. *Shephard's lemma* can also be applied to obtain the factor demand functions from (39) as

$$x_i = \partial C/\partial p_i, \qquad 1 \leqq i \leqq n. \tag{40}$$

The profit of the firm will be maximized when the products are sold (in the competitive markets) by the usual rules

$$\partial \Pi/\partial Y^j = \pi_j - (\partial C/\partial Y^j) = 0, \qquad 1 \leqq j \leqq m, \tag{41}$$

where the π_j are the prices of Y^j and $\Pi = \pi_j Y^j - C(p, Y)$ is the profit equation. Solving the foregoing for Y^j, we obtain the supply functions of Y^j as

$$Y^j = k^j(p, \pi), \qquad 1 \leqq j \leqq m, \tag{42}$$

which are homogeneous degree zero with respect to p and π. Substitution of (42) into the x_i in (37) yields the factor demand functions as

$$x_i = g^i(p, Y(p, \pi)) = \phi^i(p, \pi) \tag{43}$$

which are also homogeneous degree zero in p and π. The (maximized) profit function is derived by substituting (42) and (43) into $\Pi = \pi_j Y^j - C(p, Y)$ as

$$\Pi = \Pi(p, \pi) = \pi_j Y^j(p, \pi) - C(p, Y(p, \pi)), \tag{44}$$

which is homogeneous degree one in p and π with $\partial\Pi/\partial\pi_j > 0$ for $Y^j > 0$, and $\partial\Pi/\partial p_i < 0$ for $x_i > 0$. *Hotelling's lemma* and the derivative property will also hold for this *general* case, since we can show that

$$\begin{aligned} \partial\Pi/\partial\pi_j &= Y^j(p, \pi), \qquad 1 \leqq j \leqq m, \\ -\partial\Pi/\partial p_i &= x_i(p, \pi), \qquad 1 \leqq i \leqq n, \end{aligned} \tag{45}$$

from

$$\frac{\partial\Pi}{\partial\pi_j} = Y^j + \left(\pi_k - \frac{\partial C}{\partial Y^k}\right)\frac{\partial Y^k}{\partial\pi_j} = Y^j, \qquad 1 \leqq k, j \leqq m$$

[$\pi_k = \partial C/\partial Y^k$ from (41)], and

$$\frac{\partial\Pi}{\partial p_i} = \left(\pi_j - \frac{\partial C}{\partial Y^j}\right)\frac{\partial Y^j}{\partial p_i} - p_s S_{si} - x_i = -x_i$$

($p_s S_{si} = 0$ because of the homogeneity-of-zero property for x).

Existence and Recovery of "Aggregate" (or Surrogate) Production Function

The duality principle may be applied to show the existence of an "aggregate" or "surrogate" production function corresponding to the cost function (39). The dual function of (39) is the *aggregate* (*or surrogate*) production (transformation) function.[9] The reader can show that *the cost function is* not *separable with respect to the aggregate output even when all the individual technologies are homothetic* (*or homogeneous*). (It is certainly not separable

[9] The reader is asked to show the other properties of the duality principle, such as concavity and monotonicity, of the cost and "aggregate" production functions.

with respect to the individual output.) This is in direct contrast with the case where there exists no externality.[10]

The recovery of the aggregate production function poses no problem, if we can observe market behavior of the x_i. Substituting these into the cost equation, we can immediately obtain the cost function, from which the marginal cost functions may be derived. Those will be used to construct the aggregate production function. The direct recovery of the aggregate production function may be obtained by using the market behavior of the aggregate marginal rates of substitution. Thus, if we can express the factor price ratios as functions of factor inputs and outputs, we have the partial differential equations corresponding to the total differential equation for the aggregate output function. All the discussions in the previous sections on the necessary and sufficient conditions of integrability will be directly applied.

Simultaneous Recovery of All the Individual Production Functions

22. First, it is important to note that the price ratios comprise only one set of information necessary to recover individual technologies. In order to recover m production processes, we need additional $(m - 1)$ sets of information. Let us assume that market observations have uncovered (through the demand functions and other information) a system of partial differential equations for the marginal products of all factor inputs in m processes.

$$\partial Y^j/\partial x_i = G_i^j(x; Y), \qquad i = 1, \ldots, n, \quad j = 1, \ldots, m, \quad n > m, \tag{46}$$

in some neighborhood of a point $(a; b) = (a^1, \ldots, a^n; b^1, \ldots, b^m)$. The simultaneous recoverability problem is to find a solution consisting of functions $Y^j = f^j(x)$, $j = 1, \ldots, m$, which satisfy the system of Eqs. (46) with the initial conditions $f(a) = b$. Define an n-dimensional submanifold of $\mathbb{R}_+^{n+m} = \mathbb{R}_+^n \times \mathbb{R}_+^m$ given by $(x) \to (x : f(x))$ whose tangent plane at the point $(x : Y)$ is spanned by n vectors,

$$\begin{aligned} X_1 &= (1, 0, \ldots, 0; G_1^1, \ldots, G_1^m), \\ &\vdots \\ X_n &= (0, 0, \ldots, 1, G_n^1, \ldots, G_n^m). \end{aligned} \tag{47}$$

We then present

Theorem 6 (*Simultaneous Integrability Conditions*) (i) *If and only if*

$$[X_\alpha, X_\beta] = c_{\alpha\beta}^\gamma(x, Y)X_\gamma \qquad (1 \leqq \alpha, \beta, \gamma \leqq n, \quad \text{summation on } \gamma), \tag{48}$$

then m technologies are completely recoverable.

[10] The existence of the aggregate technology may justify the use of an implicit transformation function when there are m outputs.

(ii) *If and only if the following simultaneous integrability conditions are met,*

$$\frac{\partial G_i^j}{\partial x_k} + \frac{\partial G_i^j}{\partial Y^s} G_k^s = \frac{\partial G_k^j}{\partial x_i} + \frac{\partial G_k^j}{\partial Y^r} G_i^r \qquad \text{(summation on } s \text{ and } r\text{)}$$

$$(i, k = 1, \ldots, n, \quad j, s, r = 1, \ldots, m), \tag{48'}$$

then m technologies $f^j = Y^j$ *are completely recoverable.*

Proof This is the direct application of the Frobenius theorem. Q.E.D.

Remark One of the obvious methods of deriving (46) or its equivalent is to use the factor demand functions. By setting $\gamma^j = 0$ for each j $(1 \leqq j \leqq m)$ in the demand functions, we can obtain a system of m total differential equations, from which m technologies are recoverable.

Two-Stage Simultaneous Recoverability Problems

23. In many cases we may observe only the Slutsky equations, the substitution terms, and output (income) terms. Here we must first recover the underlying system of demand functions in order to recover the technologies which have generated the observed behavior—the two-stage recoverability problem. Suppose that at each level of Y the observations are first given by

$$\partial x_i/\partial p_k = S_{ik}, \qquad 1 \leqq i, k \leqq n, \tag{49}$$

where the S_{ik} are the substitution effects. The first stage is to recover the underlying demand functions from (49). They are completely recoverable if and only if

$$\partial x_i/\partial p_k = S_{ik} = S_{ki} = \partial x_k/\partial p_i, \qquad 1 \leqq i, k \leqq n. \tag{50}$$

The second stage is to recover the underlying production functions using the recovered system of demand functions and other information such as (46).

VI. Recoverability of Dynamic Systems: Recovery of Optimal Growth Models

General Recoverability Problem

24. Over the past half century, many theoretical economists have shown keen interest in the study of optimal dynamic systems. Stimulated by Ramsey's [1928] now most celebrated paper on the mathematical theory of saving, the analysis of optimal dynamic behavior of an economic system has become one of the leading research topics in theoretical economics. Among topics discussed include optimal capital accumulation (turnpike theory), optimal economic growth, optimal population, optimal technical progress, and other related problems (e.g., Samuelson and Solow [1956], Morishima [1964], Burmeister and Dobell [1970], Cass [1965], Koopmans [1965], Sato and Davis [1971], Sato and Ramachandran [1978]). The calculus of variations and the theory of optimal control (including dynamic programming) have served as the most accepted and most exploited tools of modern economic analysis.

The purpose of Part VI is to study the inverse optimal problem as another aspect of the general theory of observable behavior. After presenting a general formulation of the dynamic recovery problem, we analyze in detail the recoverability of simple neoclassical optimal growth models. As the methodology used here is quite general, it has a wide appeal for applicability in many different research areas of dynamic optimality.

Suppose that we are given with a system of $2n$ differential equations of price (implicit price) and quantity change as

$$\dot{q}_i = \psi^i(p, q, t), \qquad \dot{p}_i = \psi^{n+i}(p, q, t), \qquad 1 \leqq i \leqq n. \tag{51}$$

In order that these observations may be *consistent* with and generated from some underlying dynamic optimization behavior, they must satisfy

$$\psi^i(p, q, t) = \partial H/\partial p_i, \qquad \psi^{n+i}(p, q, t) = -\partial H/\partial q_i, \qquad 1 \leqq i \leqq n. \tag{52}$$

If, in addition, we can also observe $\partial H/\partial t$ as

$$\partial H/\partial t = \psi^{2n+1}(p, q, t), \tag{53}$$

then the underlying Hamiltonian can be recovered from

$$dH = \psi^i \, dp_i + \psi^{n+i} \, dq_i + \psi^{2n+1} \, dt, \tag{54}$$

provided that the total differential equation (54) satisfies the *integrability conditions*

$$[\psi^k, \psi^l] = \gamma_{kl}^s \psi^s, \qquad k, l, s = 1, \ldots, 2n + 1. \tag{55}$$

Sometimes it is more reasonable to assume that we observe[11] a system of the second-order differential equations in terms of q, $\dot{q}$, and t, as

$$\phi^i(q, \dot{q}, \ddot{q}, t) = 0, \qquad 1 \leqq i \leqq n. \tag{56}$$

[11] In general, it may be impossible to observe $\partial H/\partial t$ in economic analysis, since there is no observable data for this partial derivative. In fact, the implicit prices p may *not* in general be observable. Hence it is more plausible to begin with the second-order differential equation system consistent with the underlying Lagrangian function.

In order that Eqs. (56) may be the Euler–Lagrange equations of some underlying Lagrange function, they must satisfy the restrictions imposed by (55). Sometimes we may observe the transformed variables $P_i(p, q, t)$ and $Q_i(p, q, t)$, but again the transformed Hamiltonian may be recoverable, provided that they are canonical variables. (The general transformation problem will be studied in Part VII.)

Recoverability of Optimal Growth Models

25. First we restrict the analysis to the simplest case of $n = 1$, where there always exists a solution. Assume a situation in which we observe the equation of motion for the (aggregate) capital–labor ratio q and the differential equation for the (implicit) price $(-p)$ of investment $\dot{q}$ by

$$\dot{q} = h^1(p, q, t), \tag{56-i}$$

$$\dot{p} = h^2(p, q, t). \tag{56-ii}$$

In many cases, since the (implicit) price may not be directly observable, we must indirectly estimate (56), through the behavior of the control variable such as the savings ratio. It is actually more convenient to assume that we observe the behavior in terms of the equivalent form of a single differential equation of the second order in the quantity variable

$$\ddot{q} = F(\dot{q}, q, t). \tag{56'}$$

In many cases, (56) and therefore (56′) may be autonomous.

We want to ask *which optimal growth model generates the observed market behavior consistent with Eq.* (56) *or* (56′). That is to say, we want to determine which utility and welfare function is the true underlying function that is the basis for the observable behavior. More specifically, we ask which Lagrangian L or Hamiltonian H leads to (56′) as a necessary condition for

$$\int_{t_0}^{t_1} L(\dot{q}, q, t)\, dt \to \text{maximum}. \tag{57}$$

In other words, for which function $L = L(\dot{q}, q, t)$ does (56′) coincide with the Euler–Lagrange equation

$$\frac{\partial L}{\partial q} - \frac{d}{dt}\left(\frac{\partial L}{\partial \dot{q}}\right) = 0.$$

This is the so-called *inverse optimal problem* of the calculus of variations and optimal control. The following theorem gives a general answer to the problem

Theorem 7 *(Recovery of a General Optimal Growth Model)* (i) *If the market observation of the capital–labor ratio is given by the second-order differential equation* (56′), *then the most general optimal growth model in terms of its Lagrangian, which might have generated* (56′) *as the Euler–Lagrange equation for* (57), *can be expressed as*

$$L(\dot{q}, q, t) = \int_a^{\dot{q}} (\dot{q} - \sigma)u(\sigma, q, t)\, d\sigma + \int_b^q F(a, s, t)u(a, s, t)\, ds + \frac{d}{dt}[\phi^1(q, t) + \phi^2(t)], \tag{58}$$

where ϕ^1 *and* ϕ^2 *are arbitrary functions, and u is given by*

$$u(\dot{q}, q, t) = A[\alpha(\dot{q}, q, t), \beta(\dot{q}, q, t)]M(\dot{q}, q, t),$$

$$M(\dot{q}, q, t) = \exp\left(-\int^t F_{\dot{q}}[f_\tau(\tau, \alpha(\dot{q}, q, t), \beta(\dot{q}, q, t)), f(\tau, \alpha(\dot{q}, q, t), \beta(\dot{q}, q, t)), \tau]\, d\tau\right) \tag{59}$$

$$f(t, \alpha, \beta) = q(t) \qquad [\textit{solution to } (56')], \tag{60}$$

$$f_t(t, \alpha, \beta) = \dot{q}(t), \tag{61}$$

$$\alpha = \alpha(\dot{q}, q, t) \tag{62}$$

$$\beta = \beta(\dot{q}, q, t) \tag{63}$$

[*solution to* (60) *and* (61)].

(ii) *Alternatively, the corresponding Hamiltonian can be expressed as*

$$H[\dot{q}(p, q, t), q, t] = H(p, q, t) = \int_a^{\dot{q}} \sigma u(\sigma, q, t)\, d\sigma - \int_b^q F(a, s, t)u(a, s, t)\, ds - \frac{\partial}{\partial t}[\phi^1(q, t) + \phi^2(t)], \tag{64}$$

where $\dot{q}$ *is related to p by*

$$p = \frac{\partial L}{\partial \dot{q}} = \int_a^{\dot{q}} u(\sigma, q, t)\, d\sigma + \frac{\partial \phi^1}{\partial q}. \tag{65}$$

Proof See Section 28. Q.E.D.

In order to guarantee the concavity of the recovered utility function, we impose the restrictions on the Lagrangian as

$$L_{\dot{q}\dot{q}} = u < 0 \qquad \text{and} \qquad \begin{vmatrix} L_{\dot{q}\dot{q}} & L_{\dot{q}q} \\ L_{q\dot{q}} & L_{qq} \end{vmatrix} > 0, \tag{66}$$

where

$$L_{\dot{q}\dot{q}} = u(t, q, \dot{q})$$

$$L_{\dot{q}q} = \int_a^{\dot{q}} \frac{\partial u}{\partial q}\, d\sigma + \frac{\partial^2 \phi^1}{\partial q^2}$$

$$L_{qq} = \int_a^{\dot{q}} (\dot{q} - \sigma) \frac{\partial^2 u}{\partial q^2}\, d\sigma + \frac{\partial F(t, a, q)}{\partial q} u(t, a, q) + \frac{\partial u(t, a, q)}{\partial q} F(t, a, q)$$
$$+ \dot{q} \frac{\partial^3 \phi^1}{\partial q^3} + \frac{\partial^3 \phi^1}{\partial q^2\, \partial t}.$$

One important aspect of the recovered utility function in terms of (58) is that *there are infinitely many Lagrangians or Hamiltonians corresponding to the given observable differential equation* (56′). This is due to the fact that there are arbitrary factors in integration resulting from

(i) the integration limits a and b,
(ii) the total time derivative $d(\phi^1 + \phi^2)/dt$,
(iii) the arbitrary factor A in $u = AM$.

The first two factors are not important since we may set $a = b = 0$ and since $d(\phi^1 + \phi^2)/dt$ may be considered as a null term giving the same Euler–Lagrange equation as the original one[12] (see Chapter 7). *However, the third factor is not so trivial, for by choosing different functions for A, the resulting utility function can be made to have entirely different and unrelated forms.* For instance, the same differential equation of observable market behavior may result in both time-independent and time-dependent Lagrangian functions, which are not related. This property may be used to advantage in a recoverability problem since it may suffice to recover only time-independent Lagrangian as a *surrogate* utility function. The optimal behavior exhibited in (56′) is actually too general, and therefore, we now turn to more manageable cases.

[12] The first case (i) is a dynamic counterpart of the so-called transformation problem in static utility and welfare maximization, in that any monotonic transformation of a utility function gives the same observable demand behavior.

Local Recoverability of the Ramsey–Koopmans–Cass and Liviatan–Samuelson Models

26. The observable equation in many optimal growth models does *not* contain time t explicitly.[13] The global form of the observable market behavior consistent with the general Liviatan–Samuelson model is

$$\ddot{q} = \psi_1(\dot{q}, q) + \rho\psi_2(\dot{q}, q) - \psi_3(\dot{q}, q)\dot{q}, \tag{67}$$

where ρ is the discount rate,

$$\psi_1 = U'g_q/A, \qquad \psi_2 = U'g_{\dot{q}}/A, \qquad \psi_3 = (U''g_{\dot{q}}g_q + U'g_{\dot{q}q})/A,$$

$A = U''g_{\dot{q}}^2 + U'g_{\dot{q}\dot{q}}$, $U(g)$ is the utility function, and the (consumption) transformation function between $\dot{q}$ and q. A special case of the foregoing, when $g_{\dot{q}q} = 0$, $g_{\dot{q}\dot{q}} = 0$, and $g_{\dot{q}} = -1$, is the global form of the Ramsey–Cass model,

$$\ddot{q} = \varepsilon(\dot{q}, q)(g'(q) - \rho) + g'(q)\dot{q}, \tag{68}$$

where $\varepsilon(\dot{q}, q) = U'/U''$. [It is perhaps more convenient to write $g'(q) = f'(q) - n$, where n is the sum of growth rate of population and efficiency increase of labor.]

Consider the following special case of (67) or (68):

$$\ddot{q} = F(q, \dot{q}) = \rho\dot{q} + dG(q)/dq. \tag{69}$$

Then since $F_{\dot{q}} = \rho$, from Theorem 7 we have

$$M = e^{-\rho t} \qquad \text{and} \qquad u = A(\alpha(\dot{q}, q, t), \beta(\dot{q}, q, t))e^{-\rho t}. \tag{70}$$

Let us set $A = -1$, and therefore,

$$u = -e^{-\rho t}, \tag{71}$$

so that the first term of (66) be satisfied for strict concavity. Using the general expression in (58), we obtain one of the time-dependent Lagrangian as

$$L = -e^{-\rho t}[\tfrac{1}{2}\dot{q}^2 + \gamma\dot{q}q - a\dot{q} + a\rho q - \tfrac{1}{2}\gamma\rho q^2 + G(q)], \tag{72}$$

where a and b are arbitrary constants of integration and ϕ^1 and ϕ^2 in (58) are set to,[14]

$$\phi^1 = -\tfrac{1}{2}\gamma e^{-\rho t}q^2, \qquad \phi^2 = Ce^{-\rho t}, \qquad \rho C = -\tfrac{1}{2}a^2 + ab\rho + G(b).$$

[13] An exception to this is Samuelson's model [1976], where the optimal behavior is periodic. Also see the model in Chapter 7, Section 17.

[14] Since a, b, and γ are all arbitrary constants, the inside of the bracket of (72) can be rewritten in the form free of the discount rate ρ. By choosing $\phi^1 = e^{-\rho t}h(q)$, L can be assumed to take a more general form.

In order that (72) may be meaningful as an economic objective function, the conditions for strict concavity require that

$$\begin{vmatrix} -1 & \gamma \\ \gamma & -\gamma\rho + G''(q) \end{vmatrix} = \gamma\rho - G''(q) - \gamma^2 > 0. \tag{73}$$

The Hamiltonian corresponding to (72) is given by

$$H = e^{-\rho t}[-\tfrac{1}{2}\dot{q}^2 + a\rho q - \tfrac{1}{2}\gamma\rho q^2 + G(q)], \tag{74}$$

where $\dot{q}$ is a solution to

$$p = L_{\dot{q}} = e^{-\rho t}(-\dot{q} - \gamma q + a) \qquad \text{or} \qquad \dot{q} = a - \gamma q - e^{\rho t}p.$$

Next we shall consider *forms of the time-independent Lagrangian* which might have also generated (69). To facilitate calculations, first we assume that (69) is a linear differential equation, i.e., a *linear approximation of observable behavior near the steady-state solution.* Consider the form used in Chapter 7, Eq. (41) (see also Samuelson [1972, Eq. (47)]), which generates a typical turnpike path to the steady state, i.e.,

$$\ddot{q} = F(\dot{q}, q) = \rho\dot{q} + (1 + \gamma\rho)q. \tag{75}$$

[The local equation for the Ramsey–Cass model is a special case of the foregoing when $(1 + \gamma\rho) > 0$, $1 + \gamma\rho = \varepsilon g'' > 0$ in (68).] This is obtained from (69) by setting

$$dG(q)/dq = (1 + \gamma\rho)q \qquad \text{or} \qquad G(q) = \tfrac{1}{2}(1 + \gamma\rho)q^2. \tag{76}$$

The corresponding time-dependent Lagrangian is

$$L = -e^{-\rho t}[\tfrac{1}{2}\dot{q}^2 + \gamma\dot{q}q - a\dot{q} + a\rho q + \tfrac{1}{2}q^2]. \tag{77}$$

When $a = 0$, (77) reduces to the form

$$L = -e^{-\rho t}[\tfrac{1}{2}\dot{q}^2 + \gamma\dot{q}q + \tfrac{1}{2}q^2], \tag{78}$$

which is exactly the identical with Eq. (40), Chapter 7, and also to Eq. (46) of Samuelson [1972]. However, (77) is *not* the only Lagrangian which might have generated the observable behavior (75). There are time-independent Lagrangians. First, by solving (75), the turnpike path is given by

$$q = f(t, \alpha, \beta) = \alpha e^{\lambda_1 t} + \beta e^{\lambda_2 t}, \tag{79}$$

where λ_1 and λ_2 are the characteristic roots of

$$\lambda^2 - \rho\lambda - (1 + \gamma\rho) = 0,$$

i.e.,

$$\lambda_1 = \tfrac{1}{2}(\rho + \sqrt{\rho^2 + 4(1 + \gamma\rho)}) = \tfrac{1}{2}(\rho + \sqrt{\delta}),$$
$$\lambda_2 = \tfrac{1}{2}(\rho - \sqrt{\rho^2 + 4(1 + \gamma\rho)}) = \tfrac{1}{2}(\rho - \sqrt{\delta}), \qquad \delta = \rho^2 + 4(1 + \gamma\rho).$$

Unlike the time-dependent case, the value of A is not a constant. Suppose we set α and β in (62) and (63) as the turnpike constants

$$\alpha(t, q, \dot{q}) = (\lambda_2 q - \dot{q})e^{-\lambda_1 t}/\sqrt{\delta}, \qquad \beta(t, q, \dot{q}) = (\dot{q} - \lambda_1 q)e^{-\lambda_2 t}/\sqrt{\delta}. \quad (80)$$

Then we have

$$u = AM = A(\alpha(t, \dot{q}, q), \beta(t, \dot{q}, q))e^{-\rho t}. \quad (81)$$

First, we express

$$\frac{\alpha^k}{\beta^{1+(1+k)\lambda_1/\lambda_2}} = e^{\rho t}\,\delta^{[1-k+(1+k)\lambda_1/\lambda_2]/2}\,\frac{(\lambda_2 q - \dot{q})^k}{(\dot{q} - \lambda_1 q)^{1+(1+k)\lambda_1/\lambda_2}}.$$

Then if we choose $A(\alpha, \beta)$ as

$$\begin{aligned} A(\alpha, \beta) &= \sum_{k=0} C_k^1 \frac{\alpha^k}{\beta^{1+(1+k)\lambda_1/\lambda_2}} = e^{\rho t} \sum_k C_k \frac{(\lambda_2 q - \dot{q})^k}{(\dot{q} - \lambda_1 q)^{1+(1+k)\lambda_1/\lambda_2}}, \\ C_k &= C_k^1\,\delta^{[1-k+(1+k)\lambda_1/\lambda_2]/2}, \end{aligned} \quad (82)$$

then the general form of time-independent Lagrangian will become

$$\begin{aligned} L = &\int_a^{\dot{q}} (\dot{q} - \sigma) \sum_k C_k \frac{(\lambda_2 q - \sigma)^k}{(\sigma - \lambda_1 q)^{1+(1+k)\lambda_1/\lambda_2}}\, d\sigma \\ &+ \int_b^{q} [a\rho + (1 + \gamma\rho)s] \sum_k C_k \frac{(\lambda_2 s - a)^k}{(a - \lambda_1 s)^{1+(1+k)\lambda_1/\lambda_2}}\, ds \\ &+ \frac{d}{dt}[\phi^1(t, q) + \phi^2(t)]. \end{aligned} \quad (83)$$

There are two special cases of interest. First, by setting $C_0 \neq 0$ and all the other $C_k = 0$, and also $a = b = 0$, we derive

$$L_1 = C[(\dot{q} - \lambda_1 q)^{1-\lambda_1/\lambda_2} - (1 - \lambda_1/\lambda_2)\dot{q}(-\lambda_1 q)^{-\lambda_1/\lambda_2}]. \quad (84)$$

Second, by setting $C_k \neq 0$ for $k = -1 - \lambda_2/\lambda_1$ and all the other $C_k = 0$, we obtain

$$L_2 = C\left[(\dot{q} - \lambda_2 q)^{1-\lambda_2/\lambda_1} - \left(1 - \frac{\lambda_2}{\lambda_1}\right)\dot{q}(-\lambda_2 q)^{-\lambda_2/\lambda_1}\right]. \quad (85)$$

It is easy to show that L_1 and L_2 are not independent because

$$H_2 = (\lambda_2/\lambda_1)C[(1/C)(\lambda_2/\lambda_1)H_1]^{-\lambda_2/\lambda_1}, \quad (86)$$

where H_1 and H_2 are the Hamiltonians corresponding to L_1 and L_2,

$$\begin{aligned} H_i &= C(\lambda_i/\lambda_j)(\dot{q} - \lambda_j q)(\dot{q} - \lambda_i q)^{-\lambda_i/\lambda_j}, \\ p &= C(1 - \lambda_i/\lambda_j)[(\dot{q} - \lambda_i q)^{-\lambda_i/\lambda_j} - (-\lambda_i q)^{-\lambda_i/\lambda_j}], \\ &\quad i = 1, 2, \quad j = 1, 2, \quad i \neq j. \end{aligned} \quad (87)$$

If a priori we can determine that the time-dependent Lagrangian (77) is the *true* Lagrangian, then (84) or (85) is a *surrogate* Lagrangian function, which gives the same observation behavior as (75). The foregoing result may have an important economic implication. We usually begin economic analysis by introducing a discount factor $e^{-\rho t}$ as represented by (72) or (77). *But the same behavior can be explained by the optimal control of a completely time-independent (no discount factor) program.* Obviously, the surrogate Lagrangian may or may not satisfy all the requirements of concavity and other conditions. The concavity conditions are met if

$$-a(1-a)CA^{-a-1} < 0, \tag{88-i}$$

$$[(1+a)\dot{q}A^{-a-1}B^{-a-2} + 2A^{-a-1}B^{-a-1} - B^{-2a-2}] > 0, \tag{88-ii}$$

where

$$A = (\dot{q} - \lambda_i q), \qquad B = (-\lambda_i q), \qquad a = \lambda_i/\lambda_j, \qquad i \neq j, \quad 1 \leqq i, j \leqq 2. \tag{89}$$

(We may choose either L_1 or L_2 such that $A > 0$ and $B > 0$.)

In summary, we present

Theorem 8 *(Local Recoverability of Optimal Growth Models)* (i) *A time-dependent utility function (Lagrangian) corresponding to the observable market behavior of the capital–labor ratio* (69) *is expressed as* (72).

(ii) *A time-independent utility function (Lagrangian) corresponding to the local linear approximation of the Ramsey–Cass and Liviatan–Samuelson models* (75) *is expressed as* (84). *The above time-independent Lagrangian may be used as a "surrogate" utility function to the time-dependent form* (77).

Other Applications

27. Theorems 7 and 8 may be used to recover (or justify the existence of) other (underlying) optimal models. Consider as an example the so-called Marshall–Walrasian (quantity-price) adjustment mechanism in a single market (Beckmann and Ryder [1969]). The observable behavior is expressed by the system of differential equations

$$\dot{p} = f(p, q), \qquad \dot{q} = g(p, q). \tag{90}$$

Assume that p is related to the implicit price of the underlying optimal behavior by some mechanisms of expectation formation. Then in order to justify the existence of optimal dynamic behavior, which might have generated the foregoing system of differential equations, we may use the recovered Lagrangians with appropriate economic interpretations.

Proof of Theorem 7

28. This is the simplest type of the so-called *inverse optimal problem of the calculus of variations* (Logan [1977], Yan [1978]). Expanding the Euler–Lagrange expression as

$$L_q - L_{\dot{q}t} - L_{\dot{q}q}\dot{q} - L_{\dot{q}\dot{q}}\ddot{q} = 0$$

and using (56′), we write the foregoing

$$L_q - L_{\dot{q}t} - L_{\dot{q}q}\dot{q} - L_{\dot{q}\dot{q}}F = 0. \tag{91}$$

If this equation is differentiated with respect to $\dot{q}$, it becomes

$$L_{\dot{q}t\dot{q}} + \dot{q}L_{\dot{q}q\dot{q}} + L_{\dot{q}\dot{q}}F_{\dot{q}} + L_{\dot{q}\dot{q}\dot{q}}F = 0. \tag{92}$$

Assuming that L has continuous partial derivatives of the third order, we can find a differential equation for u,

$$u = u(t(t, q(t), \dot{q}(t)) = L_{\dot{q}\dot{q}}, \tag{93}$$

from (92) as

$$u_t + \dot{q}u_q + Fu_{\dot{q}} + F_{\dot{q}}u = 0. \tag{94}$$

Equation (94) is a first-order linear partial differential equation in the unknown u, which can be solved by the standard method of characteristics. Once the solution is known, by twice integrating u, L can be determined from (93) by simple quadrature. Introducing the implicit price variable $p = \partial L/\partial\dot{q}$ ($p = -$the implicit price) and a Hamiltonian $H = p\dot{q} - L$, one obtains a set of canonical equations $\dot{q} = \partial H/\partial p$, $\dot{p} = -\partial H/\partial q$, which is equivalent to (56′), and closely related to (56).

Noting that the first three terms of Eq. (94) can be written as

$$\frac{du}{dt} = \frac{\partial u}{\partial t} + \frac{\partial u}{\partial q}\dot{q} + \frac{\partial u}{\partial \dot{q}}\ddot{q} = u_t + u_q\dot{q} + Fu_{\dot{q}},$$

we obtain

$$\frac{du}{dt} + F_{\dot{q}}u = 0. \tag{95}$$

Now the observable behavior (56′) implies that we may express the observable time path of $q(t)$ as a general solution of (56′), and its time derivative $\dot{q}$ as

$$q(t) = f(t, \alpha, \beta), \tag{96-i}$$

$$\dot{q}(t) = f_t(t, \alpha, \beta), \tag{96-ii}$$

where α and β are arbitrary constants of integration determined by the initial conditions.

Substituting these into q and $\dot{q}$ in u and integrating (95) with respect to t, we obtain

$$
\begin{aligned}
u(t, \dot{q}(t), q(t)) &= u[t, f_t(t, \alpha, \beta), f(t, \alpha, \beta)] \\
&= A(\alpha, \beta) \exp\left(- \int^t F_{\dot{q}}[\tau, f(\tau), f_\tau(\tau)]\, d\tau \right),
\end{aligned} \tag{97}
$$

where $A(\alpha, \beta)$ is an arbitrary parametric function of α and β. Using (96), we can also express α and β as solutions of $q = f(t, \alpha, \beta)$ and $\dot{q} = f_t(t, \alpha, \beta)$ as

$$
\alpha = \alpha(\dot{q}, q, t), \tag{98-i}
$$

$$
\beta = \beta(\dot{q}, q, t). \tag{98-ii}
$$

Using (98), we finally express u as $u(t, \dot{q}, q) = A[\alpha(\dot{q}, q, t), \beta(\dot{q}, q, t)]M(\dot{q}, q, t) = L_{\dot{q}\dot{q}}$, where

$$
\begin{aligned}
M(\dot{q}, q, t) = \exp\Big(- \int^t F_{\dot{q}}[\tau, f(\tau, \alpha(t, q, \dot{q}), \beta(t, q, \dot{q})),& \\
f_\tau(\tau, \alpha(t, q, \dot{q}), \beta(t, q, \dot{q}))]\, d\tau \Big).&
\end{aligned} \tag{99}
$$

Finally, direct integration of (93) with respect to $\dot{q}$ twice gives

$$
L_{\dot{q}} = \int_a^{\dot{q}} u(t, \theta, q)\, d\theta + C_1(t, q)
$$

and

$$
\begin{aligned}
L &= \int^{\dot{q}} L_{\dot{q}}(t, \gamma, q)\, d\gamma + C_2(t, q) \\
&= \int^{\dot{q}} \left[\int_a^{\gamma} u(t, \theta, q)\, d\theta \right] d\gamma + \int^{\dot{q}} C_1(t, q)\, d\gamma + C_2(t, q) \\
&= \int_a^{\dot{q}} (\dot{q} - \sigma) u(t, q, \sigma)\, d\sigma + \dot{q} C_1(t, q) + C_2(t, q),
\end{aligned} \tag{100}
$$

where the integration constants C_1 and C_2 must be chosen to satisfy the Euler–Lagrange expression (91). Calculating L_q, $L_{\dot{q}t}$, $L_{\dot{q}q}\dot{q}$, and $L_{\dot{q}\dot{q}}\ddot{q}$ from the foregoing as

$$
L_q = \int_a^{\dot{q}} (\dot{q} - \sigma) \frac{\partial u}{\partial q}\, d\sigma + \dot{q} \frac{\partial C_1}{\partial q} + \frac{\partial C_2}{\partial q}, \qquad L_{\dot{q}t} = \int_a^{\dot{q}} \frac{\partial u}{\partial t}\, d\sigma + \frac{\partial C_1}{\partial t},
$$

$$
L_{\dot{q}q}\dot{q} = \dot{q} \int_a^{\dot{q}} \frac{\partial u}{\partial q}\, d\sigma + \dot{q} \frac{\partial C_1}{\partial q}, \qquad L_{\dot{q}\dot{q}}\ddot{q} = Fu,
$$

and using (91), we obtain

$$Fu = -\int_a^{\dot{q}} \left[\sigma \frac{\partial u}{\partial q} + \frac{\partial u}{\partial t}\right] d\sigma + \frac{\partial C_2}{\partial q} - \frac{\partial C_1}{\partial t}.$$

Next, using (94), $\dot{q}\, \partial u/\partial q + \partial u/\partial t = -(Fu_{\dot{q}} + F_{\dot{q}}u) = -\partial(Fu)/\partial \dot{q}$, we get

$$Fu = \int_a^{\dot{q}} d(Fu) + \frac{\partial C_2}{\partial q} - \frac{\partial C_1}{\partial t} = Fu\,|_a^{\dot{q}} + \frac{\partial C_2}{\partial q} - \frac{\partial C_1}{\partial t};$$

therefore

$$F(t, q, a)u(t, q, a) = \frac{\partial C_2}{\partial q} - \frac{\partial C_1}{\partial t}.$$

By setting $C_1(t, q) = \partial \phi^1/\partial q$, we can express $C_2(t, q)$ as

$$C_2(t, q) = \frac{\partial \phi^1}{\partial t} + \int_b^q F(t, a, s)u(t, a, s)\, ds + \frac{d}{dt}\phi^2(t),$$

where b is constant and ϕ^1 and ϕ^2 are some arbitrary functions. Substituting C_1 and C_2 into L in Eq. (100), we finally can derive the most general expression of underlying Lagrangian as in (58). The corresponding Hamiltonian is then given by (64), where $\dot{q}$ is related to p by (65). Q.E.D.

VII. The Group Structure of Optimal Dynamic Behavior

The Hamilton–Jacobi Theory and Technical Change

29. The recoverability problem of dynamic systems is only one aspect of the theory of optimal dynamic behavior. The purpose of Part VII is to present a formal analysis of the mathematical structure which is common to many branches of economic dynamics. With the exceptions of an excellent introduction to the so-called Hamilton–Jacobi transformation theory by Samuelson and Solow [1956], and of the path-breaking works on the Hamiltonian approach in economics by Cass, Shell and their associates [1976], economists have not been exposed to this aspect of the formal analysis. The central theme of the formal mathematics is, of course, the (Lie) group structure of economic transformations. Instead of regarding the Hamilton–Jacobi theory as the practical computational method of deriving solutions to the equations of motion, we use it to study the *invariant* properties of a dynamic economic system, invariant under the transformation due to "technical and/or taste change." *We may regard the Hamilton–Jacobi* *transformation as a broad type of "technical and taste change" occurring in the system.*

The Euler–Lagrange equations corresponding to the minimization of the functional[15]

$$J(q) = \int_{t_0}^{t_1} L(t, q, \dot{q})\, dt, \qquad q = (q_1, \ldots, q_n), \quad \dot{q} = (\dot{q}_1, \ldots, \dot{q}_n), \quad (101)$$

form a system of n second-order differential equations

$$L_{q_i} - \frac{d}{dt} L_{\dot{q}_i} = 0, \qquad 1 \leqq i \leqq n. \qquad (102)$$

Let the *canonical* (*shadow price*) *variables* be equal to

$$p_i = L_{\dot{q}_i}, \qquad 1 \leqq i \leqq n, \qquad (103)$$

and define the *Hamiltonian* corresponding to the functional $J(q)$ as

$$H = -L + p_i \dot{q}_i \qquad \text{(summation on } i\text{)}. \qquad (104)$$

Then from

$$\begin{aligned} dH &= -dL + p_i\, d\dot{q}_i + \dot{q}_i\, dp_i \\ &= -\frac{\partial L}{\partial t} dt - \frac{\partial L}{\partial q_i} dq_i - \frac{\partial L}{\partial \dot{q}_i} d\dot{q}_i + p_i\, d\dot{q}_i + \dot{q}_i\, dp_i, \end{aligned}$$

and using (53), we get

$$dH = -\frac{\partial L}{\partial t} dt - \frac{\partial L}{\partial q_i} dq_i + \dot{q}_i\, dp_i.$$

Hence we obtain $\partial H/\partial t = -\partial L/\partial t$, $\partial H/\partial q_i = -\partial L/\partial q_i$, $\partial H/\partial p_i = \dot{q}_i$. Using these, the Euler–Lagrange equations (102) take the form

$$\dot{q}_i = \partial H/\partial p_i, \qquad \dot{p}_i = -\partial H/\partial p_i, \qquad 1 \leqq i \leqq n. \qquad (105)$$

This is *Hamilton's canonical system* of Euler–Lagrange equations or simply *Hamilton's equations of motion.*

Next we shall show that H is "dual" to L through the *Legendre transformation.* Let $f(\xi)$, $\xi = (\xi_1, \ldots, \xi_n)$, be a function of n variables such that

$$\det \| f_{\xi_i \xi_j} \| \neq 0,$$

[15] We have already assumed that economic maximization problems have been reduced to the equivalent minimization problems and that optimal control and dynamic programming models have been reduced to the form (101) with appropriate multipliers and inversions.

and $p_i = f_{\xi_i}$ $(i = 1, \ldots, n)$. Form the function $H(p) = -f + \xi_i p_i$. The transformation from the pair ξ, $f(\xi)$ to the pair p, $H(p)$ defined in the foregoing is called the *Legendre transformation.* Then it is seen that[16]

$$f(\xi) = \operatorname*{ext}_p[-H(p) + p_i \xi_i] \qquad \text{and} \qquad \operatorname*{ext}_\xi f(\xi) = \operatorname*{ext}_{\xi, p}[-H(p) + p_i \xi_i],$$

where ext is the operation of taking an extremum with respect to the indicated variables. Hence the extremum of $f(\xi)$ is also an extremum of $-H + p_i \xi_i$ regarded as a function of $2n$ variables.[17] We now apply this basic property of the Legendre transformation to (101). Introduce the new functional

$$J[q, p] = \int_{t_0}^{t_1} [-H(t, q, p) + p_i \dot{q}_i] \, dt, \tag{101'}$$

where q and p are regarded as two independent sets of functions. This functional is obviously the same as the original functional (101), if we choose $p_i = L_{\dot{q}_i}$. Observe that the transformation, from the variables t, q, $\dot{q}$, and L to the variables t, q, p, and H defined by $H(t, q, p) = -L + p_i \dot{q}_i$ and $p_i = L_{\dot{q}_i}$, is an *involution*; i.e., if we subject $H(t, q, p)$ to a Legendre transformation, we get back $L(t, q, \dot{q})$. To prove the equivalence of the variational problems of (101) and (101′), it is sufficient to show that $J(q)$ is an extremum of $J[q, p]$ when p is varied and q is held fixed, i.e., $J(q) = \operatorname{ext}_p J[q, p]$. Since $J(q, p)$ does not contain $\dot{p}$, it is sufficient to find an extremum of the integrand in (101′) at every point in order to find an extremum of $J(q, p)$. Thus we have

$$\frac{\partial}{\partial p_i} [-H + p_i \dot{q}_i] = 0, \qquad 1 \leqq i \leqq n,$$

from which it follows that

$$\dot{q}_i = \partial H / \partial p_i, \qquad 1 \leqq i \leqq n.$$

But this implies $J[q] = \operatorname{ext}_p J[q, p]$ since $-H + p_i \, \partial H / \partial p_i = L$ by the inverse Legendre transformation applied to H. On the other hand,

$$\operatorname*{ext}_q J(q) = \operatorname*{ext}_q \int_{t_0}^{t_1} \left[-H + p_i \frac{\partial H}{\partial p_i} \right] dt = \operatorname*{ext}_q \int_{t_0}^{t_1} L \, dt,$$

[16] When ξ is a single variable, we have $f(\xi)$, $p = f'(\xi)$, and $H(p) = -f(\xi) + p\xi$, where ξ is regarded as the function of p obtained from $p = f'(\xi)$. If the Legendre transformation is applied to the pair p, $H(p)$, we get back the pair ξ, $f(\xi)$. This follows from $dH/dp = \xi = H'$ and $-H + pH' = f(\xi) - pH' + pH' = f(\xi)$. Thus the Legendre transformation is an *involution*, i.e., a transformation which is its own inverse.

[17] When $\| f_{\xi_i \xi_j} \|$ is positive definite, we can replace $f(\xi) = \max_p[-H + \xi_i p_i]$ and $\min_\xi f(\xi) = \min_\xi \max_p [-H(p) + \xi_i p_i]$. Consider the case in which $n = 1$ and $f'' > 0$: If $-H(p) + \xi p$ is regarded as a function of two variables, then $f(\xi) = \max_p [-H(p) + \xi p]$, for $(\partial/\partial p)[-H(p) + \xi p] = -H'(p) + \xi = 0$, or $\xi = H'(p)$ and $-H(p) + \xi p = -H(p) + pH'(p) = f(\xi) - pH'(p) + pH'(p) = f(\xi)$. It follows that $\min_\xi f(\xi) = \min_\xi \max_p[-H(p) + \xi(p)]$.

which implies $L_{q_i} - dL_{\dot{q}_i}/dt = -\partial H/\partial q_i - \dot{p}_i = 0$. Hence the Euler–Lagrange equations for (101) are equivalent to the Hamiltonian canonical system [Eq. (105) for (101′)].

We now turn to *canonical transformations* resulting from, say "*technical change*." Let us assume that there exists a one-to-one continuous transformation resulting from *technical and/or taste change* such that $(q, p) \to (Q, P)$:

$$Q_i = Q_i(p, q, t; \varepsilon), \qquad P_i = P_i(p, q, t; \varepsilon), \qquad \varepsilon = (\varepsilon_1, \ldots, \varepsilon_r), \quad 1 \leqq i \leqq n, \tag{106}$$

where ε is the vector of r-essential technical (or taste) change parameters.[18] In general, the canonical system of Euler–Lagrange equations corresponding to P and Q does not maintain the same form as (105). That is to say, the system of differential equations resulting from dynamic optimization *after* technical change with the new variables P and Q does not necessarily have the same expression as (105). The transformation of type (106) which preserve the same form as the canonical form

$$\dot{Q}_i = \partial K/\partial P_i, \qquad \dot{P}_i = -\partial K/\partial Q_i, \qquad 1 \leqq i \leqq n, \quad K = K(t, P, Q), \tag{107}$$

may be called *canonical transformations of technical change*. To find such canonical transformations, we depend on the fact that the Euler–Lagrange equations with the old variables are derived from

$$\delta \int_{t_0}^{t_1} \{p_i \dot{q}_i - H(p, q, t)\}\, dt = 0.$$

Corresponding to the foregoing with new variables, we must have

$$\delta \int_{t_0}^{t_1} \{P_i \dot{Q}_i - K(P, Q, t)\}\, dt = 0.$$

Next we note that the Euler–Lagrange equations are not affected even if a total differential $d\phi/dt$ is added to the preceding expression as long as we have

$$p_i \dot{q}_i - H(p, q, t) = P_i \dot{Q}_i - K(P, Q, t) + \frac{d\Phi}{dt}(P, Q, t), \tag{108}$$

where $d\Phi/dt$ is sometimes called the *term of nullity*. Thus, if a given technical change transformation (106) from (t, p, q) to (t, P, Q) is such that there exists Φ satisfying condition (108), then the transformation (106) may be called the *canonical type of technical change*. The $2n$ variables among the $4n + 1$ variables p, q, P, Q, and t included in (108) can be expressed by the

[18] If there exists no ambiguity from the context, ε will be omitted from the expressions (106).

other variables using (106). For instance, if p and P are expressed by q, Q, and t, then we have

$$\Phi = \Phi(q, Q, t). \tag{109-i}$$

By totally differentiating $\Phi = \Phi(q, Q, t)$ with respect to time,

$$\frac{d\Phi}{dt} = \frac{\partial\Phi}{\partial q_i}\dot{q}_i + \frac{\partial\Phi}{\partial Q_i}\dot{Q}_i + \frac{\partial\Phi}{\partial t},$$

and equating it to $d\Phi/dt = p_i\dot{q}_i - P_i\dot{Q}_i + (K - H)$, we obtain

$$p_i = \partial\Phi/\partial q_i, \qquad P_i = -\partial\Phi/\partial Q_i, \qquad K = H + \partial\Phi/\partial t, \qquad 1 \leqq i \leqq n. \tag{110-i}$$

This is precisely the desired canonical transformation. Hence, by formula (110-i), the canonical type of technical change (106) is *generated* from simple partial differentiations. We may call Φ in (109-i) the *generating function* of the canonical technical change. *When the optimal program does not contain t explicitly, obviously from* (110-*i*), we conclude that *the Hamiltonian before and after canonical technical change is invariant, i.e.,* $K = H$.

It may be sometimes more convenient to express the generating function as

$$\Phi = \Phi(q, P, t), \tag{109-ii}$$

$$\Phi = \Phi(p, Q, t), \tag{109-iii}$$

$$\Phi = \Phi(p, P, t). \tag{109-iv}$$

From $P_i\dot{Q}_i = (d/dt)(P_iQ_i) - \dot{P}_iQ_i$ and rewriting (108) (including P_iQ_i in arbitrary function,[19] ϕ), we can derive

$$p_i = \partial\Phi/\partial q_i, \qquad Q_i = \partial\Phi/\partial P_i, \qquad K = H + \partial\Phi/\partial t, \tag{110-ii}$$

$$q_i = -\partial\Phi/\partial p_i, \qquad P_i = -\partial\Phi/\partial Q_i, \qquad K = H + \partial\Phi/\partial t, \tag{110-iii}$$

$$q_i = -\partial\Phi/\partial p_i, \qquad Q_i = \partial\Phi/\partial P_i, \qquad K = H + \partial\Phi/\partial t. \tag{110-iv}$$

In order to study group properties of transformations, if, in Eq. (106), the parameters ε are functions of t and we treat t as a parameter affecting technical change, we can write $\delta\Phi$, using (110-i), as

$$\delta\Phi = \frac{\partial\Phi}{\partial q_i}\delta q_i + \frac{\partial\Phi}{\partial Q_i}\delta Q_i = p_i\,\delta q_i - P_i\,\delta Q_i. \tag{111}$$

[19] Here a new generating function in terms of (109-i) is $\Phi + P_iQ_i = \psi$. Hence (110-ii) is actually $\partial\psi/\partial q_i = p_i$, $\partial\psi/\partial P_i = Q_i$, and $K = H + \partial\psi/\partial t$. But since Φ and ψ are arbitrary functions, we use the same expressions.

Hence *the canonical transformation* $(p, q) \to (P, Q)$ *is the one in which* $P_i\,\delta q_i - P_i\,\delta Q_i$ *is the total differential.* The canonical type of technical change T has the following *Lie group* properties:

(i) Let $T_1: (p, q) \to (p', q')$ and $T_2: (p', q') \to (p'', q'')$ be two canonical transformations; then $(p, q) \to (p'', q'')$ is also a canonical transformation, i.e., $T_1 T_2 = T_3 \in T$ (composition);

(ii) $(T_1 T_2)T_3 = T_1(T_2 T_3)$, $T_1, T_2, T_3 \in T$ (associative law);

(iii) T includes $(p, q) \to (p, q)$ (identity);

(iv) T also includes the inverse transformation $T^{-1}: (P, Q) \to (p, q)$ (inverse).

We shall call T *the canonical group of technical change* (Rund [1973, p. 90]).[20]

Integral Invariants

30. Turning our attention to *integral invariants* of canonical transformations of technical change, we first assume that t is a parameter. Let us assume that a curve C in a $2n$ phase space with coordinates p, q is given with a parameter s. Then we can express

$$q_i = q_i(s), \qquad p_i = p_i(s) \qquad (a \leqq s \leqq b).$$

We apply a canonical transformation to the foregoing $(p, q) \to (P, Q)$ which carries C to C' with

$$Q_i = Q_i(q(s), p(s)) = Q_i(s), \qquad P_i = P_i(q(s), p(s)) = P_i(s).$$

If C is a closed curve $[q_i(a) = q_i(b), p_i(a) = p_i(b)]$, then so is C'. Consider the difference between $\int_C P_i\,\delta q_i = \int_a^b p_i(s) q_i'(s)\,ds$ and

$$\int_{C'} P_i\,\delta Q_i = \int_a^b P_i(s) Q_i'(s)\,ds.$$

Then we have from (111)

$$p_i(s) q_i'(s) - P_i Q_i'(s) = d\Phi/ds$$

which gives

$$\int_C p_i\,\delta q_i - \int_{C'} P_i\,\delta Q_i = \Phi(b) - \Phi(a).$$

If C and C' are closed curves, then we have

$$\oint_C p_i\,\delta q_i = \oint_{C'} P_i\,\delta Q_i. \tag{112}$$

[20] The group discussed here is sometimes called "contact group." Some authors make clear distinction between these two groups (see, e.g., Rund [1973, p. 84, Remarks 1 and 4]).

Hence the integral round the closed curve $\oint_C p_i\,\delta q_i$ is the *integral invariant of the canonical transformation*. Conversely, if (112) is satisfied, $(p_i\,\delta q_i - P_i\,\delta Q_i)$ is a total differential and $(p, q) \to (P, Q)$ is a canonical transformation. Using Stokes's theorem, we can write (112) as

$$\oint_{C=\partial S} p_i\,\delta q_i = \iint_S \delta p_i\,\delta q_i.$$

Hence $\iint_S \delta p_i\,\delta q_i$ is another invariant, i.e.,

$$\iint_S \delta p_i\,\delta q_i = \iint_{S'} \delta P_i\,\delta Q_i, \tag{112'}$$

where S and S' are regions bounded by C and C'. Equation (112) is often referred to as the *relative integral invariant* (relative to the closed curve), while (112′) to the *absolute integral invariant* (see Whittaker [1937]). Repeating this process n times, we can say that

$$\int \overset{2n}{\cdots} \int \delta p_1\,\delta q_1 \cdots \delta p_n\,\delta q_n = \text{const} \tag{112''}$$

is also an integral invariant. But this is nothing but a volume. Hence the volume of the phase space is invariant under canonical transformations (Liouville's theorem).

By using two parameters u and v, (112′) may be written as

$$\iint_S \sum_i \delta p_i\,\delta q_i = \iint \sum_i \frac{\partial(p_i, q_i)}{\partial(u, v)}\,du\,dv,$$

$$\text{where} \quad \frac{\partial(p_i, q_i)}{\partial(u, v)} = \begin{vmatrix} \partial p_i/\partial u & \partial q_i/\partial u \\ \partial p_i/\partial v & \partial q_i/\partial v \end{vmatrix}.$$

It is also seen that we have

$$\sum_i \frac{\partial(p_i, q_i)}{\partial(u, v)}\,du\,dv = \sum_i \left(\frac{\partial p_i}{\partial u}\,du\,\frac{\partial q_i}{\partial v}\,dv - \frac{\partial q_i}{\partial u}\,du\,\frac{\partial p_i}{\partial v}\,dv\right) = \text{const.} \tag{113}$$

Letting δ and δ' be the variations of q and p corresponding to du and dv. Then the foregoing implies that the *bilinear invariant* of the Pfaffian form $p_i\,\delta q_i$,

$$\delta p_i\,\delta' q_i - \delta' p_i\,\delta q_i \qquad \text{(summation on } i\text{)}, \tag{113'}$$

is also invariant under canonical transformations. Defining (113′) using the bracket notation

$$[\delta x, \delta' x] = \delta p_i\,\delta' q_i - \delta' p_i\,\delta q_i,$$

where

$$\delta x = (\delta q_1, \ldots, \delta q_n, \delta p_1, \ldots, \delta p_n),$$
$$\delta' x = (\delta' q_1, \ldots, \delta' q_n, \delta' p_1, \ldots, \delta' p_n),$$

we can express

$$\delta Q_i = A_{ir}\, \delta q_r + C_{ir}\, \delta p_r, \qquad \delta P_i = B_{ir}\, \delta q_r + D_{ir}\, \delta p_r \quad \text{(summation on } r\text{)}.$$

Let S be

$$S = \begin{bmatrix} A & C \\ B & D \end{bmatrix} = \begin{bmatrix} \partial Q_i/\partial q_r & \partial Q_i/\partial p_r \\ \partial P_i/\partial q_r & \partial P_i/\partial p_r \end{bmatrix} \tag{114}$$

and some vector $w = (u_1, \ldots, u_n; v_1, \ldots, v_n)$. Then $w = Sw$ leaves $[w, w'] = u_i v_i' - u_i' v_i$ invariant, where the bilinear covariant $[w, w']$ is the *exterior product* of w and w'. A linear transformation which leaves the exterior product invariant is called a *symplectic transformation* or simply *S transformation*. It is known (Abraham and Marsden [1978]) that in order for $w = Sw$ to be a symplectic transformation, we must have $S'JS = J = SJS'$, where $J = \left[\begin{smallmatrix} 0 & I \\ -I & 0 \end{smallmatrix}\right]$, $I = n \times n$ identity matrix. Rewriting this result explicitly, we must have

$$\begin{bmatrix} A & C \\ B & D \end{bmatrix}\begin{bmatrix} 0 & I \\ -I & 0 \end{bmatrix}\begin{bmatrix} A' & B' \\ C' & D' \end{bmatrix} = \begin{bmatrix} A & C \\ B & D \end{bmatrix}\begin{bmatrix} C' & D' \\ -A' & -B' \end{bmatrix} = \begin{bmatrix} 0 & I \\ -I & 0 \end{bmatrix}.$$

Substituting (114) into the above, we obtain the conditions in terms of the *Poisson brackets*,[21]

$$\begin{aligned} [Q_i, Q_s] &= \frac{\partial Q_i}{\partial q_r}\frac{\partial Q_s}{\partial p_r} - \frac{\partial Q_i}{\partial p_r}\frac{\partial Q_s}{\partial q_r} = 0, \\ [Q_i, P_s] &= \frac{\partial Q_i}{\partial q_r}\frac{\partial P_s}{\partial p_r} - \frac{\partial Q_i}{\partial p_r}\frac{\partial P_s}{\partial q_r} = \delta_{is} \qquad \text{(summation on } r\text{)}, \\ [P_i, P_s] &= \frac{\partial P_i}{\partial q_r}\frac{\partial P_s}{\partial p_r} - \frac{\partial P_i}{\partial p_r}\frac{\partial P_s}{\partial q_r} = 0. \end{aligned} \tag{115}$$

The above is the necessary and sufficient condition for the transformation (106) to be a canonical transformation.

The *Lagrange bracket* for Q_i and Q_s is defined as

$$(Q_i, Q_s) = \frac{\partial q_m}{\partial Q_i}\frac{\partial p_m}{\partial Q_s} - \frac{\partial p_m}{\partial Q_i}\frac{\partial q_m}{\partial Q_s} \qquad \text{(summation on } m\text{)}.$$

[21] The Poisson bracket is the Lie bracket on Hamiltonian vector fields (see Section 32) and is usually denoted by $\{Q_i, Q_s\}$. Here we use the same notation as the standard Lie bracket $[Q_i, Q_s]$.

The necessary and sufficient conditions of the canonical transformation are again shown to be

$$(Q_i, Q_s) = 0, \qquad (Q_i, P_s) = \delta_{is}, \qquad (P_i, P_s) = 0. \tag{116}$$

Using the Poisson brackets, we obtain

$$\partial F/\partial q_i = [F, q_i], \qquad \partial F/\partial p_i = [q_i, F] = -[F, q_i], \qquad F = F(p, q, t).$$

Hence the *Hamilton system of motion* can be expressed in the symmetric form as

$$\dot{q}_i = \partial H/\partial p_i = [q_i, H], \qquad \dot{p}_i = -\partial H/\partial q_i = [p_i, H]. \tag{117}$$

A canonical transformation in which the new variables P, Q differ from the original variables p, q by infinitesimal amounts is called an *infinitesimal canonical transformation*,

$$Q_i = q_i + \varepsilon\, \Delta q_i, \qquad P_i = p_i + \varepsilon\, \Delta p_i.$$

The most general *infinitesimal canonical transformation* of technical change is defined by

$$Q_i = q_i + \varepsilon\, \partial S/\partial p_i, \qquad P_i = p_i - \varepsilon\, \partial S/\partial q_i, \qquad 1 \leqq i \leqq n, \tag{118}$$

where S is an arbitrary function of p and q. Here S is a *generating function* of the infinitesimal transformation. Calculating the effect of the infinitesimal transformation on F which depends on p and q we obtain

$$\begin{aligned} \varepsilon\, dF &= F(P, Q) - F(p, q) = \left(\frac{\partial F}{\partial q_i}(Q_i - q_i) + \frac{\partial F}{\partial p_i}(P_i - p_i)\right) \\ &= \varepsilon\left\{\frac{\partial F}{\partial q_i}\frac{\partial S}{\partial p_i} - \frac{\partial F}{\partial p_i}\frac{\partial S}{\partial q_i}\right\} \\ dF &= [F, S]. \end{aligned} \tag{119}$$

Hence *the Poisson bracket* $[F, S]$ *represents the rate of change of* F *induced by the infinitesimal transformation*. By setting

$$S = H \qquad \text{and} \qquad \varepsilon = dt \qquad (H = \text{Hamiltonian}) \tag{120}$$

in (118), we can interpret (105) as implying that the transformation from the values of the variables at time t to their values at $t + dt$ is an infinitesimal canonical transformation. *The whole course of a dynamic system can thus be regarded as the gradual self-unfolding of a contact (canonical) transformation* (Whittaker [1937, p. 304]).

The first integral H (or in general S) is obviously invariant under the infinitesimal transformation (108). Hence (108) represents a symmetry of the dynamic system. This symmetry is often referred to as a *dynamic symmetry* of the system. Consider r generating functions S_k $(1 \leqq k \leqq r)$ and their corresponding infinitesimal transformations

$$X_k = \frac{\partial S_k}{\partial p_i}\frac{\partial}{\partial q_i} - \frac{\partial S_k}{\partial q_i}\frac{\partial}{\partial p_i}, \qquad 1 \leqq k \leqq r.$$

Assume that the X_k constitute r-parameter group. Then the dynamic system is said to have a *dynamic symmetry group* G_r. Hence, because of the basic property of the group, we have

$$[X_k, X_l] = C^{\lambda}_{kl} X_{\lambda}, \qquad k, l, \lambda = 1, \ldots, r \quad \text{(summation on } \lambda\text{)}. \tag{121}$$

where the C^{λ}_{kl} are constants. Hence *the Lie group properties of the dynamic symmetry group G_r are completely characterized by the Poisson brackets.*[22]

The Hamilton–Jacobi Equation

31. We have shown that a canonical transformation from the old variables p, q to the new variables P, Q can be defined by the new Hamiltonian [Eq. (110-i)]

$$K(Q, P, t) = H(q, p, t) + \frac{\partial \Phi(q, Q, t)}{\partial t}, \tag{122}$$

with $\dot{Q}_i = \partial K/\partial P_i$ and $\dot{P}_i = -\partial K/\partial Q_i$. Clearly, if $K \equiv 0$, we conclude that $Q_i = \alpha_i = \text{const}$, $P_i = \beta_i = \text{const}$, $1 \leqq i \leqq n$. The $2n$ constants α, β (canonical constants) are sufficient to describe the initial conditions and, in fact, may be regarded as being related to them. Moreover, for $K = 0$, the generating function must satisfy the differential equation

$$H(q, p, t) + \frac{\partial \Phi}{\partial t} = 0. \tag{123}$$

In view of $Q_i = \text{const}$, the generating function can be rewritten as

$$\Phi = \Phi(q, \alpha_1, \ldots, \alpha_n, t) \tag{124}$$

and

$$p_i = \partial \Phi/\partial q_i, \qquad P_i = \beta_i = -\partial \Phi/\partial \alpha_i, \qquad 1 \leqq i \leqq n.$$

Inserting the first part of the above expressions into (124), we obtain

$$H(q_1, \ldots, q_n, \partial \Phi/\partial q_1, \ldots, \partial \Phi/\partial q_n, t) + \partial \Phi/\partial t = 0. \tag{125}$$

[22] The concept of symmetry can also be introduced directly to a class of Pontryagin optimal control problems, by applying the symmetry group of a control system generated from a set of first integrals (see Ikeda and Sakamoto [1975]).

This equation represents a first-order partial differential equation in the $n + 1$ independent variables q, t and is known as the *Hamilton–Jacobi equation.* It is seen that the solution to (125) is (124) with $\alpha_1, \ldots, \alpha_n$ being constants of integration. Then provided that $\|\partial^2\Phi/\partial q_i\, \partial\alpha_j\| \neq 0$, we can use $p_i = \partial\Phi/\partial q_i$ and $\beta = -\partial\Phi/\partial\alpha_i$ to write the solution of the optimization problem in terms of α, β, and t as

$$q_i = q_i(\alpha, \beta, t), \qquad p_i = p_i(\alpha, \beta, t), \qquad 1 \leqq i \leqq n. \tag{126}$$

It will be instructive to examine the nature of the generating function Φ. Since in this case the Q_i are constant and in addition $K = 0$, Eq. (108) becomes

$$d\Phi/dt = p_i\dot{q}_i - H, \qquad \text{or} \qquad d\Phi = (p_i\dot{q}_i - H)\, dt. \tag{127}$$

Recalling the relation between L and H, (127) can be integrated to yield $\Phi = \int_{t_0}^{t} L\, dt$. If the path of integration and L are known, then Φ becomes a function of the end points

$$\Phi = \Phi[q(t_0), t_0, q(t), t] = \Phi[\alpha, t_0, q, t].$$

Φ is often called the *Hamilton principal function S*,

$$S = S(q, \alpha, t). \tag{128}$$

Hence *the generating function Φ is simply the Hamilton principal function.* Sometimes it is more usual to write the Hamilton–Jacobi equation as

$$H(q, \partial S/\partial q, t) + \partial S/\partial t = 0. \tag{125'}$$

In a special case when H does not contain t explicitly, we have

$$S(q, \alpha, t) = W(q, \alpha) - ht, \tag{129}$$

where $H = H(q, p) = h = \text{const}$. Then the Hamilton–Jacobi equation takes a form

$$H(q, \partial W/\partial q) = h \tag{130}$$

which is called the *modified Hamilton–Jacobi equation.*

The Hamilton–Jacobi method requires the solution of a single partial differential equation instead of $2n$ ordinary differential equations, namely, Hamilton's equations. This may not always represent an improvement, as there are no general methods for the solution of partial differential equations. A special case of *separable* system can be handled with great advantage using the Hamilton–Jacobi equation. Assume that H does not contain t explicitly and that the principal function can be written in additive form,

$$S(q, \alpha, t) = \sum_{i=1}^{n} W_i(q_i, \alpha_1, \ldots, \alpha_n) - \alpha_1 t. \tag{131}$$

If the modified Hamilton–Jacobi equation reduces to n differential equations of the form

$$H_i(q_i\ \partial W/\partial q_i, \alpha_1, \ldots, \alpha_n) = \alpha_{i+1}, \qquad 1 \leqq i \leqq n, \tag{132}$$

the system is said to be *separable*. Equations (132) represent a set of n ordinary differential equations of the type

$$\partial W_i/\partial q_i = f_i(q_i, \alpha_1, \ldots, \alpha_n), \qquad 1 \leqq i \leqq n, \tag{133}$$

which can always be integrated.

More Abstract Analysis of Dynamic Symmetries

32. The role played by transformation groups that leave an optimal dynamic system invariant can often be best understood from the more abstract, manifold point of view. The Hamilton–Jacobi transformation theory may be regarded as the study of the characteristic curves of a closed 2-form. A d-dimensional manifold M, where $d = 2n$, is said to have a *Hamiltonian* (*or symplectic*) *structure*, and M is then said to be a *Hamiltonian* (*or symplectic*) *manifold*, if there is a distinguished closed 2-form Ω of maximal rank d defined everywhere on M. The form Ω is called the *fundamental form* denoted by (M, Ω). The nondegenerate bilinear form Ω may be viewed as a linear isomorphism $\Omega_m\colon M_m \to M_m^*$ for each $m \in M$, and hence, as a bundle isomorphism $\Omega\colon TM \to T^*M$. (The fibers here are the vector space M_m and M_m^*, and * is the notation for a dual space.) For a vector field X the corresponding 1-form ΩX is given by $\Omega X = i(X)\Omega$, where $i(X)$ is the inner product operators.

We define the *Poisson bracket* of the 1-form τ and θ in terms of the corresponding fields $V\tau$ and $V\theta$ by

$$[\tau, \theta] = i([V\tau, V\theta])\Omega = \Omega[V\tau, V\theta], \tag{134}$$

where $V = \Omega^{-1}$ and τ is a 1-form on M. Then we observe that *the Poisson bracket of two closed forms is exact.* Since the fundamental form of a Hamiltonian manifold (M, Ω) is closed and rank d, it has local expressions

$$\Omega = dp_i \wedge dq_i, \qquad i = 1, \ldots, n = \tfrac{1}{2}d,$$

where p_i, q_i are called *Hamiltonian coordinates.* The Jacobian matrix of two systems of Hamiltonian coordinates, say, p_i, q_i and P_i, Q_i, is a symplectic matrix. Specifically, we have

$$\frac{\partial p_i}{\partial P_j} = \frac{\partial Q_j}{\partial q_i}, \qquad \frac{\partial p_i}{\partial Q_j} = -\frac{\partial P_j}{\partial q_i}, \qquad \frac{\partial q_i}{\partial P_j} = -\frac{\partial Q_j}{\partial p_i}, \qquad \frac{\partial q_i}{\partial Q_j} = \frac{\partial P_j}{\partial p_i}.$$

In terms of Hamiltonian coordinates p_i, q_i, the operators Ω and V are given by $\Omega(a_i\ \partial/\partial p_i + b_i\ \partial/\partial q_i) = -b_i\ dp_i + a_i\ dq_i$ and $V(f_i\ dp_i + g_i\ dq_i) = g_i\ \partial/\partial p_i$

$- f_i\, \partial/\partial q_i$. In particular, for a function f on M, we have $V\, df = \partial f/\partial q_i\, \partial/\partial p_i - \partial f/\partial p_i\, \partial/\partial q_i$. If f and g are functions on M, then df and dg are closed 1-forms and the Poisson brackets of the functions f and g is

$$[f, g] = i(V\, df)\, dg = (V\, df)g = \frac{\partial f}{\partial q_i}\frac{\partial g}{\partial p_i} - \frac{\partial f}{\partial p_i}\frac{\partial g}{\partial q_i}. \tag{135}$$

Since f and g are functions on the Hamiltonian manifold (M, Ω), we know that the following are equivalent: (a) f is constant along the integral curves of $V\, dg$; (b) g is constant along the integral curves of $V\, df$; (c) $[f, g] = 0$.

A vector field X is said to be a *Hamiltonian vector field* if it leaves the Hamiltonian structure invariant. Hence X is Hamiltonian if and only if ΩX is closed. It is seen that the Lie bracket of two Hamiltonian vector fields is also Hamiltonian. The topological limitations for the existence of a Hamiltonian structure on a manifold are quite severe. However, there is one important class of Hamiltonian manifolds, i.e., the cotangent bundles of other manifolds. The tangent bundle of a manifold is diffeomorphic to the cotangent bundle, and therefore, it also admits a Hamiltonian structure. It is seen that there is a canonical Hamiltonian structure on the cotangent bundle T^*M of a manifold M. The fundamental form $\Omega = d\theta$ of the Hamiltonian structure on T^*M is exact. (Here θ is the *canonical 1-form* and Ω, the *canonical 2-form* on T^*M.) The second-order differential equations of motion (Euler–Lagrange expressions) can be viewed as a vector field on the tangent bundle of the configuration space. Then the differential equations can be carried into first-order differential equations in T^*M.

If $q\colon T^*M \times \mathbb{R} \to T^*M$ is the Cartesian product projection, then we obtain a 1-form $q^*\theta$ on S from the canonical 1-form θ on T^*M. We call $\omega = \theta - dt$ the *canonical contact form* on $T^*M \times \mathbb{R}$. Then coordinates P_i, Q_i, u on S are *contact coordinates* if we have

$$\omega = \theta - dt = p_i\, dq_i - dt = P_i\, dQ_i - du.$$

Taking the exterior derivatives

$$\Omega = dp_i \wedge dq_i = dP_i \wedge dQ_i,$$

we see that the 2-form has the same appearance for any contact coordinate system. Suppose that P_i, Q_i are Hamiltonian coordinates on T^*M. Then $d(P_i\, dQ_i - p_i\, dq_i) = \Omega - \Omega = 0$, which implies that there exists a function f such that

$$P_i\, dQ_i - p_i\, dq_i = df.$$

Letting $u = t + f$, we have $\omega = P_i\, dQ_i - du$; i.e., P_i, Q_i, u are contact coordinates.

A manifold M of dimension $d = 2n + 1$ is said to have a *contact structure*, and M is then called a *contact manifold*, if M has a distinguished 1-form ω such that $\omega \wedge (d\omega)^n \neq 0$. The form ω is then called a *contact form*. (The power of $d\omega$ is the iterated wedge product.) By *Darboux's theorem* (Abraham and Marsden [1978, p. 371], Sternberg [1964]), we can show that there exist contact coordinates.[23] A diffeomorphism f of M onto M is said to be a *contact transformation* of M if $f^*\omega = h\omega$, where h is nowhere-zero function on M. Then a diffeomorphism of a contact manifold M maps every integral submanifold to another submanifold if and only if it is a contact transformation of M.

33. We shall briefly touch on the formal aspects of *general conservation laws*. In Chapter 7, we derived economic conservation laws using the so-called Noether theorem (Noether [1918]) on invariant optimal programs. Here we present a more abstract version of Noether's theorem for general optimal systems. Consider economic systems whose evolution is described by differential equations derivable from a variational principle with a Lagrange function depending on q, their first (partial) derivatives $\dot{q}$, and on the independent variables $t = (t^1, \ldots, t^m)$. The *histories* of an economic system may be described by cross sections of a bundle (M, E, π), where M and E are two sets and π a map of M onto E. (M is a bundle space, E a base space, and π a projection.) By a Lagrange function we mean a function L defined on the bundle space $\bar{M}$ of the first jet extension of (M, E, π). Given the Lagrange function

$$L: \bar{M} \to \mathbb{R},$$

we can form the Euler–Lagrange mapping

$$[L]: \bar{\bar{M}} \to F^*$$

defined by $[L] = (\partial L/\partial q) - \operatorname{div}(\partial L/\partial \dot{q})$, where $\bar{\bar{M}} = \bar{M} \times \ddot{F}$, $E = \mathbb{R}^m$, $M = E \times F$, $F = \mathbb{R}^n$, $\bar{M} = M \times \dot{F}$, $\dot{F} = E^* \otimes F$, $\ddot{F} = E^* \otimes E^* \otimes F$. Let $f: E \to F$ and $\bar{\bar{\phi}}_f$ be the second jet extension of the graph mapping ϕ_f of f. f satisfies the Euler–Lagrange mapping if $[L] \circ \bar{\bar{\phi}}_f = 0$. Define a *symmetry transformation* as an automorphism $\zeta = (\xi(t), \eta(t, q))$ of the bundle (M, E, π) such that

$$\text{if } f: E \to F \quad \text{and} \quad [L] \circ \bar{\bar{\phi}}_f = 0, \qquad \text{then} \quad [L] \circ \bar{\bar{\zeta}} \circ \bar{\bar{\phi}}_f = 0. \tag{136}$$

[23] Darboux's theorem states: Let ω be a 1-form defined in a neighborhood of $m \in M$. (a) If $\omega \wedge (d\omega)^k = 0$ and $(d\omega)^{k+1} = 0$ in a neighborhood of m, and $(d\omega_m)^k \neq 0$ and $\omega_m \neq 0$, then there are coordinates p_i, q_i $(i = 1, \ldots, k)$, and u^α $(\alpha = 1, \ldots, d - 2k)$ at m such that $\omega = p_i\, dq_i$. (b) If $(d\omega)^{k+1} = 0$ in a neighborhood of m and $\omega_m \wedge (d\omega_m)^k \neq 0$, then there are coordinates p_i, q_i $(i = 1, \ldots, k)$, t, and u^α $(\alpha = 1, \ldots, d - 2k - 1)$ at m such that $\omega = p_i\, dq_i - dt$. It is case (b) which applies to a contact form with $k = n$.

An important class of symmetry transformations which consists of all those automorphisms ζ of M for $[L]^{\alpha} = J(\partial\eta_{\beta}/\partial q_{\alpha})[L]^{\beta} \circ \bar{\bar{\zeta}}$, $(J\,\partial\eta_{\beta}/\partial q_{\alpha}) \neq 0$, $J = \det(\partial\xi^{i}/\partial t^{j})$ $(\alpha, \beta = 1, \ldots, n)$, is called a *generalized invariant transformation.* The necessary and sufficient condition for a bundle automorphism $\zeta\colon M \to M$ be a generalized invariant transformation is that there exists a mapping $\chi\colon M \to E$ such that

$$JL \circ \zeta + \operatorname{div} \chi = L.$$

Now introduce (ζ_{ε}) a one-parameter group of automorphisms of the bundle (M, E, π); then

$$\frac{d}{d\varepsilon}(J_{\varepsilon}L \circ \bar{\zeta}_{\varepsilon}) = J_{\varepsilon}(\bar{Z}(L) + L \operatorname{div} X) \circ \bar{\zeta}_{\varepsilon},$$

where $J_{\varepsilon} = \det(\partial\xi^{i}_{\varepsilon}/\partial t^{j})$, $\bar{Z}$ is the vector field induced on $\bar{M}$ by $(\bar{\zeta}_{\varepsilon})$, and $X = d\xi_{\varepsilon}/d\varepsilon|_{\varepsilon=0}$. It can be proved that a necessary and sufficient condition for the one-parameter group (ζ_{ε}) to consist of generalized invariant transformations of L is that there exists a mapping $V\colon M \to E$ such that $\bar{Z}(L) + L \operatorname{div} X + \operatorname{div} V = 0$. A special case of the foregoing corresponds to

$$\int_{\Omega} L \circ \bar{\phi}_{f},$$

where $\Omega \subset E$ is a compact domain and the integral is taken with respect to the Lebesgue measure. In particular Z induced by an invariant transformation satisfies the *Noether equation*

$$\bar{Z}(L) + L \operatorname{div} X = 0. \tag{137}$$

If f is a solution of the Euler–Lagrange equation and Z generates a one-parameter group of generalized transformations, then

$$\operatorname{div}(T \circ \bar{\phi}_{f}) = 0, \tag{138}$$

where

$$T = XL + \langle Y - \dot{\rho}X, \partial L/\partial\dot{q}\rangle + V,$$

$$\bar{Z}(L) + L \operatorname{div} X = \langle Y - \dot{\rho}X, [L]\rangle + \operatorname{div}(XL + \langle Y - \dot{\rho}X, \partial L/\partial\dot{q}\rangle),$$

$$Y = (\partial\eta_{\varepsilon}/\partial\varepsilon)|_{\varepsilon=0}, \qquad \rho\colon M \to F, \qquad \dot{\rho}\colon \bar{M} \to \dot{F}.$$

Formula (138) is *a conservation law.* For example, if the base space is one-dimensional, then (138) reduces to $d(T \circ \bar{\phi}_{f})/dt = 0$, which implies that T is a constant of motion (see Chapter 7).

Canonical transformations which we discussed earlier become a special case of the preceding discussion when $E = \mathbb{R}$, $F = \mathbb{R}^{n}$, $M = E \times F \times F^{*}$.

Let $z = (t, q, p)$ denote a typical element of M, $q \in F$, $p \in F^*$. The set $\mathscr{F}$ of all functions on M is a Lie algebra with respect to the Poisson bracket

$$[f, g] = \frac{\partial f}{\partial q_i}\frac{\partial g}{\partial p_i} - \frac{\partial f}{\partial p_i}\frac{\partial g}{\partial q_i}, \qquad f, g \in \mathscr{F}.$$

An automorphism ζ of (M, E, π) is called canonical transformation if $[f, g] \circ \zeta = [f \circ \zeta, g \circ \zeta]$. Let (ζ_ε) be a one-parameter group of automorphisms of M and $Z = (X, Q, P)$, the vector field induced on M by (ζ_ε). A necessary and sufficient condition for (ζ_ε) to be a one-parameter group of canonical transformation is that Z be a derivation of the Lie algebra $\mathscr{F}$, i.e., $Z([f, g]) = [Z(f), g] + [f, Z(g)]$. From this we can obtain $G \in \mathscr{F}$ such that $Q_i = -\partial G/\partial p_i$, $P_i = \partial G/\partial q_i$. Therefore, $Z(f) = X\, \partial f/\partial t + [G, f]$. In particular, if (ζ_ε) is time-independent, then $X = 0$ and Z is an inner derivation of $\mathscr{F}$.[24]

REFERENCES

Abraham, R., and Marsden, J. E. [1978]. *Foundations of Mechanics*, 2nd ed. Benjamin/Cummings, Reading, Massachusetts.

Beckmann, M. J., and Ryder, H. E. [1969]. Simultaneous price and quantity adjustment in a single market, *Econometrica*, **37**, 470–484.

Boothby, W. W. [1975]. *An Introduction to Differentiable Manifolds and Riemannian Geometry*. Academic Press, New York.

Burmeister, E., and Dobell, R. [1970]. *Mathematical Theories of Economic Growth*. Macmillan, New York.

Campbell, J. E. [1966]. *Introductory Treatise on Lie's Theory of Finite Continuous Transformation Groups*, 1903. Reprinted by Chelsea, New York.

Cass, D. [1965]. Optimum growth in an aggregative model of capital accumulation, *Review of Economic Studies*, **32**, 233–240.

Cass, D., and Shell, K. (eds.). [1976]. *The Hamiltonian Approach to Dynamic Economics*. Academic Press, New York.

Chevalley, C. [1946]. *Theory of Lie Groups*. Princeton Univ. Press, Princeton, New Jersey.

Chipman, J. S. *et al.* [1971]. *Preferences, Utility, and Demand*. Harcourt, New York.

Cohn, P. M. [1957]. *Lie Groups*. Cambridge Univ. Press, London and New York.

Eisenhart, L. P. [1933]. *Continuous Groups of Transformations*. Princeton Univ. Press, Princeton, New Jersey, 1933. Reprinted by Dover, New York, 1961.

Flanders, H. [1963]. *Differential Forms*. Academic Press, New York.

Hartman, P. [1970]. "Frobenius theorem under Carathéodory type conditions, *Journal of Differential Equations*, **3**, 307–333.

Hartman, P. [1964]. *Ordinary Differential Equations*. Wiley, New York. Corrected edition by Philip Hartman, Baltimore, Maryland, 1973.

[24] The interested reader is asked to study recent excellent contributions to differential geometric formalism and generalized canonical transformations by Nôno [1972], and Nôno and Mimura [1972, 1975].

Hermann, R. [1968]. *Differential Geometry and the Calculus of Variations*. Academic Press, New York.

Hermann, R. [1973]. *Geometry, Physics, and Systems*. Dekker, New York.

Hicks, N. J. [1971]. *Notes on Differential Geometry*. Van Nostrand-Reinhold, Princeton, New Jersey.

Hurwicz, L. [1971]. On the problem of integrability of demand functions, in *Preferences, Utility, and Demand* (J. Chipman *et al*., eds.). Harcourt, New York.

Hurwicz, L., and Richter, M. [1979]. Ville axioms and consumer theory, *Econometrica*, **47**, 603–620.

Ikeda, M., and Sakamoto, K. [1975]. On the concept of symmetry in Pontryagin's maximum principle, *SIAM J. Control*, **13**, 389–399.

Koopmans, T. C. [1965]. On the concept of optimal growth, in *The Econometric Approach to Development Planning*. Rand McNally, Chicago, Illinois.

Lang, S. [1972]. *Differentiable Manifolds*. Addison-Wesley, Reading, Massachusetts (Supersedes *Introduction to Differentiable Manifolds*. Wiley (Interscience), New York, 1962).

Liviatan, N., and Samuelson, P. A. [1969]. Notes on turnpikes: Stable and unstables, *Journal of Economic Theory*, **1**, 454–475.

Logan, J. D. [1977]. *Invariant Variational Principles*, Mathematics in Science and Engineering, Vol. 138. Academic Press, New York.

Lovelock, D., and Rund, H. [1975]. *Tensors, Differential Forms, and Variational Principles*. Wiley, New York.

Matsushima, Y. [1972]. *Differentiable Manifolds*. Dekker, New York.

Morishima, M. [1964]. *Equilibrium, Stability and Growth: A Multisectoral Analysis*. Oxford Univ. Press, London and New York.

Musgrave, R. A. [1959]. *The Theory of Public Finance: A Study in Public Economy*. McGraw-Hill, New York.

Noether, E. [1918]. Invariante variationsprobleme, *Nachr. Akad. Wiss. Göttingen, Math.-Phys. Kl. II*, 235–257. Translation by M. A. Tavel under the title of Invariant variation problems, *Transport Theory and Statistical Physics*, **1**(3), 186–207.

Nôno, T. [1972]. Generalized canonical transformations, *Bulletin of Fukuoka University of Education*, **22**, 45–65.

Nôno, T., and Mimura, F. [1972]. A differential geometric formalism for multiple integral variational problems, *Tensor N.S.*, **26**, 79–85.

Nôno, T., and Mimura, F. [1975]. Null class of the generalized system in mechanics, *Tensor N.S.*, **29**, 69–81.

Ramsey, F. [1928]. A mathematical theory of saving, *Economic Journal*, **38**, 543–559.

Rund, H. [1973]. *The Hamilton–Jacobi Theory in the Calculus of Variations*. Krieger Publ., New York.

Samuelson, P. A. [1950]. Problem of integrability in utility theory, *Economica*, **17**, 355–385.

Samuelson, P. A. [1972]. The general saddlepoint property of optimal-control motions, *Journal of Economic Theory*, **5**, 102–120.

Samuelson, P. A. [1976]. The periodic turnpike theorem, in *Nonlinear Analysis, Theory, Methods and Applications*, Vol. 1, pp. 3–13. Pergamon, Oxford.

Samuelson, P. A., and Solow, R. M. [1956]. A complete capital model involving heterogeneous capital goods, *Quarterly Journal of Economics*, **70**, 537–567.

Sato, R., and Davis, E. [1971]. Optimal savings policy when labor grows endogenously, *Econometrica*, **39**, 877–898.

Sato, R., and Ramachandran, R. [1978]. A Contribution to the Microeconomic Analysis of Biased Technical Progress. Discussion Paper, Department of Economics, Brown University, Providence, Rhode Island.

Sternberg, S. [1964]. *Lectures on Differential Geometry*. Prentice-Hall, Englewood Cliffs, New Jersey.

Varadarajan, V. S. [1974]. *Lie Groups, Lie Algebras, and Their Representations*. Prentice-Hall, Englewood Cliffs, New Jersey.

Whittaker, E. T. [1937]. *A Treatise on the Analytical Dynamics of Particles and Rigid Bodies*, 4th ed. Cambridge Univ. Press, London and New York. Reprinted by Dover, New York, 1944.

Yan, C. C. [1978]. Construction of Lagrangians and Hamiltonians from the equation of motion, *Am. J. Phys.*, **46**, 671–675.

APPENDIX

A BRIEF SURVEY OF LIE'S THEORY OF CONTINUOUS TRANSFORMATION GROUPS

The main feature of Lie's original work on transformation groups (Lie [1888–1893], [1891], Lie and Scheffers [1893]) is the study of the relation between groups and differential equations.[1] The purpose of this survey is to introduce economists to this particular aspect of Lie group theory.[2] More recent authors have extended the study to tensor analysis, Riemannian geometry, and to the application of Lie groups to new physical theories (e.g., Eisenhart [1933], Lovelock and Rund [1975]). These aspects of Lie groups are not presented here, but some of their economic applications are presented in Chapters 7–9 along with a brief reference to the mathematics used.

An abstract analysis of the theory of Lie groups and Lie algebras has been recently advanced by such authors as Chevalley [1946] and Cohn [1957] with a concommitant sacrifice of Lie's original intention to develop a "useful" mathematics. It is, however, true that although the abstract analysis

[1] I have benefited from the helpful assistance of Daniel Hofmann as a translator of parts of Lie's original publications in German.

[2] For some excellent mathematical studies of this aspect of Lie's groups, refer to Campbell [1966], Cohen [1911], Eisenhart [1933], Hermann [1974, 1975], and Markus [1961].

might have diminished the original motivation of Lie groups, it has brought about a level of prestige and abstraction common to all of the other modern branches of mathematical analysis; and thus, it has served the purpose of elevating Lie groups in the forefront of modern mathematics, especially in the field of differential geometry. Except for a brief excursion in Chapter 9, this aspect of Lie groups is not considered in this book.

I. Essential (or Effective) Parameters

Consider a set of n functions f^i of n variables $x_1, \ldots, x_n$ and r parameters $a_1, \ldots, a_r$, say

$$f^i(x_1, \ldots, x_n; a_1, \ldots, a_r) \equiv f^i(x; a) \qquad (i = 1, \ldots, n), \tag{1}$$

which are continuous in x and a, as are also their derivatives with respect to these to as high an order as desired in the subsequent discussion. The parameters a_α are said to be *essential* (or effective) unless it is possible to choose $r - 1$ functions of them, say $A_1, \ldots, A_{r-1}$, such that we have identically

$$f^i(x_1, \ldots, x_n; a_1, \ldots, a_r) = F^i(x_1, \ldots, x_n; A_1, \ldots, A_{r-1}).$$

Since A is a function of a, the Jacobian matrix $\|\partial A/\partial a\|$ is at most of rank $r - 1$, and consequently a set of functions ϕ_α of a, not all identically zero, exist which satisfy the equations

$$\sum_{\alpha=1}^{r} \phi_\alpha(a)\, \partial A_\sigma/\partial a_\alpha = 0 \qquad (\sigma = 1, \ldots, r - 1).$$

Hence A and any function of it satisfies a homogeneous linear partial differential equation of the first order in r variables

$$\sum_{\alpha=1}^{r} \phi_\alpha(a)\, \partial f/\partial a_\alpha = 0. \tag{2}$$

Consequently, since x does not appear in ϕ, the functions F^i satisfy (2), and hence the functions f^i satisfy (2). Conversely, suppose that the functions f^i satisfy an equation of the form (2). Clearly this partial differential equation admits $r - 1$ independent solutions which are functions of a alone, say $A_1, \ldots, A_{r-1}$, and any solution of (2) is a function of A. Consequently, each of the functions f^i is a function of x and A, and therefore, a is not essential. Hence we have

Theorem 1 *A necessary and sufficient condition that the r parameters a_α in* (1) *be essential is that the functions f^i do not satisfy a partial differential equation of the form* (2).

By the same reasoning it follows that, if the functions f^i satisfy a complete system of s $(<r)$ equations

$$\sum_{\alpha=1}^{r} \phi_\alpha^\sigma(a)\, \partial f/\partial a_\alpha = 0 \qquad (\sigma = 1, \ldots, s), \tag{3}$$

then f^i are functions of x and of $r - s$ independent solutions of this system, which are functions of a, and consequently are expressible in terms of $r - s$ essential parameters.

To illustrate, consider the transformation

$$f^1(x_1, x_2; a_1, a_2, a_3) = x_1 a_1^{\log a_2} + a_2^{\log a_1} + a_3,$$
$$f^2(x_1, x_2; a_1, a_2, a_3) = x_2 a_1^{\log a_2}.$$

If a_1, a_2, a_3 are not essential, it must be possible to find three functions of them, $\phi_1(a_1, a_2, a_3)$, $\phi_2(a_1, a_2, a_3)$, $\phi_3(a_1, a_2, a_3)$ such that

$$\sum_{\alpha=1}^{3} \phi_\alpha(a_1, a_2, a_3) \frac{\partial f}{\partial a_\alpha} = 0 \qquad \text{is satisfied identically by } f^1 \text{ and } f^2.$$

This implies that

$$\frac{\log a_2}{a_1}(x_1 a_1^{\log a_2} + a_2^{\log a_1})\phi_1 + \frac{\log a_1}{a_2}(x_1 a_1^{\log a_2} + a_2^{\log a_1})\phi_2 + \phi_3 \equiv 0,$$

$$x_2 a_1^{\log a_2}\left(\frac{\log a_2}{a_1}\phi_1 + \frac{\log a_1}{a_2}\phi_2\right) \equiv 0 \qquad \text{for all} \quad x_1 \text{ and } x_2.$$

These two identities are equivalent to

$$a_1^{\log a_2}\left(\frac{\log a_2}{a_1}\phi_1 + \frac{\log a_1}{a_2}\phi_2\right) = 0,$$

$$a_2^{\log a_1}\left(\frac{\log a_2}{a_1}\phi_1 + \frac{\log a_1}{a_2}\phi_2\right) + \phi_3 = 0,$$

$$a_1^{\log a_2}\left(\frac{\log a_2}{a_1}\phi_1 + \frac{\log a_1}{a_2}\phi_2\right) = 0,$$

which will be satisfied by $\phi_3 = 0$ and

$$\left(\frac{\log a_2}{a_1}\phi_1 + \frac{\log a_1}{a_2}\phi_2\right) = 0$$

for all x_1 and x_2 not identically equal to zero. A set of forms of ϕ_1, ϕ_2, ϕ_3 are thus found to be

$$\phi_1 = a_1 \log a_1, \qquad \phi_2 = -a_2 \log a_2, \qquad \phi_3 = 0.$$

Hence the three parameters a_1, a_2, and a_3 are *not* essential. To express the formulas of transformation in terms of a smaller number, one proceeds to solve the equation

$$a_1 \log a_1 \, \partial f/\partial a_1 - a_2 \log a_2 \, \partial f/\partial a_2 = 0.$$

Passing to the corresponding system of ordinary differential equations

$$da_1/dt = a_1 \log a_1, \qquad da_2/dt = -a_2 \log a_2, \qquad da_3/dt = 0,$$

one can obtain a set of solutions, $\log a_1 \log a_2 = c_1$ and $a_3 = c_2$, which implies $a_1^{\log a_2} = e^{c_1} = a_2^{\log a_1}$. Thus the transformation takes the form

$$f^1 = (x_1 + 1)e^{c_1} + c_2, \qquad f^2 = x_2 e^{c_1}$$

or, more simply,

$$f^1 = A_1 x_1 + A_2, \qquad f^2 = A_1 x_2,$$

where $A_1 = e^{c_1}$ and $A_2 = e^{c_1} + c_2$ are the two essential parameters.

There is a method of obtaining a criterion for the number of essential parameters. It depends on the maximum rank of the matrix derived from partial derivatives of f^i with respect to a_α and higher-order cross partial derivatives of f^i with respect to x_j and a_α. A more precise formulation of this criterion may be found in Eisenhart [1933]. If, however, f^i contains one variable x and two parameters a_1 and a_2, then the criterion reduces to a simple formulation, i.e., the parameters a_1 and a_2 are essential if and only if[3]

$$\begin{vmatrix} \partial f^i/\partial a_1 & \partial f^i/\partial a_2 \\ \partial^2 f^i/\partial a_1\, \partial x & \partial^2 f^i/\partial a_2\, \partial x \end{vmatrix} \neq 0.$$

Also consider the projective transformation of the straight line (Campbell [1966], Hermann [1975, p. 123]) $f = (c_1 x + c_2)/(c_3 x + c_4)$, where c_1, c_2, c_3, c_4 are four arbitrary constants. In this transformation there are only three *essential* parameters a_1, a_2, a_3, viz., $c_1 = c_4(1 + a_2)$, $c_2 = a_1 c_4$, $c_3 = -a_3 c_4$, so that $f = (a_1 + (1 + a_2)x)/(1 - a_3 x)$.

Exercise 1 Show that $f^1 = x + a_1 + a_3$, $f^2 = y + a_2$ involve only two essential parameters.

II. Groups and Groups of Transformations

Let $f^i(x_1, \ldots, x_n; a_1, \ldots, a_r)$ be n independent functions of x and r essential parameters $a_1, \ldots, a_r$, where r is *finite*. The equations $x'_i = f^i(x_1, \ldots, x_n; a_1, \ldots, a_r) \equiv f^i(x; a)$ $(i = 1, \ldots, n)$ for each set of values of a define a transformation of a point $P(x)$ in an n-dimensional space V_n into a point $P'(x')$.

[3] If f^i contains only one parameter a_1, the parameter is essential if and only if $\partial f^i/\partial a_1 \neq 0$.

Since the functions are independent and the Jacobian of f with respect to x is not zero, (1) may be solved for x, at least in the neighborhood of a certain point, to yield the *inverse* transformation of P' into P,

$$x_i = \bar{f}^i(x'; a) \qquad (i = 1, \ldots, n). \tag{4}$$

Because of the continuity assumptions of f and its derivatives, if $P'(x')$ is the transform of a point $P(x)$ for particular values of a, then for small changes in the values of a we get points in the neighborhood of P'. Accordingly, we say that the transformations are *continuous*.

We shall denote the transformations (1) and (4), respectively, for a set of values a^1 of a by the symbolic form $T_{a^1}x = x'$, $T_{a^1}^{-1}x' = x$. If we apply a transformation T_{a^1}, and then another T_{a^2}, we obtain a transformation which we indicate by $T_{a^1}T_{a^2}$, which is called the *product* of the two. From the definition of $T_{a^1}^{-1}$, it follows that

$$T_{a^1}^{-1}T_{a^1}x = x, \qquad T_{a^1}T_{a^1}^{-1}x' = x',$$

which is called the *identity*.

We shall now consider a set of operators T_a abstractly. They constitute the elements of a class of objects. The product of two operators constitutes an operation between two members of the class or the aggregate. Such a class, however its elements and the operations are defined, is said to form a *group* with respect to the operation under the following conditions:

(i) If T_a and T_b are elements of the class (or aggregate), then T_bT_a is uniquely defined and is also an element of the class.

(ii) The associative law holds for the operation; thus $T_c(T_bT_a) = (T_cT_b)T_a$.

(iii) There is in the class an identity element I, such that $T_aI = IT_a = T_a$ for every T_a.

(iv) For each element T_a of the aggregate, there is an inverse element T_a^{-1}, such that $T_a^{-1}T_a = T_aT_a^{-1} = I$.

When equations such as (1), which contain a finite number of arbitrary constants (parameters), define a group for continuous values of a, the group is said to be *finite* and *continuous*.[4]

In order that Eqs. (1) may satisfy condition (i) of a *group*, it is necessary (Hermann [1975, p. 117]) that for each set of values a_α^1 and a_α^2 there exist a set of values a_α^3, say

$$a_\alpha^3 = \phi_\alpha(a^1; a^2) \qquad (\alpha = 1, \ldots, r), \tag{5}$$

[4] When a group of transformations involves an infinite number of arbitrary constants, it is said to be *infinite*. If a group does not contain any two operations whose effects differ only infinitesimally, it is said to be *discontinuous*. If only conditions (i) and (ii) are satisfied, the elements are said to form a *semigroup* for the operation. In the subsequent discussion we shall be concerned with only *finite continuous groups*.

such that the equations

$$f^i[f(x; a^1); a^2] = f^i(x; a^3) \tag{6}$$

are identities in the x, a^1, and a^2, and thus for arbitrary values of a^1 and a^2, we have

$$T_{a^2} T_{a^1} = T_{a^3}. \tag{7}$$

When these conditions are satisfied, the inverse of any transformation is not necessarily a member of the set. That is to say, it is not necessarily true that to each set of values a_α there corresponds a set $\bar{a}_\alpha$, such that $x_i = \bar{f}^i(x'; a) = f^i(x'; \bar{a})$, i.e.,

$$T_a^{-1} x' = T_{\bar{a}} x' = x. \tag{8}$$

If this condition is satisfied, then we have

$$T_a T_{\bar{a}} x' = x', \qquad T_{\bar{a}} T_a x = x; \tag{9}$$

i.e., when the *inverse* of each transformation is a member of the set, so also is the identity. Hence there is a set of values a_α^0, such that $a_\alpha^0 = \phi_\alpha(a; \bar{a})$, and

$$f^i(x; a^0) = x_i. \tag{10}$$

Since the a_α are essential, there is only one set of values a_α^0 yielding the identity. Thus T_{a^0} denotes the identity I, and from (9) we have $T_{a^0} = T_a T_{\bar{a}} = T_{\bar{a}} T_a$, so that in addition to (10), we have

$$a_\alpha^0 = \phi_\alpha(a; \bar{a}) = \phi_\alpha(\bar{a}; a) \tag{11}$$

and also

$$a_\alpha = \phi_\alpha(a; a^0) = \phi_\alpha(a^0; a). \tag{12}$$

When these conditions are met, Eqs. (1) satisfy conditions (iii) and (iv) of a group. It is easy to check that condition (ii) is also satisfied. Hence, *when condition* (5) *is satisfied and the inverse of each transformation is a member of the set, the transformation scheme* (1) *forms a group.* This group is often referred to as a *finite, continuous* (*Lie*) *group*[5] G_r. In the Lie theory it is presupposed that the transformations of the group occur in pairs of *mutually inverse* ones. When this property is emphasized, the group is often referred to as a *Lie group.* A group involving r essential parameters is known as an *r-parameter group.*

Example 1 Consider the *translations* ($n = 2$, $x_1 = x$, $x_2 = y$)

$$x' = f^1 = x + a_1, \qquad y' = f^2 = y + a_2, \qquad a^1 = (a_1, a_2),$$
$$x'' = x' + b_1, \qquad y'' = y' + b_2, \qquad a^2 = (b_1, b_2).$$

[5] If only (5) is satisfied, the transformation scheme is said to form a *finite, continuous semigroup.*

If the first transformations are followed by the second, the result is

$$x'' = x + c_1, \qquad y'' = y + c_2, \qquad a^3 = (c_1, c_2),$$

where $c_1 = \phi_1 = a_1 + b_1$, $c_2 = \phi_2 = a_2 + b_2$. Thus we have

$$x'' = f^1[f^1(x, y; a^1), f^2(x, y; a^1); a^2] = f^1(x, y; a^3),$$
$$y'' = f^2[f^1(x, y; a^1), f^2(x, y; a^1); a^2] = f^2(x, y; a^3).$$

Solving the above original transformations for x and y, we obtain

$$x = \bar{f}^1 = x' - a_1, \qquad y = \bar{f}^2 = y' - a_2.$$

By setting $\bar{a}_1 = -a_1$, $\bar{a}_2 = -a_2$, we obtain

$$x = \bar{f}^1 = f^1 = x' + \bar{a}_1, \qquad y = \bar{f}^2 = f^2 = y' + \bar{a}_2.$$

Thus we have $x = \bar{f}^1 = f^1(x', y'; \bar{a})$, $y = \bar{f}^2 = f^2(x', y'; \bar{a})$, where $\bar{a} = (\bar{a}_1, \bar{a}_2)$. It is readily seen that for $a_1^0 = a_2^0 = 0$, $x' = x$ and $y' = y$. Hence the translations form a Lie group.

Example 2 The *general projective* transformations

$$x' = f^1 = \frac{a_1 x + a_2 y + a_3}{a_7 x + a_8 y + a_9}, \qquad y' = f^2 = \frac{a_4 x + a_5 y + a_6}{a_7 x + a_8 y + a_9}$$

constitute a group. Without loss of generality we may set $a_9 = 1$ so that $a_1, \ldots, a_8$ are the eight essential parameters. If one of the preceding transformations is followed by

$$x'' = \frac{b_1 x' + b_2 y' + b_3}{b_7 x' + b_8 y' + b_9}, \qquad y'' = \frac{b_4 x' + b_5 y' + b_6}{b_7 x' + b_8 y' + b_9},$$

there results

$$x'' = \frac{c_1 x + c_2 y + c_3}{c_7 x + c_8 y + c_9}, \qquad y'' = \frac{c_4 x + c_5 y + c_6}{c_7 x + c_8 y + c_9},$$

where

$$C = BA = \begin{bmatrix} c_1 & c_2 & c_3 \\ c_4 & c_5 & c_6 \\ c_7 & c_8 & c_9 \end{bmatrix} = \begin{bmatrix} b_1 & b_2 & b_3 \\ b_4 & b_5 & b_6 \\ b_7 & b_8 & b_9 \end{bmatrix} \begin{bmatrix} a_1 & a_2 & a_3 \\ a_4 & a_5 & a_6 \\ a_7 & a_8 & a_9 \end{bmatrix}.$$

Moreover, the result of solving the equations for x and y is

$$x = \frac{\bar{a}_1 x' + \bar{a}_4 y' + \bar{a}_7}{\bar{a}_3 x' + \bar{a}_6 y' + \bar{a}_9}, \qquad y = \frac{\bar{a}_2 x' + \bar{a}_5 y' + \bar{a}_8}{\bar{a}_3 x' + \bar{a}_6 y' + \bar{a}_9},$$

where $\bar{a}_1, \bar{a}_2, \ldots, \bar{a}_9$ are the cofactors of the corresponding elements of the determinant, $\det A = \det\{a_i\}$. The identical transformations are obtained by setting $a_1^0 = a_5^0 = a_9^0$ equal to any number different from zero, and $a_2^0 = a_3^0 = a_4^0 = a_7^0 = a_8^0 \equiv 0$. Thus the general projective transformations constitute a finite and continuous eight-parameter group G_8 (Campbell [1966, p. 18]).

Exercise 1 Show that the following sets of transformations form groups. Find the respective values of the parameters that give the inverse and those that give the identical transformations.

(a) $x' = a_1 x + a_2,\ y' = a_1 y + a_3,$

(b) $x' = (a_1 + 1)x + (a_2 - 1)y + a_3,\ y' = a_1 x + a_2 y + a_3,$

(c) (displacements) $x' = x \cos a_1 - y \sin a_1 + a_2,$

$y' = x \sin a_1 + y \cos a_1 + a_3.$

Exercise 2 A simple example of a *discontinuous group* is the set of six transformations, $x' = x, x' = 1/(1 - x), x' = (x - 1)/x, x' = 1/x, x' = 1 - x, x' = x/(x - 1)$. By denoting the six corresponding operations by T_1 (which is equal to unity), $T_2, \ldots, T_6$, respectively, verify that these operations form a group.[6]

III. One-Parameter Groups

We begin to study the properties of groups with the simplest case of two variables and one parameter. Consider the following example of the factor-augmenting type of technical progress in economics:

$$f^1 = K' = e^{\alpha t}K, \quad \alpha \geqq 0, \qquad f^2 = L' = e^{\beta t}L, \quad \beta \geqq 0,$$

where K' and L' are effective capital and labor (K and L being physical capital and labor), α and β the efficiency increase in capital and labor, respectively, and t the time is the parameter. It is easy to see that the factor-augmenting type of technical progress constitutes a Lie group G_1, for we have

$$K'' = e^{\alpha t'}K' = e^{\alpha t'}e^{\alpha t}K = e^{\alpha(t+t')}K = e^{\alpha t''}K,$$

$$L'' = e^{\beta t'}L' = e^{\beta t'}e^{\beta t}L = e^{\beta(t+t')}L = e^{\beta t''}L,$$

which satisfy conditions (5), $a_1^3 = \phi_1(a^1;\ a^2) = t'' = \phi(t;\ t') = t + t'$ and $f^i(K, L; t'') = f^i[f^1(K, L; t), f^2(K, L; t); t'], i = 1, 2$. Thus we have expressed K'' and L'' as functions of K and L with the same forms as K' and L', except with the change in the value of the parameter from t to t''. In addition, when the parameter takes the specific value, the transformations will reduce to the

[6] If some transformation schemes $T_1, T_2, \ldots$ of a group involve arbitrary functional symbols, the group is said to be an *infinite* group.

identity, i.e., $K' = K$, $L' = L$ at $t = t_0 = 0$. We can also find meaningful inverse functions of this type of technical progress as $K = e^{-\alpha t}K'$, $L = e^{-\beta t}L'$, which satisfy condition (4) with $\bar{a} = -t$. Hence the factor-augmenting type of technical progress constitutes a group G_1.

Now let us consider a general group of transformation of two variables with one parameter,

$$x' = f^1 = \phi(x, y; a), \qquad y' = f^2 = \psi(x, y; a). \tag{13}$$

Infinitesimal Transformation

Since ϕ and ψ are assumed to be generally analytic functions (Cohn [1957]), the transformation

$$x' = \phi(x, y; a_0 + \delta a), \qquad y' = \psi(x, y; a_0 + \delta a),$$

where a_0 is the value of the parameter determining the identical transformation and δa is an infinitesimal,[7] will change x and y by infinitesimal amounts. On expanding by Taylor's theorem,

$$x' = \phi(x, y; a) = \phi(x, y; a_0) + (\partial\phi/\partial a)_{a_0}\,\delta a + \cdots,$$

$$y' = \psi(x, y; a) = \psi(x, y; a_0) + (\partial\psi/\partial a)_{a_0}\,\delta a + \cdots.$$

Noting $\phi(x, y; a_0) = x$ and $\psi(x, y; a_0) = y$, the changes in x and y due to the transformation are $\delta x = x' - x$ and $\delta y = y' - y$, and are expressed as

$$\delta x = \xi(x, y)\,\delta a + \cdots, \qquad \delta y = \eta(x, y)\,\delta a + \cdots,$$

where $\xi = (\partial\phi/\partial a)_{a_0}$ and $\eta = (\partial\psi/\partial a)_{a_0}$. It is noted that since a_0 is a fixed value of the parameter, the only variables remaining in ξ and η are x and y. Higher powers of the infinitesimal δa may be neglected, provided at least one of ξ and η does not vanish identically and neither of them is infinite. In this case the transformation producing an infinitesimal change in x and y is

$$\delta x = \xi(x, y)\,\delta a, \qquad \delta y = \eta(x, y)\,\delta a. \tag{14}$$

This is known as an *infinitesimal* transformation of G_1 near the identity.[8]

[7] Whenever, it is obvious we may use the derivative operator d interchangeably with δ. See for instance, Eqs. (16′) and (19′) of this Appendix.

[8] In case ξ and η are both identically zero, or if one of them is infinite, we must choose a different value of a, say α, to be a value of the parameter for which $\partial\phi/\partial a$ and $\partial\psi/\partial a$ are finite and at least one of them different from zero. Then $T_{\bar{\alpha}}T_\alpha \equiv T_{a_0} \equiv I$, where $T_{\bar{\alpha}}$ is the inverse transformation of the group, $T_{\bar{\alpha}}T_{\alpha+\delta a}$ is an infinitesimal transformation. Also, since $k\,\delta a$, where k is any finite constant different from zero, is an infinitesimal when δa is, the latter may be replaced by the former in (14). Hence the infinitesimal transformation (14) is the same as $\delta x = k\xi(x, y)\,\delta a$, $\delta y = k\eta(x, y)\,\delta a$.

We can extend these basic results to the case of n variables without any modifications. Thus let

$$x_i' = f^i(x; a) \qquad (i = 1, \ldots, n) \tag{15}$$

be a transformation scheme which defines a group with one parameter a. Then we have $x_i' = f^i(x; a_0 + \delta a)$, where a_0 is the value of the parameter determining the identical transformation for which $\partial f^i/\partial a$ are finite and at least one of them different from zero. T_{a_0} may be equal to I or $T_{\bar{a}_0} T_{a_0}$ may be equal to I, where $T_{\bar{a}_0}$ defines the inverse of the group. Neglecting powers of δa higher than the first, we can express, using Taylor's theorem, an *infinitesimal* transformation of G_1 near the identity as

$$\delta x_i = \xi_i(x)\, \delta a, \tag{16}$$

where $\xi_i(x) = (\partial f^i/\partial a)_{a_0}$. We have thus arrived at

Theorem 2 *Every one-parameter group G_1 of transformations* (15) *has one and only one independent infinitesimal transformation* (16), *where $\xi_i(x) = (\partial f^i/\partial a)_{a_0}$ and a_0 is the value of the parameter determining the identical transformation.*

Example 1 Let us look at the infinitesimal transformation of our example, the factor-augmenting type of technical progress. Let $K = x$ and $L = y$. Then the factor-augmenting type $x' = e^{\alpha t}x$, $y' = e^{\beta t}y$ is nothing but the so-called nonuniform magnification group. The infinitesimal transformation is

$$\delta x = (\partial x'/\partial t)_0\, \delta t = \alpha x\, \delta t \qquad \text{or} \qquad \xi = \alpha x,$$

$$\delta y = (\partial y'/\partial t)_0\, \delta t = \beta y\, \delta t \qquad \text{or} \qquad \eta = \beta y.$$

Example 2 For the translations $x' = x + a$, $y' = y + a$, we have $\delta x = \delta a$, $\delta y = \delta a$; therefore $\xi = 1$, $\eta = 1$.

Exercise 1 Show that each of the following sets of equations defines a one-parameter group, and find the infinitesimal transformation in each case:

(a) $x' = ax$, $y' = a^{-1}y$;
(b) $x' = x/(1 - ax)$, $y' = y/(1 - ay)$;
(c) (rotation group) $x' = x\cos\theta - y\sin\theta$, $y' = x\sin\theta + y\cos\theta$;
(d) (uniform magnification group $\equiv$ perspective or similitudinous transformations $\equiv$ dilatations or homothetic transformations (Eisenhart [1933, p. 42])) $x_i' = ax_i$, $i = 1, \ldots, n$.

Exercise 2 Find the infinitesimal transformation of the projective group in Example 2 in Part II, assuming that all a_i $(i = 1, \ldots, 8)$ are functions of one parameter t, i.e., $a_i = a_i(t)$.

Symbol of Infinitesimal Transformation

If $f(x, y)$ is a generally analytic function of x and y, the effect of the infinitesimal transformation on it is to replace it by $f(x + \xi\,\delta a, y + \eta\,\delta a)$, which on expanding by Taylor's theorem becomes

$$\begin{aligned} f(x', y') &= f(x + \delta x, y + \delta y) = f(x, y) + \frac{\partial f}{\partial x}\,\delta x + \frac{\partial f}{\partial y}\,\delta y + \cdots \\ &= f(x + \xi\,\delta a, y + \eta\,\delta a) \\ &= f(x, y) + \frac{\partial f}{\partial x}\,\xi(x, y)\,\delta a + \frac{\partial f}{\partial y}\,\eta(x, y)\,\delta a + \cdots \\ &= f(x, y) + \left(\xi(x, y)\frac{\partial f}{\partial x} + \eta(x, y)\frac{\partial f}{\partial y}\right)\delta a + \cdots. \end{aligned}$$

Hence $\delta f = (\xi(x, y)\,\partial f/\partial x + \eta(x, y)\,\partial f/\partial y)\,\delta a + \cdots$. Let Xf or Uf be Lie's symbol for the coefficient of δa in the expansion so that $\delta f = Xf\ \delta a + \cdots = Uf\ \delta a + \cdots$, where $Xf = \xi(x, y)\,\partial f/\partial x + \eta(x, y)\,\partial f/\partial y = Uf$. We shall use Xf and Uf interchangeably. Then U (or X) is called the *infinitesimal operator*[9] and represents the operation

$$U = \xi(x, y)\,\partial/\partial x + \eta(x, y)\,\partial/\partial y.$$

It is easily seen that

$$Ux = \xi(x, y)\,\partial x/\partial x + \eta(x, y)\,\partial x/\partial y = \xi(x, y)\cdot 1 + \eta(x, y)\cdot 0 \equiv \xi(x, y)$$

and

$$Uy = \eta(x, y).$$

U, then, may be expressed as $U = Ux\,\partial/\partial x + Uy\,\partial/\partial y$.

If generally $\phi(x)$ is any analytic function of x, then if we expand $\phi(x')$ in powers of δa, neglecting terms of the order $(\delta a)^2$, we get

$$\begin{aligned} \phi(x_1', \ldots, x_n') &= \phi(x_1 + \xi_1\,\delta a, \ldots, x_n + \xi_n\,\delta a) \\ &= \phi(x_1, \ldots, x_n) + (\xi_1\,\partial\phi/\partial x_1 + \cdots + \xi_n\,\partial\phi/\partial x_n)\,\delta a. \end{aligned}$$

If we let X (or U) denote the infinitesimal operator

$$X = \sum_{i=1}^{n} \xi_i(x)\,\partial/\partial x_i, \tag{17}$$

[9] The infinitesimal operator is the simplest kind of *Lie derivative* and *Lie differentiation*. It is the Lie derivative of a scalar f, $\mathscr{L} f = Xf$. (See Lovelock and Rund [1975]).

$\phi(x')$ may be written as $\phi(x') = (1 + \delta a X)\phi(x)$. The expression

$$(1 + \delta a X) \tag{18}$$

is often referred to as the symbol of an infinitesimal transformation and X, the *infinitesimal* or *differential* operator, or simply the operator (Campbell [1966, p. 6]).

Example 3 The infinitesimal operator for the factor-augmenting type of technical progress is $X = \alpha x\, \partial/\partial x + \beta y\, \partial/\partial y$.

Exercise 3 Find the infinitesimal operator for each group in Exercises 1 and 2 in Part III. (For rotation group, $X = -y\, \partial/\partial x + x\, \partial/\partial y$.)

Group Generated by X

We shall see that any transformation of G_1 which contains the identical transformation can be obtained by *indefinite repetition* of an infinitesimal operator. If

$$x_i' = f^i(x:a) \qquad (i = 1, \ldots, n)$$

are the equations of such a group, then

$$f^i(x:a) = \lim_{m \to +\infty} \left(1 + \frac{\delta a X}{m}\right)^m x_i,$$

where X is defined by (17). This limit is equal to

$$\lim_{m \to +\infty} \left(1 + \frac{\delta a X}{m}\right)^m x_i = \left(1 + \frac{\delta a}{1!} X + \frac{\delta a^2}{2!} X^2 + \frac{\delta a^3}{3!} X^3 + \cdots\right) x_i. \tag{19}$$

This process involves the power series solution to the system of differential equations generated by X (Eisenhart [1933, p. 35]),

$$dx_1'/\xi_1(x') = dx_2'/\xi_2(x') = \cdots = dx_n'/\xi_n(x') = da/1. \tag{19'}$$

Invariants

A function $f(x)$ is said to be an (*absolute*) *invariant* of a group G_1 (or invariant under the group) if it is left unaltered by every transformation of the group, i.e.,

$$f(x') = f(x). \tag{20}$$

From

$$f(x') - f(x) = Xf \frac{\delta a}{1!} + X^2 f \frac{\delta a^2}{2!} + \cdots,$$

Eq. (20) will be satisfied if and only if

$$Xf\ \delta a + X^2 f\, \frac{\delta a^2}{2!} + \cdots \equiv 0.$$

In particular, it is necessary that

$$Xf = \sum_{i=1}^{n} \xi_i(x)\ \partial f/\partial x_i = 0. \tag{21}$$

However, since $X^2 f = X(Xf)$, $X^3 f = X(X^2 f), \ldots,$ it follows at once that (21) is also the sufficient condition that $f(x') = f(x)$ for all δa. Hence we have

Theorem 3 *The necessary and sufficient condition that a function $f(x)$ be invariant under the group G_1 is that $Xf = 0$.*

Example 4 To determine invariant functions, it is necessary to solve the partial differential equation defined by (21). Thus, for the factor-augmenting type of technical progress $X = \alpha x\ \partial/\partial x + \beta y\ \partial/\partial y$, we must solve

$$Xf = \alpha x\ \partial f/\partial x + \beta y\ \partial f/\partial y = 0.$$

The corresponding system of ordinary differential equations is $dx/\alpha x = dy/\beta y = df/0$. If $u(x, y) = const$ is the solution of the equation involving the first two members, then u, in this case, must take the form $u = x^{1/\alpha}/y^{1/\beta}$. The general solution of (21) is thus $f = f(x^{1/\alpha}/y^{1/\beta}) = f(x'^{1/\alpha}/y'^{1/\beta})$.

Remark 1 The general solution of $dx/\xi_1 = dy/\xi_2$, or $u(x, y) = const$, is often referred to as the equation of the family of *path curves* or *trajectories* of the group.

Exercise 4 Find the invariant functions for each group in Exercises 1 and 2 of Part III.

Invariant Family of Curves

A family of curves is said to be *invariant* under a group G_1, if every transformation of the group transforms each curve into some curve of the family. Making use of the relation

$$f(x') = f(x) + Xf(x)\frac{\delta a}{1!} + X^2 f(x)\frac{\delta a^2}{2!} + \cdots,$$

we see that $f(x')$ will be a function of $f(x)$ for all values of δa if and only if

$$Xf(x) = F(f(x)). \tag{22}$$

[If $Xf = F(f)$, then $X^2 f = dF/df\ F(f), \cdots$.] Hence we have

Theorem 4 *The necessary and sufficient condition that the family of curves $f(x) = c$ be invariant under G_1 is that (22) hold.*

Example 5 For the case of the factor-augmenting technical progress, the invariant family of curves is derived from the solution of the partial differential equation

$$Xf = \alpha x\, \partial f/\partial x + \beta y\, \partial f/\partial y = F(f).$$

Solving the corresponding system of ordinary differential equations $dx/\alpha x = dy/\beta y = df/F(f)$, we immediately obtain the invariant family as $f = f(y^{1/\beta}G(x^{1/\alpha}/y^{1/\beta})) = f(x^{1/\alpha}H(y^{1/\beta}/x^{1/\alpha}))$.

Exercise 5 Derive the invariant family for each group in Exercises 1 and 2 of Part III.

Canonical Variables and Normalized Parameter

From Eq. (6), $x_i'' = f^i[f(x; a); b] = f^i(x; c)$, $c = \phi(a, b)$, we have

$$\xi_i(x') = \left(\frac{\partial}{\partial b} f^i(x'; b)\right)_{b=a_0} = \left(\frac{\partial}{\partial c} f^i(x; c)\frac{\partial \phi}{\partial b}\right)_{b=a_0}$$

$$= \frac{\partial}{\partial a} f^i(x; a)\left(\frac{\partial \phi(a, b)}{\partial b}\right)_{b=a_0} = \frac{\partial x_i'}{\partial a} B(a),$$

where $B(a) = (\partial\phi(a, b)/\partial b)_{b=a_0}$ and $B(a_0) = (\partial\phi(a_0, b)/\partial b)_{b=a_0} = 1$. Since in the neighborhood of a_0, $B(a)$ is not equal to zero, by setting $A(a) = 1/B(a)$ we can express

$$\partial x_i'/\partial a = A(a)\xi_i(x'). \tag{16$'$}$$

If we define the parameter t by

$$t = \int_{a_0}^{a} A(a)\, da, \tag{23}$$

then $t = 0$ yields the identity, and Eq. (16′) becomes

$$\partial x_i'/\partial t = \xi_i(x'), \qquad 1 \leqq i \leqq n. \tag{16$''$}$$

The parameter t is called the *normalized parameter*, when $t = 0$ yields the identity and Eq. (16″).

Any solution of (16″) satisfies the equations $\delta x_1'/\xi_1(x') = \cdots = \delta x_n'/\xi_n(x')$. The general solution of these equations is given by $n - 1$ equations

$$\psi^\alpha(x') = c^\alpha \qquad (\alpha = 1, \ldots, n - 1), \tag{24}$$

where the ψ are independent and the c are constants. The last equation is obtained from

$$t + c^n = \int \frac{\partial x'_n}{\bar{\xi}_n} = \bar{\psi}^n(x'_n, c^1, \ldots, c^{n-1}) = \psi^n(x'_1, \ldots, x'_n),$$

where $\bar{\xi}_n = \bar{\xi}_n(x'_n, c^1, \ldots, c^{n-1})$ and ψ^n is the value of $\bar{\psi}^n$ when the c^α are replaced by ψ^α. If we effect the change of coordinates $y_i = \psi^i(x_1, \ldots, x_n)$ $(i = 1, \ldots, n)$ we have

$$y'_1 = y_1, \ldots, y'_{n-1} = y_{n-1}, \qquad y'_n = y_n + t. \tag{25}$$

Then (15) is transformed to a *translation* group. Alternatively, if we define

$$Xy_i = \sum_{j=1}^{n} \xi_j \, \partial y_i/\partial x_j = 0, \qquad i = 1, \ldots, n-1, \qquad Xy_n = \sum_{j=1}^{n} \xi_j \, \partial y_n/\partial x_j = 1, \tag{26}$$

then y_i in Eq. (25) is a general solution of (26). When the original transformation scheme (15) is transformed to (25) by means of (26), the group is said to be in the *canonical form.* We have

Theorem 5 *Any one-parameter group of transformations is equivalent to a one-parameter group of translations. Alternatively, any one-parameter group of transformations can be reduced to the "canonical form."*

Example 6 Consider the group of screw motions

$$\begin{aligned} x'_1 &= x_1 \cos t - x_2 \sin t, \\ x'_2 &= x_1 \sin t + x_2 \cos t, \\ x'_3 &= x_3 + mt, \end{aligned}$$

where $m = \text{const}$. The infinitesimal transformations are $\xi_1 = -x_2$, $\xi_2 = x_1$, and $\xi_3 = m$. Solving

$$\delta x'_1/-x'_2 = \delta x'_2/x'_1 = \delta x'_3/m = \delta t/1,$$

we get

$$\begin{aligned} y'_1 &= x'^2_1 + x'^2_2 = x_1^2 + x_2^2 = c^1 = y_1, \\ y'_2 &= \tan^{-1}(x'_2/x'_1) - (x'_3/m) = \tan^{-1}(x_2/x_1) - (x_3/m) = c^2 = y_2, \\ y'_3 &= x'_3/m = x_3/m + t = y_3 + t. \end{aligned}$$

Hence the group of screw motions is reduced to the group of translations.

Exercise 6 Obtain the normalized parameter for each question in Exercises 1 and 2 and reduce each group to the canonical form.

IV. Properties of Groups: Invariant Differential Equations and Extended Groups

From the finite equations of a group G_r,

$$x'_i = f^i(x; a), \tag{1'}$$

we can derive

$$dx'_i = \sum_{j=1}^{n} (\partial f^i/\partial x_j)\, dx_j. \tag{1''}$$

Equations (1′) and (1″) define a transformation in the $2n$ variables x_i and dx_i involving r parameters. From the group property [Eq. (6)] $f^i[f(x; a^1); a^2] = f^i(x; a^3)$, it follows that

$$\sum_{j=1}^{n} \frac{\partial f^i(x'; a^2)}{\partial x'_j} \frac{\partial x'_j}{\partial x_k} = \sum_{j=1}^{n} \frac{\partial f^i(x'; a^2)}{\partial x'_j} \frac{\partial f^j(x; a^1)}{\partial x_k} = \frac{\partial f^i(x; a^3)}{\partial x_k}.$$

Consequently, we obtain

$$dx''_i = \sum_{j=1}^{n} \frac{\partial f^i(x'; a^2)}{\partial x'_j} dx'_j = \sum_{j=1}^{n} \frac{\partial f^i(x; a^3)}{\partial x_j} dx_j$$

which establishes the group property for (1″). Hence it is shown that Eqs. (1′) and (1″) define a group G_r in the $2n$ variables, which is called the (*once*) *extended group* of G_r.

The infinitesimal transformation of the extended group will be obtained in the same manner as the original group (1′). We shall illustrate this for a special but very important case G_1 of $n = 2$. By defining

$$dx_2/dx_1 = p, \tag{27}$$

the number of equations is reduced to 3. Hence

$$x'_1 = f^1(x; a), \qquad x'_2 = f^2(x; a)$$

$$p' = \pi(x, p; a) = \sum_{j=1}^{2} \frac{\partial f^2}{\partial x_j} dx_j \Bigg/ \sum_{j=1}^{2} \frac{\partial f^1}{\partial x_j} dx_j = \left(\frac{\partial f^2}{\partial x_1} + \frac{\partial f^2}{\partial x_2} p\right) \Bigg/ \left(\frac{\partial f^1}{\partial x_1} + \frac{\partial f^1}{\partial x_2} p\right). \tag{28}$$

The infinitesimal transformation of the once-extended group is

$$X' = \xi_1(x) \frac{\partial}{\partial x_1} + \xi_2(x) \frac{\partial}{\partial x_2} + \xi'_2(x, p) \frac{\partial}{\partial p}, \tag{29}$$

where $\xi_2' = (\partial/\partial a)(dx_2'/dx_1')|_{a=a_0} = (\partial/\partial a)(dx_2/dx_1)$. It is seen that ξ_2' is equal to

$$\frac{\partial(dx_2/dx_1)}{\partial a} = \frac{(\partial/\partial a)\,dx_2}{dx_1} - \frac{dx_2(\partial/\partial a)\,dx_1}{(dx_1)^2}$$
$$= \frac{d(\partial x_2/\partial a)}{dx_1} - \frac{dx_2}{dx_1}\frac{d(\partial x_1/\partial a)}{dx_1}$$

and hence to

$$\xi_2' = d\xi_2/dx_1 - p\,d\xi_1/dx_1. \tag{30}$$

Or expanding the right-hand member of (30), we have

$$\xi_2' = \frac{\partial \xi_2}{\partial x_1} + \left(\frac{\partial \xi_2}{\partial x_2} - \frac{\partial \xi_1}{\partial x_1}\right)p - \frac{\partial \xi_1}{\partial x_2}\,p^2. \tag{30'}$$

Given a differential equation

$$f(x_1, x_2, p) = 0, \tag{31}$$

the effect of any transformation (1′) on the variables x_1 and x_2 is to transform (31) by the corresponding extended transformation (28). The family of integral curves of (31) is invariant under the G_1 if each integral curve is transformed into another integral curve of the same family. Hence every transformation (28) must leave Eq. (31) unaltered. The condition for this is

$$X'f = \xi_1\frac{\partial f}{\partial x_1} + \xi_2\frac{\partial f}{\partial x_2} + \left[\frac{\partial \xi_2}{\partial x_1} + \left(\frac{\partial \xi_2}{\partial x_2} - \frac{\partial \xi_1}{\partial x_1}\right)p - p^2\frac{\partial \xi_1}{\partial x_2}\right]\frac{\partial f}{\partial p} = 0, \tag{32}$$

whenever $f(x_1, x_2, p) = 0$. Hence

Theorem 6 *The family of integral curves of the differential equation $f(x_1, x_2, p) = 0$ and, therefore, the differential equation itself, is invariant under G_1 if $X'f = 0$ whenever $f = 0$.*

If $f(x_1, x_2, p)$ is an (absolute) invariant satisfying (32) $X'f = 0$, we say that it is a *differential invariant* of the first order of the group G_1. For a given G_1, the problem of finding its differential invariants reduces to the integration of $dx_1/\xi_1 = dx_2/\xi_2 = dp/\xi_2'$, where ξ_2' is given by Eq. (30′). Let $u(x_1, x_2) = c$ be a solution of $\xi_2\,dx_1 - \xi_1\,dx_2 = 0$, which is the equation of the family of path curves, and let $u'(x_1, x_2, p) = \text{const}$ be a second solution. Then the general type of differential equation invariant under the given G_1 is

$$F[u(x_1, x_2), u'(x_1, x_2, p)] = 0.$$

Starting with the r-parameter group of point transformations $x' = f(x; a)$, we can generally derive the *s-times-extended transformation*

$$\begin{aligned} x_i' &= f^i(x; a), \\ dx_i' &= d(f^i) = g^i(x; dx; a), \\ d^2x_i' &= d^2(f^i) = h^i(x; dx; d^2x; a), \\ &\vdots \\ d^{(s)}x_i' &= d^{(s)}(f^i) = z^i(x; dx; d^2x; \ldots; d^{(s)}x; a). \end{aligned} \tag{33}$$

Again restricting to the case of $n = 2$ and $r = 1$, we have

$$\begin{aligned} x_1' &= f^1(x; a), \\ x_2' &= f^2(x; a), \\ p' &= \pi(x, p; a), \qquad p = dx_2/dx_1, \qquad p' = dx_2'/dx_1', \\ &\vdots \\ z' &= \theta(x, p, q, \ldots, z; a), \qquad q = d^2x_2/dx_1^2, \ldots, z = d^{(s)}x_2/dx_1^{(s)}, \end{aligned} \tag{33'}$$

and the symbol of those infinitesimal transformation may be written

$$X^{(s)}f = \xi_1 \frac{\partial f}{\partial x_1} + \xi_2 \frac{\partial f}{\partial x_2} + \xi_2' \frac{\partial f}{\partial p} + \cdots + \xi_2^{(s)} \frac{\partial f}{\partial z}, \tag{34}$$

where

$$\xi_2^k = \frac{d\xi_2^{k-1}}{dx_1} - \frac{d^kx_2}{dx_1^k}\frac{d\xi_1}{dx_1} \qquad (k = 1, \ldots, s). \tag{34-i}$$

Then we obtain

Theorem 7 *A differential equation of the sth order*

$$f(x_1, x_2, p, q, \ldots, z) = 0 \tag{34-ii}$$

is invariant under the group Xf if and only if (34) *is equal to zero whenever $f = 0$, i.e.,*

$$X^{(s)}f = 0 \qquad \textit{whenever} \quad f = 0. \tag{34-iii}$$

Example 1 Consider the case of nonuniform factor-augmenting type of technical progress; i.e.,

$$X = \alpha x_1\, \partial/\partial x_1 + \beta x_2\, \partial/\partial x_2, \qquad \alpha = 1.$$

Here we have $\xi_1 = x_1$ and $\xi_2 = \beta x_2$; therefore $\xi_2' = (\beta - 1)\, dx_2/dx_1$, and $u = x_2/x_1^\beta$, $u' = p/x_1^{\beta-1}$, $p = dx_2/dx_1$.

Hence the general type of differential equation invariant under X is obtained from

$$X'f = x_1\, \partial f/\partial x_1 + \beta x_2\, \partial f/\partial x_2 + (\beta - 1)p\, \partial f/\partial p = 0.$$

The solution of the above partial differential equation yields

$$f(x_1, x_2, p) = f(u, u') = f(x_2/x_1^\beta, p/x_1^{\beta-1}) = 0$$

or

$$p = dx_2/dx_1 = x_1^{\beta-1}F(x_2/x_1^\beta) \qquad \text{or} \qquad x_1\, dx_2/dx_1 = x_2 F(x_2/x_1^\beta).$$

It is easy to show that the general type of differential equation of the sth-order invariant under $X = x_1\, \partial/\partial x_1 + \beta x_2\, \partial/\partial x_2$ may be obtained from *Theorem* 7, utilizing $\xi_2' = (\beta - 1)p$, $\xi_2'' = (\beta - 2)q, \ldots, \xi_2^{(s)} = (\beta - s)z$, as

$$f(x_2/x_1^\beta, p/x_1^{\beta-1}, q/x_1^{\beta-2}, \ldots, z/x_1^{\beta-s}) = 0.$$

This is characterized by being homogeneous in $x_1, x_2, p, q, \ldots, z$ when these elements are given the weights $1, \beta, \beta - 1, \beta - 2, \ldots, \beta - s$, respectively. The solution of the foregoing differential equation gives a general family of *almost homogeneous* functions of degree 1 and β.

Exercise 1 Obtain the *invariant* differential equation of the sth order for each question in Exercises 1 and 2 of Part III.

Lie Operator (Commutator or Alternant)

Let each of the r homogeneous partial differential operators be

$$X_a f = \sum_{i=1}^{n} \xi_i^a\, \partial f/\partial x_i \qquad (a = 1, \ldots, r).$$

Then

$$X_a X_b f = \sum_{i=1}^{n} \xi_i^a \frac{\partial}{\partial x_i}\left(\sum_{j=1}^{n} \xi_j^b \frac{\partial f}{\partial x_j}\right) = \sum_{j=1}^{n} \frac{\partial f}{\partial x_j} X_a \xi_j^b + \sum_{i=1}^{n}\sum_{j=1}^{n} \xi_i^a \xi_j^b \frac{\partial^2 f}{\partial x_i\, \partial x_j}.$$

Consequently,

$$(X_a, X_b)f = X_a X_b f - X_b X_a f = \sum_{j=1}^{n} (X_a \xi_j^b - X_b \xi_j^a)\, \partial f/\partial x_j. \tag{35}$$

The quantity $(X_a, X_b)f$ thus defined is called the *Lie operator* (or *Lie product*) or the *commutator* (*or alternant*) of $X_a f$ and $X_b f$.[10] It will be shown later that the Lie operator is one of the same type as $X_a f$ and $X_b f$. The following properties of Lie operators are immediate:

$$(X_a, X_b)f = -(X_b, X_a)f, \tag{36-i}$$

$$(X_a, X_a)f = 0, \tag{36-ii}$$

$$(X_a, X_b \pm X_c)f = (X_a, X_b)f \pm (X_a, X_c)f, \tag{36-iii}$$

$$(\phi(x)X_a, X_b)f = \phi(x)(X_a, X_b)f - X_b\phi(x)X_a f. \tag{36-iv}$$

Also, we can show that

$$\begin{aligned}(X_a, (X_b, X_c))f &= X_a(X_b, X_c)f - (X_b, X_c)X_a f \\ &= X_a(X_b X_c f - X_c X_b f) - (X_b X_c X_a f - X_c X_b X_a f) \\ &= X_a X_b X_c f - X_a X_c X_b f - X_b X_c X_a f + X_c X_b X_a f.\end{aligned}$$

Therefore,

$$(X_a, (X_b, X_c))f + (X_b, (X_c, X_a))f + (X_c, (X_a, X_b))f = 0 \qquad (a, b, c = 1, \ldots, r). \tag{37}$$

This equation is referred to as *Jacobi's identity*.

Example 2 In the projective group of the straight line we see that

$$(X_a, X_b)f \equiv X_a f, \qquad \text{where} \quad X_a = \partial/\partial x_1 \quad \text{and} \quad X_b = x_1\, \partial/\partial x_1,$$
$$(X_a, X_c)f \equiv 2X_b f, \qquad \text{where} \quad X_c = x_1^2\, \partial/\partial x_1,$$
$$(X_b, X_c)f \equiv X_c f.$$

Alternative Criterion for Invariance of a Differential Equation under a Group

If $\phi(x_1, x_2) = c$ is the solution of the differential equation

$$M_1\, dx_1 + M_2\, dx_2 = 0, \tag{38}$$

[10] Eisenhart [1933] calls this the *Poisson operator*, but the concept of the Poisson operator normally applies to a more general case. For example, Poisson operators apply to the so-called contact transformations. (See Part VII of this Appendix and, also Chapter 9.) The operation (X_a, X_b) is sometimes written as the (Lie) bracket operation $[X_a, X_b] = X_a X_b - X_b X_a$ (Chevalley [1946, p. 103], Cohn [1957, p. 59], Lovelock and Rund [1975, p. 346]). We shall use (X_a, X_b) and $[X_a, X_b]$ interchangeably.

then ϕ is a solution of the partial differential equation

$$A\phi = M_2 \frac{\partial \phi}{\partial x_1} - M_1 \frac{\partial \phi}{\partial x_2} = 0, \qquad \text{where} \quad A = M_2 \frac{\partial}{\partial x_1} - M_1 \frac{\partial}{\partial x_2}. \quad (39)$$

On the other hand, if $\phi(x_1, x_2)$ is the family of curves invariant under some group $X = \xi_1\, \partial/\partial x_1 + \xi_2\, \partial/\partial x_2$, then, in view of *Theorem* 4, ϕ must satisfy

$$X\phi = \xi_1\, \partial\phi/\partial x_1 + \xi_2\, \partial\phi/\partial x_2 = F(\phi) = 1, \quad \text{say.} \qquad (40)$$

Since $A = M_2\, \partial/\partial x_1 - M_1\, \partial/\partial x_2$ and $X = \xi_1\, \partial/\partial x_1 + \xi_2\, \partial/\partial x_2$ are two infinitesimal operators, we can find the Lie product of X and A

$$(X, A)f = XAf - AXf = (XM_2 - A\xi_1)\, \partial f/\partial x_1 - (XM_1 + A\xi_2)\, \partial f/\partial x_2. \qquad (41)$$

If $f = \phi$, then because of (39) and (40), $X(0) - A(1) = 0$, we have

$$(X, A)\phi = 0 \qquad \text{or} \qquad (XM_2 - A\xi_1)\, \partial\phi/\partial x_1 - (XM_1 + A\xi_2)\, \partial\phi/\partial x_2 = 0.$$

Then the coefficients of the above must be proportional to those of (39); i.e.,

$$(XM_2 - A\xi_1)/M_2 = (XM_1 + A\xi_2)/M_1 = \lambda(x_1, x_2),$$

or

$$XM_2 - A\xi_1 = \lambda M_2, \qquad XM_1 + A\xi_2 = \lambda M_1.$$

Putting these in (41), we get

$$(X, A)\phi = \lambda(x_1, x_2)(M_2\, \partial\phi/\partial x_1 - M_1\, \partial\phi/\partial x_2) = \lambda(x_1, x_2)A\phi. \quad (42)$$

Conversely if (42) holds, then $(X, A)\phi = \lambda A\phi = XA\phi - AX\phi = 0$ because of (39). Hence $AX\phi = 0$. Since every solution of (39) is a function of ϕ, we have $X\phi = F(\phi)$. This is exactly the condition for invariance of the family of curves ϕ under X. Hence

Theorem 8 *The necessary and sufficient condition that the differential equation $M_1\, dx_1 + M_2\, dx_2 = 0$ be invariant under X, and therefore, the family of curves of the differential equation of $M_1\, dx_1 + M_2\, dx_2 = 0$ be invariant under X, is that* (42) *hold, where*

$$A\phi = M_2\, \partial\phi/\partial x_1 - M_1\, \partial\phi/\partial x_2 \qquad \text{and} \qquad X\phi = \xi_1\, \partial\phi/\partial x_1 + \xi_2\, \partial\phi/\partial x_2.$$

We present four corollaries to the above theorems.

Corollary 8-1 *If the family of curves of the differential equation* (38) *is invariant under $X = \xi_1\, \partial/\partial x_1 + \xi_2\, \partial/\partial x_2$, then $\mu = (\xi_1 M_1 + \xi_2 M_2)^{-1}$ is an integrating factor of the differential equation.*

Corollary 8-2 *If μ is an integrating factor of the differential equation* (38), *and ξ_1 and ξ_2 satisfy $\mu = (\xi_1 M_1 + \xi_2 M_2)^{-1}$, then* (38) *is invariant under $X = \xi_1\,\partial/\partial x_1 + \xi_2\,\partial/\partial x_2$.*

Corollary 8-3 *The general type of group leaving* (38) *unaltered is expressed in the form*

$$X = \xi_1(x_1, x_2)\frac{\partial}{\partial x_1} + \left(\frac{1}{M_2\mu F(\phi)} - \frac{M_1\xi_1(x_1, x_2)}{M_2}\right)\frac{\partial}{\partial x_2}, \tag{43}$$

where ξ_1 and F are arbitrary functions and μ is an integrating factor.

Corollary 8-4 *Every group which leaves the differential equation* (38) *unaltered is given by*

$$X_a = F(\phi)X_b + \rho(x_1, x_2)A, \tag{44}$$

where F and ρ are arbitrary functions, and A is given by (39).

Proof First, we see that $M_1\,dx_1 + M_2\,dx_2 = 0$ implies

$$M_2\,\partial\phi/\partial x_1 - M_1\,\partial\phi/\partial x_2 = 0.$$

If ϕ is invariant under X, from

$$X\phi = \xi_1\,\partial\phi/\partial x_1 + \xi_2\,\partial\phi/\partial x_2 = 1,$$

we obtain

$$\frac{\partial\phi}{\partial x_1} = \frac{M_1}{\xi_1 M_1 + \xi_2 M_2} \qquad \text{and} \qquad \frac{\partial\phi}{\partial x_2} = \frac{M_2}{\xi_1 M_1 + \xi_2 M_2}$$

which proves *Corollary* 8-1. On the other hand, if $\mu = (\xi_1 M_1 + \xi_2 M_2)^{-1}$ is an integrating factor for $M_1\,dx_1 + M_2\,dx_2 = 0$, we must have

$$\frac{\partial}{\partial x_1}\left(\frac{M_2}{\xi_1 M_1 + \xi_2 M_2}\right) - \frac{\partial}{\partial x_2}\left(\frac{M_1}{\xi_1 M_1 + \xi_2 M_2}\right) \equiv 0,$$

which implies that $(XM_2 - A\xi_1)/M_2 \equiv (XM_1 + A\xi_2)/M_1$. Using Theorem 8 [Eq. (42)], we prove *Corollary* 8-2. *Corollary* 8-3 follows immediately from the fact that $\mu = (\xi_1 M_1 + \xi_2 M_2)^{-1}$ is the single condition containing two functions ξ_1 and ξ_2, and that one of them may be chosen arbitrarily. If μ is an integrating factor, then $\mu F(\phi)$ is also an integrating factor. Using this, we get (43) selecting ξ_1 arbitrarily. Finally, to prove *Corollary* 8-4, we note that if two (different) integrating factors are known, ϕ will be obtained simply from $\mu_a/\mu_b = F(\phi) = \text{const}$. Hence we have

$$(\xi_1^a M_1 + \xi_2^a M_2)/(\xi_1^b M_1 + \xi_2^b M_2) = F(\phi).$$

Rearranging the terms, we can express

$$(\xi_1^a - F(\phi)\xi_1^b)/M_2 = -(\xi_2^a - F(\phi)\xi_2^b)/M_1 = \rho(x_1, x_2).$$

Hence $\xi_1^a = F(\phi)\xi_1^b + \rho M_2$, $\xi_2^a = F(\phi)\xi_2^b - \rho M_1$ or $X_a = F(\phi)X_b + \rho(x_1, x_2)A$. Q.E.D.

Example 3 Consider the homothetic Cobb–Douglas function $\phi = x_1^{\alpha_1}x_2^{\alpha_2}$. The differential equation for this is $\alpha_1 x_2\, dx_1 + \alpha_2 x_1\, dx_2 = 0$ or $M_1 = \alpha_1 x_2$ and $M_2 = \alpha_2 x_1$. Hence $A = \alpha_2 x_1\, \partial/\partial x_1 - \alpha_1 x_2\, \partial/\partial x_2$. Since the Cobb–Douglas function is invariant under the nonuniform factor-augmenting technical progress

$$X_b = \beta_1 x_1\, \partial/\partial x_1 + \beta_2 x_2\, \partial/\partial x_2,$$

we get

$$\begin{aligned} X_a &= F(x_1^{\alpha_1}x_2^{\alpha_2})\left(\beta_1 x_1 \frac{\partial}{\partial x_1} + \beta_2 x_2 \frac{\partial}{\partial x_2}\right) + \rho(x_1, x_2)\left(\alpha_2 x_1 \frac{\partial}{\partial x_1} - \alpha_1 x_2 \frac{\partial}{\partial x_2}\right) \\ &= (\beta_1 F + \alpha_2 \rho)x_1 \frac{\partial}{\partial x_1} + (\beta_2 F - \alpha_1 \rho)x_2 \frac{\partial}{\partial x_2}, \end{aligned}$$

where F and ρ are arbitrary functions.

Exercise 2 Find a general expression of X_b for the homothetic CES function. Also study the properties of the CES function in the light of *Theorem* 8, *Corollaries* 8-1, 8-2, *and* 8-3. Show that the CES function is *not* invariant under the nonuniform factor-augmenting technical progress.

V. Complete Systems of Linear Partial Differential Equations

Consider the system of homogeneous linear partial differential equations

$$X_a f = \sum_{i=1}^{n} \xi_i^a\, \partial f/\partial x_i = 0 \qquad (a = 1, \ldots, r), \tag{45}$$

for which the rank of the matrix

$$M = \|\xi_i^a\| \tag{46}$$

is r, i.e., Eqs. (45) are independent. If $r = n$, the *only solution of* (45) *is* $f =$ *const*. If $r < n$, there is a possibility of solutions other than the trivial one

f = constant. From the definition of the Lie operator [Eq. (35)], it is evident that any solution of (45) satisfies

$$(X_a, X_b)f = 0 \qquad (a, b = 1, \ldots, r). \tag{47}$$

If

$$(X_a, X_b)f = \sum_{c=1}^{r} \gamma_{ab}^c X_c f \qquad (a, b = 1, \ldots, r) \tag{48}$$

where the γ are functions of x, then the system (45) and (47) is in fact equivalent to (45). We adjoin to (45) all the equations obtained by equating to zero those commutators which are *not* expressible in the form (48), and in this way we have s ($\geqq r$) independent equations. If $s > r$, we repeat this process until we obtain a system of t ($\leqq n$) equations. If $t = n$, the only solution of (45) is a trivial one f = const. If $t < n$, we thus have obtained a system of t equations

$$X_1 f = 0, \quad X_2 f = 0, \ldots, X_t f = 0 \qquad (r \leqq t < n)$$

such that

$$(X_a, X_b)f = \sum_{c=1}^{t} \rho_{ab}^c(x) X_c f \qquad (a, b = 1, 2, \ldots, t). \tag{49}$$

Such a system is said to constitute a *complete system of order t*.

Theorem 9 *The solution of a system of the form* (45) *is the same as that of a complete system in which* (49) *hold.*

Jacobian Complete System

If (45) is a complete system, so also is

$$Y_b f = \sum_{a=1}^{r} \lambda_a^b X_a f = 0 \tag{50}$$

where the λ are any functions of x such that the determinant $|\lambda_a^b|$ is not zero. Since $X_a f$ are supposed to form a complete system, the alternant

$$(Y_a, Y_b)f = \sum_{c=1}^{r} \gamma_{ab}'^c Y_c f \qquad (a, b = 1, \ldots, r) \tag{51}$$

is linear in $X_1 f, \ldots, X_r f$ and therefore also linear in $Y_1 f, \ldots, Y_r f$, which proves that (50) is a complete system.

Moreover, any common solution of $X_a f = 0$ must also be a solution of $Y_a f = 0$, and vice versa. Hence, the two systems (45) and (50) are said to be *equivalent*. Since the rank of M (46) is r, there is no loss in generality in assuming that $|\xi_b^a|$, for $a, b = 1, \ldots, r$ is different from zero. Hence we may solve (45) for $\partial f/\partial x_1, \ldots, \partial f/\partial x_r$ and write the result in the form

$$Y_a f = (\partial f/\partial x_a) + \sum_{t=r+1}^{n} \psi_t^a \, \partial f/\partial x_t \qquad (a = 1, \ldots, r). \tag{50'}$$

When a complete system is expressed in this form, it is called a *Jacobian complete system.* The Jacobian complete system has an interesting property. From (51), we have

$$(Y_a, Y_b)f = \sum_{t=r+1}^{n} (Y_a \psi_t^b - Y_b \psi_t^a) \, \partial f/\partial x_t \qquad (a, b = 1, \ldots, r).$$

Since $\partial f/\partial x_1, \ldots, \partial f/\partial x_r$ do not appear in this last expression, *it follows that* $\gamma_{ab}'^{c} \equiv 0$, *i.e., for a Jacobian complete system, we have* $(Y_a, Y_b)f = 0$. *Hence we always have*

$$Y_a \psi_t^b - Y_b \psi_t^a \equiv 0 \qquad (a, b = 1, \ldots, r; \quad t = r + 1, \ldots, n). \tag{52}$$

Integrability Conditions

Consider a system of partial differential equations

$$\partial \theta_\alpha/\partial x_i = \psi_i^\alpha(\theta_1, \ldots, \theta_m; x_1, \ldots, x_n) = \psi_i^\alpha(\theta; x)$$
$$(\alpha = 1, \ldots, m; \quad i = 1, \ldots, n). \tag{53}$$

These equations are equivalent to the system of *total* differential equations

$$d\theta_\alpha = \sum_{i=1}^{n} \psi_i^\alpha(\theta; x) \, dx_i \qquad (\alpha = 1, \ldots, m). \tag{53'}$$

The conditions of integrability of (53) *are*

$$\frac{\partial \psi_i^\alpha}{\partial x_j} + \sum_{\beta=1}^{m} \psi_j^\beta \frac{\partial \psi_i^\alpha}{\partial \theta_\beta} = \frac{\partial \psi_j^\alpha}{\partial x_i} + \sum_{\gamma=1}^{m} \psi_i^\gamma \frac{\partial \psi_j^\alpha}{\partial \theta_\gamma}$$
$$(i, j = 1, \ldots, n; \quad \alpha = 1, \ldots, m). \tag{54}$$

If these equations are satisfied identically, the system (53) is said to be *completely integrable.* We denote such a solution

$$\theta_\alpha = \zeta^\alpha(x : c_1, \ldots, c_m) \qquad (\alpha = 1, \ldots, m). \tag{55}$$

Returning to (52), we see that (52) *implies the conditions of integrability,* i.e.,

$$\frac{\partial \psi_p^b}{\partial x_a} + \sum_{q=r+1}^{n} \psi_q^a \frac{\partial \psi_p^b}{\partial x_q} = \frac{\partial \psi_p^a}{\partial x_b} + \sum_{q=r+1}^{n} \psi_q^b \frac{\partial \psi_p^a}{\partial x_q}$$
$$(a, b = 1, \ldots, r; \quad p = r + 1, \ldots, n). \tag{52'}$$

Thus the equations

$$\partial x_p/\partial x_a = \psi_p^a \qquad (a = 1, \ldots, r; \quad p = r+1, \ldots, n) \tag{56}$$

are completely integrable. Moreover, (50′) is the associated system of (56). Hence we have that Eqs. (50′), and equivalently, Eqs. (45) admit $(n - r)$ independent solutions, and that they do not admit more than $n - r$ independent solutions. [See a proof of (54) in Chapter 9, Part II.] Hence we have

Theorem 10 *A complete system of r homogeneous linear partial differential equations of the first order in n (> r) variables admits exactly n − r independent solutions.*

Exercise 1 Find solutions common to $X_a f = \partial f/\partial x_1 = 0$ and

$$X_b f = x_1\, \partial f/\partial x_1 + x_2\, \partial f/\partial x_2 + x_3\, \partial f/\partial x_3 = 0.$$

Show that they form a complete system.

Linear Partial Differential Equations Invariant under a Group

The homogeneous linear differential equation of the first order

$$Af = \sum_{i=1}^{n} a_i(x)\, \partial f/\partial x_i = 0 \tag{57}$$

is said to be *invariant* under

$$Xf = \sum_{i=1}^{n} \xi_i\, \partial f/\partial x_i \tag{58}$$

if the new equation

$$\sum_{i=1}^{n} Af^i\, \partial f/\partial x_i' = 0 \tag{57′}$$

is the same equation in the new variables x_i' as (57) in the old variables x_i, where $x_i' = f^i(x; a)$ is the transformation scheme corresponding to (58) and the Af^i are expressed in terms of x'. In view of *Theorem* 10, Eq. (57) has $(n - 1)$ independent solutions $\phi_i(x)$, $1 \leqq i \leqq n - 1$. If (57) is invariant under (58), it must also transform all the ϕ_i into some functions of themselves. Then using an extension of *Theorem* 4 ϕ_i will be invariant if and only if

$$X\phi_i = F_i(\phi_1, \ldots, \phi_{n-1}), \qquad 1 \leqq i \leqq n - 1. \tag{59}$$

Using the alternative approach stated in *Theorem* 8 and its extension, we thus have

Theorem 11 *The necessary and sufficient condition that* $Af = \sum_{i=1}^{n} a_i(x)\, \partial f/\partial x_i = 0$ *be invariant under a group* $Xf = \sum_{i=1}^{n} \xi_i\, \partial f/\partial x_i$ *is that* (59) *hold, of equivalently,*

$$(X, A)f = \lambda(x)Af, \tag{60}$$

where ϕ_i *is the independent solutions of* $Af = 0, i = 1, \ldots, n-1$, *and* (X, A) *the Lie operator of* X *and* A.

Likewise, the above theorem can be generalized to a complete system of linear partial differential equations. First, if (57) is *invariant* under two distinct groups $X_a f$ and $X_b f$, then we have

$$(X_a, A)f = \lambda^a Af \qquad \text{and} \qquad (X_b, A)f = \lambda^b Af. \tag{61}$$

By Jacobi's identity (37), we have

$$((X_a, X_b), A)f + ((X_b, A), X_a)f + ((A, X_a), X_b)f \equiv 0. \tag{62}$$

Using (61) and obvious properties of alternants, we have $((X_a, X_b), A)f = \mu Af$, where $\mu = X_a\lambda^b - X_b\lambda^a$. This process can be extended to a system of partial differential equations which constitutes a complete system,

$$A_\alpha f = \sum_{i=1}^{n} a_i^\alpha\, \partial f/\partial x_i = 0, \qquad \alpha = 1, \ldots, r. \tag{63}$$

We have

Theorem 12 *If a complete system of linear homogeneous partial differential equations is invariant under* $X_a f$ *and* $X_b f$, *it is also invariant under* $(X_a, X_b)f$.

Example 1 The partial differential equation $Af = \sum_{i=1}^{n} \partial f/\partial x_i = 0$ is invariant under the magnification group $Xf = \sum_{i=1}^{n} x_i\, \partial f/\partial x_i$, since

$$(X, A)f = -\left(\sum_{i=1}^{n} \partial f/\partial x_i\right) = -Af.$$

Example 2 To show that $Af = \sum_{i=1}^{3} \partial f/\partial x_i = 0$ is left unaltered by

$$X_a f = (x_2 - x_3)\frac{\partial f}{\partial x_2} \qquad \text{and} \qquad X_b f = x_1^2 \frac{\partial f}{\partial x_1} + x_1^2 \frac{\partial f}{\partial x_2}$$
$$+ (2x_1x_2 - x_2^2)\frac{\partial f}{\partial x_3},$$

we find that $(X_a, A)f \equiv 0$ and $(X_b, A)f \equiv -2x_1 Af$.

Exercise 2 Show that in *Example* 2 $(X_a, X_b)f$ also leaves $Af = 0$ unaltered.

Exercise 3 Show that the magnification group in *Example* 1 also leaves $Af = x_2\,\partial f/\partial x_1 - x_1\,\partial f/\partial x_2 + x_3\,\partial f/\partial x_3 = 0$ unaltered.

VI. *r*-Parameter Group of Transformations

Infinitesimal Transformations

The transformations scheme

$$x_i' = f^i(x; a), \qquad x = (x_1, \ldots, x_n), \quad a = (a_1, \ldots, a_r), \quad 1 \leqq i \leqq n, \tag{64}$$

which satisfies conditions (i–iv) in Part II, constitutes a Lie group with the r essential parameters. Then the transformation

$$x_i' = f(x; a^0 + \delta a), \qquad a^0 = (a_1^0, \ldots, a_r^0), \quad \delta a = (\delta a_1, \ldots, \delta a_r), \tag{64$'$}$$

changes x by infinitesimal amounts, where a^0 are the values of a, which determine the identical transformation. Equation (64′) may also be written as

$$x_i' - x_i = \sum_{\alpha=1}^{r} \frac{\partial f^i(x; a^0)}{\partial a_\alpha^0}\,\delta a_\alpha + \cdots \tag{64$''$}$$

or

$$\delta x_i = \sum_{\alpha=1}^{r} \xi_i^\alpha\,\delta a_\alpha + \cdots, \tag{64$'''$}$$

where $\xi_i^\alpha = \partial f^i/\partial a_\alpha^0$ is finite and not identically zero for all $1 \leqq \alpha \leqq r$. By taking δt as a standard infinitesimal of the first order, we may put

$$\delta a_\alpha = e_\alpha\,\delta t, \qquad 1 \leqq \alpha \leqq r, \quad e_\alpha = \text{finite constant}, \tag{65}$$

and

$$\delta x_i = \sum_{\alpha=1}^{r} e_\alpha \xi_i^\alpha\,\delta t + \cdots = \xi_i\,\delta t + \cdots, \tag{64$''''$}$$

where $\xi_i = \sum_{\alpha=1}^{r} e_\alpha \xi_i^\alpha$.

Introducing the symbol

$$Xf = \sum_{i=1}^{n} \xi_i\,\partial f/\partial x_i = \sum_{i=1}^{n} \left(\sum_{\alpha=1}^{r} e_\alpha\,\xi_i^\alpha\,\partial f/\partial x_i \right), \tag{66}$$

and

$$X_\alpha f = \sum_{i=1}^{n} \xi_i^\alpha\,\partial f/\partial x_i, \qquad 1 \leqq \alpha \leqq r, \tag{67}$$

we have

$$Xf = \sum_{\alpha=1}^{r} e_\alpha X_\alpha f. \tag{68}$$

We shall call (68) *the infinitesimal transformations of the r-parameter group.*

It is seen that, since the r parameters are essential by assumption, $X_\alpha f$ are *linearly independent*, i.e., it is impossible to find a set of constants $c_1, \ldots, c_r$ such that $c_1 X_1 f + \cdots + c_r X_r f \equiv 0$. In summary, we have

Theorem 13 *Every continuous Lie group involving r essential parameters contains r linearly independent infinitesimal transformations $X_1 f, \ldots, X_r f$, in terms of which every infinitesimal transformation of the group can be expressed linearly with constant coefficients as in (68). Moreover, every transformation of the type (68), for all choices of the constants $e_1, \ldots, e_r$ belongs to the group G_r.*

Group G_r generated by Xf

Starting with (68), one may be able to derive the group either from

$$dx_i' \Big/ \sum_{\alpha=1}^{r} e_\alpha \xi_i^\alpha(x') = dx_k' \Big/ \sum_{\alpha=1}^{r} e_\alpha \xi_k^\alpha(x') = dt, \qquad 1 \leqq i, k \leqq n, \tag{69}$$

or

$$x_i' = x_i + t \sum_{\alpha=1}^{r} e_\alpha X_\alpha x_i + (t^2/2!) \sum_{\beta=1}^{r} \sum_{\alpha=1}^{r} e_\alpha e_\beta X_\alpha X_\beta x_i + \cdots, \tag{70}$$

which should be identically equal to (64).

Because of Theorem 13, every transformation of the set (68) belongs to the r-parameter group. The ∞^r transformations of (70) therefore belong to the group. Moreover, every transformation of G_r is included in (70). Hence

Theorem 14 *If the $X_\alpha f$ $(1 \leqq \alpha \leqq r)$ are r-linearly independent transformations of an r-parameter group, the latter is precisely the aggregate of all the one-parameter groups generated by the ∞^{r-1} infinitesimal transformations $Xf = \sum_{\alpha=1}^{r} e_\alpha X_\alpha f$.*

Sometimes it is more convenient to derive the transformation (70) from the so-called Lie–Maurer method (Lie and Scheffers [1893, p. 194]). Having found the finite transformations of the one-parameter group generated by each $X_j f$,

$$x_i' = f_\alpha^i(x; a_\alpha), \qquad 1 \leqq \alpha \leqq r, \tag{71}$$

the result of performing successively one transformation out of each of the r groups (71) is a transformation belonging to the r-parameter group.

Example 1 *(Projective Groups)* Let

$$X = e_1\frac{\partial}{\partial x_1} + e_2\frac{\partial}{\partial x_2} + e_3 x_1\frac{\partial}{\partial x_1} + e_4 x_2\frac{\partial}{\partial x_1} + e_5 x_1\frac{\partial}{\partial x_2} + e_6 x_2\frac{\partial}{\partial x_2} + e_7\left(x_1^2\frac{\partial}{\partial x_1} + x_1 x_2\frac{\partial}{\partial x_2}\right) + e_8\left(x_1 x_2\frac{\partial}{\partial x_1} + x_2^2\frac{\partial}{\partial x_2}\right). \tag{72}$$

Then

$$X_1 f = \frac{\partial f}{\partial x_1}:\quad x_1' = x_1 + a_1,\qquad x_2' = x_2,$$

$$X_2 f = \frac{\partial f}{\partial x_2}:\quad x_1'' = x_1',\qquad x_2'' = x_2' + a_2,$$

$$\vdots$$

$$X_8 f = x_1 x_2\frac{\partial f}{\partial x_1} + x_2^2\frac{\partial f}{\partial x_2}:\quad x_1^{\text{viii}} = \frac{x_1^{\text{vii}}}{1 - a_8 x_2^{\text{vii}}},\qquad x_2^{\text{viii}} = \frac{x_2^{\text{vii}}}{1 - a_8 x_2^{\text{vii}}}.$$

The successive performance of these gives

$$x_1^{\text{viii}} = \frac{a_3 x_1 + a_4 x_2 + a_1 a_3 + a_2 a_4}{\alpha_7 x_1 + \alpha_8 x_2 + \alpha_9} = x_1'$$

$$x_2^{\text{viii}} = \frac{a_3 a_5 a_6 x_1 + (a_6 + a_4 a_5 a_6) x_2 + a_2 a_6 + a_1 a_3 a_5 a_6 + a_2 a_4 a_5 a_6}{\alpha_7 x_1 + \alpha_8 x_2 + \alpha_9} = x_2', \tag{73}$$

where

$$\alpha_7 = -(a_3 a_7 + a_3 a_5 a_6 a_8),\qquad \alpha_8 = -(a_4 a_7 + a_6 a_8 + a_4 a_5 a_6 a_8),$$

$$\alpha_9 = 1 - (a_1 a_3 a_7 + a_2 a_4 a_7 + a_2 a_6 a_8 + a_1 a_3 a_5 a_6 a_8 + a_2 a_4 a_5 a_6 a_8).$$

Fundamental Theorem

We have shown that an r-parameter group has exactly r independent infinitesimal transformations. On the other hand, starting with *any* r linearly independent operators $X_1, \ldots, X_r$, there is no reason to suppose they form an r-parameter group. A definite answer to this question is given by Lie's principal theorem

Theorem 15 *The necessary and sufficient conditions that* $Xf = \sum_{\alpha=1}^{r} e_\alpha X_\alpha f$ *constitutes a Lie r-parameter group are that*

$$(X_u, X_v)f = \sum_{\lambda=1}^{r} C_{uv}^{\lambda} X_\lambda f \qquad (1 \leqq u, v \leqq r), \tag{74}$$

where the C are constants.

Proof A detailed proof of this theorem is beyond the scope of this Appendix. Instead, we just present an outline of the steps necessary for proof. This theorem is the second of Lie's three fundamental theorems of continuous groups (Lie [1883–1893, Vol. 1, Chapter 9], Lie and Scheffers [1893, Chapter 9]). The proof begins with derivation of the *first fundamental theorem*: If a set of n functions $f^i(x; a)$ defines a group G_r of continuous transformations, then $f^i(x; a)$ are solutions of a system of partial differential equations,

$$\partial x_i'/\partial a_\alpha = \sum_{\lambda=1}^{r} \xi_i^\lambda(x') A_\alpha^\lambda(a) \qquad (i = 1, \ldots, n, \quad \alpha = 1, \ldots, r), \tag{75}$$

with the initial conditions $f^i(x; a^0) = x_i$. Equations (75) are the *fundamental differential equations* of the group (Eisenhart [1933]), where

$$\xi_i^\lambda(x') = -\left[\sum_{k=1}^{n} \psi_k^i \frac{\partial f^k(x'; a^2)}{\partial a_\lambda^2}\right]_{a^2 = a^0},$$

$$\sum_{k=1}^{n} \psi_k^i \frac{\partial f^k}{\partial x_j'} = \delta_{ij} \qquad (i, j = 1, \ldots, n), \tag{76}$$

$$A_\alpha^\lambda(a^1) = \left(\frac{\partial a_\lambda^2}{\partial a_\alpha^1}\right)_{a^2 = a^0} \qquad (\alpha, \lambda = 1, \ldots, r).$$

The next step is to show that Eqs. (75) are completely integrable, satisfying the integrability conditions

$$\sum_{j=1}^{n} \xi_j^\alpha \frac{\partial \xi_i^\beta}{\partial x_j} - \sum_{j=1}^{n} \xi_j^\beta \frac{\partial \xi_i^\alpha}{\partial x_j} = \sum_{u=1}^{r} C_{\alpha\beta}^u \xi_i^u \qquad (\alpha, \beta = 1, \ldots, r),$$

where the C are *constants* (Eisenhart [1933], p. 22, Theorem 6.1). As the third step, we calculate

$$(X_u, X_v)f = X_u X_v f - X_v X_u f = \sum_{i=1}^{n} \left(\sum_{j=1}^{n} \xi_j^u \frac{\partial \xi_i^v}{\partial x_j} - \sum_{j=1}^{n} \xi_j^v \frac{\partial \xi_i^u}{\partial x_j}\right) \frac{\partial f}{\partial x_i}.$$

Then the integrability conditions are written as in (74). Here we can show that the quantities C_{uv}^λ are the *structure constants* of the group which satisfy the *Jacobi relations*

$$C_{uv}^\lambda = -C_{vu}^\lambda, \qquad \sum_{\alpha=1}^{r} C_{uv}^\alpha C_{\alpha\beta}^\lambda + \sum_{\alpha=1}^{r} C_{v\beta}^\alpha C_{\alpha u}^\lambda + \sum_{\alpha=1}^{r} C_{\beta u}^\alpha C_{\alpha v}^\lambda = 0.$$

This is the *third fundamental theorem* of continuous groups (Cohn [1957], Chevalley [1946]). The final step is to show that the converses of the foregoing results hold (Cohn [1957, p. 96]). Hence, if the linearly independent X_α, $1 \leqq \alpha \leqq r$, satisfy (74), then they constitute a Lie r-parameter group G_r. Q.E.D.

Example 2 If $X_1 = \partial/\partial x_1$, $X_2 = x_1\,\partial/\partial x_2$, $X_3 = x_1^2\,\partial/\partial x_1$, then

$$(X_1, X_2) \equiv \partial/\partial x_2, \qquad (X_1, X_3) \equiv 2x_1\,\partial/\partial x_1, \qquad (X_2, X_3) \equiv -x_1^2\,\partial/\partial x_2.$$

Thus X_1, X_2, and X_3 do not form a three-parameter group.

Example 3 $X_1 = x_1\,\partial/\partial x_1 - x_2\,\partial/\partial x_2$, $X_2 = x_1\,\partial/\partial x_2$, $X_3 = x_2\,\partial/\partial x_1$, then

$$(X_1, X_2) \equiv 2X_2, \qquad (X_1, X_3) \equiv -2X_3, \qquad (X_2, X_3) \equiv X_1.$$

Thus, X_1, X_2, and X_3 form a three-parameter group.

Exercise 1 Show that $X_1 = x_2\,\partial/\partial x_3 - x_3\,\partial/\partial x_2$, $X_2 = x_3\,\partial/\partial x_1 - x_1\,\partial/\partial x_3$, $X_3 = x_1\,\partial/\partial x_2 - x_2\,\partial/\partial x_1$ generate a group.

Invariance of Differential Equations of the Second Order

If the differential equation of the second order is written in the form

$$\frac{d^2x_2}{dx_1^2} - F\left(x_1, x_2, \frac{dx_2}{dx_1}\right) = 0 \qquad \text{or} \qquad \frac{d^2x_2}{dx_1^2} = F\left(x_1, x_2, \frac{dx_2}{dx_1}\right), \tag{77}$$

then the condition that it be left unaltered by the group $Xf = \sum_{i=1}^{2} \xi_i\,\partial f/\partial x_i$ is, from *Theorem* 7, *that*

$$-\xi_1\frac{\partial F}{\partial x_1} - \xi_2\frac{\partial F}{\partial x_2} - \xi_2'\frac{\partial F}{\partial(dx_2/dx_1)} + \xi_2'' = 0, \tag{78}$$

whenever

$$d^2x_2/dx_1^2 = F(x_1, x_2, dx_2/dx_1),$$

where ξ_2' and ξ_2'' are defined by (34-i) with $k = 1, 2$.

Theorem 16 *If a differential equation of the second order is invariant under* X_1 *and* X_2, *it is invariant under* (X_1, X_2).

Proof If X_1 and X_2 leave (77) $d^2x_2/dx_1^2 = F(x_1, x_2, dx_2/dx_1)$ unaltered, the extended transformation X_1' and X_2' leave

$$Af \equiv \frac{\partial f}{\partial x_1} + \frac{dx_2}{dx_1}\frac{\partial f}{\partial x_2} + F\left(x_1, x_2, \frac{dx_2}{dx_1}\right)\frac{\partial f}{\partial(dx_2/dx_1)} = 0$$

unaltered. [Because the problem of solving (77) is reduced to that of finding two independent solutions of $Af = 0$.] By *Theorem* 12, and from $(X_1', X_2') \equiv (X_1, X_2)'$, we see that (X_1', X_2') leaves $Af = 0$ unaltered. Q.E.D.

Theorem 17 *The aggregate of all the infinitesimal transformations leaving a given differential equation of the second-order invariant constitute an r-parameter group,* $0 \leqq r \leqq 8$.

Proof (Outline of a proof is given in Chapter 5, Part IX.)

Remark *Theorem* 16 is true for an ordinary differential equation of any order. *Theorem* 17 is also true for a differential equation of the nth order, where $n > 2$. In this case $0 \leqq r \leqq n + 4$.

Projective Groups

The differential equation

$$d^2x_2/dx_1^2 = 0 \tag{79}$$

is a simple example of an equation that is left unaltered by the maximum number of eight infinitesimal transformations. The integral curves of (79) are the straight lines of the plane

$$x_2 = C_1x_1 + C_2, \tag{80}$$

where C_1 and C_2 are the arbitrary constants. Equation (80) is left unaltered by every "projective" transformation

$$x_1' = \frac{a_1 + a_3x_1 + a_5x_2}{1 - a_7x_1 - a_8x_2}, \qquad x_2' = \frac{a_2 + a_4x_1 + a_6x_2}{1 - a_7x_1 - a_8x_2}.$$

The projective group of the plane is the group which forms the basis for the study of projective geometry. One of the important features of projective geometry is the study of the invariance property of a point, a straight line, a conic, etc., under the projective group (see Lie [1888–1893], Campbell [1966]). The eight independent infinitesimal transformations corresponding to the foregoing are

$$\begin{aligned} &X_1 = \partial/\partial x_1, \qquad X_2 = \partial/\partial x_2, \qquad X_3 = x_1\,\partial/\partial x_1, \qquad X_4 = x_2\,\partial/\partial x_1, \\ &X_5 = x_1\,\partial/\partial x_2, \qquad X_6 = x_2\,\partial/\partial x_2, \qquad X_7 = x_1^2\,\partial/\partial x_1 + x_1x_2\,\partial/\partial x_2, \\ &X_8 = x_1x_2\,\partial/\partial x_1 + x_2^2\,\partial/\partial x_2. \end{aligned} \tag{81}$$

s-Parameter Subgroups

It is possible that a smaller number than r, say s, of linearly independent infinitesimal transformations in an r-parameter group determine a group, known as an *s-parameter subgroup* of G_r, i.e., $G_s \subseteq G_r$. We now prove

Theorem 18 *Every r-parameter group* $(r > 2)$ *contains two parameter subgroups.*

Proof Let $X_1, \ldots, X_r$ be independent operators for G_r. Let X_1 and $Y = \sum_{j=2}^{r} C_j X_j$ (C_j = const) be the bases for a two-parameter subgroup. Then by applying the alternating process

$$(X_1, Y) = aX_1 + b\left(\sum_{j=2}^{r} C_j X_j\right) = \sum_{j=2}^{r} C_j(X_1, X_j) = \sum_{j=2}^{r} C_j \sum_{k=1}^{r} a_{1jk} X_k, \quad (82)$$

we must have

$$\sum_{j=2}^{r} C_j a_{1j1} = a, \qquad \sum_{j=2}^{r} C_j a_{1jk} = bC_k \qquad (2 \leqq k \leqq r). \quad (83)$$

Conversely, if $C_2, \ldots, C_r$ can be found to satisfy r equations of the type (83) (a, b = const, not all of the C zero), Y will determine a two-parameter subgroup with X_1. Such a set of C can always be found by the $r - 1$ equations of (83) from determinental equation $|A_{1jk} - bI| = 0$, where $A_{1jk} = \{a_{1jk}\}$, $2 \leqq j, k \leqq r$. Q.E.D.

Example 4 $G_3 : X_1 = \partial/\partial x_1, X_2 = \partial/\partial x_2$, and $X_3 = x_2\, \partial/\partial x_1 + x_1\, \partial/\partial x_2$ determine a three-parameter group. (Show this!) To find a subgroup, the constants C_1 and C_2 must be so determined that

$$(X_3, C_1 X_1 + C_2 X_2) \equiv aX_3 + b(C_1 X_1 + C_2 X_2),$$

i.e.,

$$-C_1 X_2 - C_2 X_1 \equiv aX_3 + bC_1 X_1 + bC_2 X_2;$$

therefore $a = 0$, $bC_1 + C_2 = 0$, $bC_2 + C_1 = 0$ (since $(X_1, X_2) \equiv 0$, $(X_1, X_3) \equiv X_2, (X_2, X_3) \equiv X_1$). In order that the last two equations be consistent, b must satisfy $b^2 - 1 = 0$ or $b = \pm 1$ and $C_1/C_2 = \mp 1$. Hence, $X_3 = x_2\, \partial/\partial x_1 + x_1\, \partial/\partial x_2$ and $Y = \partial/\partial x_1 \pm \partial/\partial x_2$ form two two-parameter subgroups of G_3.

Exercise 2 Show that $X_1 = x_1\, \partial/\partial x_1$, $X_2 = x_2\, \partial/\partial x_1$, $X_3 = x_1\, \partial/\partial x_2$, and $X_4 = x_2\, \partial/\partial x_2$ determine a four-parameter group. And, find all of the two-parameter and three-parameter subgroups.

VII. Contact Transformations

The idea of contact transformation is derived from geometrical consideration applied to hyperspace. An element of surface at any position in a space of $n + 1$ dimensions is determined by means of $z, x_1, \ldots, x_n$, the coordinates of the position and of $p_1, \ldots, p_n$, the coordinates of the orientation, of the element. Thus, if $z, x_1, \ldots, x_n, p_1, \ldots, p_n$ is regarded as $2n + 1$ independent magnitudes, then the element of surface will be given by an equation (Pfaff's equation)

$$dz - \sum_{i=1}^{n} p_i\, dx_i = 0. \tag{84}$$

Consider transformations between $z, x_1, \ldots, x_n, p_1, \ldots, p_n$ and new variables $z', x'_1, \ldots, x'_n, p'_1, \ldots, p'_n$; if these relations are such that

$$dz' - \sum_{i=1}^{n} p'_i\, dx'_i = \rho\left(dz - \sum_{i=1}^{n} p_i\, dx_i\right), \tag{85}$$

where ρ is a nonvanishing quantity independent of differential elements, then the transformation is said to be a *contact transformation.*[11] Restricting our attention to the simplest case of $n = 1$, we present the basic properties of contact transformation. We set $z = x_2$ and $p_1 = p$. Two relations among the three coordinates x_1, x_2, p,

$$\phi(x_1, x_2, p) = 0, \qquad \psi(x_1, x_2, p) = 0, \tag{86}$$

determine ∞^1 elements. The condition that the lineal elements determined by (86) form a union is that

$$p = dx_2/dx_1 = -h_1/h_2 \qquad \text{or} \qquad dx_2 - p\, dx_1 = 0, \tag{87}$$

where $h_1 = \partial h/\partial x_1$, $h_2 = \partial h/\partial x_2$, $h = \phi(x_1, x_2, p(x_1, x_2)) = h(x_1, x_2)$, obtained from eliminating p between ϕ and ψ in (86). Of the possible transformations in the coordinates of a lineal element

$$x'_1 = X^1(x_1, x_2, p), \qquad x'_2 = X^2(x_1, x_2, p), \qquad p' = P(x_1, x_2, p), \tag{88}$$

those which transform every union of elements into a union are *contact transformations*. The condition that (88) be a contact transformation is readily seen to be

$$dx'_2 - p'\, dx'_1 \equiv \rho(x_1, x_2, p)(dx_2 - p\, dx_1), \qquad \rho \neq 0. \tag{89}$$

[11] When the transformation does not contain z, therefore contains only $2n$ variables, it is called the *homogeneous* contact transformation.

From condition (87), it follows that if a union is to be transformed into a union, $dx_2' - p'\,dx_1$ must vanish whenever $(dx_2 - p\,dx_1)$ does. Condition (89) may be alternatively written as

$$(X_1^2 - PX_1^1)\,dx_1 + (X_2^2 - PX_2^1)\,dx_2 + (X_3^2 - PX_3^1)\,dp \equiv \rho(dx_2 - p\,dx_1),$$

where $X_i^j = \partial X^j/\partial x_i$ $(i, j = 1, 2)$, and $\partial X^j/\partial p \equiv X_3^j$ $(j = 1, 2)$. This is equivalent to

$$X_1^2 - PX_1^1 = -\rho p, \qquad X_2^2 - PX_2^1 = \rho, \qquad X_3^2 - PX_3^1 = 0,$$

and hence

$$P = \frac{X_3^2}{X_3^1} = \frac{\partial X^2}{\partial p}\bigg/\frac{\partial X^1}{\partial p}, \tag{90-i}$$

$$X_3^1(X_1^2 + pX_2^2) - X_3^2(X_1^1 + pX_2^1) = 0. \tag{90-ii}$$

(90) may be put in the compact form

$$P = X_3^2/X_3^1 = (X_1^2 + pX_2^2)/(X_1^1 + pX_2^1). \tag{90$'$}$$

Introducing the *Poisson bracket*, (90-ii) is sometimes expressed as

$$[X^1, X^2] = \begin{vmatrix} X_3^1 & X_1^1 + pX_2^1 \\ X_3^2 & X_1^2 + pX_2^2 \end{vmatrix} = 0. \tag{90-ii$'$}$$

When X^1 and X^2 satisfy (90-ii), they are said to be *in involution*.

Remark The extended point transformation is evidently a special case of a contact transformation where $X_3^1 \equiv X_3^2 \equiv 0$.

If in the one-parameter group

$$x_1' = X^1(x_1, x_2, p, a), \qquad x_2' = X^2(x_1, x_2, p, a), \qquad p' = P(x_1, x_2, p, a), \tag{91}$$

condition (89) or its equivalent (90′) holds, then (91) defines a *one-parameter group of contact transformations*. Like any other group, this group has an infinitesimal transformation

$$B = \xi_1\,\partial/\partial x_1 + \xi_2\,\partial/\partial x_2 + \pi\,\partial/\partial p, \tag{92}$$

where ξ_1, ξ_2, and π satisfy

$$x_1' = x_1 + \xi_1(x_1, x_2, p)\,\delta a, \qquad x_2' = x_2 + \xi_2(x_1, x_2, p)\,\delta a,$$
$$p' = p + \pi(x_1, x_2, p)\,\delta a. \tag{91$'$}$$

Since (91′) is also a contact transformation, we must have

$$dx_2' - p'\,dx_1' = dx_2 - p\,dx_1 + (d\xi_2 - p\,d\xi_1 - \pi\,dx_1)\,\delta a \equiv \rho(dx_2 - \rho\,dx_1). \tag{93}$$

Hence we get $\rho = 1 + \sigma(x_1, x_2, p)\,\delta a$, where

$$\begin{aligned}\sigma(x_1, x_2, p)(dx_2 - p\,dx_1) &\equiv d\xi_2 - p\,d\xi_1 - \pi\,dx_1 \\ &= d(\xi_2 - p\xi_1) + \xi_1\,dp - \pi\,dx_1.\end{aligned} \tag{94}$$

Writing with Lie

$$\xi_2 - p\xi_1 \equiv -W(x_1, x_2, p), \tag{95}$$

where W is called the *characteristic function* of (92), the identity (94) may be replaced by

$$W_{x_1} + \pi = \sigma p, \qquad -W_{x_2} = \sigma, \qquad -W_p + \xi_1 = 0,$$

from which, using (95) and eliminating σ, we obtain

$$\xi_1 = W_p, \qquad \xi_2 = pW_p - W, \qquad \pi = -W_{x_1} - pW_{x_2}. \tag{96}$$

It is often convenient to write the infinitesimal transformation (92) as

$$B = W_p\,\partial/\partial x_1 + (pW_p - W)\,\partial/\partial x_2 - (W_{x_1} + pW_{x_2})\,\partial/\partial p, \tag{92′}$$

or using the Poisson bracket

$$Bf = [W, f] - W\,\partial f/\partial x_2. \tag{92″}$$

Example 1 Choose $W = \sqrt{1 + p^2}$; then

$$Bf = \frac{p}{\sqrt{1+p^2}}\frac{\partial f}{\partial x_1} - \frac{1}{\sqrt{1+p^2}}\frac{\partial f}{\partial x_2},$$

which belongs to the homothetic (dilatation) group

$$x_1' = x + \frac{tp}{\sqrt{1+p^2}}, \qquad x_2' = x_2 - \frac{t}{\sqrt{1+p^2}}, \qquad p' = p.$$

Exercise 1 Find the infinitesimal transformation corresponding to $W = \sqrt{a^2p^2 + b^2}$.

Remark When W is linear in p, the corresponding transformation is an extended point transformation. For if

$$W = \xi_1(x_1, x_2)p - \xi_2(x_1, x_2),$$

then

$$W_p = \xi_1, \qquad pW_p - W = \xi_2, \qquad \pi = \frac{\partial \xi_2}{\partial x_1} + p\left(\frac{\partial \xi_2}{\partial x_2} - \frac{\partial \xi_1}{\partial x_1}\right) - p^2\frac{\partial \xi_1}{\partial x_2}.$$

The general type of differential equation $f(x_1, x_2, p) = 0$ of the first-order *invariant* under the contact transformation group whose infinitesimal transformation is

$$Bf = W_p \frac{\partial f}{\partial x_1} + (pW_p - W)\frac{\partial f}{\partial x_2} - (W_{x_1} + pW_{x_2})\frac{\partial f}{\partial p}, \tag{97}$$

is obtained by equating

$$Bf = 0 \qquad \text{or} \qquad [W, f] = W\,\partial f/\partial x_2, \qquad \text{whenever} \quad f = 0. \tag{98}$$

On returning to the general case of $2n + 1$ variables,

$$\begin{aligned} z' &= z + \delta a\zeta(x, z, p), \qquad x = (x_1, \ldots, x_n), \quad p = (p_1, \ldots, p_n), \\ x_i' &= x_i + \delta a\xi_i(x, z, p), \\ p_i' &= p_i + \delta a\pi_i(x, z, p), \qquad 1 \leqq i \leqq n, \end{aligned} \tag{99}$$

the transformation is an infinitesimal contact transformation if the Pfaffian equation (84) is unaltered. Defining the characteristic function as

$$W = \sum_{i=1}^{n} p_i \xi_i - \zeta, \tag{100}$$

we obtain the corresponding infinitesimal contact transformation

$$B = \sum_{i=1}^{n} \frac{\partial W}{\partial p_i}\frac{\partial}{\partial x_i} - \sum_{i=1}^{n}\left(\frac{\partial W}{\partial x_i} + p_i\frac{\partial W}{\partial z}\right)\frac{\partial}{\partial p_i} + \sum_{i=1}^{n} p_i \frac{\partial W}{\partial p_i}\frac{\partial}{\partial z} - W\frac{\partial}{\partial z}. \tag{101}$$

The necessary and sufficient condition that the general type of differential equation $f(x, z, p) = 0$ of the first order should admit the infinitesimal contact transformations with the characteristic function W is that $Bf = 0$ whenever $f = 0$, or

$$[W, f] = W\,\partial f/\partial z, \qquad \text{whenever} \quad f = 0, \tag{102}$$

where $[W, f]$ is the *Poisson bracket* defined by

$$[W, f] = \sum_{i=1}^{n}\left\{\frac{\partial W}{\partial p_i}\left(\frac{\partial f}{\partial x_i} + p_i\frac{\partial f}{\partial z}\right) - \frac{\partial f}{\partial p_i}\left(\frac{\partial W}{\partial x_i} + p_i\frac{\partial W}{\partial z}\right)\right\}. \tag{103}$$

Hence we have

Theorem 19 (i) *Connected with every infinitesimal contact transformation there is a characteristic function* $W \equiv \sum_{i=1}^{n} p_i \xi_i - \zeta$, *in terms of which the transformation is given by means of* (101). *Conversely, starting with any function* W, *relations* (101) *define an infinitesimal contact transformation.*

(ii) *The necessary and sufficient condition that the general type of differential equation* $f(x, z, p) = 0$ *of the first order should admit the infinitesimal contact transformation with the characteristic function W is that* $Bf = 0$ *or* $[W, f] = W\,\partial f/\partial z$, *whenever* $f = 0$.

REFERENCES

Campbell, J. E. [1966]. *Introductory Treatise on Lie's Theory of Finite Continuous Transformation Groups.* Chelsea, New York.

Chevalley, C. [1946]. *Theory of Lie Groups I.* Princeton Univ. Press, Princeton, New Jersey.

Cohen, A. [1911]. *An Introduction to the Lie Theory of One-Parameter Groups.* Heath, Boston, Massachusetts.

Cohn, P. M. [1957]. *Lie Groups.* Cambridge Univ. Press, London and New York.

Eisenhart, L. P. [1933]. *Continuous Groups of Transformations.* Princeton Univ. Press, Princeton, New Jersey. Reprinted by Dover, New York, 1961.

Hermann, R. [1974]. *Geometric Structure Theory of Systems—Control Theory and Physics, Part A*, Interdisciplinary Mathematics, Vol. IX. Chapter 1, Lie's Theory of Groups and Differential Equations. Math. Sci. Press, Brookline, Massachusetts.

Hermann, R. [1975]. *Sophus Lie's 1880 Transformation Group Paper.* Translated by M. Ackerman with comments by R. Hermann in *Lie Groups: History, Frontiers and Applications*, Vol. 1. Math. Sci. Press, Brookline, Massachusetts.

Lie, S. [1888–1893]. *Theorie der Transformationsgruppen*, u. Mitw. v. F. Engel, Vols. I, II, III. Teubner, Leipzig. 2nd ed. Reprinted in 1930. Reprinted by Chelsea, New York, 1970.

Lie, S. [1891]. *Vorlesungen über Differentialgleichungen, mit bekannten infinitesimalen Transformationen* (G. Scheffers, ed.). Teubner, Leipzig. Reprinted by Chelsea, New York, 1967.

Lie, S., and Scheffers, G. [1893]. *Vorlesungen über continuierliche Gruppen mit geometrischen und anderen Anwendungen.* Teubner, Leipzig. Reprinted by Chelsea, New York, 1971.

Lovelock, D., and Rund, H. [1975]. *Tensors, Differential Forms, and Variational Principles.* Wiley, New York.

Markus, L. [1961]. *Group Theory and Differential Equations.* (Lecture Notes at the University of Minnesota). Department of Mathematics, University of Minnesota, Minneapolis, Minnesota.

AUTHOR INDEX

Numbers in italics refer to the pages on which the complete references are listed.

SUBJECT INDEX

J

K

L

M

N

T

U

V

W

X

ECONOMIC THEORY, ECONOMETRICS, AND MATHEMATICAL ECONOMICS

Consulting Editor: Karl Shell

UNIVERSITY OF PENNSYLVANIA
PHILADELPHIA, PENNSYLVANIA

Franklin M. Fisher and Karl Shell. **The Economic Theory of Price Indices:** ***Two Essays on the Effects of Taste, Quality, and Technological Change***

Luis Eugenio Di Marco (Ed.). **International Economics and Development:** ***Essays in Honor of Raúl Presbisch***

Erwin Klein. **Mathematical Methods in Theoretical Economics:** ***Topological and Vector Space Foundations of Equilibrium Analysis***

Paul Zarembka (Ed.). **Frontiers in Econometrics**

George Horwich and Paul A. Samuelson (Eds.). **Trade, Stability, and Macroeconomics:** ***Essays in Honor of Lloyd A. Metzler***

W. T. Ziemba and R. G. Vickson (Eds.). **Stochastic Optimization Models in Finance**

Steven A. Y. Lin (Ed.). **Theory and Measurement of Economic Externalities**

David Cass and Karl Shell (Eds.). **The Hamiltonian Approach to Dynamic Economics**

R. Shone. **Microeconomics:** ***A Modern Treatment***

C. W. J. Granger and Paul Newbold. **Forecasting Economic Time Series**

Michael Szenberg, John W. Lombardi, and Eric Y. Lee. **Welfare Effects of Trade Restrictions:** ***A Case Study of the U.S. Footwear Industry***

Haim Levy and Marshall Sarnat (Eds.). **Financial Decision Making under Uncertainty**

Yasuo Murata. **Mathematics for Stability and Optimization of Economic Systems**

Alan S. Blinder and Philip Friedman (Eds.). **Natural Resources, Uncertainty, and General Equilibrium Systems:** ***Essays in Memory of Rafael Lusky***

Jerry S. Kelly. **Arrow Impossibility Theorems**

Peter Diamond and Michael Rothschild (Eds.). **Uncertainty in Economics:** ***Readings and Exercises***

Fritz Machlup. **Methodology of Economics and Other Social Sciences**

Robert H. Frank and Richard T. Freeman. **Distributional Consequences of Direct Foreign Investment**

Elhanan Helpman and Assaf Razin. **A Theory of International Trade under Uncertainty**

Edmund S. Phelps. **Studies in Macroeconomic Theory, Volume 1:** ***Employment and Inflation.*** **Volume 2:** ***Redistribution and Growth.***

Marc Nerlove, David M. Grether, and José L. Carvalho. **Analysis of Economic Time Series:** ***A Synthesis***

Thomas J. Sargent. **Macroeconomic Theory**

Jerry Green and José Alexander Scheinkman (Eds.). **General Equilibrium, Growth and Trade:** ***Essays in Honor of Lionel McKenzie***

Michael J. Boskin (Ed.). **Economics and Human Welfare:** ***Essays in Honor of Tibor Scitovsky***

Carlos Daganzo. **Multinomial Probit:** ***The Theory and Its Application to Demand Forecasting***

L. R. Klein, M. Nerlove, and S. C. Tsiang (Eds.). **Quantitative Economics and Development:** ***Essays in Memory of Ta-Chung Liu***

Giorgio P. Szegö. **Portfolio Theory:** ***With Application to Bank Asset Management***

M June Flanders and Assaf Razin (Eds.) **Development in an Inflationary World**

Thomas G. Cowing and Rodney E. Stevenson (Eds.). **Productivity Measurement in Regulated Industries**

Robert J. Barro (Ed.). **Money, Expectations, and Business Cycles:** ***Essays in Macroeconomics***

Ryuzo Sato. **Theory of Technical Change and Economic Invariance:** ***Application of Lie Groups***

Iosif A. Krass and Shawkat M. Hammoudeh. **The Theory of Positional Games:** ***With Applications in Economics***

In preparation

Giorgio Szegö (Ed.). **New Quantitative Techniques for Economic Analysis**